STUDIES ON THE CIVILIZATION
AND CULTURE OF
NUZI AND THE HURRIANS

Volume 4

Studies on the Civilization and Culture
of Nuzi and the Hurrians

Edited by

David I. Owen
and
Martha A. Morrison

1. *In Honor of Ernest R. Lacheman on His Seventy-fifth Birthday, April 29, 1981.* Edited by M. A. Morrison and D. I. Owen. 1981.
2. *General Studies and Excavations at Nuzi 9/1.* Edited by D. I. Owen and M. A. Morrison. 1987.
3. *Joint Expedition with the Iraq Museum at Nuzi VII: Miscellaneous Texts.* By Ernest R. Lacheman† and Maynard P. Maidman. 1989.
4. *The Eastern Archives of Nuzi and Excavations at Nuzi 9/2.* Edited by D. I. Owen and M. A. Morrison. 1993.
5. *General Studies and Excavations at Nuzi 9/3.* Edited by D. I. Owen. Forthcoming.

THE EASTERN ARCHIVES OF NUZI

by

Martha A. Morrison

and

EXCAVATIONS AT NUZI 9/2

by

Ernest R. Lacheman†, Martha A. Morrison,
and David I. Owen

EISENBRAUNS
WINONA LAKE, INDIANA
1993

Library of Congress Cataloging-in-Publication Data

The eastern archives of Nuzi / by Martha A. Morrison. And, Excavations at Nuzi 9/2 / [compiled] by Ernest R. Lacheman, Martha A. Morrison, and David I. Owen.
p. cm. — (Studies on the civilization and culture of Nuzi and the Hurrians ; v. 4)
First work in English; 2nd work in Akkadian (cuneiform), with introductory material in English.
The 1st pt. of the 2nd work was published in Studies on the civilization and culture of Nuzi and the Hurrians 2, p. 355–702.
Includes bibliographical references and indexes.
ISBN 0-931464-64-1
1. Akkadian language—Texts. 2. Nuzi (Extinct city) 3. Hurrians. I. Morrison, M. A. (Martha A.) II. Lacheman, Ernest René, 1906–1982. III. Owen, David I. IV. Excavations at Nuzi 9/2. 1993. V. Series.
PJ3721.N8E18 1993
492′.1—dc20 93-20366

CONTENTS

PART 1: THE EASTERN ARCHIVES OF NUZI

MARTHA A. MORRISON

PART 2: TEXTS IN THE HARVARD SEMITIC MUSEUM EXCAVATIONS AT NUZI 9/2

E. R. LACHEMAN†, M. A. MORRISON AND D. I. OWEN

Part 3: Index

Preface

Progress toward the full publication of the Nuzi archives in the Harvard Semitic Museum has moved forward again with the publication below of the study of the Eastern Archives by Martha A. Morrison and the accompanying *Excavations at Nuzi* 9/2. The selection of texts for *Excavations at Nuzi* 9/2 was dictated by Morrison's concentration on those texts from the Eastern Archives. Her contribution demonstrates the importance of an internal analysis of the texts and how this can clarify the imperfect archeological record. It follows upon the study she contributed to SCCNH 2:167–201. Combining both archeological and philological data, she has brought some logical order to the organization of the Eastern Archives and has shown how they might have been grouped originally when excavated. She suggests, furthermore, additional avenues of research to follow in the analyses of other segments of the Nuzi archives.

Morrison's two studies serve as models for future work on the Nuzi texts. With the complete publication of the tablets nearing, significant reevaluation and study of Nuzi institutions should be undertaken. Her pioneering publications and the new texts being made available in *Excavations at Nuzi* 9 will make this possible. The third and final part of *Excavations at Nuzi* 9 will appear soon, along with a number of miscellaneous studies, in SCCNH 5. This will bring to a close the publication of most of E. R. Lacheman's legacy and open up many new possibilities for continuing research on Nuzi.

I would like to thank my student, Richard Wright (Cornell University), for his invaluable help with the word processing for this volume. Professor Maynard P. Maidman (York University) was kind enough to read through the final version of the manuscript and to offer many helpful observations and corrections. Their combined efforts greatly facilitated the completion of this volume for press. Eisenbrauns and particularly David P. Aiken and Pam Nichols continue to maintain the high standards that we have come to take for granted from this remarkable press. Finally, I would like to recognize Mrs. Eunice Lacheman once again for opening her home to us. It had served as a school, laboratory, and hostel during the many visits to Wellesley that were necessary to put this and previous volumes together.

DAVID I. OWEN
Ithaca, New York

Foreword

Shortly after Ernest R. Lacheman passed away in October of 1982, David I. Owen invited me to assist in the organization and publication of *Excavations at Nuzi* 9, Lacheman's unfinished manuscript consisting of over five hundred copies of Nuzi texts in the Harvard Semitic Museum. He had established the guidelines for "The Nuzi Publication Project" through which he planned to oversee the publication of the Lacheman legacy. In addition to Lacheman's copies of the tablets, he also had two, often conflicting, registers of the tablets, and Lacheman's original notes on the correlations between SMN numbers and room numbers in the excavations. Our first task was to produce a working catalog of the texts so that the plates could be matched to the original tablets, many of which had lost their numbers. Due to the large number of tablets requiring collations and our desire to publish the copies as soon as possible, we decided to divide the corpus into three manageable sections. While we were working on the catalog, I recognized a large number of texts assigned to rooms in the eastern area or obviously belonging to those archives. Although both the Nuzi excavation report and Lacheman's brief outline of the distribution of texts at Nuzi in HSS 16 (pp. v–viii) indicated that the Eastern Archives were sizable, the precise nature of these documents was not known. Because of their extent, coherence, and significance, these archives warranted separate consideration and were assigned to *EN* 9/2.

Thus, the idea for this volume developed, that is, to collect Lacheman's plates of the tablets from the Eastern Archives originally included in *EN* 9, to equip them with a proper register and catalog, and to present the texts in conjunction with my own analysis of the archival groups.

This volume is especially meaningful to me because I am fulfilling a debt to Ernest R. Lacheman, my teacher, advisor, and friend, by helping to complete his work. At the same time, I hope to honor his memory by building upon his accomplishments and by advancing our understanding of Nuzi civilization and culture.

While I was preparing this volume, I was invited to teach a graduate seminar on Nuzi at Yale University. The study and discussion in that seminar of some of the texts included here helped to elucidate their content and to open certain avenues of investigation that I have followed. I am grateful to the Department of Near Eastern Languages and Literatures at Yale University for allowing me that opportunity and to the students in that seminar for their observations, questions, and insights.

Earl Ostroff and Joel Hunt, my former students at Brandeis University, were dedicated participants in the *EN* 9 project from its inception. While their sorting and collating of tablets facilitated the progress of our work, their contributions extended well into substantive areas of research related to the issues considered here.

I am deeply grateful to David I. Owen for inviting me to participate in "The Nuzi Publication Project" and for agreeing to include the plates from the Eastern Archives in this volume. Among these are many loan documents from the Eastern Archives, transliterations and studies of which appeared first in his 1969 Brandeis University dissertation and which formed the core of that work. While we were working on *EN* 9, he identified those texts, confirmed their numbers, and collated them. I am also especially thankful for his critical insights and unfailing editorial assistance from the inception of this work through its publication. Of more far-reaching significance, we are all deeply indebted to him for his dedicated perseverance in the monumental task of managing Ernest Lacheman's academic estate. Because of his leadership, *EN* 9 will finally appear, the texts, insofar as possible, will be collated, and the Nuzi Tablet Fragments will be organized and made available to Assyriologists. Not the least of the results of his efforts has been the close collaboration of a number of Nuzi scholars through the two "Nuzi Symposia" during which information, ideas, and genuine good fellowship have been shared. The first results of those symposia have already been appearing in "Nuzi Notes" in the SCCNH series and will continue to be forthcoming in future volumes.

I would also like to thank Maynard P. Maidman who carefully read the manuscript of this volume and offered numerous suggestions for improvement. I am also indebted to my colleagues outside of Nuzi studies who listened patiently to my ideas and offered wise advice. Among them, Professors Luis Yglesias, Pierre Jacopin, and Leonard Muellner, all of Brandeis University, deserve special thanks. Of course, any errors or omissions are mine alone.

MARTHA A. MORRISON
Topsfield, Massachusetts

Abbreviations

AAN	E. Cassin and J.-J. Glassner, *Anthroponymie et Anthropologie de Nuzi*, volume 1: *Les Anthroponymes* (Malibu, 1977)
AASOR 16	R. H. Pfeiffer and E. A. Speiser, "One Hundred New Selected Nuzi Texts," Annual of the American Schools of Oriental Research 16 (1935–36)
AfO	*Archiv für Orientforschung*
AHw	W. von Soden, *Akkadisches Handwörterbuch* (Wiesbaden, 1958–81)
AO	sigla for tablets in the Musée du Louvre
AOAT	Alter Orient und Altes Testament
AOS	American Oriental Series
CAD	*The Assyrian Dictionary of the University of Chicago* (Chicago/Glückstadt, 1956–)
CPN	R. E. Hayden, *Court Procedure at Nuzi* (Diss., Brandeis University, 1962)
CT	Cuneiform Texts from Babylonian Tablets
EN	*Excavations at Nuzi* (for volumes 1–8, see HSS)
	9/1 E. R. Lacheman†, D. I. Owen, M. A. Morrison, et al., SCCNH 2 (1987) 355–702
	9/2 E. R. Lachemant†, M. A. Morrison, and D. I. Owen, SCCNH 4 (1992) 131–398.
Gadd	C. J. Gadd, "Tablets from Kirkuk," *RA* 23 (1926) 49–161
HSS	Harvard Semitic Series (Cambridge, Massachusetts)
	5 *Excavations at Nuzi 1*: E. Chiera, "Texts of Varied Contents" (1929)
	9 *Excavations at Nuzi 2*: R. H. Pfeiffer, "The Archives of Shilwa-teshub Son of the King" (1932).
	13 *Excavations at Nuzi 4*: R. H. Pfeiffer and E. R. Lacheman, "Miscellaneous Texts from Nuzi" (1942)
	14 *Excavations at Nuzi 5*: E. R. Lacheman, "Miscellaneous Texts from Nuzi, Part II: The Palace and Temple Archives" (1950)
	15 *Excavations at Nuzi 6*: E. R. Lacheman, "The Administrative Archives" (1955)
	16 *Excavations at Nuzi 7*: E. R. Lacheman, "Economic and Social Documents" (1958)
	19 *Excavations at Nuzi 8*: E. R. Lacheman, "Family Law Documents" (1962)
IM	sigla for tablets in the Iraq Museum, Baghdad

IN — B. Eichler, *Indenture at Nuzi: The Personal Tidennūtu Contract and Its Mesopotamian Analogues* (New Haven/London, 1973)

JAOS — *Journal of the American Oriental Society*

JBL — *Journal of Biblical Literature*

JCS — *Journal of Cuneiform Studies*

JEN — *Joint Expedition with the Iraq Museum at Nuzi* (American Schools of Oriental Research, Publications of the Baghdad School)
- 1 texts 1–100: E. Chiera, "Inheritance Texts" (Paris, 1927)
- 2 texts 101–221: E. Chiera, "Declarations in Court" (Paris, 1930)
- 3 texts 222–320: E. Chiera, "Exchange and Security Documents" (Paris, 1931)
- 4 texts 321–427: E. Chiera, "Proceedings in Court" (Philadelphia, 1934)
- 5 texts 428–559: E. Chiera, "Mixed Texts" (Philadelphia, 1934)
- 6 texts 560–673: E. R. Lacheman, "Miscellaneous Texts" (New Haven, 1939)
- 7 texts 674–884: E. R. Lacheman† and Maynard P. Maidman, "Miscellaneous Texts," SCCNH 3 (Winona Lake, Indiana, 1989)

JNES — *Journal of Near Eastern Studies*

LDN — D. I. Owen, *The Loan Documents from Nuzu* (Diss., Brandeis University, 1969)

MPND — D. Cross, *Movable Property in the Nuzi Documents* (AOS 10; New Haven, 1937)

NCBT — sigla for tablets housed at Yale University

NGN — L. R. Fisher, *Nuzu Geographical Names* (Diss., Brandeis University, 1959)

NIP — J. Paradise, *Nuzi Inheritance Practices* (Diss., University of Pennsylvania, 1972)

NPN — I. J. Gelb, P. M. Purves, and A. A. MacRae, *Nuzi Personal Names* (Oriental Institute Publications 57; Chicago, 1943)

NRUA — P. Koschaker, *Neue keilschriftliche Rechtsurkunden aus der El-Amarna-Zeit* (Leipzig, 1928)

Or — *Orientalia*

RA — *Revue d'Assyriologie*

RATK — A. Fadhil, *Rechtsurkunden und administrativ Texte aus Kurruḫanni* (Magister-Arbeit, University of Heidelberg, 1972)

RÉS — *Revue des Études Semitiques*

RLLA — C. Zaccagnini, *The Rural Landscape of the Land of Arrapḫe* (Rome, 1979)

SCCNH — Studies on the Civilization and Culture of Nuzi and the Hurrians (edited by D. I. Owen and M. A. Morrison; Winona Lake, Indiana, 1981–)
- 1 *In Honor of Ernest R. Lacheman on His Seventy-Fifth Birthday, April 29, 1981* (1981)

	2 *General Studies and Excavations at Nuzi 9/1* (1987)
	3 *Joint Expedition with the Iraq Museum at Nuzi VII: Miscellaneous Texts*, by E. R. Lacheman† and M. P. Maidman (1989)
	4 *The Eastern Archives of Nuzi and Excavations at Nuzi 9/2* (1993)
SCTN	E. R. Lacheman, *Selected Cuneiform Texts from Nuzi in the Harvard Semitic Museum* (2 vols.; Diss., Harvard University, 1935)
SEANFA	M. P. Maidman, *A Socio-Economic Analysis of a Nuzi Family Archive*. (Diss., University of Pennsylvania, 1976)
SMN	Semitic Museum Nuzi—signature of the Nuzi tablets at the Semitic Museum, Harvard University, Cambridge, Massachusetts
STPPKA	A. Fadhil, *Studien zur Topographie und Prosopographie der Provinzstadte des Königreichs Arrapḫe* (Baghdader Forschungen 6; Mainz am Rhein, 1983)*
TF	sigla for tablets from Tell el-Faḫḫar
UCP	University of California Publications in Semitic Philology
WO	*Die Welt des Orients*
ZA	*Zeitschrift für Assyriologie*

* Fadhil's book appeared after the initial manuscript of this book was finished. Fadhil discusses Unapšewe, among many other locales found in the Nuzi corpus and related sources. Under Unapšewe he collects all the Urḫi-kušuḫ and Muš-apu family materials known at the time, along with all of the other related Unapšewe evidence. There is, therefore, considerable overlap between his discussion of the archives and Morrison's. His intent, however, is to discuss a whole city. Morrison focuses on a single archive. For the sake of completeness, therefore, Morrison has included her original treatment of the previously published texts along with the new texts and has endeavored to acknowledge throughout where Fadhil discusses the same materials. It is gratifying to note that they are in essential agreement about Urḫi-kušuḫ and the Muš-apu family.

PART 1
THE EASTERN ARCHIVES OF NUZI

by

Martha A. Morrison

CHAPTER 1

Introduction

The excavation of the ancient city of Nuzi (modern Yorghan Tepe) and its thousands of cuneiform documents between 1925 and 1931 inaugurated a period of intense scholarly activity that produced an extraordinary volume of research.[1] In rapid succession six volumes of texts from the western suburban mound (*JEN* I–VI), two volumes of texts from the eastern suburban mound (HSS 5 and 9), and a volume of "selected texts" primarily from the eastern suburban mound and the city (AASOR 16) appeared.[2] Similar texts from clandestine digs in the area of Nuzi were known,[3] but Nuzi provided a large provenanced corpus for analysis. On the basis of these and the other materials, the dialect of the Nuzi tablets was identified as a kind of "Peripheral Akkadian" heavily influenced by Hurrian.[4] The social and economic institutions documented by texts introduced by the formulas, *ṭuppi mārūti*, *ṭuppi titennūti*, and the like, were recognized as either reflections of or variations on standard Mesopotamian practices.[5] The results of this first phase of Nuzi studies became a fundamental part of Assyriological literature and were used heavily for comparative purposes for many decades, especially in Old Testament studies.

[1] For a distribution of publications on Nuzi by year up to 1972, see M. Dietrich, O. Loretz, and W. Mayer, *Nuzi-Bibliographie* (AOAT 11; 1972). For an update of this work, see Fadhil, STPPKA, 346–50.

[2] See abbreviations for dates of publication.

[3] C. J. Gadd, "Tablets from Kirkuk," *RA* 23 (1926) 49–161. Note his references to texts found earlier and discussion of the origin of the documents, pp. 49–52 and nn. 1–8. See also the bibliography in G. Wilhelm, AOAT 9:2–3.

[4] See M. Berkooz, *The Nuzi Dialect of Akkadian, Orthography and Phonology* (Language dissertations [Supplement to Language] 23; Philadelphia, 1937); C. Gordon, "The Dialect of the Nuzu Tablets," *Or* n.s. 7 (1938) 32–63, 215–32. Most recently, see G. Wilhelm, AOAT 9.

[5] See such fundamental works as P. Koschaker, *NRUA*; idem, "Fratriarchat, Hausgemeinschaft und Mutterrecht in Keilschriftrechten Arrapha," *ZA* 41 (1933) 13–45; E. Cassin, *L'adoption à Nuzi* (Paris, 1938); C. H. Gordon, "The Status of Women Reflected in the Nuzi Tablets," *ZA* 43 (1936) 146–49; H. Lewy, "The *aḫḫūtu* Documents from Nuzi," *Or* n.s. 9 (1940) 362–73; idem, "The *titennūtu* Texts from Nuzi," *Or* n.s. 10 (1941) 313–36; idem, "Miscellanea Nuziana," *Or* n.s. 28 (1959) 1–25, 113–29; A. L. Oppenheim, "Métiers et professions à Nuzi," *RÉS* 1939: 49–61; A. Saarisalo, "New Kirkuk Documents Relating to Slaves," *StOr* 5/3 (1934); E. A. Speiser, "New Kirkuk Documents Relating to Family Laws," AASOR 10 (1932) 1–73; F. R. Steele, *Nuzi Real Estate Transactions* (AOS 25; 1943).

When sites such as Mari, Alalaḫ, and Ugarit were unearthed, new avenues of investigation opened in Assyriology and other areas of ancient Near Eastern studies. Soon, research on Nuzi and its texts waned to a trickle. Text publications continued, however, with Ernest R. Lacheman's HSS 13 (with R. H. Pfeiffer), 14, 15, 16, and 19 and other smaller collections of documents.[6] The HSS volumes contained more texts from the suburban mounds, hundreds of documents from the palace, and a few from the city of Nuzi itself. Indeed, these volumes present the bulk of the texts from the eastern suburban mound and from the palace, and most of the documents are administrative and economic in nature. These texts laid the foundation for and helped to maintain the continuity of Nuzi studies to the present day.

Since the first phase of Nuzi studies, the fields of Assyriology and ancient Near Eastern studies have expanded and changed dramatically. The vast amount of information that has come to light through excavations both in the field and in museum basements has traced the broad outlines of ancient Near Eastern history and civilization generally and has provided detailed data for numerous areas, particularly in the "peripheral" regions of Mesopotamia. Whole new disciplines, such as Ebla and Emar studies, among others, have been born. Moreover, new research directions, shaped in part by the increased information available and in part by disciplines such as anthropology, economics, and sociology, require that scholars ask new questions of older materials. Nuzi illustrates very well these developments. In a number of recent studies the Nuzi evidence underlies or contributes to linguistic, historical, anthropological, and socioeconomic studies that consider issues of significance ranging far beyond Nuzi and its environs.[7] Others combine the wealth of Nuzi evidence with that of texts from Kirkuk, unprovenanced texts, and the materials from Tel el-Faḫḫar to collect data concerning cities and towns as yet unexcavated for regional analyses of the land of Arrapḫe.[8]

A significant amount of recent research focuses on Nuzi itself and what can be learned about the social and economic structures, the internal dynamics, and the history of that community. Nuzi is particularly suitable for research of this sort because of the broad exposure of the site accomplished during the excavations. Though we lament the techniques employed to uncover such a large area

[6] N. B. Jankowska, *Legal Documents from Arrapḫa in the Collections of the U.S.S.R.* (Peredneaziatskij sbornik; Moscow, 1961) 424ff.; E. Cassin, "Tablettes inédites de Nuzi," *RA* 56 (1962) 424ff.; E. R. Lacheman, "Les tablettes de Kerkouk au Musée d'Art et d'Histoire de Genève," *Genava* 15 (1967) 5–22; idem, "Tablets from Arrapḫe and Nuzi in the Iraq Mušeum," *Sumer* 32 (1976) 113–48, and idem and D. I. Owen, "Texts from Arrapḫa and from Nuzi in the Yale Babylonian Collection," SCCNH 1:377–432.

[7] For examples, see SCCNH 1 and 2 in which the articles cover a broad range of topics. In particular, note the articles of M. Astour in both volumes; I. M. Diakonoff, E. Gaál, V. Haas, H. Hoffner, T. Kendall, W. Mayer, C. Saporetti, and H. J. Thiel in vol. 1; and M. L. Khačikyan, and I. Wegner in vol. 2.

[8] See A. Fadhil, *Rechtsurkunden und Administrative Texte aus Kurruḫanni* (Magister-Arbeit, University of Heidelberg, 1972).

in only five seasons of excavation, the result is that we have the material remains, including texts, from most areas of the ancient city and from two suburban mounds. Further, the majority of the texts has been published. Thus, it is possible to collect both the epigraphic and archeological evidence relating to the various social and economic groups that composed the community and thereby examine the cross-section of Nuzi society.

Much of this work involves the analysis of the materials according to family and administrative archives.[9] One benefit of this sort of work arises from the broader meaning that any individual tablet takes on when it is studied within its archeological and archival context. The histories of families and the operations of administrative centers can be reconstructed through the study of their respective archives or spheres of activity. Additionally, individuals whose patronymics do not appear in a text can often be identified with confidence on the basis of other materials within an archive or from the same area. As a result, texts that may not offer much information of any significance when isolated can become especially meaningful.[10]

Another important aspect of this sort of research relates to the archeology of Nuzi. Because the texts were separated from their archeological contexts almost immediately, the study of the texts proceeded in one direction and the study of the archeological remains in another. The outstanding artifacts were identified and incorporated into the wider corpus of materials from the ancient Near East. Some of the best-known Nuzi finds are unique, rare, or extraordinary examples of their genre and appear in nearly every handbook of ancient Near Eastern art and archeology. The fragments of wall painting, Nuzi ware, the ceramic lions, and the seal of Sauštattar are outstanding examples. Beyond treatments of individual objects, Nuzi glyptic studies have been a productive and exciting area of study. Other possible groups of material have been neglected, however. The temple area's yield of a sizable body of material over a number of stratums might offer a fruitful topic of investigation. The remains of the residential areas, too, require a broad-ranging investigation directed at establishing the interrelationships among various parts of the city, the socioeconomic patterns of the city, and the like. Such studies may not be possible on the basis of the archeological material alone. The city was sacked at its destruction, so "status goods" are

[9] Among recent works, see G. Wilhelm's *Das Archiv des Šilwa-Teššup*, parts 2–3: *Rationenlisten I–II* (Wiesbaden, 1980–85); M. Maidman, *A Socio-economic Analysis of a Nuzi Family Archive* (Diss., University of Pennsylvania, 1976); idem, "A Nuzi Private Archive: Morphological Considerations," *Aššur* 1/9 (1979) 179–86; G. Dosch, *Die Texte aus Room A34 des Archives von Nuzi* (Magister-Arbeit, University of Heidelberg, 1976); W. Mayer, "Nuzi Studien I: Die Archive des Palastes und die Prosopographie der Berufe," AOAT 205/1 (1978); M. Morrison, "The Family of Šilwa-Tešub *mār šarri*," *JCS* 30 (1979) 3–29; idem, "Evidence for Herding and Animal Husbandry in the Nuzi Documents," SCCNH 1:257–96; and idem, "The Southwest Archives of Nuzi," SCCNH 2:167–201. A brief survey of the distribution of all of the documents from Nuzi appears in Lacheman, HSS 16:v–viii.

[10] See remarks concerning this matter in Wilhelm, *Das Archiv des Šilwa-Teššup*, 22ff.; Morrison, *JCS* 30:4 and idem, review of Wilhelm, *Das Archiv des Šilwa-Teššup*, *AfO* 29–30 (1983–84) 114.

scarce. The remaining ceramic and other artifacts appear to be of a fairly uniform nature. Thus, the archives found in the various architectural units are particularly valuable for interpreting the archeological data and understanding the growth, development and organization of the city.

Reconstructing Nuzi archives can be problematic, however, for a number of reasons that have been discussed elsewhere.[11] Briefly, the excavation was a relatively early one, so retrieving certain data from the reports and field records is difficult. For instance, it is often noted in the excavation report that a certain number of tablets or simply that tablets came from a particular room. Information as to which tablets originated in which rooms was recorded in such a manner that confusion arose in the field and at every stage in the processing of the tablets for publication.[12] Tablet registers in the text publications often preserve erroneous room and museum numbers for the tablets, both of which can be misleading in the reconstruction of the archives. Most often, misassigned tablets can be reunited with their archives only on the basis of content, but this method presumes a large-enough body of material originating in a room or a house to justify reassigning a stray text to that group.[13] Unfortunately, the misplacing of some texts may never be detected because of their unique personal names or subject matter.

The evidence used in reconstructing the archives comes from two sources: the archeological record and the notes, lists, and tablet registers associated with the tablets.[14] Both the Nuzi excavation report and the other sources identify rooms in which tablets were found. However, the two sources of information do not always agree.[15] While the excavation report preserves observations of an "eyewitness" nature, tablet registers and other papers contain for the most part the information received at the museum when the tablets arrived. Careful comparison of the two sources ofttimes demonstrates the source of the confusions and allows for a reorganization of the materials along archival lines. An especially important source of information for some of the tablets is Lacheman's Harvard doctoral dissertation in which he treated the tablets and fragments num-

[11] See Morrison, *AfO* 29–30, 114 and SCCNH 2:168ff.

[12] For a full discussion of the issues involved here, see Morrison, SCCNH 2:193ff.

[13] A working assumption is that a reasonable percentage of the texts are assigned correctly. Thus, a cluster of documents belonging to the same individual and assigned to the same building identifies the home of the archive. An individual text belonging to that individual and assigned elsewhere has most likely been confused. Single texts, on the other hand, do not establish archives unless they can be related to the larger body of material within a building.

[14] The tablet registers appear in each published volume of texts. Among Prof. Lacheman's papers are many hand-written lists and catalogs dating from the 1930s and later. These appear to have been the sources for the published tablet registers and would have served as the basis for the catalog of *EN* 9.

[15] For examples, see Morrison, SCCNH 2:168ff., 193ff., and 197–201. Also, see below, pp. 11–20 nn.

bered SMN 2149 to 3026. This work is the earliest fixed source for the identification of tablets and fragments with SMN numbers and room numbers (where they were known). As such, it has proved of inestimable value in the organization of the *EN* 9 materials and the Nuzi tablet fragments.[16]

Here it is important to note that the well-known Nuzi archives, those of the family of Teḫip-Tilla son of Puḫi-šenni, the family of Katiri, and Šilwa-Tešup DUMU LUGAL, conform to certain patterns of composition. Family archives include those texts that were kept by families and individuals because of their legal value as proof of ownership or protection against future action. Such archives can include texts of previous generations insofar as they have current value to the last generation of the archives. As a result, wills, personnel documents, records of judgments in court and the like from early times at Nuzi can appear in last-generation archives because they served as "deeds" to property. Texts belonging to totally unrelated individuals may be included in an archive because the archive owner or his family acquired the property involved. Thus, an archival group can include texts relating directly to a particular individual along with texts of previous generations of his family and the people with whom they conducted business.[17] Administrative archives are composed of the texts that document the inflow and outflow of goods, services, personnel, and equipment from a central agency such as the palace or a large estate. Among such texts are letters, receipts, ration lists, contracts that relate to the business of the agency, and the memoranda.[18] By nature, these texts have a more limited lifespan. The principles by which such archives were maintained, that is, how long the texts were kept and under what circumstances they were cleared, if at all, require further study.[19] Of course, the two types of archives are not mutually exclusive. The archives of a private land owner with a large estate can include the documents that both proved ownership of property and recorded the activities of the estates.[20]

Archives are dated mainly through correspondences with individuals whose positions in the relative chronology of Nuzi are known. The standard skeleton upon which the chronologies are based is the five-generation scribal "family" of Apil-Sin whose members encompass the Nuzi corpus.[21] Throughout this volume, roman numerals in parentheses following the names of scribes refer to the

[16] Lacheman, *SCTN* 1, passim.

[17] See Maidman, *Aššur* 1/9, for a full analysis of the composition of family archives.

[18] These include, among others, the palace archives and parts of those of Šilwa-Tešup *mār šarri*.

[19] For instance, the reasons for retaining ration lists and other disbursement documents long after they appear to have had any value are not known.

[20] Perhaps the best example are the archives of Šilwa-Tešup. Note that the two types of archives may have been stored separately in the house of Šilwa-Tešup (Lacheman, HSS 16:vii).

[21] See Lacheman, "The Word *šudutu* in the Nuzi Tablets," *ACIO* 25:237ff.; and Wilhelm, AOAT 9:10, for the genealogy of the Apil-Sin family.

generations of the family of Apil-Sin. In addition, the family of Teḫip-Tilla son of Puḫi-šenni which has been traced for six generations, offers another chronological framework for the Nuzi corpus.[22] Comparison of the genealogies documented by archival groups to these two well-established genealogies allows for the relative dating of other families and individuals within the internal chronology of Nuzi.[23] Further, scribes and witnesses who do not belong to any known genealogy can be associated with certain generations through their appearances in texts that can be located within the chronology of the Nuzi corpus. In turn, other texts in which they appear can be dated with some accuracy.[24]

This volume considers the texts from the area called the North Eastern Area in Starr's excavation report and the Eastern Archives by Lacheman. Long known as an important source of documents, the area east of the palace has been incompletely represented in the publications to date. The chief figures of those archives were identified early, but tantalizingly limited evidence has been available for them.[25] Lacheman's manuscript of *EN* 9 included over 170 tablets which were either assigned to the eastern area in his rough catalog of the texts or can be located there because of their content. Part 2 of this volume includes his autographs of those texts, copied according to the system that he developed,[26] as *EN* 9/2. As in *EN* 9/1, collations have been added to the plates as necessary.[27] A complete catalog of the tablets and a reverse index by SMN precedes the copies. Many of the loan documents and some of the personal *titennūtu*s and legal texts have been known in transliteration or through references to them in various dissertations and publications.[28] These are identified in the catalog. The new texts, particularly the real estate contracts, offer a hitherto unsuspected wealth of evidence concerning the individuals attested in the eastern area, so they figure

[22] See Lacheman, *ACIO* 25:237 and M. Maidman, "The Teḫip-Tilla Family of Nuzi: A Genealogical Reconstruction," *JCS* 28 (1976) 141. A corrected chart of the family tree appears in *JCS* 29 (1977) 64.

[23] Work is progressing on establishing a wider framework for the Nuzi corpus. See D. Stein, SCCNH 2:225–320, for the glyptic evidence and A. Friedman, SCCNH 2:109–29, for a different proposal concerning the relative chronology of Nuzi.

[24] There are always questions raised about "third-party" linkages because an individual's lifetime could span the end of one person's adult life and the beginning of another's. Single linkages, therefore, are not as secure as multiple overlaps with parties, witnesses, and scribes.

[25] Puḫi-šenni son of Muš-apu and Pula-ḫali are mentioned by R. F. S. Starr, *Nuzi* 1:313, 316ff., and 318. E. R. Lacheman locates Purna-zini and his son Muš-apu along with "three more generations," the family of Ḫuya son of Šimika-atal, Ar-tura son of Kuššiya and his family, and Šeḫal-Tešup son of Teḫup-šenni, in this area in his survey of the Nuzi archives (HSS 16:viii). Some of the texts belonging to these individuals appear in AASOR 16 and HSS 14, 15, 16, and 19 (see pp. 11–20 below).

[26] E. R. Lacheman, "New Nuzi Texts and a New Method of Copying Cuneiform Tablets," *JAOS* 55 (1935) 429–31 with pls. 1–6.

[27] See E. R. Lacheman†, D. I. Owen, and M. A. Morrison, "Texts in the Harvard Semitic Museum, *EN* 9/1," SCCNH 2:357–702.

[28] Most notably in Owen, *LDN*; Eichler, *IN*; and Hayden, *CPN*. See catalog of *EN* 9/2 for references for individual texts.

prominently in the discussions in Part 1 of the volume. Throughout, transliterations and/or translations of the more significant texts are offered. The catalog includes page references for these texts.

Part 1 of this volume is based on a reconstruction of the Eastern Archives involving both the *EN* 9/2 texts and those published previously. This reconstruction follows the method employed for the Southwest Archives at Nuzi.[29] Texts assigned to the same rooms were examined in order to determine the group or groups of individuals represented in them. Those individuals were tracked through the Nuzi corpus of published and unpublished materials.[30] Other texts in which they appeared were considered for inclusion in the primary groups on the basis of the individual's role in the text. Once collected, the archives are located within the chronological framework of the Nuzi corpus. The parties involved in the texts are dated and their family associations, when available, are established. The contents of the archives are described and conclusions drawn as to the history, status, and position of the family and its individual members. Finally, the texts are compared with the archeological record.

The Eastern Archives of Nuzi include three hundred tablets identified so far. These texts cluster in three buildings in the area: Groups 17, 18A, and 19 of Starr's North Eastern Section.[31] Located across a street from the northeastern side of the palace, this area was considerably eroded so that the plan of stratum II, the level with which the tablets were associated, is not entirely preserved. The nature of the architectural remains in the area, however, led the excavator to observe a number of characteristic features: (1) the lack of a compact and orderly plan for the individual groups; (2) the presence of large, paved courtyards in three of the groups; (3) the inclusion of separate groups of rooms capable of independent existence within the confines of the main group; and (4) the inferior quality of the construction.[32] Thus, the area is described in the excavation report as "a less desirable location for private homes than the Southwestern Section."[33] The people of the area were "of lesser wealth," and "of a humbler class"; families of such individuals were thought to have resided in the units within the buildings and shared the courtyards and common areas.[34]

Throughout the description of the area, however, there are other features that deserve further comment. Group 19, as noted by the excavator, is built against the wall of the palace.[35] Group 15 represents a house of substance, well planned and similar to that of Šilwa-Tešup DUMU LUGAL and Group 3 of the Southwestern

[29] See Morrison, SCCNH 2:189ff.

[30] The basic tools for doing so are *NPN*, *AAN*, and K. Deller, "Indexes to Part II," SCCNH 1:471–94. In addition, Lacheman compiled a massive personal name directory including much of the unpublished material. Though incomplete, it has been helpful in tracing personal names in *EN* 9.

[31] R. F. S. Starr, *Nuzi* (Cambridge, 1939) 1:304ff. See catalog below.

[32] Ibid., 321.

[33] Ibid.

[34] Ibid.

[35] Ibid.

Area.[36] Group 16 may have been a chapel.[37] Group 18, which may have included 18A in its final configuration, evidences extensive alterations and renovations.[38] Group 19 also bears witness to rebuilding operations that conformed in part to an earlier plan.[39] Groups 17 and 18A are incompletely preserved, so conclusions about their plans cannot be based on complete data. In light of the archives' contents, as we shall demonstrate below, these features appear to be considerably more significant than previously believed.

As noted above, the archives of the eastern area are divided among three buildings. Group 17 includes two archival groups, the family of Ar-tura and Šeḫal-Tešup son of Teḫup-šenni. Group 18A contains records relating to the family of Ḫuya. The texts from Group 19 are divided primarily between those of the Muš-apu family and those of the Pula-ḫali family, but a number of smaller groups originates in this building as well.

It is interesting that the buildings which are the most haphazardly designed are the very buildings that produced tablets. As the chapters below indicate, the tablets from this area do not describe poor and humble people but rather individuals of property, wealth, and power. From the outset, then, the character of this area in the end was hardly that surmised on the basis of the architectural evidence.

The catalog that follows presents the distribution of texts in the eastern area. Within each group tablets are arranged by the room to which they are assigned in tablet registers and other materials. SMN numbers and publication numbers of the texts are provided along with the principal parties of the documents. After the buildings belonging to the eastern area, there appear texts assigned to other buildings and texts that lack room numbers and SMN numbers altogether but clearly belong to the Eastern Archives. A brief survey of the catalog indicates that the texts of this area underwent the same sort of confusion as those in other areas. The details with respect to individual groups are discussed in the chapters below. It is important to note that the excavation report provides no details as to how many tablets came from any room in the eastern area, unlike the southwestern area, so comparison between the excavation report and other sources of information is possible in only the most general terms, as indicated at the beginning of each group.[40] Notes to the catalog describe discrepancies within the materials available for locating the texts.

[36] Ibid., 306–7.

[37] Ibid.

[38] Ibid., 310–12.

[39] Ibid., 313ff.

[40] In the southwest area the disagreements between the excavation report and tablet registers are more noticeable because Starr gave figures for the numbers of texts found in various rooms and the registers diverged markedly from those figures. Here there is no such information, so it is not possible to assess whatever problems there might be in this regard. However, the mixing of tablets throughout the area is similar to what was noted in the southwest area. (See n. 15 above.)

TABLE 1. *Provenance of Tablets in the Eastern Area*

Group	*Room*	*SMN*	*Reference*	*Principal party; Comments*
15[1]	S150	2480[2]	HSS 15 64	
17	S110[3]	2085	AASOR 16 58	Utḫap-tae son of Ar-tura
		2105	HSS 19 113	Utḫap-tae son of Ar-tura
		2108	*EN* 9/2 363	Utḫap-tae son of [ ]
		2127	*EN* 9/2 450	Utḫap-tae son of Ar-tura
		2157[4]	*EN* 9/2 322	Utḫap-tae son of Ar-tura
		2158	*EN* 9/2 354	Utḫap-tae son of Ar-tura
		2159[5]	HSS 19 114	Utḫap-tae son of Ar-tura
		2160[6]	*EN* 9/1 351	Ar-tura
17	S113[7]	2001	*EN* 9/2 360	Šeḫal-Tešup son of Teḫup-šenni
		2008	HSS 19 110	Ar-tura son Kizzi, Teḫiya son of Kuššiya
		2011	*EN* 9/2 298	Šeḫal-Tešup son of Teḫup-šenni
		2012	*EN* 9/2 393	Arip-šeriš
		2013	*EN* 9/2 156	Šeḫal-Tešup son of Teḫup-šenni
		2086	HSS 19 112	Šeḫal-Tešup son of Teḫup-šenni
		2093	AASOR 16 76 (= HSS 14 20)	Šeḫram-mušni for Šeḫal-Tešup
		2110	HSS 19 10	Ar-tura son of Kuššiya
		2163[8]	HSS 19 50	Ḫutiya son of Puḫiya
		2190	HSS 16 83	Tarmiya son of Ḫuya listed
		2191	HSS 16 458	
		2192	HSS 15 294	Šeḫal-Tešup son of Teḫup-šenni
		2193	*EN* 9/2 27	ᶠTulpunnaya
		2194	*EN* 9/2 163	Puḫi-šenni son of Muš-apu
		2195	HSS 15 29 (= *RA* 36 194)	military text
		2196	HSS 14 26	letter

[1] No tablets are mentioned in the excavation report for any of the rooms in this Group.

[2] S150 may be a typographical error in Lacheman, *SCTN*. SMN numbers directly before and after are assigned to S151.

[3] No tablets mentioned in the excavation report.

[4] Assigned to S112 in dissertation but changed to S110 in catalogs.

[5] Assigned to S112 in dissertation but changed to S110 in catalogs.

[6] Assigned to S112 in dissertation but changed to S110 in catalogs.

[7] "Several tablets in bad condition," according to the excavation report.

[8] Assigned to S112 in dissertation but changed to S110 in catalogs.

TABLE 1. *Continued*

Group	*Room*	*SMN*	*Reference*	*Principal party; Comments*
		2198	HSS 16 238	Ar-tura
		2199	HSS 14 21	Šeḫram-mušni for Šeḫal-Tešup
		2200		fragment
		2201		fragment
		2202		fragment
		2203		fragment
		2204		fragment
		2700+?	*EN* 9/2 18	Muš-apu son of Purna-zini
18	S131[9]	2346	HSS 16 374	list of names
		2347[10]		fragment
		2348[11]		fragment
18A	S151[12]	2089	AASOR 16 63	Šukriya son of Ḫuya
		2128	*EN* 9/2 16	Tarmiya son of Ḫuya
		2130	HSS 16 228[13]	Šilwa-Tešup family grain rations
		2133	*EN* 9/2 29	Bēl-šadūni *wardu*
		2134	AASOR 16 56	sons of Ḫuya
		2474	*EN* 9/2 38	Muš-apu
		2479	*EN* 9/2 187	Tarmiya son of Ḫuya
		2481	*EN* 9/2 392	Tarmiya son of Ḫuya
		2483	HSS 16 376	list of names
		2484		text concerning horses
		2485	*EN* 9/2 34	Ḫanukka son of Tarmiya
		2486	*RA* 36 86–87	school text
		2487	*EN* 9/2 101	Tarmiya son of Ḫuya
		2488	*EN* 9/2 35	Ḫuya son of Šimika-atal
		2489	HSS 16 377	list of names
		2490	*EN* 9/2 234	Teḫip-Tilla son of Šukriya
		2491	HSS 16 232	Tarmiya son of Ḫuya included
		2492	HSS 19 42	Ḫanaya son of Šešwe
		2493	*EN* 9/2 153	Tarmiya
		2494	HSS 19 5	Šukriya son of Ḫuya
		2495	*EN* 9/2 395	declaration in court concerning Ḫašuar's orchard

[9] No tablets mentioned in the excavation report.

[10] Assigned to S131 in dissertation. HSS 16 374 is located in room A34 in the tablet register of the volume.

[11] Assigned to S131 in dissertation. HSS 16 374 is located in room A34 in the tablet register of the volume.

[12] Sixty-five tablets, scattered perhaps from S307.

[13] Belongs to the archives of Šilwa-Tešup.

TABLE 1. *Continued*

Group	*Room*	*SMN*	*Reference*	*Principal party; Comments*
		2496	HSS 16 233	Ḫašip-Tilla LÚ.DAM.GÀR
		2497	*EN* 9/2 36	Tarmiya son of Ḫuya
		2498	*EN* 9/2 76	Šukriya son of Ḫuya
		2499	*EN* 9/2 273	Tarmiya
		2500	*EN* 9/2 204[14]	Eḫli-Tešup
		2501	*EN* 9/2 40	Tarmiya
		2502	HSS 16 419[15]	Šilwa-Tešup grain list
		2503	HSS 19 126	Paššiya son of Pula-ḫali
		2504	*EN* 9/2 106	Tarmiya son of Ḫuya
		2505	*EN* 9/2 130	grain receipt
		2506	*EN* 9/2 528	fragmentary
		2507		fragmentary witness list
		2508		fragment
		2509		fragmentary witness list
		2510	*EN* 9/2 103	Pai-Tilla
		2511	*EN* 9/2 177	Šarteya
		2512	*EN* 9/2 96	list of fields
		2513	*EN* 9/2 279[16]	Eḫli-Tešup
		2514	*EN* 9/1 425	lawsuit concerning a horse
		2515		Tarmiya son of Ḫuya
		2516		fragment
		2517	*EN* 9/2 39	Tarmiya son of Ḫuya
		2518	*EN* 9/2 185	Tarmiya
		2520	*EN* 9/2 206	Ḫuya
		2521		fragment
		2522	HSS 16 321[17]	Tarmiya son of Ḫuya
		2523		Tarmiya
		2524		Šekaru son of Šuk[riya]
		2525	*EN* 9/1 461	Ḫuya
		2526	*EN* 9/2 455	Puḫi-šenni
		2527–2552		fragments
19[18]	S112[19]	1854	HSS 16 449[20]	Zikarru LÚ.SIPA (*bulla*)
		2050	AASOR 16 98(C 112)	seal of Elḫip-tašenni
		2078	AASOR 16 62	Urḫi-kušuḫ DUMU LUGAL

[14] Most likely belongs to the Southwest Archives. See Morrison, SCCNH 2:177, 185, and 201.

[15] Belongs to the archives of Šilwa-Tešup.

[16] Most likely belongs to the Southwest Archives. See Morrison, SCCNH 2:177, 185, and 201.

[17] HSS 16 321–323 are misnumbered in the register in HSS 16 as 320–322. HSS 16 321 = SMN 2522 (S151); HSS 16 322 = SMN 2164 (S112); HSS 16 323 = SMN 2177 (S112).

[18] The excavation report also notes in Group 19 one tablet each from S137B and S138–39.

[19] "A large number" of tablets, with a "large quantity" on a lower pavement, according to the excavation report.

[20] Starr (*Nuzi* 1, 316–17) places this text in S112.

TABLE 1. *Continued*

Group	*Room*	*SMN*	*Reference*	*Principal party; Comments*
		2082	AASOR 16 61	Kula-ḫubi son of Arteya
		2083	*EN* 9/2 20	Puḫi-šenni son of Muš-apu
		2096	HSS 16 311[21]	Puḫi-šenni son of Muš-apu
		2097	AASOR 16 67	Muš-apu son of Purna-zini
		2098	AASOR 16 66	Muš-apu son of Purna-zini
		2112	*EN* 9/2 186	Tarmiya son of Ḫuya
		2161	*EN* 9/2 359	Šeḫal-Tešup son of Teḫup-šenni
		2162	*EN* 9/2 338	Puḫi-šenni son of Muš-apu
		2164	HSS 16 322[22]	Puḫi-šenni son of Muš-apu
		2165	HSS 16 456	list of individuals and grain
		2166		fragmentary witness list
		2167	*EN* 9/2 321	Urḫi-kušuḫ DUMU LUGAL
		2168+?	*EN* 9/2 28	Muš-apu son of Purna-zini
		2169	HSS 14 31	Tarmiya
		2170	HSS 19 93	Puḫi-šenni son of Atal-Tešup
		2171+2176	HSS 19 55	Elḫip-šarri?
		2174	*EN* 9/2 458	
		2175		fragment
		2176+2171		see SMN 2171
		2177	HSS 16 323[23]	herding contract
		2178	*EN* 9/2 421	fragmentary adoption text
		2179	*EN* 9/2 142	Muš-apu son of Purna-zini
		2180	*EN* 9/2 341	Paššі-Tilla son of Pula-ḫali
		2181		fragment
		2182		fragment
		2183		fragment
		2184		Šeḫal-Tešup
		2185		fragment
		2186		fragment
		2187		fragment
		2188		fragment
		2189		fragment
		2197	HSS 16 457	GAL 11 Tupki-šenni
19	S124[24]	2007	*EN* 9/2 19	Puḫi-šenni son of Muš-apu
		2009+?	HSS 19 111	Urḫi-Kušuḫ DUMU LUGAL
		2173+2316	*EN* 9/2 77	Puḫi-šenni son of Muš-apu
		2206		fragment

[21] Starr (*Nuzi* 1, 316–17) places this text in S112. Catalogs locate HSS 16 311 in S129.
[22] See n. 17.
[23] See n. 17.
[24] No tablets mentioned in the excavation report.

TABLE 1. *Continued*

Group	*Room*	*SMN*	*Reference*	*Principal party; Comments*
		2300	HSS 16 229	Urḫi-Kušuḫ
		2301	*EN* 9/2 189	Hašip-Tilla son of Šeḫliya
		2302	*EN* 9/2 17	Muš-apu son of Purna-zini
		2303	*EN* 9/2 327	Puḫi-šenni
		2304	*EN* 9/2 526	Muš-apu son of Purna-zini
		2305	HSS 16 230	grain receipt
		2306		fragment; Unapšewe mentioned
		2307	*EN* 9/2 23	Puḫi-šenni son of Muš-apu
		2308	*EN* 9/2 493	Puḫi-šenni son of Muš-apu
		2309	*EN* 9/2 419	Puḫi-šenni son of Muš-apu
		2310		fragment
		2311	*EN* 9/2 175	Hanaya son of Tae
		2312	*EN* 9/2 171	Puḫi-šenni son of Muš-apu
		2313	*EN* 9/2 143	Muš-apu son of Purna-zini
		2314	*EN* 9/2 74	Puḫi-šenni son of Muš-apu
		2315	*EN* 9/2 334	Puḫi-šenni son of Muš-apu
		2316		see SMN 2173
		2317		fragmentary grain loan
		2318		fragment
		2319+2321	*EN* 9/2 146	Puḫi-šenni
		2320	*EN* 9/2 527	Puḫi-šenni son of Mu[š-apu]
		2321		see SMN 2319
		2322		fragment
		2323	*EN* 9/2 49	Muš-apu son of Purna-zini
		2324		fragment
		2325		fragment
		2326		fragment
		2327		fragment
		2328		fragment
		2329		fragment
		2330		fragment
		2331		fragment
		2332	HSS 19 8	Muš-apu son of Purna-zini
19	S129[25]	1854	HSS 16 449	Puḫi-šenni son of Muš-apu
		2091	*EN* 9/2 22	Puḫi-šenni son of Muš-apu
		2095	*EN* 9/2 21	Puḫi-šenni son of Muš-apu
		2333[26]	*EN* 9/2 490	Urḫi-kušuḫ
		2334	*EN* 9/2 323	Puḫi-šenni son of Muš-apu
		2335	*EN* 9/2 362	Puḫi-šenni son of Muš-apu

[25] "Several tablets in bad condition," according to the excavation report.

[26] Assigned to both S127 and S129 in notes. No room labeled S127 is listed in the excavation report.

TABLE 1. *Continued*

Group	*Room*	*SMN*	*Reference*	*Principal party; Comments*
		2336	*EN* 9/2 358	Puḫi-šenni
		2337	*EN* 9/2 73	Paya son of Elḫip-šarri
		2338	*EN* 9/2 158	Urḫi-šarri son of Ḫanaya
		2339		Puḫi-šenni?
19	S130[27]	2010	*EN* 9/2 83	statement in court (?)
		2124	*EN* 9/2 297	Ariḫ-ḫamanna son of Ḫamutta
		2126	HSS 19 145	Ḫašip-apu son of Nūr-abu
		2343		fragment
		2344	HSS 14 155	Unap-Tešup
		2345	*EN* 9/2 236	Ḫašip-tilla
19	S132[28]	2075	*EN* 9/2 384	Irašu son of Akitte
		2077	*EN* 9/2 329	Puḫi-šenni
		2079	*EN* 9/2 340	Pašši-Tilla son of Pula-ḫali
		2081	*EN* 9/2 342	Pašši-Tilla son of Pula-ḫali
		2104	HSS 19 67	Tarmiya son of Ḫuya
		2141	AASOR 16 79	Hašip-Tilla son of Kipuya
		2349	*EN* 9/2 352	sons of Pula-ḫali
		2350	*EN* 9/2 331	Eteš-šenni son of Ḫapira
		2351	*EN* 9/2 452	Wuḫḫura
		2352	*EN* 9/2 357	Ḫašip-Tilla son of Kip-ukur
		2353		Tieš-urḫe and Urḫi-Tilla mentioned
		2354	*EN* 9/2 93	list of fields
		2355	HSS 16 313	livestock record
		2356		Pašši-Tilla son of Pula-ḫali
		2357	*EN* 9/2 478	list of horses
		2358	*EN* 9/2 324	Minaššuk
		2358A	*EN* 9/2 371	[Šeḫ]al-tešup son of [Teḫ]up-šenni
		2359	*EN* 9/2 339	Pula-ḫali
		2360		Hašip-Tilla
		2361	*EN* 9/2 111	fragmentary letter
		2362	*EN* 9/2 31	Arikkaya son of Eteš-šenni
		2363	*EN* 9/2 337	Taika son of A[ ]
		2364		
		2365	*EN* 9/2 292	Pašši-Tilla son of Pula-ḫali
		2366	*EN* 9/2 32	Huziri son of Arikkaya
		2367	*EN* 9/2 157	Muš-apu
		2368	*EN* 9/2 209	Pula-ḫali

[27] No tablets mentioned in the excavation report.
[28] "A large number" of tablets, according to the excavation report.

TABLE 1. *Continued*

Group	*Room*	*SMN*	*Reference*	*Principal party; Comments*
		2369	HSS 19 97	sons of Pula-ḫali
		2370	*EN* 9/2 291	Hašip-Tilla son of Kip-ukur
		2371	*EN* 9/2 387	Šamaš-dayyānu (?)
		2372	*EN* 9/2 440	Pašši-Tilla son of Pula-ḫali
		2373	*EN* 9/2 505	Pašši-Tilla son of Pula-ḫali
		2374	*EN* 9/2 441	lawsuit
		2375	HSS 19 43	^{f}Šušenna
		2377	*EN* 9/2 207	Hašip-Tilla
		2378	HSS 19 36	^{f}Ulūlîtu
		2379	*EN* 9/2 374	Pašši-Tilla son of Pula-ḫali
		2380	*EN* 9/2 102	Kipa-lenni son of Pula-ḫali
		2381	*EN* 9/2 344	Pašši-Tilla son of Pula-ḫali
		2382	*EN* 9/2 347	Waḫra son of Paššiya
		2383		Pašši-Tilla son of Pula-ḫali
		2384	*EN* 9/2 346	Pašši-Tilla son of Pula-ḫali
		2385	*EN* 9/1 134	Elḫip-Tilla
		2386		fragment
		2387	*EN* 9/2 325	[ ]wiya son of [ ]
		2388	*EN* 9/1 233[29]	Šerta-ma-ilu
		2389		Eteš-šenni son of Ḫabira
		2390	*EN* 9/2 10	Utḫap-tae son of Ar-tura
		2391	*EN* 9/2 477	Etes-šenni son of Ḫabira
		2392	*EN* 9/1 350	record of horses and chariots
		2393	*EN* 9/2 364	Paššiya
		2394		fragment
		2395		fragment
		2396		Pašši-Tilla son of Pula-ḫali
		2397		fragment
		2398		fragment
		2399		fragmentary text concerning chariots
		2400	HSS 16 420[30]	grain ration text
		2401	*EN* 9/2 283	Pašši-Tilla son of Pula-ḫali
		2402		Niḫriya
		2403	HSS 16 231	Pašši-Tilla son of Pula-ḫali
		2404	HSS 19 60[31]	Paikku son of Ariḫ-ḫarpa
		2405	*EN* 9/2 513	Pašši-Tilla
		2406–2413		fragments
		2414	*EN* 9/2 356	Tupkiya
		2415–2417		fragments
		2418	*EN* 9/2 289	[ ] son of Ar-tura

[29] Most likely belongs to the Southwest Archives. See Morrison, SCCNH 2:177, 185, and 201.
[30] Belongs to the archives of Šilwa-Tešup.
[31] Most likely belongs to the Southwest Archives. See Morrison, SCCNH 2:177, 185, and 201.

TABLE 1. *Continued*

Group	*Room*	*SMN*	*Reference*	*Principal party; Comments*
		2419–2425		fragments
		2429		Utḫap-tae son of Siabi
		2519	*EN* 9/2 145	Muš-apu son of Purna-zini
19	S133[32]	2099	AASOR 16 59(C 133)	Ḫuya
		2426	*EN* 9/2 212	Šamaš-iluni son of Bēl-aḫḫē
		2427	HSS 19 13	Ila-nîšū son of Šurukka
		2428	*EN* 9/2 268	Paššiya son of Pula-ḫali
		2430	HSS 13 143	Niḫriya son of Ḫuziri
		2431	HSS 19 137	fragmentary text
		2432		fragment
		2433		Puḫi-šenni?
		2434	*EN* 9/2 348	Kipal-enni son of Pula-ḫali
		2435	HSS 19 99	Pašši-Tilla son of Pula-ḫali
		2436		Ḫašiya?
		2437		fragment of large tablet
		2438	*EN* 9/2 110	seal of Teḫip-Tilla son of Puḫi-šenni
		2439	*EN* 9/2 97	Kipal-enni son of Pula-ḫali
		2440		fragment
		2441		fragment
		2442		fragment
		2443	*EN* 9/2 224	Pašši-Tilla
		2444	HSS 16 375	list of names
		2445	*EN* 9/2 349	Paššiya son of Pula-ḫali
		2446	*EN* 9/2 529	Pašši-Tilla son of Pula-ḫali
		2477–2473		fragments
19	S136[33]	2125+2476	*EN* 9/2 176	Zikaya son of Hu[ziri]
		2475	*EN* 9/2 129	letter
		2476+2125		see SMN 2125
		2477–2478		fragments
19	S152[34]	2132	*EN* 9/2 172	Gimil-abi son of Akip-apu
		2376	*EN* 9/2 33	Pašši-Tilla
Tablets with no room numbers				
		1448	*EN* 9/2 524	sons of Pula-ḫali
		1684	*EN* 9/2 128	Muš-apu
		1700+2817	HSS 19 19	Tarmiya son of Ḫuya
		2002	*EN* 9/2 188	Puḫi-šenni son of Muš-apu

[32] The excavation report simply mentions "tablets."
[33] "A few tablets," according to the excavation report.
[34] No tablets mentioned in the excavation report.

TABLE 1. *Continued*

Group	*Room*	*SMN*	*Reference*	*Principal party; Comments*
		2004	*EN* 9/2 184	Šeḫal-Tešup son of Teḫup-šenni
		2102	*EN* 9/2 152	Utḫap-tae son of Ar-tura
		2117	HSS 19 134	Utḫap-tae son of Ar-tura
		2142	*EN* 9/2 343	Paššі-Tilla son of Pula-ḫali
		2143	*EN* 9/2 200	Tarmiya son of Ḫuya
		2250	*EN* 9/2 515	Paššі-Tilla
		2340		fragment
		2341		fragment
		2342		fragment
		2509		fragment
		2690	*EN* 9/2 345	Paššі-Tilla son of Pula-ḫali
		2702	HSS 14 22	Šeḫal-Tešup son of Teḫup-šenni
		2706	*EN* 9/2 81	Ennaya son of Eteš-šenni
		2708	*EN* 9/2 264	Tarmiya
		2709	HSS 19 30	Tarmiya son of Ḫuya
		2719		sons of Pula-ḫali
		2733	*EN* 9/2 45	Paya son of Elḫip-šarri
		2773	*EN* 9/2 267	sons of Pula-ḫali
		2777	*EN* 9/2 275	Puḫi-šenni son of Muš-apu
		2803	*EN* 9/2 144	Muš-apu
		2821	*EN* 9/2 168	Tarmiya
		3538	*EN* 9/2 512	Paššі-Tilla son of Pula-ḫali
		3543	*EN* 9/2 525	[Puḫi-šen]ni son of Muš-a[pu]
Tablets assigned to rooms outside of eastern area				
	C28	3145	HSS 19 120	Utḫap-tae son of Ar-tura
	F24	3483	*EN* 9/2 46	Arikkaya son of Eteš-šenni
	G73	3657	*EN* 9/2 118	Eḫlip-apu son of Apeya
	N120[35]	2094	AASOR 16 97(C 120)	sons of Pula-ḫali
		2107	*EN* 9/2 262	Utḫap-tae son of Ar-tura
		2113	*EN* 9/2 336	Puḫi-šenni son of Muš-apu
		2114	*EN* 9/2 67	Utḫap-tae son of Ar-tura
		2116	*EN* 9/2 353	sons of Pula-ḫali
		2208	*EN* 9/2 125	Šeḫal-Tešup
		2221	*EN* 9/2 250	Paššiya
		2237	HSS 19 11	Utḫap-tae son of Ar-tura
		2244	HSS 19 86	Utḫap-tae son of Ar-tura

[35] N120 is the source of the ^{f}Tulpunnaya archives. Note the ^{f}Tulpunnaya text (*EN* 9/2 27) assigned to S113, a reverse example of confusion among these archives. See also HSS 15 29 (SMN 2195) assigned to S113 in Lacheman's dissertation but to N120 in the register to HSS 15.

TABLE 1. *Continued*

Group	*Room*	*SMN*	*Reference*	*Principal party; Comments*
		2245	*EN* 9/2 166	Paya son of Elḫip-šarri
		2246	*EN* 9/2 391	Pašši-Tilla son of Pula-ḫali
		2248	*EN* 9/2 401	son of Kuššiya
	P382[36]	2579	*EN* 9/1 99	letter mentioning Tarmiya; Southwest or Eastern Archives?
	P428[37]	2620	*EN* 9/2 301	Puḫi-šenni son of Muš-apu
	P465[38]	2674	*EN* 9/2 326	Muš-apu son of Purna-zini
	P480[39]	2680	*EN* 9/2 333	Puḫi-šenni son of Muš-apu
	P485[40]	2681	*EN* 9/2 299	Pašši-Tilla son of Pu[la-ḫali]

[36] Confusion between the southwest area and the eastern area has been shown. See n. 14 above. On the basis of the personal names and contents of these texts they probably originated in the Eastern Archives.

[37] See n. 36.

[38] See n. 36.

[39] See n. 36.

[40] See n. 36.

CHAPTER 2

The Family of Ḫuya: Texts from Group 18A

The Archeological Context of the Tablets

The building known as Group 18A (including rooms N163–N337, N343, N364, N316, S151, S307, and S304), like many of the Nuzi buildings, offers primarily architectural rather than artifactual evidence (see fig. 1). The artifacts from Group 18A are rather poor: ordinary pottery from the large room and a potstand from S151. Even the architectural information is incomplete because Group 18A was not exposed entirely during the excavations (see fig. 1).[1] What does exist of the building presents certain archeological problems. First, the room apparently comprised of N337 and N163 probably was a courtyard because it is exceptionally wide, but its entryway and others in the building are poorly preserved.[2] Further, it is not clear whether or how this large room was separated from S153, part of Group 18, which itself is a most-irregularly shaped cluster of rooms. It is possible, therefore, that Group 18A is a wing of Group 18. An important feature of the building is the stepped corridor, room S151, that leads down some 26 cm from the paved courtyard N316 to S307 and appears to connect earlier construction in the area to the later parts of Group 18A.[3] In this corridor, according to the excavation report, sixty-five tablets were found. Like the potstand mentioned above, they were probably stored originally in S307 and were "thrown out of that room during the looting of the building."[4] Tablet registers and other materials, however, record only forty-two tablets and thirty-four fragments associated with S151.[5]

The majority of these texts refers to members of the family of Ḫuya son of Šimika-atal, Tarmiya son of Ḫuya in particular. As might be expected, some texts assigned to this room belong to other individuals whose archives are located in the eastern area and elsewhere.[6] In addition, a few texts whose parties

[1] R. F. S. Starr, *Nuzi* 1:296 and 312.

[2] Ibid., 312–13.

[3] Ibid., 313.

[4] Ibid.

[5] See Group 18A in table 1 above, pp. 12–13.

[6] Among them, *EN* 9/2 455 belonging to Puḫi-šenni [son of Muš-apu], HSS 19 126 belonging to Pašši-Tilla son of Pula-ḫali, *EN* 9/2 38 belonging to Muš-apu, HSS 16 228 and 419 belonging to the archives of Šilwa-Tešup (like HSS 16 420, for which see below, p. 67). *EN* 9/2 204 and 279 mention an Eḫli-Tešup. In light of the frequent confusion among texts belonging to the southwest and eastern areas, these two should probably be assigned to the archives of Eḫli-Tešup

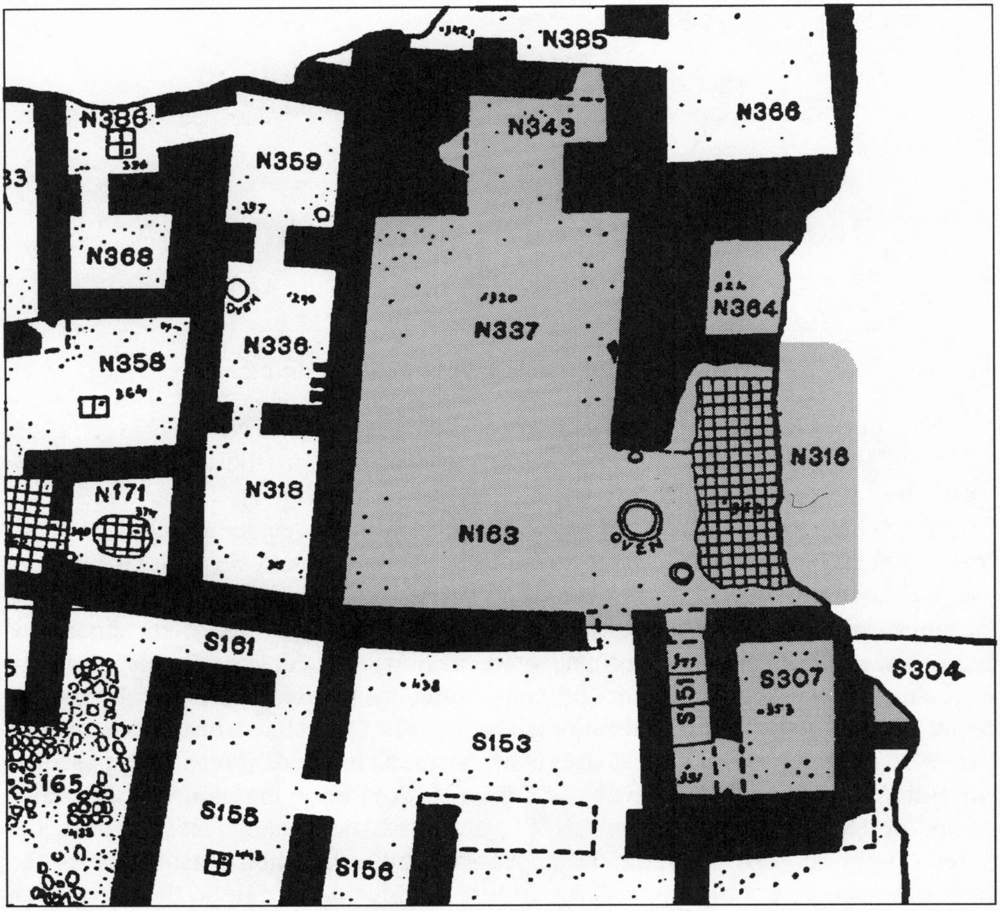

FIGURE 1. *Group 18A* (from Starr, *Nuzi II*)

are not known to have been involved with the family of Ḫuya son of Šimika-atal[7] and some miscellaneous administrative documents and fragments[8] are assigned to S151. On the other hand, texts belonging to members of this family have been associated with rooms in Group 19 in the area east of the palace[9] and elsewhere at Nuzi[10] or lack room numbers altogether.[11]

---

son of Taya. (On this individual and his family, see M. A. Morrison, "The Southwest Archives at Nuzi," SCCNH 2:169–74.)

[7] E.g., *EN* 9/2 177, HSS 19 42, HSS 16 233, and *EN* 9/2 395.

[8] HSS 16 232, 376, and 377; SMN 2480, 2484, 2507–2509, 2515, 2516, 2521, 2523, 2524, 2527–2552.

[9] AASOR 16 59 (C133), *EN* 9/2 186 (S112), HSS 14 31 (S112), HSS 19 67 (S132), *EN* 9/2 34.

[10] Probably *EN* 9/1 99 (P382) and possibly HSS 14 8. The latter is testimony in court and could well have not been kept in the archives of the family.

[11] HSS 19 19, 30; *EN* 9/2 168, 200, 262, 264, 372(?).

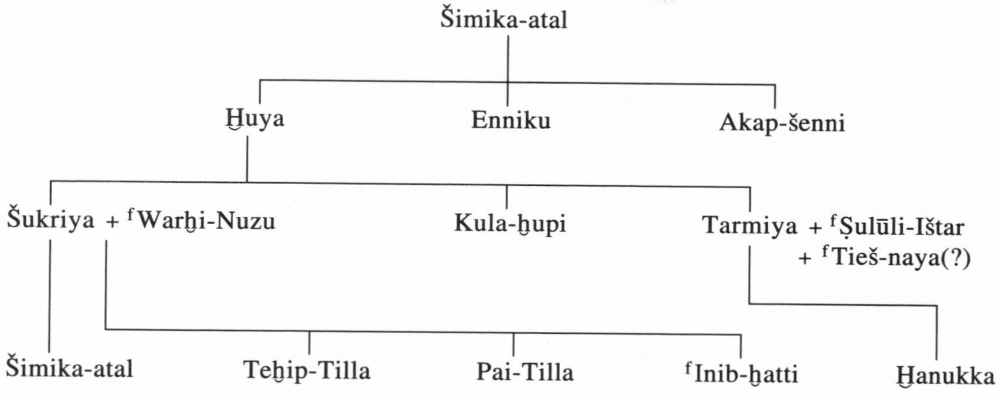

FIGURE 2. *Genealogy of the Family of Ḫuya*

The Genealogy and Chronology of the Family of Ḫuya

The archives of S151 combined with texts that undoubtedly were originally stored with this Group provide evidence for four generations of the family of Ḫuya son of Šimika-atal and offer considerable insight into this family's history. The will of Šukriya son of Ḫuya (HSS 19 5) gives the names of his wife ᶠWarḫi-Nuzu and his sons Teḫip-Tilla, Pai-Tilla and Šimika-atal, apparently Šukriya's son by another woman. Pai-Tilla's sister, ᶠInib-ḫatti, appears in a tablet recording testimony in court (HSS 14 8).[12] Proceedings from yet another court case (AASOR 16 56) provide the names of ᶠṢulūli-Ištar, an *amtu* given to Tarmiya as a wife (lines 15–16), and Kula-ḫupi, brother of Šukriya and Tarmiya (lines 3–4).[13] Though badly broken and lacking a room number, HSS 19 19 may be Tarmiya's will. If so, it gives the name of his wife Tieš-naya.[14] Ḫuya's patronymic is reconstructed on the basis of the texts from the archives that involve Ḫuya son of Šimika-atal (*EN* 9/2 35 and 206[?], and *EN* 9/1 461). AASOR 16 59 is the source for the names of Ḫuya's brothers. Ḫanukka son of Tarmiya is included in the family because the adoption text involving him (*EN* 9/2 34) is assigned to room S151 of Group 18A. The genealogy of this family, to the extent that it is now known, can be reconstructed as shown in fig. 2.[15]

[12] For discussion of HSS 19 5, see J. Paradise, *NIP*, text C-22, pp. 96–101; and, more recently, K. Deller in SCCNH 1:48–57. The resolution of Šimika-atal's status is based on the fact that he is prohibited from inheriting ᶠWarḫi-Nuzu's property (lines 57–58). For HSS 14 8, see n. 63 below.

[13] On this text, see E. A. Speiser, "I Know Not the Day of My Death," *Oriental and Biblical Studies* (Philadelphia: University of Pennsylvania, 1967) 91–92.

[14] Paradise, *NIP*, text C-16, pp. 74–79. Paradise observes that ᶠTieš-naya was a second wife of the Tarmiya in question (p. 78), a fact that would square with the existence of ᶠSululi-Ištar. Alternatively, E. Cassin (*AAN*, p. 146 *sub* ᶠTieš-naya) identifies this woman as Tarmiya's daughter or wife.

[15] See Paradise, *NIP*, 388, chart 12, for an earlier version of this genealogy.

The chronological positions of members of this family within the larger framework of the Nuzi documents may be established by reference to the scribes who write texts in which they are involved and who associate with individuals whose generations are known. The scribes who write for Ḫuya include:

Arim-matka	*EN* 9/2 35
^{d}AK-DINGIR.RA [son of Sîn-napšir] (III)	AASOR 16 59

These scribes also write for members of families that are well known at Nuzi ^{d}AK-DINGIR.RA, who belongs to the third generation of the scribal family of Apil-Sîn,[16] writes for Teḫip-Tilla son of Puḫi-šenni,[17] Akkuya son of Katiri,[18] Akap-šenni son of Zike,[19] Šilwa-Tešup DUMU LUGAL,[20] ^{f}Tulpun-naya,[21] and for the Kušši-ḫarbe trial.[22] Arim-matka writes for Akkuya son of Katiri,[23] Ar-šatuya son of Šellapai,[24] and for Taya son of Arim-matka.[25] In addition, Ḫampizi son of Ar-šatuya, whose documents are found in the southwest area and who dates to the third and fourth generations of the scribal family of Apil-Sîn,[26] appears as a witness in AASOR 16 59:18, 37.

The scribes who write texts in which the sons of Ḫuya appear include:

Abī-ilu son of ^{d}AK-DINGIR.RA (IV)	*JEN* 105 (Šukriya)
Akap-šenni [most likely son of Šukriya] (IV)	HSS 16 321 (Tarmiya)
Arip-šarri[27]	HSS 19 5 (Šukriya), *EN* 9/2 186 (Tarmiya and Kula-ḫubi son of Ḫuya), *EN* 9/2 187 (Tarmiya, Teḫip-Tilla, and ^{f}Warḫi-Nuzu)
Baltu-kašid [most likely son of Apil-Sîn] (II)	*EN* 9/2 392 (Tarmiya)
Enna-mati [son of Puḫi-šenni][28]	*EN* 9/2 101 (Tarmiya)
Iluya son of Sîn-napšir (III)	AASOR 16 56 (Tarmiya and his brothers)

[16] Only one scribe ^{d}AK-DINGIR.RA is known, the son of Sîn-napšir, hence his identification here.

[17] *JEN* 137, 149, 152, 175, 178, 194, 474, 480, and 481.

[18] HSS 5 84.

[19] HSS 5 101.

[20] HSS 9 151.

[21] AASOR 16 15, 16, and 17.

[22] AASOR 16 4.

[23] HSS 5 64:21.

[24] HSS 19 9:33–35. This individual dates at least to the second generation of the scribal family of Apil-Sîn. See Morrison, SCCNH 2:176.

[25] *EN* 9/1 75. On this individual, see Morrison, SCCNH 2:179–81 and fig. 1.

[26] See Morrison, SCCNH 2:176 and fig. 1.

[27] On Arip-šarri, see Deller, SCCNH 1:50. See also HSS 14 593 where an Arip-šarri is identified as DUB.SAR (line 44) and ÌR É.GAL (line 59).

[28] Three scribes of this name are attested at Nuzi: son of Itḫ-apiḫe, son of Puḫi-šenni, and son of Šamaš-ilu-ina-māti. Enna-mati son of Puḫi-šenni is known to have written in Ar-šalipe where this text originated (see *JEN* 403). See also p. 81 for this scribe in Unapšewe.

Nanna-adaḫ	AASOR 16 63 (Šukriya)
Niḫriya[29] (?)	*EN* 9/2 273 (Tarmiya)
Rim-Sîn[30]	*EN* 9/2 76 (Šukriya)
SAG-AN.KI	*EN* 9/2 168 (Tarmiya and Teḫip-Tilla)
Sîn-šadūni (most likely son of Amur-šarri; V of the family of Inb-Adad)	HSS 19 67 (Tarmiya), HSS 19 30 (Tarmiya and Teḫip-Tilla, Pai-Tilla and ^{f}Warḫi-Nuzu), *EN* 9/2 264.
Šimanni-(Adad) son of ^{d}AK-DINGIR.RA (IV)	*JEN* 370 (Tarmiya), *EN* 9/2 40 (Tarmiya)
[Ši-ma-]-an-ni[31]	*EN* 9/2 185 (Tarmiya)
Turar-Tešup[32]	*EN* 9/2 16 (Tarmiya)

These scribes also write texts for and concerning individuals whose chronological positions are well known. From the family of Teḫip-Tilla son of Puḫi-šenni some of these scribes write for Teḫip-Tilla and Ḫaiš-Tešup (third generation),[33] Enna-mati son of Teḫip-Tilla (fourth generation),[34] the sons of Teḫip-Tilla (fourth generation),[35] Tarmi-Tilla son of Šurki-Tilla (fifth generation),[36] and Tieš-urḫe son of Takku (fifth generation).[37] The members of the family of Katiri for whom some of these scribes write are Zike son of Akkuya (third generation),[38] Akap-šenni son of Zike (fourth generation),[39] Akawatil son of Zike (fourth generation),[40] and from the same archives of room A34, Ilānu son of Taiuki.[41] In the archives of Šilwa-Tešup DUMU LUGAL a number of these scribes write for his servants.[42] Individuals from the Southwest Archives who employ some of the same scribes include Ḫampizi son of Ar-šatuya, who dates to the third and fourth scribal generations,[43] Eḫli-Tešup son of Taya who dates to

[29] Read from the left edge: NA$_4$ *Ni-iḫ-ri-ya* DUB.S[AR].

[30] Attested elsewhere only on HSS 19 22:29. See G. Wilhelm, AOAT 9:11 n. 13.

[31] Šimanni [son of ^{d}AK-DINGIR.RA]?

[32] Two scribes of this name are attested: son of Itḫ-apiḫe and son of Kel-Tešup. Either is possible chronologically.

[33] Balṭu-kašid son of Apil-Sîn: *JEN* 2, 24, 63, 72, 75, 76, 148, 170, 173, 183, 187, 203, 210, 235, 240, 244, 250, 258, 260, 263, 275, 406, 417, 439, 484, 555; and NCBT 1934 = Yale Text 16 [SCCNH 1:396]; Iluya son of Sîn-napšir: *JEN* 226 and 438.

[34] Nanna-adaḫ: *JEN* 618.

[35] Akap-šenni: *JEN* 470.

[36] Šimanni-Adad son of ^{d}AK-DINGIR.RA: *JEN* 115, 296, 370, 573, 608, 663.

[37] Šimanni-Adad son of ^{d}AK-DINGIR.RA: *JEN* 669.

[38] Nanna-adaḫ: HSS 5 7, 60, 67.

[39] Nanna-adaḫ: HSS 5 43.

[40] SAG-AN.KI: HSS 5 14, 39.

[41] Abī-ilu: HSS 9 107; Arip-šarri: HSS 9 97 and 102; SAG-AN.KI: HSS 5 12:case, 31; 16:35; 18:47; 89:36, 41; 91:case, 42; 95:21; 98:20; HSS 9 105:40, 45; 106:45; 110:39; 155:21; Šimanni-Adad son of ^{d}AK-DINGIR.RA: HSS 9 101.

[42] For Pai-Tešup: Abī-ilu son of ^{d}AK-DINGIR.RA: HSS 9 19; Sîn-šadūni son of Amur-šarri: HSS 9 22; Šimanni-Adad son of ^{d}AK-DINGIR.RA: HSS 9 20 (Šimanni-Adad also appears in HSS 9 27 with Šilaḫi son of Šilwa-Tešup). For Bēl-aḫḫēšu the shepherd: Nanna-adaḫ: HSS 9 11. For ^{f}Ḫinzuraya the *amtu*: Šimanni-Adad son of ^{d}AK-DINGIR.RA: HSS 9 145.

[43] Abī-ilu son of ^{d}AK-DINGIR.RA: HSS 19 21 and 35. For the generations of the individuals from the Southwest Archives, see Morrison, SCCNH 2: fig. 1 and discussions of the families.

the third and fourth scribal generations,[44] fŠarum-elli daughter of Eḫli-Tešup who dates to the fourth generation,[45] Ar-taya son of Pui-tae who dates at least to the fourth generation and probably the third also,[46] fYamaštu daughter of Ninu-atal,[47] and Taya son of Arim-matka.[48] Some of these scribes are also associated with individuals who appear in the eastern area: Pašši-Tilla son of Pula-ḫali,[49] Šeḫal-Tešup son of Teḫup-šenni,[50] and Utḫap-tae son of Ar-tura.[51]

In addition, there are direct connections between some of these individuals and some well-known Nuzi figures. In one case (*JEN* 105), property is taken back from Šukriya son of Ḫuya and given to the sons of Teḫip-Tilla son of Puḫi-šenni. Further, Tarmi-Tilla son of Šurki-Tilla takes Tarmiya son of Ḫuya to court in *JEN* 370.

Members of the last generation of Ḫuya's family—Teḫip-Tilla and Pai-Tilla—appear in texts with their uncle Tarmiya, so they can be associated with some of the scribes above. Other scribes who write for the last generation of the family of Ḫuya son of Šimika-atal include:

Ar-puruša [most likely son of Tarmi-Tilla]	*EN* 9/2 34 (Ḫanukka son of Tarmiya)
Kaluppani son of Aḫu-šini	*EN* 9/2 234 (Teḫip-Tilla son of Šukriya)

Ar-puruša also writes for the wife and a servant of Šilwa-Tešup (HSS 5 66:36, 37, 40). Further, Ḫanukka son of Tarmiya witnesses a text of Eḫli-Tešup son of Taya (HSS 19 82:39).

Ḫuya is associated with a third-generation scribe and one who writes for people associated with the second generation; one of his witnesses is a third- and fourth-generation individual. The sons of Ḫuya are linked primarily with third- and fourth-generation scribes and interact with the fourth and fifth generations of the family of Teḫip-Tilla son of Puḫi-šenni. Ḫanukka son of Tarmiya witnesses a text of a third- and fourth-generation individual. It appears that Ḫuya's sons are to be located in the third and fourth generations. Ḫuya would, therefore, belong to the second and third generations and his grandson to the fourth. Within this schema, the appearance of Sîn-šadūni son of Amur-šarri of the last generation of his family might be dated in Tarmiya's later period. In any case, it ties him more firmly to a later date in the chronology. Balṭu-kašid son of Apil-Sîn who represents the second generation of his family, then, was active into the third generation, a reasonable supposition in light of the normal spans of activity for individuals at Nuzi.[52]

[44] Nanna-adaḫ: AASOR 16 64 and *EN* 9/1 196.

[45] Akap-šenni: HSS 19 89.

[46] Akap-šenni: HSS 19 127 and 128; SAG-AN.KI: HSS 19 118.

[47] Arip-šarri: HSS 19 12.

[48] Balṭu-kašid son of Apil-Sîn: *EN* 9/1 43.

[49] Abī-ilu son of dAK-DINGIR.RA: *EN* 9/2 349.

[50] Abī-ilu son of dAK-DINGIR.RA: *EN* 9/2 184.

[51] Arip-šarri: AASOR 16 58 and HSS 19 68; Šimanni-Adad son of Nabû-ila: HSS 19 113. On Arip-šarri, see Deller, SCCNH 1:50.

[52] See D. Stein, SSCNH 2:228, fig. 1.

On the basis of this chronology, the archives of room S151 line up nicely with the archives of the southwest area. First, the bulk of the texts from the Southwest Archives belongs to individuals who were active in the third and fourth generations. So, too, the majority of the texts in S151 dates to the third and fourth generations because they belong to Tarmiya son of Ḫuya. Such a concentration in the later periods in both areas is not surprising in light of the purpose and function of archives (as discussed in the introduction above). Also, the individuals from the two areas used some of the same scribes, and frequently witnessed each other's texts. With respect to the suburban mounds, the major part of the archives of S151 dates to the era of Šilwa-Tešup DUMU LUGAL and of the sons and grandsons of Teḫip-Tilla. As noted above, a few connections exist between the residents of the suburban mounds and Tarmiya's family. The implications of the relationships between the various parts of the city will be discussed further in the final chapter.

Ḫuya Son of Šimika-atal

Aside from the reference to Ḫuya in AASOR 16 56, in which Tarmiya testifies that Ḫuya gave him ᶠṢulūli-Ištar, Ḫuya appears in four texts in the archives: *EN* 9/2 35, *EN* 9/2 206, *EN* 9/1 461, and AASOR 16 59. In the first, *EN* 9/2 35,[53] Ḫuya receives houses in the heart of Nuzi from Wantip-šarri and Makuya sons of Zike through a standard real estate adoption:

> Tablet of adoption by which Wantip-šarri and Makuya the sons of Zike adopted Ḫuya the son of Šimi‹ka-a›tal. Whatever houses in the heart of Nuzi, they have given houses to Ḫuya as his inheritance share, and to these brothers he has given ten shekels of silver as their "gift." Whoever breaks the contract will pay one mina of silver and one mina of gold. ELEVEN WITNESSES. THREE SEALS.

In *EN* 9/2 206 Akkul-enni and Ar-teššše sons of Ar-[tirwi][54] give him two ANŠE of fields *ana titennūti* in return for grain and metal. If the patronymic is correct for these brothers, one of them, Ar-tešše, also adopts Teḫip-Tilla son of Puḫi-šenni and gives him houses in Turša.[55] *EN* 9/1 461, the lower part of the obverse of which is still preserved, records the debt of one Šaḫluya son of Tuliya[56] who owes Ḫuya "X" talents and thirty-one minas, presumably of some

[53] Some of the witnesses to this text are known elsewhere: line 13 Taiuki DUMU Eteš-šenni, see also HSS 13 490:23, *EN* 9 355:12, *JEN* 234:32; line 16 Eteš-šenni DUMU Wantiya, see also HSS 19 130:17; line 18 Taya DUMU Araya, see also HSS 14 111:32 and AASOR 16 10:6; line 17 Kizziri son of Ariḫ-Ḫarpa, see also *EN* 9 15:19, 26; line 21 Arim-matka the scribe, see p. 24 above.

[54] This name is tentatively restored on the basis of Lacheman's transliteration in *SCTN*: line 2 ù ᴵ*Ar-te-eš-še* DUMU.MEŠ ᴵ*Ar-[di-ir]-wa*. At the time the transliteration was made the *wa* sign appears to have been preserved.

[55] *JEN* 24:2, 11, 12. Balṭu-kašid son of Apil-Sîn and Itḫ-apiḫe son of Taya appear in that text as scribe and witness, respectively.

[56] The name is restored on the basis of *EN* 9/2 91:2 (N120), a memo recording a transaction concerning two ANŠE of Šaḫluya's fields.

sort of metal, a hefty sum, indeed. Preceding the reference to Šahluya it appears that another loan was recorded.

AASOR 16 59 is a particularly interesting document. Assigned to room S133 (at the time of its publication still called C133) in Group 19, it involves a Ḫuya and two men, Enniku and Akap-šenni sons of Šimika-atal. It records the penalty to be imposed if: (1) the two men raise a claim against Ḫuya or Ḫuya's descendants concerning the property of Šimika-atal; or if (2) Ḫuya forces the two men to do the *ilku* on the property of Šimika-atal. Apparently, this text refers to a transaction whereby Ḫuya took ownership of houses and fields of Šimika-atal with the agreement that he would bear the *ilku*. The text reports that the tablet was given to Ḫuya (line 17). Ḫuya son of Šimika-atal is the only Ḫuya in the eastern area, so it is most likely that this text represents the completion of the division of Šimika-atal's property among his heirs.[57] Thus, Enniku and Akap-šenni would be Ḫuya's brothers. These two men do not appear elsewhere at Nuzi, however, so their circumstances are not known.

Šukriya Son of Ḫuya

Šukriya son of Ḫuya is attested in six texts: HSS 19 5, AASOR 16 56 and 63, *JEN* 105, *EN* 9/2 76, and UCP 9. Though few in number, these texts indicate that Šukriya was a man of substance who was active in the standard forms of exchange at Nuzi. AASOR 16 63 is a personal *titennūtu* by which Artešše son of Ḫanaya enters Šukriya's house for twenty years in exchange for a "three-cubit" slave from the land of Lullu.[58] *JEN* 105 is the statement of Innikaya son of Šekar-Tilla who takes property back from Šukriya son of Ḫuya in order to give it to the sons of Teḫip-Tilla. Apparently, Šukriya had received it from Innikaya's father, Šekar-Tilla, who had seized it from the sons of Teḫip-Tilla. Although not all of the circumstances of this case are clear,[59] it does point to Šukriya's activity in real estate acquisitions and competition among families acquiring real estate. One wonders how and why Šukriya received this property whose title surely must have been problematic. *EN* 9/2 76 also involves real estate and records the exchange of fields between Šukriya and Šekar-Tilla son of Tarwa-zaḫ:[60]

[57] See Paradise, *NIP*, 234ff. on the *ilku* obligations of heirs. See also texts concerning the division of property (*RA* 23 6, 7, 15; HSS 5 99; HSS 13 114; HSS 19 61) and *NIP*, 343ff.

[58] Eichler, *IN*, 122–23, text 26.

[59] On this text, see Maidman, *SEANFA*, 599 n. 16 and 604 n. 56, where the pertinent bibliography is cited.

[60] Line 2: Šekar-Tilla son of Tarwa-zaḫ is known as well from *RA* 23 69, a note concerning four ANŠE of his real estate in the *dimtu* of Arip-abulliwe cut by the road of Kizzuk. HSS 16 20:2 includes him as a *rākib narkabti*, and in HSS 16 377:10 he appears in a list of names, including that of Tarmiya son of Enna-mati. HSS 13 300:15 lists him as one of a number of men who reaped *iškari* ⟨fields⟩ of the palace. Among the witnesses, Ḫui-Tešup son of Maliya (line 19) is known from HSS 19 14:30, written in Nuzi; Tae son of Ar-teya (line 26) from HSS 5 30:20; HSS 13 4 321:24, 35; HSS 19 46:56, 68, written in Nuzi; Turari son of Šimika (line 27) from AASOR 16 63:21, 27 and *EN* 9/1 47:26, 37.

4 8 GIŠ.APIN A.ŠÀ *i+na* AN-*ta-nu* AN.ZA.GÀR *ša* ^{I}*Ḫu-ya*
5 [*i+n*]*a šu-pa-al* A.ŠÀ *ša* ^{I}*Ka*$_4$*-na-a-a*
6 ^{I}[*Še-ka*$_4$]*-ar-til-la a-na* ^{I}*Šúk-ri-ia*
7 [*it-ta-*]*din* ^{I}*Šúk-ri-ia ip-le-tù-šu ša Še-ka*$_4$*-ar-til-la*
8 [*i+na* A]N.ZA.GÀR *Ḫa-ša-ri im-ta-la-šu-nu-ti-ma*
9 *a+na* ^{I}*Še-ka*$_4$*-ar-til-la it-ta-din*

Eight *awēḫaru* of fields north of the district of Ḫuya, west of the field of Kanaya Šekar-Tilla gave to Šukriya, and Šukriya has fulfilled the compensation payment of Šekar-Tilla in the district of Ḫašari and has given (it) to Šekar-Tilla.

He also pays an *Ú-ti* [61] payment, either the "balance" or an excess amount, of an ox, a sheep, four ANŠE of grain, and four BÁN of wheat. Kula-ḫupi son of Ḫuya, Šukriya's brother, witnesses the text (lines 30, 34).

The Sons and Wife of Šukriya

Šukriya's will (HSS 19 5) speaks of his wife ^{f}Warḫi-Nuzu and his three sons, Teḫip-Tilla, Pai-Tilla, and Šimika-atal. The first two sons were sons of Šukriya's wife ^{f}Warḫi-Nuzu, but Šimika-atal appears to have been born to another woman.[62] In the will, Šukriya identifies Teḫip-Tilla as his chief heir and Pai-Tilla as the secondary heir. Teḫip-Tilla receives the DINGIR.MEŠ *ša* SAG.DU GAL (lines 10–12), and Pai-Tilla receives the DINGIR.MEŠ *ša* SAG.DU TUR (lines 21–22), presumably the household gods of Šukriya.[63] Additionally, Teḫip-Tilla receives a double share of the property remaining after the specific allotments of the will (lines 31–35), and Pai-Tilla receives a share according to his rank of *tertennu* (lines 36–37). Šimika-atal also receives property, but he cannot share in ^{f}Warḫi-Nuzu's estate. ^{f}Warḫi-Nuzu receives a house which she can keep until her death, after which Teḫip-Tilla will take it.

Šimika-atal son of Šukriya is not attested again either in S151 or in other Nuzi documents, so what happened to him and his property is not known. Similarly, Šukriya's economic condition and the circumstances his heirs faced at the time of his death are not attested directly in the texts. However, the documents in which Teḫip-Tilla and Pai-Tilla appear suggest that they had to struggle with growing adversity. Both Teḫip-Tilla and Pai-Tilla engage in real estate transactions whereby their transfer property to Tarmiya son of Ḫuya, their uncle (see below).

61 For this term see Maidman, *SEANFA*, 132–33 and nn. 222–27.

62 See n. 12.

63 This text is one of the Group of texts cited in connection with HSS 14 8 in which Pai-Tilla son of Šukriya goes to court with Akip-tašenni son of Tae concerning his family gods, his mother, and his sister. Among the studies treating this text and the issue of the household gods, see K. Deller, SCCNH 1:59ff.; E. Cassin, SCCNH 1:37; A. Draffkorn, "*Ilāni/Elohim*," *JBL* 76 (1957) 216–24; M. Greenberg, "Another Look at Rachel's Theft of the Teraphim," *JBL* 81 (1962) 239–48; M. Gevaryahu, "A Clarification of the Nature of Biblical Teraphim," *Beth Miqra* 3 (1963) 81–86; and Paradise, *NIP*, 237ff.

Teḫip-Tilla appears to have inherited not only real estate but also at least one debt which he had to clear. *EN* 9/2 234 is a *ṭuppi tamgurti* between Teḫip-Tilla on the one hand and Kaya and Zimmari sons of Qîšteya on the other concerning payment of eighteen ANŠE of grain borrowed by Šukriya from Qîšteya:[64]

> [Tablet of agree]ment whereby Teḫip-Tilla son of Šukriya agrees with Kaya and with Zimmari sons of Qîšteya concerning eighteen *imer*s of loaned grain. Thus (says) Teḫip-Tilla: "Šukriya my father received eighteen *imer*s of grain on loan from Qîšteya and now I, for the eighteen *imer*s of grain, give ten (shekels) of silver *ḫašaḫu*[*šen*]*nu* to Kaya and to Zimma[ri]." Thus (says) Kaya and thus (says) Zimmari: "From (this) day Teḫip-Tilla is not indebted to me. Formerly the loan tablets . . . of the loaned grain [of Šuk]riya and of . . . [Teḫ]ip-Tilla(??) I have broken this tablet and . . . they have broken [it]." Whoever breaks the contract will pay one mina of silver and one mina of gold. The tablet was written after the proclamation at the Tišša Gate. FIVE WITNESSES. SCRIBE: Kaluppani son of Aḫu-šini. FIVE SEALS.

Pai-Tilla son of Šukriya is known as well from HSS 14 8. This text preserves his testimony in a suit against Akip-tašenni son of Tae concerning the loss of his gods, his mother, and his sister.[65] The circumstances surrounding this case are clouded, but at the very least it indicates that Pai-Tilla was in serious difficulty, perhaps caused by economic problems. Another reference to Pai-Tilla may occur in *EN* 9/2 103 which lists twenty-five men of the city of Nuzi to whom a Pai-Tilla gave A.MEŠ *ba-a-*tu_4.[66] Perhaps Pai-Tilla, like his uncle Tarmiya, was involved with the administration of irrigation.

^{f}Warḫi-Nuzu began her life as a widow with a house that she inherited from Šukriya and an "estate" of her own of indeterminate size and composition. In

[64] Kaya son of Qišteya is also known as a witness to a statement involving a real estate transfer to Teḫip-Tilla son of Puḫi-šenni (*JEN* 154:20) and to a *ṭuppi mārūti* by which Tarmi-Tilla son of Šurki-Tilla received property (*JEN* 402:32, 43).

[65] HSS 14 8 is assigned to P470 of the southwest area, but appears to be out of place there in light of the other materials in the area (see Morrison, SCCNH 2:201 n. 5). For discussions of this text, see the works cited in n. 63.

[66] The individuals listed include [Ša]r-Tešup son of Ut[ḫap-tae] (line 4), also known from HSS 14 37:1, 22 (identified as an *atuḫlu* in *AAN*, though the term follows the name of the other individual); HSS 15 57:4, 116:2, 12; HSS 19 119:4, 12, 14; *EN* 9/1 84:1ff. (*ṭuppi šupeʾʾulti* between Šar-Tešup and Kanaya son of Ikiya), 430:1ff., 434:1ff., 436:5ff. (three lawsuits), and 445:3ff.; *JEN* 321:70; [Ḫu]ite son of Akap-[tukke] (line 5), also known as a witness to *EN* 9/1 5:46; Kipa-urḫe son of Ḫu[pita] (line 6), also known as a witness in *JEN* 78:38; [E]ḫli-Tešup son of Kipa[ya] (line 7), also known from AASOR 16 58:1ff. and *EN* 9/2 262:1ff., and as a witness to *EN* 9/2 297:17 (see chap. 3 for Utḫap-tae son of Ar-Tura); [Tu]ra[r-Te]šup son of Kel-Tešup] (line 10 and left edge), known as a scribe who writes for sons of Zike (HSS 5 59:36, 41), for Ḫampizi son of Ar-šatuya (HSS 19 46:63), for the sons of Teḫip-Tilla and Ḫaiš-Tešup (*JEN* 324), and for Tarmi-Tilla son of Šurki-Tilla (*JEN* 102, 105, and 542); he is also known as the scribe of HSS 13 143:47 and *RN* 9 9:37, 42, and from CT 2 21:25, 32; Ḫerri son of Nanip-ukur (line 17), known also from HSS 9 101:2 (a *titennūtu* with Ilānu son of Taiuki) and HSS 16 466:15–16; Šellu son of Wantiya (line 18), also known from CT 2 21:23, 34. Note line 11: [ ] *Šúk-ri-ia*, possibly referring to a member of the family considered here.

addition, she figures in two of her son's real estate transactions (HSS 19 30 and *EN* 9/2 187). The first is a text in which Teḫip-Tilla and Pai-Tilla give Tarmiya real estate in return for movable property. The property in question was located in *dimtu* Ḫuya, where Šukriya's family holdings were located (see below). Clearly the land was part of the brothers' inheritance from Šukriya. In this text, she states: (20) *a-n*[*a* DUMU.MEŠ-*ya*] (21) *a-na a-bu-ti la ep-ša-ku-m*[*i*], 'I do not exercise the *abbūtu* right over [my sons].'[67] This could indicate either that she did not have the *abbūtu* right or that she chose not to exercise it. In the second text she and Teḫip-Tilla arrange for a *titennūtu* with Tarmiya concerning property in *dimtu* Šimika-atal, most likely linked to Šukriya's family. It is hard to imagine how ᶠWarḫi-Nuzu fell into the desperate circumstances described by the last text in which she appears, HSS 14 8, in which her son Pai-Tilla testifies about the loss of his gods and the sale of ᶠWarḫi-Nuzu and her daughter ᶠInib-ḫatti into a foreign land.

The assemblage of texts concerning Šukriya's heirs opens an array of questions not only about family law and inheritance practices but also about the personalities and relationships among these individuals. The dramatic decline of the family fortunes in a single generation and the seemingly anomalous behavior of members of the family might suggest that factors beyond those captured in the legal language of the texts were at work. Some efforts to untangle these matters appear on pp. 44ff. below.

Kula-ḫupi Son of Ḫuya

The second son of Ḫuya, Kula-ḫupi, is not particularly active in the texts that have been preserved at Nuzi. Aside from his participation in the court case, AASOR 16 56, he witnesses the exchange document of his brother Šukriya (*EN* 9/2 76:30, 34) and may possibly show up in *EN* 9/2 168, a text involving his other brother Tarmiya (line 30: IGI *Kul-la-ḫu-pi* D[UMU]). Like other members of the family, he engaged in a *titennūtu* with Tarmiya his brother (*EN* 9/2 186). In this transaction, he gave two parcels of land for five years *ana titennūti* in return for twelve ANŠE, one pi, one BÁN of grain, one ANŠE of wheat, four sheep, one goat, and one TÚG of standard weight,[68] all of which he received from Tarmiya *ana titennūti*. Located in the *dimtu* of Ḫuya, this property was probably part of Kula-ḫupi's inheritance.

Tarmiya Son of Ḫuya

The youngest of the three brothers according to AASOR 16 53, Tarmiya, is the best represented among the texts of S151. As the youngest, he would not be

[67] On this problem, see Deller, SCCNH 1:59; Cassin, SCCNH 1:39. For *abbūtu*, see Paradise, *NIP*, 285ff.; *CAD* A/1 48 s.v. *abbūtu*.

[68] Lines 10:13: 1 TÚG SIG$_5$-*qú na-aš-qú* 15 *i+na am-ma-*⟨*ti*⟩ *mu-ra-ak-šu* 5 *i+na am-ma-ti ru-pu-us-su* 4 *ku-duk-tu šu-qú-ul-ta-a ša* TÚG *an-nu-tu*. See C. Zaccagnini, SCCNH 1:353 and 359.

expected to receive a substantial share of his father's property.[69] Indeed, the court case suggests that his brothers begrudged him the *amtu*, ᶠṢulūli-Ištar, whom they apparently considered a part of their father's estate. Whatever his beginnings, Tarmiya built a sizable estate for himself, as his numerous transactions testify.

Tarmiya is known as a ᴸᵁ́*gugallu* 'irrigation officer'[70] from *EN* 9/2 392 and *JEN* 370. In the first he is the guarantor of a loan made by Šata son of Itḫ-apiḫe.[71] In the second he goes to court and loses to Tarmi-Tilla son of Šurki-Tilla in a case involving irrigation proceedings and an ox.[72] Litigation concerning irrigation certainly was not uncommon. Another text from the eastern area, HSS 14 31 (S112), is the response to judges who appear to be considering a complaint concerning the irrigation of a field:

> To the judges say: "Thus (says) Tarmiya the *alaḫḫinnu* of the palace of Ṣilliawe: 'The king gave those fields to me, and I spoke to Taya. He cut the border of those fields and water was released into the heart of the fields. Why does the owner of the fields complain about the fields?' "

The term *alaḫḫinnu* is understood to be an official of some sort who usually appears in connection with receipts of grain and the like.[73] Here, he is clearly a palace official testifying about irrigation problems. Tarmiya is, of course, a common name in the Nuzi texts. In light of the nature of the problem and the location of the tablet, the Tarmiya of this letter might be Tarmiya son of Ḫuya, known as an irrigation officer. However, Tarmiya would then be associated with the city of Ṣilliawe, a connection otherwise unattested. If Tarmiya did become an official of the palace whose responsibilities went beyond irrigation, the letter, *EN* 9/1 99, which concerns grain and straw to be given to a Tarmiya, may really belong to the Eastern Archives and relate to Tarmiya son of Ḫuya's official position. At least one other text from S151, *EN* 9/2 96, which lists fields held by certain individuals,[74] might relate to Tarmiya's irrigation responsibilities.

The texts documenting Tarmiya's personal activities testify to the normal range of real estate and personnel acquisitions, livestock ownership, and agreements concerning payments and the like. HSS 19 67 is a *ṭuppi aḫātūti* by which ᶠAzum-naya daughter of Ḫašeya takes Tarmiya son of Ḫuya as a brother, and Tarmiya agrees to arrange for her marriage.[75] *EN* 9/2 153 is the statement of

[69] Without Ḫuya's will the division of his estate is not known. While there are wills that divide paternal property equally, it is assumed that this was not the normal order of distribution. See Paradise, *NIP*, 258ff.

[70] *CAD* G 121 s.v. *gugallu*; W. Meyer, *Nuzi Studien* 1:129–31. Perhaps ᴸᵁ́*gugallu* is to be restored in *EN* 9/2 528:4 after Tarmiya's name.

[71] Šata son of Itḫ-apiḫe is known also from HSS 16 331:26 and 332:28.

[72] See C. Zaccagnini, *RLLA*, 63–65, for the text and bibliography.

[73] *CAD* A/1 295 s.v. *aliḫinnu*; Meyer, *Nuzi Studien*, 177.

[74] See also *EN* 9/2 93, from S132. These texts are reminiscent of HSS 9 32, concerning the lands irrigated or not irrigated by the *gugallu* of Anzugalli.

[75] Mentioned in Cassin, SCCNH 1:39 n. 15.

Ay-abāš who places his son Wantiš-še *ana titennūti* with Tarmiya.[76] Both of these texts were written in Nuzi.

Among Tarmiya's real estate transactions are three adoptions. In the first, *EN* 9/2 16,[77] Tarmiya receives from Wantiš-šenni son of [ ]:

4 [x+3] GIŠ.APIN A.ŠÀ *i-na šu-p[a-al ša* KASKAL-*ni*]
5 *ša* [URU]*Ta-ar-ku-ul-l[i-we]*

X+three *awēḫaru* of fields west of the road of Tarkulli

In the second, *EN* 9/2 36,[78] Tarmiya received from Ḫani-ašḫari son of [ ]:

2′ *ki-ma* ḪA.LA-*šu* 5 GIŠ.APIN A.[ŠÀ.MEŠ]
3′ *i+na* AN.ZA.GAR *Ka-az-zi-bu-u[z-zi]*
4′ *i+na il-ta-na-an-nu a-tap-pí*
5′ *ša Ar-ta-ma-aš-ši*

. . . as his inheritance share five *awēḫaru* of fields in the district of Kazzibuzzi, north of the Canal of Ar-tamašši. . . .

With a second parcel of one *awēḫaru* (lines 10–11), he received a total of six *awēḫaru* of fields (line 16).The last text, *EN* 9/2 106,[79] is understood as a real estate adoption because of the reference to the "gift" (line x+3) given by Tarmiya. The amount and location of the land are not preserved. All three of these adoption texts were written in Nuzi.

An interesting real estate document is *EN* 9/2 40:[80]

[76] Eichler, *IN*, text 13.

[77] On lines 4–5 the road of Tarkulli, see also *JEN* 134:6, 344:3, 355:3, 526:6, 591:6; L. R. Fisher, *NGN*, 41 no. 287; and most recently Fadhil, *STPPKA*, 151 and 285. Note line 27 Ḫuziri son of Šat[tu-marti] (cf. HSS 13 6:43).

[78] Line 5 the *dimtu* of Kazzibuzzi also occurs in *JEN* 126:7 and HSS 14 106:6. The second texts suggests that this *dimtu* was near Nuzi (line 9). Witnesses include line 33 Innabi son of Nuza (cf. HSS 16 188:5; *EN* 9 124:23); line 38 [E]ḫli-Tešup son of Keliya(?) (cf. HSS 19 127:3ff.); line 39 [Er]wi-šarri son of En-šukru (cf. *EN* 9/2 285:18 and *EN* 9/1 433:30).

[79] It is interesting that this text seems to have been the statement of Tarmiya in light of the verb form in line 6′ (*at-ta-din-mi*) used with respect to the goods given to the men ceding the property. The patronymic(s) of the three individuals contracting with Tarmiya are missing in the break at the beginning of the text. It is possible, however, that Šelluni (lines 5′, 8′, 11′) and Akawatil (lines 1′, 5′, 8′, 12′) were brothers, the sons of Akap-šenni, known from HSS 5 74:3–5. If so, this text would relate as well to the family of Katiri.

[80] Line 4 *paiḫu* 'unbuilt plot'; lines 4 and 5 *kirḫu*: for discussion of these terms and bibliography see Maidman, *SEANFA*, 376ff. and 413ff.; and Zaccagnini, *RLLA*, 113ff. and 26ff. Maidman translates *kirḫu* as 'citadel' in keeping with *CAD* K 405 s.v. Zaccagnini argues for "inner area of the rampart . . . [over which] in some cases, a proper wall might be erected." The BÀD sign restored in line 5 is based on a collation in Lacheman's notes made on 28/12/61, which indicates that the text was still preserved at that time (kindly pointed out to me by D. I. Owen). It recalls AASOR 16 58:4–10 in which a wall is mentioned in connection with the *kirḫu* of Nuzi. If BÀD was written in this text, it was the BÀD *ša kirḫi* 'wall of the *kirḫu*.' Whether this wall is to be distinguished from the city wall remains unclear. In any case, as noted below, p. 50, AASOR 16 58 does not offer any remarkable information concerning its interpretation.

EME-*šu ša* ^{I}*En-ni-ké* [DUMU Wantip-LUGAL?]
a-na pa-ni LÚ.MEŠ *ši-bu-*[*ti ki-a-am*]
iq-ta-bi mi-nu-um-me-e q[*a-aq-qáru*]
pá-i-ḫu i+na ŠÀ ^{URU}*Nu-zi i+na k*[*í-ir-ḫi*]
i+na šu-pa-al BÀD *ša kí-ir-ḫi i+na* [*il-ta-an*]
É.MEŠ *ša* ^{I}*Ar-tù-ra i+na su-ta-an* [É.ḪI.]A
ša ^{I}*Tar-mi-ya ù i+na e-li-en* É.MEŠ [ ]
iš-[*tu*] É.ḪI.A.MEŠ *ša* ^{I}*Wa-an-ti-ip-*L[UGAL]
ḪA.LA-*ya ša a-na li-qì-ya it-ti* ŠEŠ-[*ya*]
[*ša ni?-zu*]*-uz-zu ki-i-ma zi-me-e š*[*a*]*-a*
[*ù i-na-*]*an-na a-na-ku a-na* ^{I}*Tar-mi-ya* [DUMU *Ḫu-ya at-ta*]*-din*
[ù?] *a+na be-li-šu-ma un-te-eš-*[*še-er-šu-nu-ti*]
[*ù a-na-ku*] 20 MA.NA AN.NA.MEŠ *ù*
[ ] *ki-ma* ḪA.LA[-*ya*]
[*a-šar* ^{I}*Tar-mi-ya el*]*-te-qè*
[*ša l*]*i-qí-ya*
[ ] *ù a-na-ku*
[*a+n*]*a* ^{I}*Tar-mi-ya*
[*m*]*a-an-nu*
[*ša i+na be-ri-šu-nu*] KI.BAL-tu_4
[1 MA.NA KÙ.BABBAR 1 MA.NA KÙ.GI] DIRI

The statement of Ennike [son of . . .] before witnesses. He stated: "Whatever unbuilt plot in the heart of the city of Nuzi in the *kirḫu*, west of the wall of the *kirḫu*, [north] of the houses of Ar-tura, south of the [houses] of Tarmiya, and east of the houses of . . . , from the houses of Wantip-šarri, my inheritance share which as my portion with my brothers . . . [which we divided] for a price? . . . , now I have given to Tarmiya [and] to its owner I have released them. Twenty minas of tin and . . . as my inheritance share . . . from Tarmiya [I] have taken . . . of my inheritance share . . . and I . . . to Tarmiya . . . Whoever among them breaks the contract will pay [one mina of silver and one mina of gold]."

Six fragmentary names appear on the reverse, including that of the scribe [ ]-ni son of ^{d}AK-DINGIR.RA. The text is broken, so difficult to follow, but it seems to be more complicated than a typical adoption. Indeed, Ennike's father was probably Wantip-šarri who appears in line 8. He may be the Wantip-šarri who, with his brother, transferred houses in Nuzi to Ḫuya in *EN* 9/2 35 (see above). Perhaps this text records a settlement of some sort regarding the earlier agreement.

Two fragmentary *titennūtu* texts, *EN* 9/2 185[81] and *EN* 9/2 264,[82] record transfers of fields to Tarmiya. In the first text only the names of owners of

[81] In line 12 of this text it is clear that more than one individual leases the property to Tarmiya. The land is located south of the field of Paya (line 10). See *EN* 9/2 273 in which Paya son of Elḫip-šarri and Pai-Tešup son of Arteya exchange fields, Paya's plot bordering property of members of the family of Ḫuya. Note also *EN* 9/2 175. On line 30 [Aki]p-Tilla son of Nanip-[ukur], see HSS 5 36:23; on line 31 [Aka]watil son of Ellu, see HSS 5 8:3ff.; 19:9, 12; 26:4, 8, 13; 28:7, 8, 12; 40:5ff.; HSS 9 27:26; HSS 13 21:94; HSS 19 39:39, 41.

[82] Line 4 reads [*ni*]*-ra-*[*aš-ši ša* É.]GAL-*lì* or [*ni*]*-ra-*[*aš-ši ša An-zu*]*-gal-lì*. The second is known (*JEN* 154:6–6a), but there does not seem to be enough space between *ra* and *gal* for the

neighboring fields are provided (Wantiš-šenni, Paya, and Šabbire [lines 9–11]), but in the second, the land is located:

[GI]Š.APIN [A.]ŠÀ [*i+n*]*a e-le-en a-tap-pí*
[*ni-*]*ra-*[*aš-ši ša* É].GAL-*lì i+na*
[*e-le-en* A.ŠÀ *ša*] ^{I}*Tar-mi-ya*
[*i+na šu-pa-al* A.ŠÀ] *ša* ^{I}*A-mur*-GAL
[*i+na il-ta-an* A.ŠÀ] *ša* ^{I}*Ú-nap-ta-e*

EN 9/2 200 is a *tamgurtu* between Tarmiya and Ḫaiš-Tešup concerning the redemption of property that Tarmiya held in *titennūtu* from Zaziya son of Aittara. If Ḫaiš-Tešup does not produce the appropriate goods for Tarmiya, he will pay the *išpiku* of eight *awēḫaru* of fields to Tarmiya.[83]

By far the most interesting of Tarmiya's real estate activities are his arrangements with members of his family. The *titennūtu* with his brother Kula-ḫupi (*EN* 9/2 186) is discussed above. HSS 19 30, which involves Teḫip-Tilla and Pai-Tilla sons of Šukriya in either an exchange of "shares" or a real estate adoption, has long been linked with HSS 14 8 and other texts of this family.[84] *EN* 9/2 39 appears to be a *ṭuppi mārūti* because of the fragmentary beginning and the phrases ḪA.LA-*šu* and NÌG.BA-*šu* (lines 10 and 14):

[*ṭup-pí ma-ru-ti ša* ^{I}*Te-ḫi-ip-til-la*] *ù ša*
[^{I}*Pa-i-til-la* DUMU.MEŠ *Šúk-ri-ya*]
[*Tar-mi-ya* DUM]U *Ḫu-ya*
[*a-na ma-ru-t*]*i i-pu-us-sú*
[X ANŠE] A.ŠÀ *i+na* A.GÀR *ša* ^{URU}*Nu-zi*
[*i+na su-*]*pa-al* A.ŠÀ *ša* ^{I}*Pil-*[ ]
[*i+na il-ta-an*] A.ŠÀ *ša* ^{I}*Tar-m*[*i-ya*]
[*i+na su-ta-*]*an* A.ŠÀ *ša* ^{I}[ ]
[*ù i+na e-*]*le-en* A.ŠÀ *ša* ^{I}[ ]*-du-*[ ]
[*ki-ma*] ḪA.LA-*šu* ^{I}*Te-ḫi-ip-til-l*[*a*]
[*ù* ^{I}]*Pa-i-til-la a-na* ^{I}*Tar-mi-y*[*a id-di-nu*]
[*ù* ^{I}*Ta*]*r-mi-ya* 1 TÚG 1 ANŠE [ ]
[ ] 8 MA.NA AN.NA
[*ki-ma* NÌG.]BA-*šu-nu a+ne* ^{I}*Te-ḫi-*[*ip-til-la*]
[*ù a+na*] ^{I}*Pa-i-til-la it-ta-*[*din*]

[Tablet of adoption whereby Teḫip-Tilla and Pai-Tilla the sons of Šukriya] have [adopted Tarmiya] son of Ḫuya. A field in the *ugāru* of the city of Nuzi, west of the field of Pil[ ], [north] of the field of Tarmiya, [sou]th of the field of [ ], [and ea]st of the field of [ ]du[ ], Teḫip-Tilla and Pai-Tilla [have given] to Tarmiya [as] his

necessary signs. The first is reminiscent of HSS 19 30:3 *atappi* [*ša* É.G]AL-*lì*, as restored by Deller, SCCNH 1:57.

[83] This is a complicated arrangement. Apparently Tarmiya held the property that Ḫaiš-Tešup was acquiring. In order to do so, he had to pay whatever Tarmiya had given Zaziya for the land. Default is punished by Ḫaiš-Tešup's turning over the produce of the fields to Tarmiya.

[84] See discussions cited above in n. 63 and below in n. 85.

inheritance share. Tarmiya has given one garment, one *imer* . . . , and eight minas of tin [as] their "[gi]ft" to Teḫip-[Tilla] and Pai-Tilla.

The few remaining lines contain the normal prohibitions against changing the size of the field and the clearing of the claim.

A comparison of HSS 19 30 with *EN* 9/2 39 raises some interesting questions. They accomplish essentially the same purpose, that is, Tarmiya's receipt of land from his nephews in exchange for "liquid assets." The existence of *EN* 9/2 39 in which members of the same family engage in a real estate adoption contract might support the thesis that HSS 19 30 is an adoption text, not an exchange of "shares."[85] HSS 19 30 does refer to shares being given by each party, however. If the texts are taken at face value, one is cast in the language of inheritance and the other in the form of "real estate adoption" that has its roots, but not its reality, in inheritance practice. Is the first a true "exchange of shares"? If so, do the qualitatively different shares accurately reflect the shares originally received by the parties involved? Were the brothers and/or Tarmiya obligated to express the first transaction in terms of shares or did they choose to for personal reasons? Why is ᶠWarḫi-Nuzu involved in the first and not in the second?

If the first text is a true exchange of inheritance shares, an estate to which both Tarmiya and his nephews had claim must be found. Šukriya's will makes no mention of Tarmiya. We would hardly expect it to since Šukriya had his own family, and relations between Šukriya and Tarmiya may not have been all that good in light of the court case between the two. Both Tarmiya and his nephews, through their father Šukriya, were heirs to Ḫuya's estate, however. It is possible that the division of Ḫuya's estate lingered even after Šukriya's death and the first text represents the conclusion of the inheritance arrangements to the satisfaction of both Tarmiya and his nephews who had succeeded to their father's share of the estate. Perhaps Tarmiya as the youngest son did not receive real estate, certainly not a substantial amount, and found his inheritance, if any, to be primarily in the form of movable property. The brothers received real estate but needed movable property as their other records indicate. Alternatively, and more likely, it may be that the real estate involved belonged to family holdings dating back to a common ancestor of the parties to the contract, most likely Ḫuya. Transactions among family members involving such property might be transferred by means of "shares" texts without any need for establishing the recipient's right, however fictitious, to receive through an adoption text. If this is so, the second text represents a transfer of property acquired after Ḫuya's time. Tarmiya could legitimately be considered an heir to property of Ḫuya but was not directly in the line of inheritance for property acquired by his brother or nephews. In either possibility, the issue of ᶠWarḫi-Nuzu's *abbūtu* right might be involved in the first but not the second text because the shares text relates explicitly to the issue of her husband's inheritance position.

[85] See Deller, SCCNH 1:59.

In addition to the above-mentioned texts, members of the family engage in other real estate transactions with Tarmiya. *EN* 9/2 168 is a *titennūtu* whereby Teḫip-Tilla, undoubtedly the son of Šukriya, gives fields to Tarmiya:[86]

> . . . silver Tarmiya has given to Teḫip-Tilla. As soon as the years of the field are fulfilled and Teḫip-Tilla returns to Tarmiya whatever the silver (is) according to the word of this tablet, he will take his field. . . .

EN 9/2 187 is also a *titennūtu*, but this one involves both Teḫip-Tilla and ^{f}Warḫi-Nuzu, Šukriya's wife:[87]

[*ṭup-pí*] *ti-te-en-nu-ti ša* ^{I}*Te-ḫi-ip-til-la*
DUMU *Šúk-ri-ya ù ša* ^{f}*Wa-ar-*[*hi-nu*]*-zu*
aš-ša-at ša ^{I}*Šúk-ri-ya* 1 ANŠE 1 GIŠ.APIN A.ŠÀ *ši-qú-ú*
i+na AN.ZA.GÀR *ša* ^{I}*Ši-mi-ka*$_{4}$*-tal*
i+na e-le-en A.ŠÀ *ša* É.GAL*-lim*
i+na su-ta-na-nu a-tap-pí ni-ra-aš-ši
i+na il-ta-na-nu a-tap-pí ši-in-na-za-bul-ti
i+na šu-pa-al [A.ŠÀ] *ša* ^{I}*Tar-mi-ya*
a+na ti-te-[*en-nu-t*]*i a+na* 5 MU.MEŠ*-ti a+na*
[^{I}*Tar*]*-mi-ya* [DUMU *Ḫu*]*-ú-ya* SUM*-nu ù* ^{I}[*Tar-mi-ya*]
[x+] 1 ANŠE [ŠE 1 GU$_{4}$.]NITA SIG$_{5}$*-qá* [4 *na*]*-ar-bu*
[*a+n*]*a* ^{I}*Te-ḫi-ip-til-la ù a-na* ^{f}*Wa-*[*ar-ḫi*]*-nu-zu* SUM*-nu*
e-nu-ma 5 MU.MEŠ *im-ta-*[*lu ù* 1 ANŠE ŠE]
1 GU$_{4}$.NITA SIG$_{5}$*-qá du-um-na-a*[*r-bu-ú*]
^{I}*Te-ḫi-ip-til-la ù* ^{f}*Wa-ar-*[*ḫi-nu-zu*]
GUR*-ru*^{MEŠ} *ù* A.ŠÀ*-šu-nu i-liq-*[*qú-ú*]

> *Titennūtu* [tablet] whereby Teḫip-Tilla son of Šukriya and ^{f}War[ḫi-Nu]zu wife of Šukriya lease one *imer* one *awēḫaru* of irrigated fields in the district of Šimika-atal, east of the field of the palace, south of the *nirašši* canal, north of the *šinnazabulti* canal, west of the [field] of Tarmiya, for five years to [Tar]miya [son of Ḫ]uya. [Tarmiya] has given one+ *imer* of [grain and one] good [four-year]-old ox to Teḫip-Tilla and to Warḫi-Nuzu. When the five years are completed and Teḫip-Tilla and ^{f}War[ḫi-Nu]zu return [the grain] and the good four-year-old ox, they will take their field.

The usual clauses concerning claimants, size of field, and penalty for breach of contract appear. The tablet was written in Nuzi and witnessed by seven individuals, four of whom were surveyors.

Tarmiya's transactions with members of his family are summarized in Figure 3. Kula-ḫupi in *EN* 9/2 186 and Teḫip-Tilla in *EN* 9/2 168 act independently in leasing their land to Tarmiya. This certainly suggests that they were sole owners of the property transferred. The other transactions, however, involve combinations of family members of Šukriya's line. Efforts to understand

[86] Note that *Ku-la-ḫu-pi* D[UMU *Ḫu-ya*?] appears as a witness in line 23.

[87] On line 7 *atappi šinnazabulti* and line 32 Inna[bi DUMU Nuzza] see, n. 77 above. On line 36 Kelteya DUMU Taya, see HSS 9 12:31 (*manzatuḫlu*).

Text	Type of Text	Family Member(s)	Location of Property
HSS 19 30	"shares" or adoption	Teḫip-Tilla and Pai-Tilla (fWarḫi-Nuzu mentioned)	*dimtu* Ḫuya
EN 9/2 39	adoption	Teḫip-Tilla and Pai-Tilla	Nuzi
EN 9/2 168	*titennūtu*	Teḫip-Tilla	
EN 9/2 186	*titennūtu* (5 years)	Kula-ḫupi	*dimtu* Ḫuya
EN 9/2 187	*titennūtu* (5 years)	Teḫip-Tilla and fWarḫi-Nuzu	*dimtu* Šimika-atal

FIGURE 3. *Tarmiya's Transactions with Members of His Family*

why the parties contract jointly underscore the complexity of land tenure and inheritance at Nuzi.

The members of Šukriya's family share an interest in the estates of Šukriya and fWarḫi-Nuzu. Part or all of Šukriya's land was his inheritance share from his father Ḫuya. The extent and location of fWarḫi-Nuzu's property are not known. In his will Šukriya divides his estate among his sons and leaves his wife a house in which she can live until her death, after which Teḫip-Tilla will receive it. Teḫip-Tilla and Pai-Tilla are to share her other property. Against this background we can postulate reasons for the various combinations of family members in their dealings with Tarmiya. As for fWarḫi-Nuzu's participation with her son Teḫip-Tilla in *EN* 9/2 187, there are two possibilities: the property may have been owned jointly by fWarḫi-Nuzu and Teḫip-Tilla as a result of some transaction for which the contract has not survived; or the land may have been some of the property that Teḫip-Tilla would ultimately inherit from fWarḫi-Nuzu according to the terms of Šukriya's will (lines 51–57). In this case, the property would have been hers at the time of the transaction and Teḫip-Tilla participated so as to avoid complications at a later date. However, the property in this text is in *dimtu* Šimika-atal, which points to Šukriya's estates (see below), but it is not inconceivable that fWarḫi-Nuzu owned property in that *dimtu* either because she and Teḫip-Tilla acquired land near family property or because her own property was there. As for the brothers' joint contracts, perhaps they did not divide their father's property immediately. After Šimika-atal's share was removed, they may have chosen to work together, keep the family property intact, and, so, not diminish the estate's potential. Another possibility is that they were prevented from dividing the estate either because there were claims to the property or because someone else, specifically ᶠWarḫi-Nuzu, controlled it. As discussed above, HSS 19 30, the possible "shares" text, might be interpreted as a transfer of property from Ḫuya's estate within the family. Throughout, one can see evidence for ᶠWarḫi-Nuzu's continued involvement in her sons' activities both in HSS 19 30 where she speaks of the *abbūtu* right and in her text with Teḫip-Tilla. In all, these joint transactions further complicate the picture of Šukriya's family's interrelationships.

Other texts of Tarmiya include *EN* 9/2 273, a *tamgurtu* whereby he agrees with Puḫi-šenni son of [ ]-e concerning the payment of grain and metals. *EN* 9/2 101 is the statement of Eniš-tae son of Tauka concerning eight ANŠE ŠE.MEŠ *ša iš-pi-ku*$_8$ which he will give to Tarmiya.[88] This text was written in Ar-šalipe. The background of these texts is not known. Likewise, the context of HSS 16 321 by which Tarmiya gives livestock to Šekar-Tilla son of Hašiya and Akapurḫe son of Šata is not clear.[89]

In other texts, "six men of Tarmiya son of Ḫuya" appear among twenty-six LÚ.MEŠ *ša* Ḫanigalbat in HSS 16 232:4, a list of grain receipts assigned to S151.[90] Tarmiya himself appears in HSS 16 457:7, a list of men of whom Tupki-šenni is the GAL.11;[91] it is assigned to S113. Tarmiya also appears in HSS 16 83 in connection with Šennaya ÍR É *ḫurizatu* (lines 12–13) and with Akip-tašenni ÍR É.GAL (lines 24–25).[92]

[88] This may indicate a real estate arrangement between the two men. Note *EN* 9/2 200.

[89] The Group of witnesses includes some well-known individuals: line 20 Turari DUMU Taya, known as a scribe in HSS 9 17:24, 27; HSS 19 112:26; and also from HSS 5 45:2ff., HSS 13 163:30, and *EN* 9/1 149:28; line 21: Šeḫal-Tešup DUMU Ḫurpi-šenni, HSS 19 30:33; line 23: Ilaya DUMU Ḫapira, HSS 5 4:1; HSS 9 100:34, 47; HSS 15 56:8ff. (*emantuḫlu*); HSS 16 188:12 (GAL.10); 461:2; HSS 19 7:1ff., 100:6, 7; 124:9ff.; 125:5ff.; *EN* 9 182:9ff.; line 24 Niḫriya DUMU Ir-šuḫḫe, HSS 19 32:23, *JEN* 294:31, 35, and 435:47, 48; line 27 Kinniya DUMU Ikkiya, HSS 5 20:18, 22, and 82:39, 45.

[90] Others in the list include Šarteya DUMU Šekaru (see *JEN* 513:5, 12) and Ar-tura DUMU Kuššiya (see pp. 54ff. below).

[91] Others include Kewi-tae DUMU Kula-ḫupi (see HSS 16 435:14), Kirruke DUMU Akip-Tilla (see HSS 19 114:34 where he is a *šangu* and *EN* 9/2 450:22), Kip-ukur DUMU Ḫupita (see HSS 13 52:13, HSS 14 37:6, and 38:3; HSS 15 332:15; HSS 16 83:7), Ḫerši DUMU Naniya (see HSS 9 25:9, 32; *EN* 9/2 10:1ff. and 152:39?), and [ ]-Tešup DUMU Ar-tura (either Šeḫal-Tešup or Turar-Tešup). For Ḫerši and the son of Ar-tura, see pp. 48ff. below.

[92] As in the previous text, a number of the individuals are well known. Note in line 3 Tarmi-Tilla DUMU Šurki-Tilla; line 4 Nanteya DUMU Ḫutiya (see HSS 14 623:4, 20; HSS 15 307:12; *EN* 9/1 285:1, 12; and *Gadd* 66:8); line 7 Kip-ukur DUMU Ḫupita (see above n. 90); line 15 Ḫutip-šimika DUMU Teššuya (see AO 15.543:2 where he is a *rākib narkabti*; *JEN* 663:33 where he appears to be a judge; and HSS 16 331:24, 332:25, and *JEN* 370:50, the suit brought by Tarmi-Tilla son of Šurki-Tilla against Tarmiya); line 21 Utḫap-tae DUMU Šennaya (see HSS 9 145:38); line 32 Nula-zaḫi DUMU Ataya (see HSS 13 460:3, 7); line 34 Ḫasuar DUMU Minaya (see HSS 5 96:23, 29); line 35 Arik-kušuḫ DUMU Sîn-napšir (see HSS 19 114:31); line 37 Paite⟨ya⟩ DUMU Ataya (see HSS 19 75:26); line 38 Eḫli-Tešup DUMU Waqar-bēli (see HSS 16 331:8 and 332:9); line 39 Šurki-Tilla DUMU Amur-rabi (see HSS 13 58:2); line 41 Tarmip-tašenni DUMU Wirrištanni (see HSS 5 26:29–31; 56:37, 49; 91:32, 48; and HSS 19 51:25, 39).

Ḫanukka son of Tarmiya

Ḫanukka son of Tarmiya is attested in one adoption text, *EN* 9/2 34,[93] in which five sons of Keliya transfer houses in Nuzi to him. As mentioned above, Ḫanukka son of Tarmiya is included here as a member of the family because this text was assigned to the S151 archives in which the only Tarmiya is Tarmiya son of Ḫuya. If he was, indeed, the representative of the last recorded generation of this family, he continued the practice of acquiring houses in Nuzi established early in the family's history. Otherwise, Ḫanukka is known as a witness to texts of Tarmiya son of Ḫuya, *EN* 9/2 36 and 106.

The Real Estate Holdings of the Family of Ḫuya

Transactions in which members of the family of Ḫuya give or receive property involve real estate in the *dimtu* of Ḫuya. In descriptions of other land in the *dimtu* the names of members of Ḫuya's family—Tarmiya, Šukriya, Kula-ḫupi—recur. Certainly, then, this was a center of the real estate holdings of his family. Moreover, the *dimtu* undoubtedly takes its name from Ḫuya son of Šimika-atal.[94]

In HSS 19 30, Teḫip-Tilla and Pai-Tilla sons of Šukriya give their uncle Tarmiya two parcels of land totaling seven *awēḫaru* in the *dimtu* of Ḫuya. The description of the first is broken, except for its western boundary: "west of the 'canal of the palace'" (line 3). The second is three *awēḫaru* of field "east of the field of [ ], north of the field of Niḫriya, south of the field of Tarmiya, west of the field of [ ]-niya" (lines 5–8).

Kula-ḫupi son of Ḫuya also owned property east of the *dimtu* of Ḫuya and gave it to Tarmiya in *EN* 9/2 186. A description of only one portion of the property involved is preserved: "One parcel of three *awēḫaru* of field reaches the Nirašši Canal, east of the *dimtu* of Ḫuya, west of the field of Šukriya . . . " (lines 16–19). The second piece also borders property of Šukriya (line 21). In *EN* 9/2 76, Šukriya acquired a field north of the *dimtu* of Ḫuya through exchange.

Tarmiya, of course, received property in the *dimtu* of Ḫuya through the acquisitions discussed above. In the descriptions of neighboring fields in HSS 19 30:7, a Tarmiya appears, most likely Tarmiya son of Ḫuya. Also, in *EN* 9/2 177, which comes from S151, a Tarmiya holds the field south of the property in question. In this text, Šarteya son of [ ] receives the property, but the name of the party transferring real estate to him is lost. DUMU Šúk-[ ] is preserved in line 2, so this may be another transaction involving either Teḫip-Tilla or Pai-Tilla.[95]

[93] The sons are Tenteya, Umpiya, Iwišti, Ennike, and Puḫiya. Umpiya DUMU Keliya is also known from *JEN* 13:43 where he witnesses a Teḫip-Tilla son of Puḫi-šenni adoption. Witnesses in *EN* 9/2 34 include line 22 [IGI ^{I}*Tu-r*]*a-ri* DUMU *Ar-te-šup*; line 25 [IGI ^{I}*Aš-tar-t*]*e-šup* DUMU *Wa-ar-du*; line 26 [IGI ^{I}*Ma-li*]*-ya* DUMU *Be-la-nu* (see HSS 9 70:3ff.). Reconstructions are based on the preserved seal names.

[94] See Deller, SCCNH 1:58.

[95] The text is a *titennūtu* agreement for two years.

The land is described as "five *awēḫaru* of fields reaching the road of the city of [Unap]-šewe. [ ] of the field of [ ], and [ ] five *awēḫaru* of fields north of the field of Tarmiya and east of the field of the palace: [a total of ten?] *awēḫaru* of fields of the *dimtu* of Ḫuya" (lines 5–11).

Another reference to property in the *dimtu* of Ḫuya may occur in *EN* 9/2 73, an exchange between Paya son of Elḫip-šarri and Pai-Tešup son of Arteya (from S129). Here the orchard of Kula-ḫupi and houses of Šukriya are mentioned:[96] "West of the orchard of Kula-ḫupi, south of the houses of Šukriya, north of the road of the city of Ḫamena . . ." (lines 8–11).

Far more tenuous possibilities for property in the *dimtu* occur in *EN* 9/2 175 (S124), 185, and 16. In the first Ḫanaya son of Tae receives property from Šeḫliya son of Purna-[zini] and Ḫašip-Tilla son of Šeḫliya. The nine *awēḫaru* of fields involved in that transaction are located "west of the field of Šukriya, south of the field of Paya, east of the field of Muš-a[pu], north of the field of Kaya-pa[ ] . . ." (lines 5–9). Perhaps the Paya of line 7 is the Paya son of Elḫip-šarri involved in the previous transaction. A Paya also owns land bordering that transferred *ana titennūti* to Tarmiya in *EN* 9/2 185 above (line 10). Another neighbor in that text is Wantiš-šenni (line 9). He may be the individual who adopted Tarmiya in *EN* 9/2 16 and transferred land located west of the road of the city of Tarkulli (lines 4–5) to him.

Members of the family also owned property in the *dimtu* of Šimika-atal, perhaps named for Ḫuya's father. In *EN* 9/2 187, Teḫip-Tilla and ᶠWarḫi-Nuzu transfer a parcel of real estate there to Tarmiya *ana titennūti*. That property was east of the field of the palace, south of the Niraššі Canal,[97] north of the Šin-nazabulti canal, and west of a field of Tarmiya.

It is possible that the land received *ana titennūti* by Tarmiya in *EN* 9/2 264 was located in or near the *dimtu* of Ḫuya. It was located east of the *atappi nir-ašši ša ekallim* (lines 3–4), a canal name similar to two in the *dimtu* of Ḫuya: *atappi ša ekalli* (HSS 19 30:3′) and *atappi niraššі* (*EN* 9/2 186:17). Further, it was adjacent to a piece of his own property (line 5).

Members of the family also owned or acquired real estate in Nuzi. One piece of land owned by Teḫip-Tilla and Pai-Tilla and transferred through adoption to Tarmiya in *EN* 9/2 39 was located in the A.GÀR of the city of Nuzi (line 5′) and next to a field of Tarmiya (line 7′). Property (A.ŠÀ *paiḫu*) in the city of Nuzi was acquired by Tarmiya in *EN* 9/2 40. These apparently had been received as part of his inheritance by Ennike son of Wantip-šarri (lines 8–9). They bordered houses of both Ar-tura and Tarmiya. This property may be related to the houses in the city of Nuzi received by Ḫuya in *EN* 9/2 35 from Wantip-šarri and Makuya sons of Zike. Ḫanukka son of Tarmiya also acquires houses in Nuzi (*EN* 9/2 34).

[96] See p. 126 below for this text.

[97] See discussions of Niraššі in Maidman, *SEANFA*, 405ff. n. 699; Zaccagnini, *RLLA*, 58ff.; and Fadhil, *STPPKA*, 40 and 44.

Tarmiya also acquired property north of the canal of Ar-tamašši in the *dimtu* of Kazzipu[zzi] (*EN* 9/2 36).

There is a clear pattern in most of the real estate transactions of the family of Ḫuya. It is quite obvious that the exchange of real estate by Šukriya (*EN* 9/2 76) was designed to consolidate his holdings in the region of the *dimtu* of Ḫuya. In two texts (HSS 19 30 and *EN* 9/2 186) Tarmiya acquired property bordering his or Šukriya's property in the *dimtu* of Ḫuya and in one (*EN* 9/2 187) property in the *dimtu* of Šimika-atal was transferred to him. These transactions of Tarmiya represent transfers within the family and result in increases in Tarmiya's real estate holdings in the two *dimtu*s in which the family's land was located. *EN* 9/2 16 and 185 may refer to property in the same area, perhaps also the *dimtu* of Ḫuya. The first is an expansion beyond land owned by the family, but the parties to the second are not identified. *EN* 9/2 264 also augments Tarmiya's holdings beyond the original family estate, but the location of this property in one or the other *dimtu* is uncertain.

Both the *dimtu* of Ḫuya and the *dimtu* of Šimika-atal have canals. Interestingly, these canals are called *atappi ša ekalli* (HSS 19 30); *atappi nirašši* (*EN* 9/2 186), both in the *dimtu* of Ḫuya; and *atappi nirašši* and *atappi šinnazabulti* (*EN* 9/2 187) in the *dimtu* of Šimika-atal. If the property in *EN* 9/2 264 was in one of the *dimtu*s, the canal name *atappi nirašši ša ekalli* can be added to this Group. In fact, the *atappi nirašši*, the *atappi ša ekalli*, and the *atappi nirašši ša ekalli* may well have been one and the same canal. At the least, the *dimtus* and property bordering the canals were linked by the canal system. The *atappi nirašši* appears elsewhere in numerous texts, but its location is indefinite.[98] The city of Artiḫe is the only one linked clearly with a canal of this name, but it is also associated with Anzugalli, Nuzi, and Zizza. Further, it is mentioned in connection with the road of Tarkulli. Specifically, the *nirašši* canal appears to have "linked Artiḫe with Anzugalli and Nuzi, probably passing through the territory of Tarkulli."[99] In this light, the property acquired by Tarmiya in *EN* 9/2 16, west of the road of Tarkulli (line 5), might be in the same area as the family's other property. If the property in *EN* 9/2 73 is also in the *dimtu* of Ḫuya (as suggested by the holdings of Kula-ḫupi and Šukriya in lines 9–10), further topographical information is available. That property is located on the road of the city of Ḫamena and the tablet was written in the city of Akip-apu. The city of Akip-apu was located in the district of Ḫurazina-rabu along with other cities, including Artiḫe. While other texts recording the transfer of property in the *dimtu*s of Ḫuya and Šimika-atal were written in Nuzi,[100] where members of the family owned property and did business, this text in conjunction with the other toponyms connected with the *dimtu* of Ḫuya suggests

[98] Zaccagnini, *RLLA*, 58. See also Fadhil, *STPPKA*, 40.

[99] Fadhil, *STPPKA*, 9–10 (Akip-apu), 35–58 (Artiḫe).

[100] *EN* 9/2 186 and HSS 19 30 were written in Nuzi. Tarmiya's archives were located in Nuzi and Pai-Tilla's court case was found there.

that the *dimtu* was located in the district of Ḫurazina-rabu, perhaps in the city of Artiḫe.

Wherever the *dimtu*s of the family were located, the properties acquired by Tarmiya were located in areas well provided with water. It certainly is not surprising that Tarmiya the irrigation officer should acquire such real estate. Indeed, either his profession attuned him especially to irrigation concerns, or his familiarity with such properties because of his family's holdings in the *dimtu*s of Ḫuya and Šimika-atal equipped him for his position.

The original extent of the properties of this family is not known. Clearly there was a division of real estate in the generation of Ḫuya, Enniku, and Akap-šenni, another in the generation of Šukriya, Kula-ḫupi, and Tarmiya, and yet another in the generation of Šimika-atal, Teḫip-Tilla, and Pai-Tilla. In each generation there were also acquisitions and transfers that enlarged or decreased various family members' estates. We have no way of knowing how the individuals who disappear from the archives after an appearance or two fared over the long run. For those who appear frequently, specifically Tarmiya and the line of Šukriya, we have the impression that Tarmiya was successful in broadening his land base from both original family property and new acquisitions. Šukriya's family, on the other hand, appears to have dispersed its holdings. If Pai-Tilla's testimony in court (HSS 14 8) reflects serious financial difficulty, this line must have lost its basis of wealth, that is, its land. The texts in which Tarmiya acquires real estate from Šukriya's line probably do not describe all of their holdings, given the references to Šukriya's property in other documents. Thus, one wonders what happened to the rest of Šukriya's property. Presumably, it was transferred to other people whose records we do not have, probably because they were not located at Nuzi but nearer the *dimtu*s involved. It is worth noting that the individual, Akip-tašenni son of Tae, whom Pai-Tilla sues to regain his gods, mother, and sister, is not known elsewhere in the Nuzi texts.

The Nuzi properties mentioned in the texts are fewer in number, and they point primarily to urban real estate, that is, houses and *paiḫu*-plots, though at least one piece of land in the A.GÀR of the city is attested. Among the houses transferred by these texts may be the very building in which the tablets were found. It is especially interesting that Tarmiya received houses in Nuzi north of houses of Ar-Tura (*EN* 9/2 40:5–6). Perhaps this Ar-Tura is Ar-Tura son of Kuššiya whose archives were located in Group 17 and whose family is discussed in chapter 3.

Summary

The family of Ḫuya son of Šimika-atal has long been an object of attention because of the publication of some of its most interesting texts, specifically Šukriya's will and Pai-Tilla's testimony, both of which involve the household gods. Moreover, Pai-Tilla's statements combined with what was known of the family allude to a sort of drama not often easily traced at Nuzi or elsewhere.

This "human-interest" factor arouses curiosity about the family's history and interactions. The *EN* 9 texts do not disappoint us in our desire to learn more about this family; they enlarge our knowledge of the parties involved and describe more fully the family interactions. At the same time, these texts help to clarify the nature of the archives of S151.

In the first documented generation, the major figure, Ḫuya son of Šimika-atal, was a landowner who acquired his property through inheritance and acquisition. His resources were sufficient for him to make loans, and he had at least one servant over whom his sons went to court. He is the first member of the family to be recorded as an owner of property, that is, houses, in Nuzi, but his major holdings appear to have been elsewhere.

In each of three generations of this family, there were three sons: Ḫuya, Enniku, and Akapšenni, sons of Šimika-atal; Šukriya, Kula-ḫupi, and Tarmiya, sons of Ḫuya; and Teḫip-Tilla, Pai-Tilla, and Šimika-atal, sons of Šukriya. One son in each of the second two generations was unusual: Tarmiya, because he was the youngest who had to go to court with his brothers concerning a premortem "inheritance" of a slave-girl from his father; and Šimika-atal, because he was a stepbrother whose inheritance rights were clearly not those of his brothers. In both generations, there is a clear concern that the father's estate be divided correctly, even if this resulted in litigation. If HSS 19 30 is a tablet of "shares" reflecting inheritance issues from an earlier generation, it would be quite in keeping with other family behavior.

Among all of the brothers of the two generations, Kula-ḫupi and Šimika-atal are the most poorly attested. The lack of texts concerning them could mean that their spheres of activity were elsewhere, where their records would have been stored, perhaps closer to the *dimtu*s where their real estate was located. Otherwise, their situations may have been stable with neither acquisition nor sale of property. Hence, there would be no texts to trace the growth or decline of their estates.

The materials that are available focus on Tarmiya and the line of Šukriya. On the basis of the texts of S151, the history of the family of Šukriya is clear. After Šukriya's death, the family estate began to disintegrate. Šimka-atal disappears; the remaining sons (with their mother, on occasion) sell off or lease their property, Šukriya's estate. What began apparently as a prosperous land-based family was reduced to the situation described in Pai-Tilla's testimony in court: the loss of his gods and the sale of his mother and sister. A troubling question in this outline of Šukriya's family is: what happened to Teḫip-Tilla? He was the chief heir and recipient of the largest share of both his father's and mother's estates. He was specifically linked to his mother after his father's death: he was to inherit the house left to her. One would expect that he, not Pai-Tilla, would be responsible for his mother and sister. Presumably, he was already ruined or dead at the time of Pai-Tilla's testimony, and Pai-Tilla's efforts were a last gasp at saving the family's integrity. As discussed above, the brothers contracted jointly for any of a number of reasons. However, Teḫip-Tilla did make one contract on his own. This text indicates that he owned land independently. Surely, then, he either acquired it on his own or received his share of his father's estate at some point. Even with his apparent independence at some stage, he appears not to have been present when he was most needed.

Within Šukriya's family, the figure of ᶠWarḫi-Nuzu is both interesting and problematic because of her prominence in family affairs and the unclear nature of her status in the family. First, her husband provided for her in his will and protected her estate from Šimika-atal, believed to be her stepson. If she had real estate of her own, she would have received it as a dowry, as an inheritance, or through her own business activities. Real estate dowries and women active in business usually are found among wealthy families. Female inheritance of real estate usually points to a lack of male relatives whose claims to estates would supersede those of female family members. Her final situation, sale into a foreign land according to Pai-Tilla's testimony, might well indicate that she had no possible guardian but her second son. Second, Šukriya's will does not grant her the *abbūtu* right, yet she mentions it in HSS 19 30. At the same time, she participated in property contracts, albeit ones that reduced land holdings in which she had an interest. We can imagine, in light of subsequent events, that she was attempting to better her family's circumstances, which appear to have been declining. Her involvement in family affairs suggests that she did have some sort of authority or at least legal interest in her sons' disposition of land. There may have been a separate document, now missing, that established ᶠWarḫi-Nuzu's rights over her sons. But normally such considerations are included in wills. There certainly is the possibility that ᶠWarḫi-Nuzu's prerogatives were simply "understood" in the family and community, either at Šukriya's behest or through her own force of personality. To whatever extent she was involved in trying to keep the family intact or to manage her husband's estate, she was unsuccessful, as her fate indicates. In any case, her appearances in her husband's will and elsewhere suggest that she was at least respected by those around her and escaped the relative anonymity of many Nuzi women.

The beneficiary of the misfortunes of the family of Šukriya was Tarmiya, who had become an official of the government, perhaps because he was not destined through inheritance to be a landowner of any significance. The land that he acquired was well located with respect both to his own holdings and to the irrigation system. It appears that he was motivated more by a sense of gain than by kindness in his dealings with his brother's family. That is, he seems not to have made any efforts to intercede in order to prevent Pai-Tilla's great difficulties. That a man of his station and ultimate wealth would allow his sister-in-law and niece to be sold off suggests that he held them in rather little affection. One can only wonder whether his actions, or rather lack thereof, can be traced to the incident in which his brothers took him to court. In light of that suit, it is ironic that Tarmiya ultimately should become the owner or lessor of his father's property from both of his brothers' holdings.

Finally, the archives of S151 appear to be the archives of Tarmiya son of Ḫuya. Most of the texts mentioning other members of the family refer to transactions for which Tarmiya would receive the tablets. Other documents, including Šukriya's will and other contracts, might have been transferred to him in conjunction with one or another of the agreements that he made with Šukriya's sons and wife or be related to his own inheritance, whatever that might have been.[101] These archives, then, would represent the personal documents of an official of the palace who was able to develop his own estate in the course of his career.

[101] See discussion of the principles of archive-keeping in chapter 1.

CHAPTER 3

The Family of Ar-tura and Šeḫal-Tešup Son of Teḫup-šenni: Texts from Group 17

The Archeological Context and Distribution of Tablets

Group 17, like Group 18A, is incomplete, but three rooms were excavated: S108, S110, and S113 (fig. 4). On the basis of the contents of the rooms, an offering stand and glass eye beads, in particular, R. F. S. Starr concluded that the building had a religious function. According to this interpretation, the storage jars and pottery found in S110 are gifts for the chapel.[1]

Starr mentions "several tablets in bad condition" found in S113.[2] Tablet registers and other materials list twenty-three tablets and fragments from S113 and eight from S110. Of the latter, three were originally assigned to S112 in Lacheman's dissertation, but were reassigned to S110 in materials relating to *EN* 9.[3] The majority of these texts belong to the family of Ar-tura son of Kuššiya and to Šeḫal-Tešup son of Teḫup-šenni. As is usually the case, some of the texts assigned to rooms in Group 17 belong to other individuals in the eastern area and elsewhere.[4] In addition, some texts that cannot be related to the principal parties in Group 17 appear there.[5] Further, a number of texts clearly belonging to the family of Ar-tura and to Šeḫal-Tešup are assigned elsewhere or have no room number.[6]

It is possible that these two corpora of texts were not stored together in antiquity. The documents of the family of Ar-tura son of Kuššiya, which are more-widely dispersed in the tablet registers, may have originated elsewhere. In light

[1] R. F. S. Starr, *Nuzi* 1:309–10.

[2] Ibid., 309.

[3] See Group 17 in table 1 above, pp. 11–12.

[4] From the eastern area: Puhi-šenni son of Muš-apu (*EN* 9/1 338, *EN* 9/2 163) and Muš-apu son of Purna-zini (*EN* 9/2 18). From the palace (N120): ᶠTulpun-naya (*EN* 9 27).

[5] E.g., *EN* 9 393, HSS 15 29, and HSS 14 26.

[6] Texts assigned elsewhere include Ar-tura son of Kuššiya: *EN* 9/2 458 (S112) and *EN* 9/2 401 (N120/1); Utḫap-tae son of Ar-tura: *EN* 9/2 10, 298, and 387 (S132); HSS 19 11 and 86; *EN* 9/2 67, 262, and 401 (N120); HSS 19 120 (C28); Šeḫal-Tešup son of Teḫup-šenni: *EN* 9/2 359 (S112) and *EN* 9/2 125 (N120). Texts with no room number: Utḫap-tae son of Ar-tura: HSS 19 134 and *EN* 9/2 152; Šeḫal-Tešup son of Teḫup-šenni: HSS 14 22 and *EN* 9/2 184, 371.

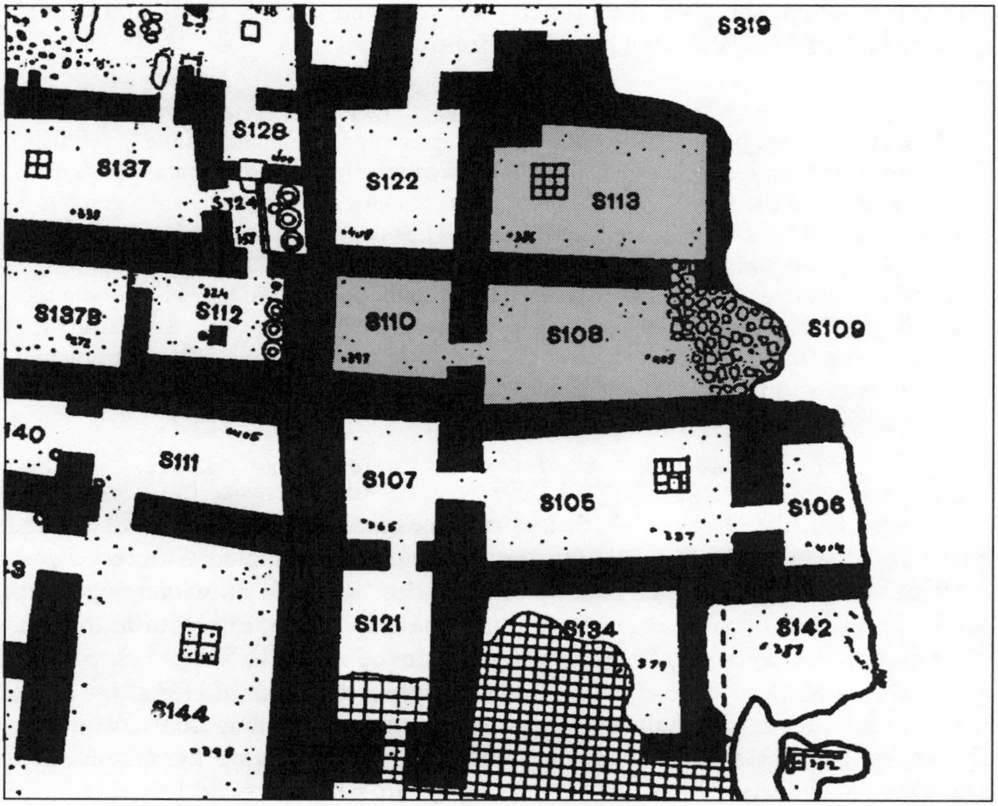

FIGURE 4. *Group 17* (from Starr, *Nuzi II*)

of the descriptions of the real estate owned by this family (see below), however, their texts obviously were located within the eastern area. Because most of their texts are concentrated in Group 17, the family is treated here.

The Genealogy and Chronology of the Family of Kuššiya

The will of Ar-tura son of Kuššiya (HSS 19 10) and a statement of ^{f}Šilwa-turi (HSS 19 11) are the primary evidence for reconstructing one line of this family. The first provides the names of Ar-tura's father Kuššiya, his wife ^{f}Šilwa-turi, five daughters, and a son, Turar-Tešup.[7] The second reiterates the name of ^{f}Šilwa-turi, Ar-tura's wife, and the name of his daughter ^{f}Tieš-menni. It also names both Utḫap-tae son of Ar-tura, presumably the son of Ar-tura son of

[7] See Paradise, *NIP*, 145ff., text C-34.

Kuššiya, to whom she gives the property she received in HSS 19 10, and fTeḫeš-menni as a "sister." HSS 19 11 reads as follows:[8]

> Thus (says) fŠilwa-turi wife of Ar-tura: "I have given to Ut[ḫap-tae] son of Ar-tura whatever itemized property my husband Ar-tura willed to me and I have given the É *ubārūti* with its É *rukbu* and with its *amri* from the houses of Ar-tura which are [in the heart] of the *kirḫu*. fTeḫeš-menni, [my] daughter, as a sister I have given to Utḫap-tae and [as a wife] he will give [her]." Thus (says) [fŠilwa-turi]: "The tablet of ite[mization] which Ar-tura wrote for me I have given to Utḫap-t[ae]." As long as fŠilwa-turi lives, Utḫap-tae will respect her and will provide her with food and clothing. When she dies, he will weep [over her] and bu[ry her]. Ši[lwa-turi's] clothing and [food] . . . yearly he will give (her). Of Utḫap-tae. . . . Whoever breaks the contract will pay a [mina of silver] and a mi[na of gold]. SIX SEALS (including those of the scribe and fŠilwa-turi).

In addition to Turar-Tešup and Utḫap-tae, Ar-tura seems to have had one or more sons. His will (HSS 9 10) refers to "his sons" (lines 33, 35, and 38) and Turar-Tešup's "brothers" (line 32). Among the texts associated with this family two individuals with the patronymic Ar-tura can be found as witnesses. Akap-šenni son of Ar-tura appears as guarantor in HSS 16 238:13, 18, a loan document that seems to have belonged to Ar-tura son of Kuššiya; Šeḫal-Tešup son of Ar-tura seals HSS 19 134:13, a text concerning the daughter of Utḫap-tae son of Ar-tura.[9] It is common practice for family members to witness contracts or participate in transactions involving their relatives, so it is very likely that these sons of Ar-tura were Utḫap-tae's and Turar-Tešup's brothers.

It is of interest that fŠilwa-turi's statement (HSS 19 11) does not identify Utḫap-tae as her son or as fTeḫeš-menni's brother. Ar-tura's will certainly was designed to make special provisions, albeit with restrictions, for fŠilwa-turi and certain of his children while dividing the bulk of his estate among his sons in the traditional manner (lines 26–30). Further, fŠilwa-turi's text (HSS 19 11) reads much like an adoption, along the lines of HSS 9 22. Thus, it is possible that fŠilwa-turi was neither Ar-tura's first or only wife nor Utḫap-tae's mother.

As for Utḫap-tae's family, only one daughter is known. HSS 19 134 attests to the consummation of the marriage of fAze daughter of Utḫap-tae and Karrate son of Pui-tae:[10]

[8] For "itemized property" (line 3) see Deller, SCCNH 1:55. For "tablet of itemization" (line 16) see HSS 13 143:28. Utḫap-tae's responsibilities are expressed by clauses standard for adoption texts.

[9] These two texts are discussed below. For other instances in which the name of Šeḫal-Tešup son of Ar-tura can be restored with confidence see below.

[10] Karrate DUMU Pui-tae appears as well in HSS 19 86:2ff., HSS 19 113:21, 25, and *EN* 9/2 262:18 (see below), all texts involving Utḫap-tae son of Ar-tura. Šeḫal-Tešup DUMU Ar-tura appears as a witness in line 13. Other witnesses include Taena DUMU Eniš-tae (line 15; see also HSS 16 221:10, where he is one of four sons of fŠuma[ ], and HSS 16 384:6).

The statement which Karrate son of Pui-tae spoke before witnesses: "The daughter of Utḫap-tae son of Ar-tura, ^{f}Aze, my wife, I have lain with her and. . . . Now for her *terḫatu* from Utḫap-tae I have taken . . . minas of bronze for five shekels of silver." FOUR SEALS. The hand of Šamaš-damiq.

Yet another branch of Kuššiya's family may be traced through *EN* 9/2 10, the statement of Ḫerši and Urḫi-Tilla sons of Naniya, who transfer houses in the *kirḫu* of Nuzi, their inheritance share from the houses of Kuššiya to Utḫap-tae son of Ar-tura. Reminiscent of the *ṭuppi zitti* formula, the "price" of the property is called ḪA.LA.[11] The houses are located west of the wall, as is the property in AASOR 16 58, discussed below, and next to houses of Ar-tura, presumably Utḫap-tae's father. Therefore, it seems that Ḫerši and Urḫi-Tilla sons of Naniya were related to Utḫap-tae as cousins, and that this text represents a division of family properties. *EN* 9/2 10 reads as follows:[12]

[*um-m*]*a* ^{I}*Ḫé-er-ši-ma ù*
[*um-m*]*a* ^{I}*Ur-ḫi-til-la-ma* DUMU.MEŠ *Na-ni-ya*
[*mi-nu*]*-um-me-e* ḪA.LA*-ni iš-tu*
É.ḪI.A.MEŠ *ša* ^{I}*Ku-uš-ši-ya ša a-bi-ni uš-tu*
kí-ir-ḫi i+na URU *Nu-zi*
36 *i+*[*na*] *am-ma-ti mu-ra-ak-šu-nu*
4 *i+na a*[*m-m*]*a-ti i+na e-le-en*
5 [*i+na*] *am-m*[*a-t*]*i i+na* [*šu-pa-al*]
i+na il-ta-na-an É.ḪI.A.MEŠ *ša* [^{I}]
i+na su-ta-na-an É.ḪI.A.MEŠ *ša* ^{I}*Ar-tu-*[*ra*]
i+na šu-pa-[*al*] BÀD*-ri ù i+na*
e-le-[*en*] É.ḪI.A.MEŠ *ša* ^{I}*Ar-ši-mi-ka*$_4$
GÍR*-pí-*[*ni*] *uš-tu* ŠÀ*-bi* É.ḪI.A.MEŠ *an-ni-ti*
uš-[*te*]*-li-mi ù* GÍR*-šu ša* ^{I}*Ut-ḫap-ta-e*
DUMU [*Ar*]*-tù-ra aš-ta-ka*$_4$*-an-mi a-na*
^{I}*Ut-ḫap-ta-e a-na-a-din ki-ma*
ḪA.LA*-šu ni-it-ta-din-šu-nu-ti*
ù ^{I}*Ut-ḫap-ta-e* 1 TÚG S[IG$_5$]
12 MA.NA AN.NA.MEŠ 3 MA.NA U[RUDU]
[É.ḪI.A].MEŠ DÙ*-šu* KÙ.BABBAR.[MEŠ] *an-nu-tu*$_4$
ḪA.LA*-šu-nu a-na* ^{I}*Ḫé-er-ši* [*ù a-na*]
^{I}[*U*]*r-ḫi-til-la it-ta-di*[*n-šu-nu-ti*]
[*šum-m*]*a* É.MEŠ GAL *la i+na-ak-*[*is*]

[11] See Paradise, *NIP*, 343ff.

[12] Line 1 Ḫerši son of Naniya also appears with Tarmiya son of Ḫuya in HSS 457:6, HSS 9 25:29, 33 (a text of ^{f}Šašuri wife of Šilwa-Tešup DUMU LUGAL), and *EN* 9/2 152 (an Utḫap-tae son of Ar-tura text). Line 37 Šeḫal-Tešup son of Sukriya is known from *JEN* 78:32, 46. Line 38 Naniya son of Kip-ukur, see n. 49 above. Line 39 Zikaya son of Ḫuziri is also known from HSS 13 169:2, HSS 16 407:11 and HSS 19 65:2ff. Line 41 Utḫap-tae son of Ariḫ-ḫaya is known from HSS 13 58:1, HSS 15 307:3ff., HSS 16 87:12, 16 and *EN* 9/2 176, below.

Left Edge

[*šum-ma*] TUR *la ú-*[*ra*]*-ad-dá*
[*šum-ma* É].MEŠ *pa-q*[*í-ra-na* TÚK*-ši*]

Reverse

[^{I}*Ḫé-er-š*]*i ù* ^{I}*U*[*r-ḫi-til-la*]
[*ú-za-a*]*k-*[*ka*$_4$*-m*]*a a-na* ^{I}[*Ut-ḫap-ta-e*]
[*i-n*]*a-an-din i-lik-šu-nu*
[^{I}*Ḫ*]*é-er-š*[*i*] *ù* ^{I}*Ur-ḫi-*[*til-la*]
[*na*]*-šu-ú ù* ^{I}*Ut-ḫap-t*[*a-e*]
[*la na-ši m*]*a-an-nu-um-me-e*
[*i-na be-ri*]*-šu-nu* KI.BAL*-kat*
1 MA.[NA] KÙ.BABBAR 2! MA.NA KÙ.GI DIRI*-la*
ṭup-p[*u i+n*]*a* EGIR*-ki šu-du-ti*
i+na ba-[*ab*] É.GAL*-lì i+na* URU *Nu-zi*
ša$_{10}$*-ti-ir*
IGI *Še-ḫal-*[*Te-šup*] DUMU *Šúk-ri-ya*
[IGI] *Na-ni-*[*ya*] DUMU *Ki-pu-kùr*
IGI *Zi-ka-*[*a*]*-a* DUMU *Ḫu-zi-ri*
IGI *Ut-ḫap-t*[*a-e* DU]MU *A-ri-ḫa-a-a*
IGI *Tu-r*[*a-* DUMU *-e*]*n-n*[*i*]
IGI *Pu-i-*[*ta-e* DUMU]
IGI *T*[*ù-r*]*a-ri* [DUMU]
[IGI]*-ip-*LUGAL [DUMU]
[8 L]Ú.MEŠ *an-nu-t*[*i š*]*a* É.MEŠ *mu-šal-mu-ú*
[*na*]*-dì-na-nu ša* KÙ.BABBAR.MEŠ
[NA$_4$ DUB].SAR*-rù* NA$_4$ ^{I}*Tu-ra-ri*

Upper Edge

[NA$_4$ ^{I}*Pu-i*]*-ta-e* NA$_4$ ^{I}*Ut-ḫap-ta-e*

Left Edge

NA$_4$ ^{I}*Še-*[*hal*]*-Te-šup*
[NA$_4$ ^{I}*Na-ni-*]*ya* NA$_4$ *Zi-ka-a-a* NA$_4$ ^{I}*Tu-ra-ri*

Thus (say) Ḫerši and Urḫi-Tilla sons of Naniya: "[What]ever our inheritance share from the houses of Kuššiya, of our father, from the *kirḫu* in Nuzi, thirty-six cubits their length, four cubits on the east, five cubits on [the west], north of the houses of [ ], south of the houses of Ar-tura, west of the wall, east of the houses of Ar-šimika, we have lifted [our] feet from those houses and the foot of Utḫap-tae son of Ar-tura I(!) have placed and I(!) have given to Utḫap-tae (and) as his inheritance share we have given. And Utḫap-tae one fine cloth, twelve minas of tin, three minas of copper, his built houses ??, this silver, their inheritance share, he has given to Ḫerši [and] Urḫi-Tilla. [If] the houses are larger, they will not diminish them. [If] the houses are smaller, they will not add to them. [If] the houses have a claim[ant], Ḫerši and Urḫi-Tilla will clear (them) and give them to [Utḫap-tae]. Their *ilku* Ḫerši and Urḫi-Tilla will bear and Utḫap-tae [will not bear]. Whoever [among] them breaks the contract will pay one mina of silver and two! minas of gold. The tablet was written after the proclamation at the gate of the palace in the city of Nuzi. EIGHT WITNESSES. These [eight] men are the surveyors of the houses and givers of the silver. EIGHT SEALS.

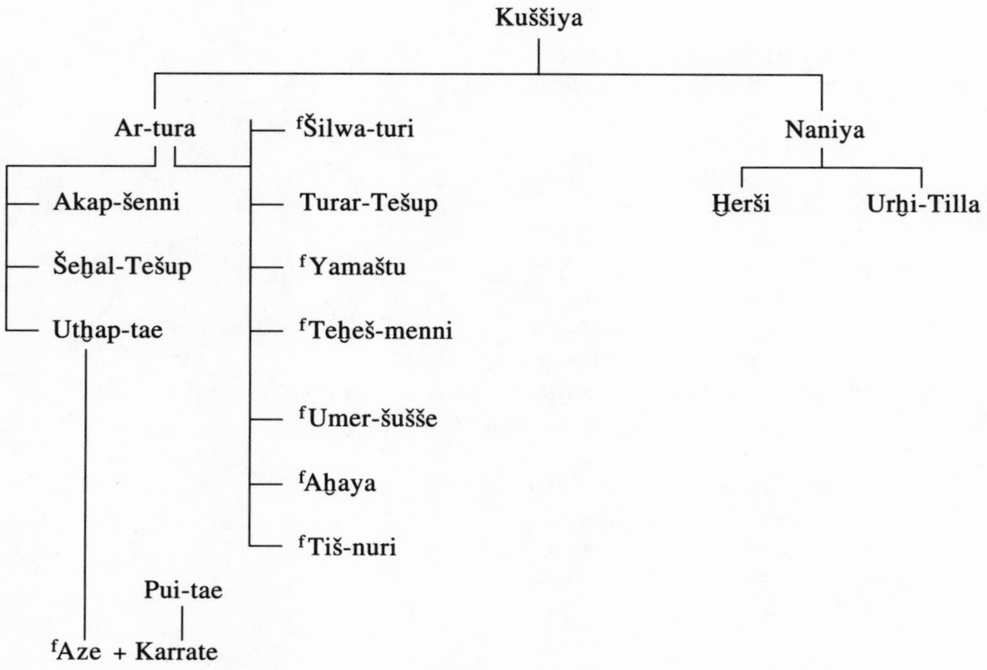

FIGURE 5. *Genealogy of the Family of Kuššiya*

On the basis of the genealogical information traced above, the family can be reconstructed as shown in figure 5.[13] This family's chronological position is documented by the scribes who write for its members and by the individuals of known generations with whom they appear. Scribes who write texts in which Ar-tura son of Kuššiya appears include:

Nirāri son of Taya (III)	HSS 19 10
Turar-Tešup[14]	*EN* 9/1 351
Turar-Tešup son of Itḫ-apiḫe (IV)	*JEN* 826
Zini (most likely son of Kiannipu) (III)	*EN* 9/2 401

These scribes are also involved with prominent figures at Nuzi. Nirāri son of Taya writes for Eḫli-Tešup son of Taya in the southwest archives,[15] Tarmi-Tilla son of Šurki-Tilla,[16] Akawatil son of Ellu,[17] and Pai-Tešup *wardu* of Šilwa-Tešup.[18] Turar-Tešup son of Itḫ-apiḫe also writes for Tarmi-Tilla son of Šurki-Tilla,[19]

[13] See Paradise, *NIP*, 190, chart 18, for an earlier version of this genealogy.

[14] Two scribes named Turar-Tešup are known: a son of Itḫ-apiḫe and a son of Kel-Tešup. Either is possible chronologically. A Turar-Tešup also writes for Tarmiya son of Ḫuya (see p. 25 above).

[15] AASOR 16 96.

[16] *JEN* 108.

[17] HSS 5 40.

[18] HSS 9 29.

[19] *JEN* 535, 540, 549, 550. 562.

Ilānu son of Taiuki,[20] ᶠUzna wife of Enna-mati,[21] and Takku son of Enna-mati.[22] Ar-tura also appears in texts with known figures: Tarmiya son of Ḫuya in HSS 16 232:3 and possibly Tarmi-Tilla son of Šurki-Tilla.[23]

A number of scribes are associated with Utḫap-tae son of Ar-tura and his brothers. The scribes listed below wrote for Utḫap-tae, except as noted in parentheses:

Arip-šarri[24]	AASOR 16 58, *EN* 9/2 10, *EN* 9/2 262, HSS 19 86
Aḫa-ay-amši[25]	*EN* 9/2 363
Bēlaya son of Ḫanukka[26]	HSS 19 114
Ḫašip-Tilla son of Enna-pali[27]	*EN* 9/2 387
Ḫeltip-kušuḫ[28]	*EN* 9/2 67
Ipša-ḫalu[29]	*EN* 9/2 322
Pui-tae[30]	*EN* 9/2 152
Sîn-šaduni (son of Amur-šarri)[31]	HSS 15 144 (Akap-šenni)
Šamaš-damiq (son of Itḫ-apiḫe)[32] (IV)	HSS 19 134 (Utḫap-tae and Šeḫal-Tešup)
Šamaš-rešuya son of Turar-Tešup (V)	HSS 9 25
Šimanni son of ᵈAK-DINGIR.RA (IV)	HSS 19 113
Tarmi-Tešup[33]	*EN* 9/2 450
Tarmiya son of Kuari	HSS 19 120
Urḫi-Tešup son of Šata	HSS 5 34
[ ]-nu	*EN* 9/2 354

Arip-šarri also writes for Ilānu son of Taiuki,[34] for Šukriya, Tarmiya, and Kula-ḫupi sons of Ḫuya, for Šukriya's family,[35] and for ᶠYamaštu daughter of Ninu-atal.[36] Sîn-šadūni son of Amur-šarri also writes for Pai-Tešup servant of

[20] HSS 5 22; 9 98.
[21] AASOR 16 52.
[22] HSS 13 241.
[23] See p. 39 above and p. 55 below.
[24] See p. 24 n. 27 above.
[25] An Aḫa-ay-amši, scribe, is identified as the son of Azena in HSS 19 138:28. Aḫa-ay-amši also appears in HSS 16 593:44 with Arip-šarri, Tarmi-Tešup, and Unap-Tešup, all identified as DUB.SAR (line 44) and ÌR É.GAL (line 59). An Aḫa-ay-amši also writes HSS 19 90.
[26] Bēlaya son of Ḫanukka is attested only here.
[27] See also AASOR 16 64.
[28] Ḫeltip-kušuḫ is attested only here.
[29] An Ipša-ḫalu the scribe also appears in HSS 5 28:22, 26 (an Akawatil son of Ellu text); HSS 9 30:8 (a Pai-Tešup *wardu* of Šilwa-Tešup text); HSS 19 75:31; *EN* 9/2 169, 249:18; and *JEN* 402:36 (a text of Tarmi-Tilla son of Šurki-Tilla).
[30] Pui-tae the scribe appears only here.
[31] Only one scribe Sîn-šaduni is known, i.e., the son of Amur-šarri.
[32] Only one scribe named Šamaš-damiq is known, i.e., the son of Itḫ-apiḫe. See *NPN*, 124, and *AAN*, 118, *sub* Šamaš-damiq.
[33] Three scribes named Tarmi-Tešup are known: son of Itti-šarri, son of Rîm-Sîn, and son of Šarru-malik. Any of these is possible chronologically.
[34] See p. 25 n. 41 above.
[35] See p. 24 above.
[36] See p. 26 n. 47 above.

Šilwa-Tešup DUMU LUGAL,[37] and for members of the family of Ḫuya.[38] Šamas-damiq son of Itḫ-apiḫe also writes for Ilānu son of Taiuki,[39] the sons of Keliya,[40] Enna-mati son of Teḫip-Tilla,[41] ᶠUzna wife of Enna-mati,[42] and Ḫutiya son of Kuššiya.[43] Šimanni son of ᵈAK-DINGIR.RA also writes for Tarmi-Tilla son of Šurki-Tilla,[44] Tieš-urḫe son of Takku,[45] Ilānu son of Taiuki,[46] Pai-Tešup *wardu* of Šilwa-Tešup,[47] and Tarmiya son of Ḫuya.[48] Tarmiya son of Kuari writes for Eḫli-Tešup son of Taya.[49] Urḫi-Tešup son of Šata writes for both Ilānu son of Taiuki[50] and his son Ili-ma-aḫḫe.[51]

Aside from scribal connections with known figures in the Nuzi corpus, Utḫap-Tae son of Ar-tura also appears as a witness for a text of Šilwa-Tešup DUMU LUGAL (HSS 9 25). In HSS 5 34, he borrows tin from Ilānu son of Taiuki. One of Utḫap-tae's brothers, [ ]-Tešup appears with Tarmiya son of Ḫuya in HSS 16 457.

These associations place Ar-tura son of Kuššiya in the third and fourth generations and his son in the fourth and fifth. Their appearances with other known individuals at Nuzi confirms these dates. Note especially that Ar-tura and his son [ ]-Tešup appear with Tarmiya son of Ḫuya. Thus, their texts are contemporaneous with those of the family of Ḫuya discussed in chapter 3 and fit into the Nuzi chronology in the same way.[52]

Ar-tura Son of Kuššiya

Aside from his will, rather little is known of Ar-tura son of Kuššiya. The will does indicate that he owned real estate which his sons would divide. Further, houses of Ar-tura in Nuzi are mentioned in *EN* 9/2 10:10 and in *EN* 9/2 40:5–6, where they border houses received by Tarmiya son of Ḫuya (see p. 34 above). In *EN* 9/1 351 he loans two ANŠE of grain to Inki-Tilla son of Ḫutip-erwi and Arim-matka son of Ḫašip-Tilla; HSS 16 238 may be another of Ar-tura's

[37] HSS 9 22.
[38] HSS 19 30 and 67.
[39] HSS 5 99.
[40] HSS 13 380.
[41] *JEN* 649.
[42] *JEN* 192.
[43] *JEN* 644.
[44] See p. 25 n. 36 above.
[45] See p. 25 n. 37 above.
[46] See p. 25 n. 41 above.
[47] See p. 25 n. 42 above.
[48] See p. 25 above.
[49] AASOR 16 65 and *EN* 9/1 192, 195, 203, 213, 251. Tarmiya son of Kuari also writes *EN* 9/2 176, another text from the eastern area.
[50] HSS 5 34.
[51] HSS 5 36. In HSS 5 17, which he also writes, Turar-Tešup son of Itḫ-apiḫe (IV) is a witness.
[52] See pp. 26–27 above.

loans.[53] In the fragmentary lawsuit *EN* 9/2 458 he goes to court concerning a field and summons witnesses, most likely to his defense.[54] Another court case occurs in *EN* 9/2 401.[55] He is a witness to *JEN* 826, possibly a Tarmi-Tilla son of Šurki-Tilla text. Finally, two men of Ar-tura appear in HSS 16 232, a list of men of the land of Ḫanigalbat.[56]

fŠilwa-turi Wife of Ar-tura

As mentioned above, fŠilwa-turi may have been a second wife of Ar-tura. In his will (HSS 19 10) he leaves her a house and their(?) daughters (lines 5–10). Presumably, this meant that she had the right to arrange for their marriages. Ar-tura also confirms that fŠilwa-turi can keep the possessions she received from her father (undoubtedly her dowry; lines 11ff.). She is, however, barred from taking anything else from Ar-tura's estate should she remarry (lines 23ff.) or from selling anything to anyone (lines 37ff.). Should she do either, Ar-tura's sons are to "strip her of her clothing and send her out," that is, she will be alienated from the family property. There is a clause suggesting that Ar-tura's sons must pay a penalty if they do not conform in some way to fŠilwa-turi's status according to the will (lines 33ff.).

Apparently, Ar-tura's will was not sufficient to guarantee fŠilwa-turi security. She enters into an adoption agreement with Utḫap-tae son of Ar-tura (HSS 9 11) through which she cedes both the property left to her and a daughter, perhaps the one remaining unmarried daughter, in return for food and clothing for life. In addition, he will perform the filial responsibilities for her: he will respect her and will weep over her and bury her when she dies. fŠilwa-turi also gives Ar-tura's will to Utḫap-tae. This should place it among his texts which are

[53] For *EN* 9/2 351, see Owen, *LDN*, 122–23 (= *EN* 9 364). In HSS 16 238 an Elḫip-šarri of Āl-ilāni receives 10 ANŠE 1 KA 1 BÁN of grain from Ar-tura and Paya and will repay it in the *dimtu* of Ilu-malik. Akap-šenni son of Ar-tura, presumably Ar-tura's son, is a witness (line 13) and guarantor (line 18) in the text. Interestingly, Elḫip-šarri is also a guarantor (line 16). Note the existence of an individual named Paya son of Elḫip-šarri in the Eastern Archives (see p. 126 below). On this text and Akap-šenni as Ar-tura's son, see Fadhil, *STPPKA*, 91. In Ilu-malikwe, ibid., pp. 89–91.

[54] Among the witnesses are [ ]-*še-en-ni* [ ] (line 11), Akaya DUMU [ ] (line 12), Utḫap-tae DUMU Kipaya (line 13; see HSS 19 67:19, a Tarmiya son of Ḫuya text), Ḫaniku DUMU Tai-šenni (line 14; see *JEN* 472:25, where he appears with his brothers), Ḫašip-Tilla DUMU Kipukur (lines 15–16; see HSS 5 15, an Ili-ma-aḫḫe text; HSS 19 10:44, discussed above; *EN* 9/2 354, an Utḫap-tae son of Ar-tura text; ASSOR 16 79:1ff.; *EN* 9/2 207 and 291, discussed below), Šellumpa DUMU Nirā[ri] (line 17), Ariḫ-ḫaya DUMU Šuru[kaya] (see HSS 5 43:11, an Akap-šenni son of Zike text; 48:19, which involves Šuriḫa-ilu son of Ellaya; and ASSOR 16 55:52, 59), and Kupata DUMU Akap-šenni (line 21). These witnesses further support the chronological relationships established above by scribe.

[55] Noted by Hayden, *CPN*, 149. See [*Ku*]-*uš-ši-ya* (line 2) and *Ar-tu-ra* (lines 5 and 19). On the reverse are the seals of Šurki-Tilla son of Ipsa-ḫalu, [Akip-ta]šenni son of Ḫutip-šarri (see also HSS 9 9:25), and Iriri-Tilla son of Šeš[we] (see also HSS 9 140:12 and *JEN* 123:24).

[56] For this text, see p. 39 above and n. 90.

located either in this building or elsewhere in the eastern area even though it is assigned to N120 in the tablet registers.

ᶠŠilwa-turi's situation is rather different from that of ᶠWarḫi-Nuzu in chapter 2. While she is explicitly prohibited from dealing in family property, she does find a guardian who will provide for her needs. ᶠWarḫi-Nuzu, on the other hand, is involved in the disposition of her husband's estate, but ends up in dire circumstances. The comparison between the two illuminates the situation of women at Nuzi. They could be secure either with substantial resources of their own or in the care of a guardian of substance whom they could be secure. Without one or the other, their fates were uncertain.

Utḫap-tae and Other Sons of Ar-tura

Only brief references exist for Akap-šenni, Turar-Tešup, and Šeḫal-Tešup sons of Ar-tura. Turar-Tešup is mentioned only in Ar-tura's will. Akap-šenni is a guarantor of a loan, apparently made by his father (HSS 16 238:13, 18), is a witness in HSS 15 144:23, a text not obviously related to the family, and is listed as one of many surveyors (*JEN* 872:14). Šeḫal-Tešup also appears as a witness to a document belonging to his brother Utḫap-tae (HSS 19 134:13) and among other men in the list HSS 16 407:8. A Šeḫal-[Tešup(?)] son of Ar-tura LÚ.[ ]-*za*(?)*allu* appears in the statement *EN* 9/2 289:4–5. Of course, there is the reference to [ ]-Tešup son of Ar-tura, either Turar-Tešup or Šeḫal-Tešup, in the list HSS 16 457:5. Archives belonging to these sons of Ar-tura have not been found, but there is always the possibility that they were stored in unexcavated areas. The building in which Utḫap-tae's records are concentrated is not complete, after all. The existing evidence however, suggests that these sons of Ar-tura led stable lives (that is, were not engaged in transactions whereby their property changed) and participated in the ongoing life of the Nuzi community.

Utḫap-tae is better attested than his father and brothers. His surviving contracts indicate that his activities are fairly typical of the later generations at Nuzi. He engages in personnel contracts, of which HSS 19 113 and 114 are the best known.[57] In these matching texts, he receives ᶠMerallu and her son from Tuḫmiya son of Arim-matka, who is identified as the Tuḫmiya *warad ekalli* of other texts. *EN* 9/2 152 is a personal *titennūtu*.[58] Another personnel transaction is attested in *EN* 9/2 354:[59]

[57] For texts and discussion, see P. Negri-Scafa, SCCNH 1:325ff.

[58] For the text and comments, see Eichler, *IN*, 128, text 35.

[59] The witnesses include (lines 18–19) [Na]niya DUMU [Ki]p-ukur, known from HSS 16 384:6, 19 113:8, and *EN* 9/2 10:39, the last two being texts of Utḫap-tae son of Ar-tura; (lines 20–21) Elḫip-Tilla DUMU Ḫanaya, known from HSS 16 384:10, where he appears with his brother Ḫal-šenni and is identified as ᴸᵁ́SIPA, and *EN* 9/2 450; (lines 22–23) Ḫašip-Tilla son of Kip-ukur, for whom, see n. 54 above and below; (lines 24–25) Wantiš-šenni son of Kip-ukur, found also in HSS 16 384:2, HSS 19 117:31, *EN* 9/2 152 (an Utḫap-tae text), and AASOR 16 61:38, 53, also from the eastern area.

Thus (says) Pal-Tešup son of Ḫutiya: "We have taken one slave girl with Utḫap-tae son of Ar-tura for a price. I, the slave girl *ma-ḫi-lu-um-ma* DÙ(-uš) . . . and I owe thirty minas of tin, the share of Utḫap-tae, and I will pay (it) to Utḫap-tae. This tin Utḫap-tae will take from the price and he will be paid in full." FIVE SEALS.

An additional personnel transaction, but of a different nature, is attested in HSS 19 86, in which Karrate son of Pui-tae gives his daughter ^{f}Nūru-māti into "daughtership" to Utḫap-tae. Karrate and Utḫap-tae were related by the marriage of Utḫap-tae's daughter to Karrate. Here, it is not stated whether ^{f}Nūru-māti was Karrate's daughter by ^{f}Aze or by another woman. Intra-family adoptions of women were fairly common at Nuzi, and such transactions certainly would strengthen the relationship between the two men.[60]

Utḫap-tae was also active in real-estate acquisitions. AASOR 16 58 is a *ṭuppi mārūti* by which Eḫli-Tešup son of Kipaya adopts Utḫap-tae and gives him property in the *kirḫu* of Nuzi, south of property of Kizzari (line 7), north of property of Šeḫal-Tešup (line 8), west of the wall (line 9), and east of property of Šeḫal-Tešup (line 10). This text presents numerous difficulties, but it is clear that Eḫli-Tešup agrees to convert a *paiḫu* plot for Utḫap-tae. The transaction was understood in AASOR 16 as involving "woods" (GIŠ.ḪI.A.MEŠ) throughout the text, but the related document, *EN* 9/2 262, indicates quite clearly that Eḫli-Tešup was to build "houses" (É.ḪI.A.MEŠ):[61]

um-ma ^{I}*E-ḫé-el-te-šup*
DUMU *Ki-pa-a-a a-ni-na*
A.ŠÀ *pa-i-ḫu i+na* ŠÀ-*bi* ^{URU}*Nu-zi*
i+na kí-ir-[*ḫi*] *a-na* É.MEŠ
a-na e-pè-ši a-na ^{I}*Ut-ḫap-ta-e*
DUMU *A*[*r-tù*]*-ra ša aq-bu-ú*
ù i+[*na*]*-an-na tup-ki-in-na-tù*
ša A.ŠÀ *pa-i-ḫi ša-a-šu*
ša pa-ni-šu ù ^{I}*Ut-ḫap-ta-e*
i-[*ta*?]*-bal mi-nu-um-me-e*
[ ]*-šu ar-ku-uš a-du-ma*
[A.ŠÀ *pa-i-ḫi š*]*a-a-šu ù*
^{I}*Ut-*[*ḫap*]*-ta-e* SIG$_4$.MEŠ
i-la-ab-bi-in
ma-an-nu-um-me-e

[60] Aside from Karrate's marriage to Utḫap-tae's daughter and this arrangement, Karrate witnesses texts for Utḫap-tae (see n. 10 above). On the social implications of "daughtership" contracts, see K. Grosz, SCCNH 2:140–41, 152.

[61] Lines 1–2: Eḫli-Tešup son of Kipaya is known as well from *EN* 9/2 297:17, 21, also from the eastern area. Line 7: *tupqinnātu* 'corners'? See K. Deller, SCCNH 1:54 for discussion of *tubqu* in HSS 19 5 where it is also associated with a *paiḫu* plot. Line 18: on Karrate son of Pui-tae, see n. 10. Line 19: on Awiš-tae son of Utḫap-tae, see HSS 19 10:42, 47 (Ar-tura's will); 51:24, 33; 79:33, 45 (a Paikku son of Ariḫ-ḫarpa text from the southwest area); and 117:29, 35. Line 20: on Ulmi-Tilla son of Akip-šenni, see HSS 15 25:39; HSS 19 81:1ff.; *EN* 9/1 454:4ff.

ša KI.BAL-*kat*
1 GU$_4$ SIG$_5$-*qú* DIRI-*la*
IGI *Kàr-ra-te* DUMU *Pu-i-ta-e*
IGI *A-wi-iš-ta-e* DUMU *Ut-ḫap-ta-e*
IGI *Ul-mi-til-la* DUMU *A-kip-še-en-ni*
[IGI *A-ri-i*]*p*-LUGAL DUB.SAR
[IGI *A-i-tù-ur-t*]*a* DUMU *Nu-ḫu-ya*
NA$_4$ DUB.SAR-*rù*
NA$_4$ DUB.SAR NA$_4$ *E-ḫé-el-*[*te-šup*]

Upper Edge
NA$_4$ ^{I}*A-i-tù-ur-ta*

Lower Edge
NA$_4$ ^{I}*Ul-mi-til-la* NA$_4$ ^{I}[*A-wi-iš-ta-e*]

Thus (says) Eḫli-Tešup son of Kipaya: "Yes, the unbuilt plot is in the heart of Nuzi in the *kirḫu* on which I said (I would) build houses for Utḫap-tae son of Ar-tura. Now the *tupqinnātu* of that unbuilt plot are as before and Utḫap-tae is 'satisfied'. . . . Whatever . . . afterwards . . . as long as . . . that unbuilt plot and Utḫap-tae will do the brickwork." Whoever breaks the contract will pay one good OX. FIVE WITNESSES. FIVE SEALS.

In this text Eḫli-Tešup and Utḫap-tae contract further concerning the building project. It appears that the original contract has been modified in that Utḫap-tae now will do the brickwork on the houses. In light of other texts found in the Eastern Archives, it is noteworthy that this property is located in the *kirḫu* of Nuzi, west of the wall, and neighboring houses of Šeḫal-Tešup.

In *EN* 9/2 67 Utḫap-tae and Ar-tašenni son of Arik-kewar contract for the planting and harvesting of a field, the proceeds of which they will share:[62]

Thus (says) Ar-tašenni son of Arik-kewar: "Three *imer* of fields in the *ugāru* of the city of Nuzi, east of the field of Šaten-šuh, west of the field of Ḫutip-šimika, which the dike of the queen cuts in two, I have given to Utḫap-tae son of Ar-tura for six years *šutadu.* Seed for seed, harvest for harvest we will divide equally." Thus (says) Utḫap-tae: "I . . . owe and I will give . . . one ox. . . ." Whoever breaks the contract will pay one ox. Thus (says) Ar-tašenni: "The grain that is written we will divide on the threshing floor. I will carry (it) away and Utḫap-tae will carry (it) away." FIVE SEALS.

Otherwise, Utḫap-tae is known from the loan texts of Nuzi, among them *EN* 9/1 450[63] (in which Hišm-apu son of Tarmiya is the borrower), *EN* 9/1 322[64] (which involves Enna-mati son of Ḫabira), *EN* 9/1 363[65] and *EN* 9/2

[62] The *ekū šarrati* 'the queen's dyke' (line 5) clearly was located in Nuzi (see line 3).
[63] = *EN* 9 375 in Owen, *LDN*, 127.
[64] Owen, *LDN*, 108.
[65] Owen, *LDN*, 19, 122.

387[66] (involving Teḫip-Tilla son of Taya). In these transactions Utḫap-tae lends grain, metal, and oxen. HSS 19 120 is the partially preserved record of a sale to Utḫap-Tae.[67]

Šeḫal-Tešup Son of Teḫup-šenni

Šeḫal-Tešup son of Teḫup-šenni is known from few documents signed by scribes, but those few indicate that he, like Utḫap-tae son of Ar-tura, was active in the last period at Nuzi. Scribes who write for him include:

Abī-ilu (most likely son of ᵈAK-DINGIR.RA) (IV)	*EN* 9/2 184
Ḫutip-apu[68]	*EN* 9/2 359
SAG-⟨AN⟩.KI	*EN* 9/2 298
ᵈUTU-PAB (most likely son of Akiya) (V)	*EN* 9/2 360

Abī-ilu also writes for Ilānu son of Taiuki,[69] Pai-Tešup *wardu* of Šilwa-Tešup,[70] Ḫampizi son of Ar-šatuya,[71] Paššši-Tilla son of Pula-ḫali,[72] and Šukriya son of Ḫuya.[73] SAG-AN·KI also writes for Ilānu son of Taiuki and Akawatil son of Zike.[74] ᵈUTU-PAB also writes for Šilwa-Tešup DUMU LUGAL,[75] Ili-ma-aḫḫe son of Ilānu,[76] and Paššši-Tilla son of Pula-ḫali.[77]

Three letters offer some insight into Šeḫal-Tešup's position and operations.[78] In HSS 14 22 Zike notifies Irkipa, *ḫazannu* of the city of Ḫušri, that Šeḫal-Tešup son of Teḫup-šenni has been appointed the *gugallu* of the city of Hušri.[79] According to AASOR 16 76 (=HSS 14 20), Šeḫal-Tešup had a "household" (line 4 *nīš bīti*^{MEŠ}), some of whose members had stolen grain and were to be sent before the king. The recipient of that letter is Šeḫram-mušni, apparently a ranking servant or representative of Šeḫal-Tešup, judging from his responsibilities concerning the household. In HSS 14 21, he writes to Akip-tašenni concerning

[66] Owen, *LDN*, 27, 129–30.

[67] A witness in this text, Akiya son of Nu[pa]na[ni] (line 18), also appears in HSS 14 595:18, 24; HSS 19 49:45, 53; *JEN* 472:26, 34; 662:74.

[68] Ḫutip-apu the scribe is attested only here.

[69] See p. 25 n. 41 above.

[70] See p. 25 n. 42 above.

[71] See p. 25 n. 43 above.

[72] See p. 25 n. 49 above.

[73] See p. 24 above.

[74] See p. 25 above and nn. 40–41.

[75] HSS 9 26:13.

[76] HSS 5 15:50 and 87:37, 43.

[77] See p. 98 below.

[78] See discussion of these letters in Fadhil, *STPPKA*, 87–88.

[79] For the text see Zaccagnini, *RLLA*, 60–61, and Fadhil, *STPPKA*, 87. For Ḫušri see Fadhil, *STPPKA*, 83–88, and L. R. Fisher, *NGN*, 57 no. 411.

members of the household of Šeḫal-Tešup who have been sold in the land of Lullu:[80]

> To Akip-tašenni say: "Thus (says) Šeḫam-mušni: 'People from the household of Šeḫal-Tešup have been stolen and have been sold in the land of Lullu. Now, take him in hand and let him see them. You, seize whichever men from the city of Nuzi go to Lullu but do not carry a tablet and a seal, and bring them to me. The king will not pronounce judgement. Whichever men are lost, accordingly I will report to the king.' "

These letters indicate not only that Šeḫal-Tešup was an official but also that he had his own household large enough to require the services of Šeḫam-mušni, who appears to have been Šeḫal-Tešup's major-domo. These references suggest that Šeḫal-Tešup had estates with which his *nīš bīti* were associated. HSS 14 21 refers to "men of Nuzi" going to Lullu under questionable circumstances. This might indicate that Šeḫal-Tešup's lost dependents were normally located at Nuzi and that Šeḫal-Tešup's properties were there. On the basis of the archeological evidence, that is, the building in which Šeḫal-Tešup's texts were found, any large holdings that he had were certainly not in the city of Nuzi, though they might have been in the surrounding area. Ḫušri, too, is a strong candidate for the location of Šeḫal-Tešup's property. He was appointed *gugallu* there and acquired real estate there as well (see below).

It appears that Šeḫal-Tešup had no heirs, since he adopted Ḫutiya son of Puḫiya and gives him all of his property in HSS 19 50.[81] Should Šeḫal-Tešup's wife bear a son, Ḫutiya would become *tertennu*, or secondary heir. Ḫutiya's family had further business with Šeḫal-Tešup in HSS 19 112, in which ᶠḪalb-abuša daughter of Ḫutiya son of Puḫiya sells a *ṣuḫārtu* GÉME *t*[*a-ar*]*-ku-li* 'slave girl of Tarkuli(?)' to Šeḫal-Tešup and three other men, including Akip-tašenni son of Ḫutiya and Šurkip-šarri son of Ḫutiya. This tablet was written in Nuzi.

Šeḫal-Tešup also engaged in a personal *titennūtu* with Minaš-šuk son of Keliya and ᶠUnuš-kiaše the wife of Keliya, who give Appuziki son of Keliya to him for four years (*EN* 9/2 156).[82] This mother-and-son team of contracting parties is reminiscent of ᶠWarḫi-Nuzu and Teḫip-Tilla of the family of Šukriya.

The property involved in the single real estate *titennūtu* (*EN* 9/2 184) of Šeḫal-Tešup is in Ḫušri, the city of which he was the *gugallu*:[83]

[80] The problem of runaway or stolen slaves was a common one in the second millennium. From the Code of Ḫammurabi to the treaties of Alalaḫ and Ugarit, practices of repatriating such individuals are described. Here, Šeḫam-mušni tries to prevent their leaving the country.

[81] For text and discussion, see Paradise, *NIP*, 47ff., 193ff. Note the seal of Utḫap-tae [son of Ar-tura?] on the upper edge.

[82] For text and discussion, see Eichler, *IN*, 111, text 6.

[83] For Ḫušri, see n. 79. Among the witnesses are (line 22) Akiya DUMU Tarmiya (see HSS 19 126:35, a text involving the sons of Pula-ḫali) and (line 25) Utḫap-tae DUMU Tarmiya (see HSS 15 144:28, 31).

(Property . . .) in the plain of the city of [Ḫu]šri, [we]st of the field of Zikašu?, south of the field of Teḫeš-šenni, east of the field of Mezazu, and north of the field of Zaḫḫabu, for lease to [Šeḫ]al-Tešup son of Teḫup-šenni [Marru] has given. Šeḫal-Tešup [has given Marru one once-shorn ewe. As soon as] Marru [returns] the once-shorn ewe to Še[ḫal-Tešup], he will take his field. If the field is larger, [it will not be diminished]. If the field is smaller, it will not be increased. If the field is plowed, Šeḫal-Tešup will not take it. If the field has a claim, Marru will clear (it). The tablet was written after the proclamation in the city of Ḫušri. Five witnesses who surveyed the field and gave the sheep. The hand of Abī-ilu the scribe. FOUR SEALS.

Two of Šeḫal-Tešup's texts involve livestock. In *EN* 9/2 360, he lends a ewe to Šekar-Tilla son of Mušteya:[84]

The statement of Šekar-Tilla son of Mušteya before these witnesses. Thus he spoke: "Previously, I borrowed one twice-shorn good ewe from Šeḫal-Tešup son of Teḫup-šenni and did not return (it). Now, one sheep according to the authority of this tablet to Šeḫal-Tešup he(!) will give. If he(!) does not, it will be shorn and will be credited my account." FOUR SEALS.

The second (*EN* 9/2 298) is the statement of Ipša-ḫalu son of [ ] and Paya son of Ni-[ ] who receive sheep for herding from Šeḫal-Tešup:

Thus (say) Ip[ša]-ḫalu son of [ ] and Paya son of Ni[ ]: "Five male sheep and five ewes we received from [Šeḫal-Tešup] son of Teḫup-šen[ni] for herding. At the beginning of the month of Impur[tanni] ten sheep Ipsa-ḫalu and Paya will give to Šeḫal-Tešup. Whoever remains will pay and give them to Šeḫal-Tešup. Two sheep . . . Šeḫal-Tešup son of Te[ḫup-šĕnni]." Thus (say) Ip[ša-ḫalu] and Paya: "Those sheep from Nuzi we took and to Nuzi we will return before these witnesses."

The witness list on the reverse is largely broken. Seals of El-[ ], Akiya, Šellu, Šen-[ ]-ni Akiya, Šennaya, and SAG-⟨AN⟩.KI the scribe can be identified. The sheep are taken from and are to be returned to Nuzi. This might indicate that Šeḫal-Tešup had certain agricultural holdings in the vicinity of Nuzi.[85]

In addition to the texts above, Šeḫal-Tešup appears in *EN* 9/2 359,[86] his statement concerning the repayment of grain to Ḫeltip-apu. HSS 15 294 is the

[84] Šekar-Tilla son of [Mu]šteya appears in HSS 15 8:16. Among the witnesses is Ilaya son of Ḫabira (line 19), for whom see p. 39 n. 89 above. Note that wool and young are the expected produce of the sheep charged against the borrower. See Morrison, SCCNH 1:257–96.

[85] That the sheep were received in Nuzi and would be returned in Nuzi (lines 16–21) most likely reflects the semi-transhumant character of the herding profession. It is interesting that the two livestock documents of Šeḫal-Tešup are formal contracts spelling out the specific responsibilities of the herdsmen. As such, they differ from the herding documents of Šilwa-Tešup whose contracts are far more abbreviated. This might suggest that the relationship between Šeḫal-Tešup and the men who herded for him was less well established than that of Šilwa-Tešup and his herdsmen. See Morrison, SCCNH 1:257–96.

[86] For the text, see Owen, *LDN*, 121.

statement of Ḫizzuri son of Unap-Tešup concerning the repair of chariot wheels for Šeḫal-Tešup.[87] On the basis of this text, Šeḫal-Tešup has been identified as a *rākib narkabti*.[88]

Utḫap-tae and the Šeḫal-Tešups

The quest for understanding the relationship between Utḫap-tae son of Ar-tura and Šeḫal-Tešup son of Teḫup-šenni, if any beyond that of neighbors in the eastern area, is complicated by the fact that there are two Šeḫal-Tešups attested in the records of Group 17: son of Ar-tura and son of Teḫup-šenni. It is not at all likely that they were one and the same individual. Šeḫal-Tešup son of Teḫup-šenni was a sufficiently prominent person that his patronym would not be confused, even if he had some familial relationship to the family of Ar-tura.[89]

One issue is the identity of the Šeḫal-Tešup who owned the houses in the eastern area. Houses of Ar-tura and houses of Utḫap-tae are attested in the area. Šeḫal-Tešup's houses might simply have been Šeḫal-Tešup son of Ar-tura's share of his father's estate. There are no archives belonging to Šeḫal-Tešup son of Ar-tura, however, in the eastern area. On the other hand, Šeḫal-Tešup son of Teḫup-šenni did store at least some of his records in this area. Does this mean that he owned the building in which his tablets were found?

There are some intriguing materials that may or may not illuminate the problem of Utḫap-Tae's relationship to Šeḫal-Tešup son of Teḫup-šenni. The first is the text *EN* 9/2 125, which includes both the names Šeḫal-Tešup and Utḫap-tae.

1 3 ANŠE A.ŠÀ *i+na šu-pa-al*
mi-is-ri ša URU *Ar-ta-iš*
4 GIŠ.APIN A.ŠÀ *i+na e-le-en* A.ŠÀ
ša [I]*Un-te-e-a iš-tu* KASKAL *ša* Ka_4-[ ]

87 This text is sealed by Taizi son of Nanteya (see *JEN* 102:48, 54, a Tarmi-Tilla son of Šurki-Tilla text), Unaya son of Šeḫliya, Akip-Tilla son of Ḫašuar (see AO 15:543:4, where he is a *rākib narkabti*; and HSS 16 83:10, discussed above in connection with Tarmiya son of Ḫuya on p. 40 n. 92), and Puḫi-šenni son of Kipaya (see HSS 9 108:22, an Ilānu son of Taiuki text; and HSS 16 461:3 where he may appear as an *emantuḫlu*).

88 See Fadhil, *STPPKA*, 87. It is, perhaps, worth noting that it is not clear all *rākib narkabti* had chariots and that all people with chariots were members of the *rākib narkabti* class.

89 There is an instance of confusion of patronymics when the individuals involved worked closely together. The herdsman Ṣill-kubi son of Puḫi-šenni is also identified as Ṣill-kubi son of Kawinni (HSS 13 427) in a text in which he was working with Tae son of Kawinni (HSS 13 427). He also collaborates with Šimika-atal son of Tae (HSS 9 62). He must have been either a relative or close associate, and the scribe simply identified him as the brother of the man with whom he was working. It is interesting, however, that the name of Šeḫal-Tešup son of Ar-tura is followed in *EN* 9/2 289:5 by [LÚ][ ] ZA-*a*[*l?*]-*lu*. The text is broken, so the reading is not certain. Perhaps this is, in fact, *gugallu*. Thus, there are four possibilities: (1) the family included two Šeḫal-Tešups, both of whom held offices; (2) the family included two Šeḫal-Tešups, both of whom were *gugallus*; (3) Šeḫal-Tešup son of Teḫup-šenni and Šeḫal-Tešup son of Ar-tura were one and the same individual; (4) the two are entirely unrelated. The third possibility is remote because he would appear well-enough established on his own to avoid such confusions.

4 GIŠ.APIN A.ŠÀ *iš-tu* GIŠ.KIRI$_{6}$
ša ^{I}*Šu-ku-ur-te-šup i+na il-ta-[an]*
ŠU.NÌGIN 3 ANŠE 8 GIŠ.APIN A.ŠÀ URU *[Ar-ta-iš]*
ḪA.LA-*šu ša* ^{I}*Ut-ḫap-ta-e*
[a+n]a ^{I}*Š[e-ḫ]a-al-te-šup* ŠEŠ-*šu*
[i]t-ta-din ma-an-nu
[i+na EGIR*]-ki an-nu-u a+na an-ni-i*
[la i]-ša-aš-ši iš-tu
break
[IGI *Tar]-mi-til-[la*]
NA$_{4}$ ^{I}*Tu-ra-ri* NA$_{4}$ ^{I}*Ma-[at-t]e-šup*
NA$_{4}$ ^{I}*Tar-mi-til-la*
NA$_{4}$ ^{I}*Ut-ḫap-ta-e*
NA$_{4}$ [DUB].SAR

Three *imer*s of fields west of the border of the city of Artaiš, four *awēḫaru* of fields east of the field of Unteya, from the road of Ka-[ ], four *awēḫaru* from the orchards of Šukri-Tešup in the north: a total of three *imer*s and eight *awēḫaru* of fields in the city of [Artaiš], the inheritance share of Utḫap-tae to his brother Šeḫal-Tešup, he has given. Afterward one shall not hail the other into court. FIVE SEALS (including those of Utḫap-tae and the scribe).

Neither party to this contract is identified by patronymic, and the text is assigned to N120. Other texts belonging to both Utḫap-tae son of Ar-tura and Šeḫal-Tešup son of Teḫup-šenni were assigned to N120, though, so the text might very well have belonged to the archives of Group 17. The circumstances behind this transaction are not known, but an Utḫap-tae transfers property called his "inheritance share" to a Šeḫal-Tešup who is called his "brother," a term used for a blood relative, an adopted brother, or even, apparently, a "business associate" of some kind.[90]

This text is similar to those in which family members divide their property.[91] If there were other elements to the division or a reciprocal arrangement of some sort, they are lost in the break. Given the placement of the prohibition against raising claims (lines 10ff.), however, it is doubtful that any other real estate is involved.

This text probably is a transaction between Utḫap-tae and Šeḫal-Tešup sons of Ar-tura as part of the settlement of Ar-tura's will. There is, however, hardly any evidence for Šeḫal-Tešup's archives, to which this text would belong, in the area. It is interesting that there may have been a family relationship between Utḫap-tae son of Ar-tura and Šeḫal-Tešup son of Teḫup-šenni. This link is made through Ḫerši and Urḫi-Tilla sons of Naniya, identified as relatives of the family of Ar-tura on the basis of *EN* 9/2 10. A Teḫup-šenni son of Naniya is attested in HSS 5 58:19, a text of Zike son of Akkuya written by Alki-Tešup son of Waqar-Bēli. This scribe belongs to the fourth generation of the family of Apil-Sîn, and so

[90] *CAD* A/1 s.v. *aḫu*. See also *JEN* 467 discussed by Maidman, *Aššur* 1/9 (1979) 2 n. 3.
[91] See p. 28 n. 57 above.

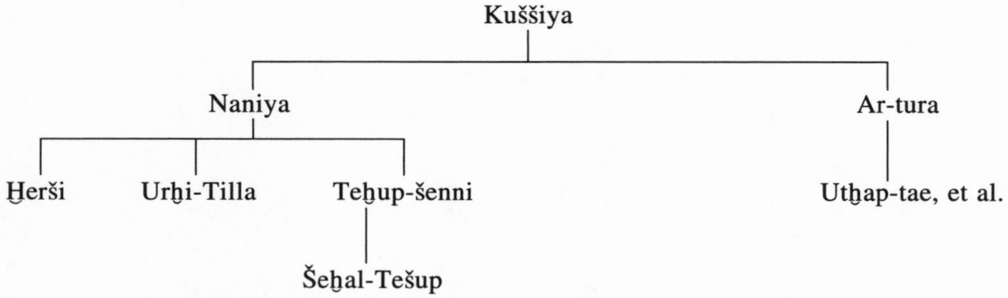

FIGURE 6. *Revised Genealogy of Kuššiya*

aligns Teḫup-šenni son of Naniya with Utḫap-tae son of Ar-tura. If Teḫup-šenni son of Naniya was, indeed, the brother of Ḫerši and Urḫi-Tilla, then Kuššiya's family might be expanded as in figure 6, showing Šeḫal-Tešup as Utḫap-tae's first cousin "once removed." Thus, *EN* 9/2 125 could have involved a transaction between the two men whose archives appear together at Nuzi.

Summary

The archives discussed above clearly belonged to Utḫap-tae son of Ar-tura and Šeḫal-Tešup son of Teḫup-šenni. The activities of these two men are not as well documented as those of Tarmiya son of Ḫuya (chapter 2), but they are similar to his and those of other members of the latter generations at Nuzi as shown by the texts of the eastern and southwestern areas. In addition, Šeḫal-Tešup, like Tarmiya son of Ḫuya (chapter 2), was a *gugallu*, an official of the palace. He was assigned to the city of Ḫušri where he also acquired land. Indeed, his own estates might have been there. He does seem to have been active in Nuzi where he may have owned property. These references suggest that the primary archive owner was Utḫap-tae.

Utḫap-tae's profession is not known, but he owned a number of houses and other property in Nuzi, so he was a man of some means directly associated with Nuzi. In fact, his real-estate transactions seem to have been designed to consolidate his holdings in the city of Nuzi. Some of these holdings he inherited from his father; another part came from his grandfather's property by way of Ḫerši and Urḫi-Tilla. The rest was non-familial property acquired from others.

A major question concerning the archives discussed above is why they are located in the same building. Central to this issue is the reference to "houses of Šeḫal-Tešup" in AASOR 16 58. If both Šeḫal-Tešup son of Teḫup-šenni and Utḫap-tae son of Ar-tura owned houses in Nuzi, one would expect their archives to be stored separately in their own houses. Of course, the archives might have become mixed together either at the destruction of the city or in the excavation and/or its reports. The little information provided in the excavation report concerning the neighboring Groups 15 and 18 does not illuminate this issue; the relatively small number of tablets belonging to Šeḫal-Tešup son of Teḫup-šenni and the scattered attributions for some of them preclude a definite conclusion regarding this possibility.

If the "houses of Šeḫal-Tešup" belonged to Šeḫal-Tešup son of Ar-tura, not Šeḫal-Tešup son of Teḫup-šenni, the latter is left without any attested houses in the city of Nuzi. In fact, his primary area of activity might have been Ḫušri. Throughout the eastern area there are individuals whose properties and official responsibilities were elsewhere but who kept their documents in Nuzi. If Šeḫal-Tešup son of Teḫup-šenni was one of these individuals and at the same time was related to the family of Ar-tura, he might have stored his texts in his relative's (i.e., Utḫap-tae's) house.

Some of the texts of Group 17 along with one from Group 18A shed some light on the configuration of the city and patterns of urban real estate acquisition. Houses and *paiḫu* plots acquired by Tarmiya son of Ḫuya (*EN* 9/2 40) and Utḫap-tae son of Ar-tura (*EN* 9/2 10 and AASOR 16 58) and owned by Ar-tura (HSS 19 11) were located in the *kirḫu* of the city. Furthermore, those in three texts (*EN* 9/2 10 and 40 and AASOR 16 58) are "west of the wall" or "west of the wall of the *kirḫu*. The eastern area is, of course, the part of the city west of the city wall of Nuzi.[92] So, the texts refer to buildings in the area in which the tablets were found. This area, then, was part of the *kirḫu* or area inside the wall of Nuzi. In the time of Tarmiya and Utḫap-tae there were *paiḫu* or unbuilt plots remaining next to the wall. Both Tarmiya and Utḫap-tae acquired properties bordering their own or their family's. The holdings of both Tarmiya and the family of Ar-tura extended to the wall itself in the eroded area into which their existing buildings continued. Property belonging to Tarmiya and to the family of Ar-tura became contiguous at the area of the wall with Tarmiya's acquisition of *paiḫu* land south of his own property and north of houses of Ar-tura (*EN* 9/2 40). These materials point to expansion and consolidation of properties by two of the principal figures of the area.

Group 17 was presumed to have some cultic purpose, but it appears to have been a private house owned by one or the other of the individuals, most likely Utḫap-tae, whose archives are discussed above. Therefore, the contents of the house would either belong to that individual or be in that individual's keeping for some reason. The artifacts of "cultic" significance might have been for private use or—perhaps in the case of the eye beads, for commerce—related to some religious responsibility of the owner of the house.

[92] R. F. S. Starr, ibid, 324–332.

CHAPTER 4

Urḫi-kušuḫ DUMU LUGAL and the Family of Muš-apu: Texts from Group 19 (Part 1)

The Archeological Context and Distribution of Tablets

Unlike Groups 17 and 18A, the entire plan of Group 19 is preserved (fig. 7). Composed of eighteen rooms,[1] it is arranged in an orderly fashion with separate Groups of rooms that Starr interpreted as independent dwelling units within the larger structure.[2] A particularly interesting feature of Group 19 is the multi-leveled nature of the structure. Room S137 is about a meter lower than the courtyard S133. Rooms S129 through S137B slope down with steps between S128 and S124 and a single step between S124 and S112 to about a meter and a half below the level of the courtyard. A series of six steps connects S137B to S167 on the upper level. Starr suggests that the lower rooms belonged to an earlier level and were reused in the later building.[3]

The finds in this building were fairly typical pottery, some cultic and ceremonial objects, storage vessels, and the like. In addition, Starr mentions tablets in S133 (the courtyard), S129, S112, S137B, S138–139, S132, and S135. Aside from the single texts noted in connection with S137B and S138–139, the excavation report provides only general information concerning the quantity and condition of tablets found in these rooms. The excavation report records finding "tablets" (S133), "several tablets in bad condition" (S129), "a large number" (S112), a "large quantity" (S112 lower pavement), "large numbers" (S132), and "a few" tablets (S136).[4] It is interesting that some of the texts from S112 come from a lower pavement associated with an earlier phase of the room.[5]

Tablet registers and other materials list 181 tablets and fragments from Group 19.[6] As Starr notes, these documents relate for the most part to Puḫi-šenni son of Muš-apu and the family of Pula-ḫali.[7] The few records of Urḫi-

[1] S152, 183, 133, 182, 137, 129, 128, 124, 112, 137B, 167, 130, 160, 166, 139–138, 141, 132, and 136. See R. F. S. Starr, *Nuzi* 1:313–18.

[2] Ibid., 313, 318.

[3] Ibid., 314–15.

[4] Ibid., 314, 316, 318.

[5] Ibid., 317. It is most unfortunate that these tablets cannot be identified, as they might provide stratified evidence concerning the history of this area.

[6] See Group 19 in table 1 above, pp. 13–18.

[7] Ibid., 313, 318.

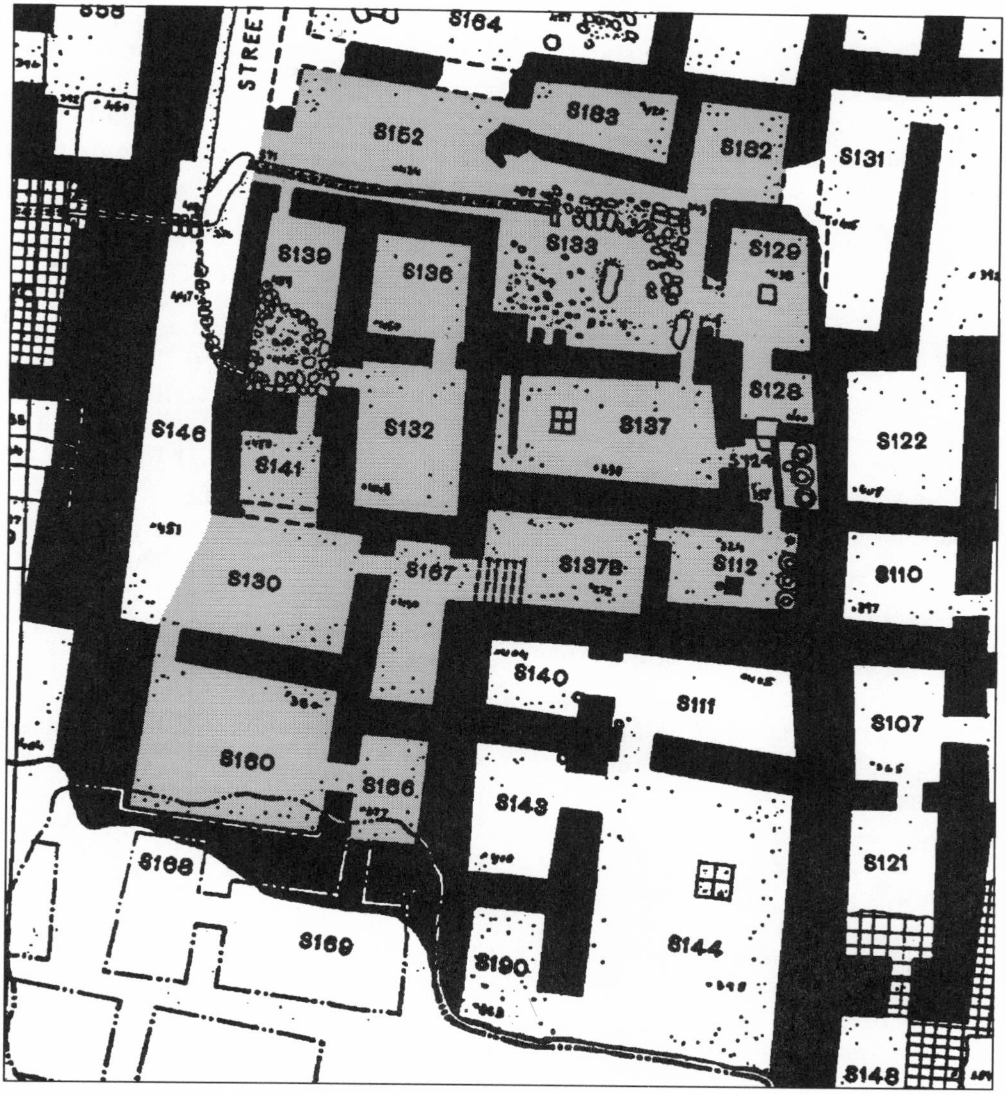

FIGURE 7. *Group 19* (from Starr, *Nuzi II*)

kušuḫ DUMU LUGAL are also located in Group 19. Of course, texts belonging to other individuals in the eastern area[8] and elsewhere[9] are assigned to Group 19. Further, texts belonging to the families of Muš-apu and Pula-ḫali are assigned to

[8] E.g., Ḫuya (AASOR 16 59), Tarmiya (HSS 14 31, 19 67), Tarmiya son of Ḫuya (*EN* 9/2 186), Šeḫal-Tešup son of Teḫup-šenni (HSS 14 21, *EN* 9/2 359), Utḫap-tae son of Ar-tura (*EN* 9/2 10, 289, 387).

[9] Šerta-ma-ilu (*EN* 9/1 233); Šilwa-Tešup DUMU LUGAL (HSS 16 420).

rooms in other buildings[10] or have no room numbers.[11] Within Group 19, the records of Urḫi-kušuḫ DUMU LUGAL and the family of Muš-apu cluster in rooms S112, S124, and S129, and those of the family of Pula-ḫali in S132 and S133 (see chap. 5). In addition to these two large Groups of tablets, some individual texts and small Groups of documents belonging to other individuals are found in Group 19. These are discussed in chapters 5 and 6.

Urhi-kušuḫ DUMU LUGAL

Urḫi-kušuḫ DUMU LUGAL is known from only five texts in the eastern area.[12] Two of these are grain loans: *EN* 9/2 321 and 490.[13] One (HSS 16 229) is a *ṭuppi taḫsilti* recording distributions to various individuals including skilled workers, Eḫli-Tešup DUMU LUGAL, and three men identified by patronymic.[14] HSS 19 111 is a personnel document by which Turar-Tešup son of Puḫi-šenni enters the *niš bīti* of Urḫi-kušuḫ for three years. The tablet was written in the city of Unap-šewe and witnessed by six men, including Puḫi-šenni son of Muš-apu, Elḫip-Tilla son of Kel-Tešup the scribe, and Eḫlip-apu son of Abeya.[15] The final text is AASOR 16 62, a personal *titennūtu* by which Akip-Tilla son of Šarriya gives his son Kinniya to Urḫi-kušuḫ for five years in return for three ANŠE of emmer and one ANŠE of barley. Akip-Tilla states that he has received the grain from Puḫi-šenni son of Muš-apu, the *amumiḫḫuru* 'representative' of Urḫi-kušuḫ.[16] Two of the witnesses are Akip-šarri and Kanna son of Ḫabira, the first of whom also witnesses *EN* 9/2 21, a Puḫi-šenni son of Muš-apu text written in Unapšewe. The presence of this man and Puḫi-šenni son of Muš-apu suggest that AASOR 16 62 was also written in that city. However, it is clear that Urḫi-kušuḫ and

[10] The Muš-apu family: S113: *EN* 9/2 18, 163; N120: *EN* 9/2 336; S151: *EN* 9/2 38, 455; P428: *EN* 9/2 301; P465: *EN* 9/2 326; P480: *EN* 9/2 333. The Pula-ḫali family: C120 (= N120): AASOR 16 97; *EN* 9/2 353, 391; S151: HSS 19 126; P485: *EN* 9/2 299.

[11] The Muš-apu family: *EN* 9/2 19 and 144. The Pula-ḫali family: *EN* 9/2 188, 267, 275, 343, 345, 512, 513, 515, 524.

[12] A complete survey of the Urḫi-Kušuḫ materials appears in Fadhil's *STPPKA*, 296 and 319.

[13] For the texts see Owen, *LDN*, 107–8, where *EN* 9/2 490 appears as *EN* 9 323.

[14] Among the recipients, Puḫi-šenni son of Artašenni (line 16) also borrows grain from Puḫi-šenni son of Muš-apu (*EN* 9/2 338), and Haiš-Tešup son of Erwi-šarri witnesses *JEN* 469. Eḫli-Tešup DUMU LUGAL also appears in HSS 15 21:4, 34:23, and 36:1, all military contexts (see Fadhil, *STPPKA*, 296).

[15] Note that only SMN 2009 is probably the correct number for this text. SMN 2319 and 2321 are definitely not used in the join. A transliteration and commentary appear in Fadhil, *STPPKA*, 316, where it is suggested that Turar-Tešup is most likely the son of Puḫi-šenni son of Muš-apu. On Elḫip-Tilla son of Kel-Tešup the scribe, see below. Eḫlip-apu son of Abeya witnesses many texts belonging to Puḫi-senni son of Muš-apu (see p. 88 below). Another witness is Akip-Tilla son of Kikkiya who also appears in CT 51:3 as a leather-worker.

[16] For a translation of the text and comments, see Eichler, *IN*, 138, text 52. On *amumiḫḫuru* see ibid. and *CAD* A/2 90 and *AHw* 45, *sub amumiḫḫuru*. The term *amumiḫḫuru* appears to mean 'representative' on the basis of context. Whether or not it is an official position or office is not known. Also note Fadhil, *STPPKA*, 316.

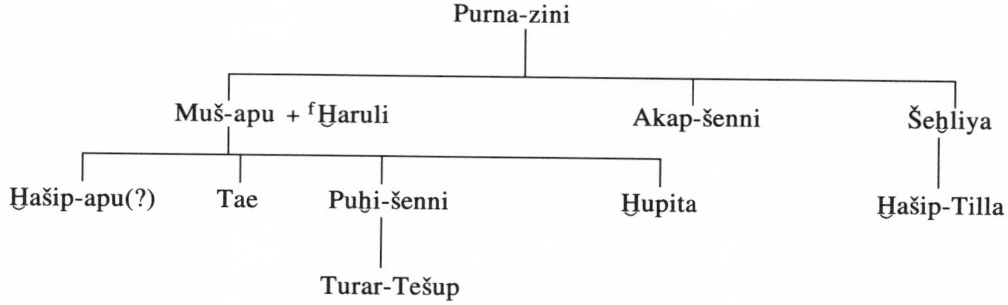

FIGURE 8. *Genealogy of Purna-zini*

Puḫi-šenni son of Muš-apu were associated outside this text. Puḫi-šenni witness one of Urḫi-kušuḫ's texts. Furthermore, their documents were stored together. HSS 19 111 and possibly AASOR 16 62 were written in Unapšewe where the activities of the family of Muš-apu were centered.

The Family of Muš-apu Son of Purna-zini

EN 9/2 includes a large number of texts relating to the family of Muš-apu son of Purna-zini. Combined with materials published previously, they allow for the reconstruction of this family and many of its activities. HSS 19 8, the will of Muš-apu son of Purna-zini, provides the names of Puḫi-šenni, Tae, and Ḫupita, his sons, and ᶠḪaruli, his wife, and indicates that Tae was the chief heir.[17] A Ḫašip-apu son of Muš-apu is the principal party in HSS 19 145:3–4, a text assigned to S130 in Group 19. He is mentioned only here, but the room number is troublesome in that no tablets for the room are noted in the excavation report. Hence, his connection with the family must be considered tentative. *EN* 9/2 143 gives the name of Akap-šenni son of Purna-zini, and *EN* 9/2 175 the names of Šeḫliya son of Purna-z[ini] and his son Ḫašip-Tilla, perhaps members of this family.[18] The Turar-Tešup son of Puḫi-šenni, who appears above in connection with Urḫi-kušuḫ, may be the son of Puḫi-šenni son of Muš-apu, as noted above. The family tree of Purna-zini can be reconstructed as in figure 8.[19] AASOR 16 67

[17] For text and comments, see Paradise, *NIP*, 102ff., text 23. Line 2 should read DUMU Pur-ra-[zi-ni]. See Fadhil, *STPPKA*, 313.

[18] These individuals were active in Unapšewe as *EN* 9/2 143 and the numerous attestations of Hašip-Tilla son of Šeḫliya indicate. The preserved portion of the name of Šeḫliya's father, *Pur-na-*[ ] might be restored as Purn-apu or Purna-zini. If it is Purna-zini, Šeḫliya undoubtedly belonged to this family. The name Purna-zini is not common. In fact, it is otherwise attested only as the patronymic of Akap-šenni and Muš-apu. It is unlikely that there were two men named Purna-zini in Unapšewe whose sons were contemporaneous.

[19] Revised from Paradise, *NIP*, 388, chart 13. Fadhil also discusses the family of Muš-apu, *STPPKA*, 314.

mentions an individual named Enna-pali son of Šennaya, brother of Muš-apu son of Purna-zini. He also appears in *JEN* 63:1ff. in a *ṭuppi mārūti* by which he transfers property in Unapšewe to Teḫip-Tilla son of Puḫi-šenni but there is no mention of Muš-apu in that text. Enna-pali was probably either a distant relative or a close associate of Muš-apu.[20]

Muš-apu son of Purna-zini

Aside from his will, Muš-apu son of Purna-zini is attested in numerous real-estate and personnel transactions and loans. AASOR 16 66 is a *ṭuppi titennūti* by which Pui-tae son of Eteya gives eight *awēḫaru* of fields in the city of Unapšewe to Muš-apu son of Purna-zini for five years in return for five ANŠE of grain, one ANŠE of wheat, three minas of tin, two male spring lambs with their wool, and one female lamb with its wool.[21] AASOR 16 67 is the statement of Mannu-māḫiršu son of Nai-šeri who gives two ANŠE of fields in Unapšewe to Muš-apu after the latter paid a four-year-old ox in place of forty minas of copper. The property had previously been given to Ḫamanna son of Šurki-turi, Mannu-māḫiršu's grandfather by Enna-pali son of Šennaya, "brother" of Muš-apu.[22]

Among the *EN* 9/2 texts, Muš-apu acquires property through adoption on numerous occasions, in some instances from the same individual more than once. In *EN* 9/2 17 Ḫanie son of Teḫip-apu adopts Muš-apu and gives him three ANŠE of fields in Unapšewe:[23]

> Tablet of adoption by which Ḫanie son of Teḫip-apu has adopted Muš-apu son of Purna-⟨zi⟩ni. Three *imer*s of fields in the *ugāru* of the city of Unapšewe, south of the field of Ili-pazza, north of the field of Nai-še[ri], west of the field of Ili-pazza, east of the road of the *dimtu* of Puzawe, and cut by the road of the city of Ḫamena, Ḫanie has given to Muš-apu as his inheritance share. Muš-apu has [given as a gift] to Ḫanie seven *imer*s of [grain], three *imer*s of wheat, twenty minas of . . . , five minas of copper, one garment, and one *zi*[*anātu*]. If the field [has a claimaint], Ḫanie will clear (it) and will give (it) to Muš-apu. Ḫanie will [bear] the *ilku* of the field

[20] See p. 63 and n. 90.

[21] Pui-tae son of Eteya and his brother adopt Teḫip-Tilla son of Puḫi-šenni in *JEN* 586. Among the witnesses to AASOR 16 66, Eteš-šenni son of Âtanaḫ-ili (line 34) witnesses a number of Muš-apu and Puḫi-šenni texts. Others include Ḫanaya son of Taya (line 35), Ḫerriya son of Teḫip-apu (line 36), Mušuya son of Ḫašin-nawar (line 37), and Kelip-šarri son of Abeya (line 38). Tarmi-Tilla is the scribe (line 39). For attestations of the parties, scribes, witnesses, and others who appear in the texts of Group 19, see the appendix to this chapter.

[22] The property in this text borders the *dimtu* of Irribiya and the road of the city of Apenaš.

[23] Nai-šeri who owned a neighboring field perhaps is Nai-šeri son of Ḫamanna of *JEN* 243:29, father of Mannu-māḫiršu of AASOR 16 67. For *dimtu* Puzawe, see also HSS 19 93:3: *i+na* KASKAL *ša Pu-za-we* (see Fadhil, *STPPKA*, 292). For URU Ḫamena, see also HSS 14 123:11 and HSS 15 74:4 and 286:18. See Fisher, *NGN*, 54 no. 390; and Fadhil, *STPPKA*, 83. Among the new texts, see also *EN* 9/2 73:11. *Dimtu* Ḫamena appears in HSS 16 464:8. Witnesses include Eteš-šenni son of Âtanaḫ-[ili] (line 29), Ḫerriya son of (Teḫi[p-apu]) (line 31), and Iriri-Tilla son of Arip-a[pu] (line 34), all known in other texts (see the appendix).

and Muš-apu will not bear (it). If the field is larger, he will not diminish (it); if the field is smaller, he will not add to (it). Whoever breaks the contract will pay one mina of silver and one mina of gold. The tablet was [written] after the proclamation at the gate of the city of U-napšewe. SEVEN WITNESSES (including Amumiya the scribe). FIVE SEALS.

Eḫlip-apu son of Abeya engages in three transactions with Muš-apu: *EN* 9/2 18, 28, and 49. The first is clearly a *ṭuppi mārūti* involving real estate in Unapšewe. *EN* 9/2 49 also appears to be a *ṭuppi mārūti* because of the terminology of the text, that is, the appearance of the terms ḪA.LA (*zittu*) and NÌG.BA *(qištu)*. It also involves property in Unapšewe, as evidenced by the *dimtu* name, Ḫamanna.[24] *EN* 9/2 28 is less well preserved, but the term ḪA.LA does appear. In light of the other two texts, it is likely that this is a *ṭuppi mārūti* as well and was written in Unapšewe. *EN* 9/2 18[25] reads as follows:

Tablet of adoption by which Eḫlip-apu [son] of Abeya has adopted Muš-apu son of Purna-zini. One [*imer*] of field ea[st . . .] (there follows a break in which the location of the first parcel and information concerning another parcel of property appeared). . . . A total of [three *imer*s of fields] in the *ugāru* of the cit[y of Unapšewe] as his inheritance share Eḫli[p-apu] has given to Muš-apu. Mu[š-ap]u has given as a gift to Eḫlip-apu ten *imer*s of grain, X+two *imer*s of wheat, ten minas of tin, and four garments. If those three *imer*s of fields have a claimant, Eḫlip-apu will clear (them) and given (them) to Muš-apu. If the field is larger or smaller, he will not take (them) and he will not give (them). Eḫlip-apu will bear the *ilku* of the field and Muš-apu will not bear (it). He will not take a portion of the fields. The statement of Eḫlip-apu. Thus he spoke: "Silver according to the record of this tablet from Muš-apu I have taken and I am paid in full." Whoever breaks the contract will pay one mina of silver and one mina of gold. The tablet [was written in the month? at the gate of the city of Unapšewe]. THREE WITNESSES. FOUR SEALS.

The first translation below is of *EN* 9/2 28,[26] the second of *EN* 9/2 49.[27]

[. . . houses] and *paiḫu* land as his inheritance share [to Muš-apu Eḫlip-apu has given]. Muš-apu [has given] to Eḫlip-apu [as his gift . . .] and one robe. If the houses and the *paiḫu* [land] have a claimant, Eḫlip-[apu] will clear (them) and will give (them) to Muš-apu. Eḫlip-apu will bear the *ilku* of the houses [and *paiḫu*

[24] See *JEN* 92:5–7; Fisher, *NGN*, 55 no. 391; Fadhil, *STPPKA*, 288.

[25] See the appendix for the numerous appearances of Eḫlip-apu son of Abeya. In lines 35–37 the standard formula, "this tablet was written at the gate of the city of Unapšewe," should appear. Perhaps a month name was included in line 36 (AŠ I[TU?]), but this would be very unusual. Witnesses include Šipki-[Tešup], restored on basis of *EN* 9/2 157:25 and 28. There he is the son of [ ]-ri-a.

[26] Lines 3′ and 11′ refer to the same property, restored on the basis of traces. The seal owner in line 26 may be [Akip]-šarri son of [Ḫabira] restored on the basis of AASOR 16 62:30.

[27] For *dimtu* Ḫamanna (line 6) see n. 24. Iriri-Tilla (line 7) was probably the son of Akip-apu. Ḫerriya (line 8) was probably the son of Teḫip-apu. See the appendix for these men.

land] and Muš-apu will not bear (it). Whoever breaks the contract will pay one mina of silver and one mina of gold. FOUR WITNESSES. [The tablet was writ]ten after the proclamation in the city of Unapšewe at the gate of the city. TWO WITNESSES. THREE SEALS.

[Tablet of adoption by which Eḫlip-apu son of] Abeya [has ad]opted [Muš-apu son of] Purna-[zini]. X *awēḫaru* of fields in the *ugāru* of the [city of Unapšewe], west of the *dimtu* of Ḫamanna, east of the field of Iriri-Tilla, west of the field of Ḫerriya, south of the field of Ḫuti[p-], north of . . . , as his inheritance share Eḫlip-a[pu] has give to Muš-apu. Muš-apu has given as his gift to Eḫli[p-apu] one pair of [object of wood] and five minas of worked bronze. Eḫlip-apu will bear the *ilku* of the field and Muš-apu will not bear (it). (If) the field is larger he will not dim[inish it]; (if) [the field] is smaller, he will not add [to it]. [If the field has a claimant, Eḫlip-apu will clear it and will give it to Muš-apu.]

In addition to AASOR 16 66, mentioned above, Muš-apu also engaged in a number of real-estate *titennūtu*s, the most interesting of which is *EN* 9/2 143, which involves Akap-šenni son of Purna-zini, who probably was Muš-apu's brother, in a transaction concerning property in the *ugāru* of Unapšewe. Others include *EN* 9/2 145 with Wantiya son of Ar-nuzu, who gives property in Unapšewe for four years, and the fragmentary *EN* 9/2 142, which appears to be a renewal by Unnuni of a *titennūtu* made previously by his father Waqar-bēli. The two following translations are of *EN* 9/2 143[28] and *EN* 9/2 145:[29]

Tablet of lease by which Akap-šenni son of Purna-zini has given for five years to Muš-apu three *imer*s of fields in the *ugāru* of the city of Unapšewe [south of] the field of [ ] north of the field of Eḫli-Tešup, east of the field of Tulpi-šenni, and west of the field of At-[ ]-kalluni. [Mu]š-apu has given [moveable property including grain, sheep and goats to Akap-šenni]. [When Akap-še]nni returns [this property to Muš-apu], he will return that [field]. [The tablet] was written after the proclamation [at the gat]e of the city of Unapšewe. SIX WITNESSES (including the scribe). FOUR SEALS.

Seal of Pai-Tilla. Tablet of le[ase] by which Wantiya son of Ar-nu[zu] has given on lease for four years nine *awēḫaru* of fields in the *ugāru* of the city of Unapšewe, north of the field of Teḫip-apu the smith(?), [bordering] the road of the city of Ḫamena, . . . of Teḫip-apu, . . . of the city of Unapšewe, . . . [bordering] the road of the *dimtu* of Puza [to Mu]š-apu son of Purna-zini. Muš-apu has given to Wantiya on lease [for that fie]ld X minas of tin and . . . refined silver. [If the] field is larger,

[28] Tulpi-šenni the landowner (line 7) is probably the son of Zikuki. Among the witnesses are the brothers Kimparu and Alteya sons of Adad-rabū (lines 34–35). Others are the familiar Eteš-šenni son of Âtanaḫ-ili (lines 25–26), Mušuya [son of Ḫašin-nawar] (line 27; restored on the basis of AASOR 16 66:37), and Abeya [son of Paip-purni] (line 28; restored on the basis of HSS 19 8:40).

[29] Wantiya son of Ar-Nuzu (line 3) may have been the son of Ar-Nuzu son of Arim-matka (*JEN* 214:28, 34). For URU Ḫamena (line 7) see n. 23. Teḫip-apu (line 8) may have been the father of Ḫerriya (see the appendix). *For dimtu* Puza (line 10) see n. 23.

he will not diminish it; [if the] field is smaller, he will not add to it. [If] that field has a claimant, Wantiya will clear (it). [As soon] as the four years are [completed], and he [returns] the silver [mentioned in this tablet, Wantiya will take that field.]

Four more texts, all quite broken, refer to real-estate transactions of Muš-apu: *EN* 9/2 38,[30] 128,[31] 157, and 526. *EN* 9/2 526 is clearly a *ṭuppi titennūti*.[32] *EN* 9/2 157 is especially interesting because it refers to a previous arrangement, perhaps a *titennūtu* and it involves Ḫanie son of Teḫip-apu who transferred property to Muš-apu through the adoption text *EN* 9/2 17. Here, it is possible that the original agreement that Ḫanie extends was made by his father, Teḫip-apu.[33] *EN* 9/2 157 reads as follows:

> [Tablet of lease whereby a field . . .] Teḫi[p-apu son of] . . . has given [to Muš-apu son of Purna-zini]. Now . . . four minas and thirty shekels of worked [bronze] in addition to the previously mentioned silver I have received from Muš-apu. [When] he returns the previous silver of the field and Ḫanie [returns] to Mus-apu the four minas and thirty shekels of worked bronze with it, [he will take his] field . . . . and [the field . . .] Whoever [among the]m breaks the contract and [the field? . . .]. FIVE WITNESSES (including the scribe). FOUR SEALS.

As might be expected in light of the real-estate acquisitions of Muš-apu, he had also a "household" into which he received at least one individual on a personal *titennūtu* (*EN* 9/2 144). Akip-tašenni agrees to work for Muš-apu for three years in return for twenty minas of wrought copper and two ANŠE five BÁN of grain.[34] Muš-apu also borrows grain in the city of Unapšewe (*EN* 9/2 326).[35] Otherwise, he is attested as a witness in HSS 19 93, a *terḫatu* contract between Pal-Tešup son of Šukriya and Puḫi-šenni son of Atal-Tešup.[36]

[30] The party to this contract was a Ḫanakka (line 11), perhaps son of Milkiya (see catalog). Note [ ] son of Purna-zini in line 24 and [Ḫašip-Tilla] son of Šeḫliya in line 25, both possible members of Muš-apu's family.

[31] Perhaps the Šeḫliya of this text is Šeḫliya son of Purna-zini, Muš-apu's brother. Land owners include Ninu-atal (line 4), [ ]-ri DUMU DINGIR-ni (line 8), Unapu (line 9), Tešup-nirari (lines 10, 11, and 14), Amur-atal (line 12), the palace (line 15), Tainšuḫ (line 16), and Tupkiya (line 17). Note *dimtu* Tainšuḫ in *EN* 9/2 22.

[32] The party here is Pui-[ ] son of Ikkiya (lines 2–3). Note line 4, *ᴵNu-ša-pu* DUMU *Pu-ri-z[i-ni]*.

[33] Teḫi[p-apu] appears at the beginning of the preserved portion of the tablet with space remaining after his name where his patronymic could fit.

[34] For text and comments, see Eichler *IN*, 114, text 11 (= SMN 2803).

[35] For the text see Owen, *LDN*, 109. The lender is Tupki-Tilla son of Unaya, to whom Muš-apu has returned the grain. Lines 9ff. should be restored: *iš-tu* U_4 *an-ni-i i+na* EGIR *sa ᴵMu-ša-pu la a-ša-as-si*.

[36] HSS 93:11 *Mu-ša-pu* DUMU *Pu-na-zi-nu*. Note that the property is on the road of Puzawe (line 3), like that in *EN* 9/2 17 and 145. The witnesses include Iriri-Tilla son of Arip-apu (line 19), well known at Unapšewe (see the appendix). Also, Fadhil has demonstrated that the three men who survey the field with Muš-apu are known as judges, *STPPKA*, 314.

Without patronymic, a Muš-apu appears as a judge in four texts: *JEN* 631:21, involving Teḫip-Tilla son of Puḫi-šenni, and *JEN* 107:63, 651:52, and 673:46, all involving Enna-mati son of Teḫip-Tilla.[37] Such a position would be in keeping with the social and economic status that Muš-apu clearly held.[38] Also without patronymic, a Muš-apu receives oil for the gods of the city of Tilla in AASOR 16 48 and horses from merchants for the palace in AASOR 16 100. Though these texts do not come from Group 19, it is possible that they refer to Muš-apu son of Puḫi-šenni.[39]

Puhi-šenni Son of Muš-apu

Puḫi-šenni son of Muš-apu is known through a variety of texts in the Nuzi corpus, the most famous of which are the matching herding contract and *bulla* mentioned first by Starr and then discussed by many others.[40] Further activities involving livestock are attested in HSS 16 322.[41] In other contexts, he is the *amumiḫḫuru* and witness for Urḫi-kušuḫ DUMU LUGAL,[42] and he figures prominently as a lender of grain in the loan texts of Nuzi.[43] The *EN* 9/2 texts include a substantial Group of real-estate transactions that demonstrate that he, like his father, was active in real-estate acquisitions in the city of Unapšewe. These real-estate contracts include *ṭuppi mārūti*s, *ṭuppi šupe*ʾʾ*ulti*s, and *ṭuppi titennūti*s.

[37] Observed by Fadhil, *STPPKA*, 313ff., with discussion of the judges with whom Muš-apu appears.

[38] Fadhil identifies Muš-apu as a member of the *rākib narkabti* class at Unapšewe (*STPPKA*, 313). Indeed, judges appear in the *rākib narkabti* listings. E.g., HSS 13 6, in which Niḫriya son of Akap-tukke (line 8), Akap-tukke son of Kakki (line 22), Utḫap-tae son of Zike (line 24), all known as judges, are listed along with the sons of Teḫip-Tilla son of Puḫi-šenni (line 21), the sons of Ḫaiš-Tešup (line 11), and two scribes of the family of Apil-Sîn, Waqar-bēli son of Taya, and ᵈAK.DINGIR.RA son of Sîn-napšir.

[39] See p. 109 below for AASOR 16 100 which may suggest a connention between Muš-apu and others in Group 19.

[40] Starr, *Nuzi* 1:316–17; A. L. Oppenheim, "On an Operational Device in Mesopotamian Bureaucracy," *JNES* 18 (1959) 127; D. Schmandt-Besserat, *Syro-Mesopotamian Studies* 1 (1977) 31–70; idem, *Scientific American* 238/6 (June 1978) 50–59; and T. Abusch, SCCNH 1:1–9. These two records and the accounting system they represent have been variously interpreted in these works. Yet another possibility exists, i.e., that two parallel systems of accounting were used, the contract and the bulla. They simply served different purposes within the livestock owner's accounting procedures. The contract would be the legal document, the bulla the counting record.

[41] This text comes from Group 19, so the Puḫi-šenni mentioned is undoubtedly Puḫi-šenni son of Muš-apu. He gives a ewe (presumably) with its lamb to Ḫašikke son of Zike who gives them in turn to Waḫri-šenni son of Eḫliya. The text would be a most-unusual herding contract since Puḫi-šenni is to clear any claim on the animals in question. A fine for noncompliance is also involved. The "farming out" of livestock from one herdsman to another is known, however (see Morrison, SCCNH 2:269ff.). More likely, this text represents a payment of some kind.

[42] See page 69 above.

[43] Many of Puḫi-šenni's loan documents appear in Owen, *LDN*: *EN* 9/2 301, pp. 98–99, *EN* 9/2 323, p. 108 (= *EN* 9 324 in *LDN*); *EN* 9/2 327, p. 109; *EN* 9/2 329, p. 110; *EN* 9/2 333, pp. 109–10 (= *EN* 9 328 in *LDN*); *EN* 9/2 334, p. 110 (= *EN* 9 333 in *LDN*); *EN* 9/2 336, p. 111; *EN* 9/2 338, p. 112. For others, see below.

Puḫi-šenni is adopted twice by Naite son of Ḫanaya and once by Naite son of Ḫanaya and Ḫatarte son of Âtanaḫ-ili in the next three texts.

EN 9/2 20[44]

Tablet of adoption by which Naite son of Ḫanaya has adopted Puḫi-šenni son of Muš-apu. One *awēḫaru* of field and a full *kumānu* of field, a threshing floor in the suburbs of the city of Unapšewe, south of the road of Tupšarriniwe, north of the houses of Nui-šeri, east of the road of Apenaš, west of the threshing floor of Muš-apu, Naite has given to Puḫi-šenni as his inheritance share. Puḫi-šenni has given as a gift to Naite one *pi* and three BÁN of grain. Naite will bear the *ilku* of the field and Puḫi-šenni will not bear (it). If the field has a claimant, Naite will clear that field and will give (it) to Puḫi-šenni. Whoever breaks the contract will pay one mina of silver and one mina of gold. The tablet was written after the proclamation before the gate of the city of U[napšewe]. THREE MEN (who surveyed the field and gave the silver). FOUR WITNESSES (including Elḫip-Tilla the scribe). FOUR SEALS. Houses and a well are on the threshing floor. If the field is larger, they will not diminish it. If the field is smaller he will not add to it. SEAL OF THE SCRIBE.

EN 9/2 21[45]

Tablet of adoption by which Naite son of Ḫanaya has adopted Puḫi-šenni son of Mu[š-apu]. Naite has given as his inheritance share to Puḫi-šenni one *imer* and two *awēḫaru* of fields in the *ugāru* of the city of Unapšewe, south of the field of Naite, east of the field of Naite, north of the field of Pu[ḫi-še]nni, west of the field of Bēlu-[ ]. Puḫi-šenni has given as a gift to Naite one ox and three once-shorn male sheep. Naite will bear the *ilku* of the field and Puḫi-šenni will not bear (it). (If) the field has a claimant, Naite will clear (it) and will give (it) to Puḫi-šenni. If the field is larger, they will not diminish (it); (if) the field is smaller, he will not add (to it). He will not take the *kaška*-land from the field. Whoever breaks the contract will pay one mina of silver and one mina of gold. The tablet was written after the proclamation in front of the gate of the city of Unapšewe. FIVE WITNESSES (including Elḫip-Tilla the scribe). These men surveyed the field and gave the silver. TWO WITNESSES. SEVEN SEALS.

44 Naite son of Ḫanaya also borrows from Puḫi-šenni (*EN* 9/2 334). Lines 5–6 read *ma-ag-ra-at-tu* AŠ *ṣe-ri-tu ša* URU *Ú-nap-še-we*, translated here as 'a threshing floor in the suburbs of Unapšewe' following Maidman *SEANFA*, 147 and nn. 345–50, where *ṣēru* is nicely translated as 'suburbs'. For another interpretation, see Zaccagnini, *RLLA*, 32ff., where the term is translated as 'steppe'. Fadhil notes the "road of Tupšarriwe" (line 7) in *JEN*u 371:5, a text concerning land in Unapšewe, and the "road of Apenaš" (line 9) in AASOR 16 67 (*STPPKA*, 292, 291). Witnesses include Ari[p-šarri son of Ku]ntanu (line 26), Ḫaši[nna son of A]kip-apu (line 27), Enšu[ya son of] Enna-mati (line 28), all surveyors, and Akkul-en[ni] and Zike sons of Kurru (line 31), Akkul-enni [son of] Zike (line 32; the previous Zike's son?), and Kaya son of Šennaya (line 33). See the appendix for these men.

45 Witnesses include Tešup-atal son of Kula-ḫupi (line 29), Teḫiya son of U[kur-atal] (line 30), Karrate son of Teḫiya (line 31), Wurteya son of Šuk-[ ], and the scribe Elḫip-Tilla as surveyors and givers of the silver, and Zikarru son of Šalliya (line 36) and Akip-[šarri son of] Ḫabira (line 37). Zikarru son of Šalliya is the herdsman of the *bulla* and contract noted above in n. 40.

EN 9/2 23[46]

Tablet of [adoption by which Ḫatarte] son of [Ât]anaḫ-[ili and] Naite son of Ḫa[naya] have adopted Puḫi-šenni s[on of Muš-apu]. They have given as his inheritance share one *imer* and four *awēḫaru* of field . . . , east of the canal . . . , north of the field of Šur-[ ], west of the field of Šur-[ ], and nine *awēḫaru* of field west of the field of . . . , south of the field of Nai([te?), east of the field of Zi[ku]ki, north of the border of the *dimtu* of Ir[ribiya], a total of two *imer*s and three *awēḫaru* of fields in the *ugāru* of the city of Unapšewe. Puḫi-šenni has given to Ḫatarte [and to] Naite as their gift one new, good-quality garment, x + four *imer*s of grain, three sheep, and six minas of tin. Ḫatar[te] and Naite [will bear the *ilku* of] the field and Puḫi-šenni will not bear (it). (If) the field has a claimant, Ḫatarte and Naite will clear that field and will give it to Puḫi-šenni. (If) the field is larger they will not diminish it; (if) the field is smaller, they will not add to it. They will not take the *kaška*-land from the fields. Whoever breaks the contract will pay one mina of silver and one mina of gold. This [ta]blet [was written] after the proclamation [at the gate] of the city of Unapšewe. FIVE MEN who surveyed [the field and gave] the silver. THREE WITNESSES (including Elḫip-Tilla the scribe). SEVEN SEALS.

In *EN* 9/2 188[47] Puḫi-šenni enters into a *titennūtu* agreement with Ḫatarte son of Âtanaḫ-ili known from the previous text:

Tablet of lease by which Ḫatarte son of Âtanaḫ-ili has given on lease to Puḫi-šenni son of Muš-apu one *imer* and eight *awēḫaru* of fields in the *ugāru* of the city of Unapšewe, south of the field of Akip-tašenni, east of the road of the city of Apenaš, north of the field of Ḫatarte which Ḫašip-Tilla holds, and west of the field of Urḫi-kušuḫ. Puḫi-šenni has given to Ḫatarte five *imer*s of grain, one ewe, and one she-goat. When Ḫatarte returns the five *imer*s of grain, the ewe, and the she-goat to Puḫi-šenni, he will take his field. If [the field] is plowed, he will not take it. The tablet was written after the proclamation at the gate of the city of Unapšewe. SIX WITNESSES (including Elḫip-Tilla the scribe). SIX SEALS.

[46] The joint ownership of the field may suggest that Ḫatarte son of Atanaḫ-ili and Naite son of Ḫanaya were related. The field is located south of the field of *Na-i-*[*te*?]. "Naite" would not be surprising in light of texts above, but the traces of signs remaining in the line indicate that something followed. The landowner Zi[ku]ki may be the father of Tulpi-šenni (*EN* 9/2 17:30). For *dimtu* Irribiya (l. 13) see Fadhil, *STPPKA*, 288. Among the witnesses, Eḫlip-apu (line 35) may be the son of either Abeya or Šatta-u̯azza (see the appendix). Pui-tae (line 36) may be the son of either Eteya or Ḫaniu, though the latter is more likely since he witnesses other texts of Puḫi-senni (*EN* 9/2 25 and 146). Other witnesses include Ḫašinna [son of Akip-apu] (line 37), Ḫuti son of [Gimil-šuabi] (line 38), Ḫašip-Til[la son of either Šeḫliya or Akawa-til], but the first is more likely because of his many appearances with Puḫi-šenni, all surveyors and givers of the silver, and [Ke]lip-[šarri son of Abeya] (line 42), Arik-[kamari son of Ziliya?] (line 43), and Elḫip-Tilla the scribe. See the appendix for these men.

[47] One of the neighboring fields is "held" by one Ḫašip-Tilla. See *EN* 9/2 189 for a *titennūtu* between Ḫatarte and Ḫašip-Tilla. Note that the field borders property of Urḫi-kušuḫ DUMU LUGAL (line 9). Among the witnesses are Teḫiya son of U[kur]-a[tal] (line 23), Ḫašip-[Til]la son of Še[ḫ]liya (line 24), Ari[ya] son of Naniya (line 25), Taula son of Ḫanatu (line 26), Utḫap-tae son of Ennamati (line 27), and Elḫip-Tilla the scribe.

Another of Puḫi-šenni's *titennūtu* agreements is preserved in *EN* 9/2 171:[48]

[The statement] of Attilammu son of Tur-šenni before these [witnesses thus he spo]ke: "X + one *awēḫaru* of field in the *ugāru* of the city of U[napšewe], west of the field of [ ]e, east [of the field of . . .], and south of . . . on lease I have gi[ven for] three years to Pu[ḫi-šenni] son of Muš-apu. I have rec[eived] fifteen minas of tin [from] Puḫi-šenni. When the three years are com[pleted, I will return] the fifteen minas of tin to Puḫi-šenni and my field I wi[ll take]. If the field is plo[wed], I will not take (it)." If Attilammu bre[aks the contract] he will pay one cow. FIVE WITNESSES (including Elḫip-Tilla the scribe). FIVE SEALS.

In *EN* 9/2 19[49] Ḫanukka son of Zilip-Tilla adopts Puḫi-šenni:

Tablet of adoption by which Ḫanukk[a] son of Zilip-Tilla has adopted Puḫi-šenni son of Muš-a[pu]. Eight *awēḫaru* of fields in the *ugāru* [of] the city of Unapšewe, west of [the field] of Urḫa-tati, so[uth] of the field of Eḫli-Tešup son of [ ], north of the field of A-[ ], east of the field of Ḫanukk[a,] Ḫanukka has given as his inheritance share to Puḫi-šenni. And Puḫi-šenni as [his] gift has given to Ḫanukka(!). If the [fie]ld has a claimant, [Ḫ]anukka will clear that field and will give (it) to Puḫi-šenni. Ḫanukka will bear the [*il*]*ku* of the field [and P]uḫi-šenni will not bear (it). (If) the field is [larger], they will not diminish (it); [(if) the field is smaller, they will not add (to it)]. (The penalty clause probably occurred here in the break.) [This tablet was written after the proclamation at the gate of the city of] Unapšewe. FIVE MEN (who surveyed the field and gave the grain). THREE WITNESSES (including Elḫip-Tilla the scribe). FIVE SEALS.

EN 9/2 22[50] records the adoption of Puḫi-šenni by Ḫanakka son of Milkiya who transfers property bordering land of Zilip-Tilla, perhaps the father of Ḫanukka in the adoption immediately above:

Tablet of adoption by which Ḫanakka son of Milkiya has adopted Puḫi-šenni son of Muš-apu. X *awēḫaru* and one full *kumānu* of fields in the *ugāru* [of the city] of

[48] Attilammu son of Tur-šenni may be the son of Zilip-kanari (*JEN* 651:10). See also *dimtu* Tur-šenni in Unapšewe (see Fadhil, *STPPKA*, 290; Zaccagnini, *RLLA*, 157ff., Maidman, *SEANFA*, 189 and nn. 644 and 1178). Witnesses include Ḫašip-Tilla son of Še[ḫliya] (line 23), Akitt[a] son of Ili-imitti (line 24), Kelip-šarri son of Abey[a] (line 25), Pui-tae son of Ḫaniu (line 26), and Elḫip-Tilla the scribe son of Kel-Tešup. See the appendix for these men.

[49] For other appearances of Ḫanukka son of Zilip-Tilla see the appendix. The "gift" Puḫi-šenni gives to Ḫannuka is not specified. This appears to be a scribal omission as there is little space available on the tablet for its inclusion. Witnesses include [E]ḫli-Tešup son of Bē[laya] (line 25), [Ḫ]ašip-Tilla son of Še[ḫliya] (line 26), Akip-tašenni son of [ ] (line 27), Akkul-enni and Zike sons of Kurri (lines 28–29), all surveyors and givers of silver, and Šekaru son of Ḫa-[ ] (line 32), Ariya son of Na[niya] (line 33), and Elḫip-Ti[ll]a the scribe. See the appendix for these men.

[50] Ḫanakka son of Milkiya witnesses *EN* 9/2 146:33 for Puḫi-šenni. For *dimtu* Tainšuḫwe (line 7) see also HSS 15 41:15, HSS 16 394:4, and *JEN* 643:6. Cf. Fisher, *NGN*, 40 no. 278. Witnesses include Ḫašuar son of Ennamati (line 26), Ḫašip-Tilla son of Šeḫliya (line 27), [Ḫanukka?] son of Zilip-Tilla (line 28), Eḫli-Tešup son of Bēlaya (line 29), all surveyors and givers of the tin, Arip-šarri son of Kuntanu (line 32), Zike son of Kurri (line 33), Ariya so[n of Nani]ya (line 34), Eḫ[lip-apu son of] Šatta-uazza (line 35), Ḫan[e] son of Šukriya (line 36), and Elḫip-Tilla the scribe (line 37).

Unapšewe, north of the *dimtu* of Tain-šuḫ, west of the field of Bēlaya, east of the field of Zilip-Tilla, and south of the field of Zil⟨ip⟩-Tilla, Ḫanakka has given to Puḫi-šenni as his inheritance share. Puḫi-šenni has given as a gift to Ḫanakka five BÁN of grain and four minas of tin. Ḫanakka will bear the *ilku* of the field and Puḫi-šenni will not bear (it). If the [field] has a claimant, Ḫanakka will clear that field and will give (it) to Puḫi-šenni. Whoever breaks the contract will pay one mina of silver and one mina of gold. The tablet was written after the proclamation before the gate of the city of Unapšewe. FOUR MEN who surveyed the field and gave the grain and tin. SIX WITNESSES (including Elḫip-Tilla the scribe). SIX SEALS.

Other texts attesting to Puḫi-šenni's acquisition of real estate, *EN* 9/2 146, 163, and 275, are less well preserved, but they are clearly a real-estate adoption and two *titennūtu* texts, respectively. In the first, which was written in Unapšewe, Amarša gives property to Puḫi-senni son of Muš-apu.[51] In the second, [A]kaya son of Kuššiya gives property in the *ugāru* of Unapšewe bordering the road of the *dimtu* of Ibriyawe, a field of Kuššiya and the *dimtu* of Kušuḫ-erwe for five years.[52] Both of these texts were written by Elḫip-Tilla the scribe. In the third an Akaya son of Ka-[ ] gives real estate which had previously been given by his father(?) to Puḫi-senni son of Muš-apu. A Pal-Tešup is involved in this text perhaps and may have held the field in the past, but the context is too fragmentary to be certain.[53] *EN* 9/2 525 preserves only the incipit of a *ṭuppi mārūti* by which Eḫlip-apu son of Abeya adopts Puḫi-šenni. Eḫlip-apu was, as noted above, a frequent party to contracts with Muš-apu.[54]

Puḫi-šenni also engaged in at least two exchange agreements translated here:

EN 9/2 74[55]

Tablet of exchange by which Utḫap-tae son of Enna-mati ex[changed] fields in the *ugāru* of the city of Unapšewe with Puḫi-šenni son of M[uš-apu]. Five *awēḫaru* of fields south of the road of the *dimtu* of Zaziya, north of the field of Mar-[ ], east of the field of Akip-t[ašenni], Puḫi-šenni [has given] to Utḫap-tae. Five *awē-*

[51] Only one Ammarša is identified by patronymic in the Nuzi corpus: Ammarša son of Palteya (see catalog). The text contains the prohibition against taking the *kaška* land (line 21), and the tablet was written in Unapšewe (line 25). The list of witnesses contains well-known personalities at Unapšwewe: Ḫasinna son of Akip-apu (line 26), Ḫašip-Tilla son of Šeḫliya (line 27), Matteya son of Enna-mati (line 28), Ḫuti son of Gimil(šu)-abi (line 29), Pui-tae son of Ḫaniu (line 30), Ḫanakka son of Milkiya (line 33), and Elḫip-Tilla the scribe (line 34).

[52] Line 3 describes the property as being on the road of the *dimtu* of Ibriyawe, most likely Irribiyawe (see above, n. 46). For Kušuḫ, see Fisher, *NGN*, 52. Ḫašip-Tilla son of Šeḫliya appears in line 12.

[53] It would be tempting to relate this text to the preceding, but the beginning of the ka_4 sign is clearly visible before the break in line 2. [ᴵ]*Pal-te-šup* might be the Pal-Tešup son of Šukriya who is a party to HSS 19 93:1ff.

[54] This fragment does not join any of the other Eḫli-apu texts, all of which deal with Muš-apu. See p. 72 above for contracts between Eḫlip-apu and Muš-apu.

[55] For *dimtu* Zaziya (line 7) see also *JEN* 70:6 and 399:11 (Fisher, *NGN*, 70 no. 506; and Fadhil, *STPPKA*, 291). Line 20 Eḫlip-apu son of Abeya is restored on the basis of his many appearances in these texts (see catalog).

ḫaru of fields west of the field of Taya son of Warad-dūri, cut in one large parcel, Utḫa[p-tae] has given to Puḫi-šenni. Whichever field [has] a claimant, he will clear (it) and will give (it). Whoever breaks the contract will pay one mina of silver and [one m]ina of gold. (break) TWO WITNESSES (including Elḫip-Tilla the scribe). SIX SEALS.

EN 9/2 77[56]

[Tablet of ex]change by which [Ḫu]tip-Tilla [son] of Ḫuya exchanges fields in the *ugāru* of the city of Unapš[ewe] with Puḫi-šenni son of Muš-apu. One *imer* of field, south of the field of Šattu-u̯azza, west of the field of Šeḫliya, east of the field of EN-[ ]-Tešup, Puḫi-šenni has given to Ḫut[ip-Tilla]. One *imer* three *awēḫaru* of fields, north of the road of the *dimtu* of [ ]-we, south of [. . .], west of [. . .]-šup, and east of the fie[ld of . . .], Ḫutip-Til[la] has given to Pu[ḫi-šenni]. One *imer* of grain as [an *utāru* payment] over and above the field Puḫi-šenni has given to Ḫutip-Tilla. (If) the fields are la[rger], they will not diminish them. (If) the fields are [smal]ler, they will not add to (them). Whichever field has a claimant, he will clear that field. The *ilku* of their fields each will bear. Thus (says) Ḫutip-Tilla: "That field previously Ḫuya my father gave to Muš-apu and [wr]ote a tablet. Now [I] write a ta[blet for] Puḫi-šenni." Whoever breaks the contract will pay one mina of silver and one mina of gold. The tablet was written after the proclamation before the gate of the city of Unapšewe. SEVEN WITNESSES (including Elḫip-Tilla the scribe). SEVEN SEALS.

The *EN* 9/2 texts include a few new loan documents to add to the already large number already known for Puḫi-šenni:[57] *EN* 9/2 358, 362, 455, and 493. The obverse of *EN* 9/2 358 is almost entirely effaced, but the few readable lines indicate that Ḫanie son of Šukriya borrowed tin from Puḫi-šenni.[58] *EN* 9/2 455 appears to be a portion of a loan agreement whereby Ḫašinna [son of Akip-apu] borrowed an ox from Puḫi-šenni.[59] Two other grain loans, are better preserved:

EN 9/2 362[60]

Five *imer*s of gr[ain of] Puḫi-šen[ni son of Muš-apu Kinni] son of Ḫaniu took on loan. After the harvest the grain with its interest Kinni will return to Puḫi-šenni. FOUR WITNESSES (including Elḫip-Tilla the scribe). FIVE SEALS.

[56] Ḫutip-Tilla's statement indicates that the same exchange was accomplished between his father and Puḫi-šenni's father. Either the field had reverted to Ḫutip-Tilla under unknown circumstances or it was necessary to reconfirm the transaction. For the *utāru* payment, see Maidman, *SEANFA*, 132ff. The landowner Šatta-u̯azza may be the father of Eḫli-apu (see Appendix). Šeḫliya (perhaps son of Purna-zini?) is another landowner. Witnesses include Karrate son of Teḫiya (line 24), Ḫašip-Tilla son of Šeḫliya (line 25), Šekaru son of Ḫašip-apu (line 26), Arip-šarri son of Kuntanu (line 27), Šimika-atal son of Eḫli-Tešup (line 28), Arrumpa son of Umkiya (line 29), and Elḫip-Tilla the scribe (line 30).

[57] See n. 43 above.

[58] Seal names on the reverse include ᵈIŠKUR-KUR-ni, Akkul-enni, Šimika, and Kuari [son of Kuššiya?].

[59] Lines 6–9 *šum-ma* AŠ *qa-bu* U$_4$-*mi* GU$_4$ ᴵ*Ḫa-ši-in-na a+na* ᴵ*Pu-ḫi-še-en-ni la i+na-an-din.*

[60] Kinni son of Ḫaniu may have been the brother of Pui-tae son of Ḫaniu (see the appendix).

EN 9/2 493[61]

X *imers* of grain of [Pu]ḫi-šenni son of Muš-a[pu] Urḫi-kuš ⟨uḫ⟩ son of Šeḫurni took on loan. After the harvest the grain, its capital, Urḫi-kušuḫ will return to Puḫi-šenni. FOUR WITNESSES (including Elḫip-Tilla the scribe). ONE SEAL.

Lending was not without its difficulties. Puḫi-šenni goes to court with Ḫatarte son of Âtanaḫ-ili, known from the real-estate documents above, and with Teḫiya son of Ukur-atal concerning a large amount of metal they had borrowed (*EN* 9/2 419).[62] Puḫi-šenni not only lent metals, but also dispensed large amounts for manufacturing, as shown by HSS 15 300 in which Puḫi-šenni provides bronze to Tae son of Ḫaši[nna]/Ḫaši[in-nawar]:[63]

> Six minas and thirty shekels of bronze for *namu*, two minas of bronze for *ṣupra* which Puḫi-šenni son of Muš-apu (gave) for working to Tae son of Ḫašin-nawar.

Without patronymic Puḫi-šenni appears in HSS 16 230 which records the receipt of grain by Ḫašip-Tilla and the men of the city of Erḫaḫḫe from Puḫi-šenni.[64] Puḫi-šenni son of Muš-apu may be Puḫi-šenni the judge who appears without patronymic in *JEN* 399 and 668.[65] If so, he followed in his father's footsteps in this position. These texts both involve Tieš-urḫe son of Takku and Ammarša, who also appears in *EN* 9/2 146.

Šehliya Son of Purna-zini and Ḫašip-Tilla Son of Šeḫliya

Šeḫliya son of Purna-zini appears in only one text, *EN* 9/2 175, a real-estate *titennūtu* in which he and Ḫašip-Tilla son of Šeḫliya, presumably his son, give nine *awēḫaru* of fields to Ḫanaya son of Tae for three years.[66] Ḫanaya son of Tae, on the other hand, is known from a number of documents. He participates in an exchange with Teḫip-Tilla (*JEN* 287:4). As a witness, he appears in an adoption of Teḫip-Tilla son of Puḫi-šenni written by Balṭu-kašid son of Apil-Sîn (II; *JEN* 203:13); an exchange between Teḫip-Tilla and Kula-ḫupi son of Tae (Ḫanaya's brother according to *JEN* 287) written by ᵈNANNA-MA.AN.SÍ (III) (*JEN* 252:31); an adoption of Teḫip-Tilla concerning Nuzi real estate written by

[61] Presumably, Urḫi-kuš is to be understood as Urḫi-kušuḫ. Witnesses include Akitta son of Waḫḫiya (line 9), Teḫiya son of U[kur-a]tal (line 10), Zike son of [Kurri] (line 11), and Elḫip-Tilla the scribe son of [Kel]-Tešup.

[62] Noted by Hayden, *CPN*, 150. See also Fadhil, *STPPKA*, 317.

[63] Full commentary in Fadhil, *STPPKA*, 315 and 317–18, who relates Tae son of Ḫašin-nawar to Mušuya son of Ḫašin-namar the smith, known from AASOR 16 66:37, 46, and HSS 16 229:11. While this is most likely, the personal name Ḫašinna is also known at Unapšewe (see the appendix). He may be the individual who appears in *EN* 9/2 323. On the terms *namu* and *ṣupra*, see *CAD* N/1 252 s.v. and *CAD* Ṣ 250, respectively.

[64] Text transliterated and discussed in Fadhil, *STPPKA*, 319.

[65] Fadhil, *STPPKA*, 312.

[66] This text was mentioned above, p. 41, as describing land that might be in the district of Ḫuya. Note that the property borders that of Paya and Muš-a[pu]. The tablet was written in Unapšewe (line 26).

Taya son of Apil-Sîn (II); a declaration text also concerning Nuzi property written by Iniya son of Kiannipu (III); and AASOR 16 61, which comes from S112 of Group 19, a text in which Kula-ḫupi son of Arteya receives Urḫiya son of Aki-Tilla in a personal *titennūtu* written in Nuzi by Tarmi-Tešup.[67] It is interesting that Ḫanaya seems to be involved primarily with Nuzi in these other texts while his transaction with Šeḫliya is in Unapšewe.

Ḫašip-Tilla son of Šeḫliya is better attested. Along with numerous appearances as a witness to texts of the Muš-apu family (see the appendix), he engages in a real-estate *titennūtu* with Ḫatarte [son of Âtanaḫ-ili], *EN* 9/2 189, written in the city of Unapšewe by Enna-mati son of Puḫi-šenni. Ḫatarte son of Âtanaḫ-ili, as noted above, was involved frequently with Puḫi-šenni in real-estate transactions and a law suit. Ḫatarte's statement (lines 20ff.) identifies the Ḫašip-Tilla of this text as the son of Šeḫliya:[68]

um-ma ^{I}*Ḫa-tar-te-ma* (*la* erased)
a-na pa-ni-ni KÙ.BABBAR.MEŠ *ša-a-šu*
a-šar ^{I}*Še-eḫ-li-ya*
a-bi-ya(!)*ša* ^{I}*Ḫa-ši-ip-til-la*
el-te-qè-mi

Thus (says) Ḫatarte: "Previously I took that silver from Šeḫliya the father of Ḫašip-Tilla."

Puḫi-šenni son of Muš-apu witnesses the text along with other well-known parties at Unapšewe.[69]

Chronology of the Muš-apu Family

The chronology of the Muš-apu family has been deduced already on the basis of previously known materials,[70] but it is worth repeating here because the new materials support and strengthen the earlier conclusions. Also, the time span of this family is important for a fuller understanding of their activities, especially in the area of real-estate acquisition.

The evidence for the chronology of this family is not as clear-cut as that for the other families in the eastern area because the scribes who write for members of the family, with one possible exception, do not belong to the scribal families that provide the chronological skeleton for the Nuzi corpus. The following list includes the scribes who write for members of the Muš-apu family and for Urḫi-kušuḫ.

[67] For text and comments, see Eichler, *IN*, 132–33. For the scribe, see p. 53 n. 33. Tarmi-Tešup son of Itti-šarri also appears in *JEN* 78, written in Nuzi, and writes *JEN* 290, also in Nuzi.

[68] This transaction may be reflected in *EN* 9/2 188. See n. 47.

[69] Witnesses include Eteš-šenni son of Âtanaḫ-ili (line 29), Teḫiya son of Ukur-atal (line 30), Puḫi-šenni son of Muš-apu (line 31), Ḫašinna son of Akip-apu (line 32), Ḫašik-kamar son of Teḫiya (lines 33–34), and the scribe Enna-mati son of Puḫi-šenni (lines 35–36). See the appendix for these individuals.

[70] See Fadhil, *STPPKA*, 315.

Urhi-kušuḫ:	
Elḫip-Tilla son of Kel-Tešup[71]	HSS 19 111 (in Unapšewe)
Elḫip-Tilla	AASOR 16 62
Taklāk-ilu	*EN* 9/2 321
Muš-apu son of Purna-zini:	
Amumiya (son of Sîn-nādin-šumi; IV?)[72]	*EN* 9/2 17 (in Unapšewe)
Dayyān-bēl[73]	HSS 19 8
Iddin-Sîn	HSS 19 93
Kel-Tešup [74]	*EN* 9/2 326
Tarmi-Tilla[75]	AASOR 16 66 and 67 (both in Unapšewe); *EN* 9/2 157
Puḫi-šenni son of Muš-apu:	
Appa [son of Intiya][76]	*EN* 9/2 419
Elḫip-Tilla (son of Kel-Tešup)	HSS 16 322; *EN* 9/2 19, 20, 21, 23(?), 77, and 146(?) (all in Unapšewe); *EN* 9/2 163 and 188 (probably in Unapšewe); *EN* 9/2 74(?), 301(?), 323, 329, 333, 336, 358(?), 362
Elḫip-Tilla son of Kel-Tešup	*EN* 9/2 22 (in Unapšewe), 171, and 493
Kelteya (possibly Kel-Tešup)	*EN* 9/2 338
Teḫiya	*EN* 9/2 301(?)

The surviving texts of this family and Urḫi-kušuḫ were written primarily by one scribe, Elḫip-Tilla son of Kel-Tešup who appears to have been based in Unapšewe. He does not write for other individuals active at Unapšewe, but without more complete records from that city, it would be premature to suggest that he worked exclusively for the Urḫi-kušuḫ/Muš-apu Group. Among the other scribes, Tarmi-Tilla also appears in Tupšarriniwe[77] and is discussed in chapter 5 below. Only one scribe, Amumiya, may belong to the scribal family of Apil-Sîn, if his name is the hypochoristic for Amumi-Tešup.

Apart from the scribes, there are certain links that can be demonstrated for the family of Muš-apu and known figures in the Nuzi corpus. The direct correspondences include the following:

1. Akap-šenni son of Purna-zini engages in a lawsuit with Šilwa-Tešup DUMU LUGAL in HSS 9 139, written by Ila-nîšū [son of Sîn-napšir] (III). As mentioned above, Akap-šenni is otherwise unattested, but if he belongs to this family, this is an important chronological connection.

71 Ibid., 282.

72 There are two scribes named Amumi-Tešup for which Amumiya may be the hypochoristic form: son of Sîn-nādin-šumi (III) and possibly son of Šimanni-Adad (IV; G. Wilhelm, AOAT 9:10). The first is more likely, given the chronology of the scribes and Muš-apu's period of activity.

73 See Fadhil, *STPPKA*, 283.

74 Ibid., 282.

75 Ibid., 283.

76 Ibid., 282.

77 Fadhil points out that a road joined Unapšewe and Tupšarriniwe; ibid., 283.

2. Appa son of Intiya writes for both Puḫi-šenni (*EN* 9/2 419) and Enna-mati son of Teḫip-Tilla (*JEN* 369 and 653).

3. Enna-mati son of Puḫi-šenni is the scribe who writes for Ḫašip-Tilla son of Šeḫliya (*EN* 9/2 189). This text is witnessed by Puḫi-šenni son of Muš-apu. Otherwise, Enna-mati writes for Tarmi-Tilla son of Šurki-Tilla (*JEN* 403) and possibly Tarmiya son of Ḫuya (*EN* 9/1 101) and Pašši-Tilla son of Pula-ḫali (*EN* 9/2 529)

4. Enna-pali son of Šennaya is the "brother" of Muš-apu in AASOR 16 67. In *JEN* 63, written by Itḫ-apiḫe son of Taya (III), he adopts Teḫip-Tilla son of Puḫi-šenni.

5. Kelip-šarri son of Abeya appears with both Muš-apu (AASOR 16 66) and Puḫi-šenni (*EN* 9/2 171). In *JEN* 399 and 668 he is a judge in a case involving Tieš-urḫe son of Takku. Puḫi-šenni appears to be another of the judges in these texts.

6. Pui-tae son of Eteya engages in contracts with both Muš-apu (AASOR 16 66, and Teḫip-Tilla son of Puḫi-šenni (*JEN* 586).

7. As noted above, Šeḫliya son of Purna-zini appeared with an individual who dates to the second and third scribal generations. The correspondences for Muš-apu relate him to the third scribal generation, to Teḫip-Tilla son of Puḫi-šenni, and to Tieš-urḫe son of Takku. If he was, indeed, a judge, he is directly connected to both Teḫip-Tilla and his son Enna-mati. Akap-šenni is associated with Šilwa-Tešup DUMU LUGAL and the third scribal generation. Puḫi-šenni corresponds to Enna-mati son of Teḫip-Tilla, Tarmi-Tilla son of Šurki-Tilla, and Tieš-urḫe son of Takku. If he was a judge, he is directly connected to Tieš-urḫe son of Takku.

These associations suggest that Muš-apu's generation of the family overlapped with those of Teḫip-Tilla son of Puḫi-šenni and Enna-mati son of Teḫip-Tilla in the third scribal generation, and Puḫi-šenni's followed into the fourth generation and later.[78] This would make the generations of the Muš-apu family documents roughly contemporaneous with those of the other families attested in the eastern area.

Further evidence for this dating of the family of Muš-apu has been shown through some witnesses to their texts.[79] While those who appear with Muš-apu belong to the generation of Unapšewe families that appears with Teḫip-Tilla, those who are associated with Puḫi-šenni belong to the following generation at Unapšewe. The appendix at the end of this chapter lists the individuals who appear with Urḫi-kušuḫ and members of the Muš-apu family. It is immediately obvious that these names are not widely attested in the Nuzi corpus. Together with other Unapšewe texts, however, they offer the opportunity to reconstruct several genealogies of families active at Unapšewe. Such an endeavor, however, is beyond the scope of this volume.

The relatively few attestations of individuals who appear in texts of the Teḫip-Tilla family and the Muš-apu family reinforce the observation that the

[78] Ibid., 315.

[79] See Fadhil's synchronisms, ibid., p. 315.

Muš-apu family was active primarily after the period in which Teḫip-Tilla son of Puḫi-šenni acquired real estate in Unapšewe. If the Nuzi archives of Teḫip-Tilla's family are representative, his descendants appear not to have continued any major expansion of their holdings in Unapšewe, hence the limited evidence for Unapšewe in the later period.[80] The new texts illustrate that latter period and show that the strength of the Muš-apu family grew and was not fully expressed until the other large landowning family in the area had reached its peak. In the two generations of the Muš-apu family represented here, Muš-apu's texts reflect real-estate adoptions and some *titennūtu* activity. It is Puḫi-šenni's texts that demonstrate extensive acquisitions and typical consolidation practices, in *šupe*ᵓᵓ*ultū* documents.

Another interesting comparison between the Muš-apu family and the family of Teḫip-Tilla lies in the areas of Unapšewe in which the two families were acquiring property. Some familiar toponyms recur in the new texts, the *dimtu*s of Irribiya, Ḫamanna, and Zaziya, for instance.[81] The *EN* 9/2 texts also offer some the new geographical terms, however. Puzawe is identified as a *dimtu* in *EN* 9/2 17.[82] The field involved is in the *ugāru* of the city of Unapšewe, east of the road of the district of Puzawe and cut by the road of the city of Ḫamena. The *dimtu* of Tain-šuḫ appears in *EN* 9/2 22, in which the field is in the *ugāru* of the city of Unapšewe and north of that *dimtu*. The *dimtu* of Kušuḫ-erwi appears in *EN* 9/2 163. These new toponyms reflect the fact that the Muš-apu family was acquiring properties in areas of Unapšewe that had not been involved in the real-estate acquisitions of the Teḫip-Tilla family.

Summary

The common denominator of this Group of texts from Group 19 is Puḫi-senni son of Muš-apu. His records, his father's records, and possibly his nephew's single text comprise almost the entire archive. Puḫi-šenni and his father Muš-apu were important figures in the city of Unapšewe. Land and livestock owners, lenders, and judges, they held prominent social, economic, and official positions. Not much is known about the other members of the family, most likely because whatever texts they had were kept in Unapšewe. One can not help but be curious about Tae son of Muš-apu, however, who was designated as his father's chief heir. If he survived his father, he might be expected to be listed among the judges or appear in other records from Unapšewe. Moreover, Puḫi-šenni's eminence is difficult to explain.[83] Puḫi-šenni was, of course, associated with Urḫi-kušuḫ DUMU LUGAL in the city of Unapšewe, as a witness and, more significant, as his representative, in which capacity he paid out grain for Urḫi-kušuḫ. The mingling of the texts of the two men suggests that the relationship between

[80] See ibid., 297ff.; Maidman, *SEANFA*, 186–93, 234–36.
[81] For the *dimtus* of Unapšewe, see Fadhil, *STPPKA*, 286ff.; and Zaccagnini, *RLLA*, 155–62.
[82] Fadhil, *STPPKA*, 292.
[83] See ibid., 314, on this subject.

Puḫi-šenni and Urḫi-kušuḫ revealed in that transaction was not confined to a single instance but had a more-permanent nature.[84] In fact, the Urḫi-kušuḫ texts found in Puḫi-šenni's archives might all relate to Puḫi-šenni's responsibilities and/or concerns within the administration of Urḫi-kušuḫ's affairs. Certainly, AASOR 16 62 does. The others involve the distribution of grain both as rations and for loans. Finally, HSS 19 111 might involve Puḫi-šenni's son who was entering the household of Urḫi-kušuḫ. Perhaps this royal association contributed to Puḫi-šenni's success regardless of the status of his brother, Tae.

A possible parallel to Puḫi-šenni's relationship with Urḫi-Kušuḫ exists in the relationship between Ḫutiya son of Kuššiya with Šilwa-Tešup DUMU LUGAL. Ḫutiya is Šilwa-Tešup's substitute in court on two occasions (HSS 9 8 and 12). In HSS 9 41 he gives out beams of Šilwa-Tešup on loan. In HSS 9 43, he and Purn-apu, a highly placed *wardu* of Šilwa-Tešup, borrow grain in the city of Palaya and give it as rations to the *niš bīti* of Šilwa-Tešup. He also witnesses texts involving Šilwa-Tešup (HSS 9 17:19, 26; HSS 9 18:44, 59; and HSS 13 363:66) and the Purn-apu mentioned above (HSS 13 161:45, 60). Of particular interest, Ḫutiya is identified as *mār šipri ša* [*šarri*] in HSS 13 363:66.

Like Puḫi-šenni, Ḫutiya son of Kuššiya and his son Kel-Tešup maintained separate private archives. Ḫutiya's relate to Šuriniwe,[85] but were kept in Nuzi much as Puḫi-šenni's, which relate to Unapšewe. Ḫutiya's official responsibilities as *mār šipri* and possibly his association with Šilwa-Tešup brought him to Nuzi. Perhaps a similar situation obtained for Puḫi-šenni.

Though the evidence for Urḫi-kušuḫ is limited, his activities are reminiscent of those of Šilwa-Tešup DUMU LUGAL, whose archives were located at Nuzi.[86] If he was as active as Šilwa-Tešup, Urḫi-kušuḫ DUMU LUGAL would be expected to have more-extensive archives kept at his own center, possibly Unapšewe. Šilwa-Tešup certainly had households in other cities, and references to real-estate transactions belonging to him and his servants point to his ownership of fields and houses in various cities. Thus, indications that Urḫi-kušuḫ had a presence of some sort in Nuzi are not surprising.

Finally, the documents relating to the private activities of Puḫi-šenni and his father Muš-apu demonstrate a growth in wealth over the two generations to the point where Puḫi-šenni was a landowner of substance and a grain banker of some note. The multiple contracts with the same individuals at Unapšewe probably point to the same patterns of family disintegration among the landed citizens of the land as noted in other texts of this period.[87] In this family's case, the property was being acquired by individuals who appear to have had official connections, certainly positions of authority in the city involved.

[84] See ibid., 316.

[85] See G. Dosch and K. Deller, SCCNH 1:93.

[86] See Maidman, *SEANFA*, 555, for discussion of the DUMU LUGAL and pertinent bibliography, especially the possible official responsibilities of these individuals.

[87] See Morrison, "The Southwest Archives of Nuzi," SCCNH 2:167–201, for examples from Nuzi.

Appendix: The Principals of the Urḫi-kušuḫ Archive and the Muš-apu Family Archive

The *EN* 9/2 texts include the names of some individuals already known in the Nuzi corpus, along with a large number of new names. Most of these people were located in Unapšewe, the center of Urḫi-kušuḫ's and the Muš-apu family's holdings and activities. The individuals listed here appear as parties to contracts, witnesses, and landowners in the texts of Urḫi-kušuḫ DUMU LUGAL and the Muš-apu family. The party with which each appears is cited along with his or her role in the documents (P = party; W = witness; L = landowner; S = scribe; C = mentioned in contract; M = miscellaneous). The major scribes of the archive appear above on pp. 82–83. To avoid duplication, they are not repeated here. Line numbers represent the line in which he or she first appears in the text. In some instances relationships between certain individuals are clear; in other cases it is possible to deduce or suggest family relationships.[88] These are indicated where appropriate. These new names make it possible to extend certainly family genealogies known already. On pp. 94–95, at the end of the appendix, are figures 9–11, giving a few genealogies of families whose members are attested in the archives of Urḫi-kušuḫ and the Muš-apu family. Others are certainly possible on the basis of all of the Unapšewe texts, but such an endeavor is beyond the scope of this work.

A-[ ] ~ Puḫi-šenni: *EN* 9/2 19:9 (L)

Abeya son of Paip-purni ~ Muš-apu: HSS 19 8:40 (W), *EN* 9/2 143:29; probably father of Eḫlip-apu, Kelip-šarri, and Šurki-Tilla and brother of Ar-zizza (see fig. 9)

Ad-māti-il(u) (*ad-ma-ti*) son of Šulpe-nini ~ Muš-apu: AASOR 16 67:34 [corrected] (W); probably brother of Ḫalu-šenni son of Šulpe-nini; see Fadhil, *STTPKA*, 315

A[k-] ~ Puḫi-šenni: *EN* 9/2 74:26 (W)

Akap-še son of Kartiya ~ Puḫi-šenni: *EN* 9/2 336:5–6 (P)

Akap-šenni ~ Puḫi-šenni: *EN* 9/2 525:4 (W)

[Akap-šenni son of] Purna-zini ~ Muš-apu: *EN* 9/2 38:24 (W)

Akap-šenni son of Purna-zini ~ Muš-apu: *EN* 9/2 143:9 (P); see also HSS 9 139:2, 7, a lawsuit with Šilwa-Tešup DUMU LUGAL, Ila-nîšū the scribe; Akap-šenni, as noted above, was probably Puḫi-šenni's brother

Akaya son of Ka-[ ] ~ Puḫi-šenni: *EN* 9/2 275:2 (P)

Akaya son of Kuššiya ~ Puḫi-šenni: *EN* 9/2 163:8 (P); possibly brother of Kuari son of Kuššiya

[Akip]-šarri son of [Ḫabira] ~ Muš-apu: *EN* 9/2 28:26 (W)

Akip-šarri son of Ḫabira ~ Urḫi-kušuḫ: AASOR 16 62:30 (W); ~ Puḫi-šenni: *EN* 9/2 21:37 (W); probably brother of Kana son of Ḫabira

Akip-[ta?-] ~ Puḫi-šenni: *EN* 9/2 74:9 (L)

[88] The texts come from the same locale and the generations of the Muš-apu family provide a rough chronology for these individuals. Except in the case of very common names, it is possible to suggest familial connections.

Akip-tašenni ~ Muš-apu: *EN* 9/2 18:7 (L), *EN* 9/2 144:7 (P); ~ Puḫi-šenni: *EN* 9/2 19:26 (W), *EN* 9/2 188:5 (L)
Akip-tašenni son of Kawinni ~ Puḫi-šenni: *EN* 9/2 333:6–7 (P)
Akip-Tilla son of Ḫurpu ~ Puḫi-šenni: *EN* 9/2 329:3 (P)
Akip-Tilla son of Kikkiya ~ Urḫi-kušuḫ: HSS 19 111:23 (W), CT 51 3 LÚ*aškāpu*
Akip-Tilla son of Kipariya ~ Urḫi-kušuḫ: AASOR 16 62:2 (P)
Akitta ~ Puḫi-šenni: *EN* 9/2 327:13 (W)
Akitta son of Ili-imitti ~ Puḫi-šenni: *EN* 9/2 171:24 (W)
Akitta son of Waḫḫiya ~ Urḫi-kušuḫ: *EN* 9/2 321:13–14 (W); ~ Puḫi-šenni: *EN* 9/2 493:9 (W)
Akkul-enni ~ Puḫi-šenni: *EN* 9/2 358:14 (W)
Akkul-enni LÚ*aškāpu* ~ Urḫi-kušuḫ: HSS 16 229:3 (M)
Akkul-enni son of Kurri ~ Puḫi-šenni: *EN* 9/2 20:31 (W), *EN* 9/2 19:27 (W); brother of Zike son of Kurri
Akkul-enni son of Zike ~ Puḫi-šenni: *EN* 9/2 20:32 (W); see also HSS 13 340:17 and HSS 19 125:26, 36, a text of Ilaya son of Ḫabira
Alteya son of Adad-rabu ~ Muš-apu: *EN* 9/2 143:25 (W)
Ammarša ~ Puḫi-šenni: *EN* 9/2 146:7 (P); see also *JEN* 399 and 668 in which an Ammarša son of Palteya is sued by Tieš-urḫe son of Takku
Amumiya son of Ḫašip-Tilla ~ Puḫi-šenni: HSS 16 322:16 (W)
Amumiya son of Tupki-Tilla ~ Urḫi-kušuḫ: *EN* 9/2 321:17–18 (W) (see fig. 10)
Amur-atal ~ Muš-apu: *EN* 9/2 128:12 (L)
Apakkeya ~ Puḫi-šenni: *EN* 9/2 163:5 (L)
Apen-atal ~ Muš-apu: AASOR 16 67:8 (L)
Arik-[ ] ~ Puḫi-šenni: *EN* 9/2 23:43 (W)
Aril-lu son of Šakarakti ~ Puḫi-šenni: *EN* 9/2 362:9–10 (W)
Arip-šarri ~ Puḫi-šenni: *EN* 9/2 74:25 (W)
Arip-šarri son of Kuntanu ~ Puḫi-šenni: *EN* 9/2 20:26 (W), *EN* 9/2 22:32 (W), *EN* 9/2 77:27 (W)
Ariya son of Naniya ~ Puḫi-šenni: *EN* 9/2 188:25 (W), *EN* 9/2 19:32 (W), *EN* 9/2 22:34 (W)
Arrumpa son of Tupkiya ~ Puḫi-šenni: *EN* 9/2 77:39 (W)
Artašenni son of Unap-tae ~ Muš-apu: HSS 19 8:42 (W), *EN* 9/2 142:26–27 (W)
fAruna ~ Muš-apu AASOR 16 66:4 (L)
Ar-zizza son of Paip-purni ~ Muš-apu: HSS 19 93:12 (judge with Muš-apu); probably brother of Abeya son of Paip-purni (see fig. 9)
At-[ ]-kalluni ~ Muš-apu: *EN* 9/2 143:8 (L)
Attilammu son of Tur-šenni ~ Puḫi-šenni: *EN* 9/2 171:1–2 (P)

Bēlaya ~ Puḫi-šenni: *EN* 9/2 22:8 (L)
Bēliya LÚ.SIMUG? ~ Muš-apu: *EN* 9/2 18:43 (W)
Bēlu-[ ] ~ Puḫi-šenni: *EN* 9/2 21:10 (L)

Eḫlip-apu (son of Abeya) ~ Muš-apu: *EN* 9/2 18:14 (L), *EN* 9/2 28:7 (P), *EN* 9/2 49:11 (P); ~ Puḫi-šenni: *EN* 9/2 23:35 (W)

Eḫlip-apu son of Abeya ~ Urḫi-kušuḫ: HSS 19 111:22 (W); ~ Muš-apu: *EN* 9/2 18:1–2 (P); ~ Puḫi-šenni: *EN* 9/2 21:40 (W), *EN* 9/2 74:19–20? (W), *EN* 9/2 338:36 (W), *EN* 9/2 525:1–2 (P); see also *EN* 9/2 118 in which he is a party to a transaction conducted in Nuzi; probably son of Abeya son of Paip-purni and brother of Kelip-šarri and Šurki-Tilla sons of Abeya (see fig. 9)

Eḫlip-apu son of Šatta-u̯azza ~ Puḫi-šenni: *EN* 9/2 22:34 (W)

Eḫli-Tešup ~ Muš-apu: *EN* 9/2 143:6 (L); ~ Puḫi-šenni: *EN* 9/2 19:8 (L)

Eḫli-Tešup son of Bēlaya ~ Puḫi-šenni: *EN* 9/2 19:24 (W), *EN* 9/2 22:29 (W)

Eḫli-Tešup DUMU LUGAL ~ Urḫi-kušuḫ: HSS 16 229:23 (M); see also HSS 15 21:4, 34:23, 36:1

El-[ ] ~ Puḫi-šenni: *EN* 9/2 74:21; probably Elḫip-Tilla the scribe

EN-[ ]Tešup ~ Puḫi-šenni: *EN* 9/2 77:8 (L)

Enna-mati son of Puḫi-šenni ~ Ḫašip-Tilla: *EN* 9/2 189:35–36 (S)

Enna-pali son of Šennaya ~ Muš-apu: AASOR 16 67:12–13 ("brother" of Mus-apu); see also *JEN* 63 in which he adopts Teḫip-Tilla son of Puḫi-šenni

Enšuya son of Enna-mati ~ Puḫi-šenni: *EN* 9/2 20:28 (W)

Eteš-šenni son of Âtanaḫ-ili ~ Muš-apu: AASOR 16 66:34 (W), *EN* 9/2 17:29 (W), *EN* 9/2 143:26–27 (W); ~ Puḫi-šenni: *EN* 9/2 189:29 (W with Puḫi-šenni), *EN* 9/2 334:5–6 (P); ~ Ḫašip-Tilla: *EN* 9/2 189:29 (W); probably brother of Ḫatarte son of Âtanaḫ-ili

Ḫa-[ ] ~ Puḫi-šenni: *EN* 9/2 163 (W)

Ḫaiš-Tešup son of Erwi-šarri ~ Urḫi-kušuḫ: HSS 16 229:18 (M); see also *JEN* 469:17

Ḫaiš-Tešup son of Kutukka ~ Puḫi-šenni: *EN* 9/2 338:18–19 (W)

Ḫalu-šenni son of Šulpe-nini ~ Muš-apu: HSS 19 93:18 (co-witness with Muš-apu); probably brother of Ad-māti-il(u) son of Šulpe-nini; see Fadhil, *STTPKA*, 315.

Ḫalutta son of Taya ~ Puḫi-šenni: *EN* 9/2 301:11–12

Ḫamanna son of Šurki-turi ~ Muš-apu: AASOR 16 67:16 (M); father of Nai-šeri, grandfather of Mannu-māḫiršu (*NPN*, 51)

Ḫanakka ~ Puḫi-šenni: *EN* 9/2 323:15 (W)

Ḫanakka son of Milkiya ~ Puḫi-šenni: *EN* 9/2 22:1 (P), *EN* 9/2 146:35 (W)

Ḫanaya son of Šukrip-apu ~ Puḫi-šenni: *EN* 9/2 419:33 (judge)

Ḫanaya son of Taya ~ Muš-apu: AASOR 16 66:35 (W)

Ḫanianni ~ Puḫi-šenni: *EN* 9/2 329:17 (W)

Ḫanianni son of Makuya ~ Urḫi-kušuḫ: *EN* 9/2 321:4–5 (P)

Ḫanie ~ Puḫi-šenni: *EN* 9/2 525:5 (W)

Ḫanie son of Ḫanatu ~ Muš-apu: *EN* 9/2 17:33 (W)

Ḫanie son of Šukriya ~ Puḫi-šenni: *EN* 9/2 22:36 (W), *EN* 9/2 358:1–2 (P), *EN* 9/2 362:7 (W)

Ḫanie son of Teḫip-apu ~ Muš-apu: *EN* 9/2 17:2 (P)

Ḫaniu son of Aḫu-wa[qar?] ~ Muš-apu: HSS 19 93:14 (judge with Muš-apu); probably father of Kinni and Pui-tae sons of Ḫaniu (see fig. 11)

Ḫanukka ~ Puḫi-šenni: *EN* 9/2 19:10 (L)

Ḫanukka [son of]-RI ~ Muš-apu: *EN* 9/2 157:23 (W)

Ḫanukka son of Zilip-Tilla ~ Urḫi-kušuḫ: *EN* 9/2 321:15–16 (W); ~ Puḫi-šenni: *EN* 9/2 19:1–2 (P), *EN* 9/2 22:23 (W); probably son of Zilip-Tilla son of Zil-teya
Ḫašik-kamar son of Teḫiya ~ Puḫi-šenni: *EN* 9/2 189:33 (W with Puḫi-šenni); ~ Ḫašip-Tilla; *EN* 9/2 189:33 (W)
Ḫašik-ke son of Zike ~ Puḫi-šenni: HSS 16 322:4 (P)
Ḫašin-na ~ Puḫi-šenni: *EN* 9/2 20:37 (W), *EN* 9/2 455:4 (P)
Ḫašin-na son of Akip-apu ~ Puḫi-šenni: *EN* 9/2 20:27 (W), *EN* 9/2 146:28 (W), *EN* 9/2 189:32 (W with Puḫi-šenni); ~ Ḫašip-Tilla: *EN* 9/2 189:32 (W)
Ḫašin-[na-mar?] ~ *EN* 9/2 323:11 (W); probably father of Tae and Mušuya sons of Ḫašin-nawar; see Fadhil, *STPPKA*, 317–18.
Ḫašip-Tilla ~ Puḫi-šenni: HSS 16 230:2 (M), *EN* 9/2 188:8 (C)
Ḫašip-Tilla [ ] ~ Puḫi-šenni: *EN* 9/2 23:39 (W), *EN* 9/2 329:18 (W)
Ḫašip-Tilla *aškāpu* ~ Urḫi-kušuḫ: HSS 16 229:13 (M)
Ḫašip-Tilla son of [ ] ~ Muš-apu: *EN* 9/2 157:24 (W)
Ḫašip-Tilla son of Akawatil ~ Urḫi-kušuḫ: HSS 16 229:19 (M)
[Ḫašip-Tilla son of] Šeḫliya (?) ~ Muš-apu: *EN* 9/2 38:25 (W), *EN* 9/2 128:?
Ḫašip-Tilla son of Šeḫliya ~ Puḫi-šenni: *EN* 9/2 19:25 (W), *EN* 9/2 22:27 (W), *EN* 9/2 77:25 (W), *EN* 9/2 146:29 (W), *EN* 9/2 163:31 (W), *EN* 9/2 171:23 (W), *EN* 9/2 188:24 (W), *EN* 9/2 189:4 (P)
Ḫašiya ~ Puḫi-šenni: *EN* 9/2 301:44 (P)
Ḫašuar son of Enna-mati ~ Puḫi-šenni: *EN* 9/2 22:26 (W); possibly brother of Utḫap-tae, Matteya, and Tupkiya sons of Enna-mati
Ḫatarte ~ Puḫi-šenni: *EN* 9/2 188:7 (L), *EN* 9/2 189 (P with Ḫašip-Tilla son of Šeḫliya, W with Puḫi-šenni)
Ḫatarte son of Âtanaḫ-ili ~ Puḫi-šenni: *EN* 9/2 23:1–2 (P), *EN* 9/2 188:2 (P), *EN* 9/2 301:22 (P), *EN* 9/2 333:3 (P), *EN* 9/2 419:2 (P)
Ḫerriya ~ Muš-apu: *EN* 9/2 49:8 (L)
Ḫerriya son of Teḫip-apu ~ Muš-apu: AASOR 16 66:36 (W), *EN* 9/2 17:31 (W)
Ḫurazzi son of [ ] ~ Urḫi-kušuḫ: AASOR 16 62:34
Ḫuti-[ ] ~ Muš-apu: *EN* 9/2 49:9 (L)
Ḫuti-[ ] ~ Puḫi-šenni: *EN* 9/2 23:38 (W)
Ḫuti son of Gimil(šu)-abi ~ Puḫi-šenni: *EN* 9/2 146:31 (W)
Ḫutik-kewar son of Arta-pai ~ Puḫi-šenni: *EN* 9/2 329:9–10 (P)
Ḫutip-Tilla son of Ḫuya ~ Puḫi-šenni: *EN* 9/2 77:2 (P)

Ili-pazza ~ Muš-apu: *EN* 9/2 17:6 (L)
Iluni son of Puḫi-šenni ~ Puḫi-šenni: *EN* 9/2 338:20 (W)
Ipša-ḫalu son of Maṣī-ilu ~ Puḫi-šenni: HSS 16 322:18 (W)
Ipša-ḫalu son of Zike ~ Puḫi-šenni: *EN* 9/2 301:39 (P); see also HSS 19 24:26
Iriri-Tilla ~ Muš-apu: *EN* 9/2 49:7 (L)
Iriri-Tilla son of Arip-apu ~ Muš-apu: AASOR 16 67:39 (W) (*maṣṣar abulli*), *EN* 9/2 17:34 (W), HSS 19 93:19 (co-W with Muš-apu); see also IM 70726:18, 20 (TF1 107 = *WO* 9:23–26, no. 2)
ᵈIŠKUR-ŠAD-ni ~ Puḫi-šenni: *EN* 9/2 358:13 (W)

Kakkatanu ~ Puḫi-šenni: *EN* 9/2 74:24 (W)

Kana son of Ḫabira ~ Urḫi-kušuḫ: AASOR 16 62:31 (W); probably brother of Akip-šarri son of Ḫabira
Kani son of Mu-[ ] ~ Urḫi-kušuḫ: AASOR 16 62:33 (W)
Kani son of Mušeya ~ Puḫi-šenni: *EN* 9/2 301:14–15 (P)
Karrate son of Teḫiya ~ Puḫi-šenni: *EN* 9/2 21:31 (W), *EN* 9/2 77:24 (W)
Kaya son of Šennaya (?) ~ Puḫi-šenni: *EN* 9/2 20:34 (W)
Kelip-[šarri?] ~ Puḫi-šenni: *EN* 9/2 23:42 (W)
Kelip-šarri ~ Puḫi-šenni: *EN* 9/2 333:12 (W)
Kelip-šarri son of Abeya ~ Muš-apu; AASOR 16 66:38 (W); ~ Puḫi-šenni: *EN* 9/2 171:25 (W); see also *JEN* 339:43 and 668:55, where he is a judge in a court case involving Tieš-urḫe son of Takku and Ammarša (see above); probably son of Abeya son of Paip-purni and brother of Eḫlip-apu and Šurki-Tilla sons of Abeya (see fig. 9)
Keliya ? ~ Puḫi-šenni: *EN* 9/2 163 (W)
Kel-Tešup ~ Muš-apu: *EN* 9/2 326 (W); probably Kel-teya/Kel-Tešup the scribe
Kelum-atal son of Alpuya ~ Muš-apu: HSS 19 8:41 (W)
Kewar-atal ~ Muš-apu: AASOR 16 66:5 (L)
Kimparu son of Adad-rabi ~ Muš-apu: AASOR 16 67:36 (W), *EN* 9/2 143:24 (W)
Kinni son of Ḫaniu ~ Puḫi-šenni: *EN* 9/2 362:3 (P); probably brother of Pui-tae son of Ḫaniu and son of Ḫaniu son of Aḫu-wa[qar?], the judge (see fig. 11)
Kinniya son of Akip-Tilla ~ Urḫi-kušuḫ: AASOR 16 62:14 (C)
Kinzi ^{LÚ}*išpartu* ~ Urḫi-kušuḫ: HSS 16 229:5 (M)
Kuari ~ Puḫi-šenni: *EN* 9/2 358:17 (W)
Kuari son of Kuššiya ~ Puḫi-šenni: *EN* 9/2 327:4–5 (P); probably brother of Akaya son of Kuššiya
Kula-ḫupi ~ Puḫi-šenni: *EN* 9/2 323:14 (W)
Kuššiya ~ Puḫi-šenni: *EN* 9/2 163:4 (L); probably father of Kuari and Akaya

Mannu-māḫiršu son of Nai-šeri ~ Muš-apu: AASOR 16 67:1 (P); son of Nai-šeri, grandson of Ḫamanna, great-grandson of Šurki-turi (*NPN*, 95)
Mat-teya ~ Puḫi-šenni: *EN* 9/2 301:26 (P), *EN* 9/2 336:13–14 (guarantor) (M)
Mat-teya son of Enna-mati ~ Urḫi-kušuḫ: HSS 19 111:26 (W); ~ Puḫi-senni: *EN* 9/2 146:30 (W); possibly brother of Utḫap-tae, Ḫašuar, and Tupkiya sons of Enna-mati
Mušuya *nappāḫi* ~ Urḫi-kušuḫ: HSS 16 229:11 (M); same as next entry
Mušuya son of Ḫašin-nawar ~ Muš-apu: AASOR 16 66:37 (W), *EN* 9/2 143:28 (W); probably brother of Tae son of Ḫašin-nawar; see Fadhil, *STPPKA*, 317–18; same as previous entry

Nai-šeri ~ Muš-apu: *EN* 9/2 17:7 (L); most likely father of Mannu-māḫiršu; see AASOR 16 67 (*NPN*, 102)
Naite ~ Puḫi-šenni: *EN* 9/2 21:8 (L), *EN* 9/2 23:11 (L)
Naite son of Ḫanaya ~ Puḫi-šenni: *EN* 9/2 20:1–2 (P), *EN* 9/2 21:2 (P), *EN* 9/2 23:3 (P), *EN* 9/2 334:11–12 (P)
Nan-teya son of Ḫummuru ~ Muš-apu: AASOR 16 67:35 (W)

Ninu-atal ~ Muš-apu: *EN* 9/2 128:4 (L)
Nui-šeri ~ Puḫi-šenni: *EN* 9/2 20:8 (L)

Pai-Tilla ~ Muš-apu: *EN* 9/2 145:1 (W)
Pal-Tešup ~ Puḫi-šenni: *EN* 9/2 275:9 (W)
Pal-Tešup son of Šukriya ~ Muš-apu: HSS 19 93:1 (P) (Muš-apu a witness)
Puḫi-šenni ~ Urḫi-kušuḫ: *EN* 9/2 490:11 (W); ~ Puḫi-šenni: *EN* 9/2 21:9 (L)
Puḫi-šenni son of [ ]-šenni ~ Puḫi-šenni: *EN* 9/2 338:1–2 (P)
Puḫi-šenni son of [Ar-ta]šenni ~ Urḫi-kušuḫ: HSS 16 229:16 (M); ~ Puḫi-šenni: *EN* 9/2 338:1–2 (P)
Puḫi-šenni son of Atal-Tešup ~ Muš-apu: HSS 19 93:5 (P) (Muš-apu a witness)
Pu-[i? son of]-ikiya ~ Muš-apu: *EN* 9/2 526:2–3 (P)
Pui-tae [son of] ~ Puḫi-šenni: *EN* 9/2 23:36 (W)
Pui-tae son of Eteya ~ Muš-apu: AASOR 16 66:9 (P); see also *JEN* 586:2–3, in which he and his brother adopt Teḫip-Tilla son of Puḫi-šenni (Itḫ-apiḫe the scribe)
Pui-tae son of Ḫaniu ~ Puḫi-šenni: *EN* 9/2 146:32 (W), *EN* 9/2 171:26 (W); probably son of Ḫaniu son of Aḫu-wa[qar?] and brother of Kinni son of Ḫanniu (see fig. 11)
Punneya ~ Urḫi-kušuḫ: HSS 16 229:8 (M); ~ Puḫi-šenni: *EN* 9/2 301:42 (P)

Sîn-abi ~ Puḫi-šenni: HSS 16 230:9 (W)

Ša-[ ] ~ Urḫi-kušuḫ: HSS 16 229:1 (M)
Šamḫari son of Ipša-ḫalu ~ Muš-apu: HSS 19 93:17 (co-W with Muš-apu)
Šatta-u̯azza ~ Puḫi-šenni: *EN* 9/2 77:6 (L); probably father of Eḫlip-apu
Šeḫal-[te/li?] ~ Urḫi-kušuḫ: HSS 16 229:9 (M)
Šeḫal-te son of Akiya ~ Urḫi-kušuḫ: AASOR 16 62:32 (W)
Šeḫliya ~ Muš-apu: *EN* 9/2 142:34 (W); ~ Puḫi-šenni: *EN* 9/2 77:7 (L)
Šekaru son of Ḫašip-apu ~ Puḫi-šenni: *EN* 9/2 19:31 (W), *EN* 9/2 77:26 (W), *EN* 9/2 323:4–5 (P), *EN* 9/2 362:8 (W); see also HSS 14 180:2, where he and his brother Tae are identified with Unapšewe and their trip to the land of Akkad is mentioned; see Tae son of Ḫašip-apu below
Šimika ~ Puḫi-šenni: *EN* 9/2 358:16 (W)
Šimika-atal son of Eḫli-Tešup ~ Puḫi-šenni: *EN* 9/2 77:28 (W)
Šipki-[Tešup?] ~ Muš-apu: *EN* 9/2 18:44 (W)
Šipki-Tešup son of [ ]-ri-a? ~ Muš-apu: *EN* 9/2 157:25 (W)
Šukrip-[ ] ~ Muš-apu: *EN* 9/2 18:11 (L)
Šukri-Tešup ~ Puḫi-šenni: *EN* 9/2 327:1 (W)
Šukriya ~ Puḫi-šenni: *EN* 9/2 74:27 (W)
Šukriya son of Una[p-Tae] ~ Muš-apu: HSS 19 93:13 (co-W with Muš-apu)
Šur-[ ] ~ Puḫi-šenni: *EN* 9/2 23:8–9 (L)
Šurki-Tilla son of Abeya ~ Muš-apu: AASOR 16 67:37 (W); probably brother of Kelip-šarri and Eḫlip-apu sons of Abeya (see fig. 9)
Šurki-Tilla son of Tampi-kutatti ~ Urḫi-kušuḫ: *EN* 9/2 490:2–3 (P)

Šušanni ~ Urḫi-kušuḫ: *EN* 9/2 490:10 (W)

Tae son of Ḫašip-apu ~ Puḫi-šenni: *EN* 9/2 323:3–5 (P); see Šekaru son of Ḫašip-apu above

Tae son of Ḫaši[n-na]/Ḫaši[n-nawar] ~ Puḫi-šenni: HSS 15 300:6 (M with Puḫi-šenni); probably brother of Mušuya son of Ḫašin-nawar; see Fadhil, *STTPKA*, 317–18.

Tae son of Šukrip-apu ~ Puḫi-šenni: *EN* 9/2 419:37 (judge)

Tai[ ] ~ Puḫi-šenni: *EN* 9/2 74:23 (W)

Tain-šuḫ ~ Muš-apu: *EN* 9/2 128:16 (L)

Tarmiya ~ Puḫi-šenni: *EN* 9/2 301:47 (P)

Taula son of Ḫanatu ~ Puḫi-šenni: *EN* 9/2 188:26 (W)

Taya son of Warad-dūri ~ Muš-apu: AASOR 16 67:32 (W); ~ Puḫi-šenni: *EN* 9/2 74:12 (L); see also TF1 107 = IM 70726:17 (*WO* 9 [1977] no. 2)

Teḫip-apu ~ Muš-apu: *EN* 9/2 145:8 (L)

Teḫip-šarri son of Tenteya ~ Urḫi-kušuḫ: HSS 19 111:24–25 (W)

Teḫip-šarri [LÚ]*naggāru* ~ Urḫi-kušuḫ: HSS 16 229:4 (M)

Teḫiya ~ Puḫi-šenni: *EN* 9/2 163:33 (W), *EN* 9/2 301:44 (scribe?)

Teḫiya son of Ukur-atal ~ Puḫi-šenni: *EN* 9/2 21:30 (W?), *EN* 9/2 188:23 (W), *EN* 9/2 189:30 (W with Puḫi-šenni for Ḫašip-Tilla), *EN* 9/2 493:10 (W)

Teḫiya son of Unaya ~ Puḫi-šenni: *EN* 9/2 419:3 (P) (see fig. 10)

Tešup-atal son of Kula-ḫupi ~ Puḫi-šenni: *EN* 9/2 21:29 (W)

Tešup-nirari ~ Muš-apu: *EN* 9/2 128:10ff. (L)

Tuḫmiya son of Mat-Tešup ~ Puḫi-šenni: HSS 16 322:19 (W)

Tukultī-ili ~ Urḫi-kušuḫ: HSS 16 229:14 (M)

Tulpi-šenni ~ Muš-apu: *EN* 9/2 143:7 (L)

Tulpi-šenni son of Zikuki ~ Muš-apu: *EN* 9/2 17:30 (W)

Tupki-Tilla son of Unaya ~ Muš-apu: *EN* 9/2 326:1–2 (P); probably father of Amumiya (see fig. 10)

Tupkiya ~ Muš-apu: *EN* 9/2 128:17 (L)

Tupkiya son of Enna-mati ~ Puḫi-šenni: HSS 16 322: 17 (W); possibly brother of Ḫasuar, Mat-teya, and Utḫap-tae sons of Enna-mati

Turari ~ Puḫi-šenni: *EN* 9/2 301:5 (guarantor of Utḫap-šenni son of En-šaku) (M)

Turari son of [ ]-kaya ~ Puḫi-šenni: *EN* 9/2 301:8

Turar-Tešup son of Puḫi-šenni ~ Urḫi-kušuḫ: HSS 19 111:1–2 (P)

Turar-Tešup son of Tai-Tilla ~ Puḫi-šenni: *EN* 9/2 338:30–31 (W)

Unnuni son of Waqar-bēli ~ Muš-apu: *EN* 9/2 142:1–2 (P)

Ulmiya ~ Puḫi-šenni: *EN* 9/2 525:5 (W)

Ulmiya son of Šamḫari ~ Muš-apu: HSS 19 8:43 (W)

Unap-tae son of Ḫu-[ ] ~ Muš-apu: *EN* 9/2 17:32 (W)

Unapu ~ Muš-apu: *EN* 9/2 128:9 (L)

Urḫa-tati ~ Puḫi-šenni: *EN* 9/2 19:7 (L)

Urḫi-kutu son of Šeḫurni ~ Puḫi-šenni: *EN* 9/2 493:3–4 (P)

Urḫi-šarri son of Zikaya ~ Muš-apu: AASOR 16 67:33 (W)

Urḫi-Tešup ~ Muš-apu: AASOR 16 66:6 (L)
Utḫap-šenni son of En-šaku ~ Puḫi-šenni: *EN* 9/2 301:2 (P)
Utḫap-tae ~ Muš-apu: *EN* 9/2 28:28 (W)
Utḫap-tae son of Enna-mati ~ Puḫi-šenni: *EN* 9/2 74:2, *EN* 9/2 188:27 (W); see also HSS 19 124:41, where Utḫap-tae is a witness to a text involving Ilaya son of Ḫabira, and *JEN* 636:28, 38; possibly brother of Ḫasuar, Mat-teya, and Tupkiya sons of Enna-mati

Waḫri-šenni son of Eḫliya ~ Puḫi-šenni: HSS 16 322:7–8 (P)
Wantiš-šenni son of Zike ~ Puḫi-šenni: HSS 16 322:15 (W)
Wantiya son of Ar-nuzu ~ Muš-apu: *EN* 9/2 145:3 (P)
Wurteya son of Šuk[riya?] ~ Puḫi-šenni: *EN* 9/2 21:32 (W)

Zikaru son of Šalliya ~ Puḫi-šenni: HSS 16 311:11–12 (P), HSS 16 449:8 (LÚ.SIPA), *EN* 9/2 21:36 (W)
Zike son of Kurri ~ Puḫi-šenni: *EN* 9/2 19:28 (W), *EN* 9/2 20:31 (W), *EN* 9/2 22:33 (W), *EN* 9/2 493:11 (W); brother of Akkul-enni son of Kurri; possibly father of Akkul-enni son of Zike
Zi[ku]ki ~ Puḫi-šenni: *EN* 9/2 23:12 (L); probably father of Tulpi-šenni
Ziku[ki? son of]-RI ~ Muš-apu: *EN* 9/2 157:22 (W)
Zilip-[ ] ~ Puḫi-šenni: *EN* 9/2 327:14 (W)
Zilip-Tilla ~ Puḫi-šenni: *EN* 9/2 22:9–10 (L)
Zilip-Tilla son of Zil-teya ~ Puḫi-šenni: *EN* 9/2 338:21–22 (W); probably father of Ḫanukka son of Zilip-Tilla

[ ]apakeya ~ Muš-apu: *EN* 9/2 38:23 (W)
[ ]-a son of A-[ ] ~ Muš-apu: *EN* 9/2 28:25′ (W)
[ ] son of Akip-apu ~ Puḫi-šenni: *EN* 9/2 301:35 (P)
[son of Arik]-kamari ~ Puḫi-šenni: *EN* 9/2 163:24 (W)
[ ] son of Arip-apu ~ Muš-apu: *EN* 9/2 143:30 (W)
[ ] son of Ekeke ~ Puḫi-šenni: *EN* 9/2 301:29 (P)
[-ki?]ya son of Ḫaši-x-[ ] ~ Puḫi-šenni: *EN* 9/2 527:3
[ ] son of Ḫašip-apu ~ Puḫi-šenni: *EN* 9/2 333:11 (W)
[ ]-RI DUMU Ili-imitti ~ Muš-apu: *EN* 9/2 128:8 (L)
[ ] son of Pur[n-a]pu ~ Muš-apu: *EN* 9/2 28:20′ (W)
[ ] son of Purna-zini ~ Muš-apu: *EN* 9/2 38:24 (W)
[ ] son of Šehliya ~ Muš-apu: *EN* 9/2 38:25 (W)
[ ] son of Šellapai ~ Puḫi-šenni: *EN* 9/2 301:32 (P)
[ ]-pa-za-zu ~ Puḫi-šenni: *EN* 9/2 163:25 (W)
[ ]-ḫiya ~ Puḫi-šenni: *EN* 9/2 163:26 (W)
[ ]-pi-Tešup son of Urḫiya ~ Puḫi-šenni: *EN* 9/2 163:27 (W)
[ ] son of Zilip-Tilla ~ Puḫi-šenni: *EN* 9/2 22:28 (W)
[ ] son of [ ] ~ Puḫi-senni: *EN* 9/2 74 (W)

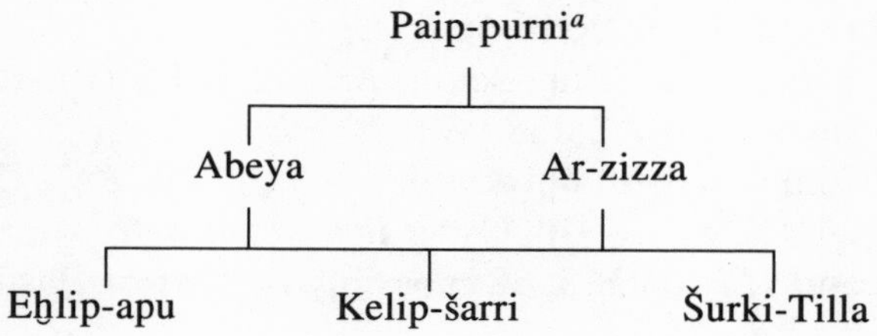

[a]See Fadhil, *STTPKA*, 137, for part of this family.

FIGURE 9. *Genealogy of Paip-purni's Family*

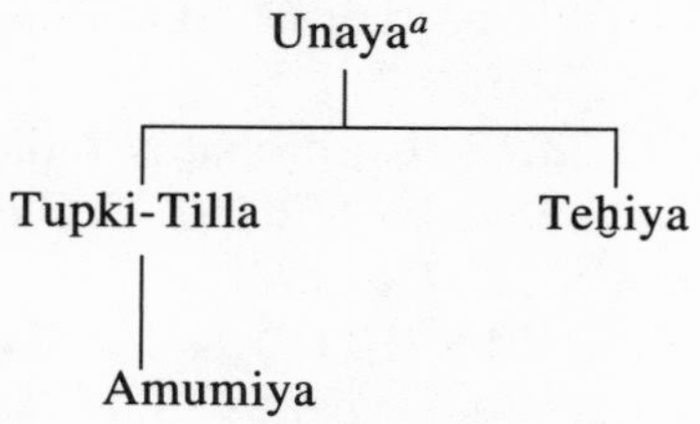

[a]See Fadhil, *STTPKA*, 137, for part of this family.

FIGURE 10. *Genealogy of Unaya's Family*

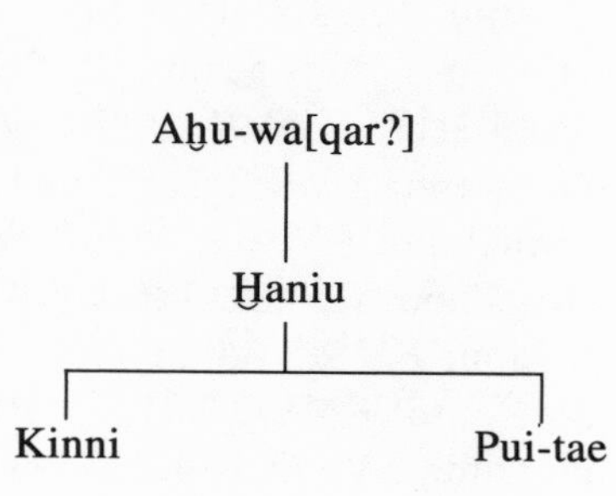

FIGURE 11. *Genealogy of Aḫi-wa[qar?]'s Family*

CHAPTER 5

The Family of Pula-ḫali and the Merchants: Texts from Group 19 (Part 2)

As noted in chapter 4, the texts from Group 19 include the archives of the family of Pula-ḫali. These documents cluster in rooms S132 and S133, rooms that belong to two of the "independent" units within Group 19 (see fig. 7 on p. 67 above). There is confusion regarding the room numbers of these texts as there is for the loci of all of the archives in the eastern area.[1] When reassembled, the records of the Pula-ḫali family describe the activities of three generations of the family.

The Family of Pula-ḫali

HSS 19 97 traces the family line for one branch, that of Akip-tura son of Pula-ḫali. In this text, one Ḫalutta son of Akiya gives five ANŠE of fields in the city of Tupšarriniwe to Pašši-Tilla and Kipal-enni the sons of Pula-ḫali and brothers of Akip-tura. Previously, the fields in question had been given to Ḫalutta's grandfather by Kamputtu son of Akip-tura as a *terḫatu*.[2] HSS 19 99 is the statement of Ilika son of Aḫiya concerning the *terḫatu* of his daughter ᶠḪaluli which he received from Pašši-Tilla son of Pula-ḫali. She may have become Pašši-Tilla's wife or Pašši-Tilla may have been arranging a marriage for somebody else.[3] An individual named Wuḫḫura son of Paššiya appears in two texts in this archive. In that Paššiya is the common hypochristic form of Pašši-Tilla in his own texts, Wuḫḫura was undoubtedly his son.[4] Yet another son of Pašši-Tilla may appear as a witness in *EN* 9/2 97:12–13, [ ]-wiya son of Pašši-Tilla. In addition to the brothers of Akip-tura, sons of Pula-ḫali, who appear in HSS 19 97, other texts mention a Šurki-Tilla son of Pula-ḫali. He is a witness in *EN* 9/2 441, a lawsuit written in the city of Tupšarriniwe (lines 29–20), and *EN* 9/1 337:16–17. Most important, he, Kipal-enni, and probably Pašši-Tilla sons of

[1] See p. 67–69 and nn. 10–11.

[2] The text is transliterated and translated with commentary by Fadhil, *RATK*, 20–21, with reference to E. Cassin, *RA* 63 (1969).

[3] Ibid., 21–22.

[4] See, among others, HSS 19 126:10, 24, 31; and *EN* 9/2 268, p. 103 below.

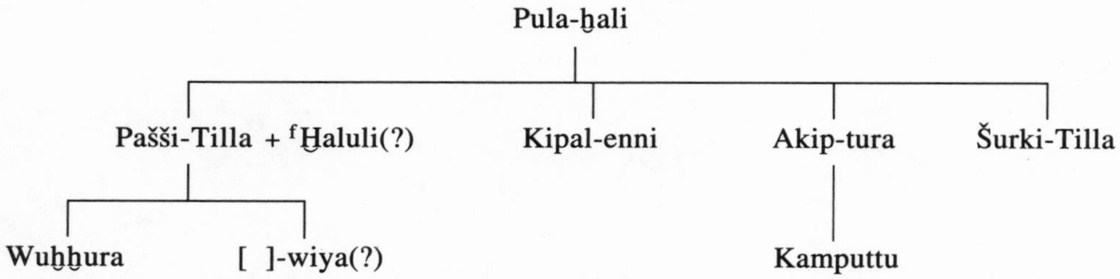

FIGURE 12. *Genealogy of Pula-ḫali's Family*

Pula-ḫali receive a field *ana titennūti* in *EN* 9/2 267. Similarly, in SMN 2719 he appears, at least with Pašši-Tilla son of Pula-ḫali in a *titennūtu* contract. This family can be reconstructed as shown in figure 12.

The chronology of this family is established by the scribes who write for its members. The scribes who write for Pula-ḫali include:

Mušteya son of Sîn-ibni	*EN* 9/2 339
Maliya	*EN* 9/2 209

Mušteya also writes for Teḫip-Tilla son of Puḫi-šenni.[5] Maliya also writes the lawsuit instituted by Ar-nawar *wardu* of ᶠAmminaya against Eḫli-Tešup son of Taya because of damage to ᶠAmminaya's property caused by Eḫli-Tešup's sheep.[6]

Scribes who write texts for the sons of Pula-ḫali or texts in which they appear include:

Abī-ilu son of ᵈAK.DINGIR.RA (V)	*EN* 9/2 349
Akkul-enni[7]	HSS 9/2 126, *EN* 9/2 440
Ariḫ-ḫamanna[8]	*EN* 9/2 441
Ḫut-Tešup [son of Eḫli-Tešup][9]	*EN* 9/2 292 and 505
Tarmi-Tilla	AASOR 16 97, HSS 19 99, *EN* 9/2 342, 343, SMN 2383

[5] *JEN* 259, 287, 587.

[6] HSS 13 310.

[7] Two scribes named Akkul-enni are known: the son of Ariḫ-ḫamanna and the son of MU-[ ]. The first writes for Tarmi-Tilla son of Šurki-Tilla in *JEN* 386:46. The second appears in *EN* 9 436:42. Otherwise a scribe named Akkul-enni also appears in HSS 5 1:25 and HSS 15 179:12. See n. 8.

[8] Ariḫ-ḫamanna writes *EN* 9/2 441, in which Šurki-Tilla son of Pula-ḫali is a witness. A scribe named Ariḫ-ḫamanna son of Ḫutiya writes for Teḫip-Tilla son of Puḫi-šenni (*JEN* 240 and 439). An Ariḫ-ḫamanna the scribe also writes *EN* 9/1 331 (also from the Eastern Archives). See n. 7 for Akkul-enni son of Ariḫ-ḫamanna. Perhaps these individuals represent three generations of a scribal family. See *RATK*, 47.

[9] Ḫut-Tešup is identified as the son of Eḫli-Tešup on the basis of HSS 19 129:12. See G. Wilhelm, AOAT 9:10, where Ḫut-Tešup is shown as a fifth-generation scribe descended from either Turari or Waqar-bēli, both sons of Taya.

Urḫi-Tešup [son of Šata][10]	*EN* 9/2 364
^{d}UTU-PAB	*EN* 9/2 207, 283, 337, 340, 341, 344, 345, 352, 353, 513, 515; IM 70985 (= TF1 426)
^{d}UTU-PAB son of Akiya (V)	HSS 19 97; *EN* 9/2 224, 250 and 299
ZU-^{d}IŠKUR	*EN* 9/2 33

Some of these scribes also write for well-known figures in the Nuzi corpus. Abī-ilu writes for Ilānu son of Taiuki, Pai-Tešup *wardu* of Šilwa-Tešup, Ḫampizi son of Ar-šatuya, Šeḫal-Tešup son of Teḫup-šenni, and the sons of Ḫuya.[11] Tarmi-Tilla writes for Muš-apu son of Purna-zini.[12] Urḫi-Tešup son of Šata writes for Ilānu son of Taiuki, Utḫap-tae son of Ar-tura, and Ili-ma-aḫi son of Ilānu; he also appears with Turar-Tešup son of Itḫ-apiḫe (IV).[13] ^{d}UTU-PAB writes for Šeḫal-Tešup son of Teḫup-šenni, Šilwa-Tešup DUMU LUGAL, and Ili-ma-aḫi son of Ilānu.[14]

The direct relationships between the sons of Pula-ḫali and fourth-and fifth-generation scribes place them in the last period of the Nuzi corpus. Indirectly, the sons of Pula-ḫali are associated with other individuals who were active at that time, including many of the figures of the Eastern Archives. No direct links exist between Pula-ḫali and the scribal family of Apil-Sîn. However, Maliya writes the lawsuit HSS 13 310 between ^{d}Aminnaya and Eḫli-Tešup son of Taya. Eḫli-Tešup son of Taya dates to the third and fourth scribal generations,[15] and ^{d}Aminnaya was the mother of Šilwa-Tešup DUMU LUGAL.[16] Thus, Pula-ḫali is comfortably associated with scribes of the appropriate generation.

The family of Pula-ḫali has been known in the Nuzi corpus mainly from the HSS 19 texts cited above, a court case,[17] a large body of loan documents,[18] two contracts concerning the payment of grain, both of which stem from Tupšarrin-iwe,[19] and texts from Tel el-Faḫḫar.[20] As was the case with the Muš-apu family, the new texts expand considerably our knowledge of the concerns and activities of the Pula-ḫali family. Further, they offer important information about the commercial life of the land of Arrapḫe.

[10] A scribe, Urḫi-Tešup son of Šata, is known from HSS 5 17:34, 40; 34:13, case; and 36:20. An Urḫi-Tešup also writes AASOR 16 68, HSS 19 116, and *JEN* 321, the last of which involves Kel-Tešup son of Ḫutiya.

[11] See p. 24 above and Chapter 2, nn. 41–43 and 50.

[12] See p. 82 above, *sub* Tarmi-Tilla.

[13] See p. 53 above and Chapter 3, nn. 50 and 51.

[14] See p. 59 above and Chapter 3, nn. 75–76.

[15] See pp. 25–26 above and Chapter 2, n. 43.

[16] See M. Morrison, "The Family of Šilwa-Tešup *mār šarri*," *JCS* 31 (1979) 14–16.

[17] *EN* 9/2 440 = SMN 2372 in Hayden, *CPN* 148–49.

[18] AASOR 16 97, and the loan documents in Owen, *LDN*: *EN* 9/1 340 (p. 113), 341 (pp. 113–14), 342 (p. 114), 343 (pp. 114–15), 344 (p. 115), 345 (p. 115), 346 (pp. 115–16), 348 (= *EN* 9 349, p. 116), 349 (= *EN* 9 348), 352 (p. 118), 353 (p. 118), 374 (p. 126). See also *EN* 9/2 97.

[19] HSS 16 231 and HSS 19 126, on which, see below.

[20] Fadhil, *RATK*, 15ff., collects and analyzes the corpus of Nuzi and Tel el-Faḫḫar materials concerning Tupšarriniwe. These include the Pula-ḫali materials known at the time.

Pula-ḫali LÚ.DAM.GÀR

Though he is attested in only a few texts, Pula-ḫali is an especially interesting figure. In *EN* 9/2 339, one Nūr-kûbi son of [ ]-šu states that he received the metals that he had given to Pula-ḫali *ana šipti u tamkarši* from Pula-ḫali and that he is paid in full.[21] This text suggested that Pula-ḫali was a *tamkāru* who engaged in the sorts of business documented for other individuals known to have been active in that occupation.[22] *EN* 9/2 209, a similar text, confirms this supposition:[23]

[EME-*š*]*u ša* ^{I}MI.NI-^{d}UTU
[DUMU *i*]*p*-LUGAL *a-na pa-ni*
[LÚ.MEŠ *ši-bu*]*-ti an-nu-ti*
[*ki-a-am iq*]*-ta-bi*
[*mi*]*-nu-me-e* [AN.NA.]MEŠ *ša* KA *ṭup-pi*^{MEŠ} *ḫu-ub-bu-li-šu*
[*ša* ^{I}]*Pu-la-ḫ*[*a-li*] LÚ.DAM.GÀR
[X MA].NA AN.NA.[MEŠ *a*]*-šar* ^{I}*Pu-la-ḫa-li*
[*el*]*-te-qì-mi ù ap-la-ku-mi*
[*ù*] *qa-an-na-su ša* ^{I}*Pu-la-ḫa-li*
[*i-na*] *pa-ni* LÚ.MEŠ *ši-bu-ti*
[*im*]*-ta-šar ù i+na* u$_4$*-mi*
[*a*]*n-ni-i* ^{I}*Pu-la-ḫa-li* [*a-n*]*a mi-im-ma*
[*a-na i*]*a-ši la ḫu-ub-ul-mi*
[*ma-na*]*-am-ma tup-pa*
[*ša ḫu-u*]*b-bu-li-šu*
[*ša* ^{I}*P*]*u-la-ḫa-li*
[*ú-te-e*]*l-li ù aš-šum*
[*mi-i*]*m-ma i+na* EGIR-*ki*
[*ša* ^{I}]*Pu-la-ḫa-li*
[*a-š*]*a-as-sí*
[X] MA.NA KÙ.GI DIRI-*la*
IGI EN-*ya* DUMU *Ka*$_4$*-ti-ri*
IGI *Zi-li-ya* DUMU
:*En-na-ma-ti*
IGI *A-ki-ya* ^{LÚ}*ḫa-za-an-nu*
IGI *Mu-šu-uš-še*
DUMU MI.NI-*še-mi*
IGI *Te-ḫi-ya* DUMU *Pa-ḫu*
IGI *Ma-li-ya* DUB.SAR

21 For text see Owen, *LDN*, 22 and 112. A revised translation appears in Zaccagnini, "The Merchant at Nuzi," *Iraq* 39 (1977) 186.

22 See Zaccagnini, *Iraq* 39:171, 185ff.

23 Line 5 AN.NA.MEŠ restored on the basis of line 7. Note that in *EN* 9/2 339 Pula-ḫali receives URUDU.MEŠ and ZABAR.MEŠ *ana* MÁŠ-*ti ù tám-kàr-ši*^{MEŠ} (lines 2–4). Here the payment is related to *ṭup-pi*^{MEŠ} *ḫu-ub-bu-li-šu*. Whether the "loan tablets" specified only interest or the sort of arrangement described in *EN* 9/2 339 is not known. In other respects, the two texts are very similar. For witnesses, scribes, etc., see catalog below.

30 [ ] NA4 ^I^*Mu-uš-[še]*
[ ] NA4 ^I^EN-*ya*

The statement of Ṣill-Šamaš son of [ ]-ip-šarri. Thus he spoke before these witnesses: "Whatever [tin] according to the word of the loan tablets of Pula-ḫali the merchant, x *minas* of tin from Pula-ḫali I have received and I am paid in full. Pula-ḫali impressed his hem before witnesses. From this day Pula-ḫali does not owe me anything. Whatever loan tablets (there were) of Pula-ḫali, he has taken (them) up. (If) I raise a case against Pula-ḫali on account of anything, I will pay x *minas* of gold." SIX WITNESSES (including Maliya the scribe). TWO SEALS.

According to *EN* 9/2 339, Pula-ḫali was a merchant who received investments from individuals who expected a return in the form of interest and commercial profit. The tin in *EN* 9/2 209 is described as a loan. The terms of the loan (i.e., the interest, time of repayment, and the like), would have appeared on the "loan tablets" mentioned in the text. These loan tablets might have referred to an investment of the sort noted in *EN* 9/2 339. On face value, though, it appears that Pula-ḫali had borrowed tin, most likely to finance up front a commercial venture.

The evidence concerning Pula-ḫali's patronymic is not clear. In *EN* 9/2 339 the text is poorly preserved precisely in line 6 where traces have been read as DUMU-*šu* ⟨⟨*šu*⟩⟩ *Nu-ša-pu*.[24] While it is tempting to see a relationship between the Pula-ḫali family and the Muš-apu family whose texts are stored in the same building, the reading remains problematic. Moreover, the Muš-apu family, as noted in chapter 4, was based in Unapšewe. Even in Pula-ḫali's generation, Muš-apu's family was connected with Turšarriniwe. One of the texts from Tel el-Faḫḫar, IM 70985 (= TF1 426), in which Pašši-Tilla son of Pula-ḫali appears as a "man of Tupšarriniwe," mentions land of Pula-ḫali (see below). The only discernible connections between the two families are that they both were engaged in lending and certain members of the families stored their records in the same building in Nuzi.

The Sons of Pula-ḫali

Pula-ḫali was a landowner and merchant who must have been quite successful. As his sons' records indicate, family members were able to extend their real-estate holdings and engage in a number of other enterprises requiring considerable capital.

The *EN* 9/2 texts include more loans made by the sons of Pula-ḫali. *EN* 9/2 97 is the fragmentary record of a tin loan by [Kipal]-enni son of Pula-ḫali (line 4) and witnessed by Pašši-Tilla son of Pula-ḫali and [ ]-wiya son of Pašši-Tilla (lines 12–13).[25] *EN* 9/2 529 records a tin loan to be paid back to Pašši-Tilla

[24] Owen, *LDN*, 112. This peculiar line yields a reading of "Pula-ḫali or his son Nuš-apu" (p. 22) and "Pula-ḫali son of Muš-apu" (Zaccagnini, *Iraq* 39:186).

[25] Other witnesses include Tukultī-ili son of Pui-tae (line 14), [U]ante son of EN-la-x[ ] (line 15), known from other texts in the archive, and Šekar-Tilla son of Bēlaya (lines 18 and 20). See the appendix below.

in the city of Zizza.[26] *EN* 9/2 364 is the statement of an individual who borrowed metal(?) from Paššiya (= Pašši- Tilla).[27] Others include *EN* 9/2 512, 513, and 515, the last of which was written in the city of Tupšarriniwe.[28]

EN 9/2 292 and 505 are particularly interesting texts since both refer to large animals used in the "journey of the palace," that is, the palace-sponsored overland trade. The translations of these texts follow:

EN 9/2 292[29]

Thus says Zunna son of Urḫiya: "One ass of Pašši-Tilla son of Pula-ḫali which for thirty minas of tin *aladumma ēpuš*. It was sent on the journey of the palace it was sent. Zunna (will give) thirty minas of tin in the month of Arkapinnu." FOUR WITNESSES. The hand of Ḫut-Tešup the scribe. The tablet was written in the city of Ulamme. SIX SEALS.

EN 9/2 505[30]

Thus says Tupkin-a‹tal› son of Ḫapiašu: "Two horses of the road from the hand of Tupki-Tilla (and) from Pašši-Tilla son of Pula-ḫali I received and I am paid in full. The horses are in the *bīt ṭuppi* of the palace." FOUR SEALS. The hand of Ḫut-Tešup the scribe. This tablet. . . . FIVE SEALS. The tablet was written at the gate of the City of Gods at the ditch.

[26] Perhaps the scribe is Enna-mati (son of Puḫi-šenni) (line 12). See pp. 24 and 83.

[27] Note lines 7–8 EN-*ri*-[ ] ^{LÚ}*ḫa-b*[*i-ru*?]. Witnesses include Tukultī-ilu son of Pui-tae (lines 9–10), Pettiya son of [ ] (line 11), Kel-Tešup son of Sīn-ibni (lines 12–13), and Urḫi-Tešup the scribe (line 14). See the appendix for these men.

[28] *EN* 9/2 512 is a statement before witnesses. Tae son of Teḫiya (lines 13 and 15) may be the party involved. At the least, he is a witness (see the appendix). *EN* 9/2 513 is the statement of Itḫ-apiḫe son of Arip-urekke who borrows bronze from Pašši-Tilla. ^{d}UTU-PAB is the scribe. The obverse of *EN* 9/2 515 is poorly preserved, but it may be a repayment note (line 13, [*ap*]-*la-ku-mi*). Witnesses include Šilaḫi-Tešup son of Elḫip-[šarri] (line 23), Ḫa-bu?(written over the DIŠ sign)-x-ŠI son of Zaziya (line 24; Zaziya is known as the father of Attaya and Ḫaniya in these texts), Akip-Tilla son of [Ir]ri[ke] (line 25), and Pal-teya son of Ward-aḫḫe (line 26). ^{d}UTU-PAB is the scribe (line 27).

[29] The meaning of *aladumma epēšu* (lines 5–6) is not known. Here, it seems to refer to a kind of financial arrangement. Perhaps Pašši-Tilla loaned/contributed the ass to Zunna's venture with the expectation of a return of 30 minas of tin. Note that the animal is used for the "road of the palace," i.e., the overland trade. The witnesses include Tae son of Elḫip-Tilla (line 13), Anin-api son of Šuk-[ ] (line 14), Ḫašip-Tilla son of Šar-teya (lines 15–16), and Ar-Tešup son of Šummuku (line 17). See the appendix for these individuals. For Ḫut-Tešup the scribe, see n. 9.

[30] A Tupkin-atal appears in HSS 15 12:16, 16:36, 20:23, 27:32, 117:28, all from N 120, and HSS 16 95:3 from C 19. In the last, he receives grain. In the HSS 15 texts he is involved with armaments, charioteers, and horses. It is possible that the Tupkin-atal of the HSS 15 texts was responsible for, or involved with, horses for the overland trade as well and, so, might be the son of Ḫapi-ašu. Among the witnesses are Nūr-[Šamaš] son of Akap-šenni (line 9), Akkul-enni son of [A]kitte (lines 10–11), P[ui]-tae son of Ḫamanna (lines 12–13), and Akawa[til] son of Elḫip-Tilla, for all of whom, see the appendix. Surely the horses were not kept in the *bīt ṭuppi* of the palace. Perhaps they were accounted for in the records stored there. If the Tupkin-atal of *EN* 9/2 505 and the HSS 15 texts are the same, then room N 120 with its large number of texts, including horse texts, might have been the *bīt ṭuppi* of the palace.

Real-estate ownership for the sons of Pula-ḫali has been attested by HSS 19 97 in which they received a *terḫatu* field in Tupšarriniwe which had originally belonged to their family. At least six other real-estate transactions are attested for the sons of Pula-ḫali. These include one text that appears to be a *ṭuppi mārūti* (*EN* 9/2 33) and five *titennūtu* arrangements (*EN* 9/2 224, 267, 268, and 524, and SMN 2719). It is noteworthy that metals figure prominently in these and other transactions of the sons of Pula-ḫali.

EN 9/2 33[31]

. . . x cubits . . . twenty cubits its circumference along the fence. East of the orchard of Ḫašip-šarri, west of the orchard of Tai-šenni, north of the threshing floor of the palace, south of the wall of Teḫiya. Tae has given this orchard to Pašši-Tilla as his inheritance share. Pašši-Tilla has given this "money"—five minas of tin, two minas of bronze, one pi of grain, two BÁN of wheat—to Tae as [his] gift. [Who]ever among them [breaks the con]tract [will pay] one mina of silver and [one mina of gold] . . . . FOUR MEN who [sur]veyed the orchard and [gave the sil]ver." FIVE WITNESSES including ZU-^{d}IŠKUR the scribe. SIX SEALS.

EN 9/2 224[32]

[Tablet of *tit*]*ennūtu* [whereby Šur]ukka [son of Ar]ip-urikke [(a field) i]n the plain of the city of [Tupšarrini]we on the road of . . . does not cut in two . . . he holds. East of the field of [. . .] "ditto," west of the field of [. . .] north of the field of . . . , south of the field of . . . on lease [for x years] to Pašši-[Til]la son of Pul[a-ḫali] I have given. Pašši-Tilla has given five BÁN of grain and two minas of tin to Šuruk[ka]. As soon as [Šurukka] returns the five BÁN of grain and two min[as of tin] to Pašši-Til[la,] he will take his field. If (the field) has a claim, Šurukka will clear (it) and will give (it) to Pašši-Tilla. This tablet (was written) after the proclamation at the gate of the city of Tupšarriniwe. FOUR WITNESSES. [The hand] of ^{d}UTU-PAB the scribe son of Akiya. [The]se men were the surveyors. SIX SEALS.

The obverse of *EN* 9/2 267 is quite broken, but it is clear that more than one individual gives property to the sons of Pula-ḫali:[33]

. . . on lea[se for six years] Šurki-Tilla and . . . have given to Šurki-Tilla, to [Pašši-Tilla], and to Kipal-en[ni sons of Pula-ḫali]. The sons of [Pula-ḫa]li have given to

[31] For "its circumference along the fence" (line 3, *li-mi-is-*[*-su i*]*-na ḫu-ub-bal-li*), see *CAD* Ḫ 213 s.v. *ḫubballa/i*. The measure of the orchard around its border is being provided. Among the witnesses are Pal-teya son of Ward-aḫḫe (line 20) restored on the basis of *EN* 9/2 353:19 et al. and Kipal-enni son of Pula-ḫali (line 27).

[32] The name of Šurukka son of Arip-urekke is restored on the basis of his multiple appearances in these texts (see the appendix).

[33] Šurki-Tilla is clearly a recipient of the field in line 5. The Šurki-Tilla in line 4 is the name of one of the individuals giving the field. For parallels to "a section (*niksa*) he will not cut," see HSS 5 33:36–37, 87:23–24, and HSS 9 101:36. Among the witnesses, Tae son of Bêliya can be restored in line 40 on the basis of his numerous appearances in texts of this Group (see the appendix).

Šurki-Tilla and . . . this silver—one ewe, plucked five times, . . . twice-plucked, three male sheep . . . , one ewe . . . , two twice-plucked male sheep, two . . . twice-plucked ewes, x+four minas of bronze. As soon as the six years "are filled," they will return [to the sons of Pul]a-ḫali [the silver according to the word] of this tablet and they will take their field. If the field has a claim, these two(?) men will clear it and will give it to the sons of Pula-ḫali. If the field is plowed, they will not take it. If the field is larger, he will not diminish it (lit., "take it"). If the field is smaller, he will not increase it. From the field he will not cut a section. Whoever among them remains will pay the silver and clear the field. Whoever among them breaks the contract will pay two oxen. This tablet was written after the proclamation [at] the gate of the city of Tupša[rriniwe]. THREE WITNESSES who were the surveyors. TWO WITNESSES.

EN 9/2 268[34]

. . . west of the field of . . . , south of the field of Ipšaya, north of the canal of Ar-šašitti, [Šekaru] has given his orchard with its well and with its threshing floor on lease for thr[ee years] to Paššiya [son of P]ula-ḫali. Paššiya has given five m[inas of tin] for his field to Šekaru. As soon as the three years have elapsed, Šekaru will return the five minas of tin [to Paššiya and will take his field].

EN 9/2 524[35]

. . . sons of Pu[la-ḫali] have given to Ak[iya si]x minas of tin on lease for his field. If the field has a claim, Akiya will clear it and will give it to the sons of Pula-ḫali. When the three years [have elapsed], Akiya will return six minas of tin to the sons of Pula-ḫali and his field [he will take]. If the field . . . from this day . . . (minas) of tin . . . he will return. If the field is [plo]wed he will not take it. Whatever . . . grain . . . he will pay.

SMN 2719 is known at present only in a transliteration that indicates that it is poorly preserved. However, it describes a *titennūtu* agreement between a Puḫi-šenni(?) and at least Paššiya and Šurki-Tilla sons of Pula-ḫali. The property is located in the *ugāru* of the city of Tupšarriniwe south of the border of the palace, and the contract is to run for six years.[36]

Among the documents of the sons of Pula-ḫali are contracts of various sorts and miscellaneous texts. In *EN* 9/2 283, for instance, Taika son of Akap-šenni states that he sold to Pašši-Tilla son of Pula-ḫali the pair of doors which he received as his inheritance share from his father's estate.[37] EN 9/2 250 is an agreement between Ḫašiya [son of Ward-aḫḫe?] and Pašši-Tilla concerning

[34] This appears to be a particularly fine piece of property; it borders a canal and includes an orchard, well, and threshing floor.

[35] The names of the sons are not preserved. Pašši-Tilla usually appears with one or both of his brothers.

[36] The transliteration of this text is in E. R. Lacheman's unpublished Harvard doctoral dissertation *SCTN* 2: 242–43.

[37] Pašši-Tilla pays six minas of tin as the price (lines 10–11) of *it-te-nu-tu*$_4$ GIŠ.IG (line 3). See the appendix for other texts involving Taika. ^{d}UTU-PAB is the scribe (line 20). This tablet does not turn in the normal way but rather side to side.

livestock that Ḫašiya[38] is to give to Paššši-Tilla. This text was written in the city of Tupšarriniwe. *EN* 9/2 299 is a *ṭuppi mārtūti* by which Uante son of *EN*[ ] gives his sister fElwin[ni] to Paššši-Tilla. According to the arrangements, which follow the normal pattern, Paššši-Tilla will arrange for her marriage and receive a portion of the *terḫatu*.[39] *EN* 9/2 391 is a wage contract through which Arnukka son of Elḫip-Tilla receives two minas of tin as wages (*ki-ma ig-ri-šu*) and three BÁN of grain for food (*ki-ma a-ka-li-šu*) from Paššši-Tilla son of Pula-ḫali. In return he will provide Paššši-Tilla two thousand and some hundred bricks.[40]

The lawsuit, *EN* 9/2 440, concerns a debt that Paššši-Tilla claims he is owed by the brothers of one of his debtors who had died. The case was tried in Tupšarriniwe.[41] Kipal-enni, too, was involved in litigation as the letter *EN* 9/2 102, from Akip-tašenni the SUKAL to Teḫip-šarri, indicates.[42]

Wuḫḫura Son of Paššši-Tilla

Wuḫḫura son of Paššši-Tilla is attested in only two texts, *EN* 9/1 347, a loan document, and *EN* 9/2 452.[43] He is identified as the son of Paššši-Tilla in the second because the text is assigned to S132 and only one Wuḫḫura, the son of Paššiya (= Paššši-Tilla) of *EN* 9/1 347, is known in the Nuzi corpus. Further, *EN* 9/2 452 is a "memorandum" text indicating the amounts of tin that the listed individuals received, presumably on loan.[44] It would be entirely appropriate that Paššši-Tilla's son continue in the lending business.

[38] This might, in fact, be Ḫašiya son of Ward-aḫḫe (see catalog). Pal-teya [son of Ward-aḫḫe] is the guarantor. Note HSS 16 317 in which Zilip-apu is the guarantor for his brother Eḫli-Tešup son of Taya in a transaction involving livestock. Written in Tupšarriniwe (lines 14–15), the text is witnessed by a number of familiar figures: Tukultī-ilu son of Pui-tae (line 16), Akiya son of Nūr-kûbi (line 17), Ḫalutta son of Akiya (line 18), dUTU-PAB the scribe (lines 20–21).

[39] This text, too, appears to have been written in Tupšarriniwe since many individuals associated with the city are mentioned: Uante, the party to the contract along with Akiya son of Šaš-tae (line 28), Attaya son of Zaziya (line 29), Ḫašiya son of Ward-aḫḫe (line 30), Zaziya son of Akkuya (line 31), Tae son of Teḫiya (line 32), Umpiya son of Zilip-apu (line 33) (known from an Unapšewe text), Šurukka son of Arip-urekke (line 38), and dUTU-PAB the scribe (line 34).

[40] Was Paššši-Tilla using or lending the bricks? No brick loans are attested for him, but they were a commodity loaned out by the palace and private individuals (see Owen, *LDN*, 28–30 and *EN* 9/2 393 below). In line 20, Akiya son of Šaš-tae witnesses the text.

[41] For the text, see Hayden, *CPN*, 148–49. The brothers Alki-Tilla and Ḫupita sons of Akitte appear elsewhere in texts belonging to the Pula-ḫali family (see the appendix). Ḫupita borrows from Paššši-Tilla in *EN* 9/2 342. Tultukka son of Akitte, whose debt is the subject of the suit, is involved in another transaction by which he collects a debt (*EN* 9/2 477).

[42] Apparently, Kipal-enni believed that his case was not properly heard. Akip-tašenni the SUKKAL is attested in other texts: HSS 15 34:18 and 36:32, both of which concern "teams" and "horses" listed for men, two of whom appear in these texts (Akip-tašenni son of Ariḫ-ḫamanna and Umpiya son of Zilip-apu) and some of whom are well-known figures at Nuzi, e.g., Tarmi-Tilla son of Šurki-Tilla. In HSS 16 111:7 he receives grain, possibly for horses.

[43] For the texts see Owen, *LDN*, 116 (*EN* 9/2 347) and 122 (*EN* 9/2 452 = *EN* 9 362).

[44] This text is similar to the "ledger texts" collected by Owen, *LDN*, 12.

The Enterprises of the Pula-ḫali Family

Numerous texts stemming from Nuzi and Tel el-Faḫḫar associate the Pula-ḫali family with the city of Tupšarriniwe both directly and through the parties, scribes, and witnesses who appear with them. Particularly explicit is IM 70985 (= TF1 426), which lists Paššši-Tilla son of Pula-ḫali among men of the city of Tupšarriniwe and describes the property involved as bordering land of Pula-ḫali.[45] The sons of Pula-ḫali added to the family holdings in Tupšarriniwe, as the real estate transactions discussed above demonstrate. Though Paššši-Tilla appears more frequently in the real-estate transactions, the other brothers sometimes acquire property with him.[46] Further, much of the non-real estate activity of the family of Pula-ḫali also occurred in Tupšarriniwe as witnessed by the loan texts and other records.

Like other individuals in the Eastern Archives, then, the Pula-ḫali family had its real-estate base and substantial interests elsewhere. Yet, at least some of their records were stored in Nuzi. This family was concerned with cities other than Tupšarriniwe. *EN* 9/2 292, 374, and 505 were written in Ulamme, Tilla, and Āl-Ilāni, respectively. *EN* 9/2 102 may refer to a court case in Tašenni, and the loan in *EN* 9/2 529 is to be repaid in Zizza.

The commercial enterprises of Pula-ḫali's sons took them to the cities mentioned above. The best-attested aspect of their commerce was lending, primarily metals but also grain and at least one ass which was used "for the road," that is, the overland trade. Another sort of financial activity is documented by HSS 16 231 and HSS 19 126.[47] In both, Paššši-Tilla gives individuals gold with the agreement that they will give him fifteen ANŠE of grain (HSS 16 231) and nineteen ANŠE of grain (HSS 19 126) at an appointed time after the harvest. In both texts, the gold is the "price" (*šīmu*) of the grain. In itself, this marks these texts as special: gold does not appear frequently in commercial transactions. These two texts appear to represent "futures" transactions by which Paššši-Tilla locks in either the price or the supply of the grain before the harvest.[48]

[45] For the text, see Fadhil, *RATK*, 24–26.

[46] Unlike other family Groups represented in the eastern area, these brothers appear to work together. Contrast this with the situations of the Ḫuya family and the Muš-apu family.

[47] Comments on both texts appear in Fadhil, *RATK*, 18–19, 22–24. See below.

[48] Note that the texts have very similar forms:

HSS 16 231:1-16

[X] SU KÙ.GI *ša* [I]*Pá-aš-ši-til-*[*la*]
[DUMU] *Pu-la-ḫa-li a-na ši-mi*
a-na 5! ANŠE ŠE.MEŠ
Te-ḫi-ip-zi-iz-za DUMU *A-ḫu-še-e*[*a*]
[I]EN-*li-ya* DUMU *Ka-ti-ri* 2 ANŠE ŠE.MEŠ
[I]DINGIR.ZAG DUMU Ka_4*-ti-ri* 2 ANŠE ŠE.MEŠ
[I]*Dūr-*[d]UTU DUMU *A-kap-še-en-ni* 2 ANŠE ŠE.MEŠ
il-qú i-na ITI *Ku-r*[*i-i*]*l-li*
15 ANŠE ŠE.MEŠ
i-na-an-din

The issue of price is complex because the data are incomplete for the Nuzi economy. The normal market rate for grain has been calculated as 1.5 shekels of silver for one ANŠE of grain,[49] but what "normal" means in this economy is not clear with respect to prices, interest rates, or rates of exchange. The rate of exchange in HSS 19 126 is 0.47 shekels of silver for one ANŠE of grain.[50] If one sheckel of gold is the price in HSS 16 231, the rate of exchange is 0.60 shekels of silver for one ANŠE of grain. Given the nature of the transactions, these prices are called "forward prices" in the language of finance. Both of these prices are considerably lower than the "normal" market rate. The texts also have different months for delivery for the grain. The first, with its 0.47 rate of exchange, is due in Ululi and the second, with its rate of exchange of 0.60, is due in Kurilli. These differing "forward prices" might well support the notion that the price of grain fluctuated according to the season and the supplies available. Moreover, from a strictly financial point of view, Pašši-Tilla would be motivated to enter into such contracts if he believed the price of the grain in the future (i.e., the months in which he wanted it) would be equal to or higher on the open market than the prices in the contracts. As for the other parties to the contract, the gold they received through the contracts would have had more value for them at the time of the contract than the grain would in the future. Further speculation about the financial implications and incentives of these contracts would require a more-detailed knowledge of interest rates and the period of time elapsing between the contracts and the harvest(s).

Certainly, other than financial factors might have been involved in these contracts. The supply of grain, for one, might have influenced the parties to engage

---

HSS 19 126

[1] SU KÙ.GI *ša* [ᴵ*Pá-aš-ši-ya*]
DUMU *Pu-la-ḫa-li* [ ] GÀR?
ᴵᵈ30-*mu-šal-li* DU[MU]
ᴵ*Še-en-na-ta-ti* DU[MU]
a-na ši-mi a-na 19 ANŠE ŠE.MEŠ
il-qú-ú ù i-na EGIR EBUR *i-na* ITI *Ú-lu-li*
19 ANŠE ŠE.MEŠ *ši-mu ša* KÙ.GI
ᴵᵈ30-*mu-šal-li ù*
ᴵ*Še-en-na-ta-ti a-na*
ᴵ*Pá-aš-ši-ya i-na-an-din*

Lines 15–25 of HSS 19 126 record another such agreement: 1 SU KÙ.GI KI.MIN (of Paššiya son of Pula-ḫali) Zime son of Ziliya and Aḫ-ummiša son of Turaše *a-na ši-mi il-qú-ú i-na* EGIR EBUR *i-na* ITI Ú-lu-li 19 ANŠE ŠE.MEŠ *ši-mu ša* KÙ.GI Zime and Aḫ-ummiša *a-na Paššiya i-na-an-din-nu*. In HSS 16 231 and HSS 19 126, a penalty clause follows the agreement: work to be done (*RATK*, 19) and interest, respectively. HSS 19 126 adds a final "escape" clause (*RATK*, 23–24. Both texts represent transactions between Pašši-Tilla and Groups of men of Tupšarriniwe (see their other attestations in the catalog). Note the alternation of the singular and plural verbs *inandin* and *inandinū* within the contracts: HSS 16 231:10 and HSS 19 126:10 vs. HSS 19 126:12, 25, 27.

[49] See Eichler, *IN*, 15 n. 29, with references to D. Cross, *MPND*, 35 n. 75 and 36 n. 81.

[50] See Eichler, ibid. With respect to relative values of goods in the Nuzi corpus, agreements that call for future delivery of commodities such as HSS 19 126 and 127 must be used with caution because of the "future value" factor that may be involved.

in these "futures" transactions. While Pašši-Tilla had his own property, presumably it did not produce enough grain to meet his needs. If he was worried about future supplies of grain, he might have been willing to commit his gold early in order to guarantee the quantities he required. The other parties, if they were unsure of the market in the future, might have been willing to commit their harvests to guarantee a buyer for their grain. There is also always the possibility of distress, that is, that the other parties needed "cash" at the time of the contract and contracted with the only thing they had, that is, their future harvests.

Although there may be unknown factors relating these texts reveal a sophisticated type of exchange not otherwise subjected to rigorous calculation until the last century. An important question, of course, is why Pašši-Tilla needed the grain. One can hypothesize that these transactions enabled him to contract for cheap grain he could convert later to other goods at the market rate. These goods most likely included the metals that were his primary lending medium. In turn, he gained a profit in the form of interest from the loans that he made.

The sons of Pula-ḫali certainly are to be counted among the wealthy private "bankers" of the land. Indeed, their loan documents are similar to those of Puḫi-šenni son of Muš-apu, Šilwa-Tešup DUMU LUGAL, and other private lenders at Nuzi.[51] That is, the loan texts of the sons of Pula-ḫali describe the metals as belonging to them and to be returned to them just as do the texts of Šilwa-Tešup DUMU LUGAL and other landowners who loan grain, even when someone else arranges the loan for them.[52] The palace is another lender at Nuzi. Some of the loan texts mention the palace specifically as the source of the item(s) loaned, and some include the name of the agent making the loan.[53]

How did the sons of Pula-ḫali acquire the metals they loaned out? Presumably, the source of the metals was the overland trade conducted by the DAM.GÀRS, 'merchants,' individuals who may have served as agents of the palace.[54] Certainly, the palace maintained DAM.GÀRS as HSS 14 593:34–35 indicates.[55] While the sons of Pula-ḫali are neither identified as private DAM.GÀRS nor listed among the commercial agents of the palace, they might, indeed, have followed in their father's profession. Relevant to this point is HSS 19 126:1–2 in which after a break following the name [Paššiya DU]MU Pula-ḫali, the GAR sign appears. It has been suggested that [LÚ] should be restored, thus identifying Pašši-Tilla as an official, possibly a "miller."[56] There is no compelling evidence that Pašši-Tilla held such a position. It is possible, however, that the term to be restored is [LÚ.DAM.GÀ]R. The GAR sign that remains might in reality be the end of the GÀR sign or a scribal misspelling of the term DAM.GÀR.[57]

[51] Owen, *LDN*, 43–44.
[52] See Owen, *LDN*, *passim*.
[53] E.g., HSS 13 120, 188; HSS 14 623; HSS 16 233.
[54] Zaccagnini, *Iraq* 39:173ff.
[55] See W. Mayer, *Nuzi-Studien* 1:159.
[56] Fadhil, *RATK*, 23.
[57] The sign appears after a long break which wraps around the tablet, so it is unclear to which line it belongs.

In any case, Pula-ḫali's title of "merchant" makes it clear that there were private merchants who might also own real estate in one or another city. The activities of his sons indicate that the overland trade was intimately connected with domestic banking. In addition, the overland trade also produced a market for animals for the use of those who were engaged in the overland trade.

If the sons of Pula-ḫali were merchants, then it would appear that individuals of that profession could be involved in trade, real estate, and banking. If they themselves were not merchants, then the financial base for their real-estate and banking activities may have been founded by their merchant father. Both generations owned real estate in their city, but we have the acquisition texts only of Pašši-Tilla's generation. Thus it appears that the growth in real-estate holdings happened at least at that time.

Whether they conducted trade abroad or simply prospered at home, it is clear that the sons of Pula-ḫali maintained active contact with the trading community. Pašši-Tilla had connections with the palace. In *EN* 9/2 505, for instance, the animals "of the road" are returned to an individual who may well belong to the palace bureaucracy. Of course, if Pašši-Tilla was a LÚ.GAR, he, too, might have belonged to the palace bureaucracy.[58] If so, the two grain texts (HSS 16 231 and HSS 19 126) may relate to an official position that Pašši-Tilla held. In this case, Pašši-Tilla might either have served as a commercial agent for the palace, and he might have continued private lending activities after he became a palace official.

Other Texts from Rooms S132 and S133

Further evidence for Pašši-Tilla's connection with the mercantile Group of Nuzi comes from other texts found in the same unit in Group 19. These relate to activities of individuals described as DAM.GÀR. HSS 14 26, for instance, is a letter concerning Akiya the LÚ.DAM.GÀR of the queen. HSS 16 233 states very clearly that Turar-Tešup son of Mālik-nāṣir, otherwise known as a LÚ.DAM.GÀR, received grain of the palace from Ḫašip-Tilla the LÚ.DAM.GÀR. In addition, a number of loan texts belonging to individuals other than the sons of Pula-ḫali come from Group 19, including *EN* 9/2 324, 325, 337, 356, 384, and 393.[59] Among these are texts that describe more than an archival relationship between Pašši-Tilla and other lenders. For example, Taika son of Akap-šenni is a lender in one of these texts and a borrower in one of Pašši-Tilla's.[60] In addition, scribes and witnesses

[58] Fadhil, *RATK*, 23.

[59] See Owen, *LDN*: *EN* 9/2 324 (= *EN* 9 371, p. 125), *EN* 9/2 325 (pp. 108–9), *EN* 9/2 337 (pp. 19 and 111–12), *EN* 9/2 356 (p. 120). *EN* 9/2 384 is the loan of a cow belonging to Irašu son of Akitte to Awilauki son of Šennatti. Ḫutiya son of Zaba-[ ] is the guarantor of the loan. Note the familiar witnesses: Muš⟨uš⟩še son of Ṣill-šēmi (line 15), Eḫliya son of Akkuya (line 16), Bēliya son of Aḫ-ummiša LÚ*nāgiru* (lines 18–19), Šura-šarri son of Akitte (line 20; perhaps related to the other sons of Akitte appearing in these texts). *EN* 9/2 393 is a brick loan involving Arip-šeriš and Ḫutiya the son of [Š]ekari. dAK.DINGIR.RA [son of Sîn-napšir] (III) is the scribe.

[60] *EN* 9/2 337 and *EN* 9/2 344.

recur in these texts and those of the Pula-ḫali family, largely because a number of the texts originate in Tupšarriniwe.[61]

Ḫašip-Tilla son of Kip-ukur is an especially interesting figure. The transaction in AASOR 16 79 in which he receives a sheep *ana šīmi ana* DAM.GÀR-*ši* suggests that he was a LÚ.DAM.GÀR.[62] He was probably the Ḫašip-Tilla LÚ.DAM.GAR of HSS 16 233, mentioned above, in which he lends grain belonging to the palace. Further, he is the lender in *EN* 9/2 357, and *EN* 9/2 291 indicates that he had given an ass to Akip-Tilla who was replacing that ass because it had been lost.[63] He is the guarantor of a loan in *EN* 9/2 297, and appears in *EN* 9/2 207, a fragmentary commercial text.[64]

This same Ḫašip-Tilla son of Kip-ukur is active as a witness for Ili-ma-aḫi son of Ilānu (HSS 5 15:54), Artura son of Kuššiya (HSS 19 10:44 and *EN* 9/2 458:15–16), and Utḫap-tae son of Ar-tura (*EN* 9/2 354:23–24). These associations place Ḫašip-Tilla son of Kip-ukur chronologically within the same period as the sons of Pula-ḫali and others of Group 19. Furthermore, Kipal-enni [son of Pula-ḫali] may be a party to *EN* 9/2 207.

Also assigned to rooms in Group 19 are some texts concerning disbursements of horses (AASOR 16 98 and *EN* 9/1 350). The latter, though fragmentary, includes reference to [LÚ.M]EŠ DAM.[GÀR] (line 2), 67 ANŠE.MEŠ (line 15), [*s*]*í-mi-it-tu*$_4$ GIŠ.GIGIR (line 17), and ANŠE.KUR.RA.MEŠ (line 18). All these are to be "returned" (line 5). It is clear from such documents as AASOR 16 99 and 100, HSS 9 149, HSS 14 12, and *JEN* 108 that the LÚ.DAM.GÀRS were active in horse trading and lending for both private individuals and the palace.[65]

Summary

Documents of the Pula-ḫali family, and those of Pašši-Tilla son of Pula-ḫali in particular, dominate the archives of rooms S132 and S133, so these materials appear to have been primarily the archives of Pašši-Tilla. He frequently worked with his brothers, though, and some of their texts are found in these archives, too. As a result, the Pula-ḫali family corpus appears to be just that, that is, archives of the sons of Pula-ḫali. In that the family was based in Tupšarriniwe, though, it is likely that there were other family archives in that city or elsewhere and that the Nuzi texts do not represent the complete archives of the family. Of

[61] See the appendix.

[62] Following Zaccagnini, *Iraq* 39:187; and Mayer, *Nuzi-Studien* 1:159 n. 3.

[63] For *EN* 9/2 357, see Owen, *LDN*, 120–21. Note that Turari son of Tai-šenni (line 12) also witnesses HSS 19 30, a text of the Ḫuya family written in Nuzi and *JEN* 472. Umpiya son of Ḫašḫarpa (line 14) witnesses *JEN* 470, a text written in Nuzi.

[64] Note that the name Kipal-enni, possibly son of Pula-ḫali, may appear in this text (lines 1, 11, 14).

[65] See texts in Zaccagnini, *Iraq* 39: *passim*. Also, Mayer, *Nuzi-Studien* 1:158–59. It is worth noting that AASOR 16 99 and 100 are assigned to N 120 (see n. 30 above). Given the confusion between N 120 and the eastern area and the similarity of texts, AASOR 16 98 and *EN* 9/2 350 may have originated there as well.

further interest are the texts belonging to a number of other individuals who were engaged in trade and commerce and originating in these rooms. It is possible that these individuals entrusted their texts to the Pula-ḫali family because of their professional associations. However, the overall character of the texts in these rooms of Group 19 suggests that the building was a depository for the documents of individuals who were engaged in trade. This commercial activity involves individuals who were contemporaries and who were affiliated with each other and possibly with some common entity, most likely the palace. However, the nature of their involvement with the palace is not as clear as has been supposed. Though some of the characters are DAM.GÀRS who work for the palace, the most active representatives, the Pula-ḫali family, appear to be private merchants. Whether the sons of Pula-ḫali were LÚ.DAM.GÀRS or not, the mixing of their texts with those of people who had a connection with the palace suggests a close relationship of the individuals who conducted the private business with those who worked for the state. Thus, while some LÚ.DAM.GÀRS worked exclusively for the palace, others did not. Some mixed palace and private activities. Others participated at various stages in the trading process. The overall view of Arrapḫean commerce is that of a complex network of financial interests in which the private and state sectors coexist and overlap.

The appearance of these texts in Nuzi, even though many have to do with other cities, is quite understandable in light of this situation. As an administrative center, Nuzi was home base for many who conducted business throughout the land and attracted others who participated in commerce in a variety of ways. The most prominent representatives of this Group, the Pula-ḫali family, are excellent examples of the kinds of individuals found in this segment of Nuzi society.

Appendix:
The Principals of the Pula-ḫali Archives

As the comments to the new texts indicate, the individuals who appear in these texts include citizens of Tupšarriniwe already known from the published materials as well as members of their families. The texts also provide a number of new names. The following catalog includes the names recorded in texts of the Pula-ḫali family and in texts in which members of the family appear. Where a city other than Tupšarriniwe is specifically stated, the city's name is provided. As in chapter 4, the individuals are also identified by their role in the documents in which they appear (P = party; W = witness; L = landowner; S = scribe; C = mentioned in contract; M = miscellaneous). Major scribes appear on pages 96–97 above and are omitted here to avoid duplication. Other texts from the Nuzi corpus in which they appear are included.

Aḫ-ummiša son of Turaše: AASOR 16 97:16 (W), HSS 19 126:17 (P)
Akawatil son of Eḫliya: *EN* 9/2 352:31 (C)
Akawatil son of Elḫip-Tilla: *EN* 9/2 505:14–15 (W) (Āl-Ilāni)

Akip-[ ]: *EN* 9/2 267:41 (W)
Akip-tašenni SUKKAL: *EN* 9/2 102:3 (M) (Tašenni); see also HSS 15 34:18, 36:32; HSS 16 111:7
Akip-tašenni son of [ ]: *EN* 9/2 33:20 (W)
Akip-tašenni son of Ariḫ-ḫamanna: *EN* 9/2 341:20–21 (W); see also HSS 15 34:19
Akip-Tilla son of Irrike: HSS 19 126:37 (W), *EN* 9/2 515:25
Akitte son of [ ]: *EN* 9/2 339 (W)
Akiya: *EN* 9/2 337:19 (W), *EN* 9/2 524:4 (P)
Akiya [LÚ]*ḫazannu* son of [ ]: *EN* 9/2 209:25 (W), *EN* 9/2 339:35 (W); see also HSS 15 125:8 in which Akiya the [LÚ]*ḫazannu* receives Akawatil who had come from Ḫanigalbat
Akiya son of [ ]: *EN* 9/2 349:13 (W)
Akiya son of Nūr-kûbi: HSS 19 97 (father of P, son of C), *EN* 9/2 250:17 (W), *EN* 9/2 349:12 (W)
Akiya son of Šaš-tae: *EN* 9/2 224:31 (W), *EN* 9/2 299:28 (W), *EN* 9/2 391:20 (W)
Akiya son of Tarmiya: HSS 19 126:35 (W); see also *EN* 9/2 184:22, a Šeḫal-Tešup son of Tehup-šenni text written in Ḫušri by Abī-ilu [son of [d]AK.DIN-GIR.RA] (IV)
Akkul-enni son of Akitte: *EN* 9/2 224:33 (W), *EN* 9/2 374:5–6 (P) (Tilla), *EN* 9/2 505:10–11 (W) (Āl-Ilāni)
Alki-Tilla son of Akitte: *EN* 9/2 349:14–15 (W), *EN* 9/2 440:3 (P)
Anin-api son of Šuk[ri?-]: *EN* 9/2 292:13 (W) (Ulamme)
Ariḫ-ḫamanna: *EN* 9/2 441–22; see also *EN* 9/2 331:25 (S)
Ariḫ-ḫamanna son of Nūr-kûbi: *EN* 9/2 331:16 (W), *EN* 9/2 440:29 (W = judge), *EN* 9/2 441:16 (W = judge); see also *EN* 9/1 424:16
Arip-Tilla son of [ ]: *EN* 9/2 33:18 (W)
Arip-uppi son of Teḫip-zizza: HSS 19 97:36 (W)
Arnukka son of Elḫip-Tilla: *EN* 9/2 291:5 (P)
Ar-šali: *EN* 9/2 268:5 (L)
Ar-Tešup son of Pai-[ ]: *EN* 9/2 267:38 (W)
Ar-Tešup son of Šumuku: *EN* 9/2 292:16 (W) (Ulamme)
Aštar-Tilla son of Bēliya: *EN* 9/2 352:21 (W)
Attaya son of Kai-Tešup: *EN* 9/2 347:11 (W)
Attaya son of Zaziya: AASOR 16 97:13 (W), HSS 19 97:35 (W), *EN* 9/2 224:34 (W), *EN* 9/2 299:29 (W), *EN* 9/2 340:17 (W), *EN* 9/2 341:18–19 (W), *EN* 9/2 344:12–13 (W), IM 70985 (= TF1 426):5

Bēliya son of Aḫ-ummeya/ummiša: *EN* 9/2 339:32–33 (W), *EN* 9/2 352:18–19 (W), *EN* 9/2 391:21 ([LÚ]*abultannu*) (W), *EN* 9/2 441:23–24 (*abultannu*) (W); see also *EN* 9/2 384:18, where he is identified as [LÚ]*nāgiru* and Bēliya [LÚ]*ab-ultannu* in *EN* 9/2 331:24 (W)
Bēliya son of Katiri: HSS 16 231:5 (P), *EN* 9/2 209:22 (W)

Dūr-Šamaš son of Akap-šenni: HSS 231:7 (P)

Eḫliya: HSS 16 231:16 (W)
Eḫliya son of Akkuya: *EN* 9/2 352:1–2 (P); see also *EN* 9/2 384:16
Elḫip-šarri son of [ ]-ya: *EN* 9/2 440:28 (W = judge)
Ellatu son of Šimika-atal: AASOR 16 97:15 (W)
fElwe daughter of EN-[ ], sister of Urate: *EN* 9/2 299:3 (C)
[Enna]-mati: *EN* 9/2 529:12 (S)
Enna-mati son of [ ]: *EN* 9/2 339:29 (W)
Ennuki son of Teḫip-Tilla (of the city of Ašuḫis): *EN* 9/2 250:18 (W)
EN-ri-[ ] LÚ*ḫa-[bi-ru*?]: *EN* 9/2 364:7–8 (W)
Eteš-šenni: *EN* 9/2 440:27 (W = judge)
Eteš-šenni son of [ ]: *EN* 9/2 441:10 (C)

Ḫa-[ ] son of Zaziya: *EN* 9/2 515:24
Ḫalutta: *EN* 9/2 362:5 (P)
Ḫalutta son of Akiya: HSS 19 97:1–2 (P), *EN* 9/2 250:19 (W), *EN* 9/2 347:3 (P), *EN* 9/2 353:18 (W), IM 70985 (= TF1 426):6
Ḫamanna son of Akawatil: *EN* 9/2 505:13–14 (W) (Āl-Ilāni)
Ḫanakka: *EN* 9/2 337:18 (W)
Ḫanakka son of Akiya: HSS 19 97:40 (W); see also *EN* 9/2 337:18–19, where he is a witness with Šurki-Tilla son of Pula-ḫali for Taika son of Akap-šenni (text written by dUTU-PAB)
Ḫanakka son of Urḫiya: HSS 19 126:33 (W)
Ḫaniya son of Zaziya: *EN* 9/2 340:16 (W)
Ḫašiya son of Ward-aḫḫe: HSS 19 97:37 (W), *EN* 9/2 299:30 (W), *EN* 9/2 353:20 (W), IM 70985 (= TF1 426):1
Ḫašip-šarri: *EN* 9/2 33:4 (L)
Ḫašip-Tilla son of Šar-teya: *EN* 9/2 292:14–15 (W)
Ḫellu: *EN* 9/2 343:1–2 (P)
Ḫišm-apu: *EN* 9/2 362:7 (P)
Ḫui-Tilla son of Akip-Tilla: HSS 19 99:17 (W)
Ḫupita son of Akitte: *EN* 9/2 342:2 (P), *EN* 9/2 440:2–3 (P)
Ḫupita son of GIŠ.MI-lurašše: *EN* 9/2 331:22–23 (W)
Ḫutip-apu son of Eḫliya: HSS 19 126:39 (W), *EN* 9/2 337 (P), *EN* 9/2 340: 1–3 (P), *EN* 9/2 343:20 (W), *EN* 9/2 352:32 (C); see also *EN* 9/2 331:21 (W)
Ḫuya son of Akik-keya: *EN* 9/2 441:23 (*abultannu*) (W)

Ikkiya son of Ar-tirwi: *EN* 9/2 346:16 (W)
Ili-imitti son of Katiri: HSS 16 231:6 (P), *EN* 9/1 441:21
Ilika son of Aḫiya: HSS 19 99:1–2 (P)
Ipšaya: *EN* 9/2 268:3 (L)
Itḫ-apiḫe son of Arip-urekke: *EN* 9/2 343:17–18 (W), *EN* 9/2 513:1–2 (P)
Iwiš-Tilla: *EN* 9/2 362:3 (P)

Ka(n)kapa son of Ḫanaya: *EN* 9/2 342:19 (W), *EN* 9/2 353:23 (W)
Kamputtu son of Akip-tura: HSS 19 97:8–9 (C)

Kel-Tešup son of Sīn-ibni: *EN* 9/2 364:12–13 (W)
Kel-teya son of Ṭāb-Arrapḫe: *EN* 9/2 331:18–19 (W)
Kennu: *EN* 9/2 341:22 (W)
Kezzi son of Pui-tae: *EN* 9/2 352:17 (W)
Kipal-enni son of Pula-ḫali: HSS 19 99:19 (W), *EN* 9/2 33:26 (W)
Kip-talili son of Zel-[ ]: *EN* 9/2 33:24 (W)
Kula-ḫupi: HSS 19 99:22 (W)
Kunuttu son of Zilip-apu: HSS 19 97:39 (W)
Kurri son of Kel Tešup: HSS 19 97:38 (W), IM 70985 (= TF1 426):15
Kušuniya son of Ka[nk]eya: *EN* 9/2 341:1–2 (P)

[Man]nu-[tāri]ssu (son of Kiribti-^{d}Enlil (?)): *EN* 9/2 97:19 (S)
Maliya: *EN* 9/2 209:9 (S)
Mat-Tešup son of [ ]-a: *EN* 9/2 441:18
Mišik-atal son of Karti-[ ]: *EN* 9/2 343:21 (W)
Mušušše son of Ṣill-šēmi: *EN* 9/2 209:26–27 (W); see also *EN* 9/2 384:15

Niḫriya: HSS 16 231:15 (W)
Ninkiya: *EN* 9/2 374:19 (S)
Nūr-kûbi son of [ ]: *EN* 9/2 339:1 (P)
Nūr-kûbi son of Mārat-Adad: HSS 19 97:10–11 (C)
Nūr-Šamaš son of Akap-šenni: HSS 16 231:7 (P), *EN* 9/2 505:9 (W) (Āl-Ilāni)
Nūrše son of Akap-šenni: *EN* 9/2 353:21 (W)

Paite: *EN* 9/2 374:15 (P)
Pal-teya son of Puḫi-šenni: *EN* 9/2 441:2 (C)
Palteya son of Ward-aḫḫe: *EN* 9/2 33:19 (W), *EN* 9/2 344:10–11 (W), *EN* 9/2 353:19 (W), *EN* 9/2 515:26, IM 70985 (= TF1 426):7
Pettiya son of [ ]: *EN* 9/2 364:11 (W)
Pilmašše son of Ababilu: *EN* 9/2 347:13 (W)
Pu-[ ]-paniya son of Tae: *EN* 9/2 267:36 (W)
Puḫi son of Akap-nanni: *EN* 9/2 331:17 (W)
Pui-tae son of Ḫamanna: *EN* 9/2 505:12–13 (W) (Āl-Ilāni)
Pusira: *EN* 9/2 374:10 (P) (Tilla)

Sîn-mušallim son of [ ]: HSS 19 126:3 (P)

Ṣill-Šamaš son of [ ]-ip-šarri: *EN* 9/2 209:1–2 (P)

Šatu-kewi son of Wirri: *EN* 9/2 347:12 (W)
Šekar-Tilla son of Bēlaya: *EN* 9/2 97:18 (W)
Šekaru: *EN* 9/2 268:14 (P)
Šennatati son of [ ]: HSS 19 126:4 (P)
Šennaya: HSS 19 99:21 (W)

Šennaya son of Ipnu[š]a$^{?}$: *EN* 339:34 (W)
Šennaya son of Papante: *EN* 9/2 440:31 (W = judge)
Šilaḫi-(Tešup) son of Elḫip-šarri: HSS 19 126:34 (W), *EN* 9/2 342:20–21 (W), IM 70985 (= TF1 426):3
Šilaḫi son of Zilip-apu: HSS 19 126:38 (W)
Šimika-atal: HSS 16 231:14 (W)
Šimika-atal son of Nūr-kûbi: *EN* 9/2 441:7–8 (P)
Šimi-Tilla: *EN* 9/2 374:13 (P) (Tilla)
Šukriya son of Kutukka: *EN* 9/2 339:31 (W), *EN* 9/2 352:16 (W)
Šurki-Tilla: *EN* 9/2 267:4 (P), *EN* 9/2 374:11 (P) (Tilla)
Šurki-Tilla son of Akawe: HSS 19 97:42 (W)
Šurki-Tilla son of Pula-ḫali: *EN* 9/2 267:5 (P), *EN* 9/2 337:16–17 (W), *EN* 9/2 441:19–20 (W)
Šurukka son of Arip-urekke: AASOR 16 97:5 (P), *EN* 9/2 224:2–3 (P), *EN* 9/2 299:38 (W), *EN* 9/2 349:1–2 (P), *EN* 9/2 353:1–2 (P); see also IM 70882 (= TF1 258 = *RATK* 18):21 (W) and IM 70981 (= TF1 436 = *RATK* 13):1–2

Tae: *EN* 9/2 33:8 (P)
Tae son of [ ]: *EN* 9/2 283:17 (W)
Tae son of Bēliya: HSS 19 97:41 (W), *EN* 9/2 33:23 (W), *EN* 9/2 267:40 (W), *EN* 9/2 340:15 (W), *EN* 9/2 342:18 (W), *EN* 9/2 349:11 (W), *EN* 9/2 352:20 (W), IM 70985 (= TF1 426):14
Tae son of Elḫip-Tilla: *EN* 9/2 292:12 (W) (Ulamme)
Tae son of Teḫiya: *EN* 9/2 299:32 (W), *EN* 9/2 515:13 and 15?
Taika: *EN* 9/2 345:15 (W)
Taika son of Akap-šenni: *EN* 9/2 283:1–2 (P), *EN* 9/2 344:4 (P); see also *EN* 9/2 337, in which Taika is the creditor
Tai-šenni: *EN* 9/2 33:5 (L)
Tarmi-Tešup son of Elḫip-Šarri: *EN* 9/2 342:20–21 (W); see also IM 70985 (= TF1 426):11
Tarmi-Tilla son of Eḫliya: *EN* 9/2 340:2–3 (P), *EN* 9/2 342:22 (W), *EN* 9/2 352:31 (C)
Teḫip-šarri: *EN* 9/2 102:1 (M)
Teḫip-zizza ^{LÚ}*naggāru*: *EN* 9/2 353:22 (W)
Teḫip-zizza son of Aḫu-šeya: HSS 16 231:4 (P), IM 70985 (= TF1 426):10
Teḫiya: *EN* 9/2 33:7 (L)
Teḫiya son of Ḫaip-šarri: *EN* 9/2 331:20 (W)
Teḫiya son of Paḫu: *EN* 9/2 209:28 (W)
Teššuya son of [ ]: *EN* 9/2 33:21 (W)
Tukultī-ilu son of Pui-tae: *EN* 9/2 97:14 (W), *EN* 9/2 250:16 (W), *EN* 9/2 340:18–19 (W), *EN* 9/2 346:15 (W), *EN* 9/2 364:9–10 (W)
Tulpi-šenni son of [ ]-ya: HSS 19 97:43 (W)
Tultukka son of Akitte: *EN* 9/2 331:1–2 (P), *EN* 9/2 440 (M)
Tupkin-a⟨tal⟩ son of Ḫapi-ašu: *EN* 9/2 505:1–2 (P) (Āl-Ilāni)
Tupkiya son of Šaš-tae: *EN* 9/2 341:16–17 (W)

Uante son of EN-[la-ya?]: *EN* 9/2 97:15 (W), *EN* 9/2 299:2 (P)
Ukkuya son of [ ]: *EN* 9/2 441:15 (W)
Umpiya: *EN* 9/2 362:14 (P)
Umpiya: *EN* 9/2 346:23 (W)
Umpiya son of Mu-[ ]: *EN* 9/2 348:10
Umpiya son of Zilip-apu: *EN* 9/2 299:33 (W); see also HSS 15 36:29 and *JEN* 399:42, a court case involving Ammarša of Unapšewe
Unaya son of Akip-Tilla: HSS 19 97:40 (W)
Urḫi-Tešup son of Yanzi-mašḫu: *EN* 9/2 441:1 (P)
Urḫiya son of Tarmiya: HSS 19 126:36 (W)

Wantiš-šenni: *EN* 9/2 374:14 (P) (Tilla)
Ward-aḫḫe: HSS 19 97:5–7 (L)
Ward-aḫḫešu son of [ ]-šenni: *EN* 9/2 33:25 (W)
Wurruku: *EN* 9/2 362:9 (P)

Zaziya son of Akkuya: *EN* 9/2 299:31 (W); see also IM 70882 (= TF1 258 = *RATK* 18):25
Zike: *EN* 9/2 374:12 (P) (Tilla)
Zike son of Akiya: *EN* 9/2 348:1–2 (P)
Zilip-apu son of Akkuya: *EN* 9/2 440:30 (W = judge)
Ziliya: *EN* 9/2 345:18 (W)
Ziliya son of Enna-mati: *EN* 9/2 209:23–24 (W)
Zil-Tešup son of Šennaya: *EN* 9/2 346:1 (P)
Zime son of Ziliya: AASOR 16 97:14 (W), HSS 19 126:16 (P), *EN* 9/2 224:32 (W), *EN* 9/2 343:19 (W), *EN* 9/2 345:4 (P)
ZU-^{d}IŠKUR: *EN* 9/2 33:27 (S)
Zunna son of Urḫiya: *EN* 9/2 292:1–2 (P) (Ulamme)

[ ] son of Sîn-mušallim: HSS 19 97:16 (W)
[ ]-mi-Tilla son of Eteš-šenni: *EN* 9/2 267:37
[ ]-la son of Ṭāb-[šarri]: *EN* 9/2 97:16 (W)
[ ]-nikiya son of Kizzi: *EN* 9/2 97:17 (W)

CHAPTER 6

The Eastern Archives: An Overview

Composition of the Archives

The majority of the texts from the eastern area belong to one or another of the archival Groups discussed in the preceding chapters: those belonging to Tarmiya son of Ḫuya, Utḫap-tae son of Ar-tura, Šeḫal-Tešup son of Teḫup-šenni, Puḫi-šenni son of Muš-apu, Urḫi-kušuḫ DUMU LUGAL, and the sons of Pula-ḫali. These archival Groups, in turn, are associated with three buildings, Groups 17, 18A, and 19. The documents of Utḫap-tae son of Ar-tura and Šeḫal-Tešup son of Teḫup-šenni share an archive in Group 17. The archive of Tarmiya son of Ḫuya is located in Group 18A. The records of Urḫi-kušuḫ DUMU LUGAL are found with those of Puḫi-šenni son of Muš-apu in one section of Group 19, and those of the sons of Pula-ḫali in another part of Group 19. Mixed together with the last texts is a particularly interesting collection of loans and commercial documents belonging to a number of other people.

In all of these cases, either a connection between the archives could be demonstrated or the individual archives were extensive enough to determine that a "presence" in the building was involved. Puḫi-šenni son Muš-apu was associated with Urḫi-kušuḫ DUMU LUGAL in such a way that the few Urḫi-kušuḫ documents found with Puḫi-šenni's could be explained. The commercial texts are substantially similar to the documents of the Pula-ḫali family with which they are located. Šeḫal-Tesup son of Teḫup-šenni and Utḫap-tae son of Ar-tura were contemporaries and both were active in Nuzi, though no direct connection between them can be firmly established.

The archives of the eastern area belonged to the individuals mentioned above; they do not, however, appear to be "family archives," that is, the repositories for all of the tablets of all members of the families. In a number of cases, there is evidence that family members owned property and conducted various activities of their own, but the nature and extent of these activities are not known because the personal archives of these people have not been found. Some of the families attested in the Eastern Archives were based in other cities, so any texts involving the non-Nuzi relatives would be found in their home cities. Even for some of the individuals who stored texts in Nuzi, there is reason to believe

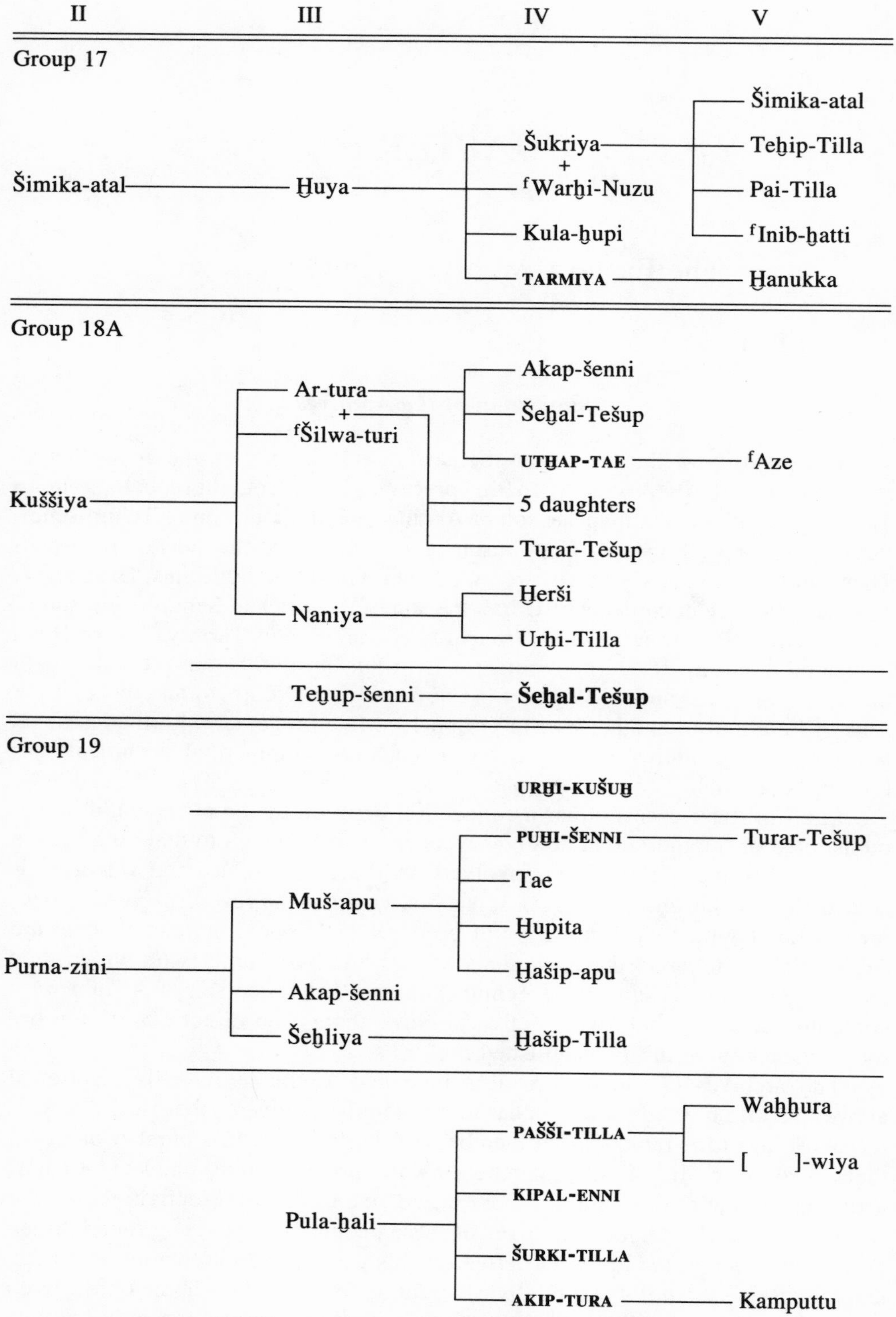

FIGURE 13. *Genealogies of Archive Owners in the Eastern Archives*

that they had other archives elsewhere. Urḫi-kušuḫ and the Muš-apu and Pula-ḫali families, for instance, undoubtedly kept records in the cities of Unapšewe and Tupšarriniwe, respectively.

Families Known through the Texts of the Eastern Area

The texts of the eastern area do offer considerable, albeit incomplete, information about the families of the men who owned the archives. As a result, it has been possible to reconstruct the family trees of the people of the eastern area over a number of generations. These families are shown in figure 13. Scribal generations are indicated by roman numerals, and the archive owners' names appear in bold capital letters.

Chronologically, the families attested in the archives of the eastern area span the second through the fifth scribal generations and are contemporaneous. The archive owners themselves date to the latter parts of the Nuzi period, since they employ scribes from the third and following generations of the scribal family of Apil-Sīn. Further, the owners of the texts of the Eastern Archives are contemporaneous with those of the Southwest Archives, the archives of Šilwa-Tešup DUMU LUGAL and his servants, and the third through fifth generations of the family of Teḫip-Tilla son of Puḫi-šenni.

Inheritance and Intra-Family Contracts in the Eastern Area

The sources of information about these families are primarily wills and intra-family transactions. Occasionally, a family member is known because one or another of his texts was stored with the archive owner's documents, but these situations are infrequent. The wills and intra-family contracts were kept, of course, because they represented the proof of ownership to real property, that is, they were the "deeds" to the property involved. These texts are valuable for us because they illustrate certain aspects of Nuzi inheritance practices and include a variety of transactions among family owners involving inherited property.

The wills of Muš-apu son of Purna-zini, Ar-tura son of Kuššiya, Šukriya son of Ḫuya, and Tarmiya son of Ḫuya all arrange for the disposition of the real property of these men. The portions for specific offspring are designated; in certain instances a "chief heir" and "secondary heir" are named. In all, provision is made for a wife; in Ar-tura's, daughters are mentioned.

Obviously, the wills serve the same purpose, but their details vary. For instance, Šukriya is concerned with his "family gods." Ar-tura indicates that he has "sons" (their names do not appear) who are to share in his property in the usual way after certain property has been given to other heirs. The specific distribution of property, of course, also differs considerably among the wills.

The variations among the wills reinforce the idea that such documents were drawn up by individuals departing from normal inheritance practices. In at least two of these cases, it appears that the composition of the family was complicated and the testator wished to provide for all members of his family, not just those who might inherit normally. Ar-tura, for example, provides for his wife, daughters, and only one son by name. Other evidence in the archive suggests that that wife was a second wife and that the daughters (hence, possibly the son) were her children. The heirs to the bulk of his estate would be his sons by another wife, that is, the "sons" not mentioned by name in this will. Šukriya also seems to deal with the issue of a son by a wife different from the one mentioned in the will. His son Šimika-atal is prohibited from sharing in his wife Warḫi-Nuzu's estate. These wills also demonstrate the authority of a property owner to dispose of his property as he or she saw fit. It is worth noting that all of the individuals involved here were wealthy people with extensive holdings. As such, they were able to provide well for their families. One of a number of houses could go to a wife, specific fields to certain sons, and the like. Among average families at Nuzi, the estates certainly were not so great as to allow for such largesse.

The importance of a will is demonstrated by the court case (AASOR 16 56) in which two sons of Ḫuya dispute the inheritance share of Tarmiya son of Ḫuya. The gift given to Tarmiya by Ḫuya apparently would not have been part of his inheritance under normal circumstances. Seemingly, Ḫuya did not commit this gift to writing, so the other heirs could contest it.

Related to the issue of inheritance is the matter of real adoption through which a property owner adopted an individual and named him the heir to his or her property. Both Šeḫal-Tešup son of Teḫup-šenni and ᶠŠilwa-turi, Ar-tura's wife, make such arrangements for their property. Šeḫal-Tešup had no heirs and chose to leave his property to an individual with whose family he had other dealings. ᶠŠilwa-turi is known to have had daughters and possibly a son, but she adopted Utḫap-tae son of Ar-tura as her heir in return for his support. She appears to have been motivated by the need for a guardian/protector. These two situations illustrate quite clearly how the same sort of text, here a "real-adoption" text, can result from significantly different circumstances. Moreover, the terms of the text vary. No mention is made of filial duties in Šeḫal-Tešup's text, and his land will pass to Ḫutiya upon his death. In ᶠŠilwa-turi's text, she cedes her property to Utḫap-tae in return for his support and filial service upon her death.

Among the texts of the Eastern Archives are a number dealing with arrangements among heirs to estates. These include a text (AASOR 16 59) stating the severe penalties imposed for questioning the division of the estate of Ḫuya's father Šimika-atal. In the real-adoption text in which ᶠŠilwa-turi adopts Utḫap-tae, the property that Utḫap-tae received was his father's. Through this text the property rejoined whatever property Utḫap-tae inherited from his father's estate. The transfer of "inheritance shares" is also attested among these texts. Property originally belonging to the estate of Kuššiya was given to Utḫap-tae son of Ar-tura (son of Kuššiya) by Ḫerši and Urḫi-Tilla sons of Naniya (sons of Kuššiya) in return for moveable property. Here, cousins engage in a transaction involving property belonging to their grandfather. Both the property and the payment for it are described as "inheritance shares." Utḫap-tae had a legitimate family relationship to the property in question, so the transaction could be cast in the language of inheritance. Teḫip-Tilla and Pai-Tilla sons of Šukriya may engage in another such exchange of inheritance shares with their uncle Tarmiya son of Ḫuya in HSS 19 30, in which real estate is transferred in exchange for moveable goods. The land involved is in one of the family *dimtu*s and probably belonged originally to Ḫuya, grandfather of Teḫip-Tilla and Pai-Tilla and father of Tarmiya. Again, all of the parties involved were related to the original owner of the property and could be considered his heirs.

Real-estate adoption also figures among family members in these texts. The same two men, Teḫip-Tilla and Pai-Tilla sons of Šukriya, transfer other property to their uncle Tarmiya by this legal device. In this case (*EN* 9/2 39), the land is in Nuzi, not in one of the family *dimtu*s. As discussed in chapter 2, an adoption text may have been necessary because the property may have been acquired by Šukriya or by his sons. If this were the case, Tarmiya would not have been in the line of inheritance for the property. On the other hand, in the family of Eteš-šenni discussed below, Ennaya son of Eteš-šenni adopts his brother Arik-kaya and transfers his inheritance share to him. In this case, the brothers are more closely related to the original owner of the property than those who engaged in the exchanges of inheritance shares above. Certainly Arik-kaya was legitimately connected to the property by his position in the family. Why did Eteš-šenni have to adopt him? This sort of intra-family adoption is reminiscent of those in the archive of Katiri from one of the suburban mounds. There the device of adoption serves to channel family real estate to a specified heir who belongs to the family but would not be in the normal line of inheritance. This heir does, however, have a legitimate family relationship to the property.[1]

Thus, through texts that are exchanges of inheritance shares, real-estate adoptions, and even real adoptions, family real estate moves from one branch of a family to another. While real adoption often establishes a continuing relationship between the parties involved or provides for the transfer of property after the owner's death, the other two types of arrangements do not appear to provide for any such extended relationship between the parties involved. Moreover, the property is transferred at the time of the writing of the text. The exchanges of shares and real-estate adoption texts, then, achieve the same end—that is, the transfer of family property between relatives—but use different formulas. Apparently there was an element of choice in the use of formula. In the exchange of shares texts, the focus is on the property; in the real-estate adoption, it is on the adoptive relationship through which the property can be transferred. Perhaps such concerns were factors in determining which formula to use. That is, the real-estate adoption formula might be chosen in cases where the parties involved wanted to guarantee that no questions might be raised later, and the exchange-of-shares format when the right to own the property was not an issue.

The numerous intra-family transfers of real estate also demonstrate the importance of the bond between a family and its land. A family's property was its means of social and economic survival in the agriculture based economy of

[1] See E. Chiera, HSS 5:vii, and G. Dosch, *Die Texte aus Room A34 des Archives von Nuzi* (Magister-Arbeit, University of Heidelberg, 1976).

Arrapḫa. Without property to cultivate and its associated livestock activities, a family was cut off from the primary mode of production in its society. Craftsmen and other skilled professionals could earn their livings through their trades, but dispossessed landowners might be forced into dependence on wealthier landowners in return for their support. The gradual impoverishment of the small landowner class and the growth of the *wardu* class in Arrapḫa have been discussed elsewhere,[2] so we need not elaborate on them here except to note that the loss of family property was a fundamental element in this process. In order to gain the basic means of survival—food, clothes, and shelter—individuals might give up their freedom with all its social perquisites. Repeatedly in the archives of both the eastern and southwest areas, to say nothing about the massive archives of the Teḫip-Tilla family, we can trace the disintegration of family lines among those who relinquish their property or those who manage the inheritance of their property poorly.[3] Of course, the most obvious example in the eastern area is the family of Šukriya, who divided his property among his sons. They, in turn, transferred portions of it to their uncle through a variety of agreements. Finally, the surviving son was left without his gods, his mother, his sister, and, one would imagine, his land. In contrast to this sort of situation, the sons of Pula-ḫali appear to have worked together both in their lending and real-estate activities. Such familial cooperation produced most successful results for the brothers, by all accounts.

Women in the Eastern Archives

The women in the Eastern Archives range from the wives in the wealthy families to slave girls purchased by the archive owners. As noted above, ᶠWarḫi-Nuzu wife of Šukriya, ᶠŠilwa-turi wife of Ar-tura, ᶠHaruli wife of Muš-apu, and, if HSS 19 19 is Tarmiya's will, his wife ᶠTieš-naya all appear in their husband's wills as beneficiaries to their estates. Their husbands' arrangements for them, however, are quite different. ᶠḪaruli receives property which she cannot sell to an "outsider." Her sons are charged with supporting her with food and clothing. ᶠŠilwa-turi receives five daughters (presumably the right to arrange their marriages), a house, and household furnishings. If she remarries, her sons "will strip her and send her out," that is, she can take nothing with her to her new household. ᶠWarḫi-Nuzu receives a house to use for as long as she lives. ᶠTieš-naya, though, was made guardian of her husband's estate for her life. His sons must wait until her death for their inheritance and they must protect her offspring. Furthermore, she has the right to disinherit Tarmiya's sons and can go free with her belongings whenever she chooses. In all cases, the husbands provided for their wives, but the degree of freedom and authority given them was quite different. These wills illustrate very well the range of economic and social independence

[2] See G. Wilhelm's *Das Archiv des Šilwa-Teššup*, part 2: *Rationenlisten I* (Wiesbaden, 1980), and *The Hurrians*.

[3] See M. Morrison, SCCNH 2:167–201.

possible for a woman from a wealthy family after her husband's death. Ideally, as a widow, a woman could be a free and equal participant in her community.

The reality of at least some of these women's situations was rather different from what their husbands intended. fŠilwa-turi resorted to a real adoption to gain support for herself in return for her property. fWarḫi-Nuzu, on the other hand, had her own property and the house left to her by her husband. Further, she was involved in her sons' real-estate transactions by which they ceded their property either permanently or on lease to their uncle. Her husband's will does not give her any guardianship rights, but, apparently, she was able to participate in her family's activities. Although she had both financial resources and personal vigor, she was sold into a foreign land.

As noted in chapter 3, these two situations demonstrate the need that most women had for a protector in the community. Throughout the Nuzi corpus, those women who successfully pursued business interests of their own or maintained households of any magnitude were backed by extensive holdings or royal connections. From the archives of the Teḫip-Tilla family come the figures of fWinnirke, fḪinzuri, and fUzna. From the archives of Šilwa-Tešup DUMU LUGAL come his mother fAmmin-naya, his wife fŠašuri, his sister fŠuwar-Ḫepa, and his *esirtu* women. Of course, fTulpun-naya's many transactions indicate that her wealth was substantial.

Aside from the wills, women figure in texts involving daughtership or sistership agreements. In HSS 19 67, fAzum-naya daughter of Ḫašeya becomes the "sister" of Tarmiya son of Ḫuya. He is to arrange for her marriage and retain only a portion of the silver he receives for her. The relationships among the parties to this contract and their circumstances are not known, so we can only speculate on their reasons for entering into such an agreement. It is clear, though, that fAzum-naya had a prominent individual in the community arrange her marriage. Elsewhere, fŠilwa-turi, Ar-tura's wife, was "given" five daughters in her husband's will, presumably so that she could arrange for their marriages. In her adoption of Utḫap-tae, she gives one of her daughters, fTeḫeš-menni, to Utḫap-tae as a "sister" with the stipulation that he will arrange for her marriage. Given fŠilwa-turi's relationship to Utḫap-tae, fTeḫeš-menni was probably Utḫap-tae's stepsister to begin with. Since fŠilwa-turi's reason for entering this agreement was to gain support and a protector for herself, the sistership arrangement for her daughter doubtless had the same motivation. In the daughtership agreement, HSS 19 86, Utḫap-tae takes fNūr-māti the daughter of Karrate son of Pui-tae as his daughter and agrees to arrange for her marriage. Karrate was Utḫap-tae's son-in-law by his marriage to Utḫap-tae's daughter, fAze. Here, Utḫap-tae adopts as a daughter either his own granddaughter, if fNūr-māti was Karrate and fAze's child, or his daughter's stepdaughter. Thus, Utḫap-tae, the senior or most prominent member of the family, found himself responsible for arranging marriages for both fTeḫeš-menni, probably his stepsister, and fNūr-māti, also a member of his family. Certainly it was desirable for these women to have such an individual as a protector and matchmaker for them. In light of the financial return for such responsibilities, one might imagine that Utḫap-tae acted out of a sense of duty or affection for these women.[4] In any case, these texts emphasize the need for a woman to be wealthy or sponsored by a wealthy person in order to assure her future well-being.

There is one instance in the Eastern Archives of the movement of real estate in connection with women. In HSS 19 97, land formerly given as a *terḫatu* by one member of the family of Pula-ḫali is reclaimed by two sons of Pula-ḫali. This text shows how women could serve as conductors of real estate beyond the limits of their families, a phenomenon well attested elsewhere at Nuzi.[5] Moreover, by undoing such a transfer of property, it demonstrates the desire of members of the family to keep family property intact. It is noteworthy that the men who retrieved their family were sons of Pula-ḫali, many of whose dealings suggest a strong sense of the unity of their family.

Genres of Texts and the Terminology of the Family

It is immediately obvious from the above discussion that a number of familiar genres of texts are represented just among the intra-family contracts and texts concerning women in the eastern archives. These include real adoption, real-estate adoption, exchange of shares, and daughtership and sistership agreements. One benefit that arises from considering these texts within the context of the archives to which they belong is that background material emerges to inform the texts' meanings. While the results of the transactions described in the texts are quite clear, the circumstances generating the various kinds of texts vary considerably. For instance, the two real-adoption texts arose from very different circumstances, and two different kinds of texts, exchanges of shares and real-estate adoption, were used to achieve the same end—transfer of real estate between family members. Among the daughtership and sistership texts, two clearly point to intra-family activity, perhaps for different reasons, while the circumstances of a third remain unknown.

All of these examples, then, illustrate the difficulty in assigning fixed definitions and legal parameters to any particular genre of text. It is clear from all of these texts, however, that the terms used to describe family relationships and traditional inheritance patterns provided the terminology for these genres of texts. The model of the family and its practices emerges as a means of describing not only social relationships but also economic and legal ones. This underscores, of course, the importance of the family unit and its practices in Nuzi society.

The Archive Owners in the Eastern Area

The individuals whose archives are the most prominent in the eastern area comprise an interesting and diverse Group. Tarmiya son of Ḫuya was an irrigation officer who is known to have owned property in Nuzi (including urban real

[4] See K. Grosz, SCCNH 2:152.

[5] See Morrison, SCCNH 2:167–201.

estate), in his family *dimtu*, and elsewhere. A younger son whose inheritance was even questioned by his brothers, he entered the officialdom of the land and prospered. His texts document the growth of his real-estate holdings, a portion of which came through transactions with the apparently beleaguered family of his brother Šukriya. The irony of his acquisition of familial property from the family of the brother who sued him over a slave girl does not escape us. Nor can we ignore his apparent lack of interest in their desperate circumstances.

Šeḫal-Tešup son of Teḫup-šenni was an irrigation officer assigned to the city of Ḫušri. He had a household with servants and, apparently, a senior servant or representative who handled his affairs. He owned property in Ḫušri, had business activities in Nuzi, and may have been a member of the *rākib narkabti*. It seems that he had no biological heirs since he adopts a man and gives him all his property.

Urḫi-kušuḫ was a son of the king with holdings in Unapšewe. Puḫi-šenni son of Muš-apu was his representative, but was also a judge, like his father, and probably a member of the *rākib narkabti*. He owned considerable property in Unapšewe and was a grain "banker." Puḫi-šenni, like Tarmiya, was not the chief heir of his father, according to his father's will. Perhaps because of the death of his older brother, he succeeded to his status.

The sons of Pula-ḫali were landowners in Tupšarriniwe and metal "bankers" of substance. Their father was a merchant and they themselves were connected to the network of trade and commerce in the land of Arrapḫe either directly or through their lending activities. They work together frequently, but Pašši-Tilla is the most prominent among them.

Utḫap-tae son of Ar-tura appears to have been based in Nuzi. His texts mention urban real estate in Nuzi. His profession is not known, but his activities are reminiscent of those of the people of the southwest area, that is, real-estate acquisitions and personnel transactions. He also engages in lending of grain, metal, and livestock. Unlike Tarmiya, whose neglect of his brother's family is apparent, Utḫap-tae acquired a number of dependent women from branches of his father's family or from his own.

These individuals, then, were prosperous officials, merchants, and private citizens, hardly the poorer members of Nuzi society as was initially thought. They held positions of authority and had private resources which, in some cases, were substantial. It is interesting to note how each of these men achieved his social and economic status. Puḫi-šenni son of Muš-apu obviously came from a wealthy and influential family and belonged to the *rākib narkabti* class of society. How he became Urḫi-kušuḫ's representative is not known, but he was already highly placed in Arrapḫean society. The sons of Pula-ḫali also began their careers with resources most likely accumulated by their father. He is known to have owned real estate, and he was a merchant engaged in the overland trade. Urḫi-kušuḫ, of course, was a son of the king. Like others of his rank, he undoubtedly had estates devoted to agriculture and livestock. Utḫap-tae received a portion of his father's real-estate holdings. By the standards of this area, his circumstances appear modest, but the extent of his inheritance is not known. The background of Seḫal-Tešup son of Teḫup-šenni is not certain, so we cannot speculate on the source of his wealth. His presumed position among the *rākib narkabti* along with his other activities suggest that he came from a landowning family of note. Finally, Tarmiya son of Ḫuya, the youngest son, must have received little from his father's estate, along with the slave girl who became his wife. His family was wealthy, however, and he became a government official. Perhaps he was able to benefit from his family's status and his position to become a landowner of means.

Thus, all of the archive owners seem to have come from wealth and position and to have built upon what they received from their families. While all emerge from landowning families, there are variations in the peak period and focus of the various families' activities. The Muš-apu family, for instance, seems secure in its social and economic position by Muš-apu's generation, and Puḫi-šenni simply augmented both. Ḫuya's family, on the other hand, seems to have reached a peak in Ḫuya's generation. His son Tarmiya appears to have had to rebuild for himself, using property acquired from his relatives and others. The Pula-ḫali family appears to have increased its resources considerably in the generation of the sons of Pula-ḫali. Ar-tura's family, like that of Ḫuya, seems to have peaked in Ar-tura's generation. Ar-tura divided his property among his sons and other heirs. While his son Utḫap-tae acquired real estate and engaged in lending as did his father, he certainly started, at least, with less than his father had. Some indication of the relative wealth of the archive owners may be found in the area of lending. Lending and commercial enterprises were certainly respectable businesses in Arrapḫe. Not only wealthy individuals, but also the palace and royalty itself, were involved in such activities. To engage in lending, individuals needed excess commodities beyond what their households required. Those who lend grain are known to have had real-estate holdings that would produce the supplies needed for lending. Metal lenders had to acquire the metals through trade either in metals and/or in other commodities. The family of Pula-ḫali clearly had commercial ties, real estate producing agricultural products, and interests in the crops produced by others. Among the archive owners, all are engaged in one or another kind of lending, with the exception of Tarmiya and Šeḫal-Tešup son of Teḫup-šenni. It may be a fluke of discovery that no loan texts have been found for these men. Alternatively, they may simply not have had the surplus means to engage in such activities.

Other Texts and Groups from the Eastern Area

In addition to the six major archival Groups, some texts belonging to individuals who are otherwise unattested in the area are assigned to Groups 17, 18A, and 19. For instance, HSS 19 42 (S151, Group 18A) involves a Ḫanaya son of Šešwe. He is otherwise known as a witness for Akap-šenni son of Zike (HSS 5 52:12) and as an *ālik ilki* (HSS 13 6:40). AASOR 16 61 is a *titennūtu* whereby Kula-ḫupi son of Arteya acquires Elḫip-tašenni son of Urḫiya. This text was written in Nuzi by Tarmi-Tešup son of Itti-šarri. Kula-ḫupi is also known from

HSS 16 336:4, where he appears in a list of names of individuals given to certain men. He also witnesses the lawsuit *EN* 9/1 430. In HSS 19 36, Urḫiya and ᶠUlūlîtu are mentioned and HSS 19 43 mentions ᶠKunna[tu], Utḫaya, ᶠZilip-šau, and ᶠSusenna. HSS 19 13 (S133, Group 19) is the will of Ila-nîšū son of Šurukka. Though these texts are assigned to rooms in the Eastern Archives, it must be remembered that they may not in fact have originated there.

Some other names appear with greater frequency. Paya son of Elḫip-šarri, for instance, appears in *EN* 9/2 73, which is assigned to S129 (Group 19). This text is a *ṭuppi šupeʾʾulti* by which Paya and Pai-Tešup son of Ar-teya exchange *paiḫu* fields. As noted in chapter 2, the property that Paya gives borders that of Kula-ḫupi and Šukriya and the road of the city of Ḫamena.[6] The text was written in the city of Akip-apu.[7] Paya also figures in *EN* 9/2 166, which is assigned to N120, texts of which room clearly belong to the Eastern Archives. In this text, a *ṭuppi titennūti*, Teḫup-šenni son of Urḫiya enters Paya's house in return for twenty minas of tin. *EN* 9/2 45 is a *ṭuppi mārūti* by which Nai-šeri adopts Paya and his brothers Ar-zizza and Alki-Tešup and gives them property in the *dimtu* of Kurriawe. This text was also written in the city of Akip-apu. Assigned SMN 2733, the text has no room number, though others in this high range clearly come from the Eastern Archives. Otherwise, Paya son of Elḫip-šarri is attested as a guard of the *bīt qaritī ša kamari* in HSS 16 356:1 and as delivering wagons in Nuzi in HSS 13 228:27. In the second, he appears with Šurki-Tilla and Enna-mati sons of Teḫip-Tilla. Likewise, he is a witness for these men in *JEN* 385:22. Paya's brothers Ar-zizza and Alki-Tešup also appear as witnesses to *EN* 9/2 73 (lines 29–30). Paya son of Elḫip-šarri appears to have been active in Nuzi but, like so many others in the eastern area, had real-estate holdings elsewhere.

Another Group of texts concerns the family of Eteš-šenni son of Ḫapira who appears in *EN* 9/2 331 and 477 (both assigned to S132, Group 19). *EN* 9/2 31 from S132 (Group 19) is a *ṭuppi mārūti* by which Ennaya son of Eteš-šenni adopts Arik-kaya his brother and gives him his inheritance share. Taya is the scribe for the text. *EN* 9/2 32 also from S132 (Group 19), records the adoption of Ḫurizi son of Akik-kaya by Ennaya son of Eteš-šenni. Taya the son of Apil-Sîn writes this text. *EN* 9/2 46, assigned to F24, is a *ṭuppi mārūti* by which Iluya son of Ipša-ḫalu and Waraduya son of Wur-Šenni adopt Arik-kaya son of Eteš-šenni and give him property. Again, Taya writes the text. *EN* 9/2 81, which has no room number, is a *ṭuppi šupeʾʾulti* between Ḫuziri son of Arik-kaya and Ennaya son of Eteš-šenni. ᵈNanna-mansi [son of Taya] writes this document. Ḫuziri son of Arik-kaya is also known as an *ālik ilki* in HSS 13 6:32.

Other members of this family may appear in *EN* 9/2 176, a *ṭuppi titennūti* by which Kel-teya son of Ḫuziri gives property, his inheritance share, to Zikaya son of Ḫuziri. Tarmiya son of Kuari is the scribe for this text, which is assigned to S136. Zikaya son of Ḫuziri appears in HSS 13 169:2, 5, in which he receives

6 See p. 41 above.

7 For the city of Akip-apu, see L. R. Fisher, *NGN*, 11 no. 23.

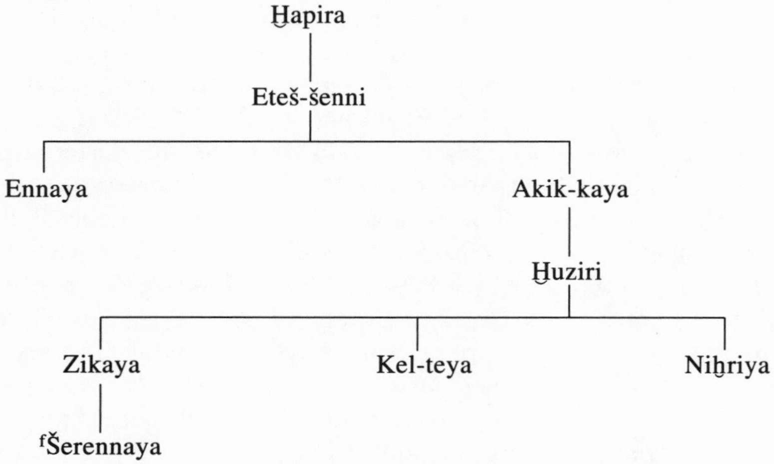

FIGURE 14. *Genealogy of Eteš-šenni's Family*

his daughter Šerennaya. The text was written in Nuzi. In HSS 16 407:11 he appears in a list of names with Šeḫal-Tešup son of Ar-tura, and in HSS 19 65, a text with a high SMN number (3758) and no room number, he appears as a principal in a *ṭuppi aḫḫūti* contract written in Nuzi by Arip-šarri. Of particular interest, Zikaya son of Ḫuziri appears as a witness to *EN* 9/2 10 (line 40), a contract involving Utḫap-tae son of Ar-tura. Yet another son of Ḫuziri many appear in HSS 13 143 (S133, Group 19), in which Niḫiya son of Ḫuziri acquires a substantial amount of property in Nuzi and elsewhere from Ewaya son of Ar-zizza. It is interesting that he also receives Ar-zizza's will as title to the property (lines 28–31). Turar-Tešup son of Kel-Tešup is the scribe for this text. The family may be reconstructed as in figure 14. This family was involved primarily with Nuzi. Scribes of the second and third generations write for Ennaya and Ḫuziri (Taya son of Apil-Sīn and ^{d}Nanna-mansi son of Taya). Ḫuziri appears with the sons of Teḫip-Tilla son of Puḫi-šenni and other second- and third-generation scribes in HSS 13 6, a text assigned to the third generation by other individuals who appear in it. Zikaya is contemporaneous with Utḫap-tae son of Ar-tura and the scribes Arip-šarri and Tarmiya son of Kuari. Thus, he would date to the third and fourth generations.[8] Niḫriya's scribe, Turar-Tešup son of Kel-Tešup, is associated with the fourth generation in the Southwest Archives.[9]

Those texts that are assigned to the Eastern Archives belong to that part of Group 19 in which archives of the Pula-ḫali family and the merchants were located. Thus, if the Group originated in the Eastern Archives, it represents another small archive mixed in with the texts of a number of individuals with whom no other relationship can be determined.

[8] See Morrison, SCCNH 2:172, 183.

[9] Ibid., 180.

Interconnections among the Archives

While certain relationships can be ascertained between the archives of individual buildings in the eastern area, there is very little interconnection among the archives of the eastern area as a whole. Only occasionally do the principal parties of the archives appear together, such as HSS 16 232, in which Ar-tura son of Kuššiya (line 2) and Tarmiya son of Ḫuya (line 4) appear, and HSS 19 10 and *EN* 9/2 354, in which Ḫašip-Tilla son of Kip-ukur witnesses the will of Ar-tura son of Kuššiya (line 44) and a text of Utḫap-tae son of Ar-tura (line 22), respectively. Likewise, there is relatively little interaction among the parties of these archives and those of the other major archives of Nuzi, for example, the archives of the family of Teḫip-Tilla son of Puḫi-šenni, Šilwa-Tešup DUMU LUGAL, Katiri, and the Southwest Archives. Among the few instances recorded, Akap-šenni son of Purna-zini goes to court with Šilwa-Tešup DUMU LUGAL (HSS 9 139), Utḫap-tae son of Ar-tura witnesses a Šilwa-Tešup text (HSS 9 25:25), and Ḫanukka son of Tarmiya witnesses a text of Eḫli-Tešup son of Taya (HSS 19 82:29). Muš-apu son of Purna-zini and his son Puḫi-šenni are listed as judges in texts involving members of the Teḫip-Tilla son of Puḫi-šenni family in Unapšewe. It does seem unusual that the individuals attested in the archives of Nuzi, especially those who clearly were based in Nuzi, did not interact more extensively.

The principal connection among all of the archives at Nuzi is, of course, the scribes who write the texts. In the Eastern Archives, for instance, Arip-šarri writes for the sons of Ḫuya and Utḫap-tae son of Ar-tura. Elsewhere, he is attested in the Southwest Archives and in the archives of the family of Katiri. Šimanni son of ^{d}AK.DINGIR.RA writes for Utḫap-tae son of Ar-tura and Tarmiya son of Ḫuya in the Eastern Archives and individuals from other parts of the city.[10] Abī-ilu son of ^{d}AK.DINGIR.RA writes for Šukriya son of Ḫuya, Šeḫal-Tešup son of Teḫup-šenni, and the sons of Pula-ḫali, in addition to other major figures in the Nuzi corpus.[11] Enna-mati son of Puḫi-šenni writes for Ḫašup-Tilla son of Šeḫliya, Tarmiya son of Ḫuya and Paššі-Tilla son of Pula-ḫali, an interesting connection in light of their respective bases of operation.[12] Finally, ^{d}UTU-PAB son of Akiya writes for Šeḫal-Tešup and the sons of Pula-ḫali, along with other well-known individuals at Nuzi.[13] The scribes, then, bind the characters of the eastern archives to the larger community.

The Character of the Eastern Area of the City

Analysis of the archives of the eastern area leads to the question of the character of the eastern area of the city. The excavator describes the area as being poorly designed and constructed and suggests that it was occupied by the poorer

[10] See pp. 24–25 and 53–54 above.

[11] See pp. 24–26 and 59 above.

[12] Ḫašip-Tilla was active in Unapšewe, Tarmiya primarily in the *dimtu* of Ḫuya and Nuzi and Paššі-Tilla in many locales. See pp. 24 and 81.

[13] See pp. 59 and 97 above.

residents of the city. As noted in the introduction, however, only portions of this area are not as well planned as other parts of the city. Those buildings that show the most reconstruction and variation in plan are the very buildings that produced the tablets. Buildings contiguous to those housing the tablets were respectable edifices similar to those elsewhere in the city.

Of the buildings producing tablets, Groups 17 and 18A were not completely excavated, so little can be said about their quality and design beyond the evidence that exists for renovations. The first Group is associated with Utḫap-tae son of Ar-tura, an individual of means though his profession is not known, and Šeḫal-Tešup son of Teḫup-šenni, an irrigation officer in another city. The second Group is associated with Tarmiya son of Ḫuya, also an irrigation officer whose private resources were considerable. Both Utḫap-tae and Tarmiya are known to have owned houses in Nuzi, most likely these very houses, and Utḫap-tae's archives include two texts concerning building activities in this part of the city of Nuzi.[14] Whether Šeḫal-Tešup owned property in Nuzi or not is not clear, but he, too, had significant properties elsewhere. If he in fact did not own property in Nuzi but stored his tablets in Utḫap-tae's house in Nuzi, his situation would be much like that of the archive owners in the major building from which tablets come, Group 19.

Group 19 is the most irregular of all of the buildings in the eastern area, of a series of "independent units."[15] Rooms S132, 136, 139 and 141 comprise one unit. The archives of this unit belonged to the sons of Pula-ḫali, who were based in Tupšarriniwe and had interests throughout the land; a Group of merchants, who also were engaged in far-flung business activities; and the family of Eteš-šenni, who appear to have been involved mostly with Nuzi, itself. This unit contained few objects, has no hearth, and offers little evidence of domestic activity. All the other rooms of Group 19 meander irregularly to form another unit. Throughout the second unit are signs of alteration and renovation, work that appears to have changed the original plan of the building. The principle archive owners of this unit of Group 19 are Puḫi-šenni son of Muš-apu and Urḫi-kušuh DUMU LUGAL, both based in Unapšewe. In fact, the Urḫi-kušuh texts were probably present in Nuzi because Puḫi-šenni was his representative and his own texts were there. This unit has two hearths, extensive storage facilities, and signicant evidence of domestic activity, especially in the courtyard S133. Thus, the archaeological and textual evidence differentiates the two "units" of Group 19 rather considerably.

Most of the individuals of Group 19 were personally involved in business whether it be banking or trading. Some of the merchants had a direct connection with the palace; others had no official connection but a commercial relationship with the palace, hence a vested interest in its activities. The presence of these individuals in Nuzi would have been necessitated by their responsibilities or business interests.

[14] See discussion on pp. 64–65.
[15] R. F. S. Starr, *Nuzi* I, pp. 64–65.

One interpretation of Group 19, then, is that it was a *pied à terre* of sorts maintained by people whose primary holdings were elsewhere but who needed space in the administrative center. This interpretation suggests that Group 19 actually housed the people who owned the tablets with the "independent" units within the building giving some privacy to the various individuals of the archives. One can imagine that Puḫi-šenni son of Muš-apu or Urḫi-Tešup DUMU LUGAL might have used the larger unit of Group 19 as a residence in Nuzi, though the arrangement of the rooms would be most inconvenient. The smaller unit, though, would seem inadequate, even on a temporary basis, for the sons of Pula-ḫali and the other merchants unless they could not find any other arrangements, that is, unless urban property in Nuzi was extremely scarce. There is evidence, however, from the texts of Groups 17 and 18A that unbuilt plots were available in this very area at the same time as the archives of Group 19.

A second interpretation of Group 19 is that it was used primarily as a text depository, that is a *bīt ṭuppi* or "tablet house," and storage facility for a Group of people related through their involvement in banking and commerce. Any domestic activity might be accounted for by dependents maintaining the building. This explanation for Group 19 rests on the fact that most of the archive owners are not based at Nuzi and are connected to each other because of their professions in banking and commerce. This view is especially appealing for the smaller of the two units but could well be extended to the building as a whole.

As for the area as a whole, it is very clear that the people of the eastern area were not poor. Instead, the principal figures were officials or private citizens with considerable resources. Most were connected in some way with the palace bureaucracy or the royal family. Quite a few participated actively in the commercial life of Arrapḫe. Thus, the area was a neighborhood associated with the administrative and commercial sectors of the population, and these sectors prospered in the later period of Nuzi.

It is particularly interesting that all of the archives of the eastern area point to increased activity during the later phase of Nuzi as the archive owners expanded their holdings in the area or moved their texts into Nuzi. The excavator believed that the reconstruction evident throughout the eastern area was necessary to meet the needs of its people.[16] In light of the identities of the archive owners and their activities, these renovations in the eastern area in the late Nuzi period would point to increasing activity in Nuzi of people largely associated with government and commerce. This might suggest a growth in the bureaucracy and an increased importance of the administrative sector of the state. In this case, the attraction to this area of private individuals engaged in commerce and profiting from business with the administration would be most understandable.

It is also worth noting that the renovations in the eastern area may have been accomplished hurriedly near the end of the life of the city in order to accomodate an influx of individuals from other cities. That is, with the threat of Assyria looming over Arrapḫe, officials and wealthy individuals from such places

[16] R. F. S. Starr, *Nuzi* I, p. 321.

as Unapšewe and Tupšarriniwe gravitated to Nuzi, the administrative center, in search of safety. Privilege of office and private wealth facilitated their entry into the area. At the very least, their archives were moved into the city to secure them for the future. This possibility is particularly attractive for Group 19, which contains the texts of individuals whose association with Nuzi is, at best, very tentative.

With respect to the rest of the city, it is obvious that the eastern area has a history different from that of the southwest area, which appears to be residential in character and occupied by middle-class individuals. Future study of the northwestern area of the city and the archives there may provide information to illuminate more fully the nature of the urban population at the end of the Nuzi period. Already, however, it is clear that two areas of the city were occupied by or associated with people of means ranging from the middle class of the southwest area to officials and bankers of greater wealth in the eastern area.

Index to Transliterations and Translations*

Text	*Page*
Translations (whole or partial)	
EN 9/2 10	51
EN 9/2 16	33
EN 9/2 17	70–71
EN 9/2 18	71
EN 9/2 19	77
EN 9/2 20	75
EN 9/2 21	75
EN 9/2 22	77–78
EN 9/2 23	76
EN 9/2 28	71–72
EN 9/2 33	101
EN 9/2 35	27
EN 9/2 36	33
EN 9/2 39	35–36
EN 9/2 40	34
EN 9/2 49	72
EN 9/2 67	58
EN 9/2 74	78–79
EN 9/2 76	29
EN 9/2 77	79
EN 9/2 125	63
EN 9/2 143	72
EN 9/2 145	72–73
EN 9/2 157	73
EN 9/2 171	77
EN 9/2 184	61
EN 9/2 187	37
EN 9/2 188	76
EN 9/2 189	81
EN 9/2 209	99
EN 9/2 224	101
EN 9/2 234	30
EN 9/2 262	58
EN 9/2 267	101–2
EN 9/2 268	102
EN 9/2 292	100
EN 9/2 354	57
EN 9/2 360	61
EN 9/2 362	79
EN 9/2 493	80
EN 9/2 505	100
EN 9/2 524	102
HSS 14 21	60
HSS 14 31	32
HSS 15 300	80
HSS 19 11	49
HSS 19 134	50
Transliterations	
EN 9/2 10	50–51
EN 9/2 16:4–5	33
EN 9/2 36:2′–5′	33
EN 9/2 39:1–15	35
EN 9/2 40	34
EN 9/2 76:4–9	29
EN 9/2 125	62–63
EN 9/2 187:1–16	37
EN 9/2 189:20–24	81
EN 9/2 209	98–99
EN 9/2 262	57–58
EN 9/2 264:3–7	104n
HSS 16 231:1–16	104n
HSS 19 126:15–25	105n

* This index was compiled by Richard M. Wright, Cornell University.

PART 2
TEXTS IN THE HARVARD SEMITIC MUSEUM

Excavations at Nuzi 9/2

by

E. R. Lacheman†, M. A. Morrison and D. I. Owen

Catalogue of Texts

This, the second part of *Excavations at Nuzi* 9, continues the pattern established in the first part, published in SCCNH 2:355–702. The texts included here have all been collated by the editors, who have also prepared the catalog. Therefore no collation signs (+) have been used in the catalog entries. There have been numerous small corrections to the copies and to the transliterations in Lacheman, *SCTN* 2, and in Owen, *LDN*. Furthermore, the copious notes and collations left by Lacheman often help to restore passages in places where the tablets have deteriorated or where parts have been lost. Regrettably, the inclusion of extensive transliterations and notes has not been possible here. At some stage in this publication project, complete transliterations, utilizing all this data, will be made available. As indicated in the introduction to *EN* 9/1 (SCCNH 2:357), the texts are published in the order assigned to them by Lacheman. For those numbers to which Lacheman had not assigned texts or where duplications necessitated the removal of a text, copies previously unassigned have been substituted. The catalog follows the same format as *EN* 9/1 with some minor changes to accommodate the information required by Morrison's study above. For abbreviations used in the catalog, see pp. xi–xiii above. We are grateful to Paola Negri Scafa for her assistance in providing corrections and clarifications for the names of scribes in broken or obscure contexts.

No.	SMN	Room	Group	Description
10	2390	S132	19	Statement of Ḫerši and Urḫi-Tilla sons of Naniya by which they adopt Utḫap-tae son of Ar-tura and give him houses in the *kirḫu* of the city of Nuzi. [Arip]-šarri [the scribe]. *SCTN* 2:112–13.
16	2128	S151	18A	*Ṭuppi mārūti* by which Wantiš-šenni son of [ ] adopts Tarminya son of [Ḫuya] and gives him x+ three *awēḫaru* of fields west of the road of the city of Tarkulli. Turar-Tešup (son of Kel-Tešup) [the scribe]. Tablet written at the Tišša gate.
17	2302	S124	19	*Ṭuppi mārūti* by which Ḫanie son of Teḫip-apu adopts Muš-apu son of Purna-zini. Property in Unapšewe. Amumiya (son of Sîn-nādin-šumi?) the scribe. *SCTN* 2:78.
18	2700+?	S113	17	*Ṭuppi mārūti* by which Eḫlip-apu son of [Abeya] adopts Muš-apu son of Purna-zini and gives him three ANŠE of fields. *SCTN* 2:233.

No.	SMN	Room	Group	Description
19	2007	S124	19	*Ṭuppi mārūti* by which Ḫanukka son of Zilip-Tilla adopts Puḫi-šenni son of Muš-apu and gives him a field in Unapšewe. Tablet written in Unapšewe by Elḫip-Tilla.
20	2083	S112	19	*Ṭuppi mārūti* by which Nai-te son of Ḫanaya adopts Puḫi-šenni son of Muš-apu and gives him property in the city of Unapšewe. Tablet written in Unapšewe by Elḫip-Tilla.
21	2095	S129	19	*Ṭuppi mārūti* by which Naite son of Ḫanaya adopts Puḫi-šenni son of Muš-apu and gives him property in Unapšewe. Tablet written in Unap-šewe by Elḫip-Tilla.
22	2091	S129	19	*Ṭuppi mārūti* by which Ḫanakka son of Milkiya adopts Puḫi-šenni son of Muš-apu and gives him property in Unapšewe. Tablet written in Unap-šewe by Elḫip-Tilla son of Kel-Tešup.
23	2307	S124	19	*Ṭuppi mārūti* by which Ḫatarte son of [Âtanaḫ-ili] and Nai-te son of Ḫanaya adopt Puḫi-šenni son of Muš-apu and give him property in Unapšewe. Tablet written in Unapšewe by El[ḫip-Tilla]. *SCTN* 2:80.
27	2193	S113	17	Statement of Akkul-enni son of [ ] by which he gives an orchard in Temtenaš to ᶠTulpun-naya. Taya the scribe. *SCTN* 2:19.
28	2168+?	S112	19	[*Ṭuppi mārūti*] by which Eḫlip-apu son of [Abeya] adopts Muš-apu son of Purna-zini and gives him houses and *paiḫu* land. Tablet written in Unapšewe by [Ta?]ya. *SCTN* 2:10.
29	2133	S151	18A	*Ṭuppi mārūti* by which Unap-tae son of Akkul-enni adopts Bēl-šaduni *wardu* of [ ]. Šamaš-uraššu son of Ṣilliya the scribe.
31	2362	S132	19	*Ṭuppi mārūti* by which Ennaya son of Ete[š-šenni] adopts Arik-kaya his brother and gives him prop-erty. Tablet written in Āl-Ilāni by Taya. *SCTN* 2:97.
32	2366	S132	19	*Ṭuppi mārūti* by which Ennaya son of Eteš-šenni adopts Ḫuziri son of Arik-kaya and gives him property. Taya son of Apil-Sīn the scribe. *SCTN* 2:99.
33	2376	S152	19	[*Ṭuppi mārūti*] by which Tae son of [ ] adopts Pašši-Tilla and gives him an orchard. ZU-ᵈIŠKUR the scribe. *SCTN* 2:105.

No.	SMN	Room	Group	Description
34	2485	S151	18A	Statement of Tenteya, Umpiya, Iwišti, Ennike, and Puḫiya sons of Keliya by which they adopt Ḫanukka son of Tarmiya and give him houses in the city of Nuzi. Ar-puruša the scribe. *SCTN* 2:132.
35	2488	S151	18A	*Ṭuppi mārūti* by which Wantip-šarri and Makuya sons of Zike adopt Ḫuya son of Šimika-atal and give him houses in the city of Nuzi. Arim-matka the scribe. *SCTN* 2:134.
36	2497	S151	18A	[*Ṭuppi mārūti*] by which Ḫani-ašḫari son of [ ] adopts Tamiya son of Ḫuya and gives him two parcels of land, one in the *dimtu* of Kazzi-buzzi. Tablet written in Nuzi. *SCTN* 2:141–42.
38	2474	S151	18A	Fragmentary text in which Muš-apu receives property in Unapšewe. *SCTN* 2:127 assigns the text to room 133. [Amumiya? the scribe.]
39	2517	S151	18A	[*Ṭuppi mārūti*] by which Pai-Tilla and Teḫip-Tilla [sons of Šukriya] adopt Tarmiya son of Ḫuya and give him property in Nuzi. *SCTN* 2:152–53.
40	2501	S151	18A	Statement of Ennike son of [ ] by which he adopts Tarmiya and gives him *paiḫu* land in the *kirḫu* of Nuzi. [Šiman]ni son of ᵈAK-DINGIR.RA the scribe. *SCTN* 2:144.
45	2733			*Ṭuppi mārūti* by which Nai-šeri adopts Paya, Ar-zizza and Alki-Tešup sons of Elḫip-šarri and gives them a field in the *dimtu* of Kurriawe. Tablet written in the city of Akip-apu. [ ]-a-[ ] son of ᵈSîn-iliya the scribe. *SCTN* 2:253.
46	3483	F24		*Ṭuppi mārūti* by which Iluya son of Ipša-ḫalu and Waraduya son of Wur-šenni adopt Arik-kaya son of Eteš-šenni and give him property. Taya the scribe.
49	2323	S124	19	[*Ṭuppi mārūti*] by which Eḫlip-apu son of [Abeya] adopts Muš-apu son of Purna-zini and gives him property in [Unapšewe]. *SCTN* 2:85: "Fragment, not transliterated." [Elḫip-Tilla? the scribe.]
67	2114	N120		Statement of Artašenni son of Arik-kewar concerning property in Nuzi which he has given to Utḫap-tae son of Ar-tura for six years. They will share the produce of the field. Tablet written by Ḫeltip-kušu⟨ḫ⟩.

No.	SMN	Room	Group	Description
73	2337	S129	19	*Ṭuppi šupe᾽᾽ulti* by which Paya son of Elḫip-šarri and Pai-Tešup son of Ar-teya exchange *paiḫu* fields. Tablet written in the city of Akip-apu. *SCTN* 2:88–89.
74	2314	S124	19	*Ṭuppi šupe᾽᾽ulti* by which Utḫap-tae son of Enna-mati and Puḫi-šenni son of Muš-apu exchange fields in Unapšewe. El[ḫip-Tilla] the scribe. *SCTN* 2:82–83.
76	2498	S151	18A	*Ṭuppi šupe᾽᾽ulti* by which Šukriya son of Ḫuya and Šekar-Tilla son of Tarwa-zaḫ exchange fields. Šukriya receives property north of the *dimtu* of Ḫuya. Rim-Sîn the scribe. *SCTN* 2:142–43.
77	2173 +2316	S124	19	*Ṭuppi šupe᾽᾽ulti* by which Ḫutip-Tilla son of Ḫuya and Puḫi-šenni son of Muš-apu exchange fields in Unapšewe. Elḫip-Tilla the scribe. *SCTN* 2:12, 83–84.
81	2706			*Ṭuppi šupe᾽᾽ulti* by which Ḫuziri son of Arik-kaya and Ennaya son of Eteš-šenni exchange fields. ^{d}Nanna-mansi the scribe. *SCTN* 2:236.
83	2010	S130	19	Statement, perhaps in court, of Akkul-enni concerning fields given to Ariḫ-ḫarpa and Kiziri.
93	2354	S132	19	List of fields and individuals who hold them. *SCTN* 2:93–94.
96	2512	S151	18A	List of *tarbie* fields owned by certain individuals. Totaled as *tarbie ša* ZAG. *SCTN* 2:149–50.
97	2439	S133	19	Tin loan of [Kipal]-enni son of Pula-ḫali. *SCTN* 2:125. [Man]nu-[tāri]ssu the scribe.
101	2487	151	18A	Statement of Eniš-tae son of Tauka concerning grain, *išpiku*, to be given to Tarmiya son of Ḫuya. Tablet written in Ar-šalipe by Enna-mati. *SCTN* 2:133.
102	2380	S132	19	Letter to Teḫip-šarri from Akip-tašenni SUKAL concerning Kipal-enni son of Pula-ḫali. *SCTN* 2:107.
103	2510	S151	18A	List of twenty-five men of Nuzi to whom Pai-Tilla gives water. *SCTN* 2:148.
106	2504	S151	18A	[*Ṭuppi mārūti*] by which Akawatil, Tai-Tilla, and Šelluni [sons of Akap-šenni?] adopt Tarmiya son of Ḫuya and give him property. Tablet written in Nuzi. *SCTN* 2:146.

No.	SMN	Room	Group	Description
110	2438	S133	19	Beginning of text lost. *SCTN* 2:125: "Fragment, not transliterated." Lacheman's notes read: x+1. *um-ma* [^{I}*wa-an-ti-ia-ma*] x+2. *a-nu-u*[*um-ma*..] x+3. ^{I}*šur-k*[*i-til-la*..] x+4. LÚ [. . . .] x+5. *ša* [. . . .] x+6. 6 ANŠE.MEŠ-*šu* x+7. 4 LÚ.MEŠ [..] x+8. *i-na* KUR *nu-ul-*[*lu-a-ú*] x+9. DU-*ak* x+10. *a-na* ŠU-*t*[*i*] x+11. *bi-ki-is-*[*mi*] x+12. *ù li-qè-*[*mi*] x+13. NA$_4$ ^{I}*wa-an-ti-*[*ia*] x+14. NA$_4$ ^{I}*te-ḫi-ip-til-la* DUMU *pu-ḫi-še-en-ni*
111	2361	S132	19	Fragmentary letter. Nanna-adaḫ mentioned. *SCTN* 2:97.
118	3657	G73		Statement of Ila-nîšū son of Ḫapira concerning the transfer of Tarmiya and Taika sons of Kula-ḫupi to Eḫlip-apu son of Abeya. The two men were debtors of Ila-nîšū; and Eḫlip-apu paid their debt to him. Tablet written in Nuzi by Muš-Tešup son of Ḫupita.
125	2208	N120		Record of a total of three ANŠE eight *awēḫaru* of fields, the inheritance share of Utḫap-tae, which he gives to his "brother," Šeḫal-Tešup. *SCTN* 2:28.
128	1684			Part of a transaction whereby fields are given to Muš-apu and Šeḫliya.
129	2475	S136	19	Letter to Eḫli[ya] from Šurki-Tilla concerning the Tiššа gate, the gathering of scribes and the people of Nuzi, and their dispatch to Anzugalli. *SCTN* 2:127–28.
130	2505	S151	18A	Statement of Tai-Tilla son of Utḫap-še concerning grain. *SCTN* 2:146–47.
142	2179	S112	19	Statement of Unnuni son of Waqar-bēli concerning the renewal of a real-estate *titennūtu* with Muš-apu son of Purna-zini made previously by his father. *SCTN* 2:14–15.

No.	SMN	Room	Group	Description
143	2313	S124	19	*Ṭuppi titennūti* whereby Akap-šenni son of Purna-zini gives a field to Muš-apu son of Purna-zini. Tablet written in Unapšewe. *SCTN* 2:82.
144	2803			Statement of Akip-tašenni who enters the house of Muš-apu son of Purna-zini in *titennūti* for three years. See *IN*, 114, text 11. *SCTN* 2:258: "Un-numbered fragment, not transliterated."
145	2519	S132	19	*Ṭuppi titennūti* by which Wantiya son of Ar-nu[zu] gives fields in Unapšewe to Muš-apu son of Purna-zini. *SCTN* 2:154.
146	2319 +2321	S124	19	[*Ṭuppi mārūti*] by which Ammarša adopts Puḫi-šenni. Tablet written in Unapšewe by [Elḫip]-Tilla. *SCTN* 2:84–85: "Fragment, not transliterated."
152	2102			*Ṭuppi titennūti* whereby Matip-apu and Akip-Tešup sons of Tarmiya receive bronze from Utḫap-tae son of Ar-tura in return for Akip-Tešup's working for Utḫap-tae for four years. Pui-tae the scribe. See *IN*, 128, text 35.
153	2493	S151	18A	Statement of Ay-abāš whereby he places his son Wantiš-še *ana titennūti* with Tarmiya son of [Ḫuya]. Tablet written in Nuzi. *SCTN* 2:137. See *IN*, 115, text 13.
156	2013	S113	17	*Ṭuppi titennūti* wherein Minaššuk son of Keliya and [f]Unuš-kiaše wife of Keliya give Appuziki son of Keliya for four years to Šeḫal-Tešup son of Teḫup-šenni in exchange for ten minas of tin and two fine ewes. Tablet written in Nuzi. [. . . the scribe]. See *IN*, 111, text 6.
157	2367	S132	19	Fragmentary text describing a *titennūtu* arrange-ment between Ḫanie son of Teḫip-apu and Muš-apu [son of Purna-zini]. A previous arrangement is mentioned. Tarmi-Tilla the scribe. *SCTN* 2:100.
158	2338	S129	19	Statement of Šurki-Tilla son of Tampi-kutati who gives his inheritance share to Urḫi-šarri son of Ḫanaya. *SCTN* 2:89.
163	2194	S113	17	Record of a *titennūtu* by which [A]kaya son of Kuššiya gives property in Unapšewe to Puḫi-šenni son of Muš-apu. Elḫip-Tilla the scribe. *SCTN* 2:20.

No.	SMN	Room	Group	Description
166	2245	N120		*Ṭuppi titennūti* by which Teḫup-šenni son of Urḫiya enters the house of Paya son of Elḫip-šarri. A[kap?/kipta?]-šenni the scribe. *SCTN* 2:69–70.
168	2821			Fragmentary *titennūtu* by which Teḫip-Tilla [son of Šukriya] gives property to Tarmiya. SAG.AN.[KI] the scribe. *SCTN* 2:258: "Unnumbered fragment, not transliterated."
171	2312	S124	19	Statement of Attilammu son of Tur-šenni whereby he gives a fields in Unapšewe to Puḫi-šenni son of Muš-apu. Elḫip-Tilla son of Kel-Tešup the scribe. *SCTN* 2:81–82.
172	2132	S152	19	*Ṭuppi titennūti* by which Keliya son of Tampuya gives fields in Nuzi to Gimil-abi son of Akip-apu for five years. SAG-AN.KI the scribe.
175	2311	S124	19	*Ṭuppi titennūti* by which Šeḫliya son of Purna[-zini?] and Ḫašip-Tilla son of Šeḫliya give a field to Ḫanaya son of Tae. Tablet written in Unap-šewe. *SCTN* 2:80–81.
176	2125 +2476	S136	19	*Ṭuppi titennūti* by which Kelteya son of Ḫuziri gives a field to Zikaya son of Ḫu[ziri]. [Tar]miya son of Kuari the scribe. *SCTN* 2:128.
177	2511	S151	18A	Statement of [Ḫupita?] son of Šuk[riya] by which he gives a field bordering the *dimtu* of Ḫuya to Šarteya. Tablet written in Nuzi by Akap-šenni son of Šukriya. *SCTN* 2:149.
184	2004			[*Ṭuppi titennūti*] by which Šeḫal-Tešup son of Teḫup-šenni receives a field in the city of Ḫušri from Marru. Tablet written in Ḫušri by Abī-ilu.
185	2518	S151	18A	Statement before witnesses by [ ] sons of [ ] concerning property apparently give *ana titennūti* to Tarmiya. [Šim]anni(?) the scribe. *SCTN* 2:153.
186	2112	S112	19	Statement of Kula-ḫupi son of Ḫuya by which he gives property east of the *dimtu* of Ḫuya to Tarmiya son of Ḫuya. Tablet written in Nuzi by Arip-šarri.
187	2479	S151	18A	*Ṭuppi titennūti* by which Teḫip-Tilla son of Šukriya and Warḫi-Nuzu wife of Šukriya give property in the *dimtu* of Šimika-atal to Tarmiya son of Ḫuya. Tablet written in Nuzi by Arip-šarri. *SCTN* 2:128–29.

No.	SMN	Room	Group	Description
188	2002			*Ṭuppi titennūti* by which Ḫatarte son of Âtanaḫ-ili gives a field in Unapšewe to Puḫi-šenni son of Muš-apu. Tablet written in Unapšewe by Elḫip-Tilla.
189	2301	S124	19	[*Ṭuppi titennūti*] by which Ḫatarte son of [Atanaḫ-ili] gives a field to Ḫašip-Tilla son of Šeḫliya. Tablet written in Unapšewe. Enna-mati son of Puḫi-šenni the scribe. *SCTN* 2:76–77.
200	2143			[Statement of] Ḫaiš-Tešup whereby he agrees to redeem property that Tarmiya [son of Ḫuya] holds in *titennūtu* from Zaziya son of Aittara. Tablet written in Nuzi.
204	2500	S151	18A	Fragmentary agreement between Zime and Eḫli-Tešup concerning the division of grain on the threshing floor. Probably belongs to Southwest Archives. *SCTN* 2:144.
206	2520	S151	18A	*Ṭuppi titennūti* by which Akkul-enni and Ar-tešše sons of Ar-[tirwi] gives fields to Ḫuya son of [Šimika-atal]. *SCTN* 2:154.
207	2377	S132	19	Fragmentary commercial text involving Ḫašip-Tilla son of Kip-ukur and Kipal-enni [son of Pula-ḫahi?]. ^{d}UTU-PAB the scribe. *SCTN* 2:106.
209	2368	S132	19	Statement of Ṣilli-Šamaš son of [ ]-ip-šarri concerning the receipt of the tin which he loaned to Pula-ḫali the merchant. Maliya the scribe. *SCTN* 2:100.
212	2426	S133	19	*Ṭuppi titennūti* by which Ḫutin-nawar son of [Šuk]ri-Tešup and Nul-aḫḫe son of Killate give a field to Šamaš-iluni son of Bēl-aḫḫē. Qaqqadu the scribe. *SCTN* 2:119–20.
224	2443	S133	19	*Ṭuppi titennūti* by which Šurukka son of Arip-urikke gives a field in Tupšarriniwe to Pašši-Tilla son of Pula-ḫali. Tablet written in Tupšarriniwe by ^{d}UTU-PAB son of Akiya. *SCTN* 2:126.
234	2490	S151	18A	[*Ṭuppi tamgur*]*ti* in which Teḫip-Tilla son of Šukriya and Kaya and Zimmari sons of Qîšteya agree to Teḫip-Tilla's payment of a large debt of Šukriya. Tablet written at the Tišša gate by Kaluppani son of Aḫu-šini. *SCTN* 2:135.

No.	SMN	Room	Group	Description
236	2345	S130	19	Fragmentary record of a *titennūtu* by which Ḫašip-Tilla receives a field from Ḫan[i]e son of Al[ki]-Tilla. *SCTN* 2:90.
250	2221	N120		Damaged sale agreement by which Ḫašiya son of [Ward-aḫḫē?] sells sheep to Paššiya. Tablet written in Tupšarriniwe by ᵈUTU-PAB son of Akiya. *SCTN* 2:42.
262	2107	N120		Statement of Eḫli-Tešup son of Kipaya concerning the *paiḫu* property in the city of Nuzi on which he agreed to build for Utḫap-tae son of Artura (as in AASOR 16 58). Arip-šarri the scribe.
264	2708			*Ṭuppi titennūti* by which [Ḫupi]ta son of Arip-ḫurra gives property to Tarmiya. Sīn-šadūni the scribe. *SCTN* 2:236–37.
267	2773			Fragmentary *titennūtu* agreement by which Šurki-Tilla and at least one other person give a field to Šurki-Tilla, Pašši-Tilla, and Kipal-enni sons of Pula-ḫali. Tablet written in Tupšarriniwe.
268	2428	S133	19	Fragmentary *titennūtu* agreement by which property with an orchard, well, and threshing floor is given by Šekaru to Paššiya son of Pula-ḫali. *SCTN* 2:121.
273	2499	S151	18A	[*Ṭuppi tam*]*gurti* whereby Puḫi-šenni son of [ ]-e and Tarmiya come to an agreement concerning the payment of grain, livestock, and metals. Niḫriya the scribe. *SCTN* 2:143.
275	2777			Fragmentary *titennūtu* by which Akaya son of Ka-[ ] gives to Puḫi-šenni son of Muš-apu property previously given him by his father(?). *SCTN* 2:258: "Unnumbered fragment, not transliterated."
279	2513	S151	18A	Record of a *titennūtu* by which Ḫašip-Tilla and the Zike sons of Ar-teya give a field to Eḫli-Tešup. [Nanna-mans]i? the scribe. Perhaps belongs to the Southwest Archives. *SCTN* 2:151.
283	2401	S132	19	Statement of Taika son of Akap-šenni by which he sells a pair of doors to Pašši-Tilla son of Pula-ḫali. ᵈUTU-PAB the scribe. *SCTN* 2:117.
289	2418	S132	19	Fragmentary statement of Ḫa/Za-[ ] son of Šerši[ya] concerning Tulpi-šenni [the ? of the] SAL.LUGAL and Šeḫal-[Tešup(?)] son of Ar-tura ᴸᵁ́[ ]-*za*(?)-*a*[*l*(?)]-*lu*. Possibly a dispute

No.	SMN	Room	Group	Description
				concerning the queen's sheep. *SCTN* 2:119: "Fragment, not transliterated."
291	2370	S132	19	Statement of [A]kip-Tilla concerning repayment of a lost ass belonging to Ḫašip-Tilla son of Kip-ukur. *SCTN* 2:102.
292	2365	S132	19	Zunna son of Urḫiya borrows an ass from Paššі-Tilla son of Pula-ḫali for the journey of the palace. Tablet written in Ulamme by Ḫut-Tešup. *SCTN* 2:98–99.
297	2124	S130	19	Šekar-Tilla son of Šelwiya borrows a shekel of gold from Ariḫ-ḫamanna son of Ḫamutta. Teḫip-Tilla the scribe.
298	2011	S113	17	Herding contract by which Ipša-ḫalu son of [ ] and Paya son of Ni-[ ] receive sheep from Šeḫal-Tešup son of Teḫup-šenni. The sheep were received and will be returned in Nuzi. SAG-AN.KI! the scribe.
299	2681	P485!		*Ṭuppi mārtūti* by which Uante son of Enna-mati gives his sister [f]Elwi[ni] to Paššі-Tilla son of Pu[la-ḫali]. [d]UTU-PAB the scribe. *SCTN* 2:219–20.
301	2620	P428!		Multiple grain loan text of Puḫi-šenni son of Muš-apu. [Elḫ]ip-Tilla or Teḫiya the scribe. *SCTN* 2:188; *LDN* (*EN* 9 301).
321	2167	S112	19	Ḫani-anni son of Makuya borrows grain from Urḫi-kušuḫ DUMU LUGAL. Taklāk-ilu the scribe. *SCTN* 2:10; LDN (*EN* 9 321).
322	2157	S110	17	Statement of Enna-mati son of Ḫapira by which he gives his son Bēlani to Utḫap-tae son of Artura in return for an ox. [Ipša]-ḫalu the scribe. *SCTN* 2:5; *LDN* (*EN* 9 322).
323	2334	S129	19	Tae and Šekaru sons of Ḫašip-apu borrow grain from Puḫi-šenni son of Muš-apu. Elḫip-Tilla the scribe. *SCTN* 2:87; *LDN* (*EN* 9 324 [= *EN* 9 323]).
324	2358	S132	19	Teḫup-šenni son of Šekaru borrows grain from Minaš-šuk. Bēl-ili the scribe. *SCTN* 2:96; *LDN* (*EN* 9 371 [= *EN* 9 324]).
325	2387	S132	19	Muš-Tešup son of Akip-tašenni borrows tin from [ ]-wiya son of [ ]. *SCTN* 2:109–10; *LDN* (*EN* 9 325). The following transliteration, based on an early Lacheman file, contains parts of the

No.	SMN	Room	Group	Description
				tablet no longer preserved when the tablet was copied. 1. [12] MA.NA *a-*[*na-ku ša*] 2. [[I]. .]-*wi-ia* DUMU [. . . .] 3. [I]*mu-uš-te-šup* 4. DUMU *a-kip-ta-še-en-ni* 5. *a-na* UR$_5$.RA *il-*[*te-qè*] 6. *i-na* EGIR[-*ki* EBUR *i-na*] 7. ITI *ḫi-in-zu-*[*ri it-ti*] 8. *sí-ip-ti-šu* 9. 12 MA.NA *a-na-ku* 10. [I]*mu-uš-te-šup ù* 11. [. . . .*ši*]-*ka* 12. [*ú-ta*]-*ar* 13. [*šum-ma i-na*] ITI *ḫi-in-zu-ri ši-im-*[*ta-mu*] 14. [. . .]*ša* MÁŠ *ša* [. . . .] rev. 15. [NA$_4$] *tar-mi-te-šup* 16. NA$_4$ *še-en-nu-un-mi* 17. DUMU *ša-li-ia* 18. NA$_4$ *pa-i-til-la* DUMU *ar-te-šup* 19. [NA$_4$ *šu*]-*ur-kip-til-la* DUMU [. . . .]
326	2674	P465!		Statement of Tupki-Tilla son of Unaya concerning the return of the grain he loaned to Muš-apu son of Purna-zini in Unapšewe. Kel-Tešup the scribe. *SCTN* 2:216; *LDN* (*EN* 9 326).
327	2303	S124	19	Kuari son of Kuššiya borrows grain from Puḫi-šenni son of Muš-apu. [Elḫip-Tilla the scribe.] *SCTN* 2:78–79; *LDN* (*EN* 9 327).
329	2077	S132	19	Akip-Tilla son of Ḫurpu and Ḫutip-kewar son of Artapai borrow grain from Puḫi-šenni son of Muš-apu. Elḫip-Tilla the scribe. *LDN* (*EN* 9 329).
331	2350	S132	19	Statement of Tultukka son of Akitte concerning silver he received from Eteš-šenni son of Ḫapira. Ariḫ-ḫamanna the scribe. *SCTN* 2:92; *LDN* (*EN* 9 331).
333	2680	P480!		Ḫatarte son of Âta⟨na⟩ḫ-ili and Akip-tašenni son of Kawinni borrow grain from Puḫi-šenni son of Muš-apu. Elḫip-[Tilla the scribe.] *SCTN* 2:218; *LDN* (*EN* 9 328 [= *EN* 9 333]).
334	2315	S124	19	Eteš-šenni son of Âtanaḫ-ili borrows barley, and Nai-Tešup son of Ḫanaya borrows wheat from Puḫi-šenni son of Muš-apu. *SCTN* 2:83; *LDN* (*EN* 9 333 [= *EN* 9 334]).

No.	SMN	Room	Group	Description
336	2113	N120		Akap-še son of Kartiya, Matte son of Enna-mati, and Taika son of Maliya borrow grain from Puḫi-šenni son of Muš-apu. Elḫip-Tilla the scribe. *LDN* (*EN* 9 336).
337	2363	S132	19	Ḫutip-apu son of [E]ḫliya borrows tin from Taika son of A[kap-šenni]. dUTU-PAB the scribe. *SCTN* 2:98; *LDN* (*EN* 9 337).
338	2162	S112	19	Puḫi-šenni son of [Ar-ta]šenni (Lacheman restored [a-kip-ta-š]e-en-ni; our restoration is suggested by the name in line 24, although it is spelled differently) borrows grain from Puḫi-šenni son of Muš-apu. Kelteya the scribe. *SCTN* 2:7; *LDN* (*EN* 9 338).
339	2359	S132	19	Statement of Nūr-kûbi son of [ ]-šu concerning the copper and bronze which he had loaned to Pula-ḫali and his son for interest and commercial profit. Muš-teya son of Sīn-ibni the scribe. *SCTN* 2:98; *LDN* (*EN* 9 339). (SMN 2369 in *LDN* is a typographical error.)
340	2079	S132	19	Ḫutip-apu and Tarmi-Tilla sons of Eḫliya borrow grain from Paššši-Tilla son of Pula-ḫali. dUTU-PAB the scribe. *LDN* (*EN* 9 340).
341	2180	S112	19	Kušuniya son of K[ank]eya borrows tin from Paššši-Tilla son of Pula-ḫali. dUTU-PAB the scribe. *SCTN* 2:15; *LDN* (*EN* 9 341).
342	2081	S132	19	Ḫupita son of Akitta borrows tin from Paššši-Tilla son of Pula-ḫali. Tarmi-Tilla the scribe. *LDN* (*EN* 9 342).
343	2142			Ḫellu borrows copper from Paššši-Tilla son of Pu[la-ḫali]. Tarmi-Tilla the scribe. *LDN* (*EN* 9 343).
344	2381	S132	19	Taika son of Akap-šenni borrows tin from Paššši-Tilla son of Pula-ḫali. dUTU-PAB the scribe *SCTN* 2:107; *LDN* (*EN* 9 344).
345	2690			Zime son of Ziliya borrows tin from Paššši-Tillla son of Pula-ḫali. dUTU-PAB the scribe. *SCTN* 2:225; *LDN* (*EN* 9 345).
346	2384	S132	19	Zil-Tešup son of Šennaya borrows bronze from Paššiya son of Pula-ḫali. Seal of the scribe. *SCTN* 2:108–9; *LDN* (*EN* 9 346).

No.	SMN	Room	Group	Description
347	2382	S132	19	Ḫalutta son of Akiya borrows tin from Waḫḫura son of Paššiya. [ ] the scribe. *SCTN* 2:108; *LDN* (*EN* 9 347).
348	2434	S133	19	Statement of Zike son of Akiya concerning repayment of grain load of Kipal-enni son of Pula-ḫali. *SCTN* 2:123; *LDN* (*EN* 9 349).
349	2445	S133	19	Šurukka son of Arip-urikke borrows grain from Paššiya son of [Pula-ḫali]. Abī-ilu the scribe son of ᵈA[K-DINGIR.RA]. *SCTN* 2:127; *LDN* (*EN* 9 348 [= *EN* 349]).
352	2349	S132	19	Eḫliya son of Akkuya borrows tin from the sons of Pula-ḫali. ᵈUTU-PAB the scribe. *SCTN* 2:91–92; *LDN* (*EN* 9 352).
353	2116	N120		Šurukka son of Arip-urikke borrows tin from the sons of Pula-ḫali. ᵈUTU-PAB the scribe. *LDN* (*EN* 9 353). (SMN 2216 in *LDN* is a typographical error.)
354	2158	S110	17	Statement of Pal-Tešup son of Ḫutiya concerning tin owed to Utḫap-tae son of Ar-tura. [ ]-nu the scribe. *SCTN* 2:5–6. *EN* 9 354 in *LDN* = *EN* 9/1 379, *not* this text.
356	2414	S132f	19	Arikku son of Šamaš-ilu borrows tin from Tupkiya. *SCTN* 2:119: "Fragment, not transliterated." *LDN* (*EN* 9 356).
357	2352	S132	19	Ḫašip-Tilla son of Tiantukku borrows yokes from Ḫašip-Tilla son of Kip-ukur. *SCTN* 2:93; *LDN* (*EN* 9 357).
358	2336f	S129	19	Ḫanie son of Šukriya borrows tin from Puḫi-šenni son of Muš-apu. El[ḫip-Tilla the scribe]. *SCTN* 2:87–88.
359	2161	S112	19	Statement of Šeḫal-Tešup son of Teḫup-šenni concerning grain which he owes to Ḫeltip-apu. Ḫutip-apu the scribe. *SCTN* 2:7; *LDN* (*EN* 9 359).
360	2001	S113	17	Šekar-Tilla son of Muš-te borrows a ewe from Šeḫal-Tešup son of Teḫup-šenni. ᵈUTU-PAB the scribe *LDN* (*EN* 9 360).
362	2335	S129	19	Kinni son of Ḫaniu borrows grain from Puḫi-šenni son of Muš-apu. Elḫip-Tilla the scribe. *SCTN* 2:87.

No.	SMN	Room	Group	Description
363	2108	S110	17	Utḫiya son of [Kel-te]ya borrows tin from Utḫap-tae son of Ar-tura. Aḫa-ay-amši the scribe. *LDN* (*EN* 9 363).
364	2393	S132	19	Fragmentary loan text of Paššiya [son of Pula-ḫali]. Urḫi-Tešup the scribe. *SCTN* 2:114.
371	2358A	S132		Fragmentary grain loan of Šehal-Tešup son of Teḫup-šenni [. . .]-ni-[. . . the scribe]. The SMN 2358 number recorded for *EN* 9 371 in Owen, *LDN* belongs to *EN* 9/2 324.
374	2379	S132	19	List of individuals with whom tin was deposited. Pašši-Tilla son of Pula-ḫali and Akkul-enni son Akitte included. Tablet written in the city of Tilla. Ninkiya the scribe. *SCTN* 2:106–7; *LDN* (*EN* 9 374).
384	2075	S132	19	Awiluti son of Šenna-tatti owes Irašu son of Akitte a cow. [T]eḫip-Tilla the scribe. Tablet missing, not collated.
387	2371	S132	19	Statement of Teḫip-Tilla son of Taya concerning the ox owed to him by Utḫap-tae and his transfer of Utḫap-tae to Šamaš-dayyānu. Tablet written in Nuzi by Ḫašip-Tilla son of Enna-pali. *SCTN* 2:203; *LDN* (*EN* 9 387).
391	2246	N120		Wage contract by which Pašši-Tilla son of Pula-ḫali agrees to pay Arn-ukka son of Elḫip-Tilla wages and food for making bricks. *SCTN* 2:70.
392	2481	S151	18A	Statement of Šata son of Itḫ-apiḫe. Tarmiya, LÚ*gugallu*, son of Ḫuya is the guarantor for the interest on a loan received from Matip-Tešup son of Muš-Tešup. Balṭu-kašid the scribe. *SCTN* 2:130; *LDN* (*EN* 9 392).
393	2012	S113	17	Ḫutiya son of Šimika-atal borrows bricks from Arip-šeriš. dAK.DINGIR.RA the scribe.
395	2495	S151	18A	Declaration in court of Erwi-ḫuta slave of Ḫašuar who testifies concerning Ḫalutta's presence in Ḫašuar's orchard. Šeršiya the scribe. *SCTN* 2:140–41.
401	2248	N120		Declaration in court of Azzina son of Tešup-nirari in a suit with [Ar-tura] son of Kuššiya. Zini the scribe. *SCTN* 2:71.

No.	SMN	Room	Group	Description
419	2309	S124	19	Lawsuit between Puḫi-šenni son of Muš-apu and Ḫatarte son of Âtanaḫ-ili and Teḫiya son of Ukur-atal concerning the bronze the two owed to Puḫi-šenni. Appa the scribe. *SCTN* 2:81; *CPN*, 270.
421	2178	S112	19	Fragmentary [*ṭuppi mārūti*] text. Sīn-liqiš the scribe. *SCTN* 2:14.
440	2372	S132f	19	Lawsuit between Pašši-Tilla son of Pula-ḫali and Ḫupita and Alki-Tilla sons of Akitte concerning the debt of Tultukka son of Akitte. Case tried in Tupšarriniwe. Akkul-enni the scribe. *SCTN* 2:103; *CPN*, 148–49.
441	2374	S132	19	Lawsuit between Urḫi-Tešup son of Yanzi-mašḫu and Pal-teya son of Puḫi-šenni concerning the payment of a servant woman owed to him. Ariḫ-ḫamanna the scribe. *SCTN* 2:104.
450	2127	S110	17	Hišm-apu son of Tarmiya borrows grain from Utḫap-tae son of Ar-tura. Tarmi-Tešup the scribe. *LDN* (*EN* 9 375).
452	2351	S132	19	*Ṭuppi taḫsilti* concerning tin borrowed from Waḫ-ḫura. *SCTN* 2:92–93; *LDN* (*EN* 9 362).
455	2526	S151	18A	Ḫašin-na borrows an ox from Puḫi-šenni. *SCTN* 2:157.
458	2174	S112	19	Lawsuit concerning a field involving Ar-tura who appears to call a number of men, probably to testify as witnesses before judges. *SCTN* 2:13.
477	2391	S132	19	Record of the sale of a horse. Eteš-šenni son of Ḫapira sells a horse to Puya son of Ḫašiya. *SCTN* 2:113.
478	2357	S132	19	List of horses received by men of Kipali, the merchant. *SCTN* 2:95.
490	2333	S127/9		Šurki-Tilla son of Tampi-kutatti borrows grain from Urḫi-kušuḫ DUMU LUGAL. *SCTN* 2:87; *LDN* (*EN* 9 323 [ ]).
493	2308	S124	19	Urḫi-kuš⟨uḫ⟩ son of Šeḫurni borrows grain from Puḫi-šenni son of Muš-apu. Elḫip-Tilla the scribe son of [Kel]-Tešup. *SCTN* 2:80.
505	2373	S132	19	Tupkin-a⟨tal⟩ son of Ḫapi-ašu receives two horses of the road which were owed to him by Pašši-Tilla

No.	SMN	Room	Group	Description
				son of Pula-ḫali. Ḫu[t-Tešup] the scribe. *SCTN* 2:103.
512	3538			Fragmentary loan of bronze made by Paššši-Tilla son of Pula-ḫali.
513	2405	S132	19	Itḫ-apiḫe son of [ ]-ip-erwi borrows bronze from Paššši-Tilla. ^{d}UTU-PAB [the scribe]. *SCTN* 2:119.
515	2250			Fragmentary text involving Paššši-Tilla and payment, perhaps for doors. Tablet written in the Tupšarriniwe gate by ^{d}UTU-PAB.
524	1448			Part of a *titennūtu* by which Akiya gives the sons of Pula-ḫali a field.
525	3543			Fragment of a *Ṭuppi mārūti* by which Elḫip-apu son of Abe[ya] adopts [Puḫi-šen]ni son of Muš-apu.
526	2304	S124	19	*Ṭuppi titennūti* by which Muš-apu son of Purna-zini receives fields from Puri-[ ] son of Ikkiya. *SCTN* 2:79.
527	2320	S124	19	Fragmentary record of the goods Puḫi-šenni son of Mu[š-apu] paid, perhaps for property. *SCTN* 2:85.
528	2506	S151	18A	Fragmentary text. Šimika-atal and Tarmiya ^{LÚ}[*gu-gallu*?] mentioned. *SCTN* 2:147.
529	2446	S133	19	Loan of tin with interest of [Pa]ššši-Tilla son of Pula-[ḫali]. [Enna]-mati the scribe. *SCTN* 2:127, where it is listed as SMN 2446 (now assigned to *EN* 9/1 372).

Index of SMN Numbers

SMN	EN 9/2
2684	128
2001	360
2002	188
2004	184
2007	19
2010	83
2011	298
2012	393
2013	156
2075	384
2077	329
2079	340
2081	342
2083	20
2091	22
2095	21
2102	152
2107	262
2108	363
2112	186
2113	336
2114	67
2116	353
2124	297
2125+2476	176
2127	450
2128	16
2132	172
2133	29
2142	343
2143	200
2157	322
2158	354
2161	359
2162	338
2167	321
2168+?	28
2173+2316	77
2174	458
2178	421
2179	142
2180	341
2193	27
2194	163
2208	125
2221	250
2245	166
2246	391
2248	401
2250	515
2301	189
2302	17
2303	327
2304	526
2307	23
2308	493
2309	419
2311	175
2312	171
2313	143
2314	74
2315	334
2319+2321	146
2320	527
2323	49
2333	490
2334	323
2335	362
2336	358
2337	73
2338	158
2345	236
2349	352
2350	331
2351	452
2352	357
2354	93
2357	478
2358	324
2358A	371
2359	339
2361	111
2362	31
2363	337
2365	292
2366	32
2367	157
2368	209
2370	291
2371	387
2372	440
2373	505
2374	441
2376	33
2377	207
2379	374
2380	102
2381	344
2382	347
2384	346
2387	325
2388	233
2390	10
2391	477
2393	364
2401	283
2405	513
2414	356
2418	289
2426	212
2428	268
2434	348
24318	110
2439	97
2443	224
2445	349
2446	529
2474	38
2475	129
2479	187
2481	392
2485	34
2487	101
2488	35
2490	234
2493	153
2495	395
2497	36
2498	76
2499	273
2500	204
2501	40
2504	106
2505	130
2506	528
2510	103
2511	177
2512	96
2513	279
2517	39
2518	185
2519	145
2520	206
2526	455

SMN	EN 9/2	SMN	EN 9/2	SMN	EN 9/2
2620	301	2700+?	18	2777	275
2674	326	2706	81	2803	144
2680	333	2708	262	2821	168
2681	299	2733	45	3483	46
2690	345	2773	267	3657	118

Index of Room Numbers

Room	EN 9/2	SMN
None	45	2733
	81	2706
	128	1684
	144	2803
	152	2102
	168	2821
	184	2004
	188	2002
	200	2143
	264	2708
	267	2773
	275	2777
	343	2142
	345	2690
	512	3538
	515	2250
	524	1448
	525	3543
F24	46	3483
G73	118	3657
N120	67	2114
	125	2208
	166	2245
	250	2221
	262	2107
	336	2113
	353	2116
	391	2246
	401	2248
P428!	301	2620
P465	326	2674
P480	333	2680
P485	299	2681
S110	322	2157
S112	20	2083
	28	2168+?
	142	2179
	186	2112
	321	2167
	338	2162
	341	2180
	354	2158
	359	2161
	363	2108
	421	2178
	450	2127
	458	2174
S113	18	2700+?
	27	2193
	156	2013
	163	2194
	360	2001
	393	2012
S124	17	2302
	19	2007
	23	2307
	49	2323
	74	2314
	77	2173+2316
	143	2313
	146	2319+2321
	171	2312
	175	2311
	189	2310
	327	2303
	334	2315
	419	2309
	493	2308
	526	2304
	527	2320
S127/9	490	2333
S129	21	2095

Room	EN 9/2	SMN
	22	2091
	73	2337
	158	2338
	323	2334
	358	2336
	362	2335
S130	83	2010
	236	2345
	297	2124
S131	298	2011
S132	10	2390
	31	2362
	32	2366
	93	2354
	102	2380
	111	2361
	145	2519
	157	2367
	207	2377
	209	2368
	283	2401
	289	2418
	291	2370
	292	2365
	324	2358
	325	2387
	329	2077
	331	2350
	337	2363
	339	2359
	340	2079
	342	2081
	344	2381
	346	2384
	347	2382
	352	2349
	356	2414
	357	2352
	364	2393
	371	2358A
	374	2379
	384	2075
	387	2371
	440	2372
	441	2374

Room	EN 9/2	SMN
	452	2351
	477	2391
	478	2357
	505	2373
	513	2405
S133	97	2439
	110	2438
	212	2426
	224	2443
	268	2428
	348	2434
	349	2445
	529	2446
S136	129	2475
	176	2125+2476
S151	16	2128
	29	2133
	34	2485
	35	2488
	36	2497
	38	2474
	39	2517
	40	2501
	76	2498
	96	2512
	101	2487
	103	2510
	106	2504
	130	2505
	153	2493
	177	2511
	185	2518
	187	2479
	204	2500
	206	2520
	234	2490
	273	2499
	279	2513
	392	2481
	395	2495
	455	2526
	528	2506
S152	33	2376
	172	2132

Index of Scribes

Scribe	EN 9/2
Abī-ilu	184
Abī-ilu son of ^{d}AK-DINGIR.RA	349
Aḫa-ay-amši	363
^{d}AK-DINGIR.RA	393
Akap-šenni son of Šukriya	177
A[kip-ta]šenni	166
Akkul-enni	440
Ammumiya	17, [38]
Appa	419
Ariḫ-ḫamanna	331; 441
Arim-matka	35
Arip-šarri	10, 186, 187, 262
Ar-puruša	34
Balṭu-kašid	392
Bēl-ili	324
Elḫip-Tilla	19, 20, 21, 23?, 74, 77, 146?, 163, 188, 301?, 323, 333?, 329, 336, 358?, 362
Elḫip-Tilla son of Kel-Tešup	22, 171, 493
Enna-mati	101, 529
Enna-mati son of Puḫi-šenni	189
Ḫašip-Tilla [son of] Enna-pali	387
Ḫeltip-kušu⟨ḫ⟩	67
Ḫutip-apu	359
Ḫut-Tešup	292, [505]
[Ipša]-ḫalu	322
Kaluppani son of Aḫu-šini	234
Kel-Tešup	326
Kel-teya	338
Maliya	209
Muš-Tešup son of Ḫupita	118
Muš-teya	339
^{d}Nanna-mansi	81, [279]
Niḫriya	273
Ninkiya	374
Pui-tae	152
Qaqqadu	212
Rim-Sîn	76
SAG-AN.KI	168, 298!
Sîn-liqiš	421
Sîn-šaduni	264
Šamaš-nāṣir	207, 283, 299, 337, 340, 341, 344, 345, 352, 353, 60, 513, 515
Šamaš-nāṣir son of Akiya	224, 250
Šamaš-uraššu son of Ṣilliya	29
[Šim]anni	185
[Šiman]ni son of ^{d}AK-DINGIR.RA	40
Taklāk-ilu	321
Tarmi-Tešup	450
Tarmi-Tilla	157, 342, 343
[Tar]miya son of Kuari	176
Taya	27, 28?, 31: 46
Taya son of Apil-Sîn	32
Teḫip-Tilla	297, 384
Teḫiya	301?
Turar-Tešup	16
Turšiya	395
Urḫi-Tešup	364
^{d}UTU-PAB	see Šamaš-nāṣir
Zini	401
ZU-^{d}IŠKUR	33
[ ]-ya	279

10

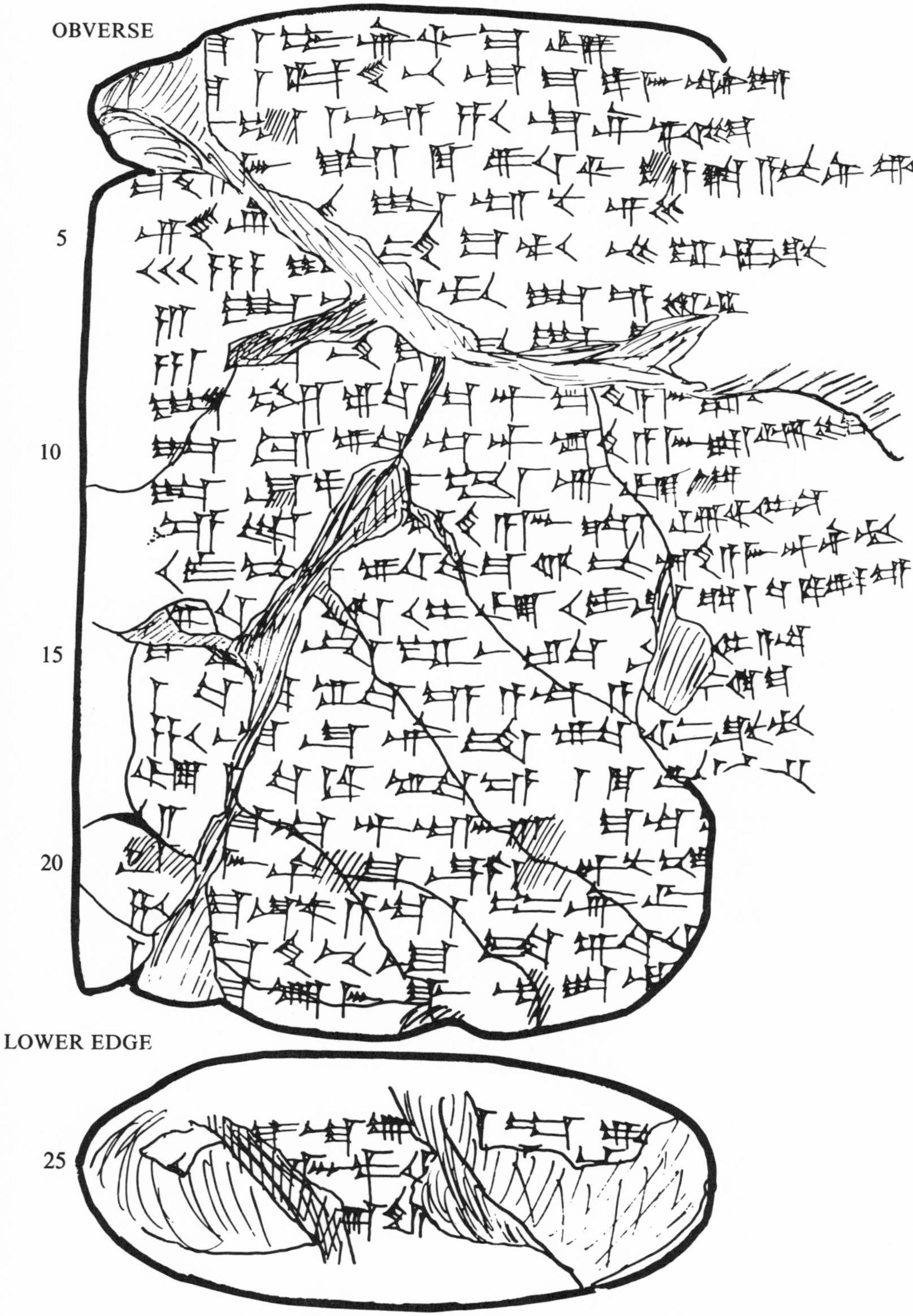

10

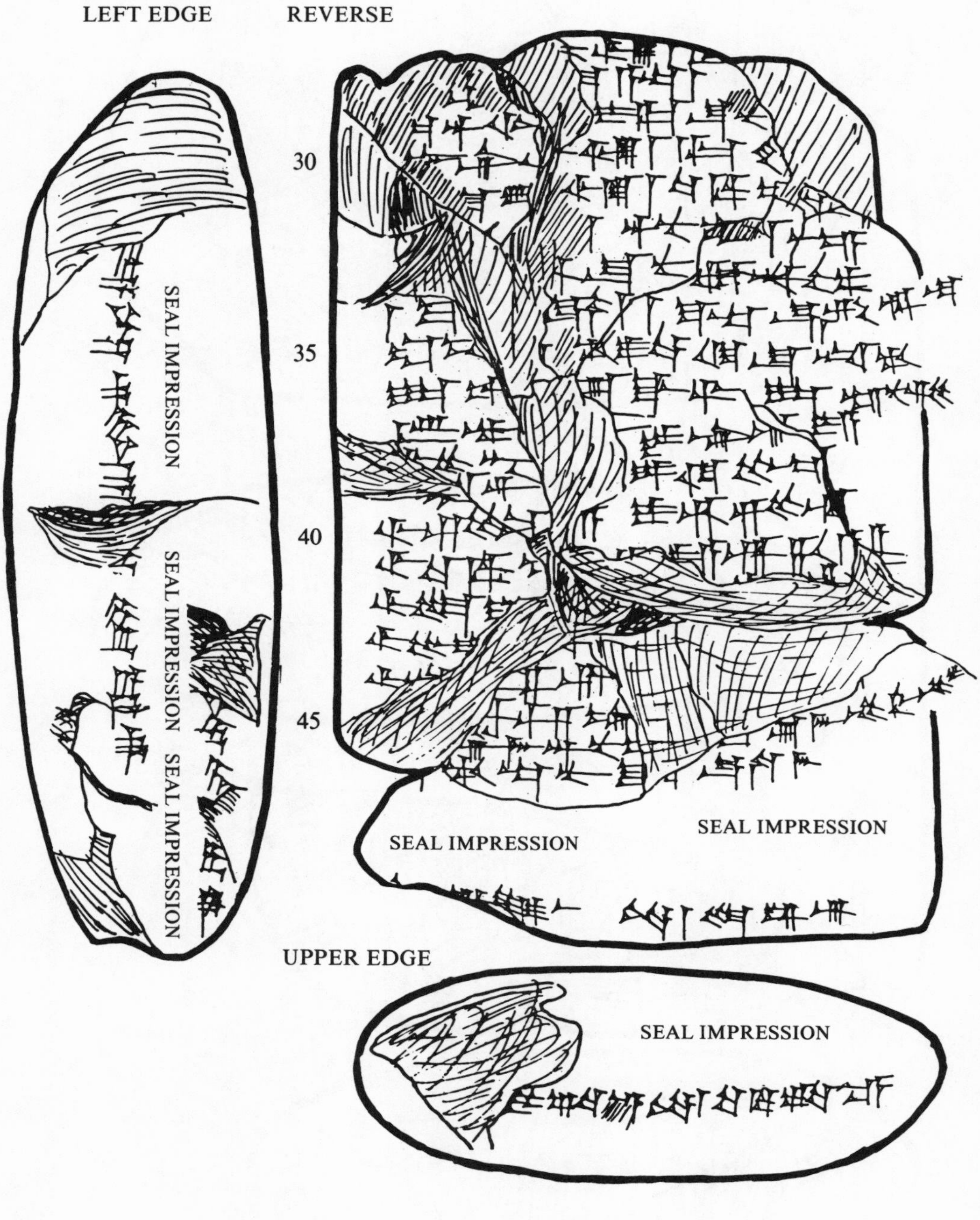
LEFT EDGE
REVERSE
SEAL IMPRESSION
SEAL IMPRESSION
SEAL IMPRESSION
SEAL IMPRESSION
SEAL IMPRESSION
SEAL IMPRESSION
UPPER EDGE
SEAL IMPRESSION

16

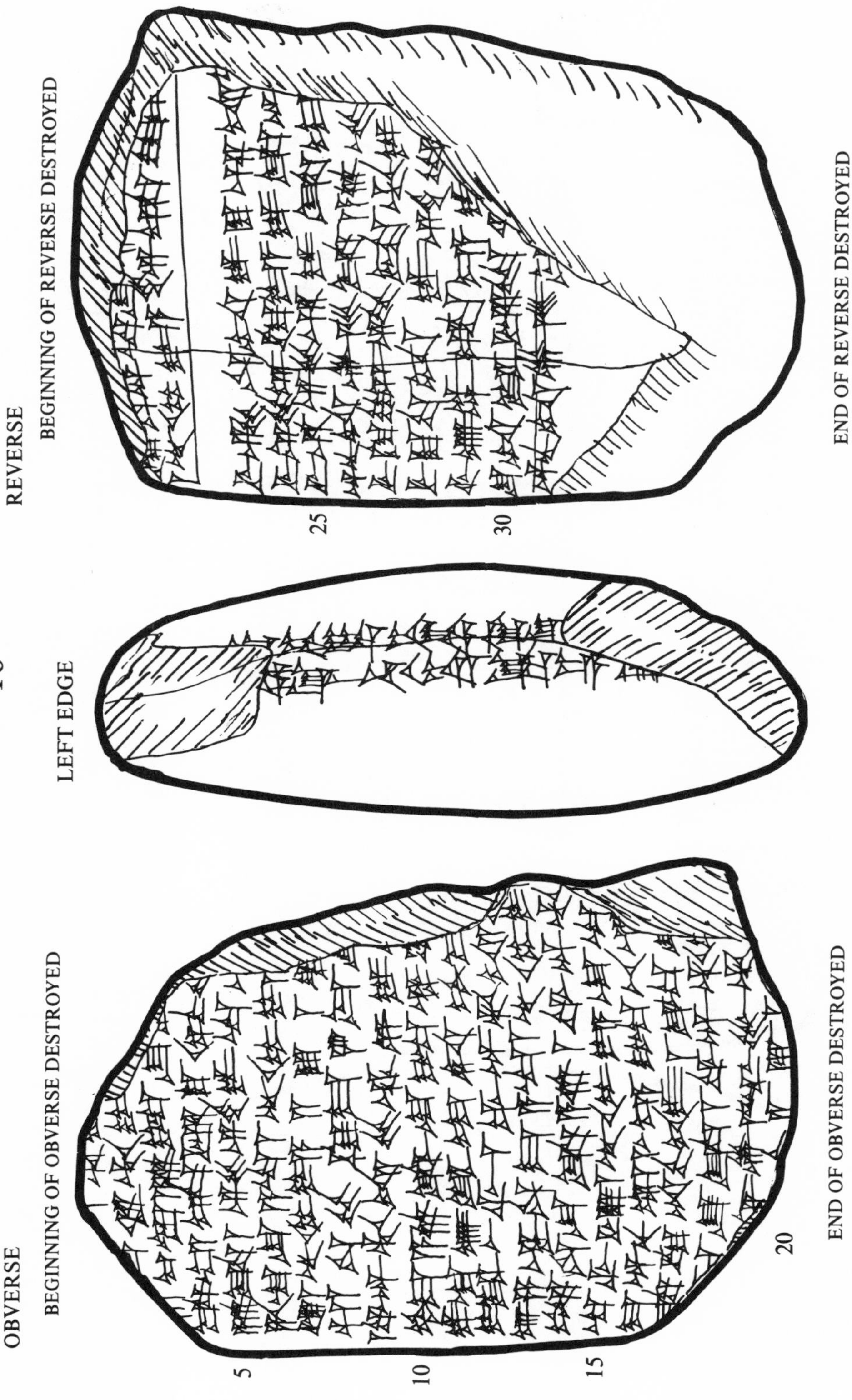
REVERSE
BEGINNING OF REVERSE DESTROYED
END OF REVERSE DESTROYED
25
30
LEFT EDGE
OBVERSE
BEGINNING OF OBVERSE DESTROYED
END OF OBVERSE DESTROYED
5
10
15
20

17

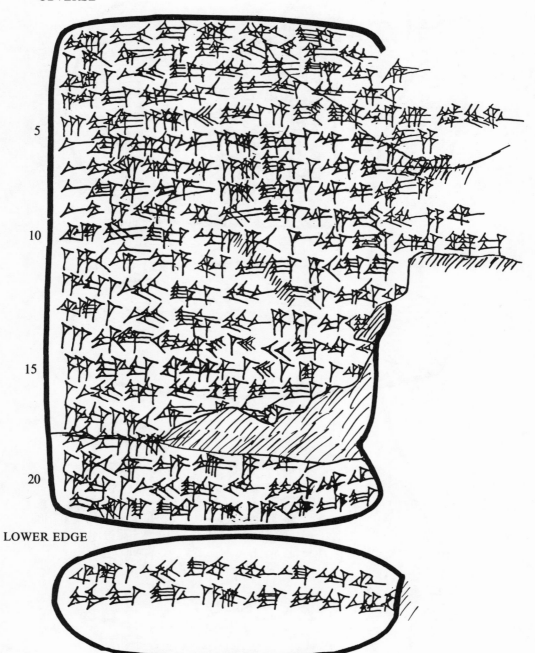

OBVERSE

LOWER EDGE

17

LEFT EDGE

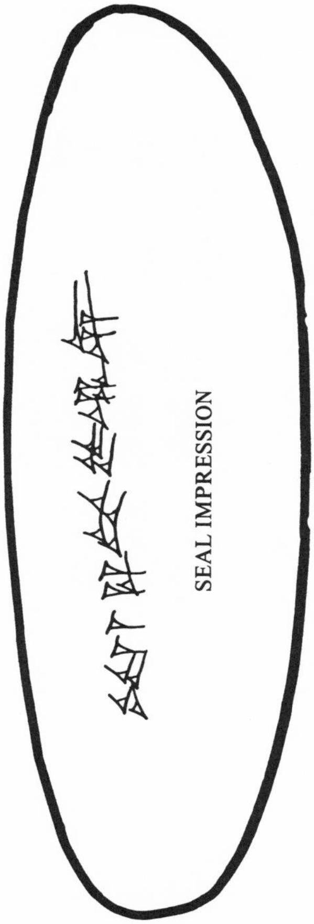

REVERSE

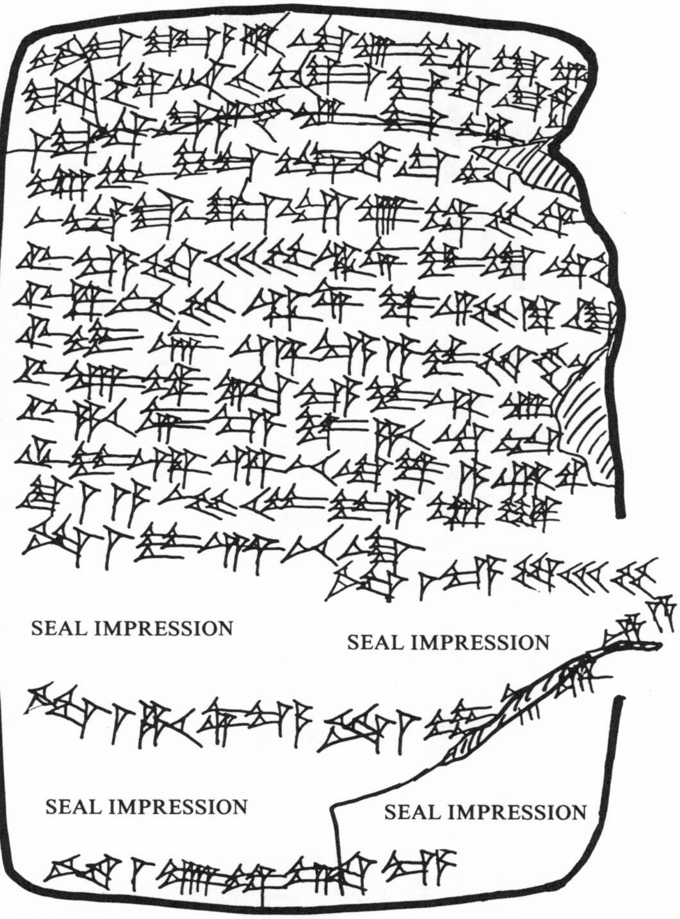

UPPER EDGE

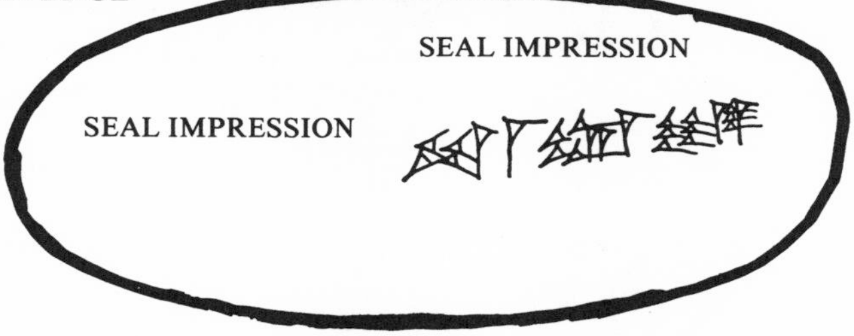

18

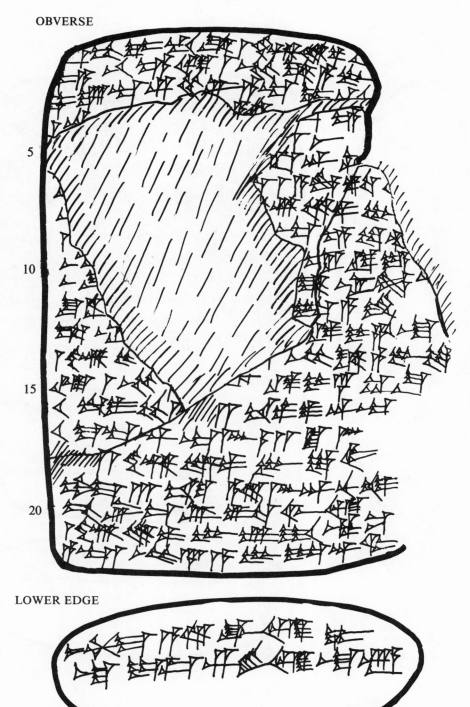

OBVERSE

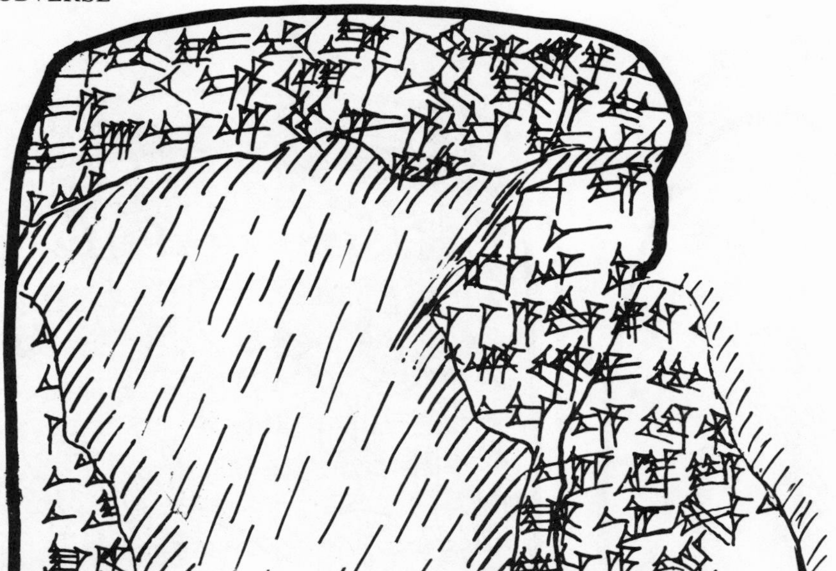

LOWER EDGE

18

LEFT EDGE

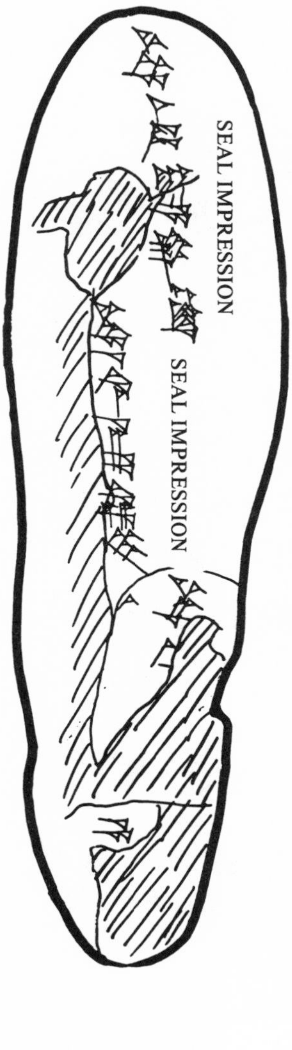

REVERSE

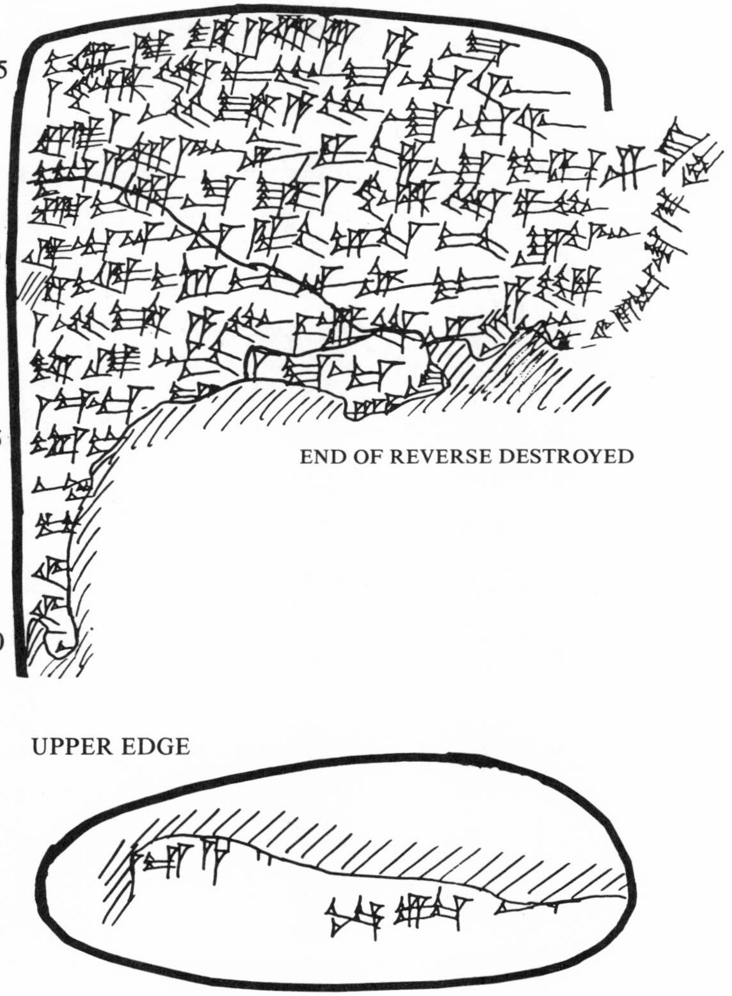

UPPER EDGE

19

OBVERSE

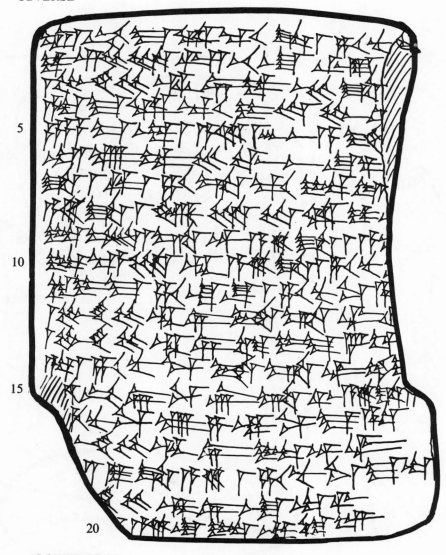

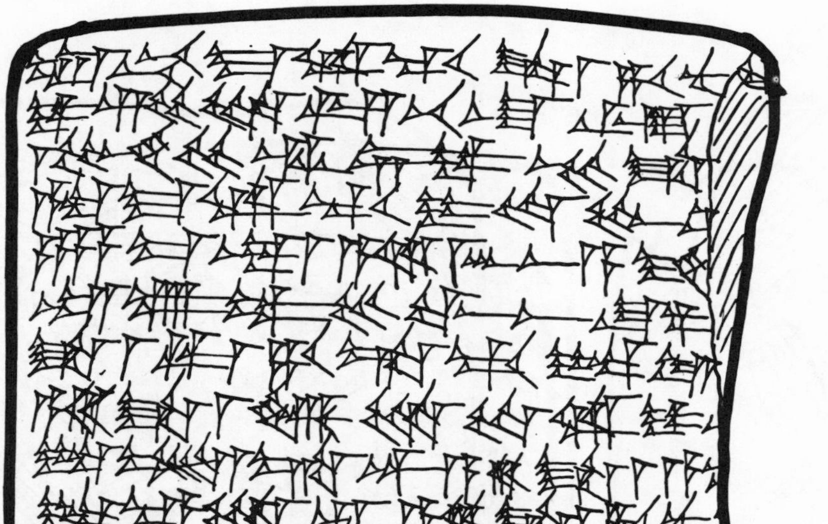

LOWER EDGE

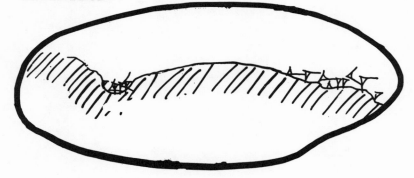

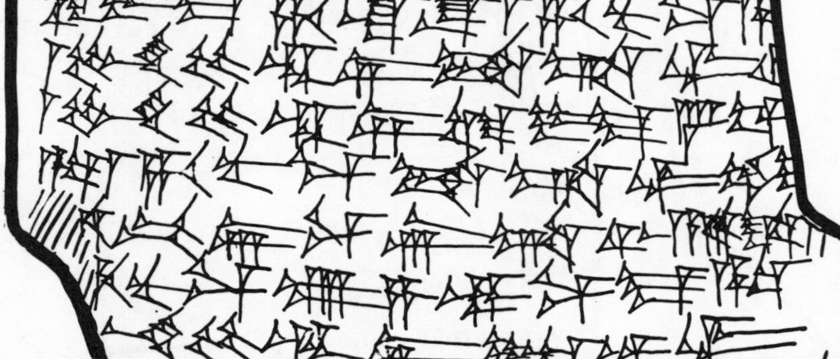

19

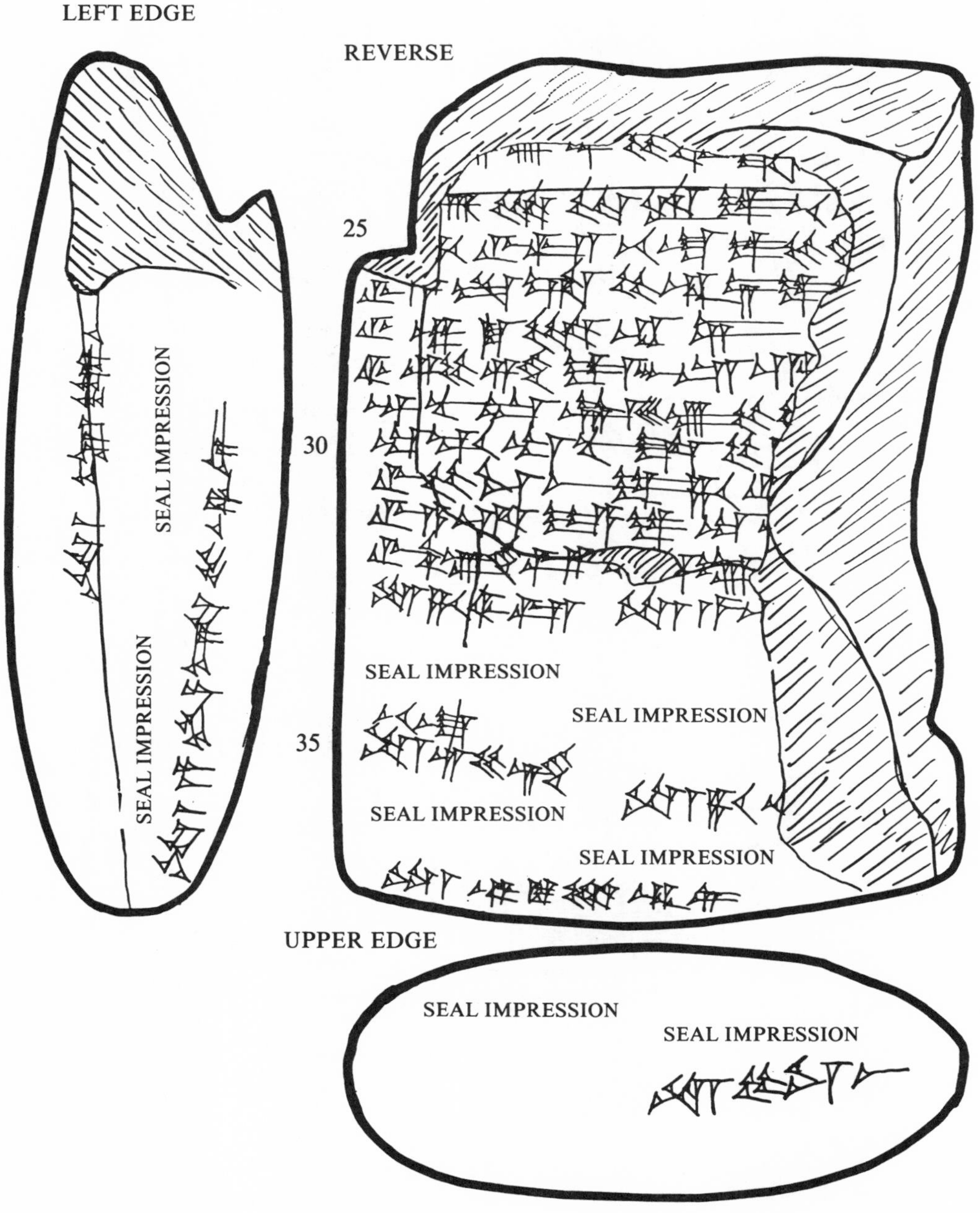
LEFT EDGE
REVERSE
25
30
35
SEAL IMPRESSION
SEAL IMPRESSION
SEAL IMPRESSION
SEAL IMPRESSION
SEAL IMPRESSION
SEAL IMPRESSION
SEAL IMPRESSION
UPPER EDGE
SEAL IMPRESSION
SEAL IMPRESSION

20

OBVERSE

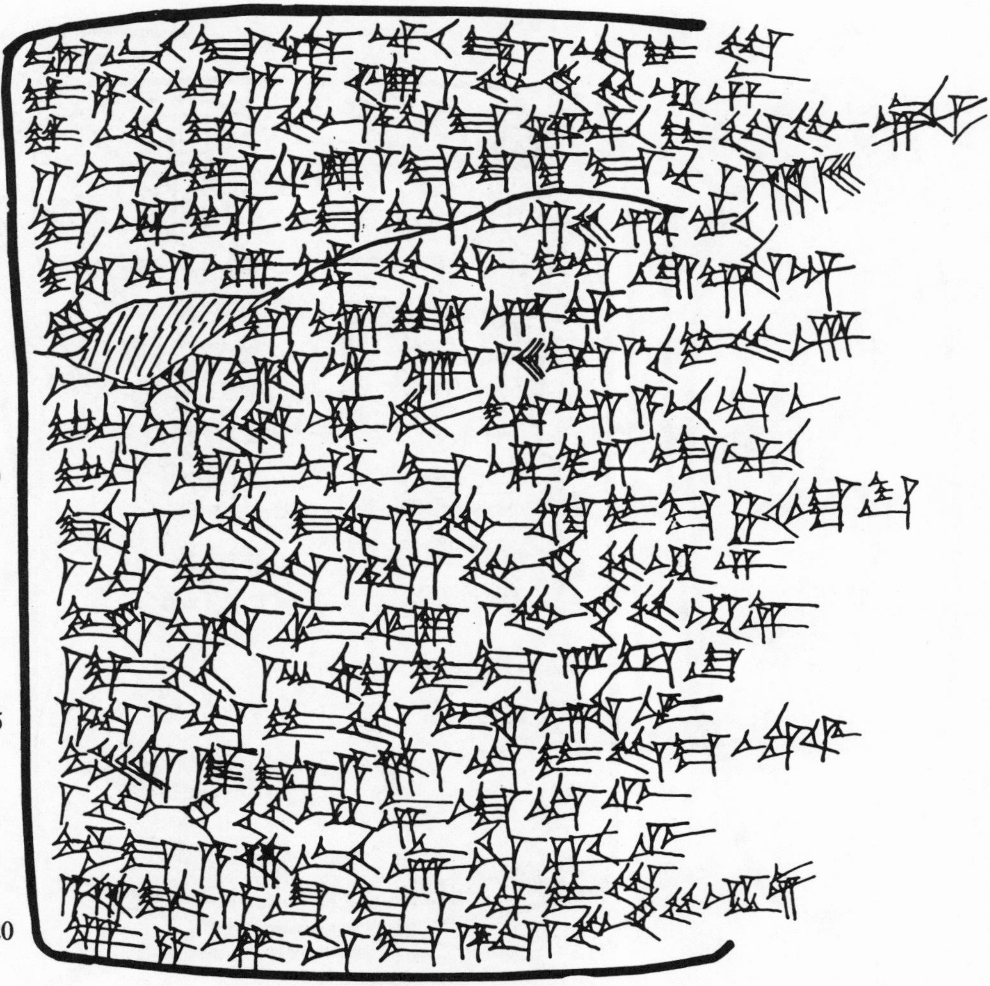

LOWER EDGE

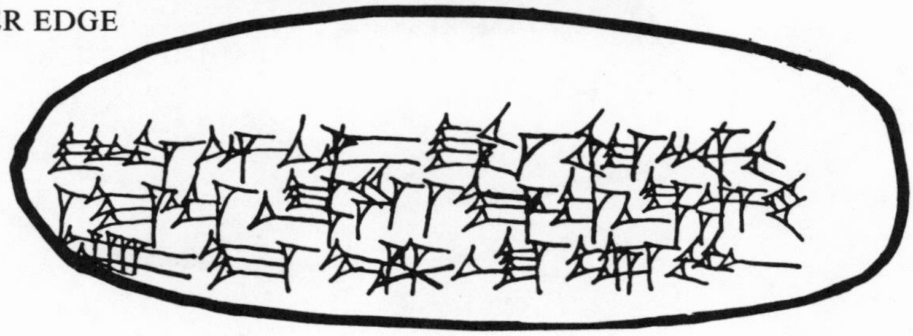

20

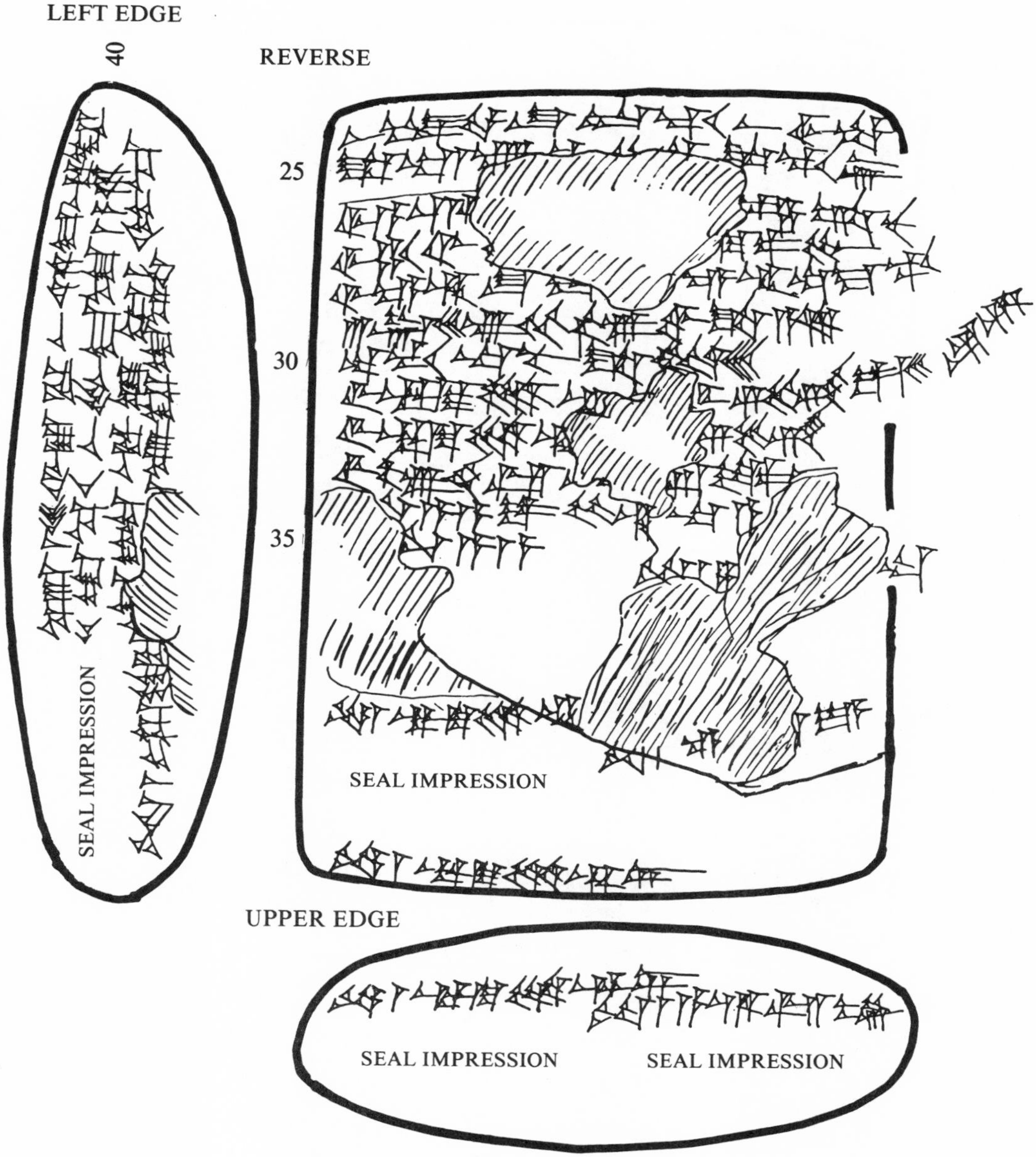
LEFT EDGE
40
REVERSE
25
30
35
SEAL IMPRESSION
SEAL IMPRESSION
UPPER EDGE
SEAL IMPRESSION
SEAL IMPRESSION

21

OBVERSE

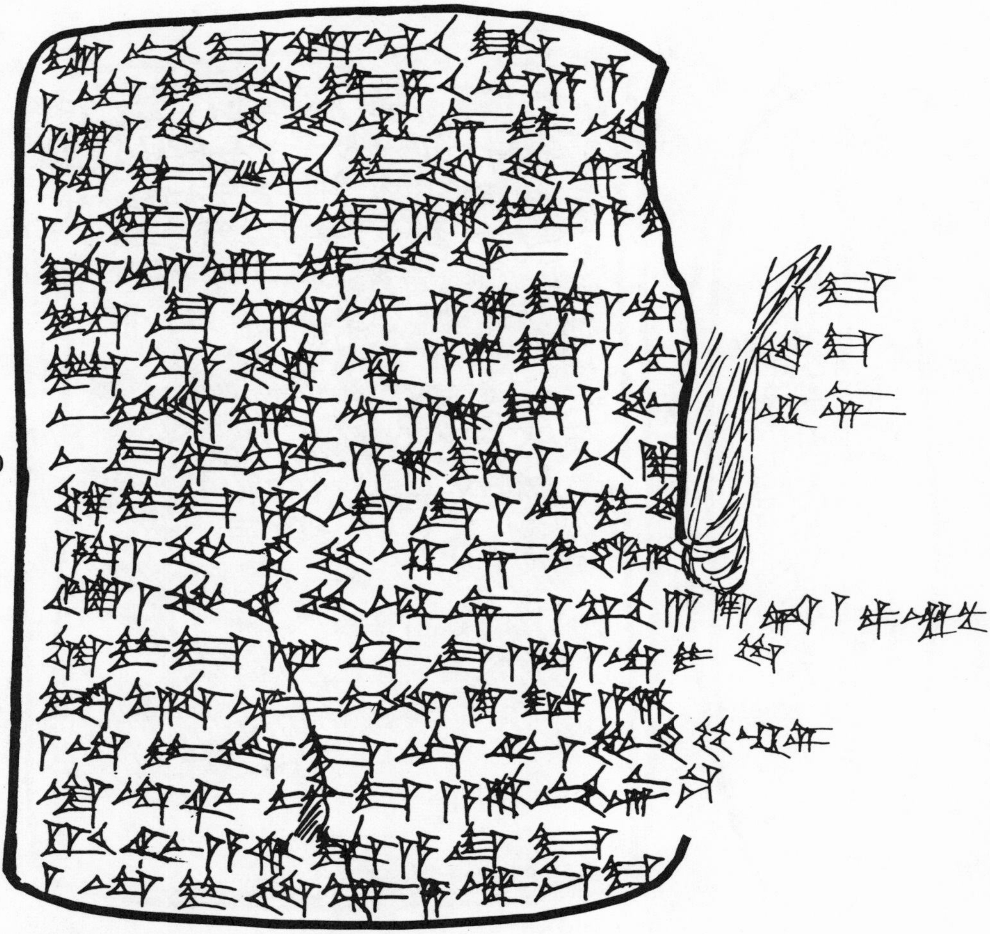

LOWER EDGE

21

LEFT EDGE

REVERSE

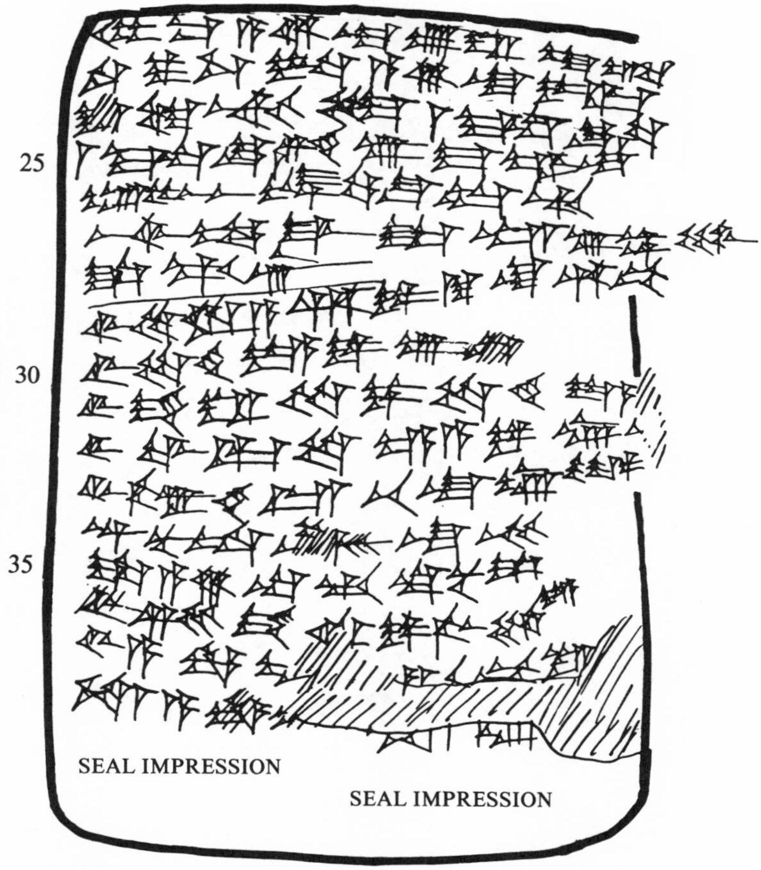

UPPER EDGE

22

OBVERSE

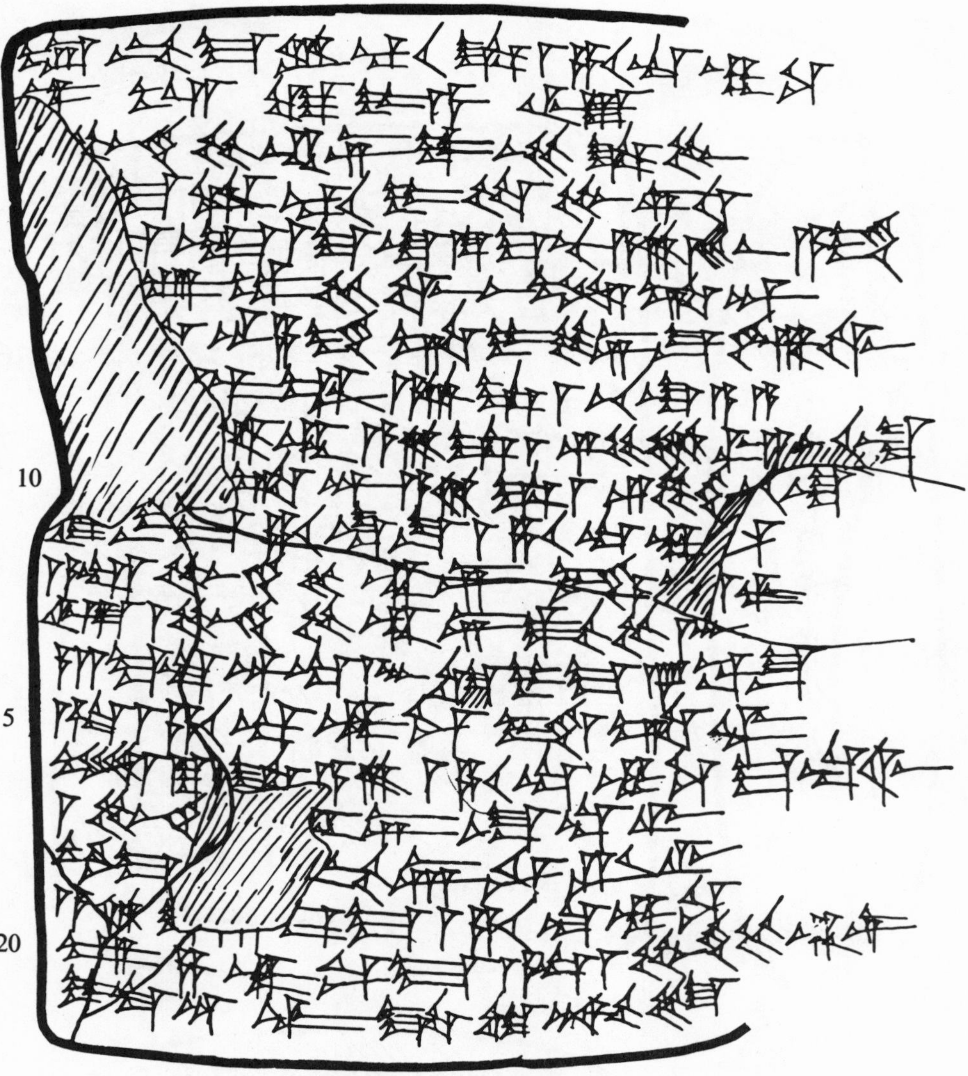

LOWER EDGE

22

REVERSE

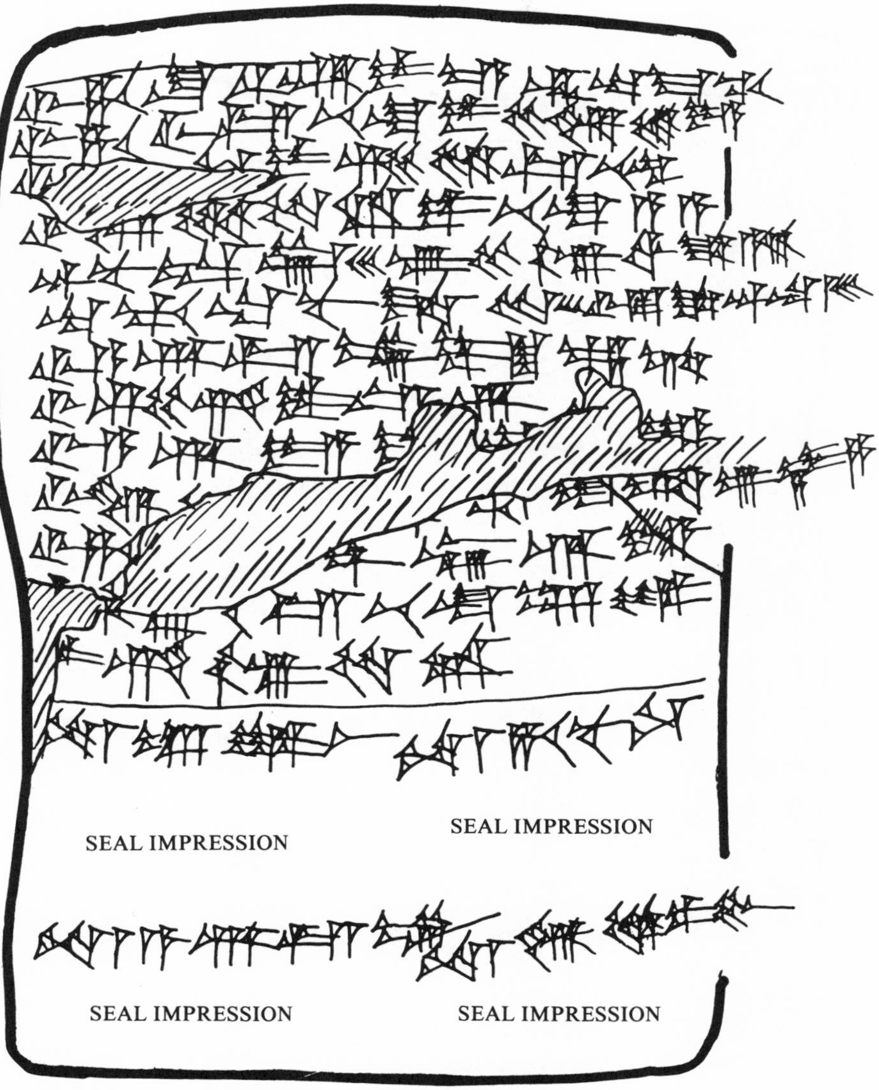

UPPER EDGE

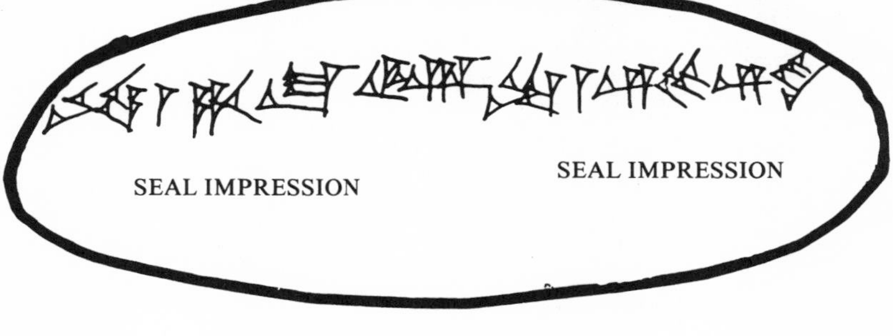

23

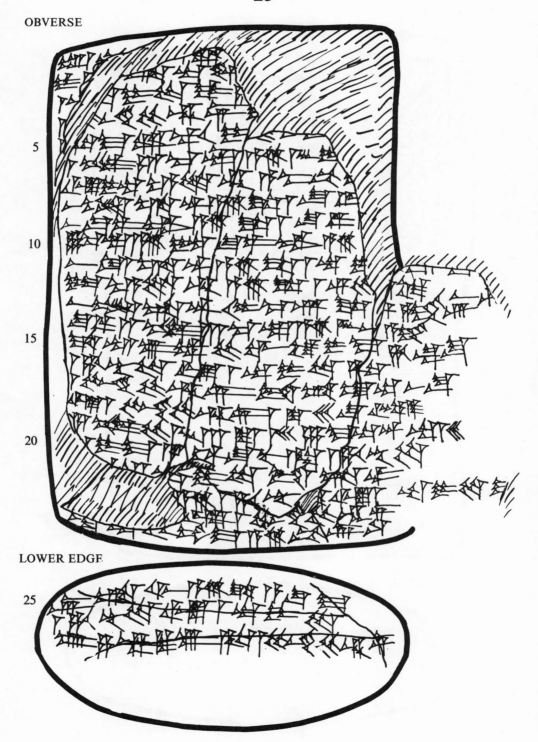

OBVERSE

LOWER EDGE

23

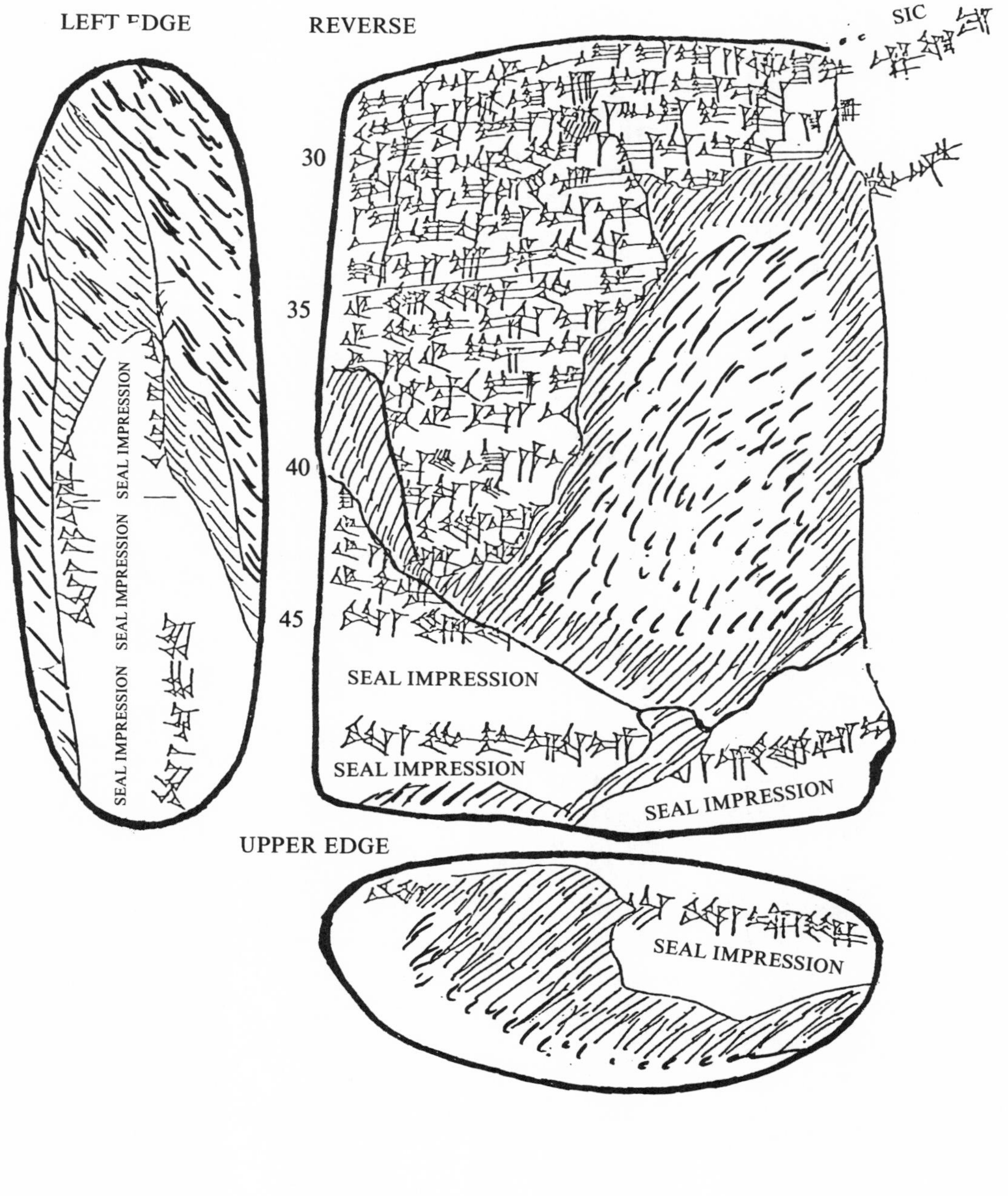
LEFT EDGE
REVERSE
SIC
30
35
40
45
SEAL IMPRESSION
SEAL IMPRESSION
SEAL IMPRESSION
SEAL IMPRESSION
SEAL IMPRESSION
SEAL IMPRESSION
SEAL IMPRESSION
UPPER EDGE
SEAL IMPRESSION

27

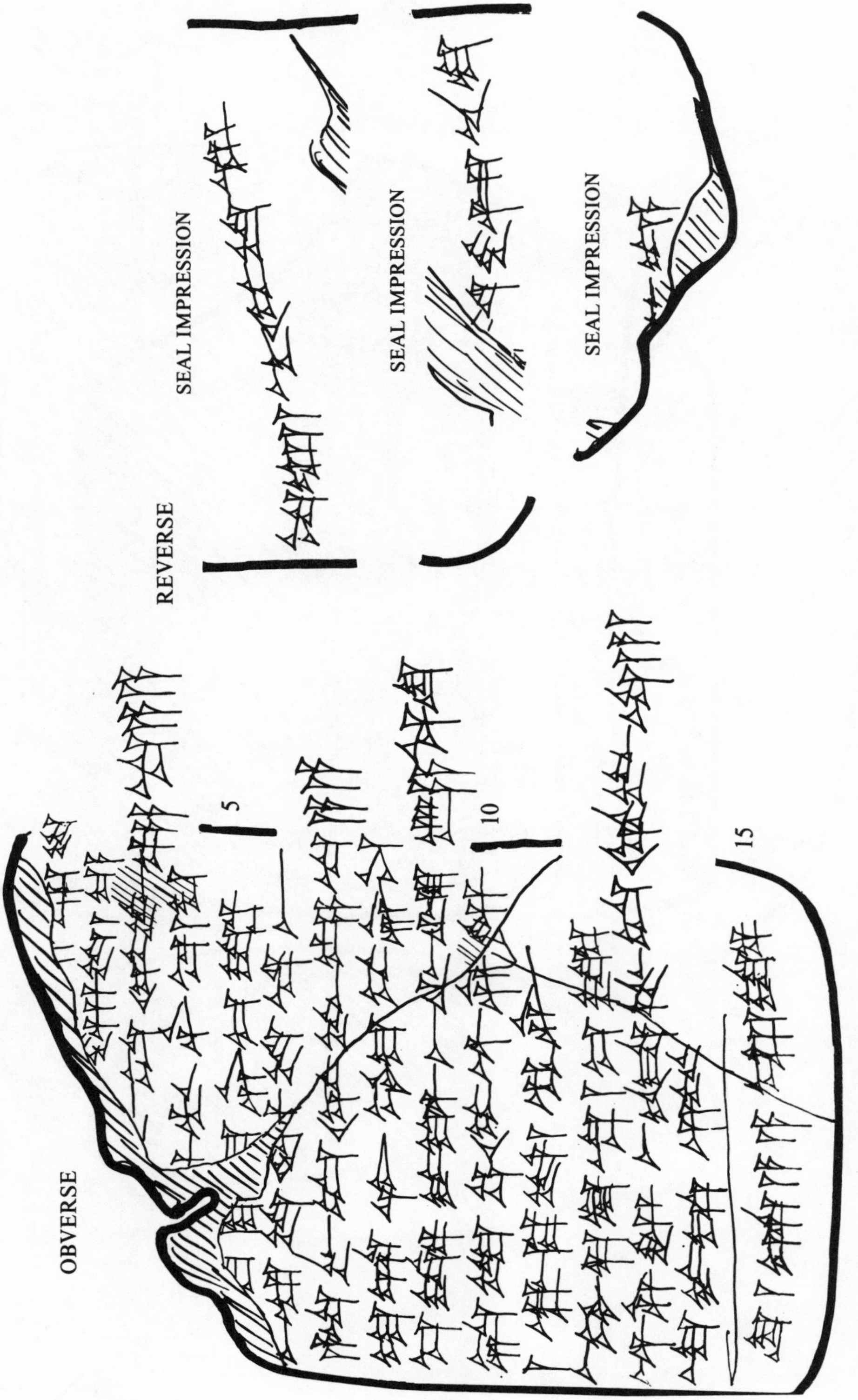
OBVERSE
REVERSE
SEAL IMPRESSION
SEAL IMPRESSION
SEAL IMPRESSION

28

OBVERSE

BEGINNING OF OBVERSE DESTROYED

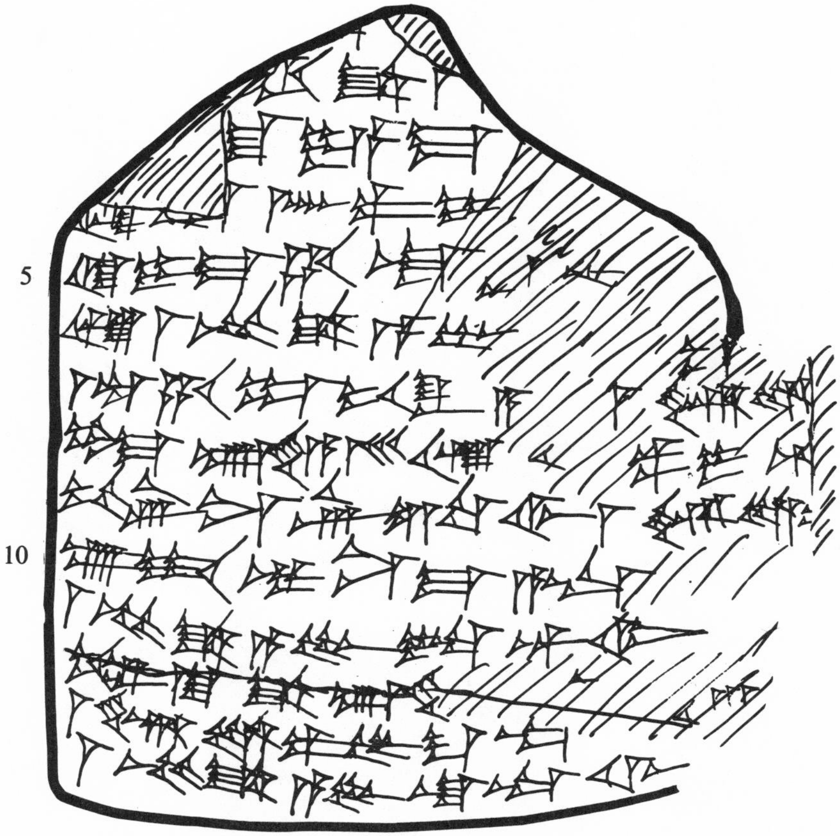

LOWER EDGE

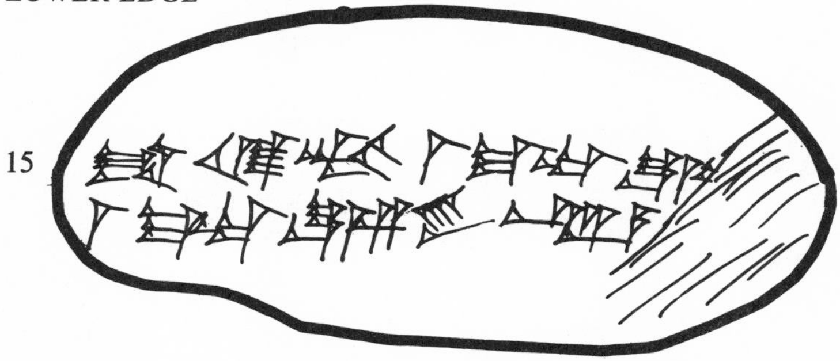

28

REVERSE

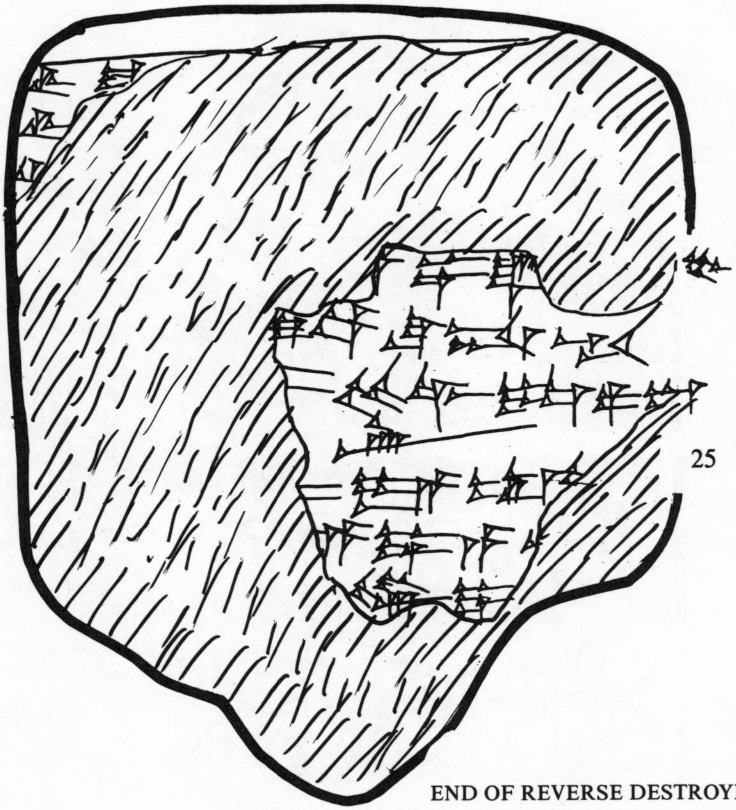

END OF REVERSE DESTROYED

LEFT EDGE

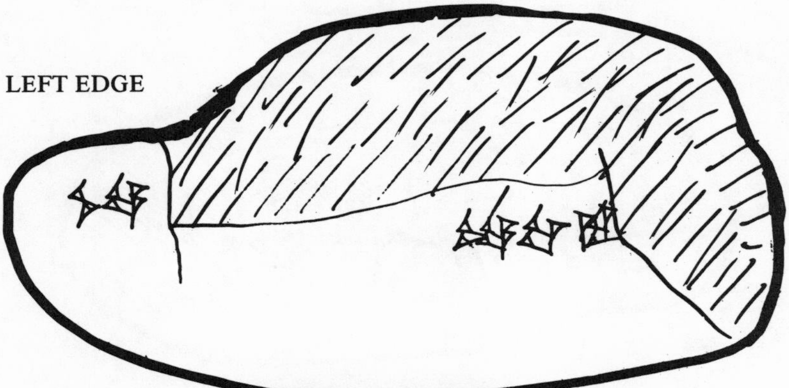

29

OBVERSE

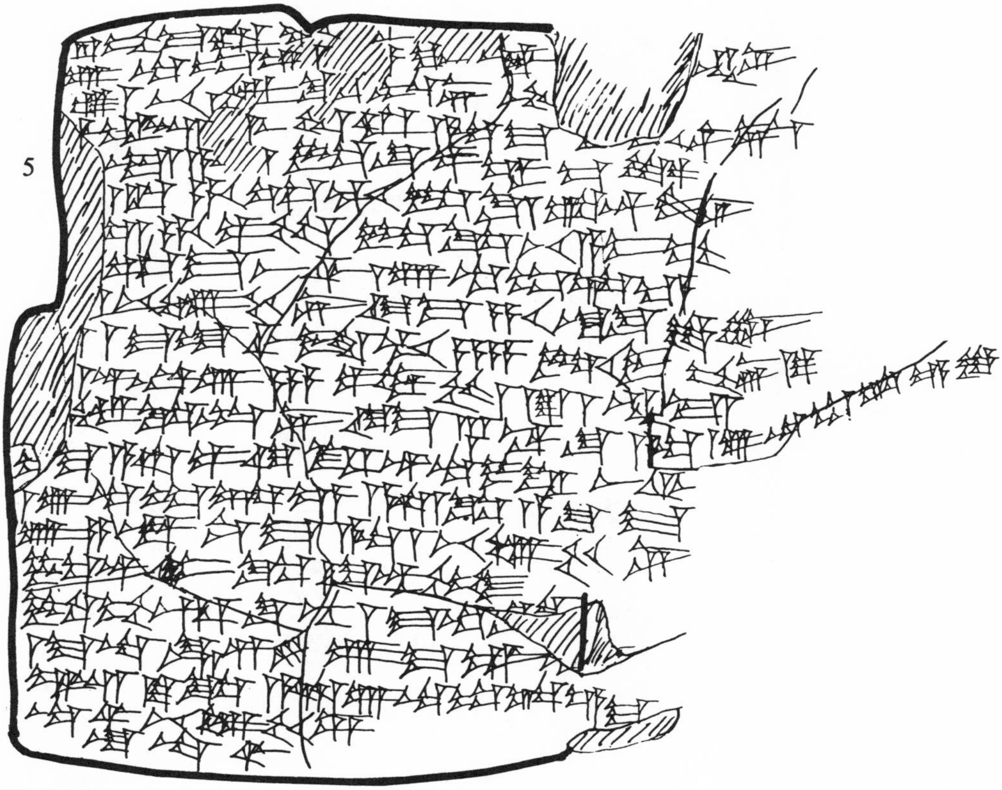

LOWER EDGE

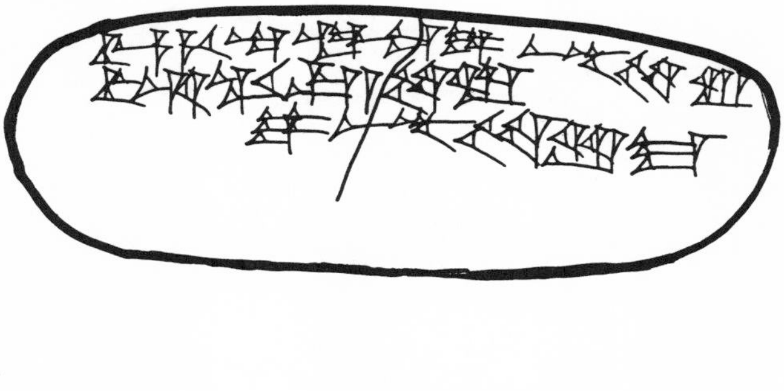

29

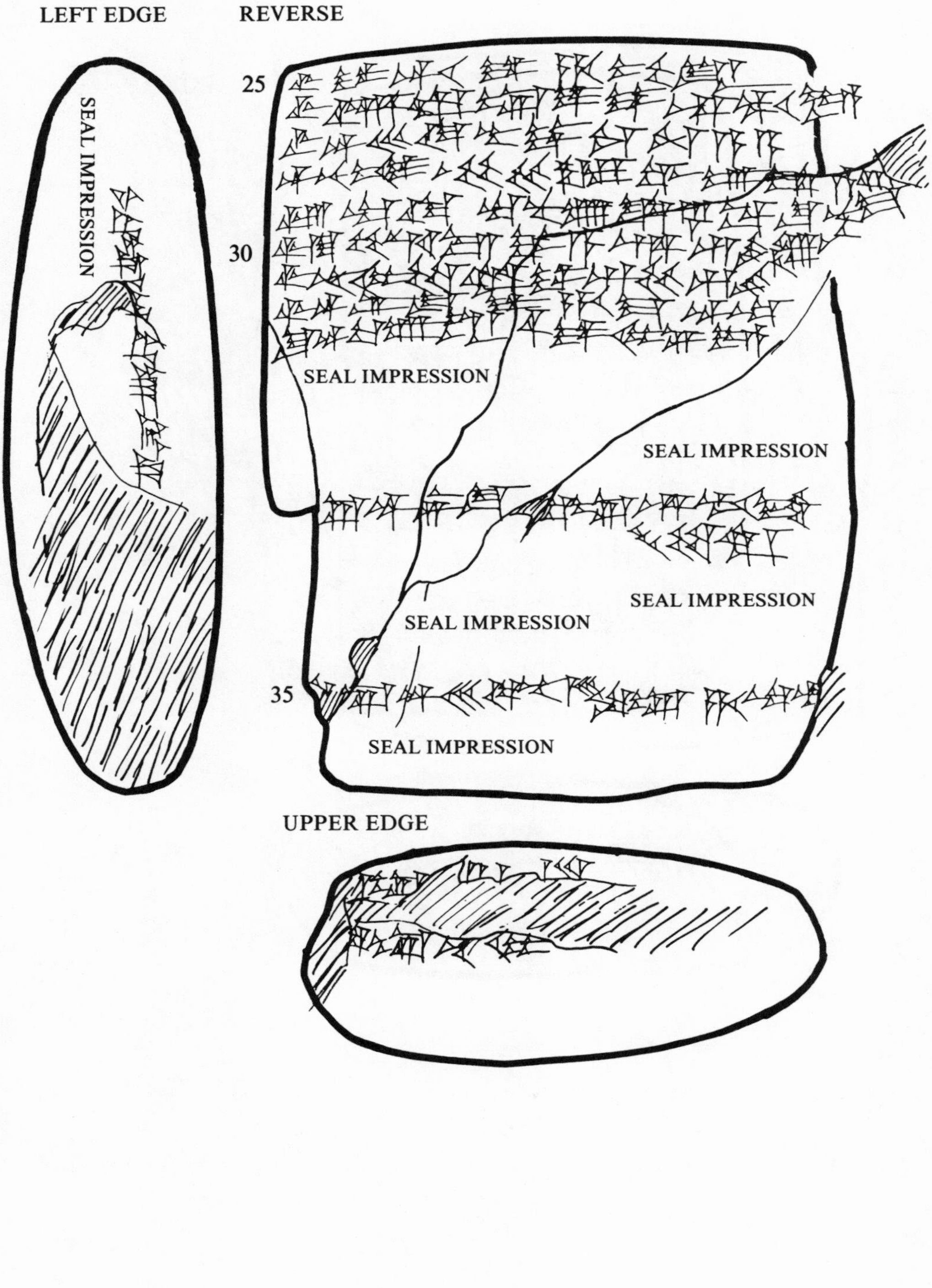
LEFT EDGE
REVERSE
SEAL IMPRESSION
SEAL IMPRESSION
SEAL IMPRESSION
SEAL IMPRESSION
SEAL IMPRESSION
SEAL IMPRESSION
UPPER EDGE

31

OBVERSE

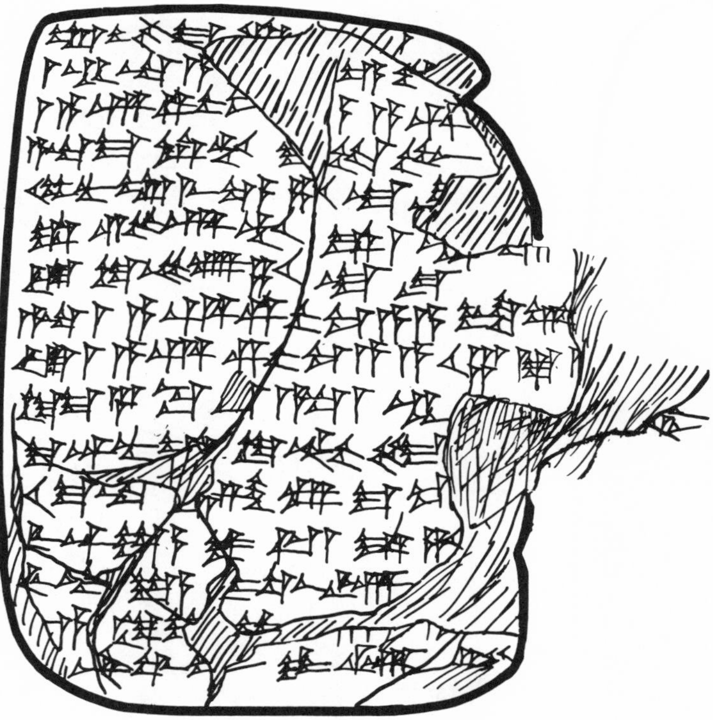

LOWER EDGE

31

REVERSE

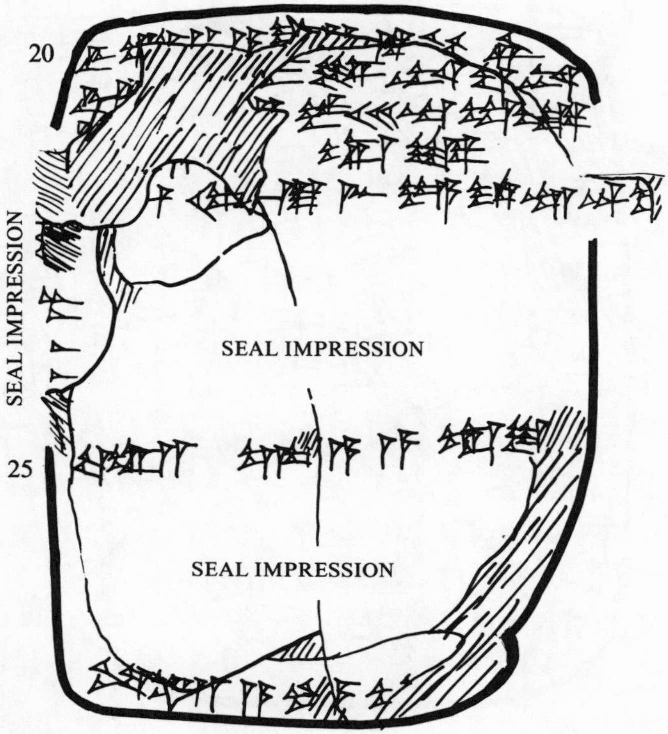

UPPER EDGE

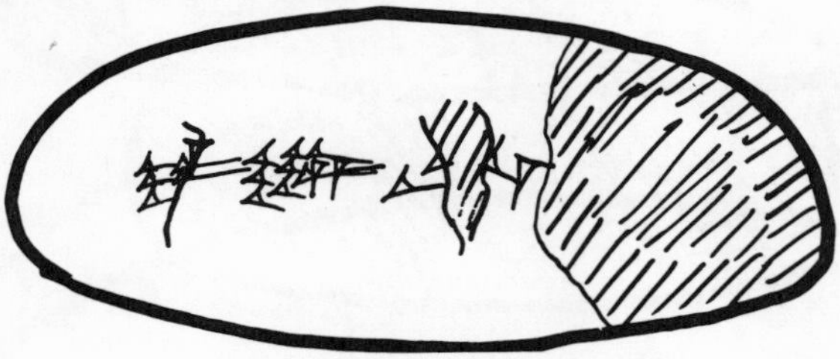

32

OBVERSE

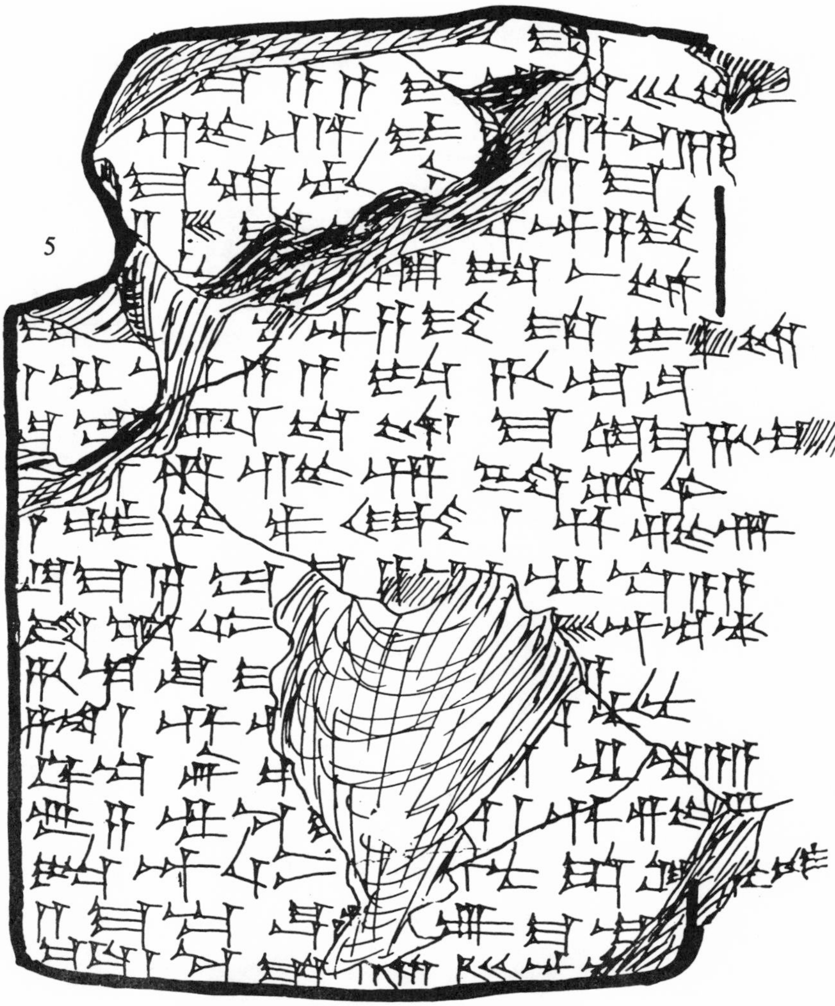

LOWER EDGE

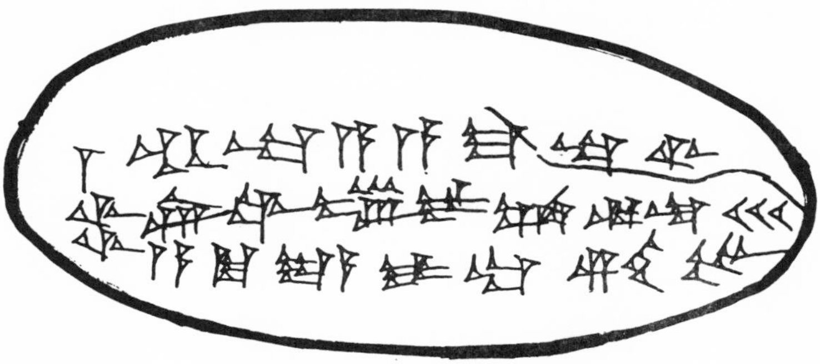

32

LEFT EDGE

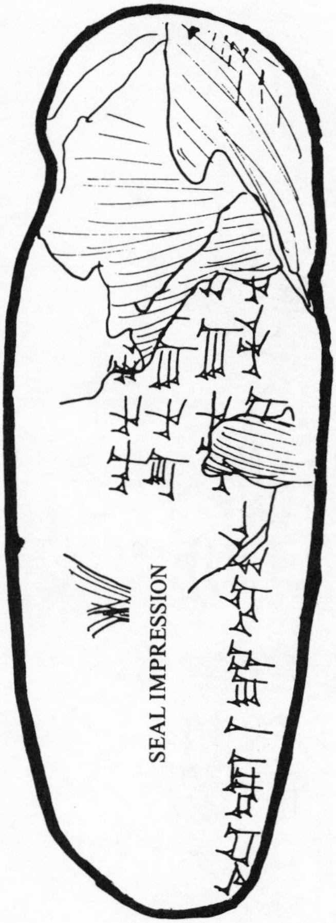

REVERSE

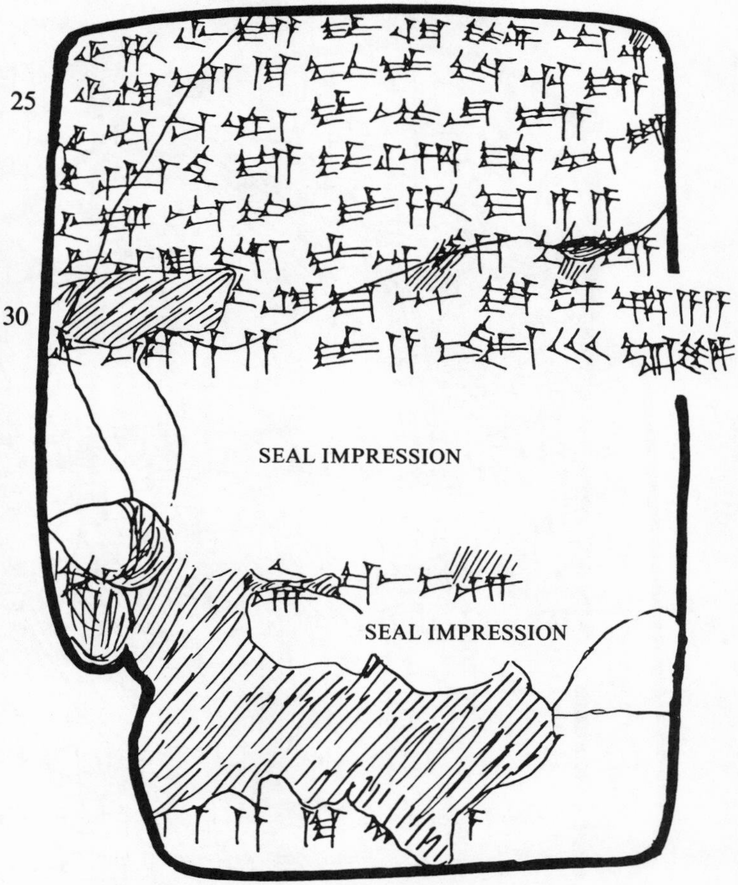

UPPER EDGE

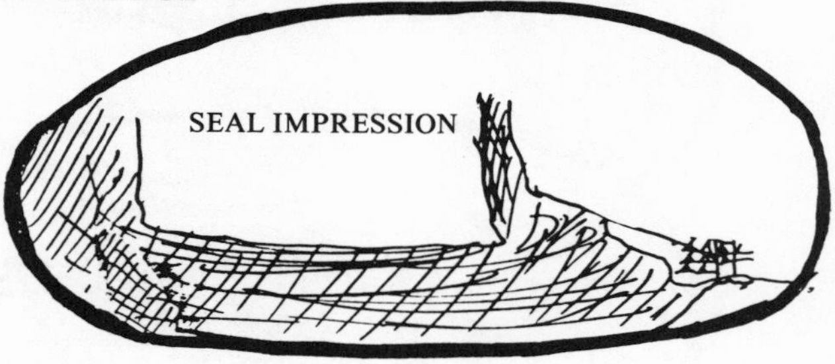

33

OBVERSE

BEGINNING OF OBVERSE DESTROYED

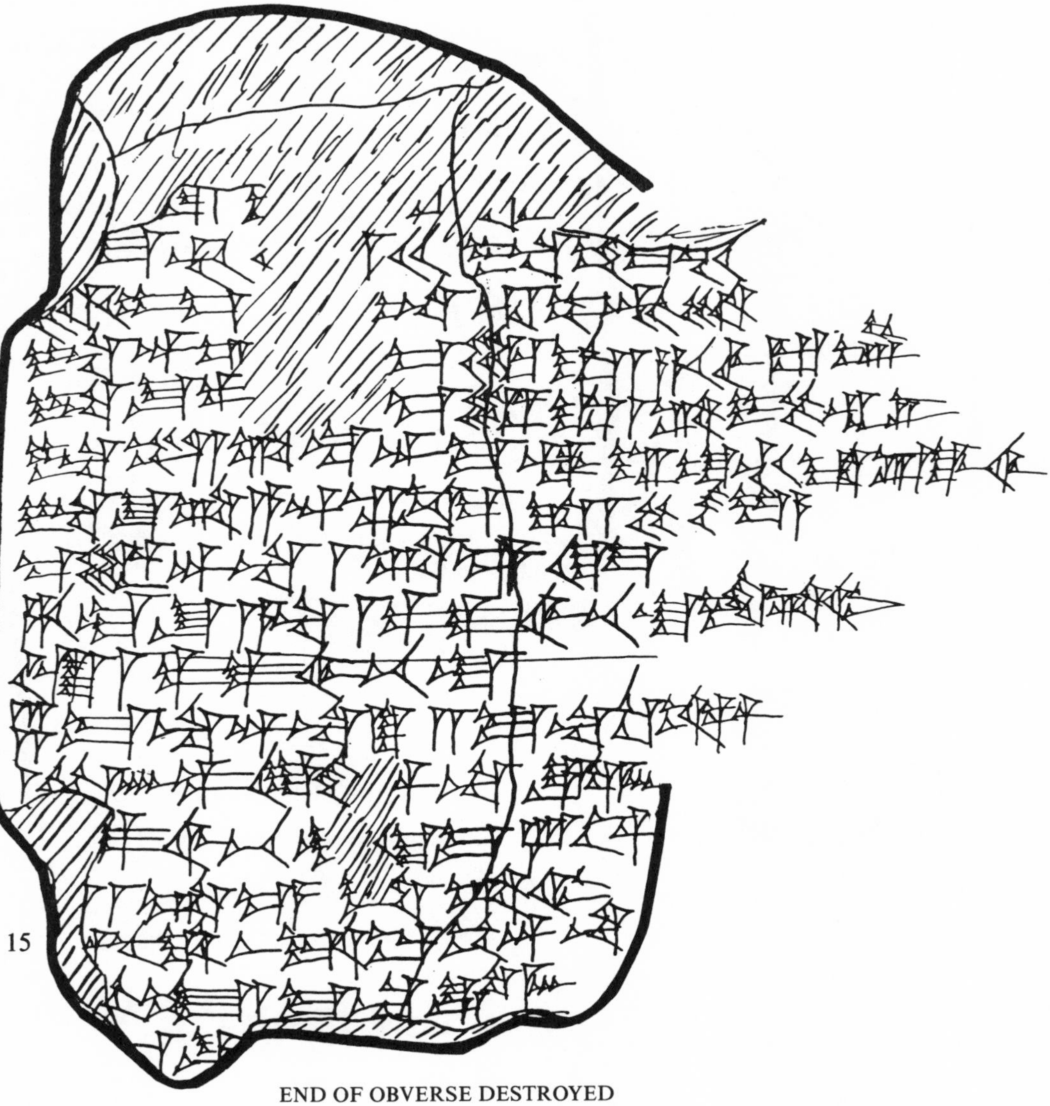

END OF OBVERSE DESTROYED

33

REVERSE

BEGINNING OF REVERSE DESTROYED

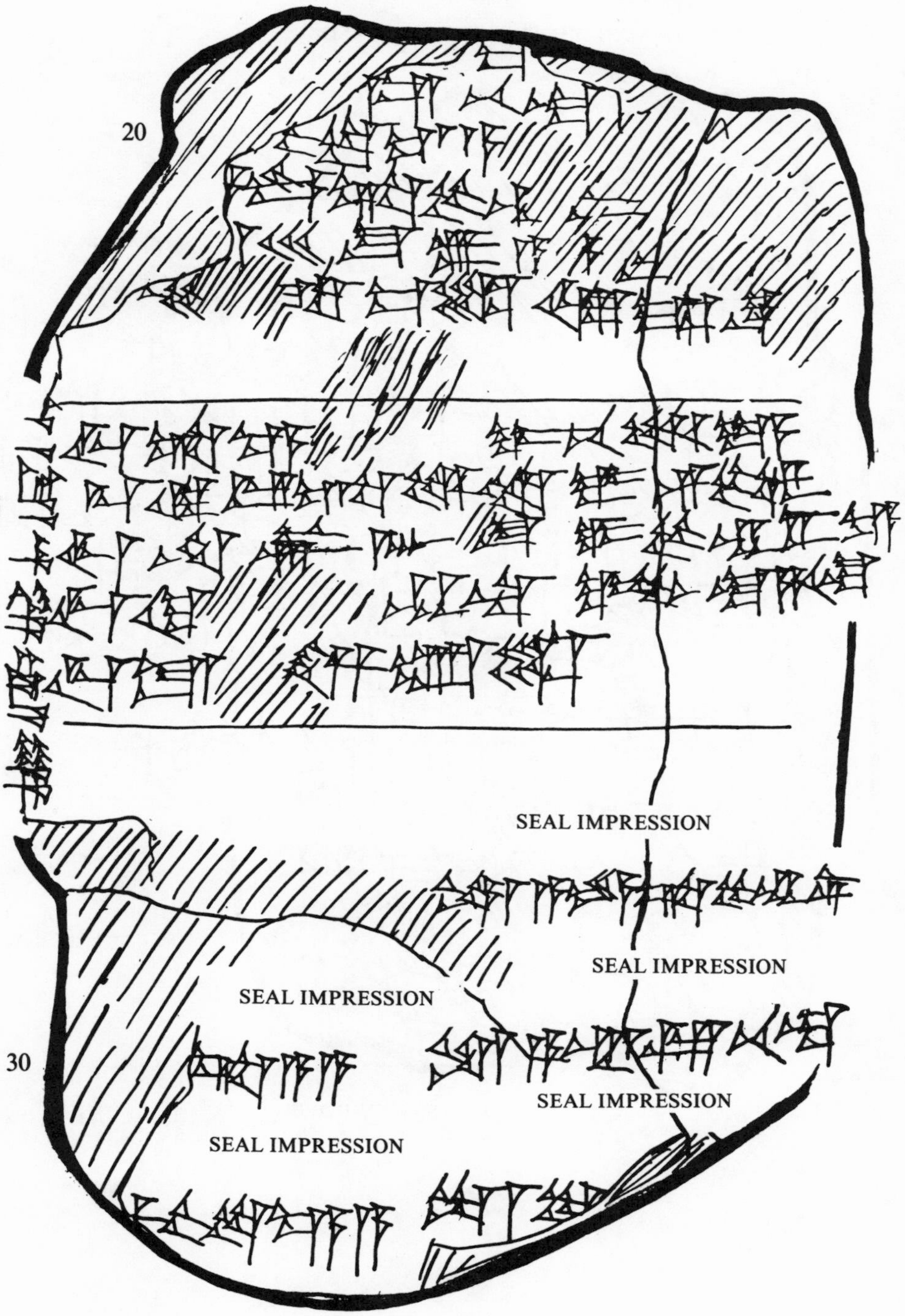

34

OBVERSE

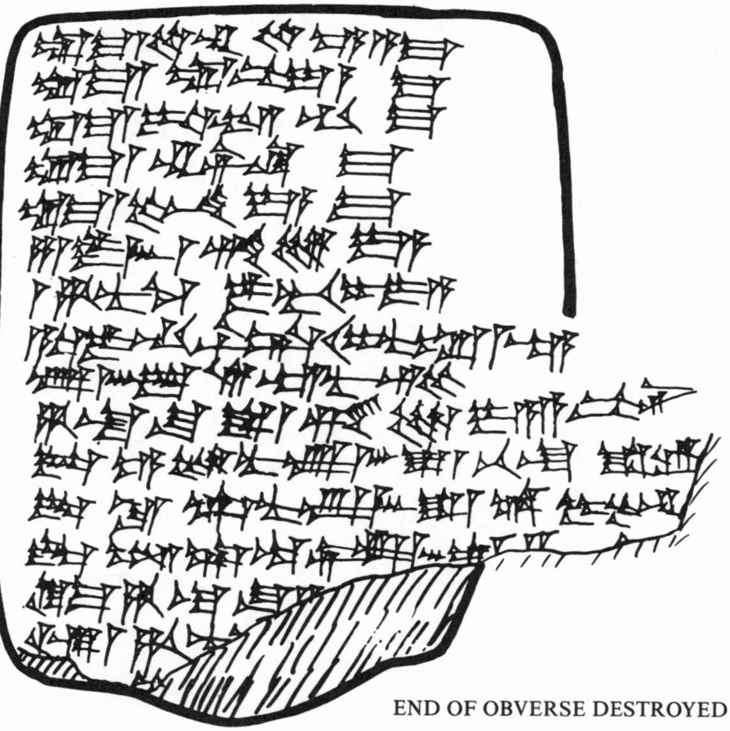

END OF OBVERSE DESTROYED

UPPER EDGE

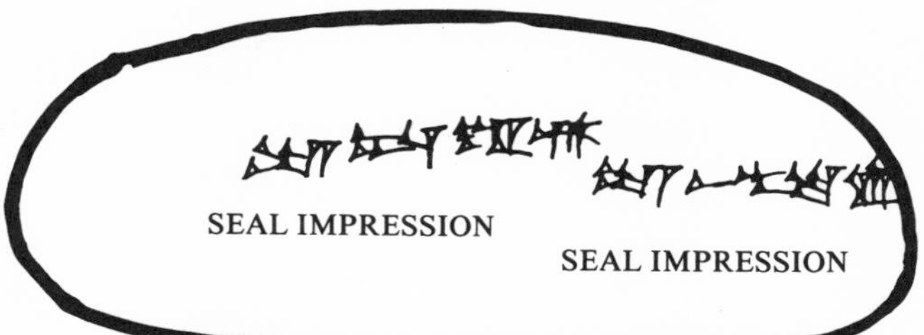

34

REVERSE

BEGINNING OF REVERSE DESTROYED

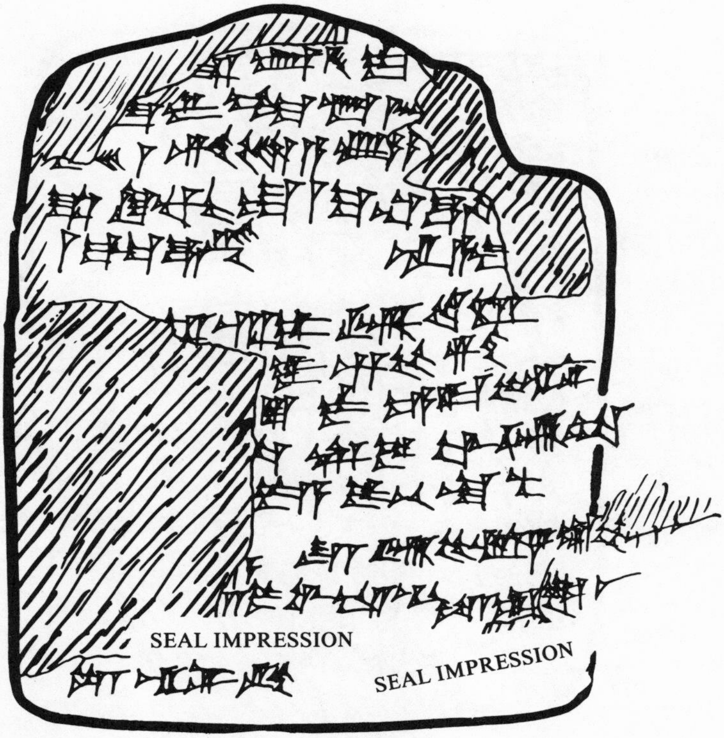

LEFT EDGE

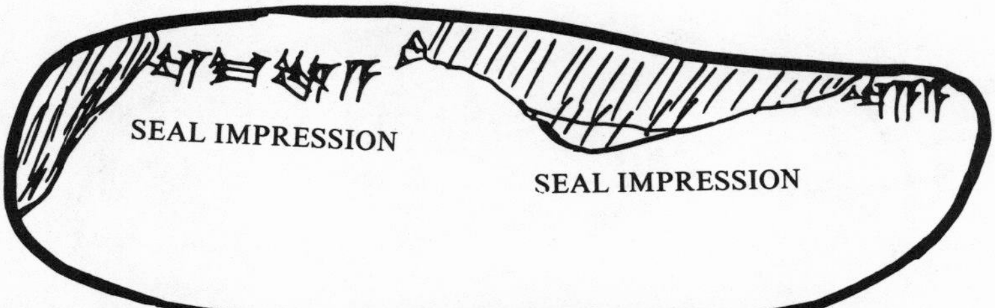

35

OBVERSE

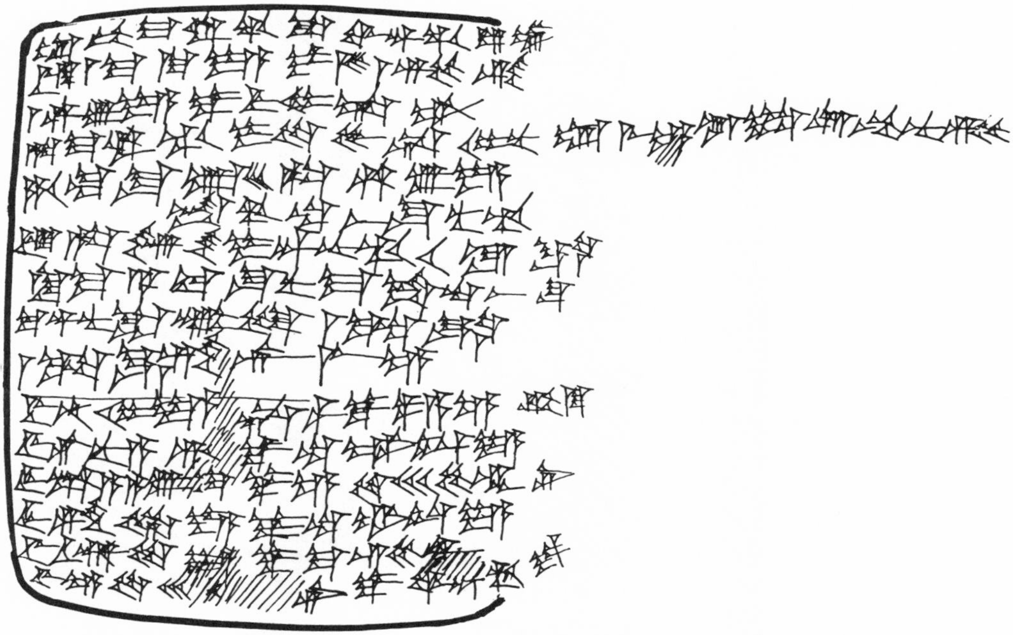

LOWER EDGE

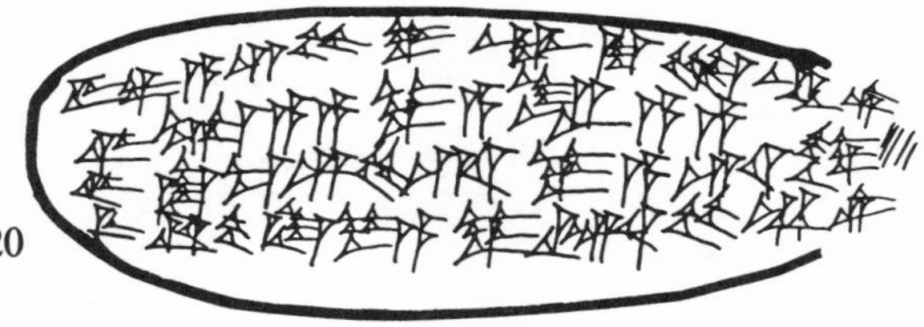

35

REVERSE

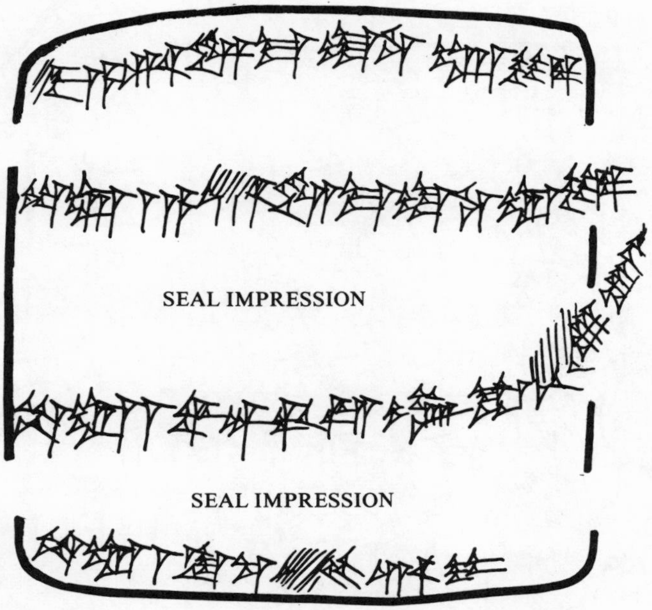

UPPER EDGE

25

36

OBVERSE

BEGINNING OF OBVERSE DESTROYED

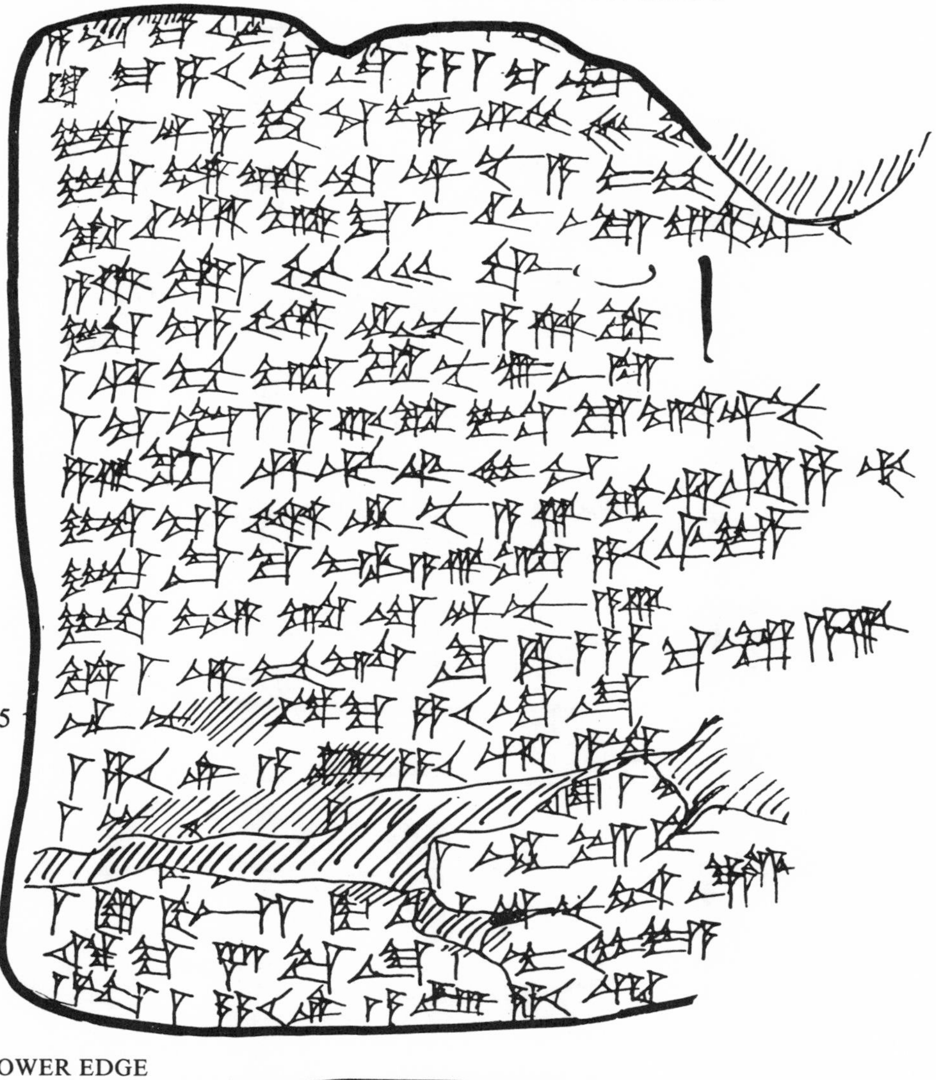

LOWER EDGE

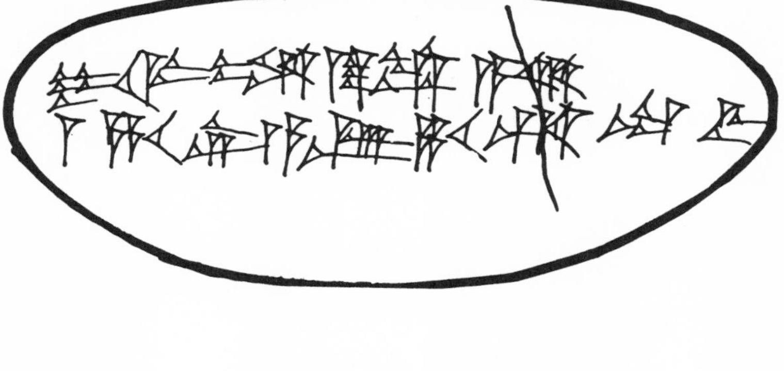

36

REVERSE

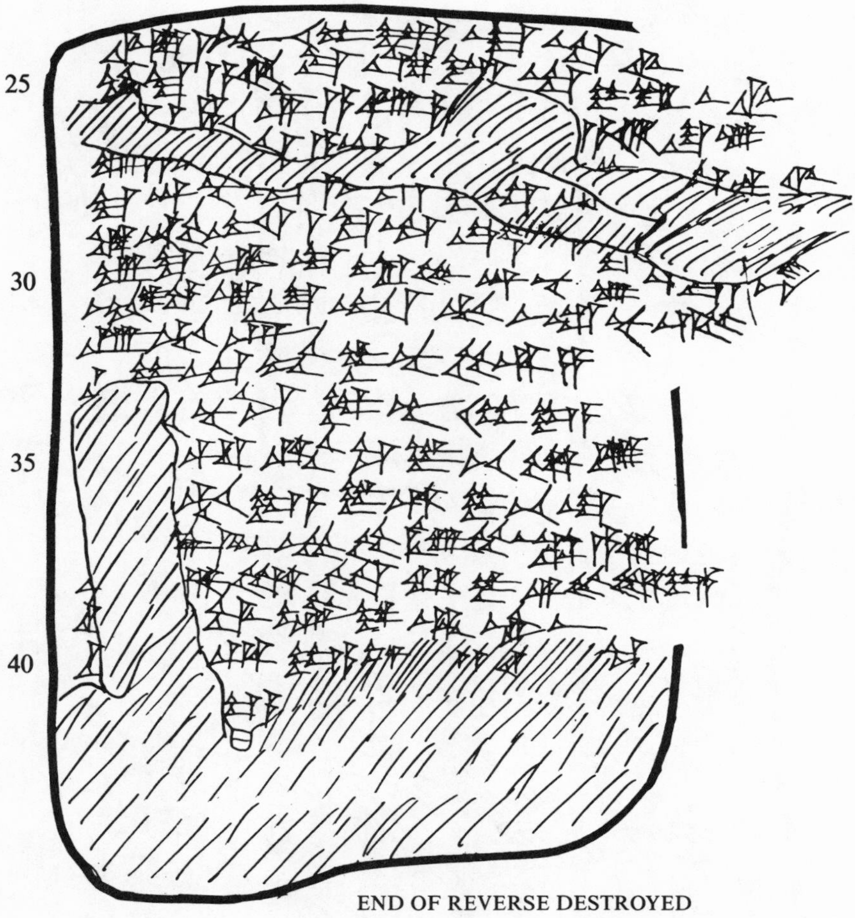

END OF REVERSE DESTROYED

LEFT EDGE

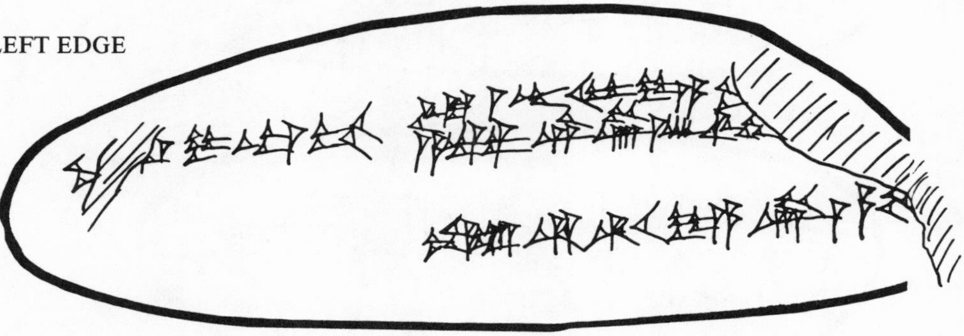

38

OBVERSE

BEGINNING OF OBVERSE DESTROYED

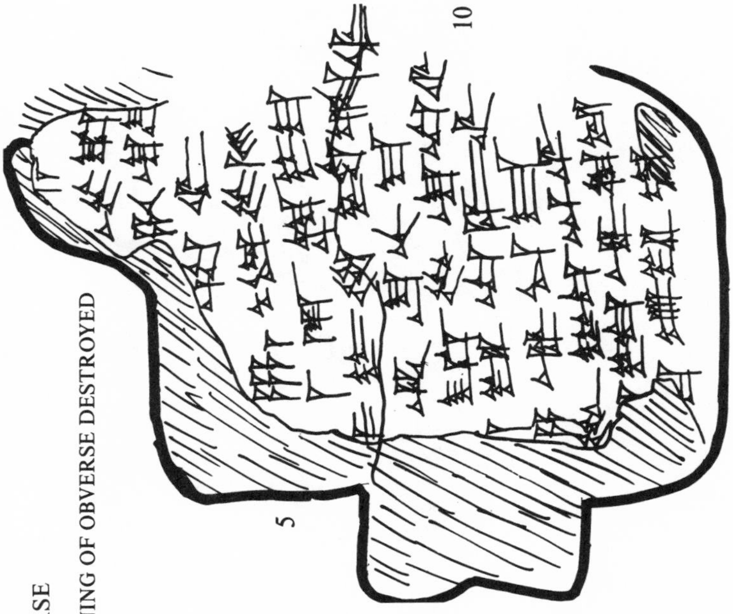

REVERSE

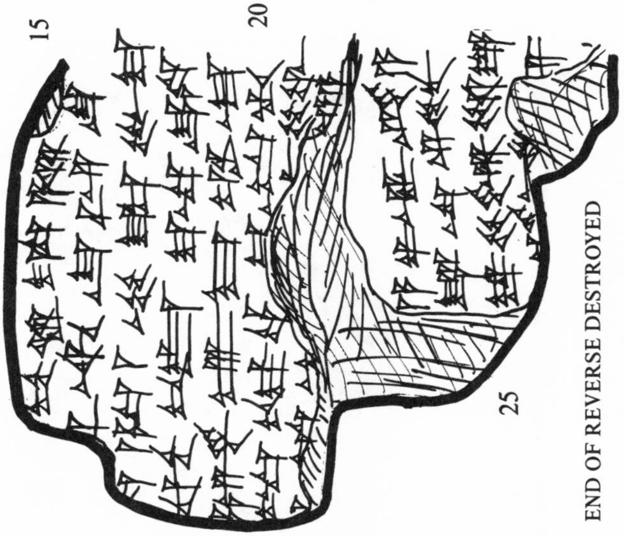

END OF REVERSE DESTROYED

39

OBVERSE

BEGINNING OF OBVERSE DESTROYED

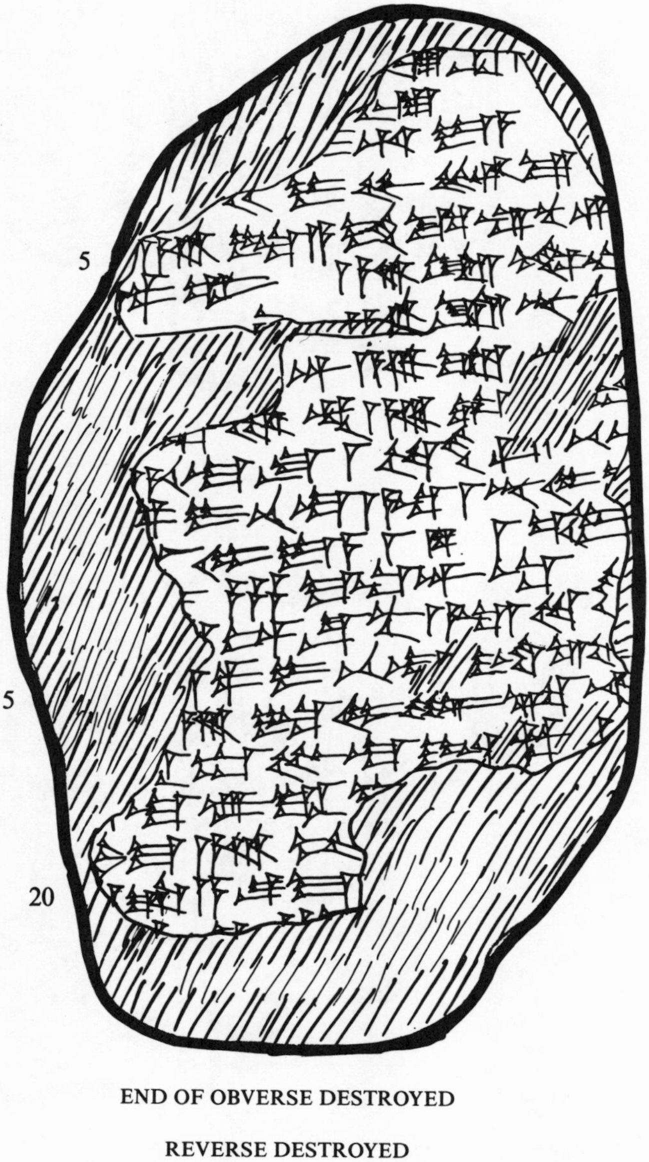

END OF OBVERSE DESTROYED

REVERSE DESTROYED

40

OBVERSE

LOWER EDGE

40

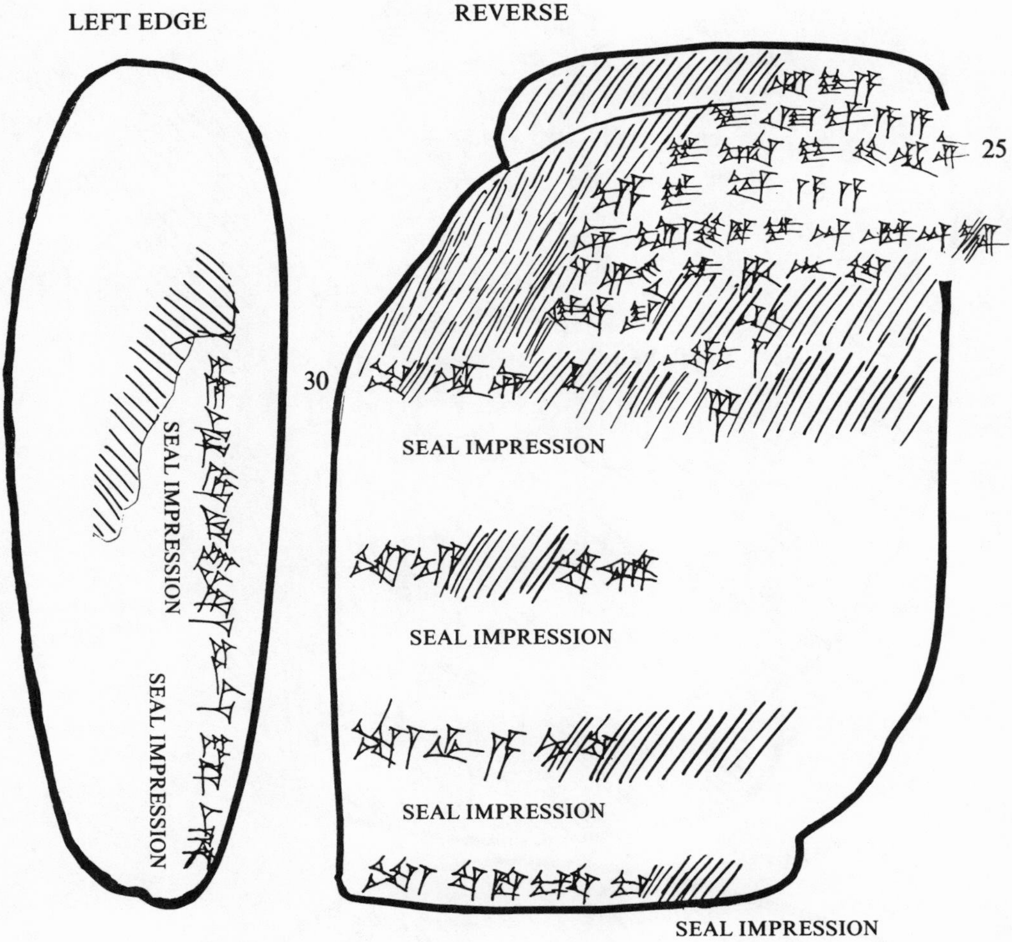
LEFT EDGE
REVERSE
25
30
SEAL IMPRESSION
SEAL IMPRESSION
SEAL IMPRESSION
SEAL IMPRESSION
SEAL IMPRESSION
SEAL IMPRESSION

45

OBVERSE

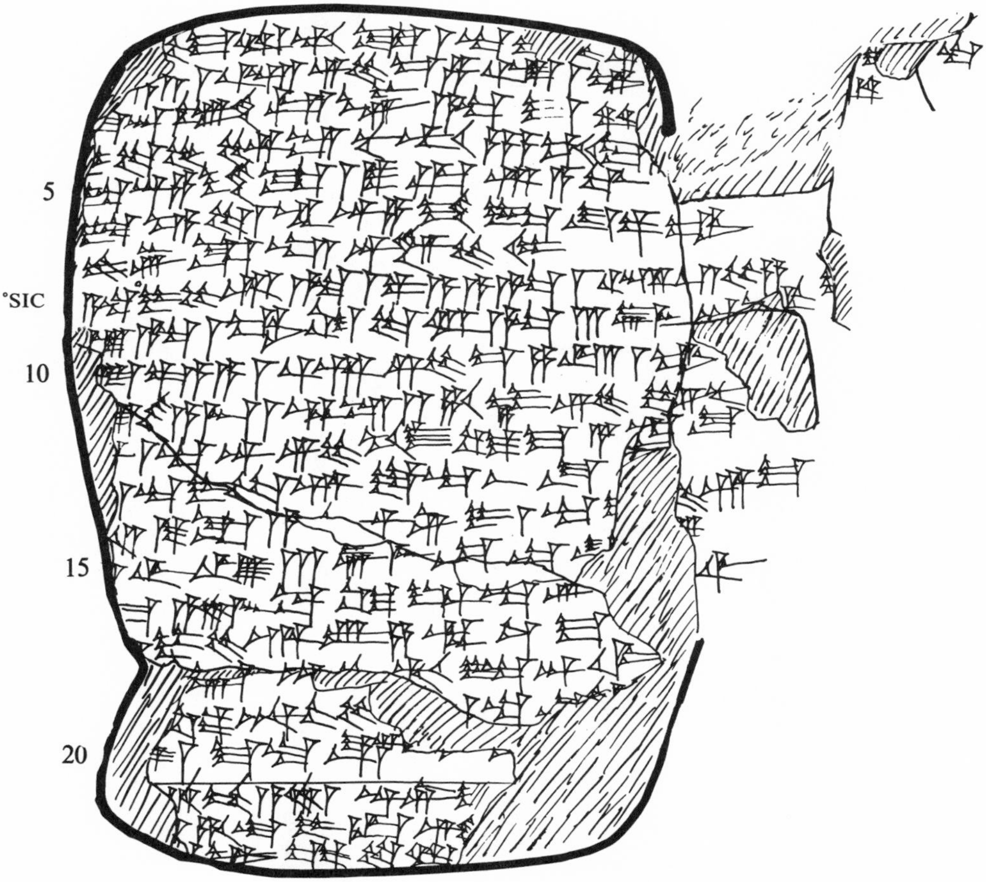

45

LOWER EDGE

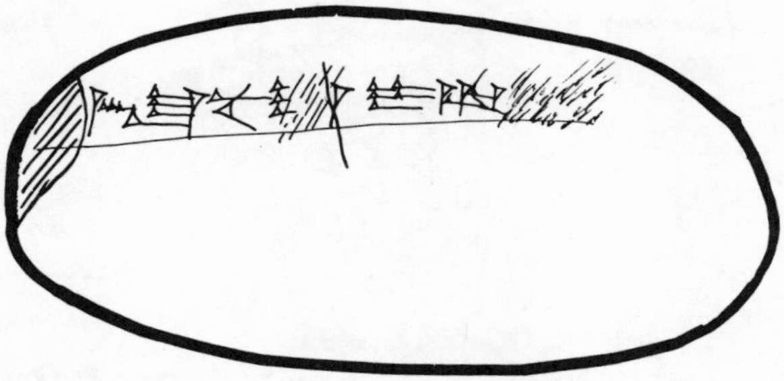

REVERSE

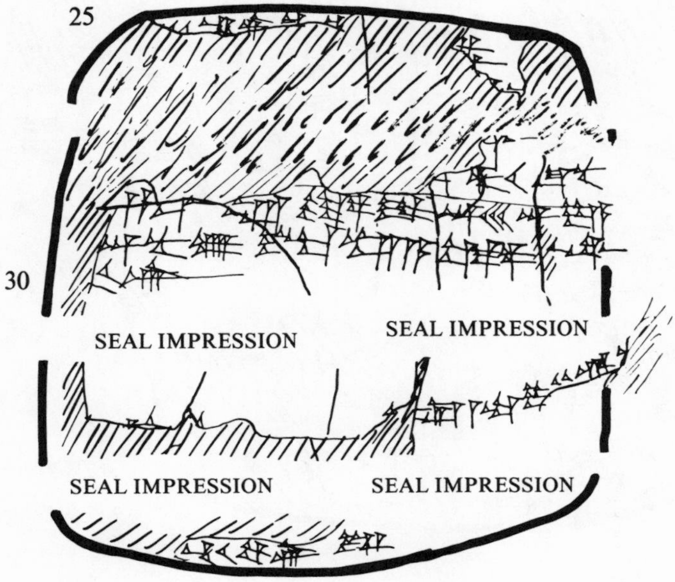

46

OBVERSE

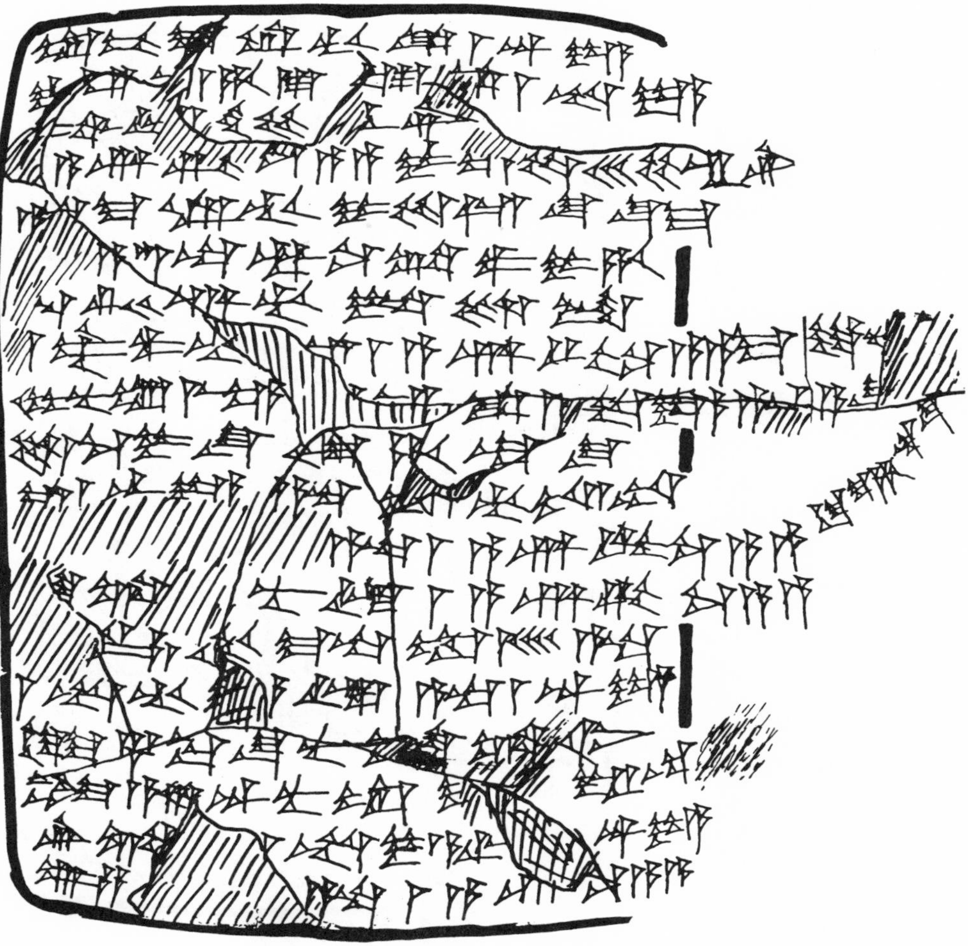

LOWER EDGE

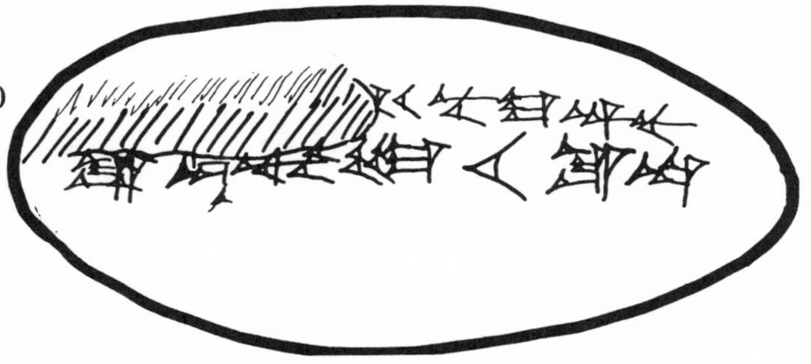

46

LEFT EDGE

REVERSE

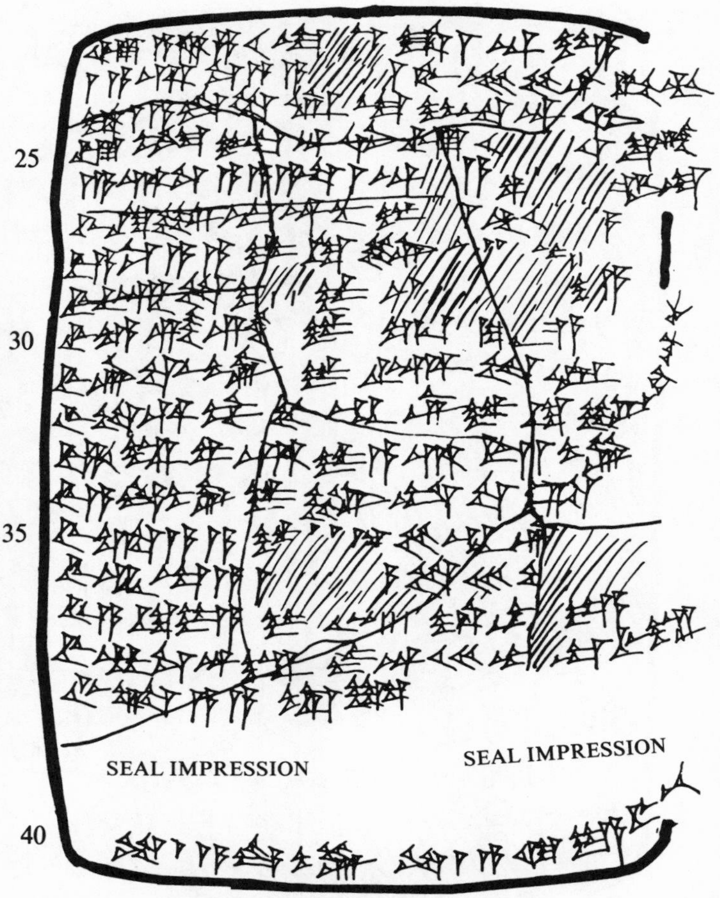

UPPER EDGE

SIC

49

OBVERSE

BEGINNING OF OBVERSE DESTROYED

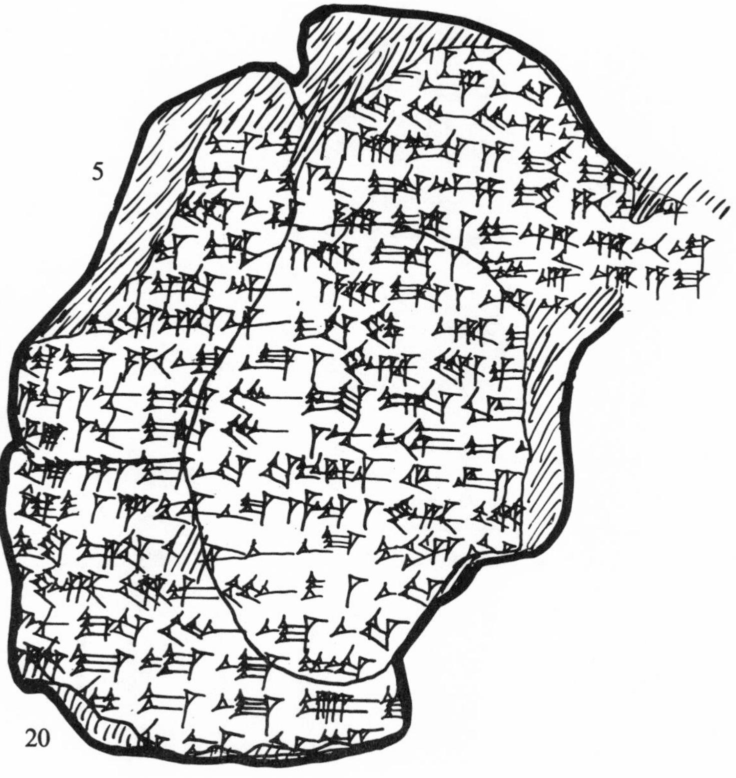

END OF OBVERSE DESTROYED

REVERSE DESTROYED

67

OBVERSE

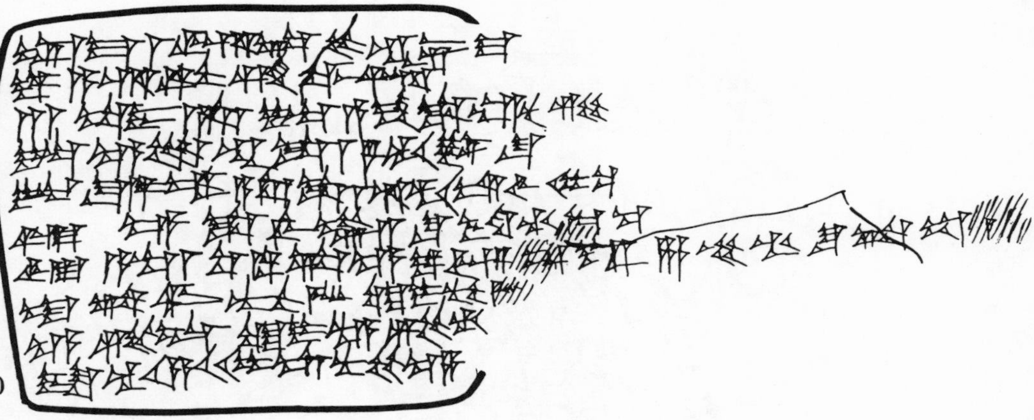

LOWER EDGE

REVERSE

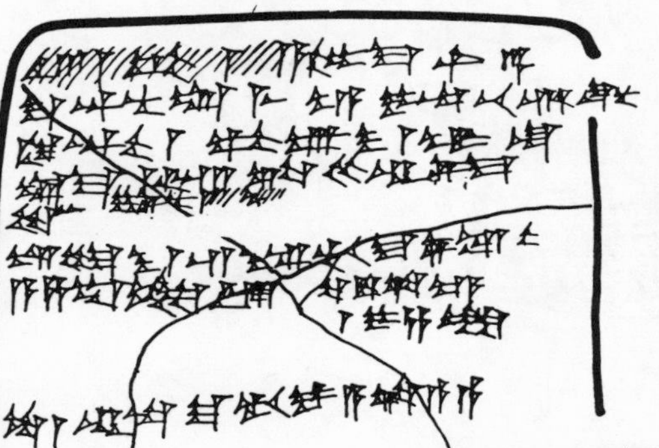

LEFT EDGE

UPPER EDGE

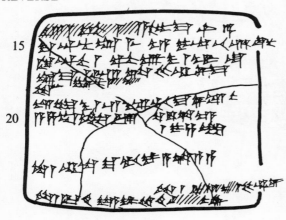

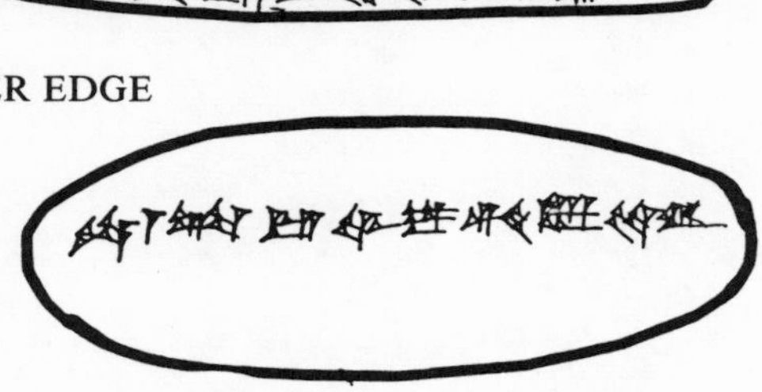

73

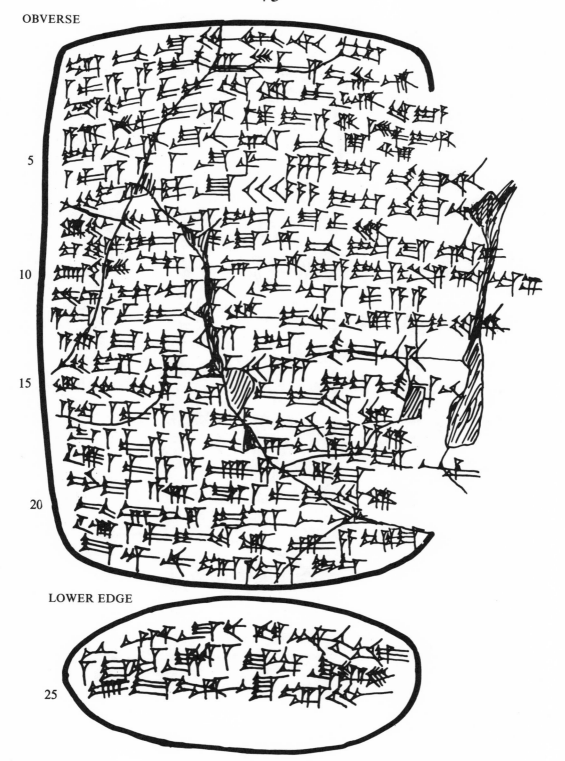

OBVERSE

LOWER EDGE

73

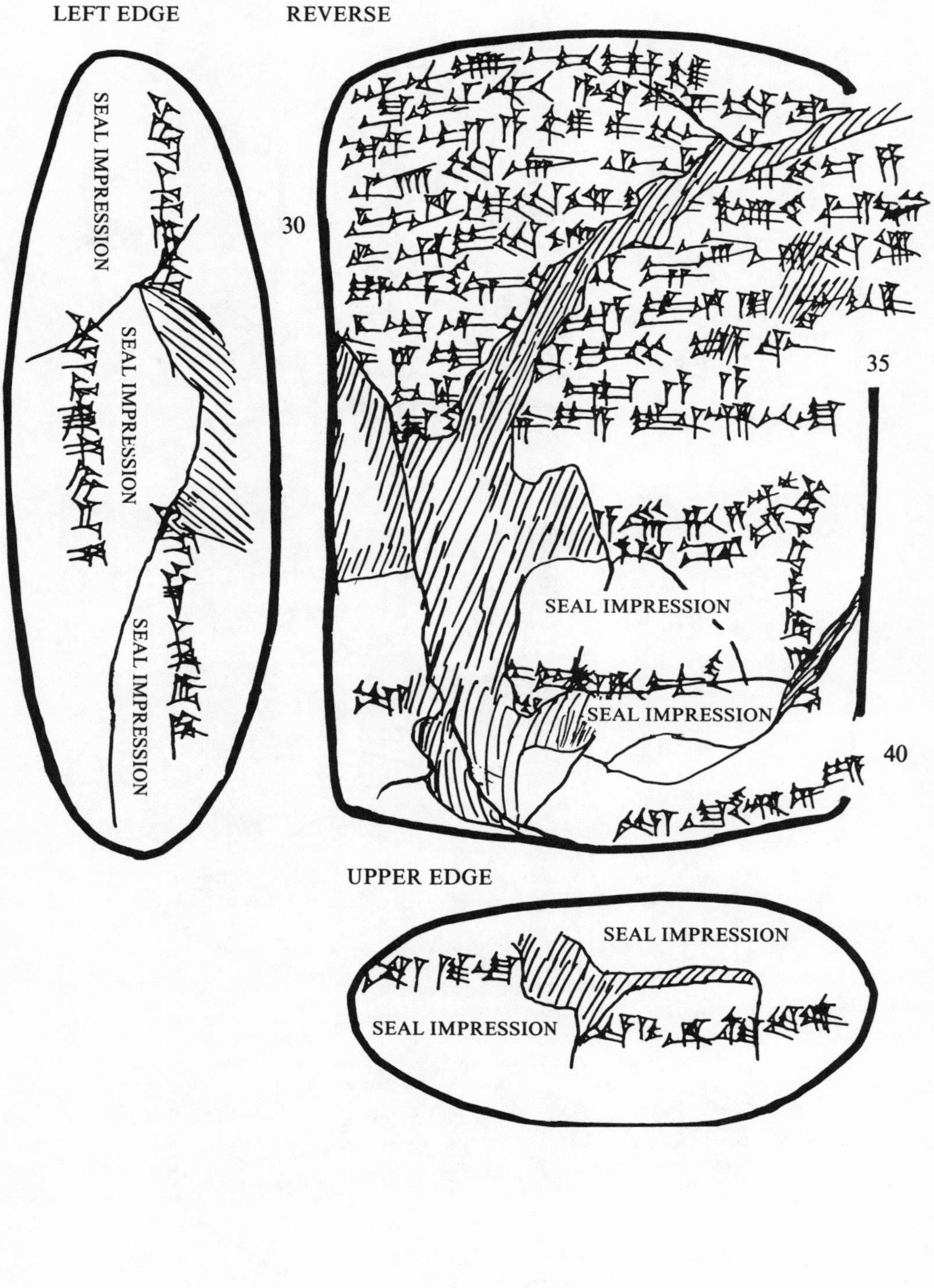
LEFT EDGE
REVERSE
SEAL IMPRESSION
SEAL IMPRESSION
SEAL IMPRESSION
30
35
SEAL IMPRESSION
SEAL IMPRESSION
40
UPPER EDGE
SEAL IMPRESSION
SEAL IMPRESSION

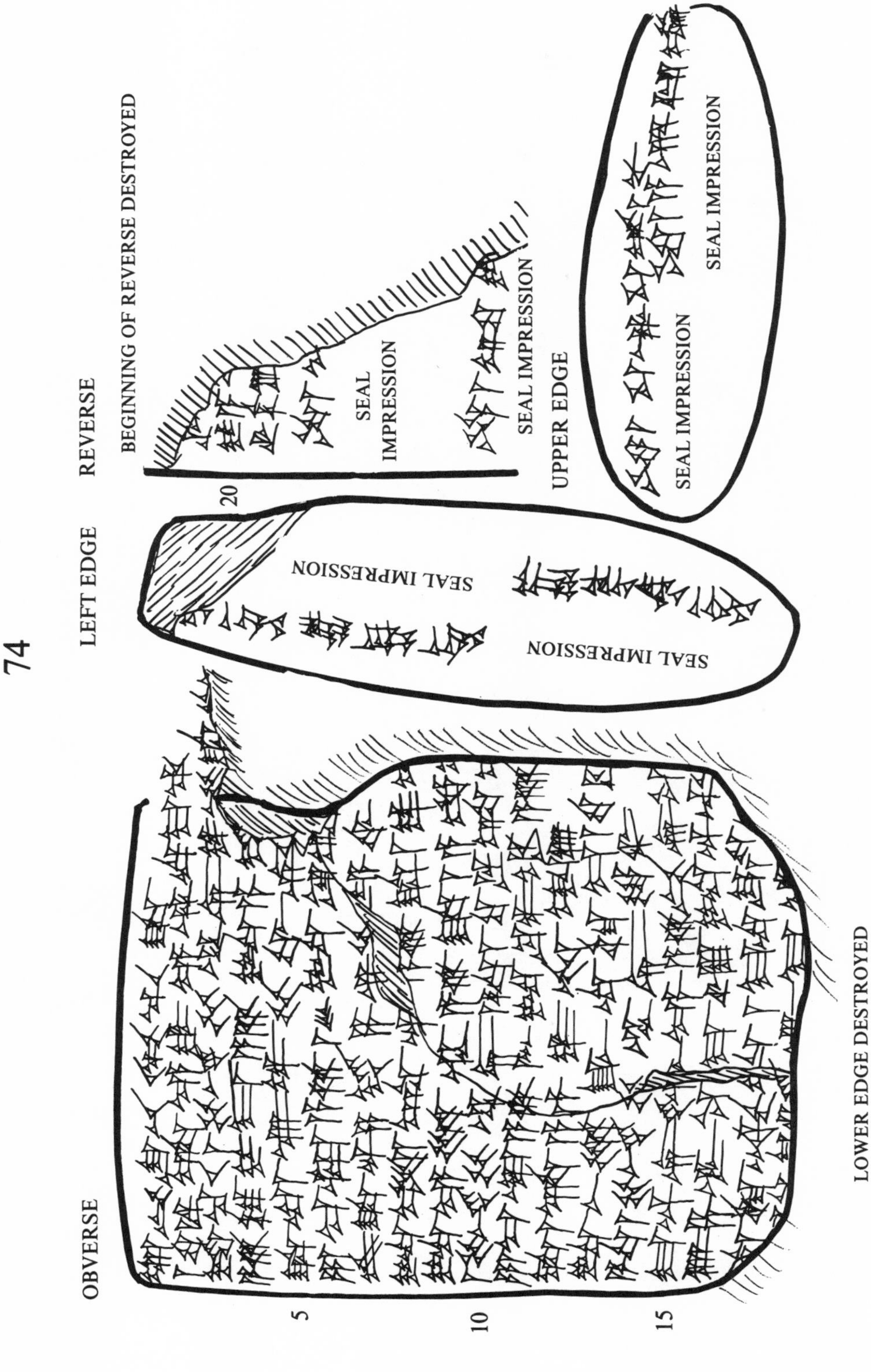
74
OBVERSE
LOWER EDGE DESTROYED
LEFT EDGE
SEAL IMPRESSION
SEAL IMPRESSION
REVERSE
BEGINNING OF REVERSE DESTROYED
SEAL IMPRESSION
SEAL IMPRESSION
UPPER EDGE
SEAL IMPRESSION
SEAL IMPRESSION

76

OBVERSE

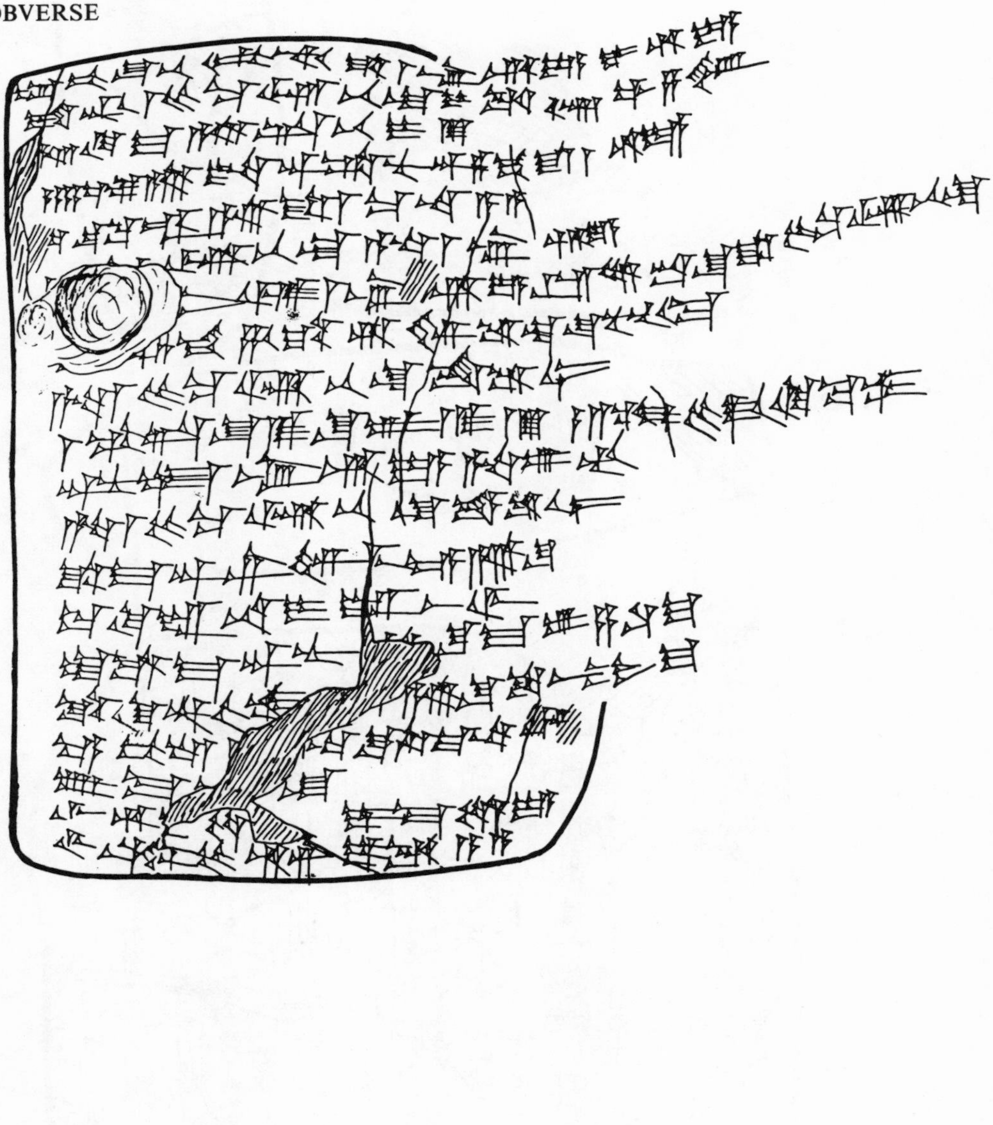

76

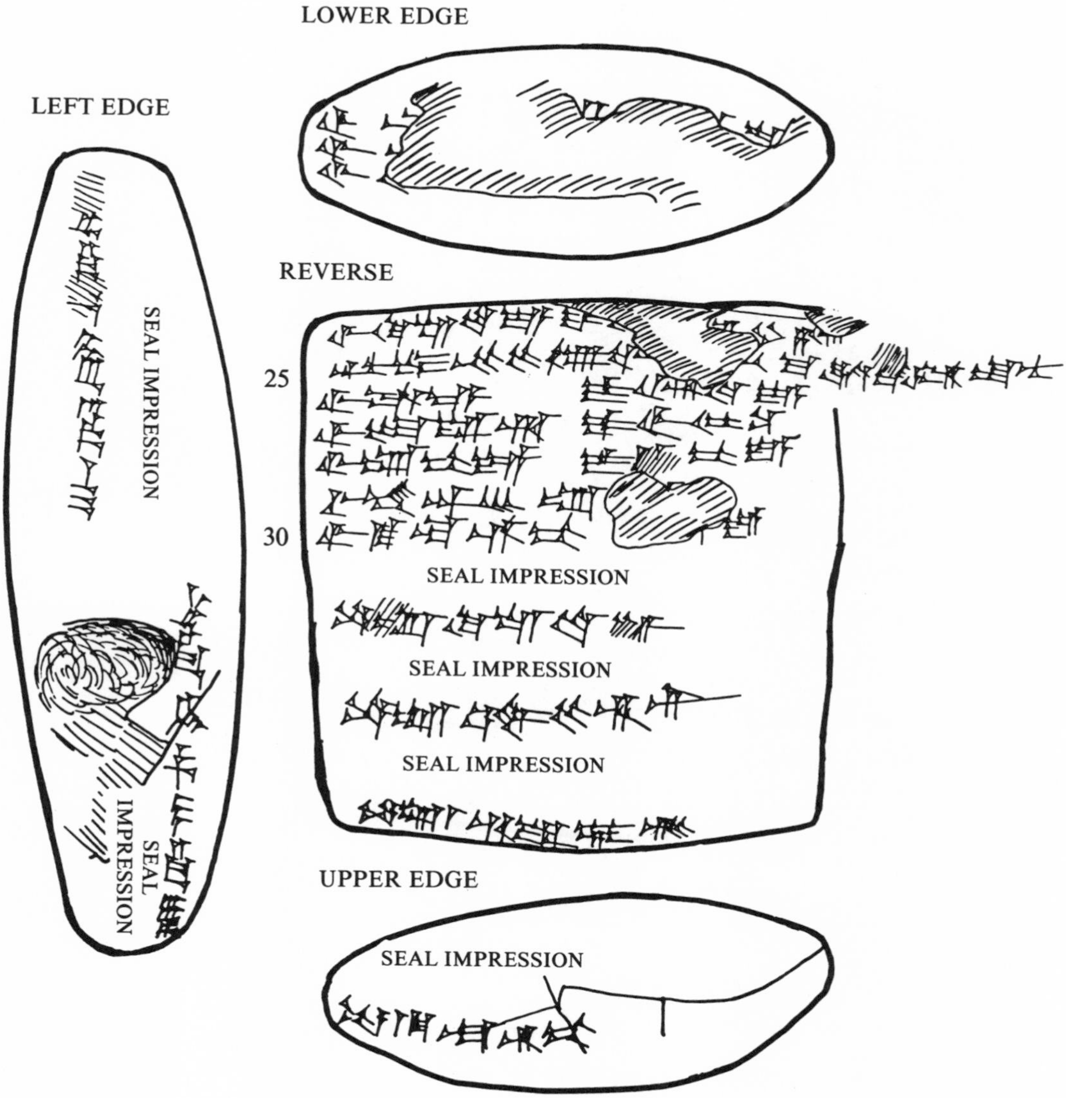
LOWER EDGE
LEFT EDGE
SEAL IMPRESSION
SEAL IMPRESSION
REVERSE
25
30
SEAL IMPRESSION
SEAL IMPRESSION
SEAL IMPRESSION
UPPER EDGE
SEAL IMPRESSION

77

OBVERSE

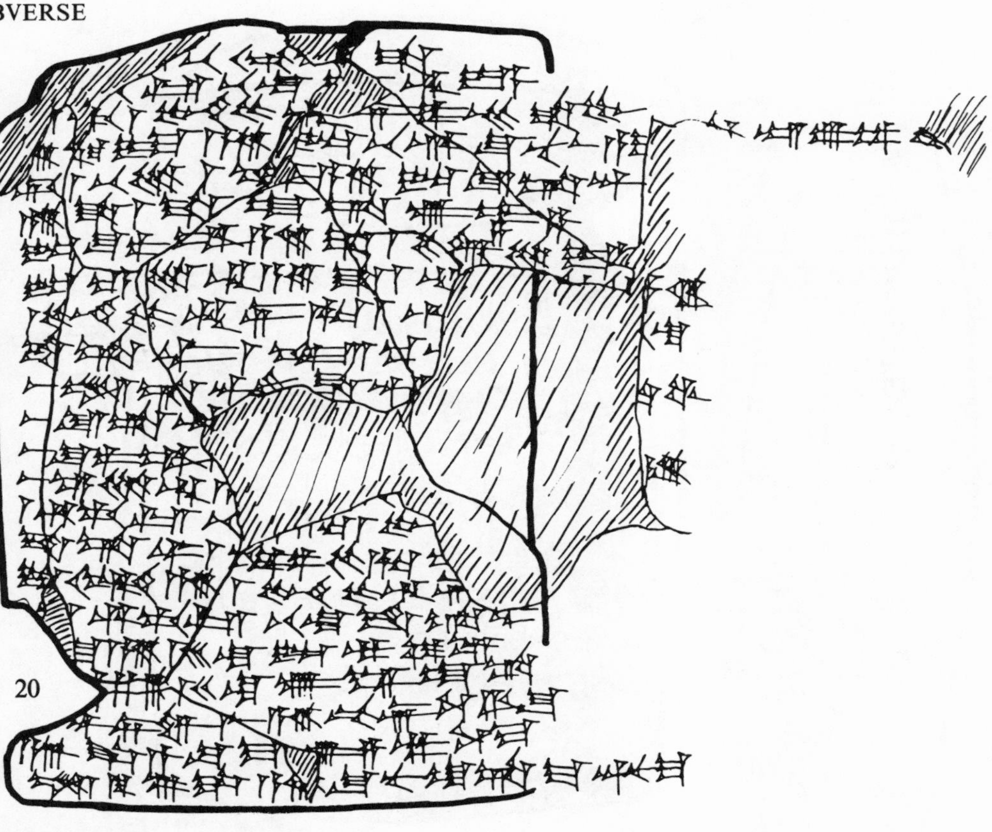

LOWER EDGE

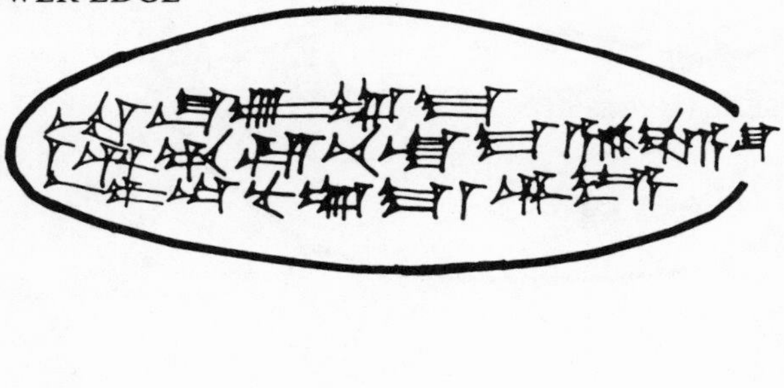

77

LEFT EDGE

REVERSE

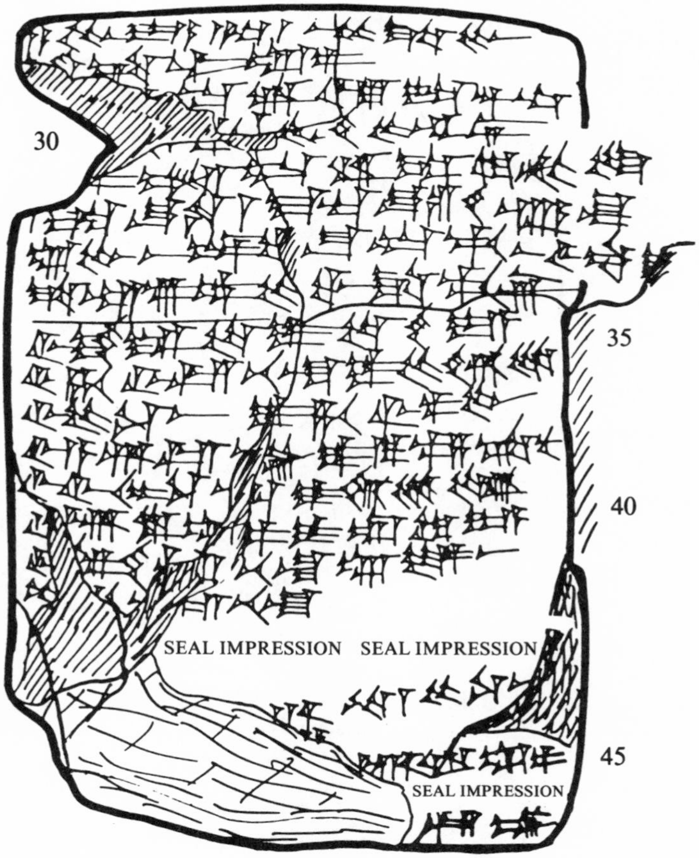

81

OBVERSE

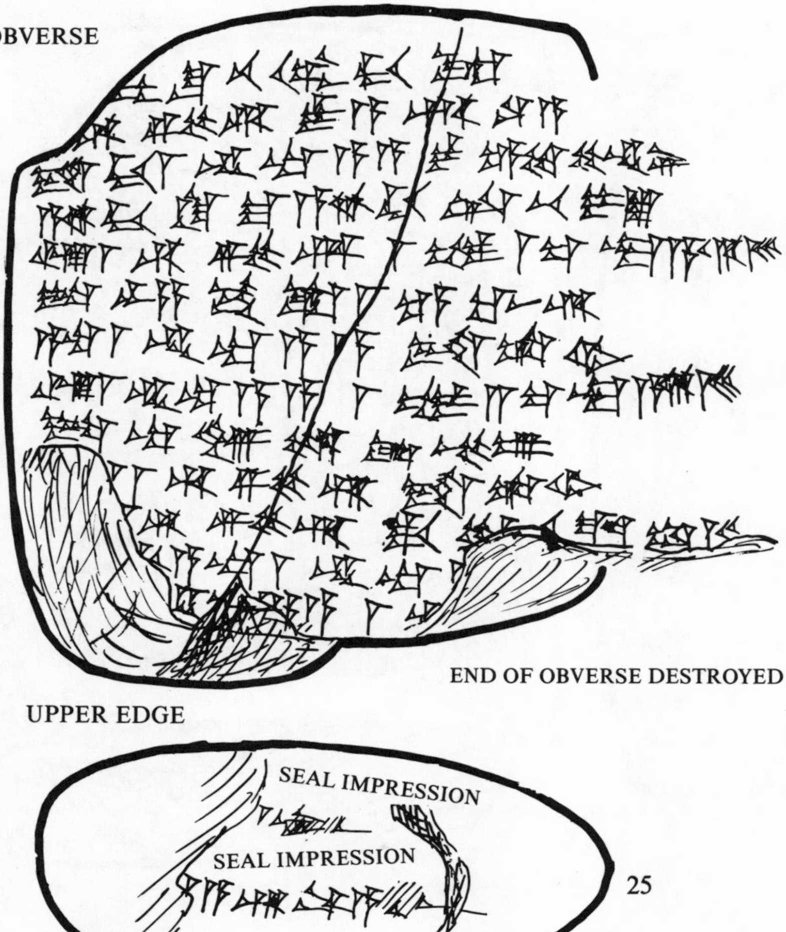

END OF OBVERSE DESTROYED

UPPER EDGE

81

REVERSE

BEGINNING OF REVERSE DESTROYED

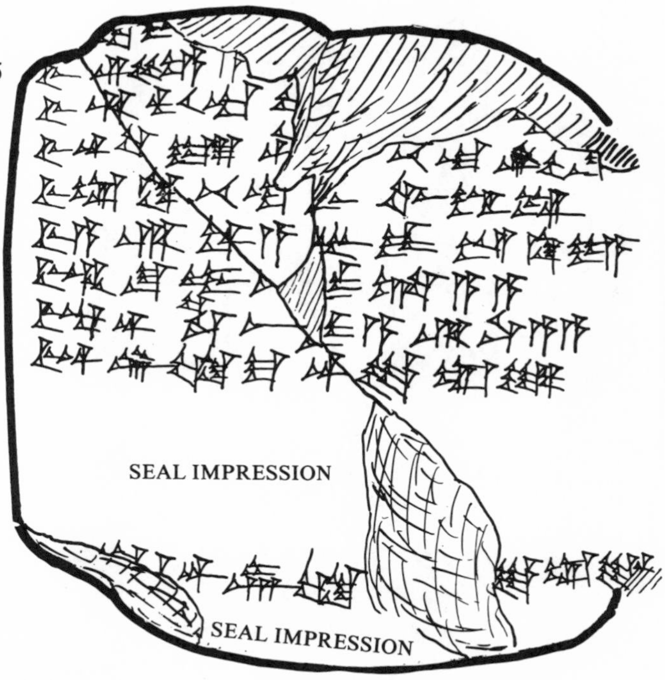

LEFT EDGE

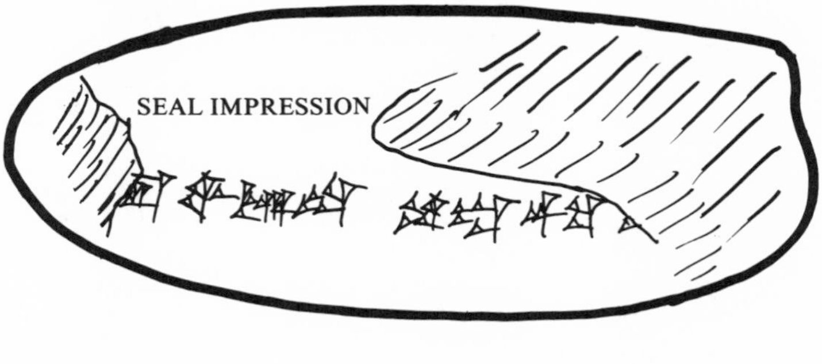

83

OBVERSE

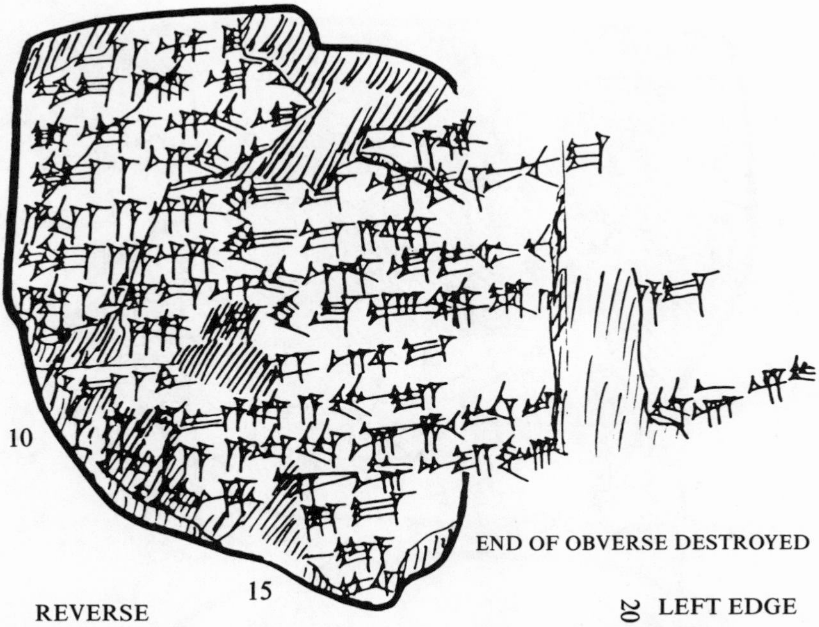

END OF OBVERSE DESTROYED

REVERSE

BEGINNING OF REVERSE DESTROYED

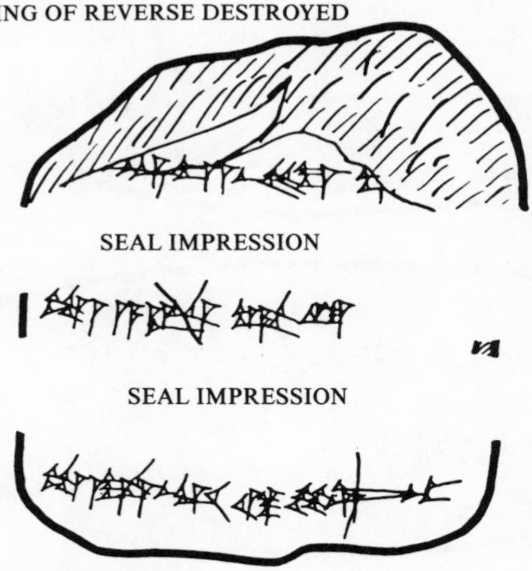

LEFT EDGE

UPPER EDGE

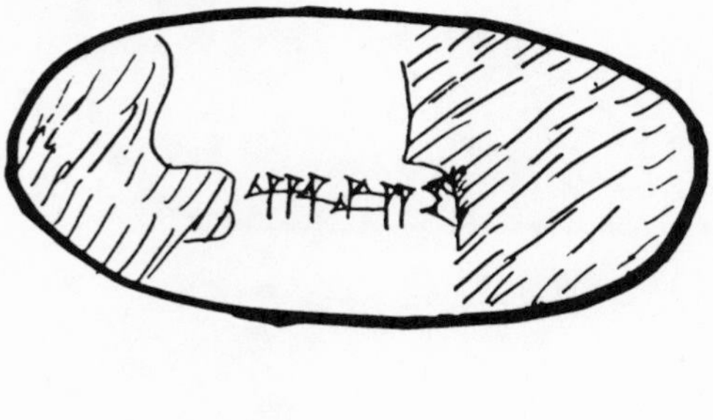

93

OBVERSE

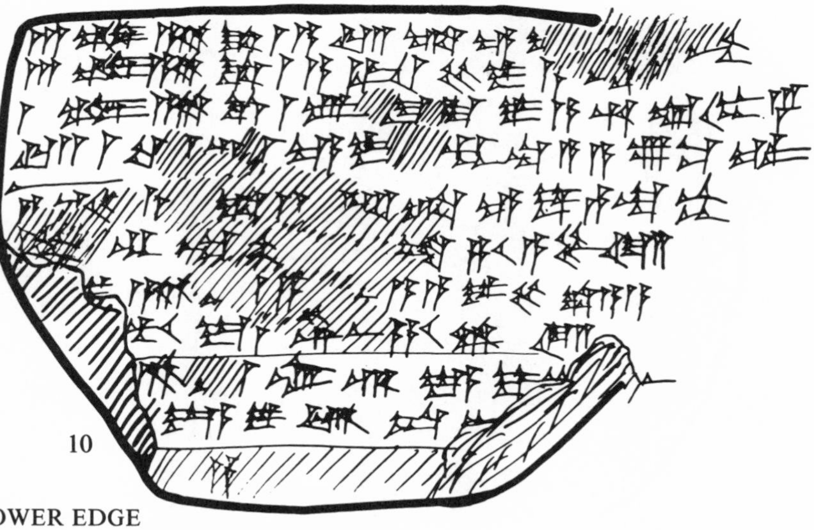

LOWER EDGE

REVERSE

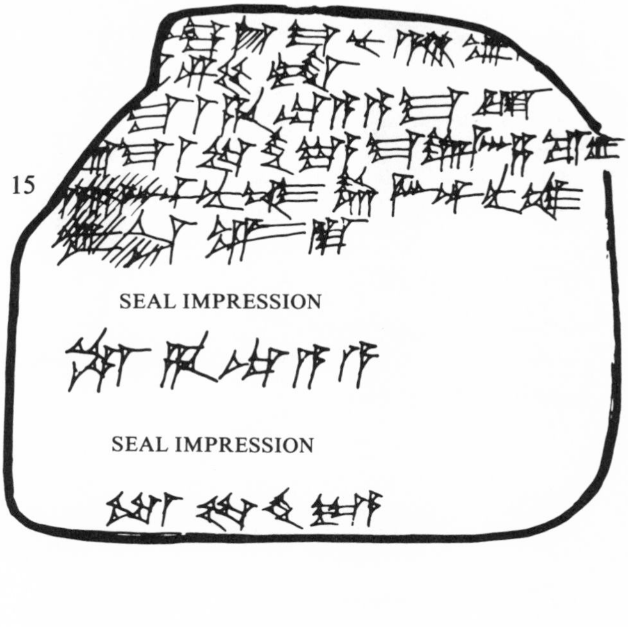

96

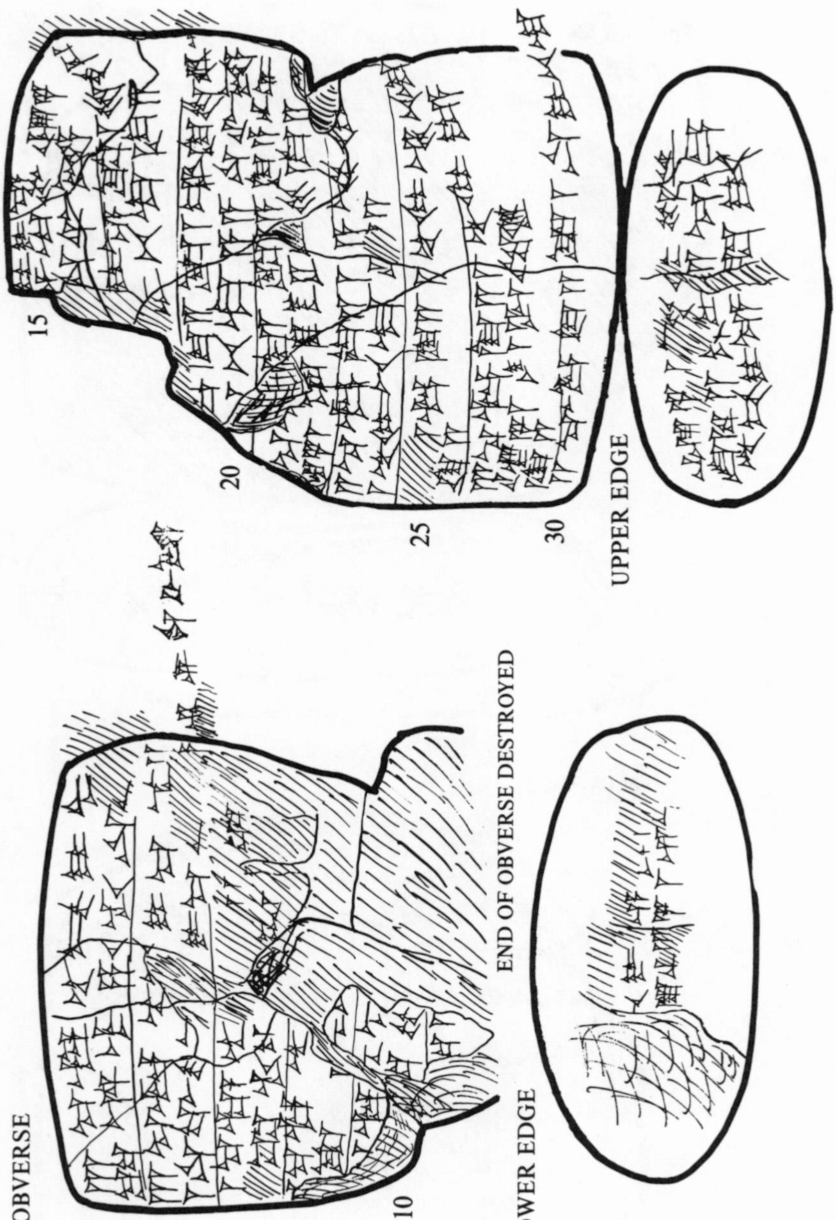
OBVERSE
REVERSE
END OF OBVERSE DESTROYED
LOWER EDGE
UPPER EDGE

97

OBVERSE

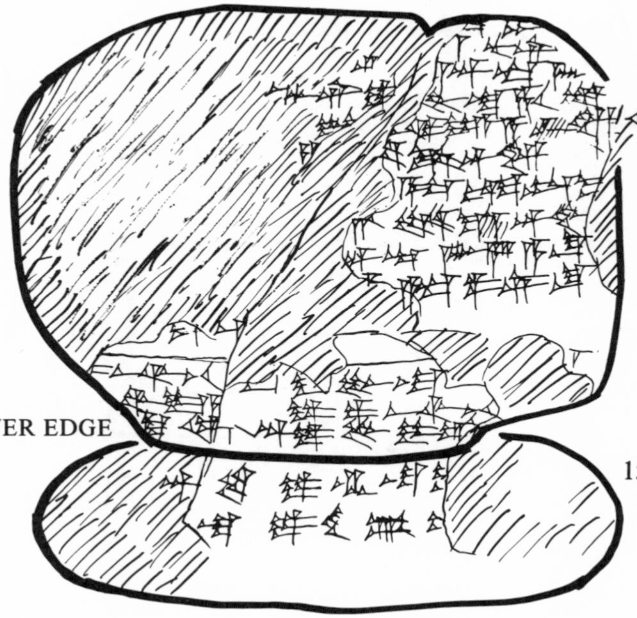

REVERSE

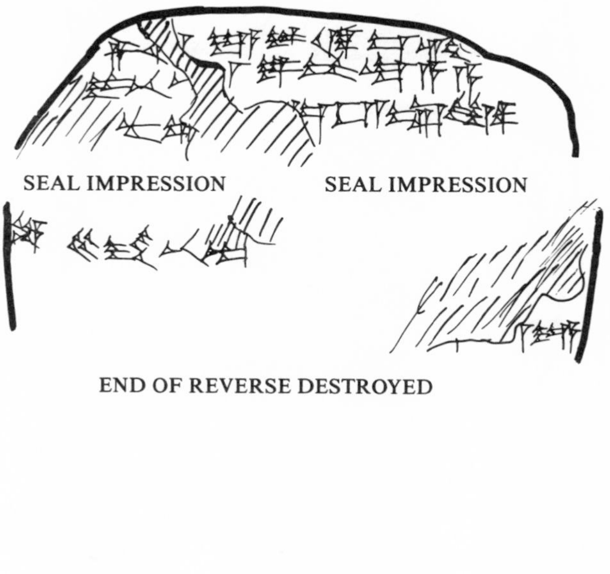

END OF REVERSE DESTROYED

101

OBVERSE

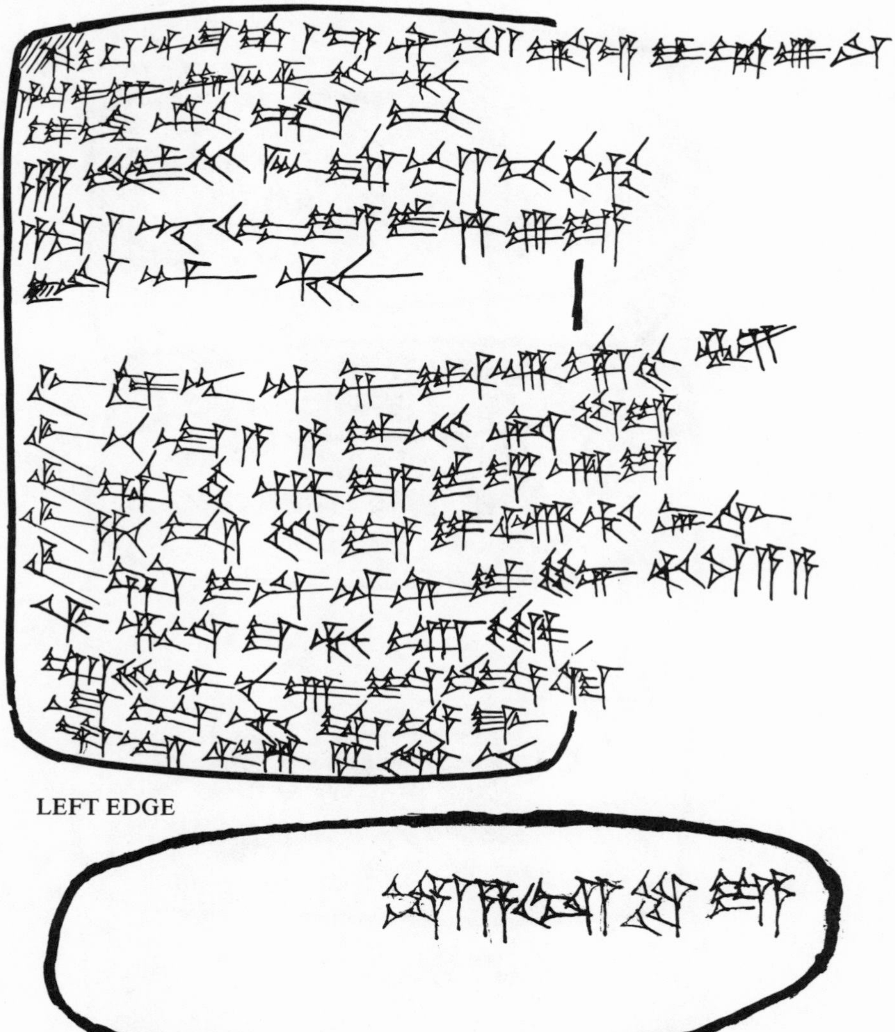

LEFT EDGE

101

LOWER EDGE

REVERSE

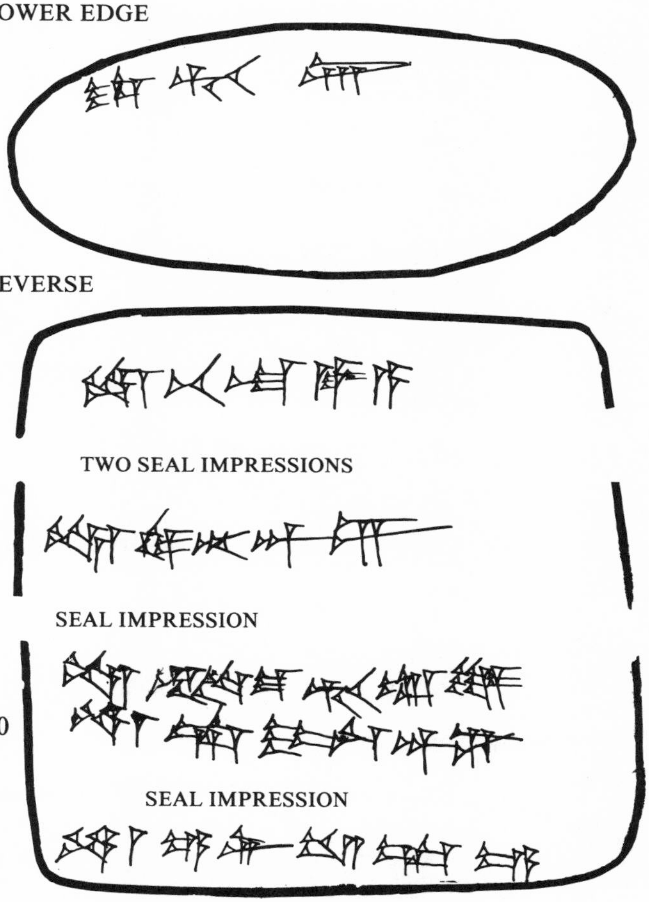

UPPER EDGE: SEAL IMPRESSION

102

OBVERSE

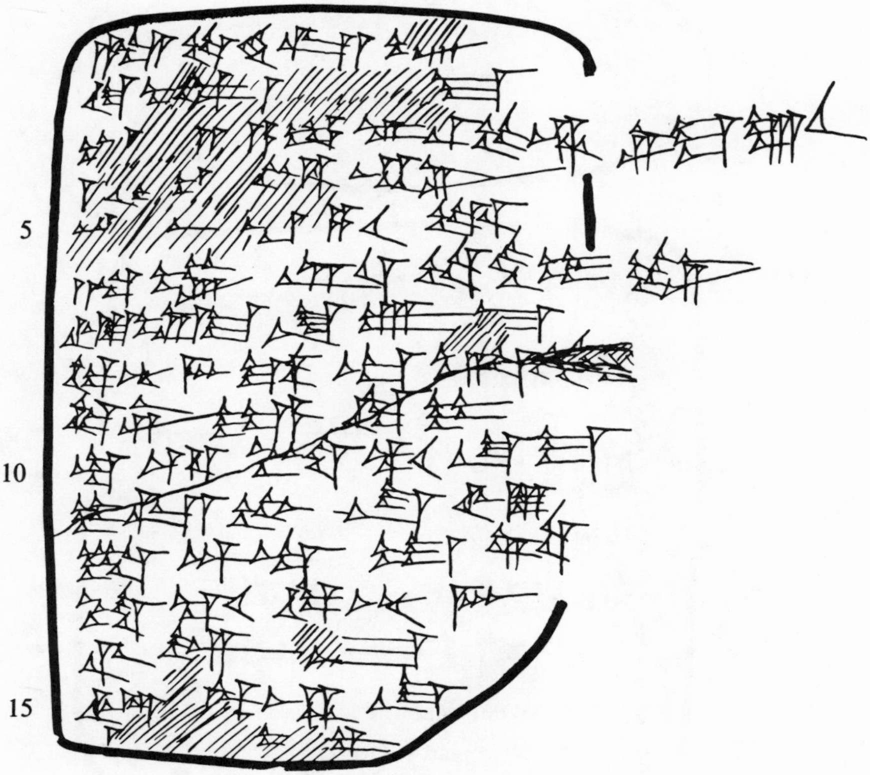

102

LOWER EDGE

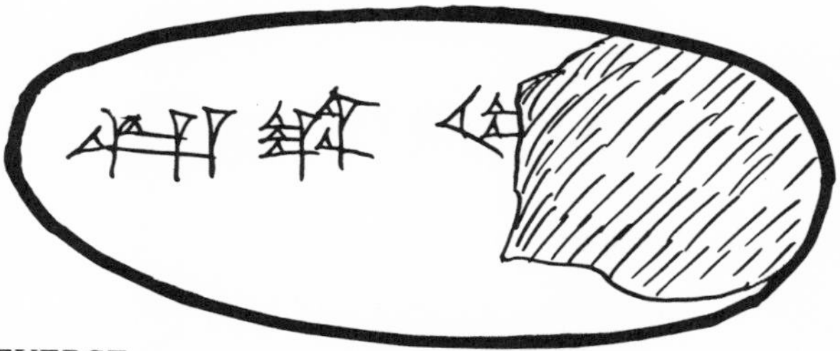

REVERSE

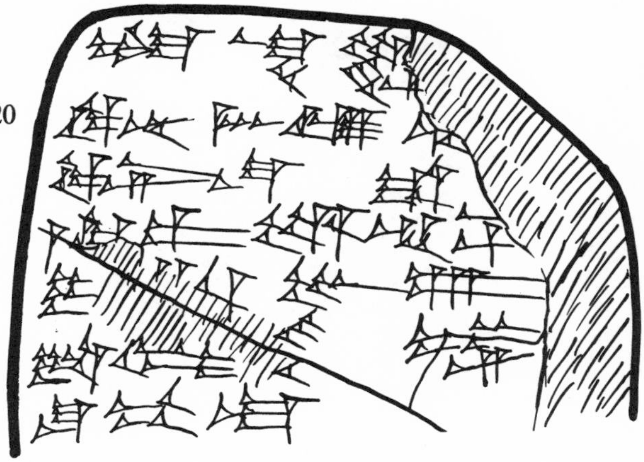

REST OF REVERSE UNINSCRIBED

103

OBVERSE

BEGINNING OF OBVERSE DESTROYED

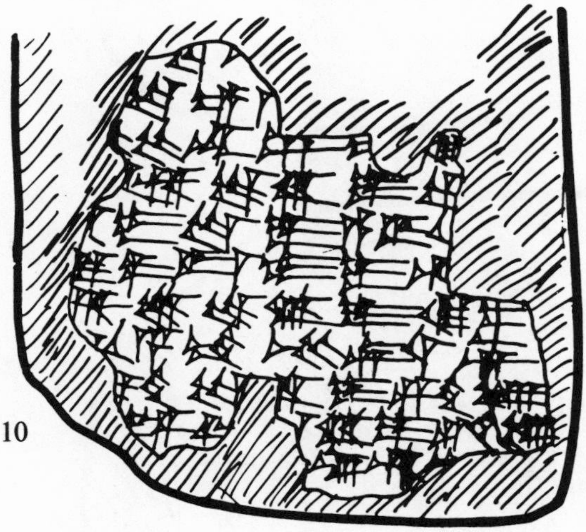

LEFT EDGE

103

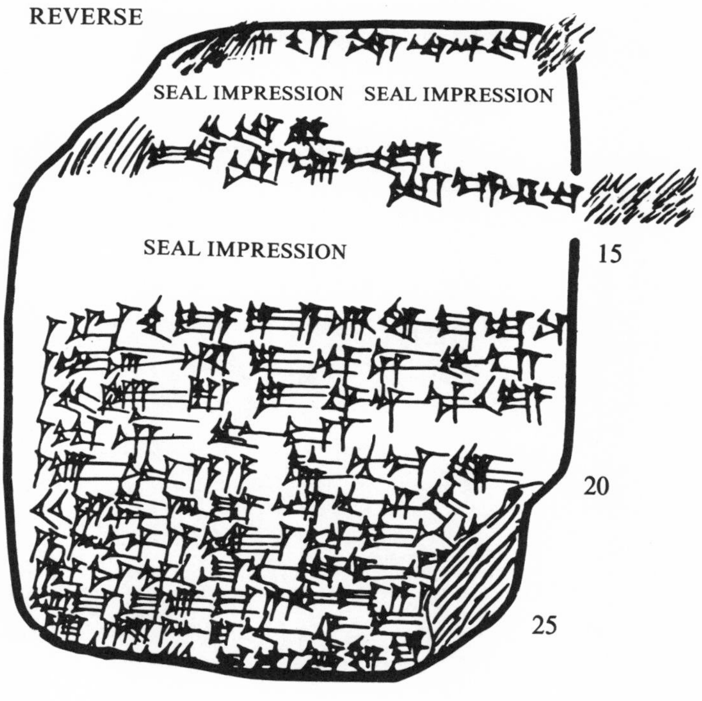
REVERSE
SEAL IMPRESSION
SEAL IMPRESSION
SEAL IMPRESSION
15
20
25

106

OBVERSE

BEGINNING OF OBVERSE DESTROYED

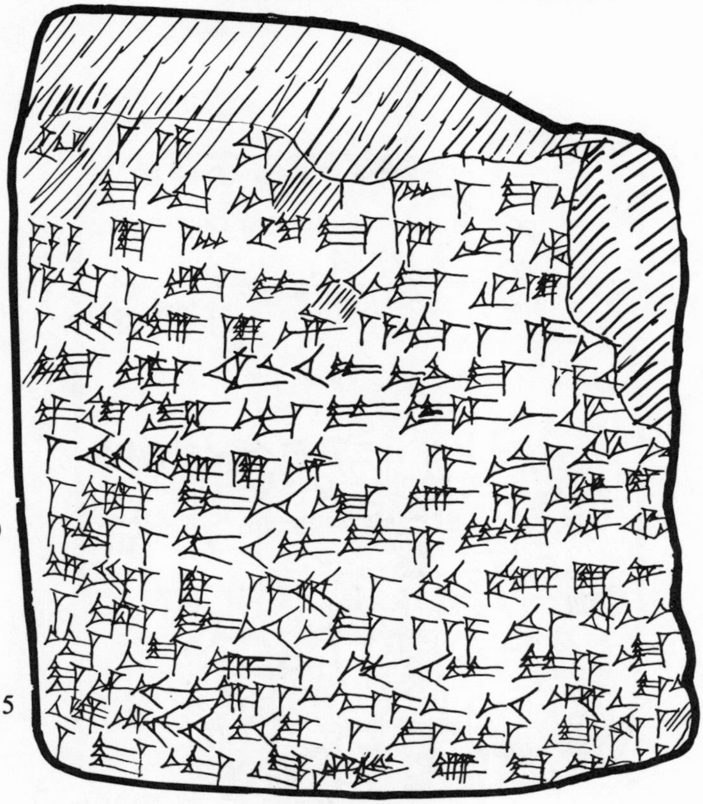

LOWER EDGE

106

REVERSE

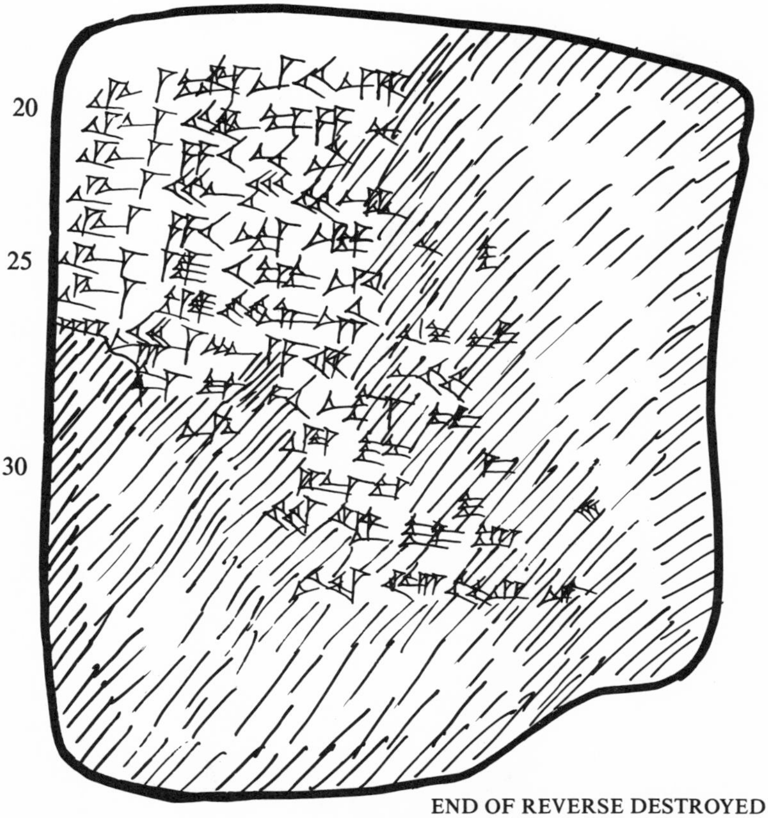

END OF REVERSE DESTROYED

LEFT EDGE

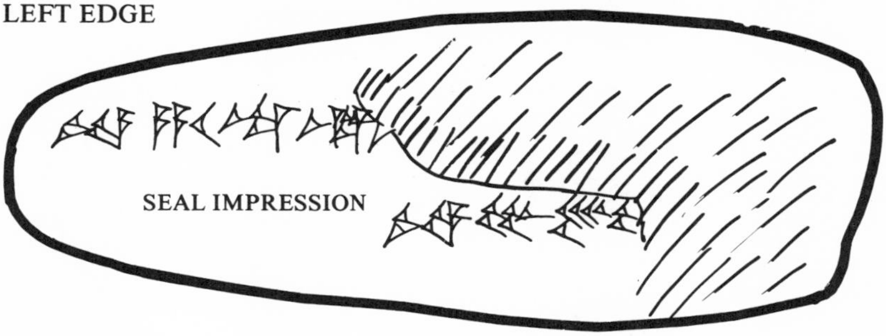

111

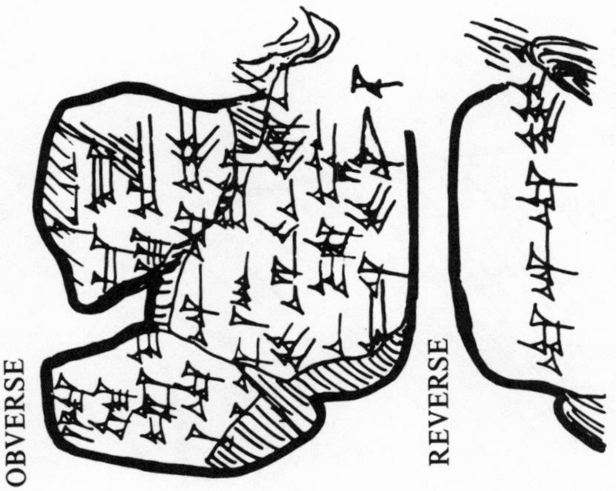
OBVERSE
REVERSE

110

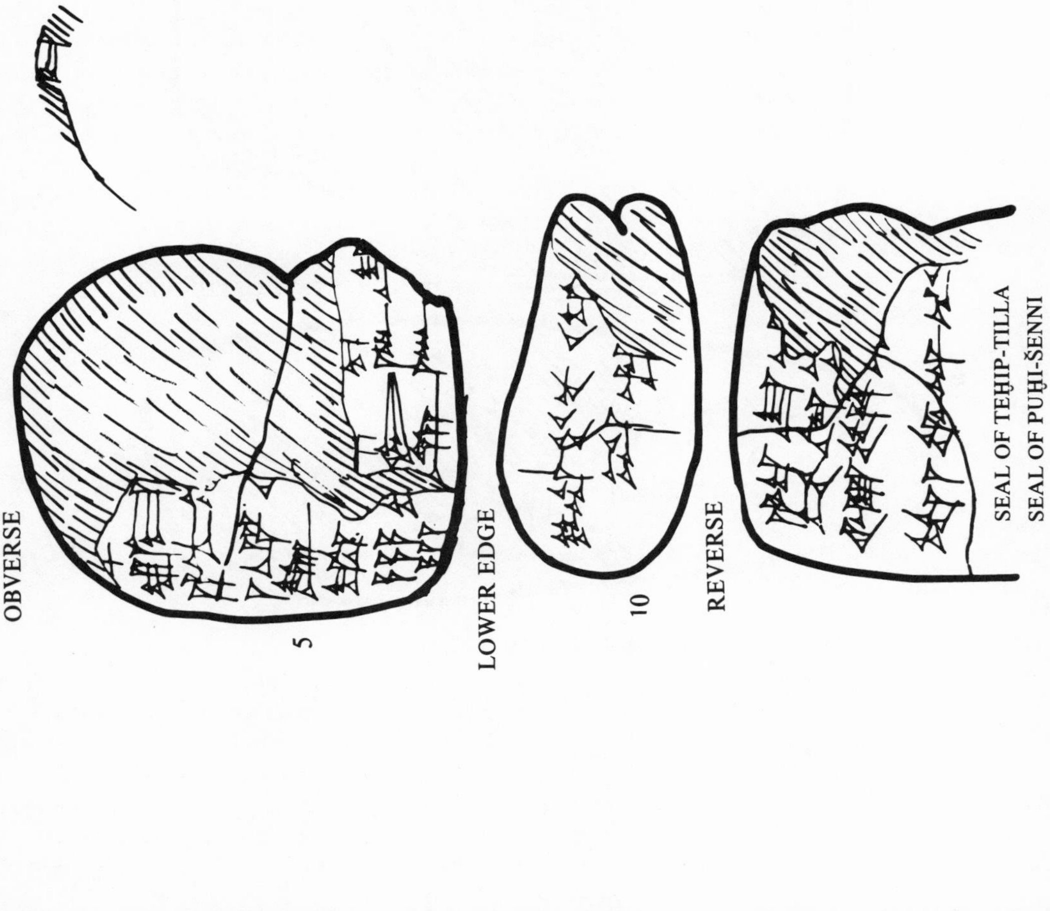
OBVERSE
LOWER EDGE
REVERSE
SEAL OF TEḪIP-TILLA
SEAL OF PUḪI-ŠENNI

118

OBVERSE

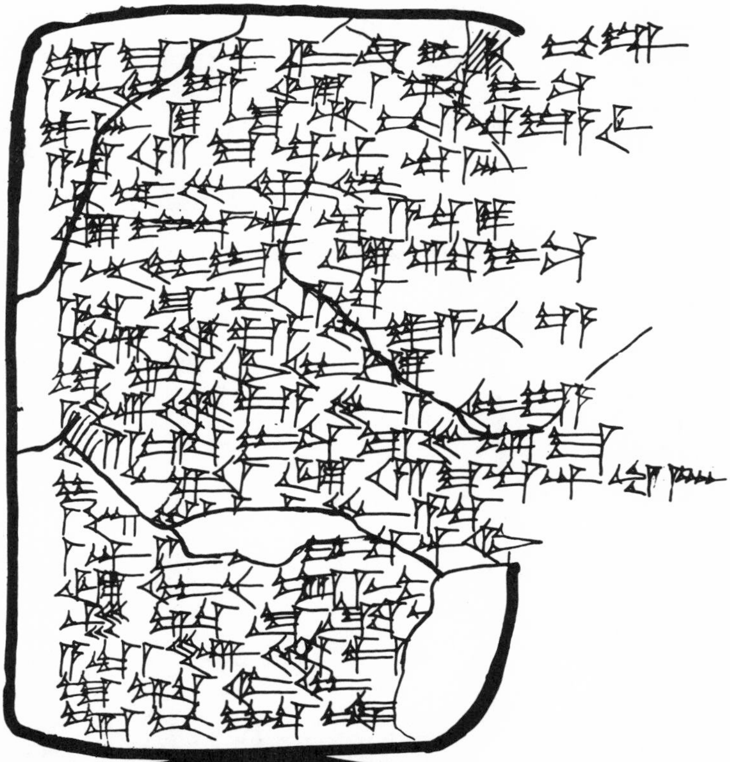

LOWER EDGE

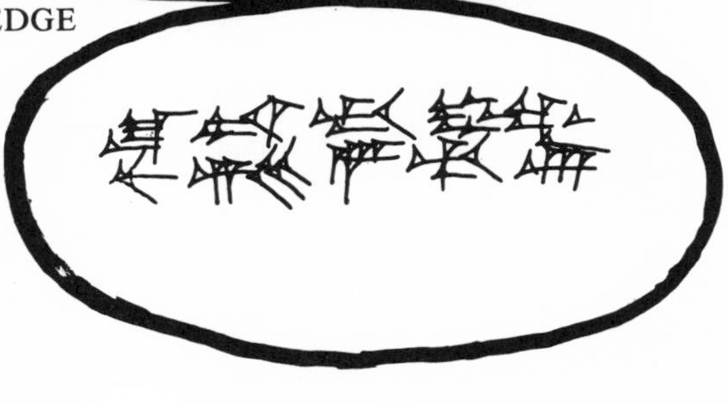

118

REVERSE

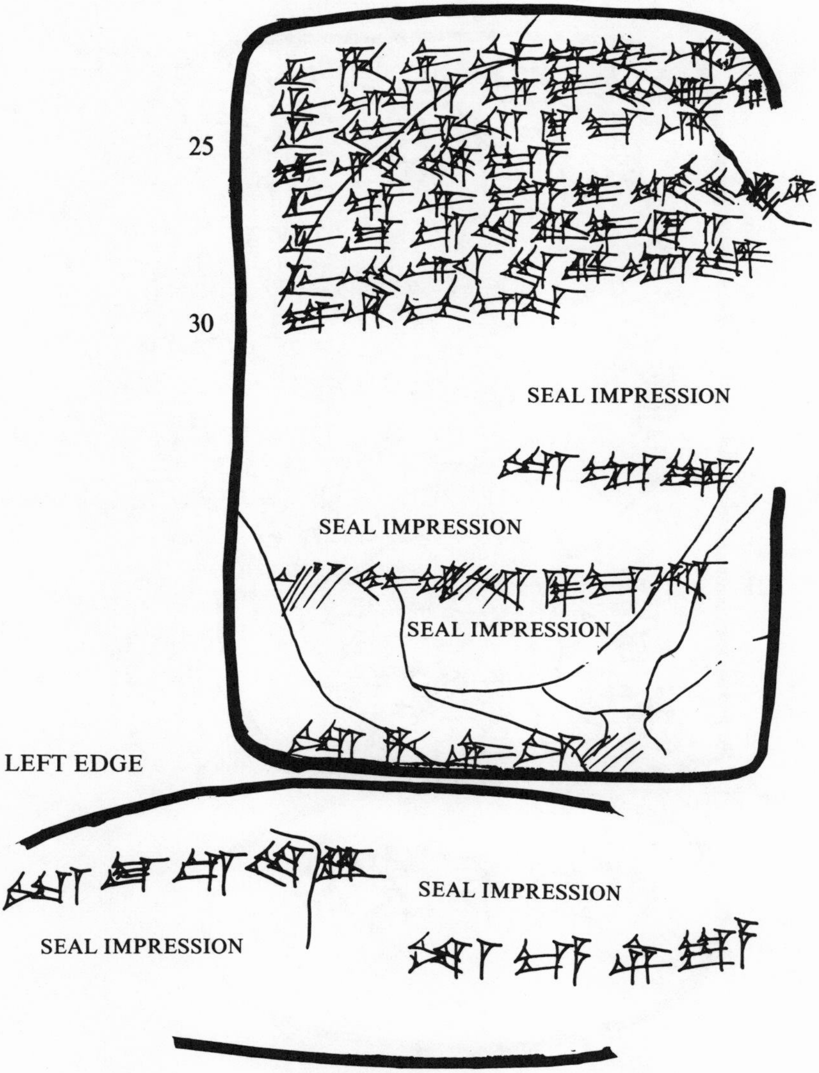
25
30
SEAL IMPRESSION
SEAL IMPRESSION
SEAL IMPRESSION
LEFT EDGE
SEAL IMPRESSION
SEAL IMPRESSION

125

OBVERSE

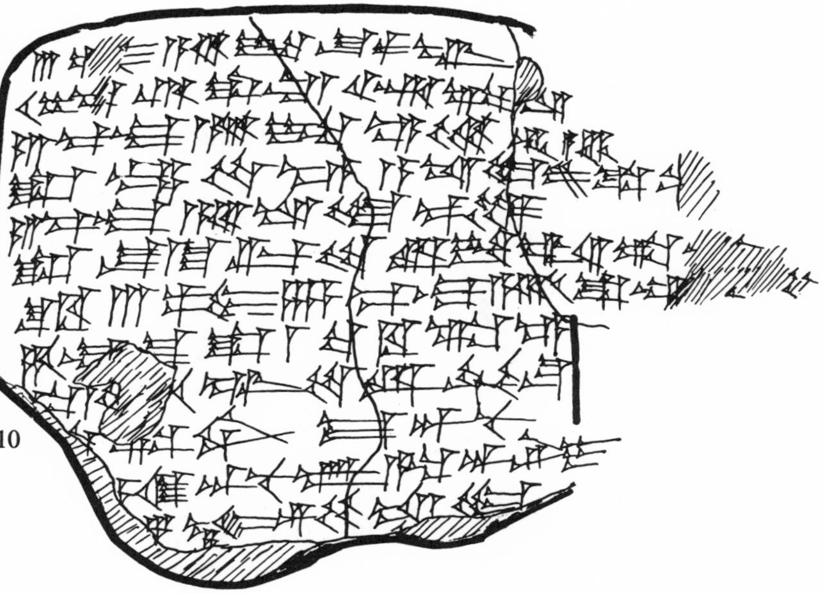

REVERSE

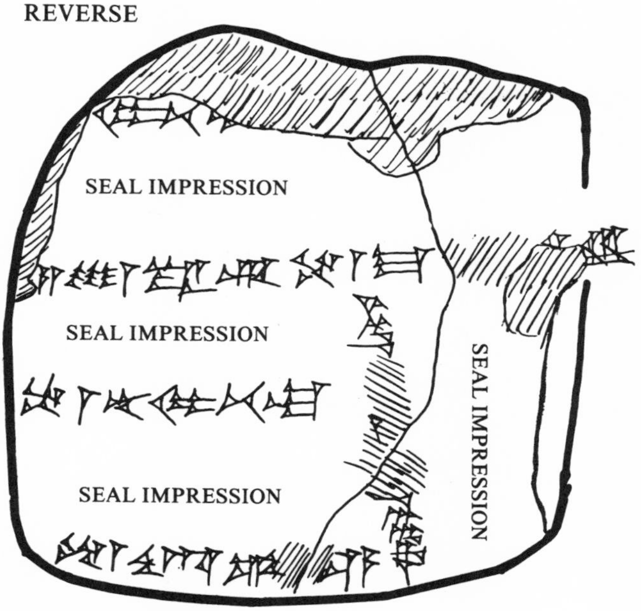

128

OBVERSE

BEGINNING OF OBVERSE DESTROYED

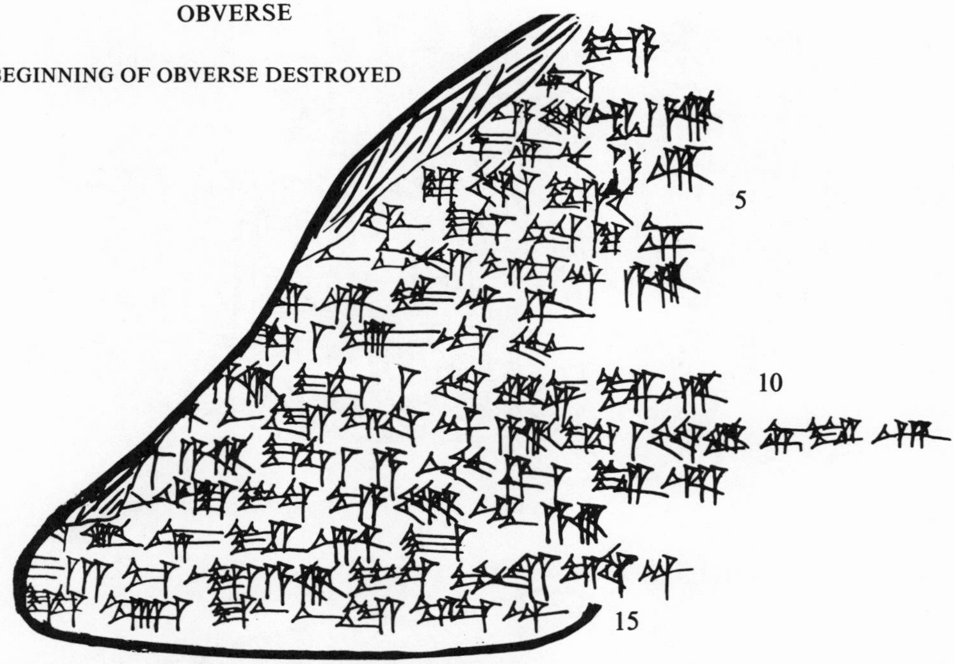

LOWER EDGE

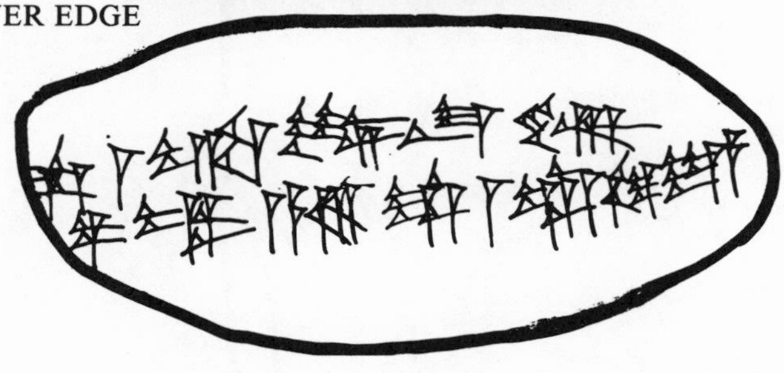

128

REVERSE

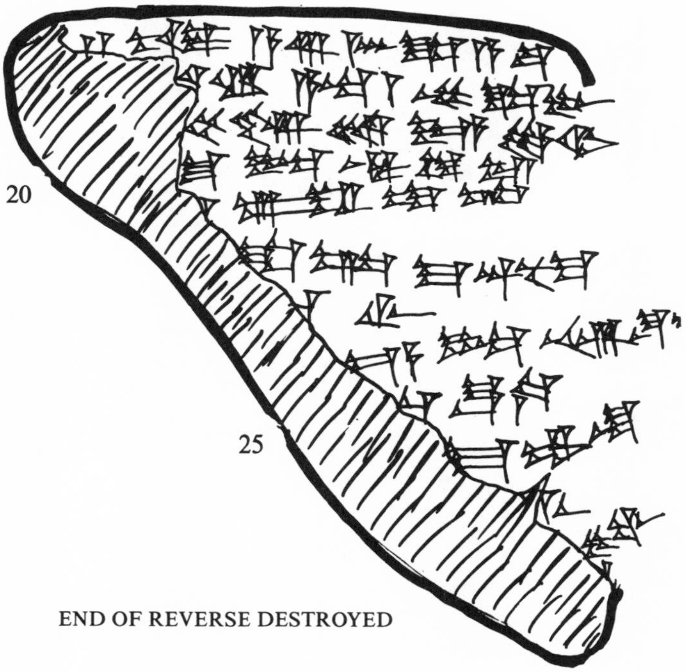

END OF REVERSE DESTROYED

129

OBVERSE

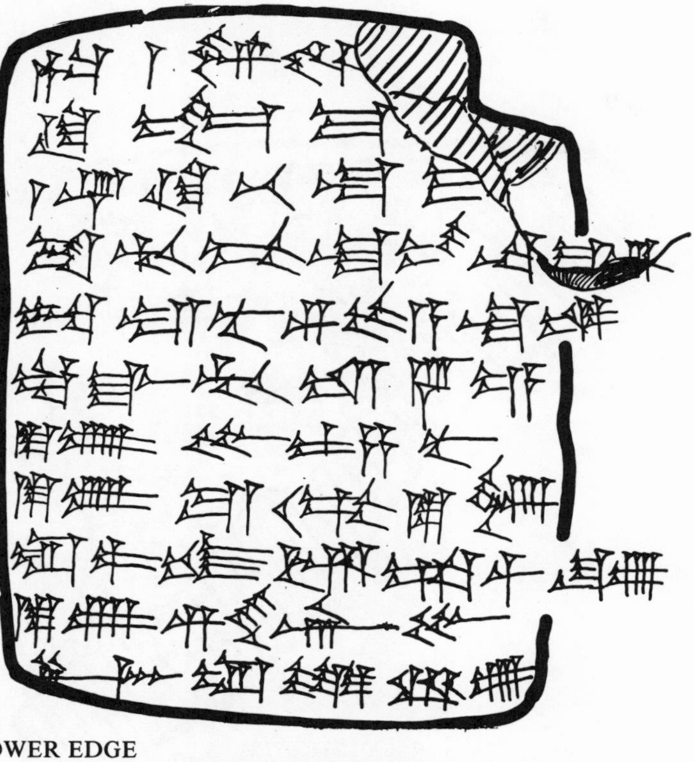

LOWER EDGE

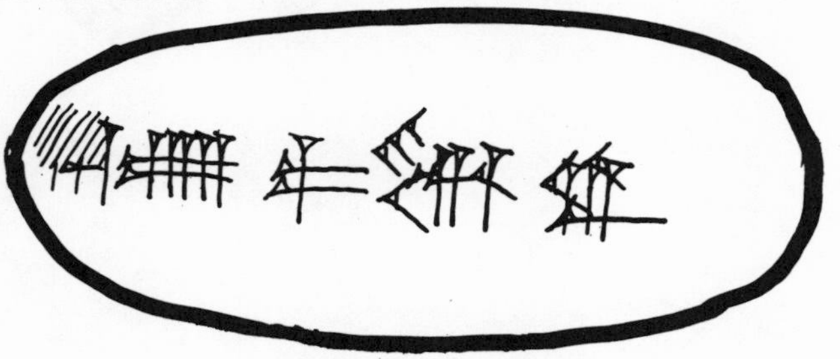

129

REVERSE

UPPER EDGE

130

OBVERSE

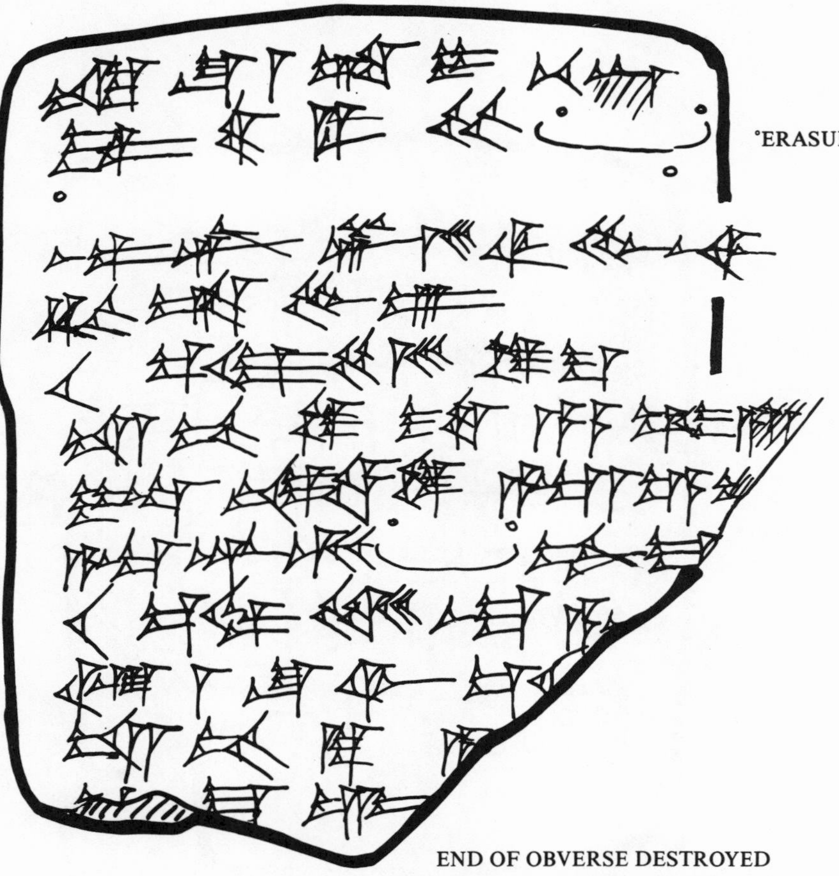

END OF OBVERSE DESTROYED

REVERSE DESTROYED

UPPER EDGE

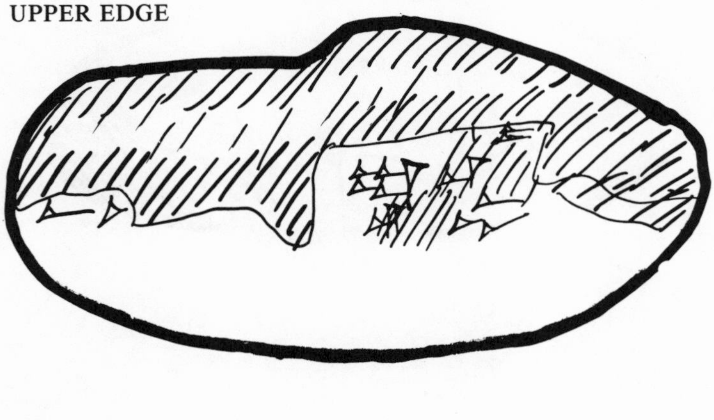

142

OBVERSE

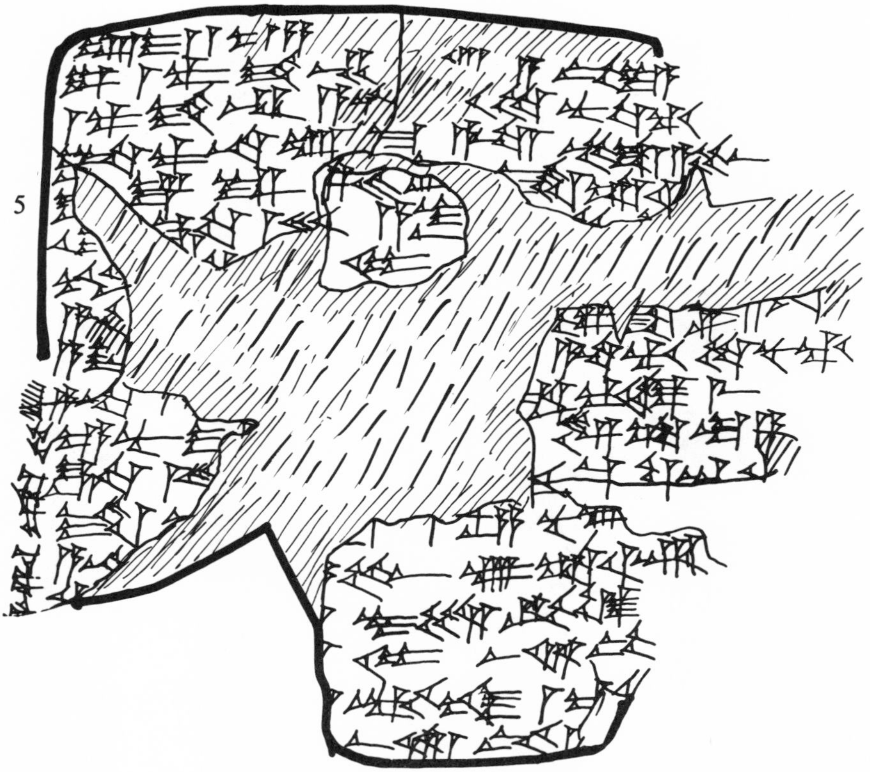

142

REVERSE

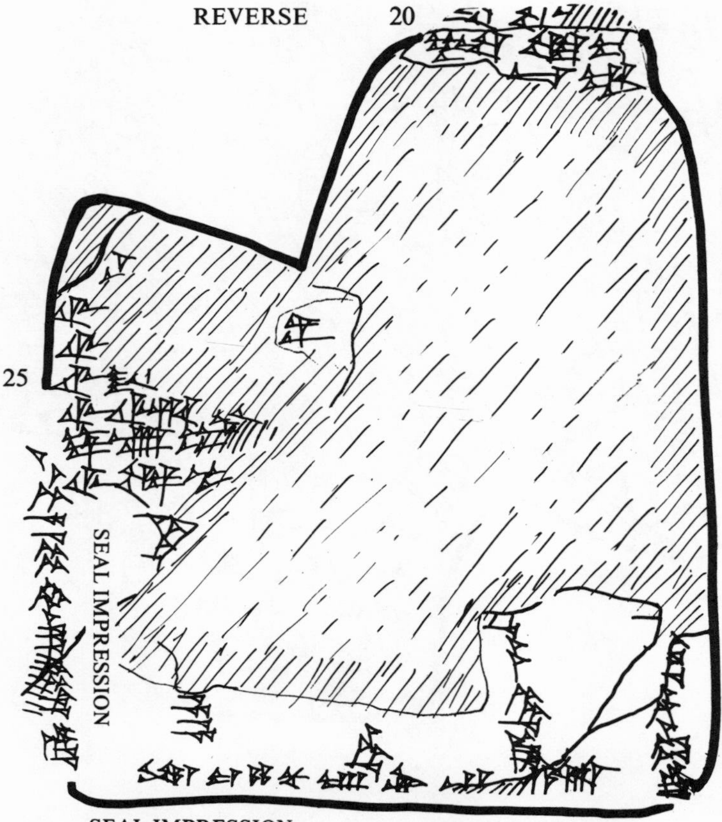

SEAL IMPRESSION SEAL IMPRESSION

143

OBVERSE

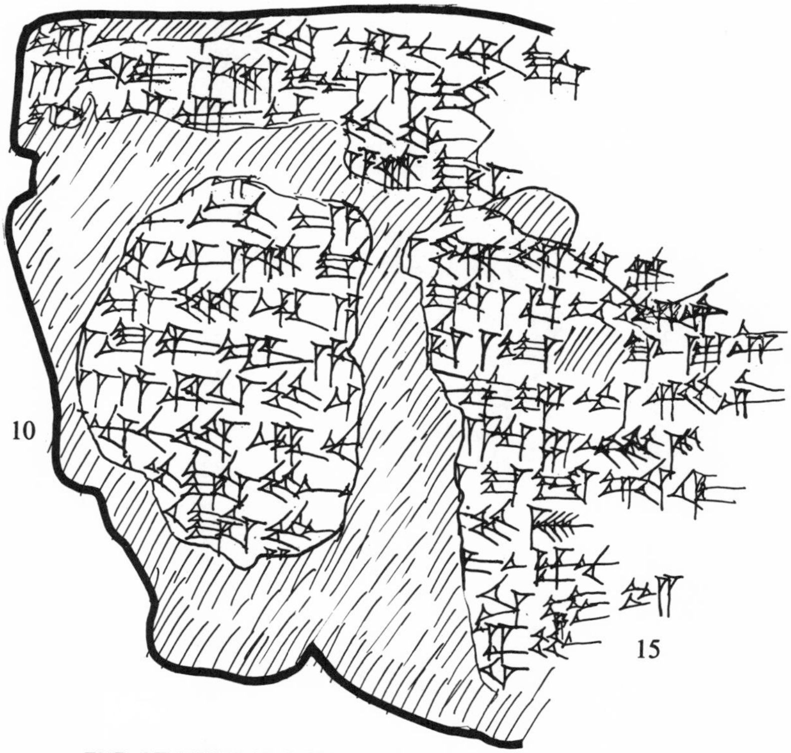

END OF OBVERSE DESTROYED

143

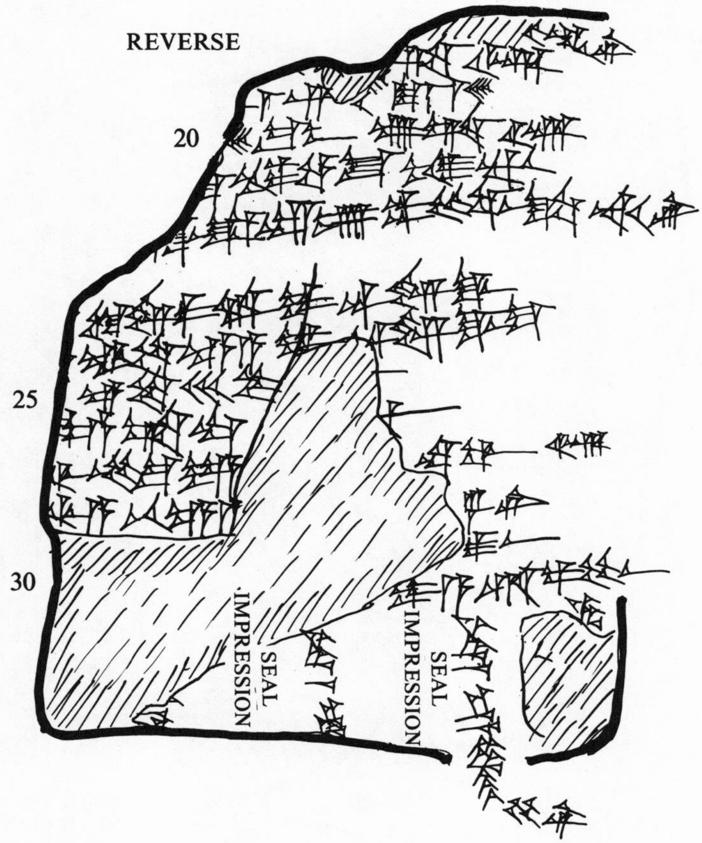

144

OBVERSE

BEGINNING OF OBVERSE DESTROYED

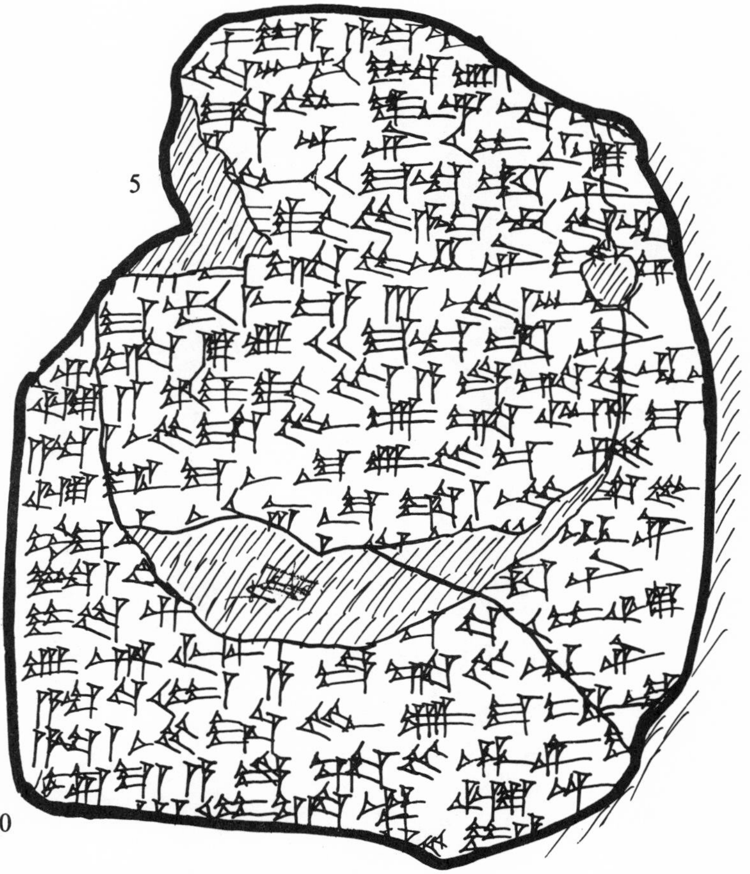

END OF OBVERSE DESTROYED

REVERSE DESTROYED

145

OBVERSE

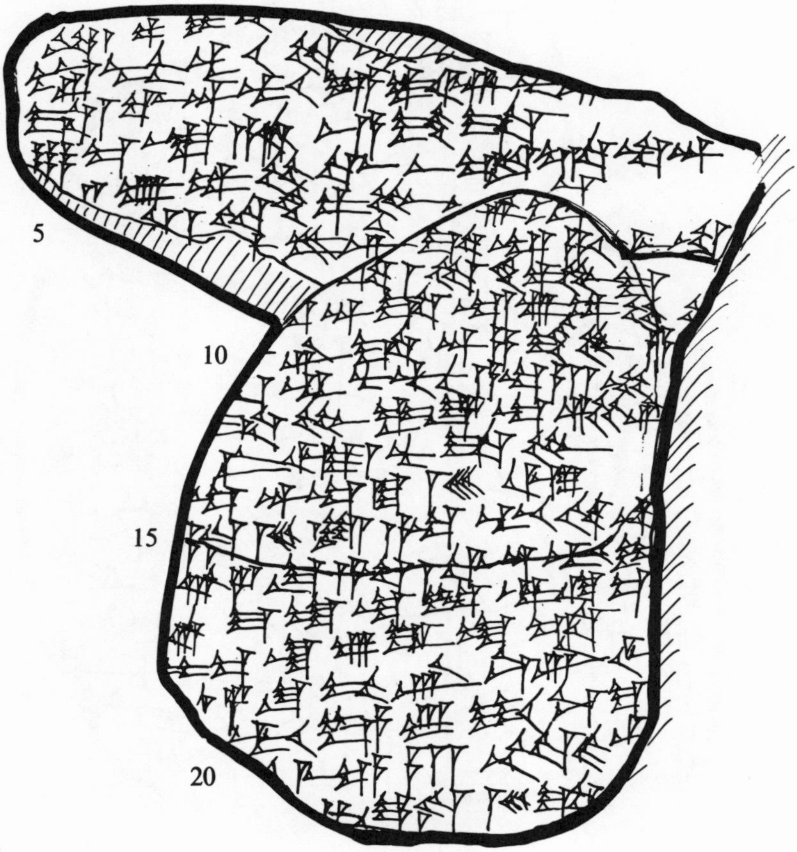

END OF OBVERSE DESTROYED

REVERSE DESTROYED

146

OBVERSE

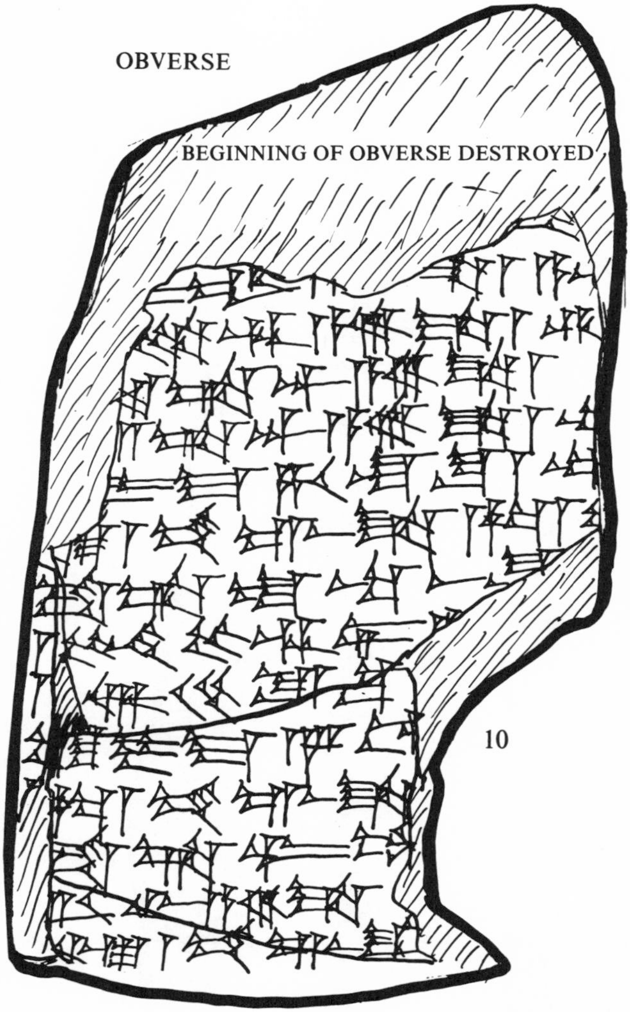

LOWER EDGE

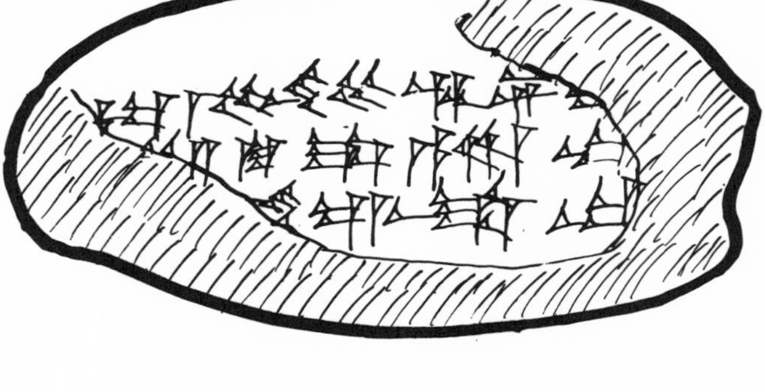

146

REVERSE

END OF REVERSE DESTROYED

152

OBVERSE

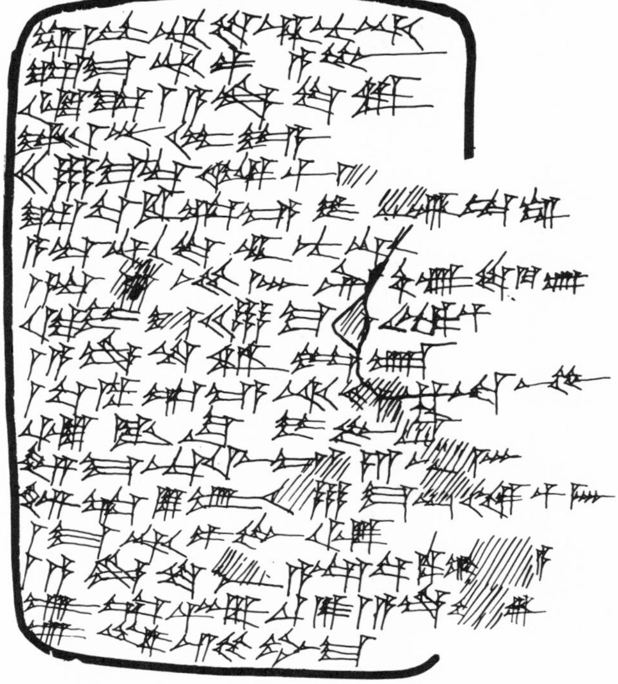

LOWER EDGE

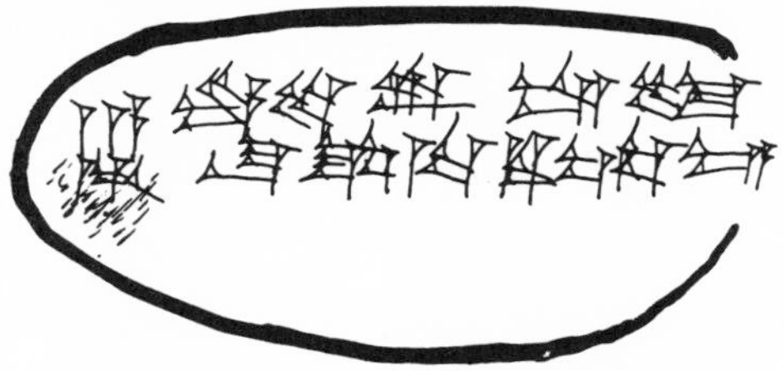

152

REVERSE

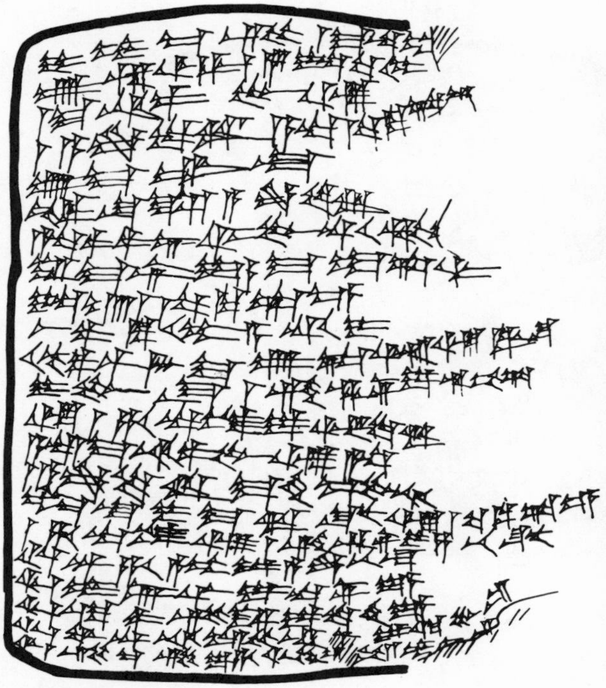

LEFT EDGE

UPPER EDGE

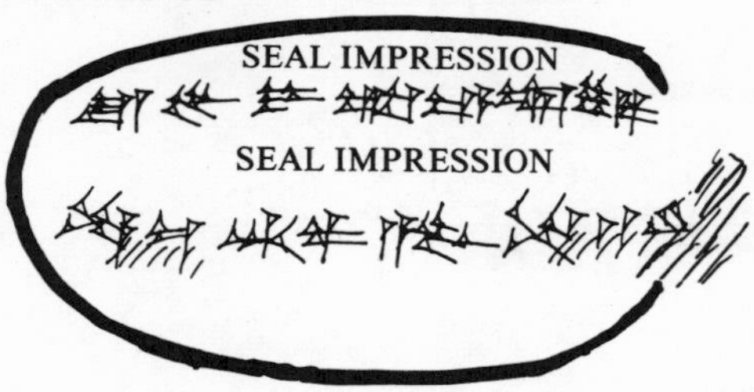

153

OBVERSE

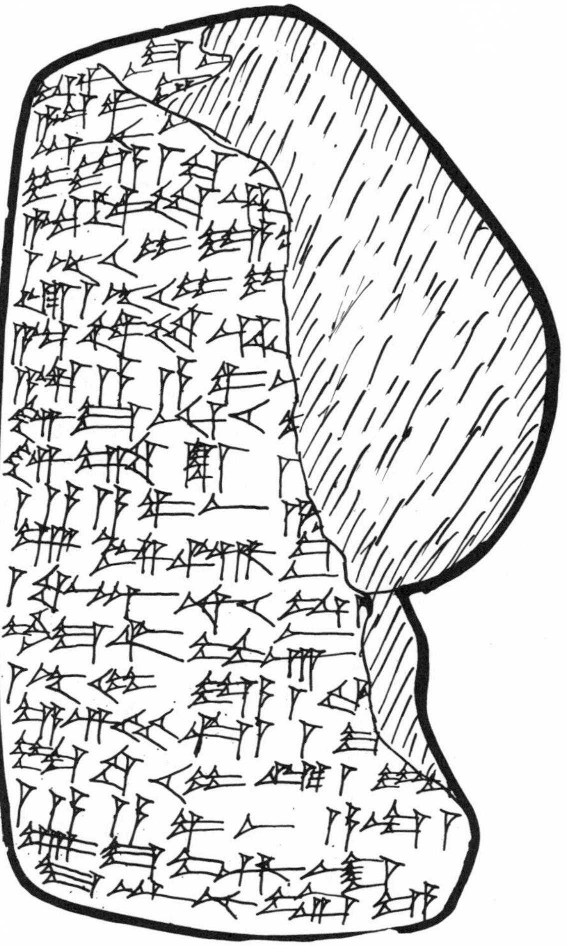

LOWER EDGE

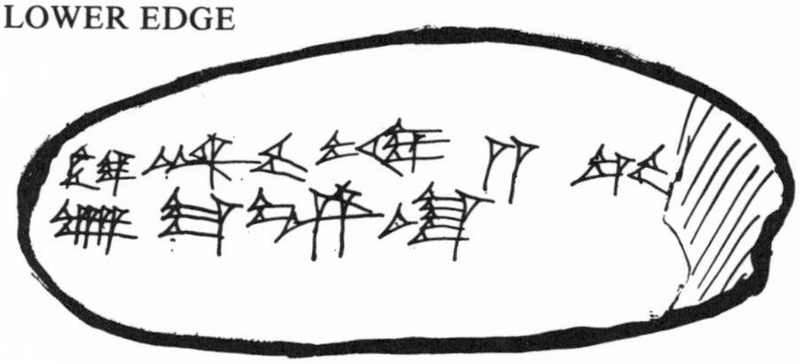

153

LEFT EDGE

REVERSE

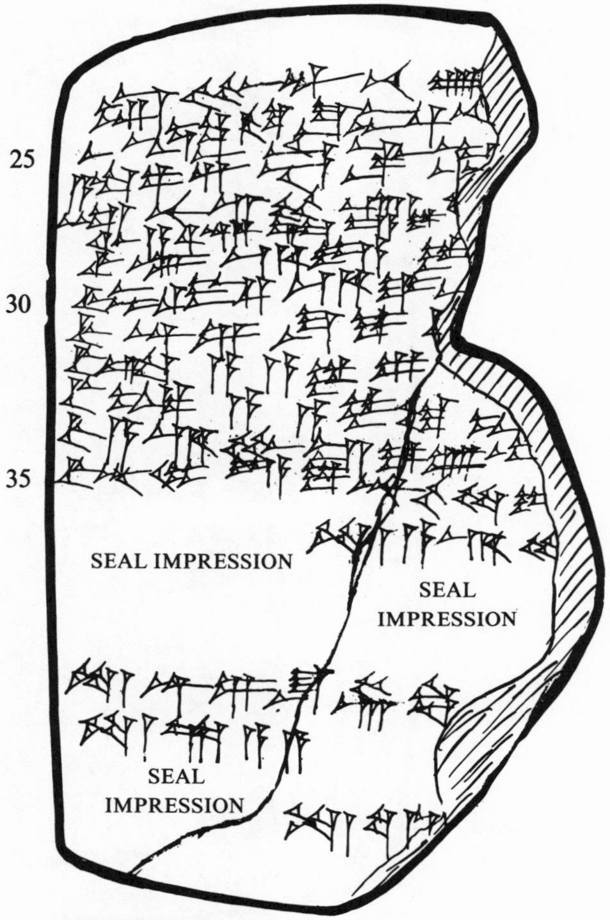

UPPER EDGE

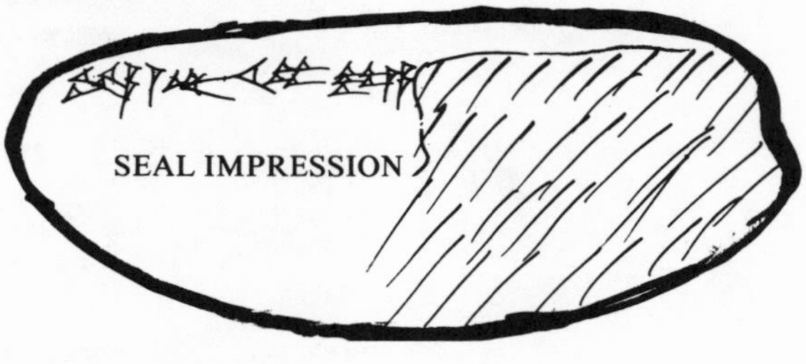

156

OBVERSE

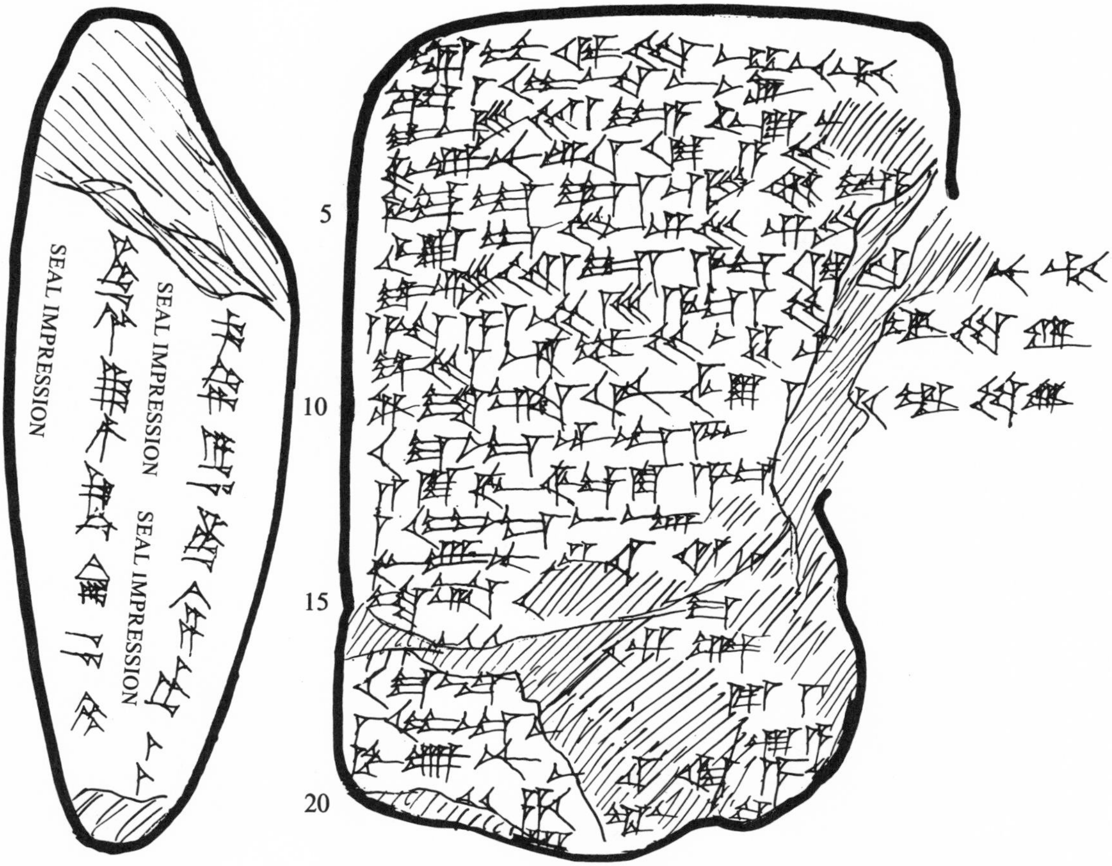

END OF OBVERSE DESTROYED

LOWER EDGE

156

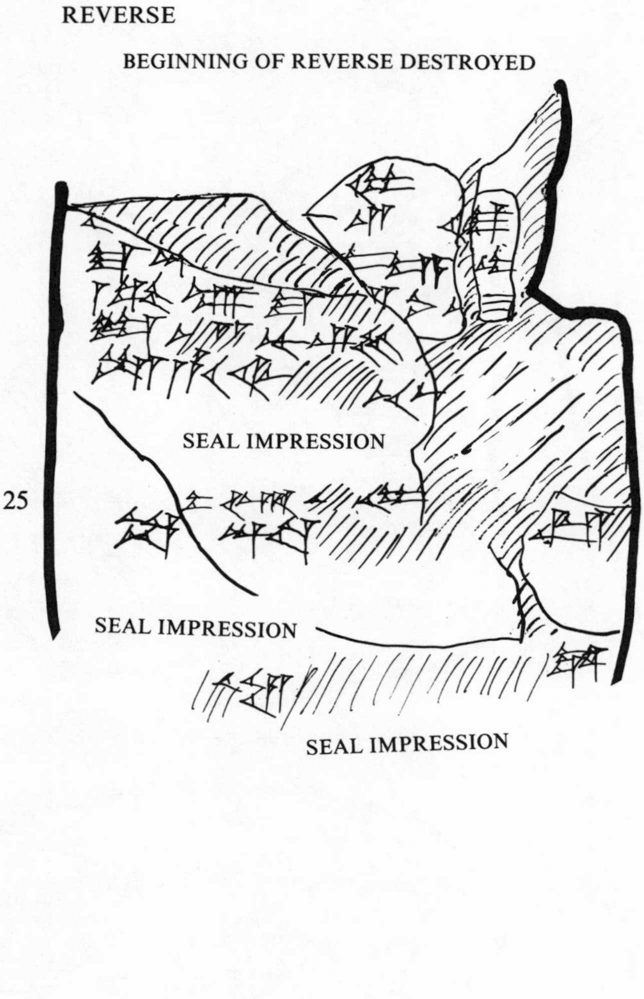
REVERSE
BEGINNING OF REVERSE DESTROYED
SEAL IMPRESSION
25
SEAL IMPRESSION
SEAL IMPRESSION

157

OBVERSE

BEGINNING OF OBVERSE DESTROYED

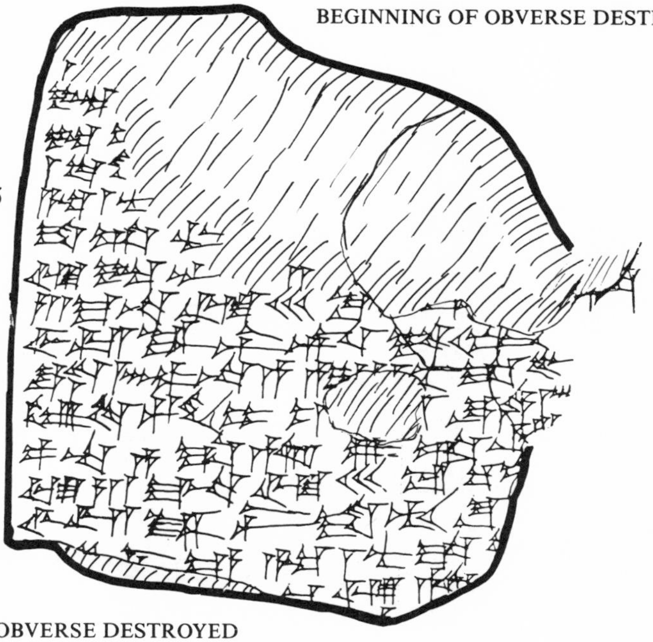

END OF OBVERSE DESTROYED

REVERSE

BEGINNING OF REVERSE DESTROYED

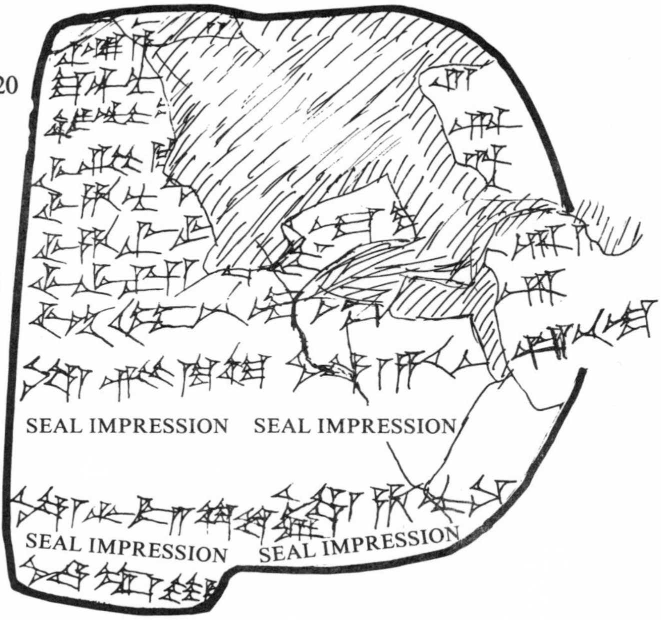

158

OBVERSE

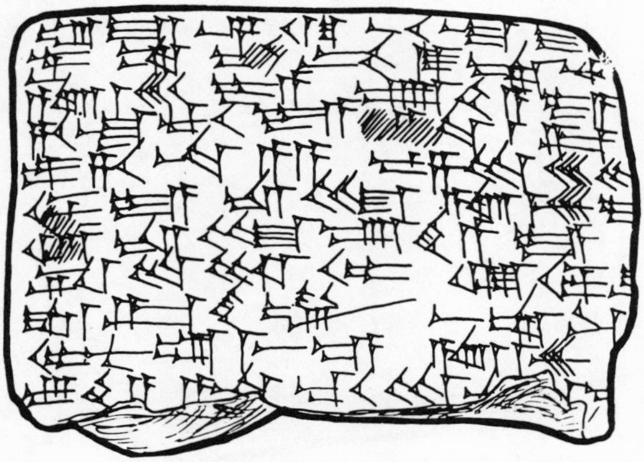

END OF OBVERSE DESTROYED

REVERSE DESTROYED

163

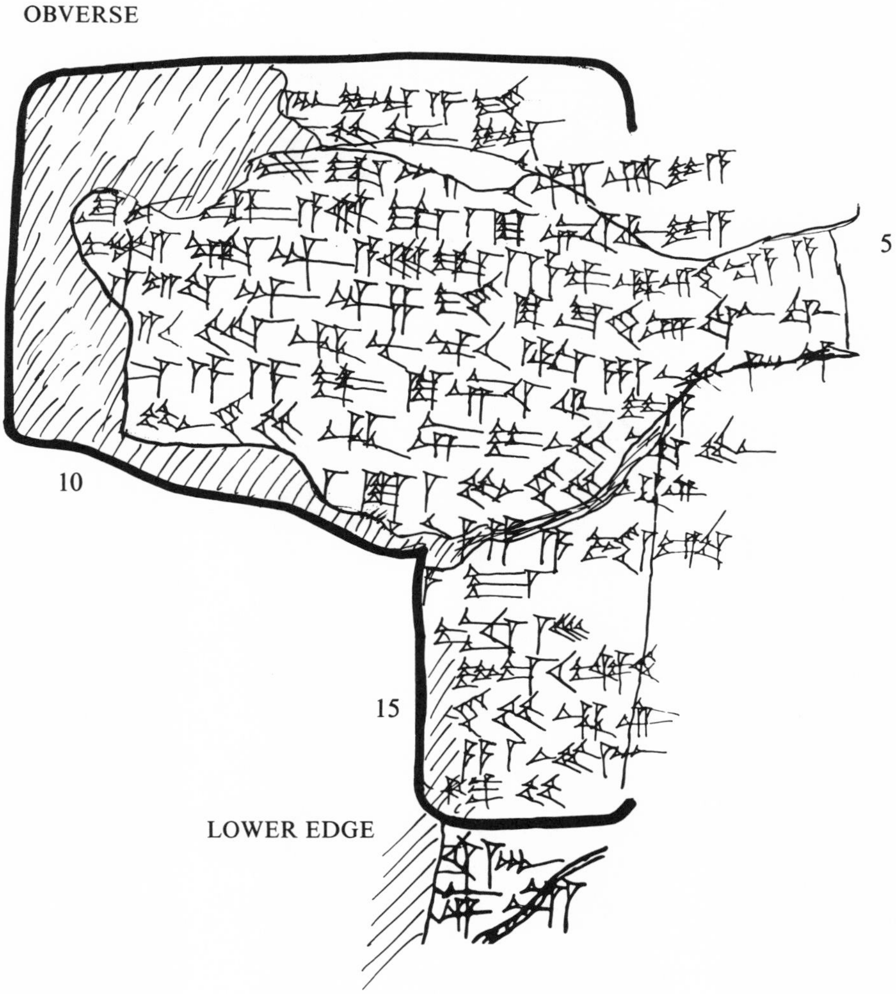

163

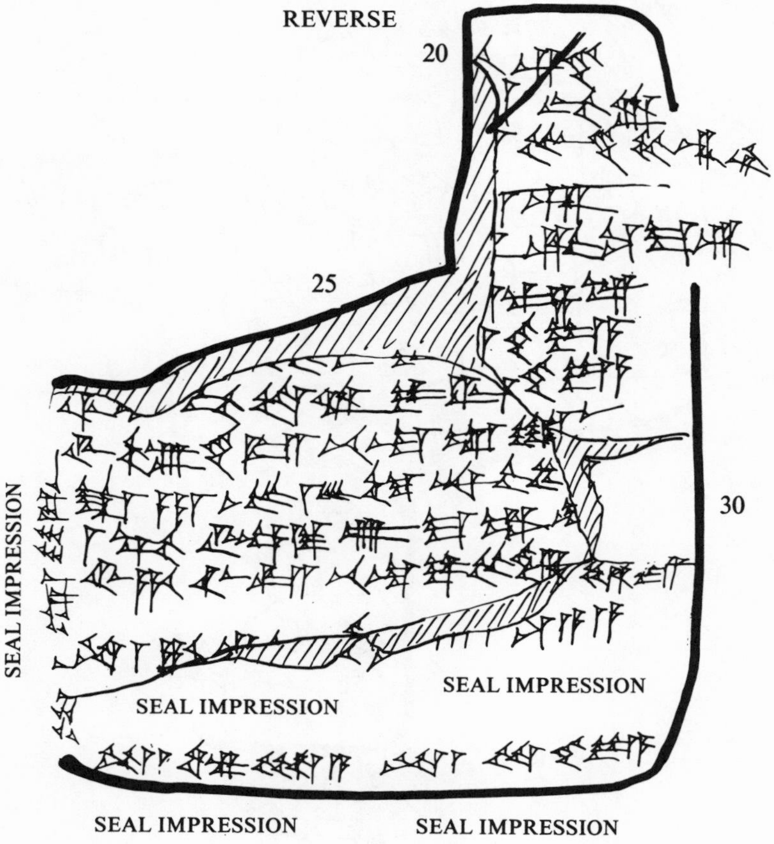
REVERSE
20
25
30
SEAL IMPRESSION
SEAL IMPRESSION
SEAL IMPRESSION
SEAL IMPRESSION
SEAL IMPRESSION

166

OBVERSE

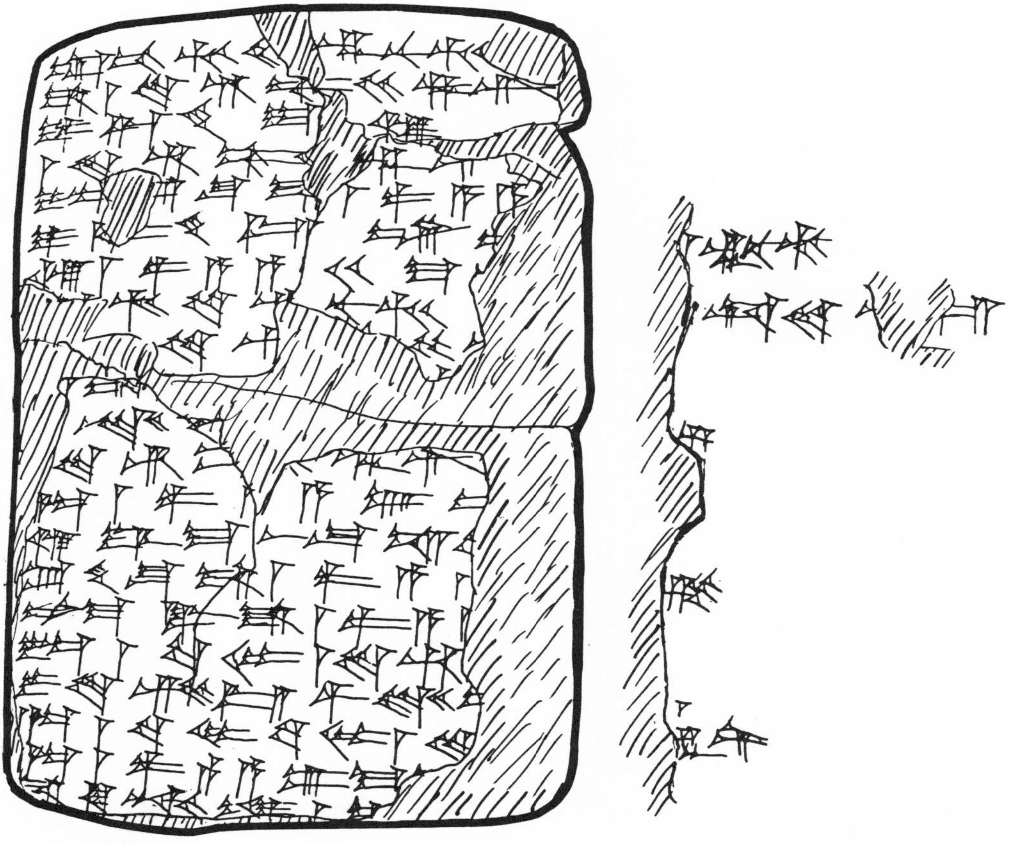

LOWER EDGE

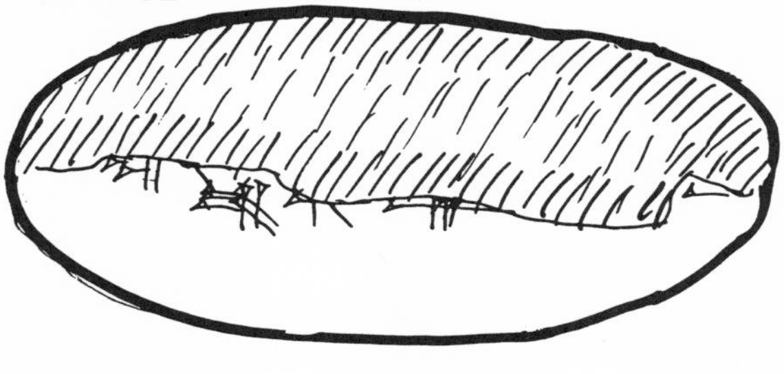

166

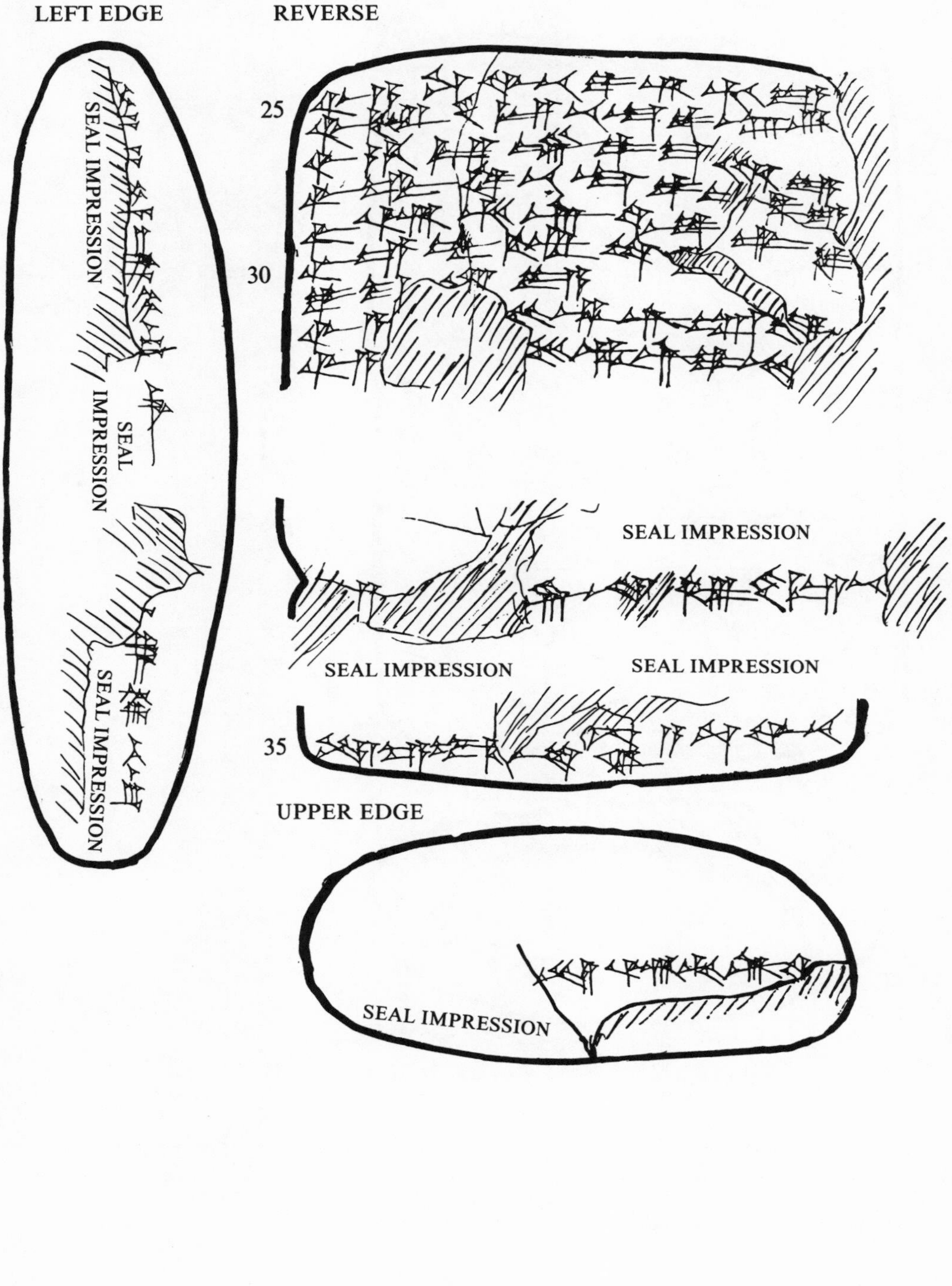
LEFT EDGE
REVERSE
25
30
SEAL IMPRESSION
SEAL IMPRESSION
SEAL IMPRESSION
SEAL IMPRESSION
SEAL IMPRESSION
SEAL IMPRESSION
35
UPPER EDGE
SEAL IMPRESSION

168

OBVERSE

BEGINNING OF OBVERSE DESTROYED

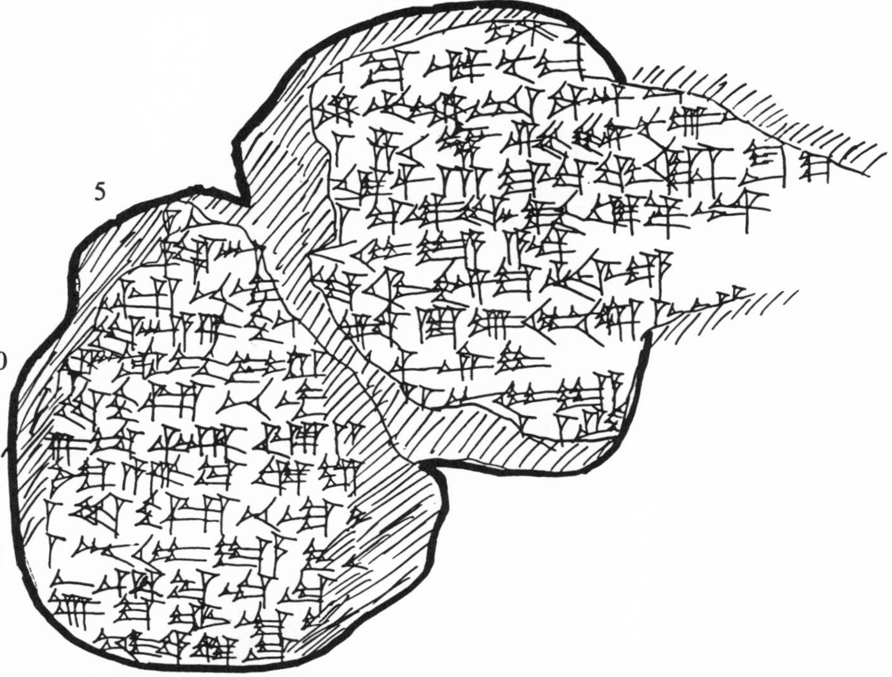

LOWER EDGE

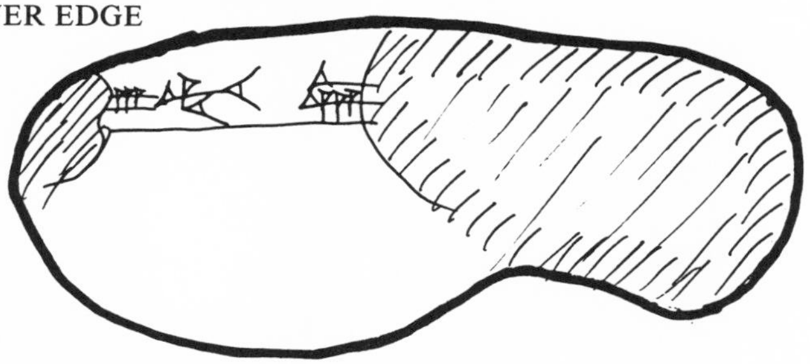

REVERSE

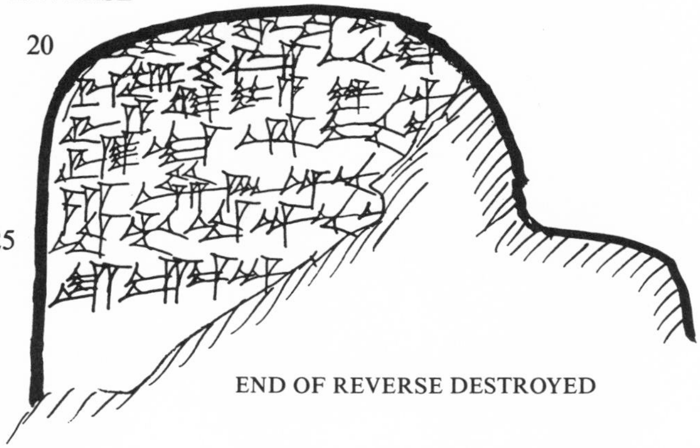

END OF REVERSE DESTROYED

171

OBVERSE

LOWER EDGE

171

REVERSE

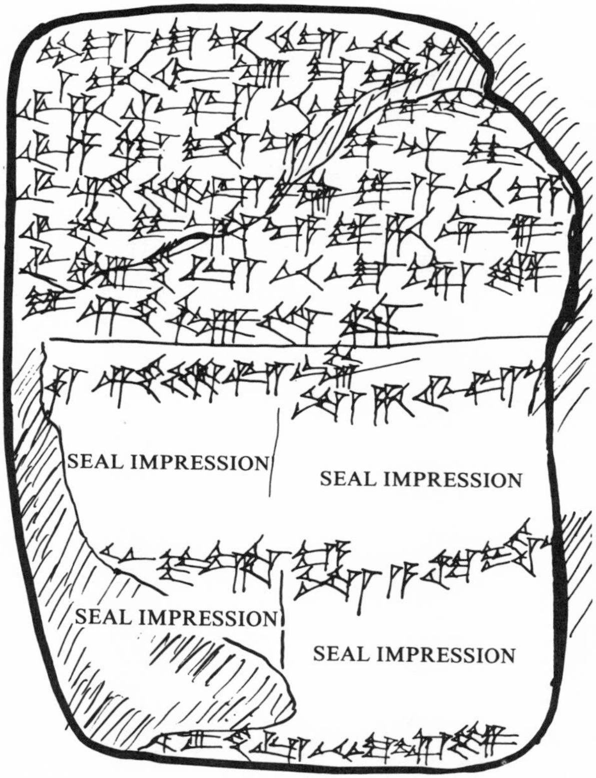
SEAL IMPRESSION
SEAL IMPRESSION
SEAL IMPRESSION
SEAL IMPRESSION

172

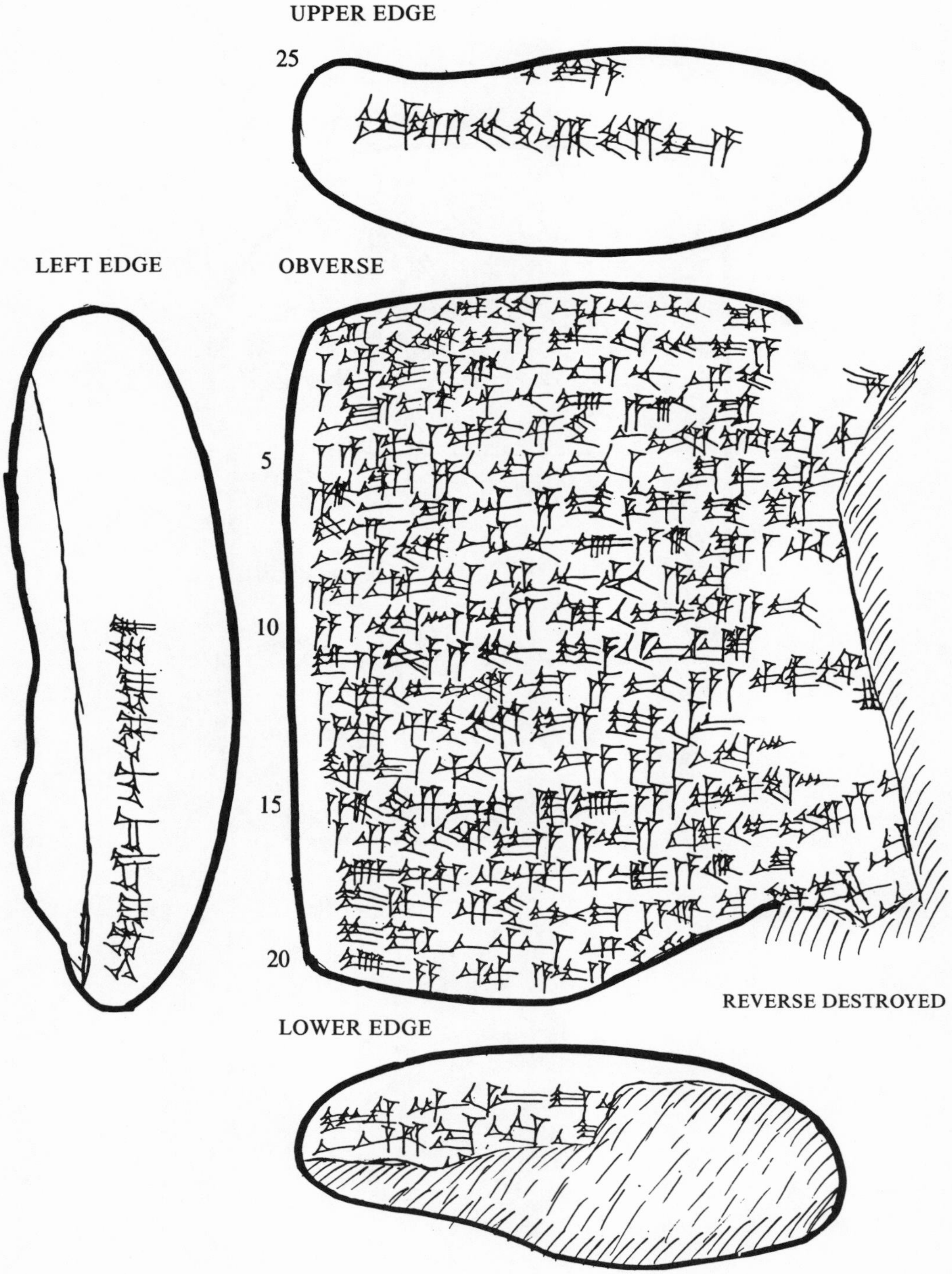
UPPER EDGE
25
LEFT EDGE
OBVERSE
5
10
15
20
REVERSE DESTROYED
LOWER EDGE

175

OBVERSE

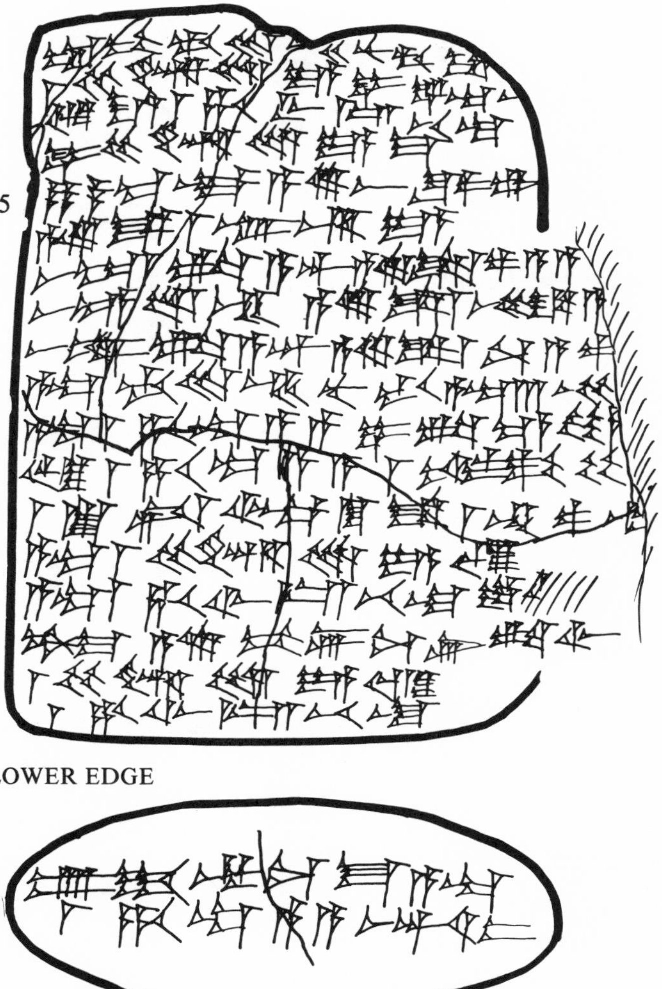

LEFT EDGE

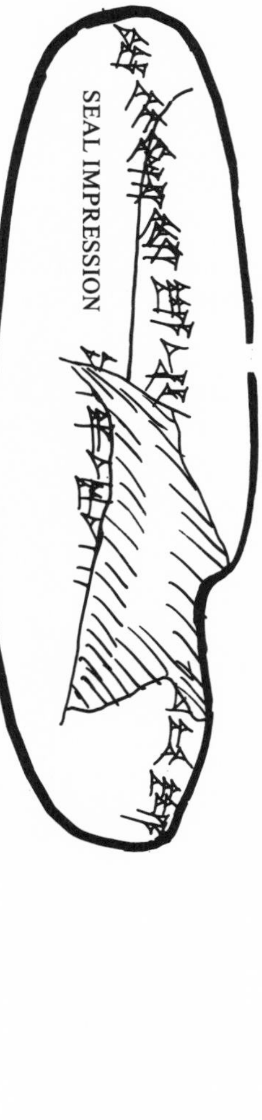

LOWER EDGE

175

REVERSE

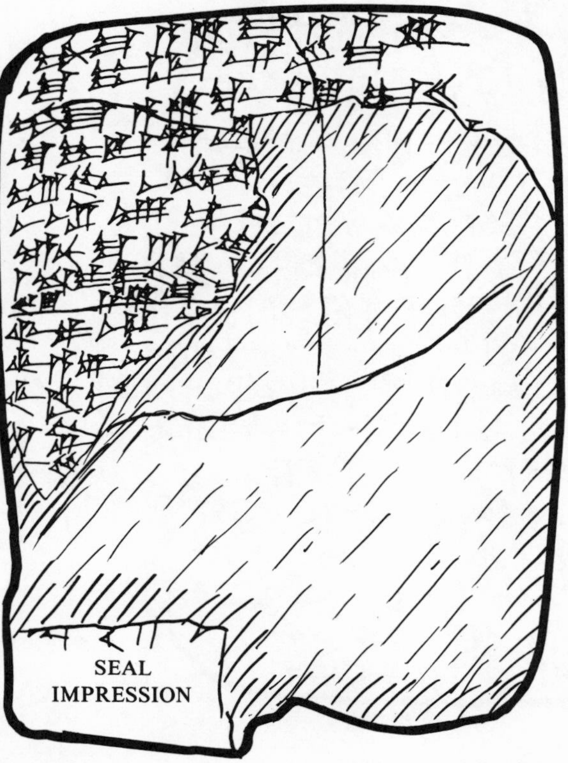

UPPER EDGE

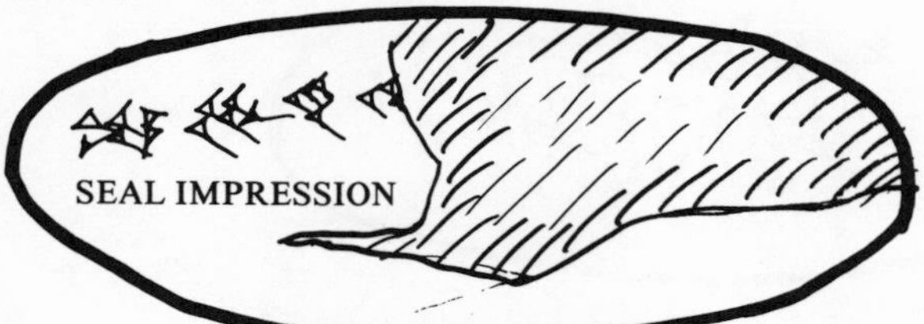

176

OBVERSE

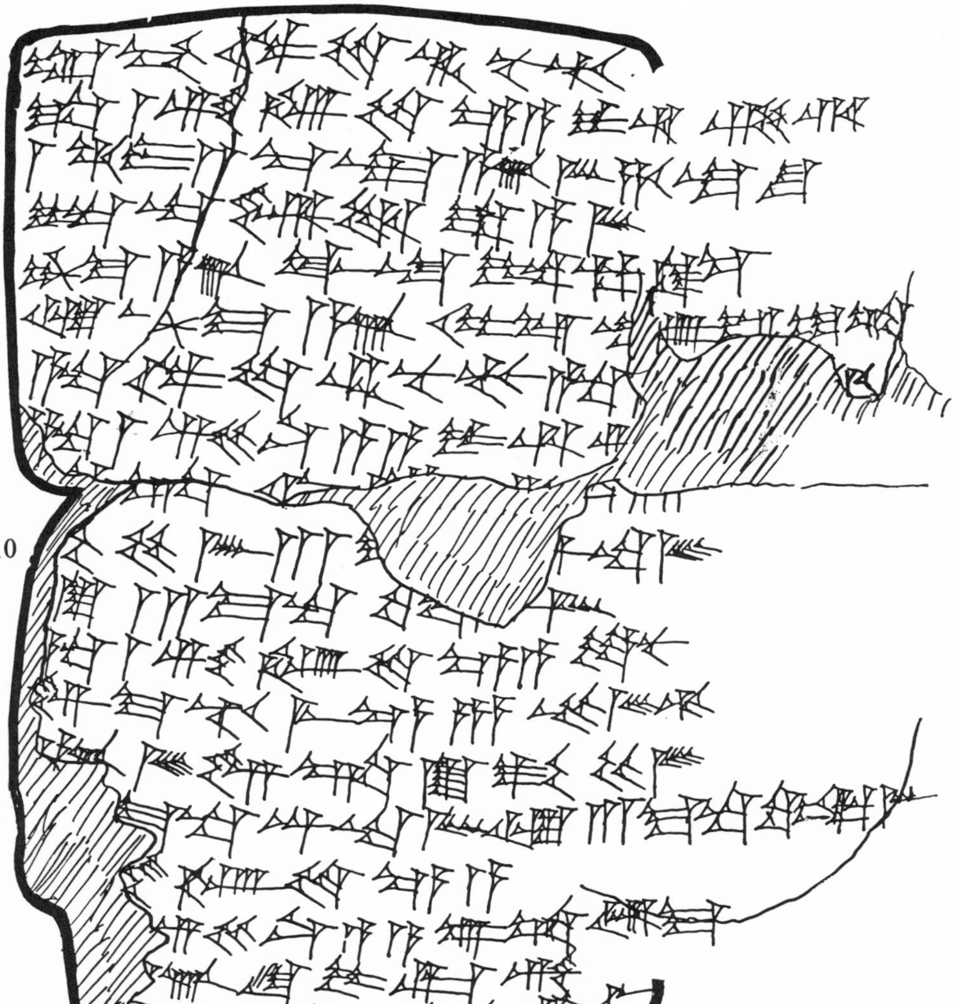

LOWER EDGE

176

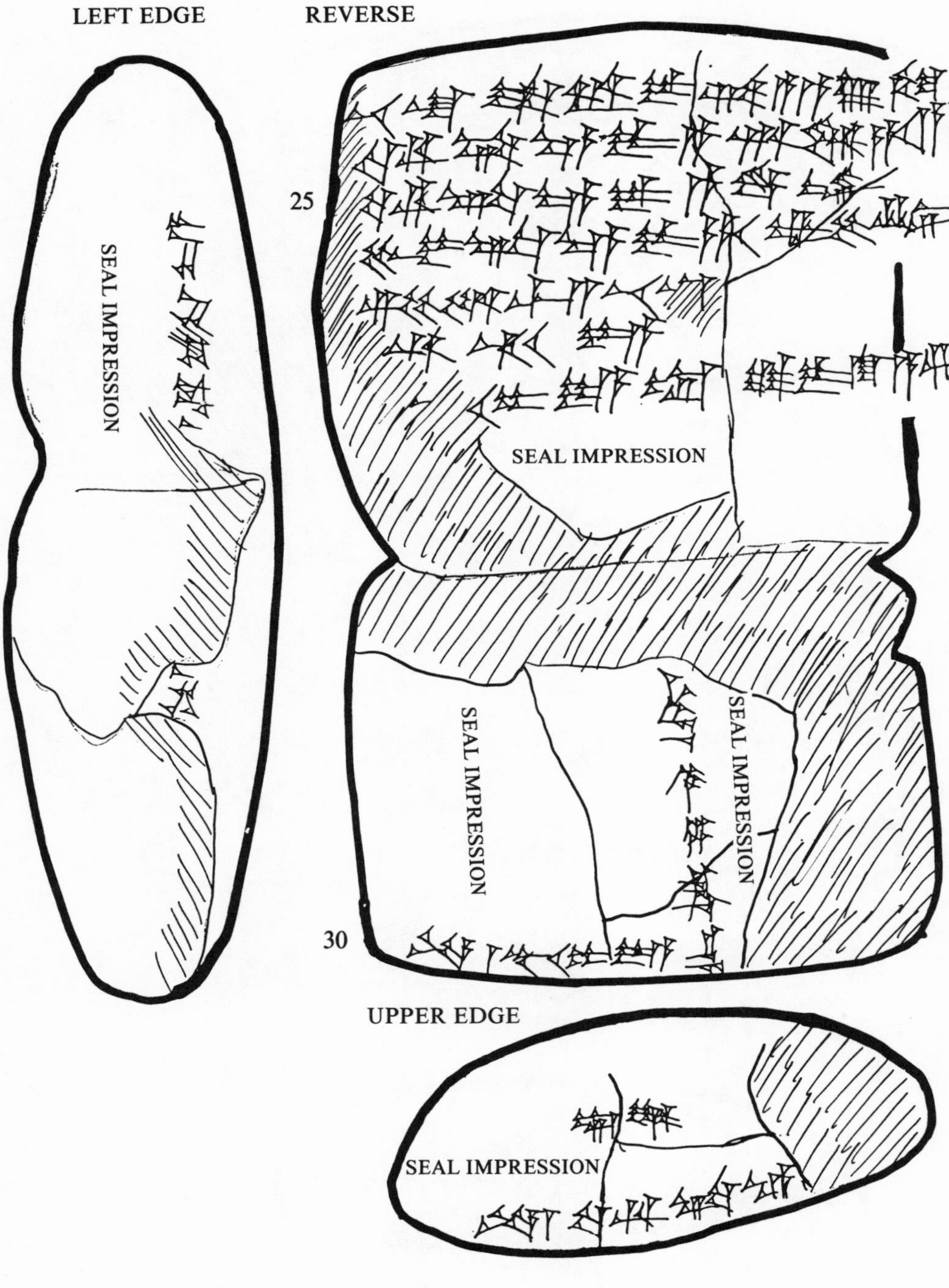
LEFT EDGE
REVERSE
SEAL IMPRESSION
25
SEAL IMPRESSION
SEAL IMPRESSION
SEAL IMPRESSION
30
UPPER EDGE
SEAL IMPRESSION

177

OBVERSE

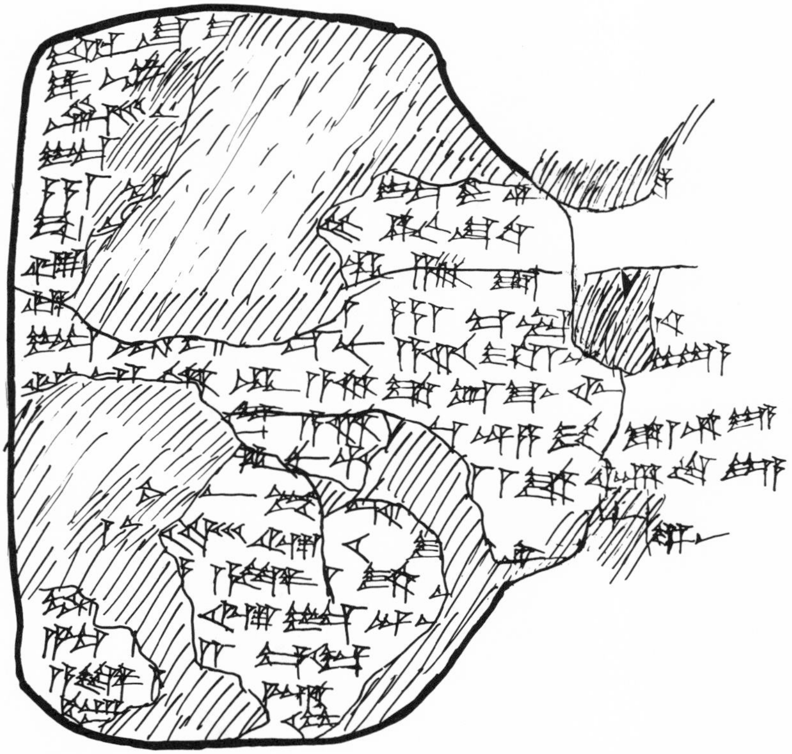

LOWER EDGE

177

REVERSE

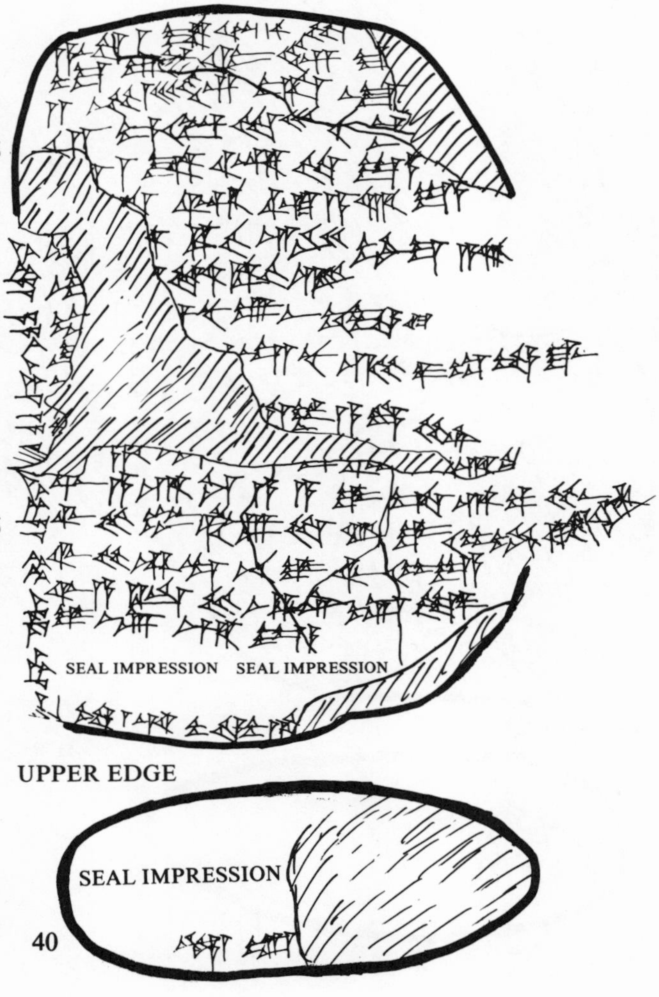

UPPER EDGE

184

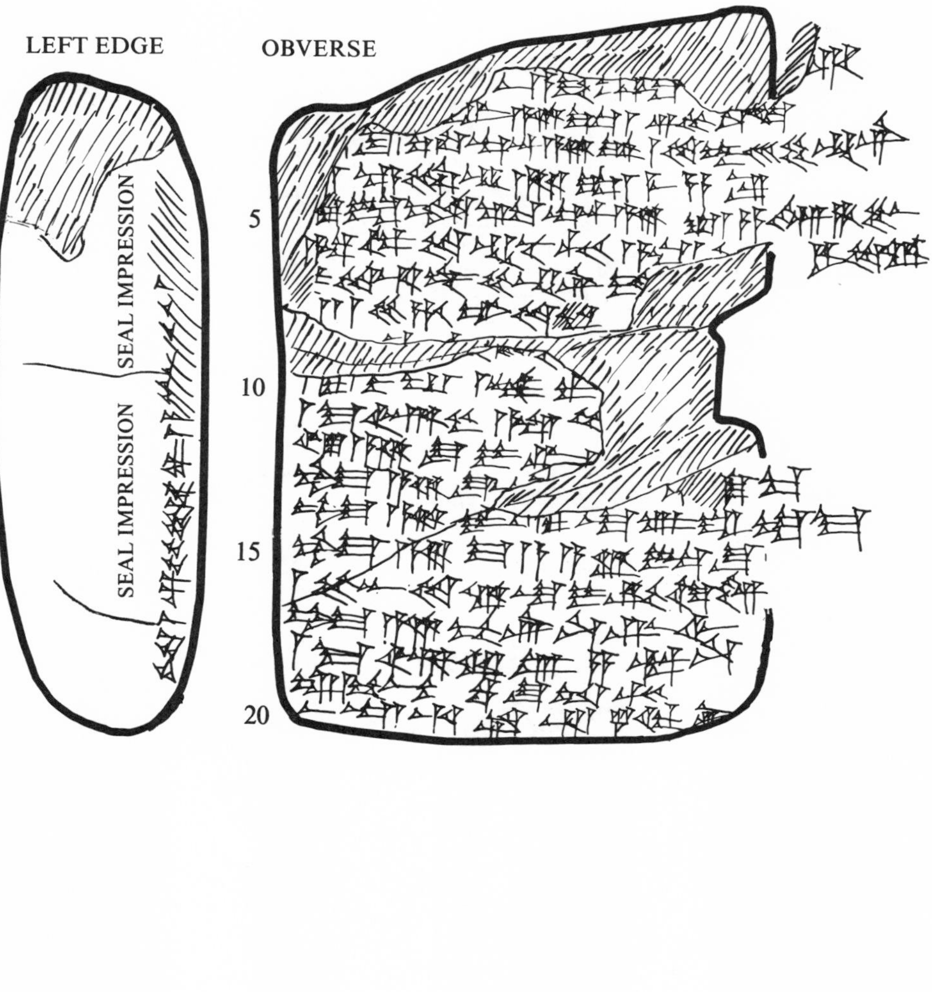
LEFT EDGE
OBVERSE
SEAL IMPRESSION
SEAL IMPRESSION
5
10
15
20

184

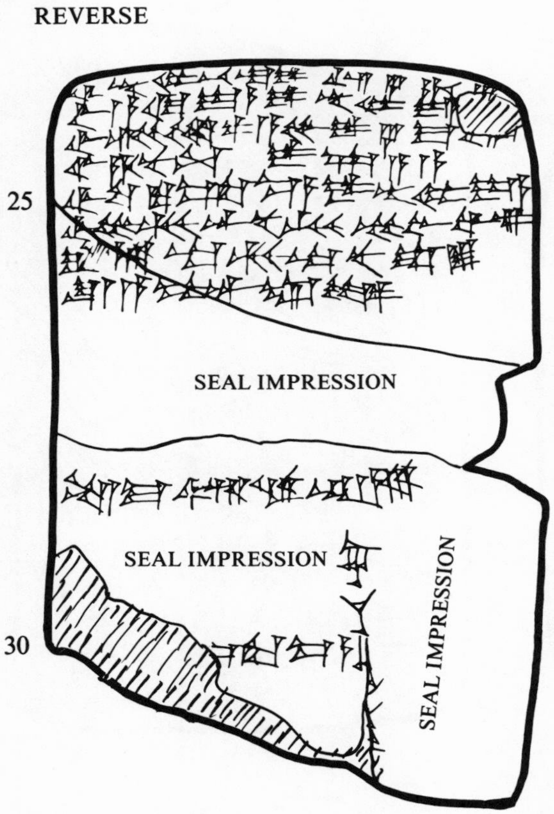
REVERSE
25
SEAL IMPRESSION
SEAL IMPRESSION
30
SEAL IMPRESSION

185

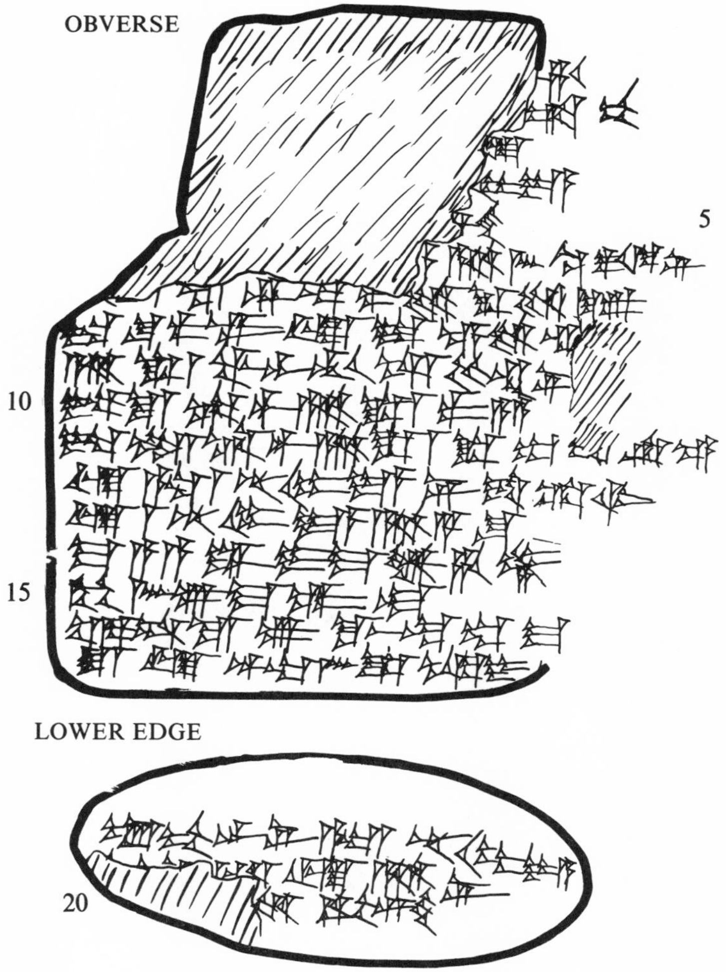

185

LEFT EDGE

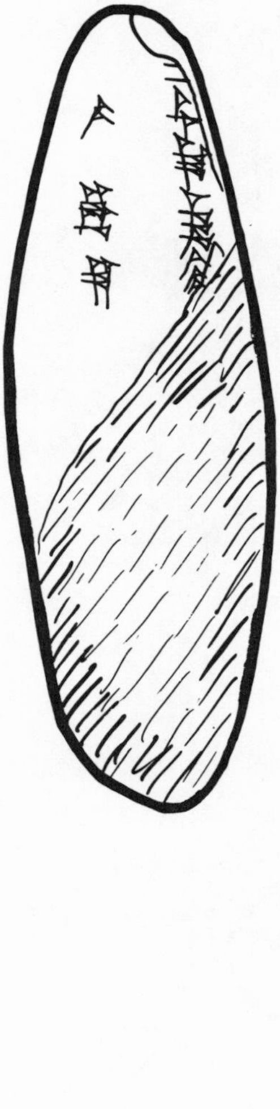

REVERSE

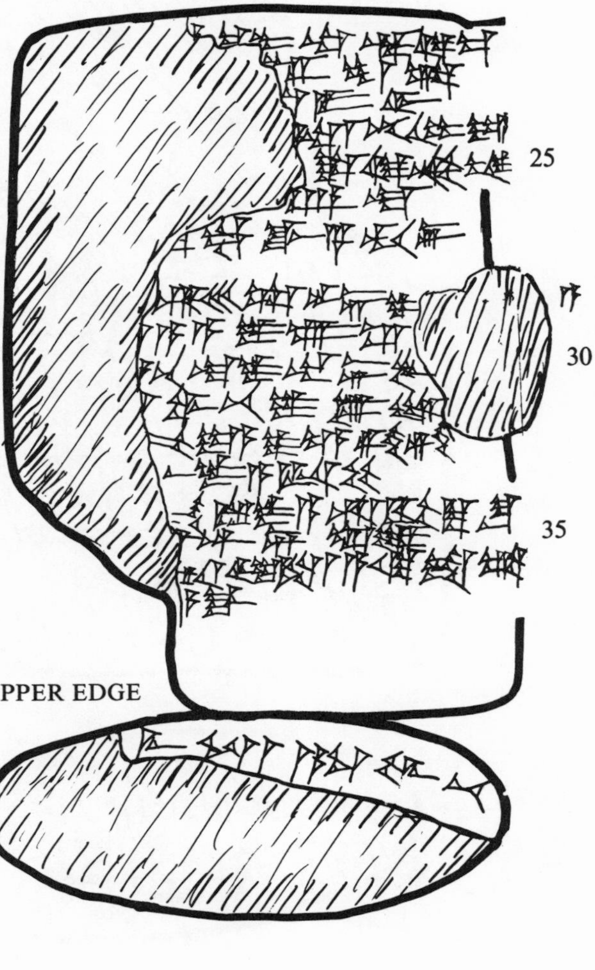

UPPER EDGE

186

OBVERSE

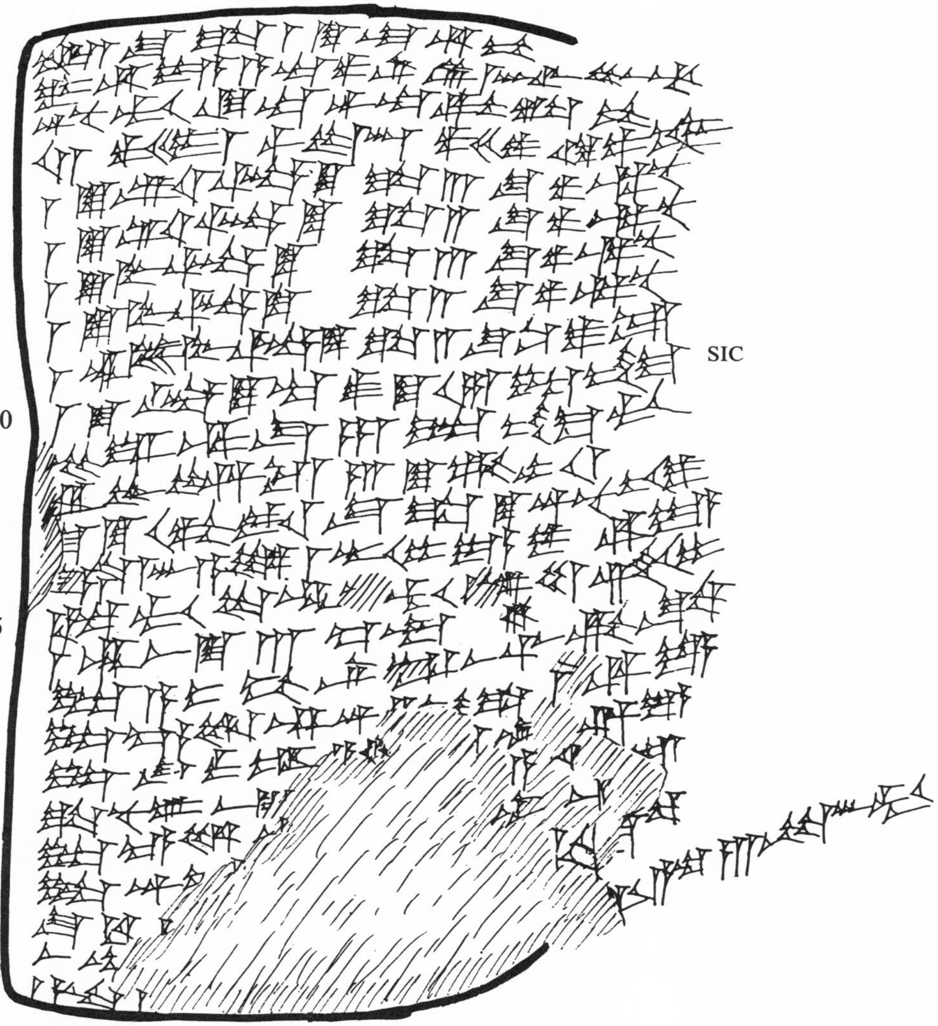

LOWER EDGE

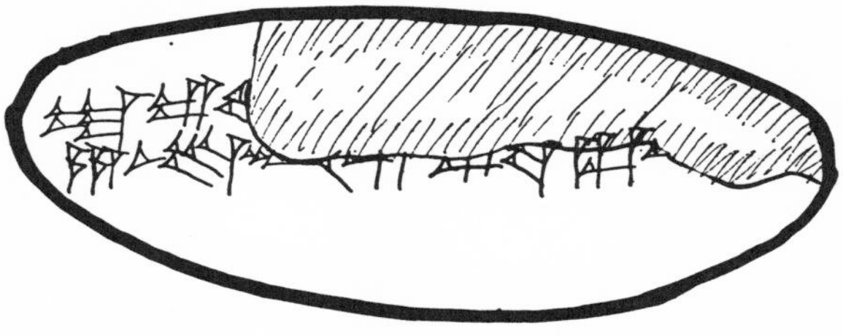

186

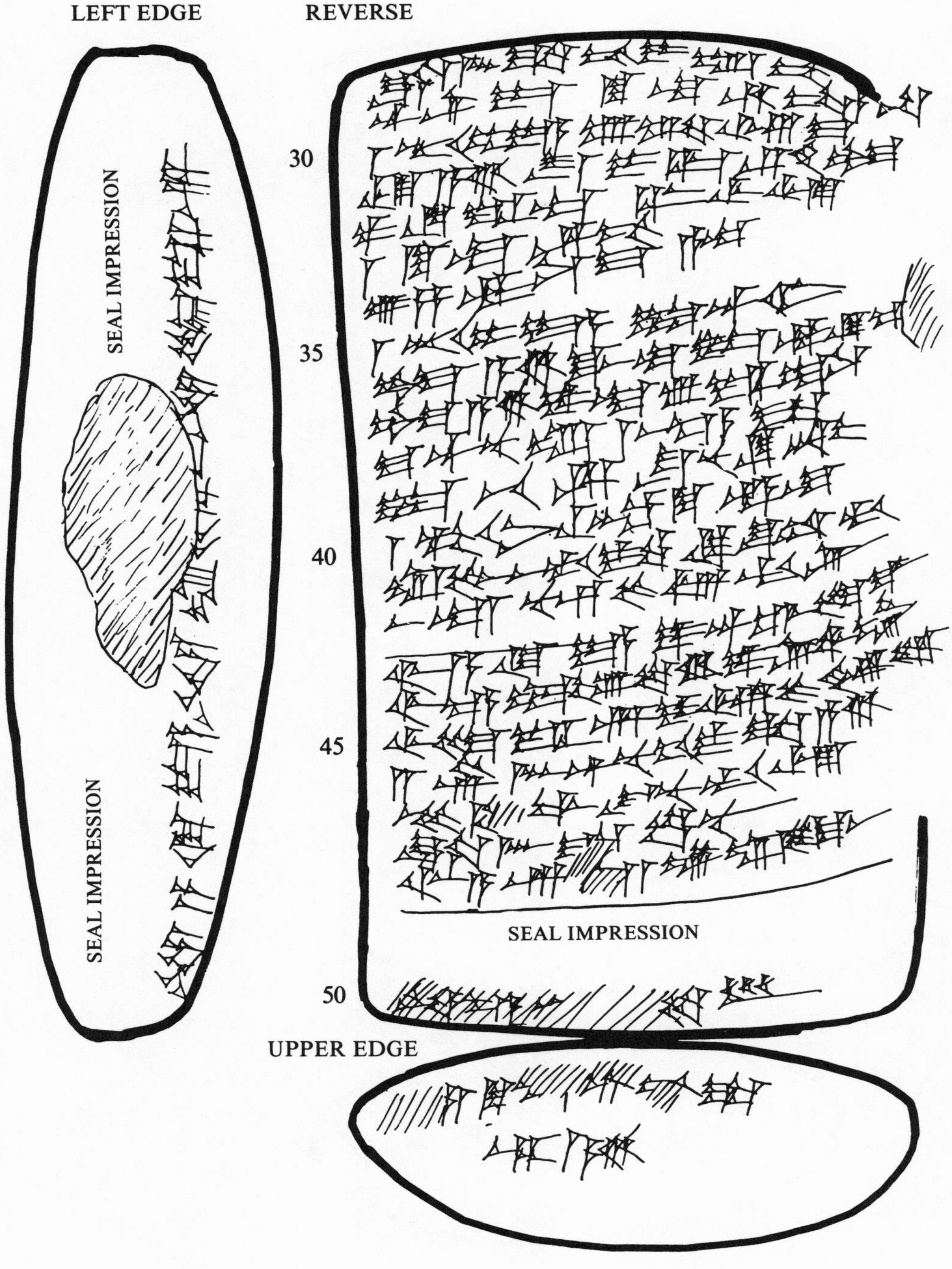
LEFT EDGE
REVERSE
SEAL IMPRESSION
30
35
40
45
SEAL IMPRESSION
SEAL IMPRESSION
50
UPPER EDGE

187

OBVERSE

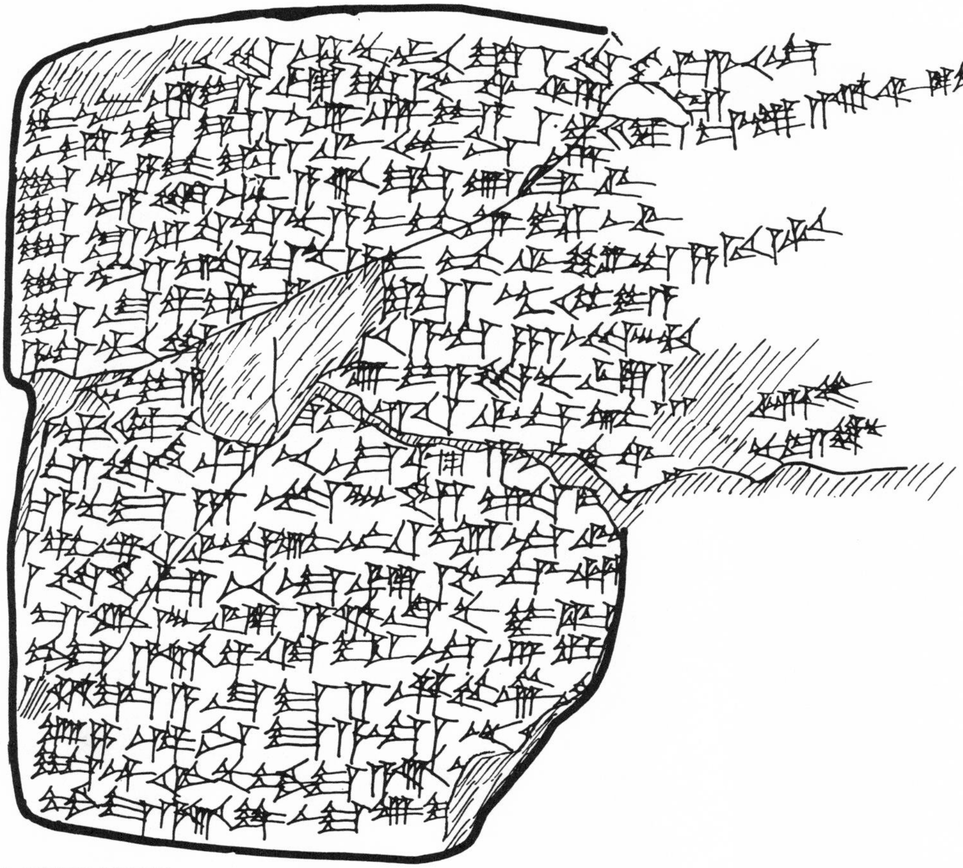

LOWER EDGE

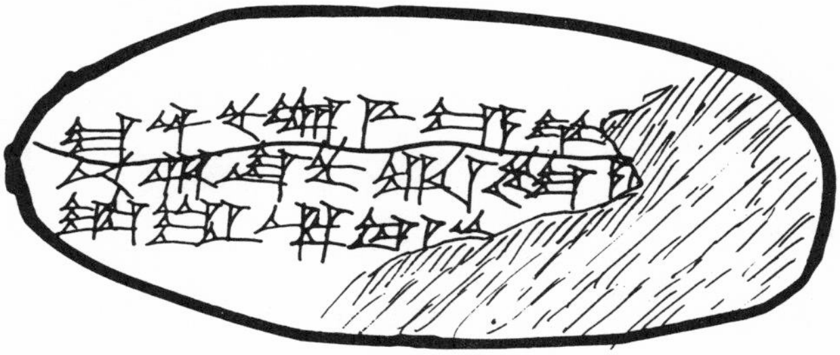

187

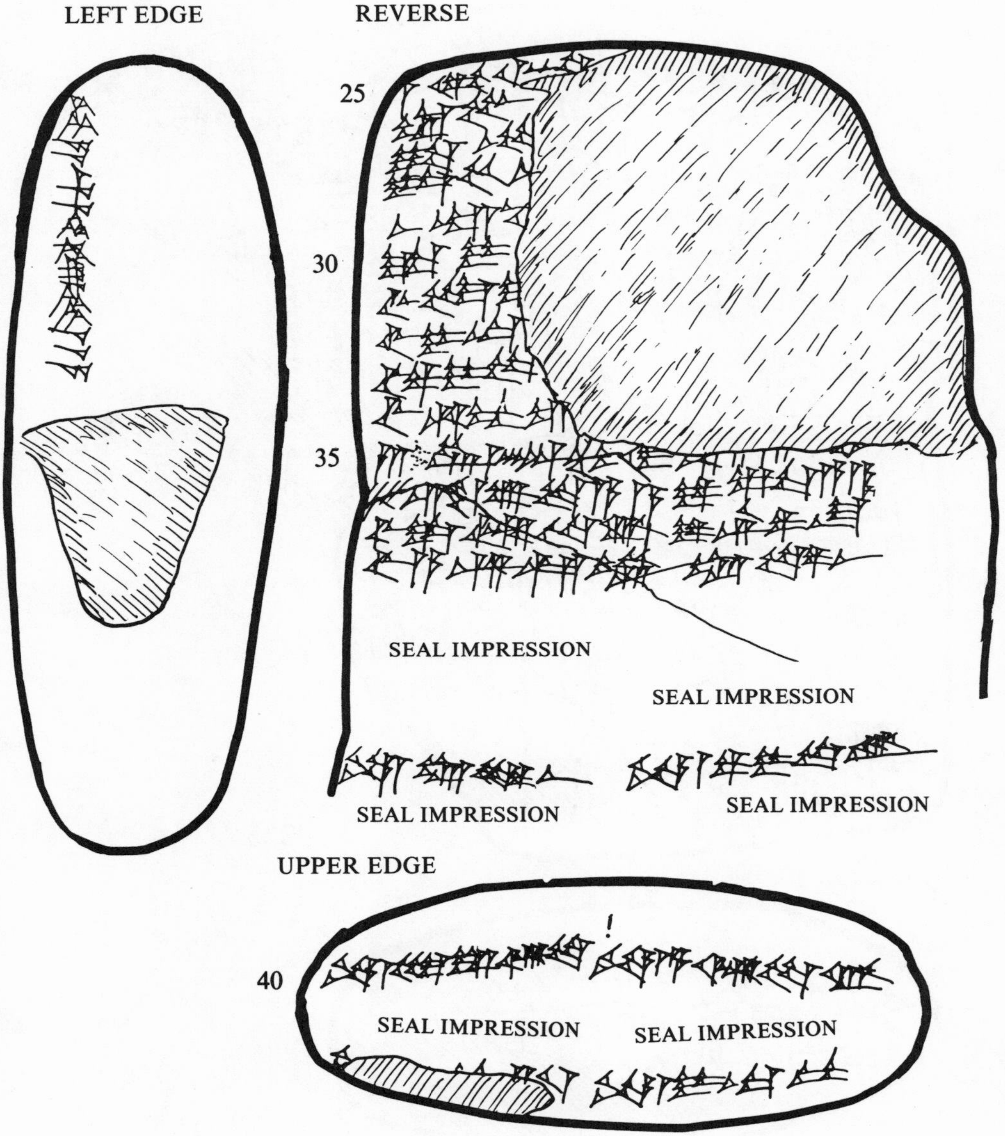
LEFT EDGE
REVERSE
25
30
35
SEAL IMPRESSION
SEAL IMPRESSION
SEAL IMPRESSION
SEAL IMPRESSION
UPPER EDGE
40
SEAL IMPRESSION
SEAL IMPRESSION

188

OBVERSE

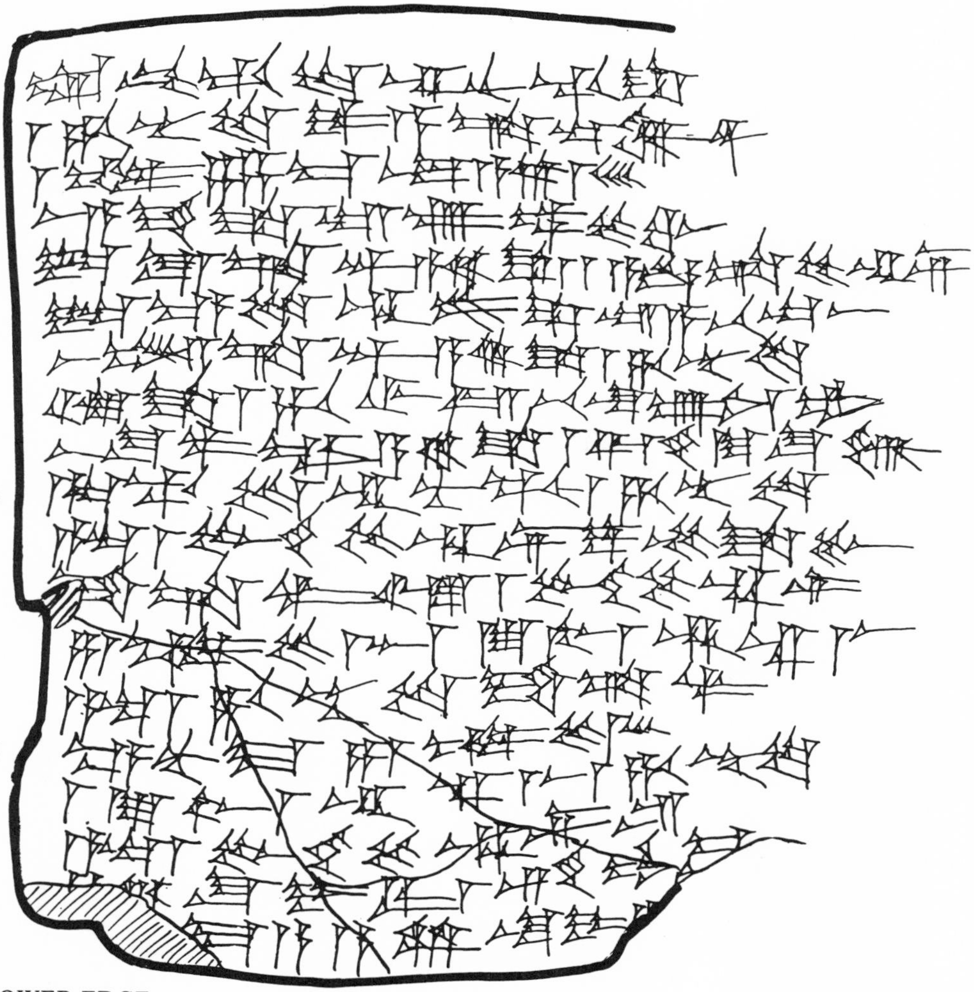

LOWER EDGE

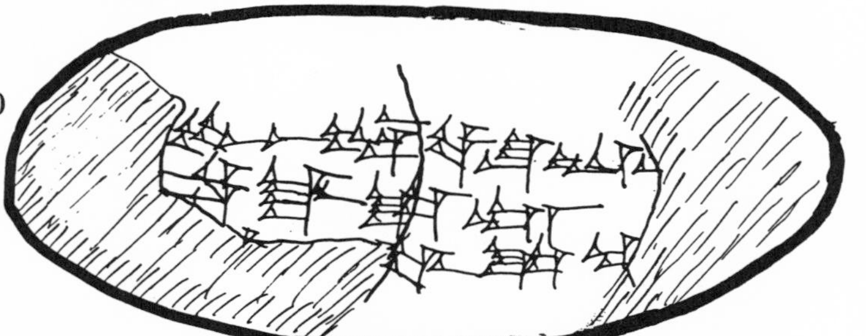

188

LEFT EDGE REVERSE

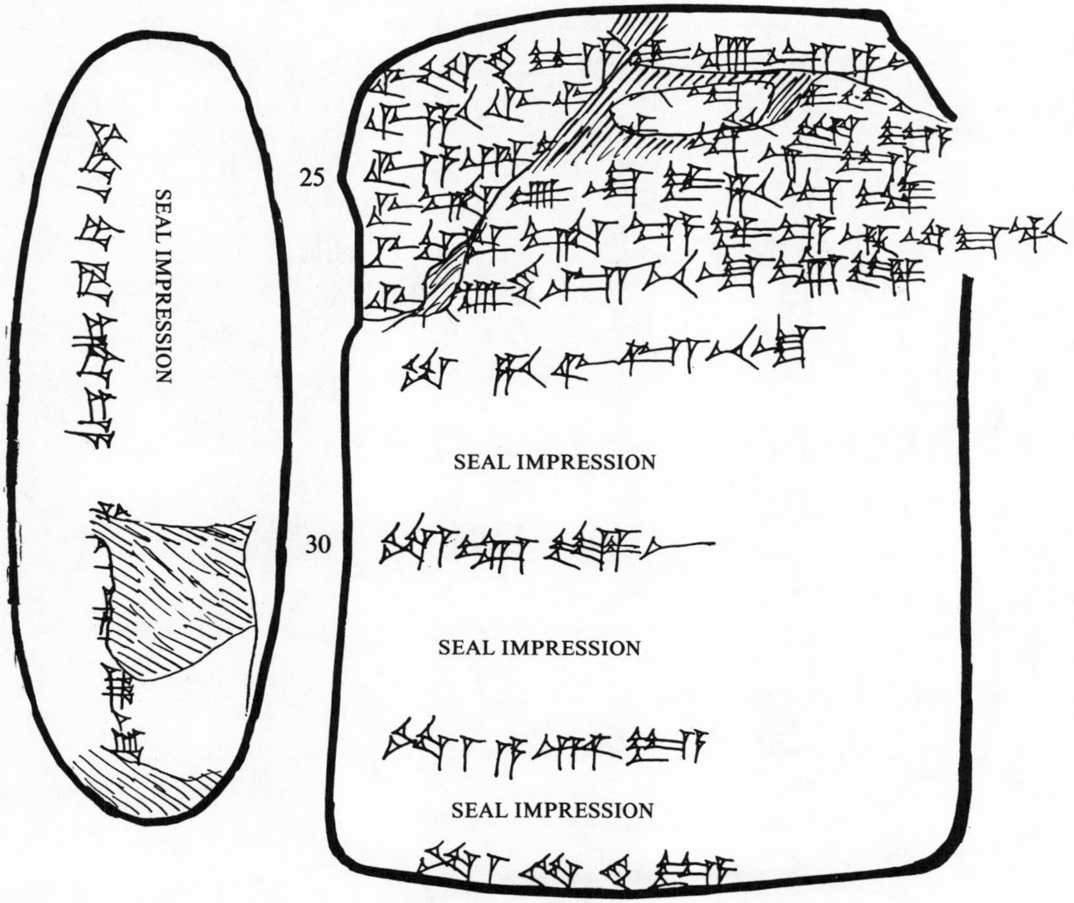

189

OBVERSE

BEGINNING OF REVERSE DESTROYED

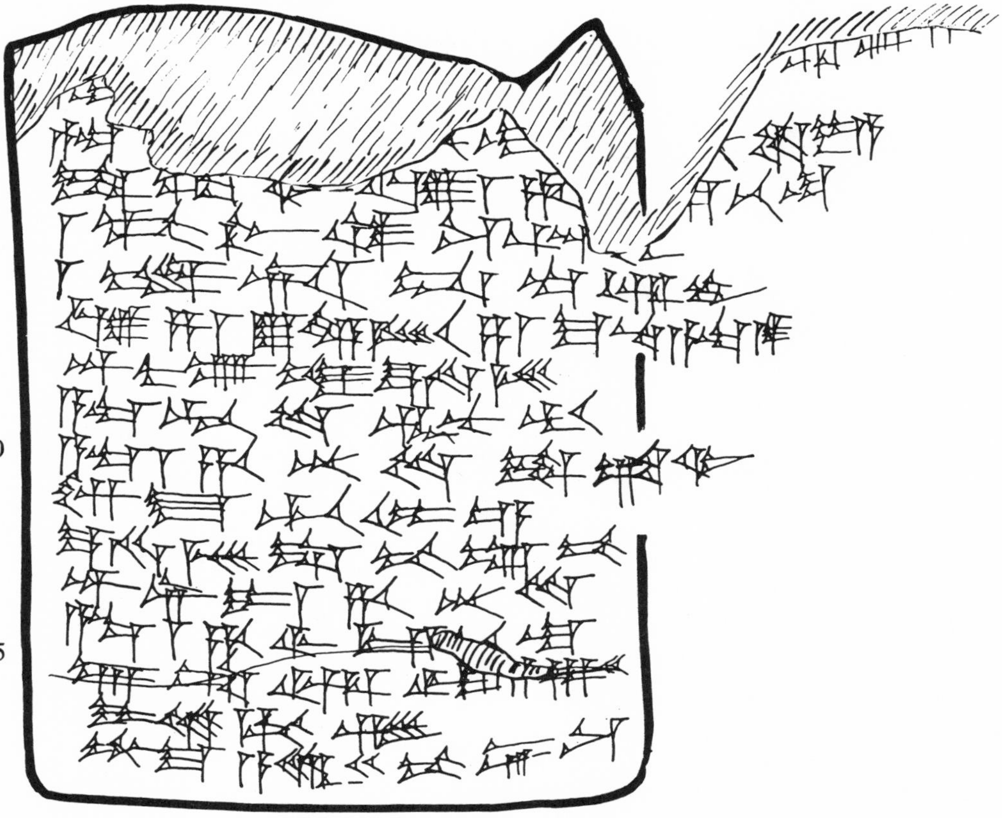

LOWER EDGE

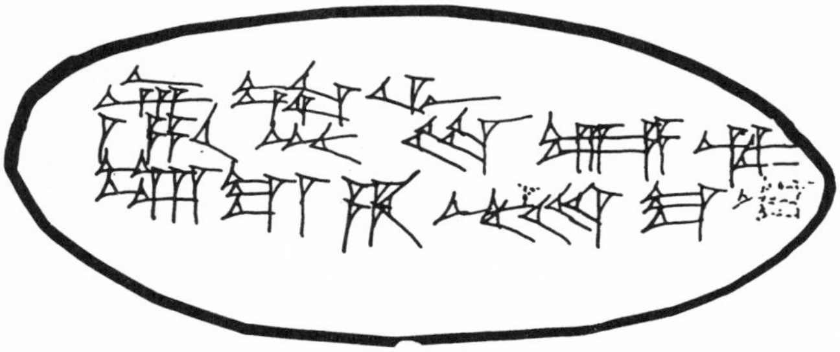

189

REVERSE

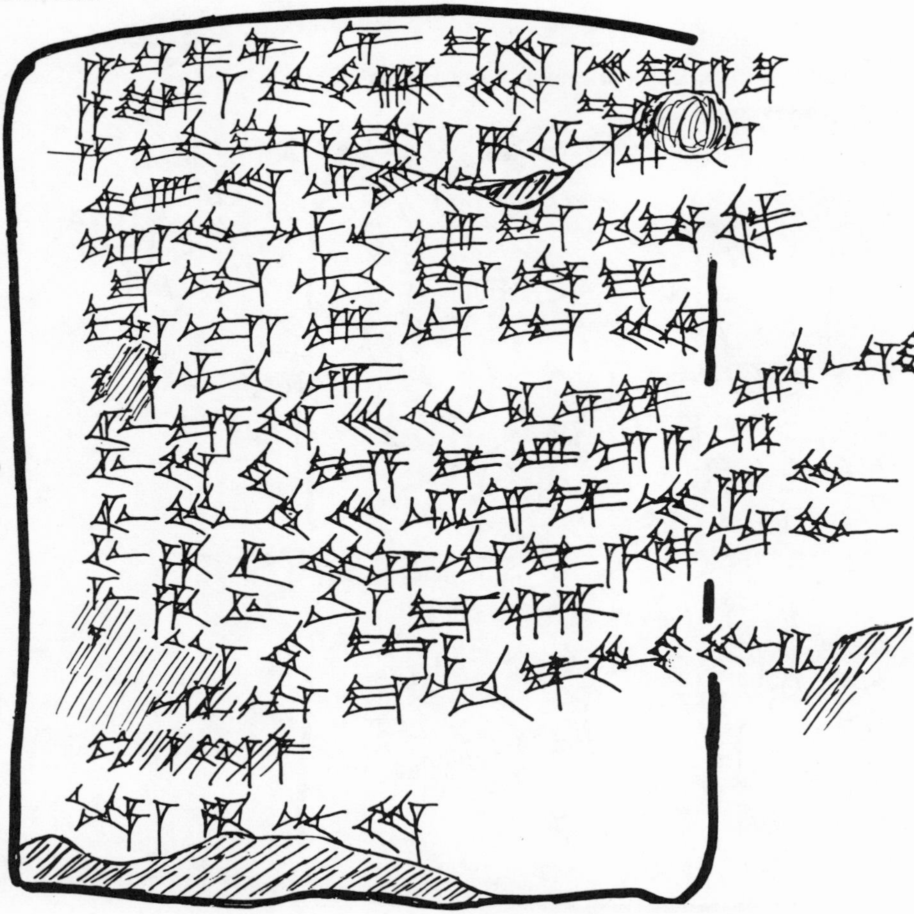

LEFT EDGE

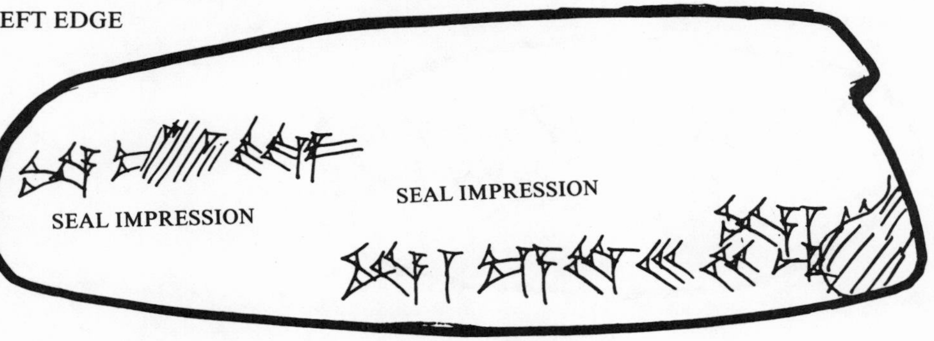

200

OBVERSE

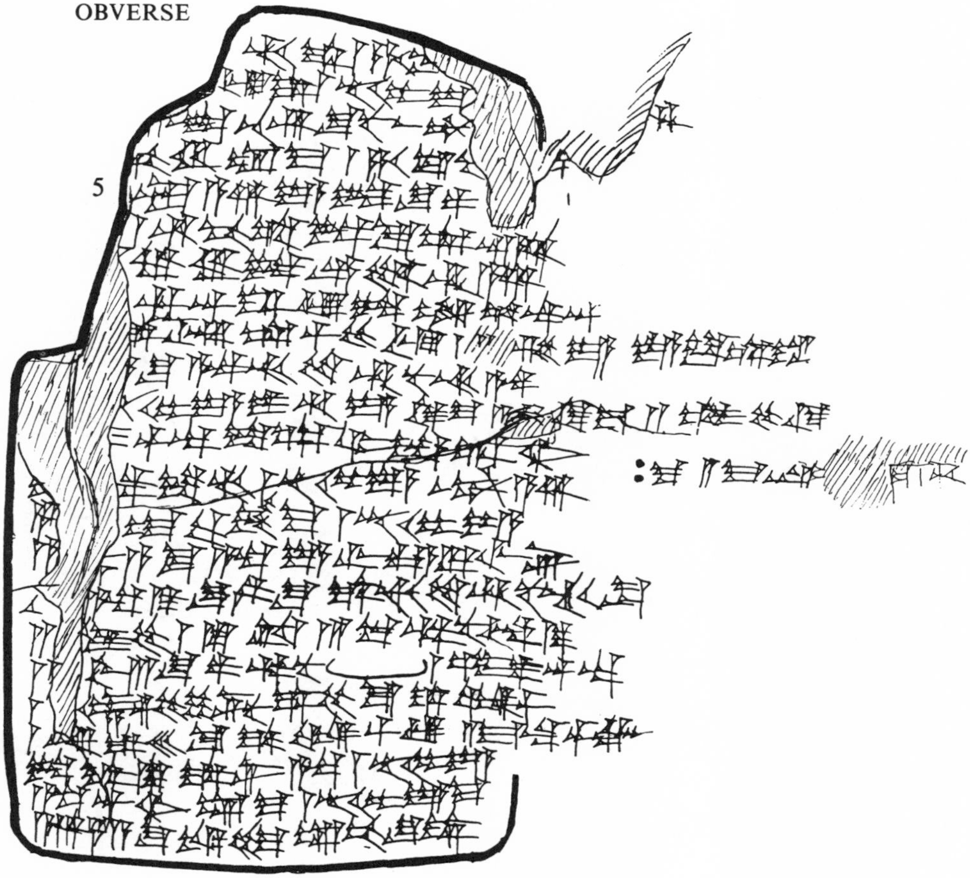

LOWER EDGE

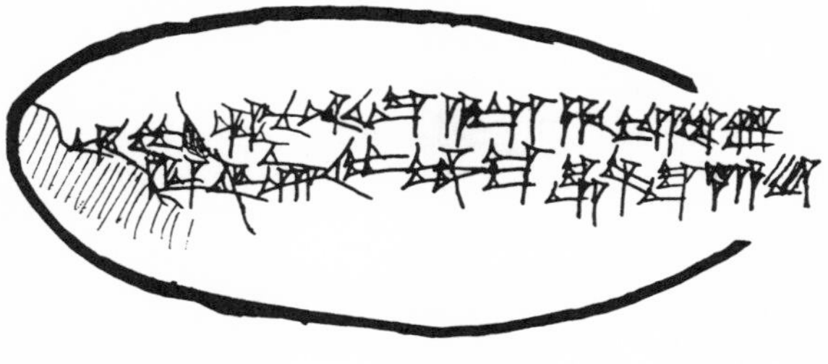

200

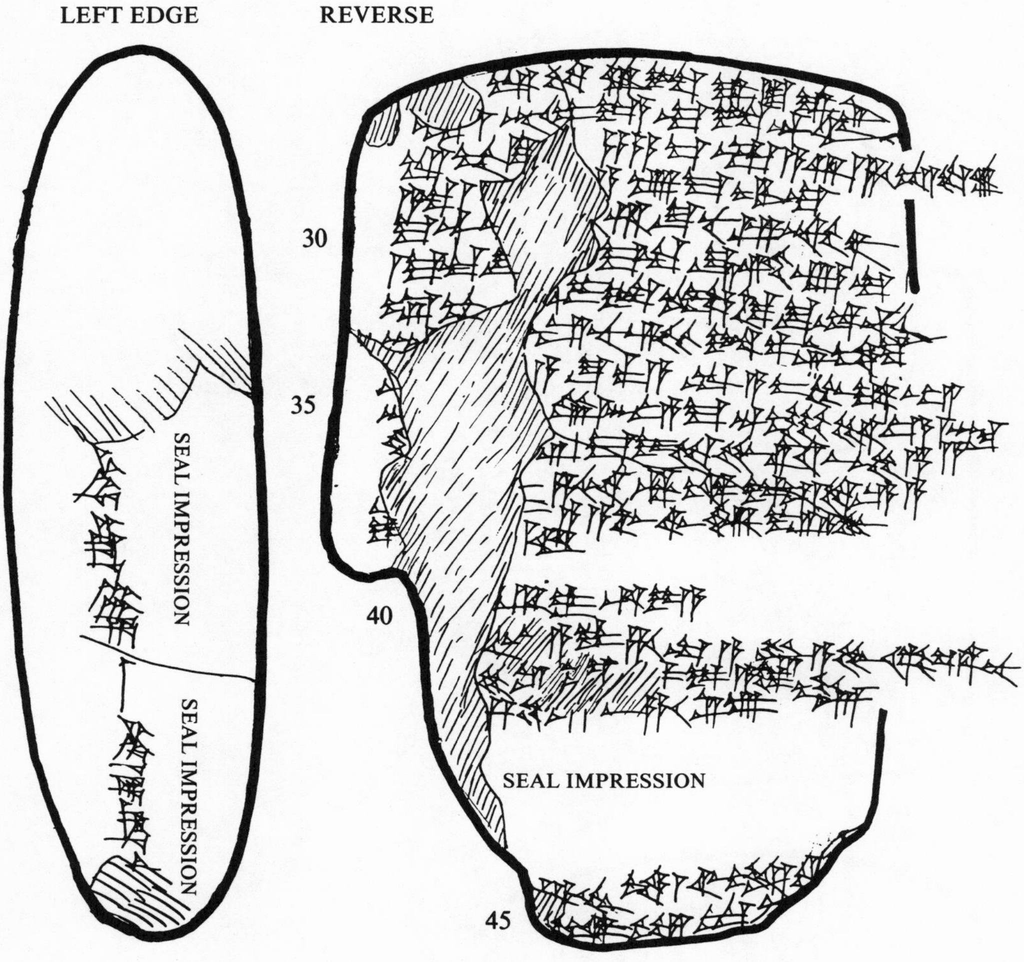

LEFT EDGE
REVERSE
SEAL IMPRESSION
SEAL IMPRESSION
30
35
40
SEAL IMPRESSION
45

204

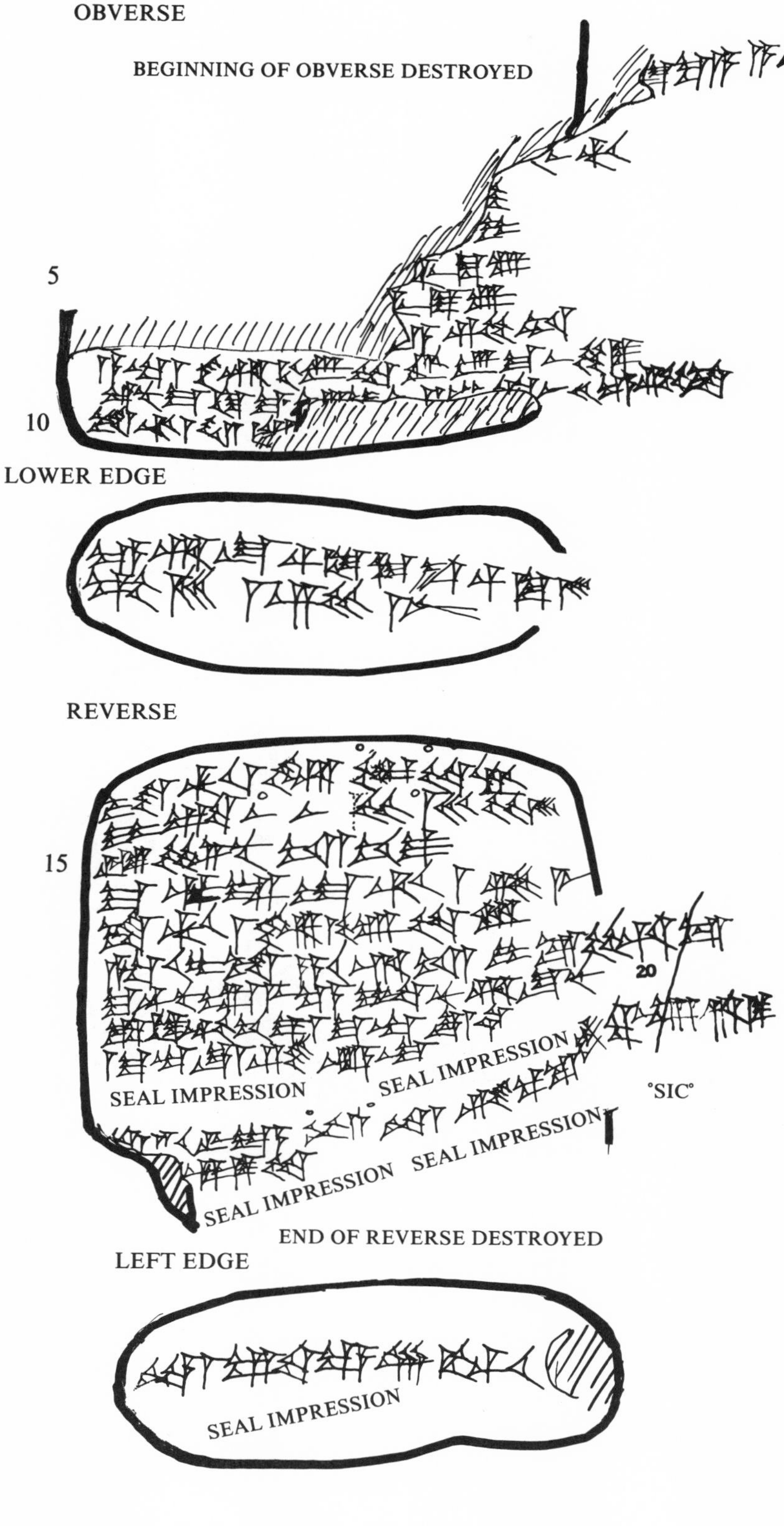
OBVERSE
BEGINNING OF OBVERSE DESTROYED
LOWER EDGE
REVERSE
SEAL IMPRESSION
SEAL IMPRESSION
°SIC°
SEAL IMPRESSION
SEAL IMPRESSION
END OF REVERSE DESTROYED
LEFT EDGE
SEAL IMPRESSION

206

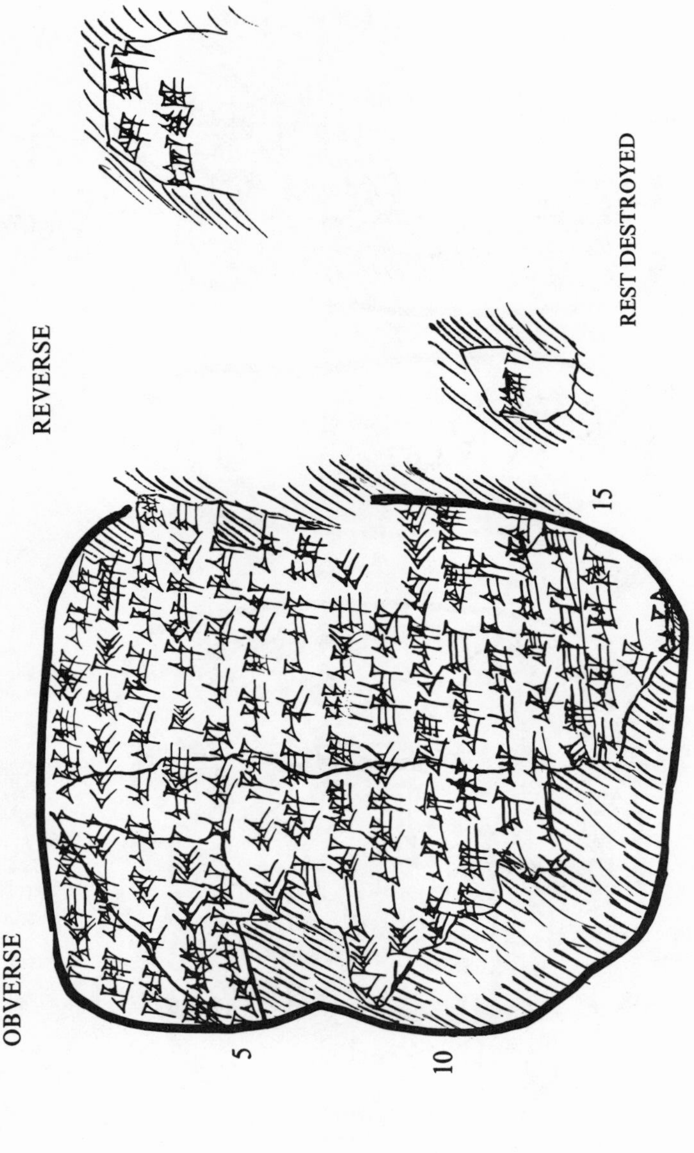

207

OBVERSE

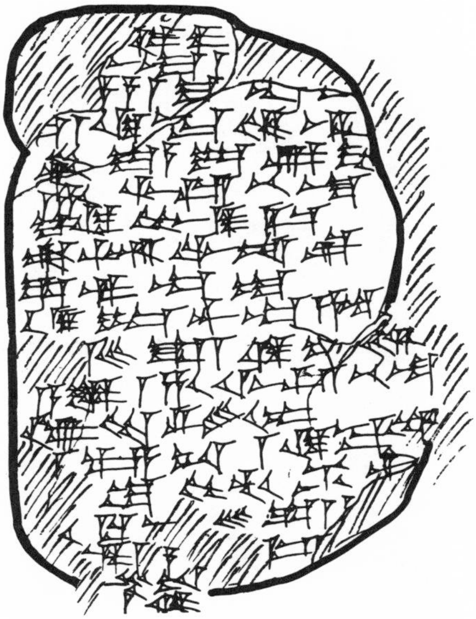

REVERSE

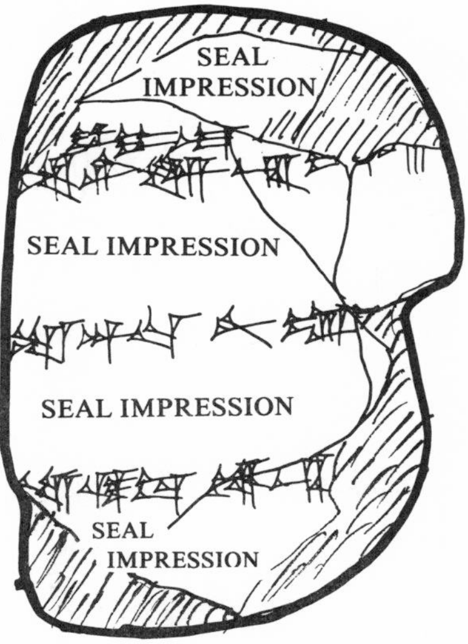

209

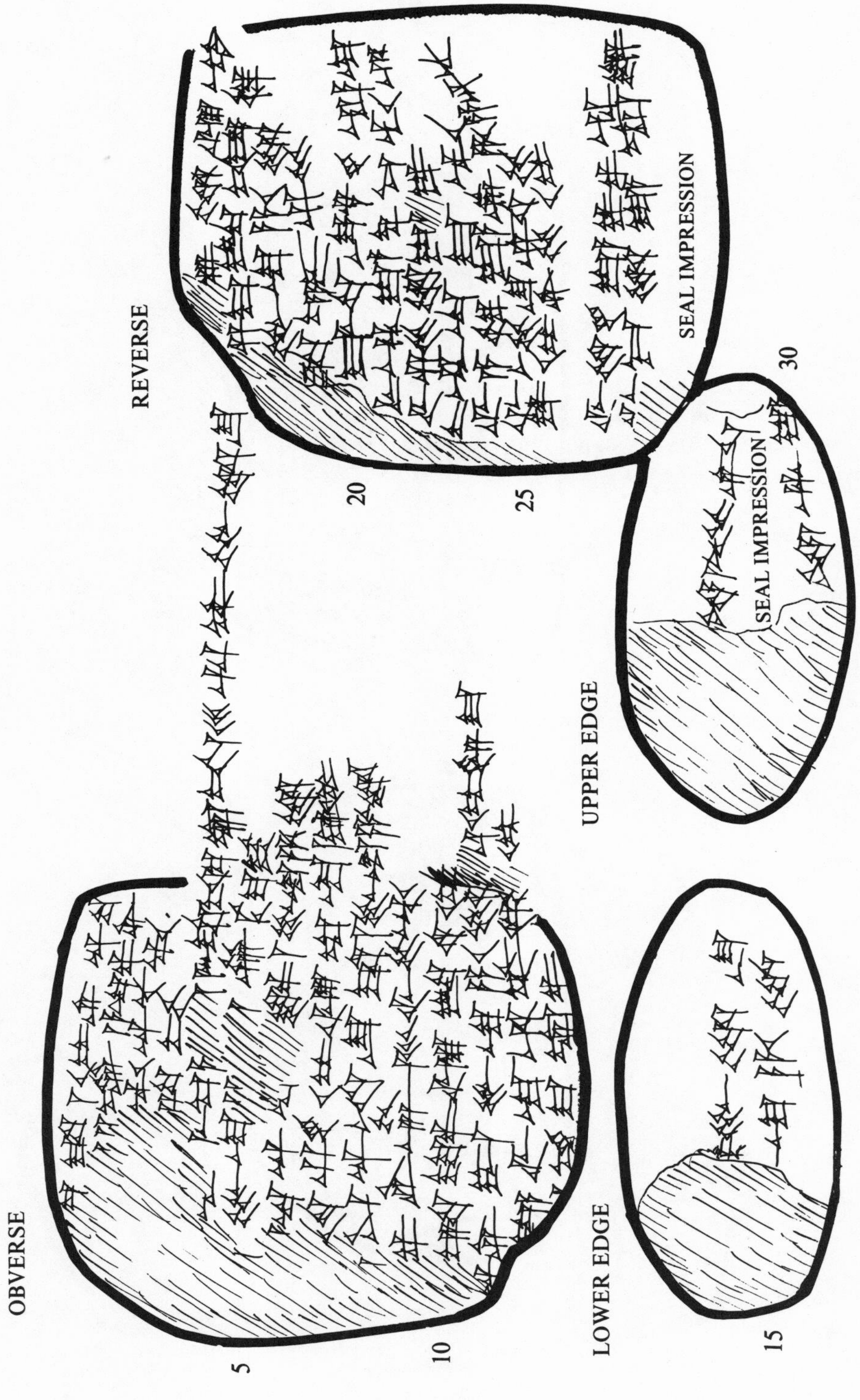

OBVERSE
REVERSE
LOWER EDGE
UPPER EDGE
SEAL IMPRESSION
SEAL IMPRESSION
5
10
15
20
25
30

212

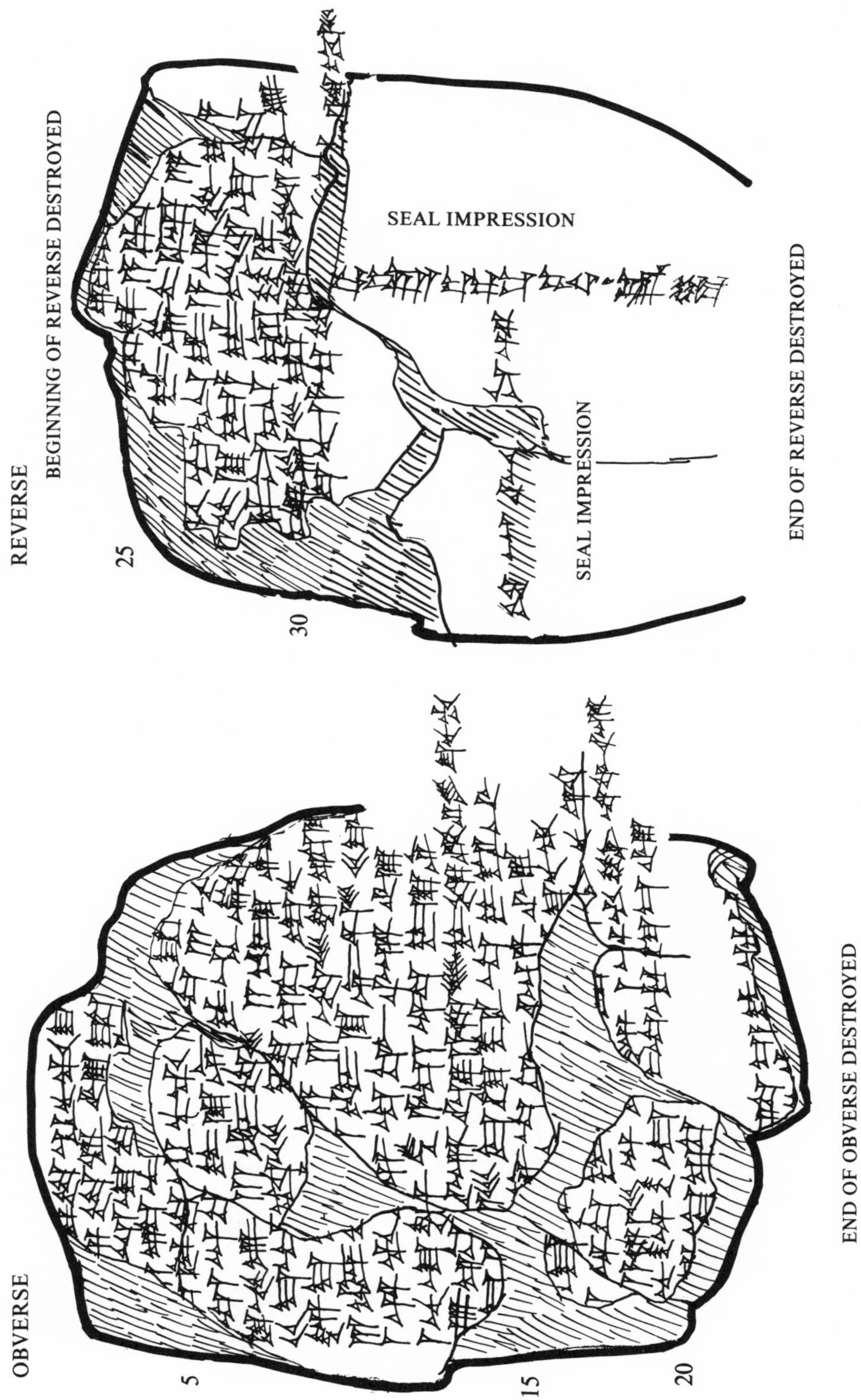
OBVERSE
END OF OBVERSE DESTROYED
REVERSE
BEGINNING OF REVERSE DESTROYED
SEAL IMPRESSION
SEAL IMPRESSION
END OF REVERSE DESTROYED

224

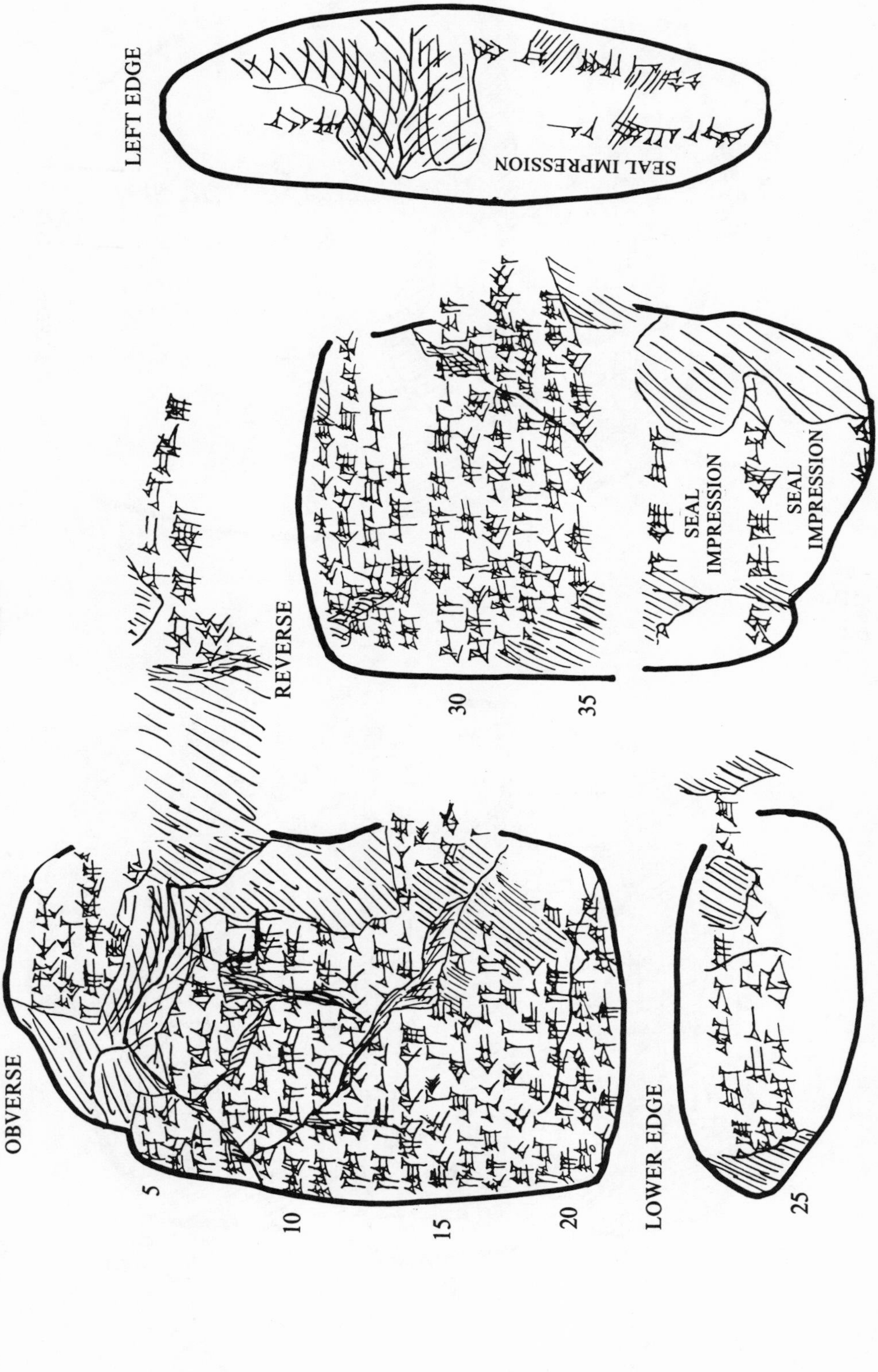

LEFT EDGE
SEAL IMPRESSION
REVERSE
SEAL IMPRESSION
SEAL IMPRESSION
OBVERSE
LOWER EDGE

234

OBVERSE

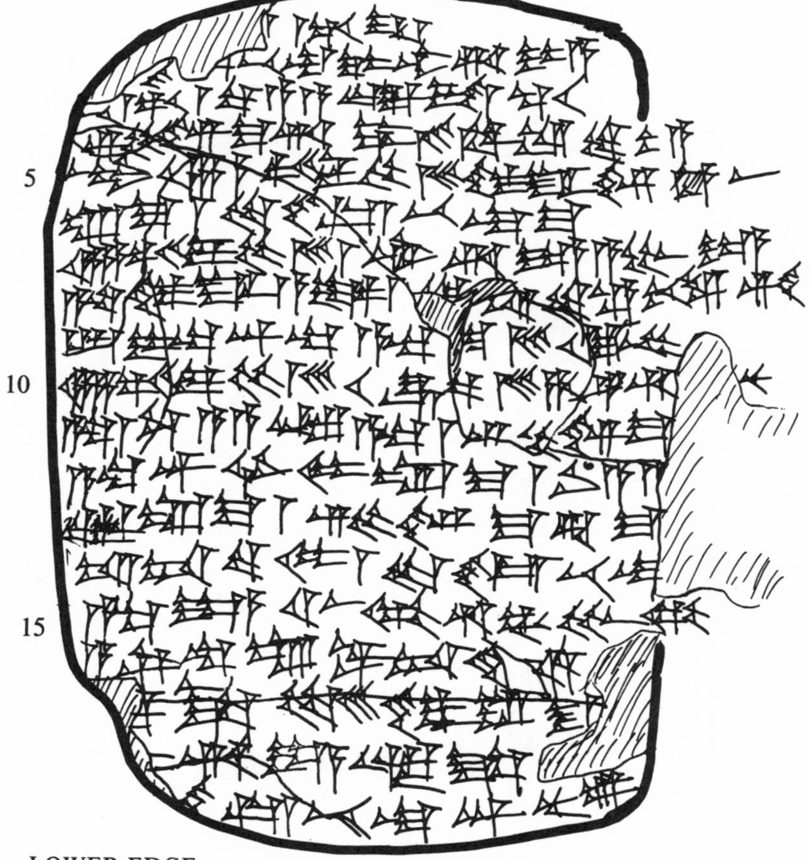

LOWER EDGE

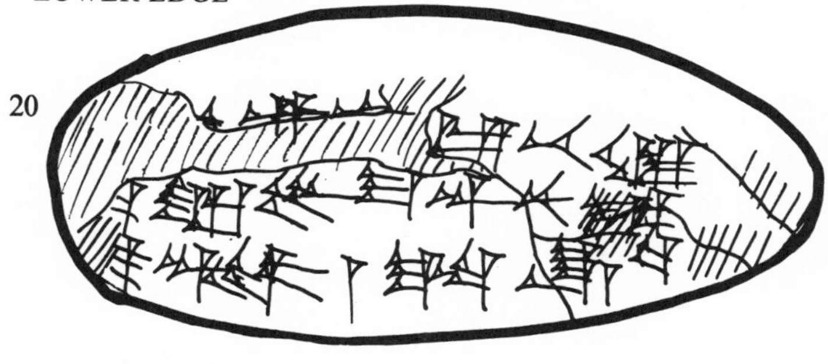

234

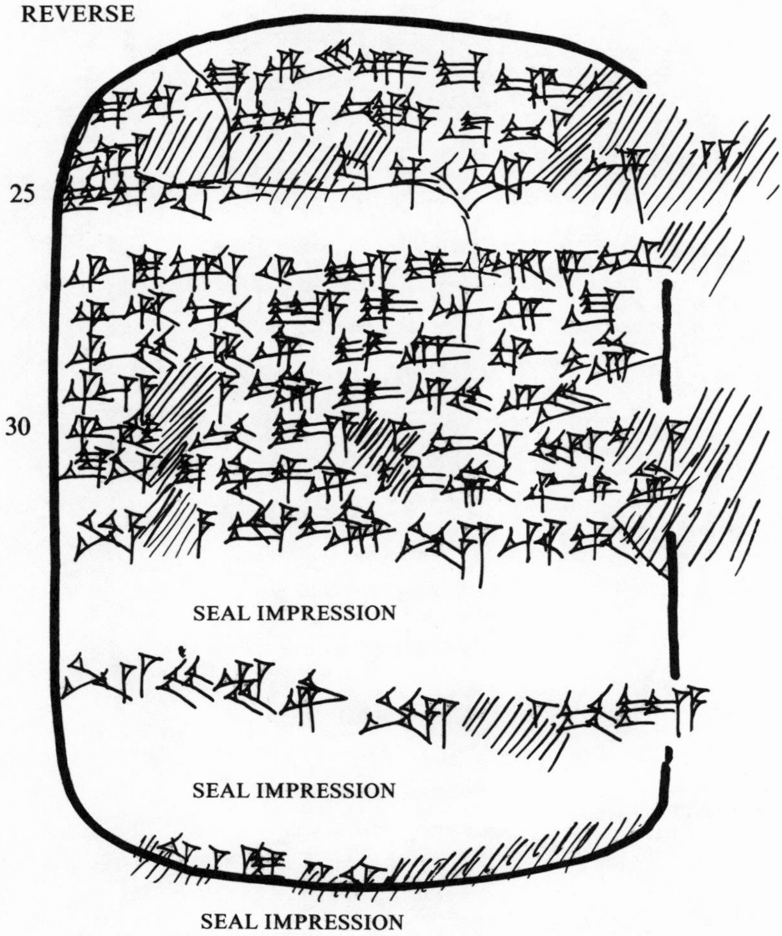
REVERSE
25
30
SEAL IMPRESSION
SEAL IMPRESSION
SEAL IMPRESSION

236

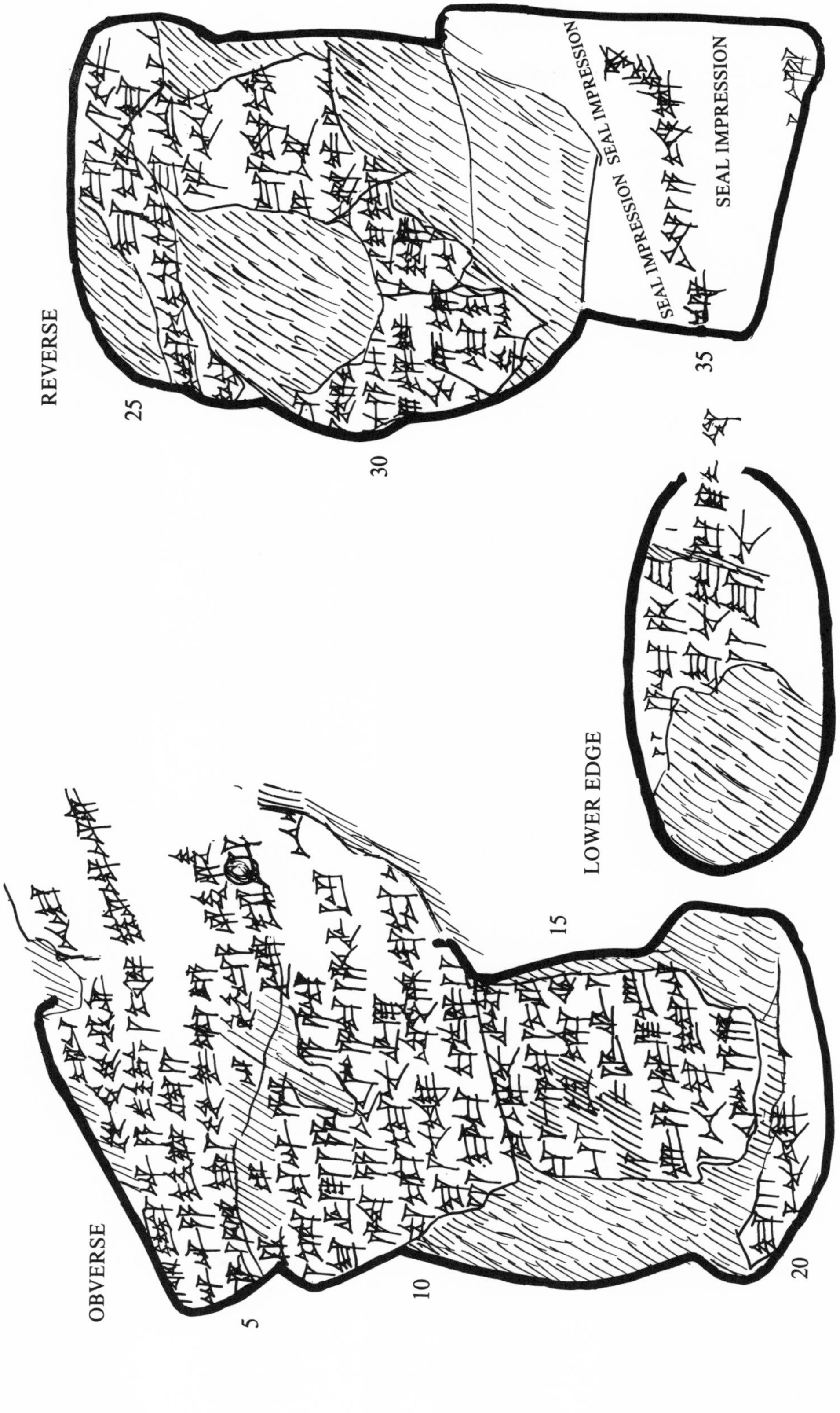
OBVERSE
5
10
15
20
LOWER EDGE
REVERSE
25
30
35
SEAL IMPRESSION
SEAL IMPRESSION
SEAL IMPRESSION
SEAL IMPRESSION

250

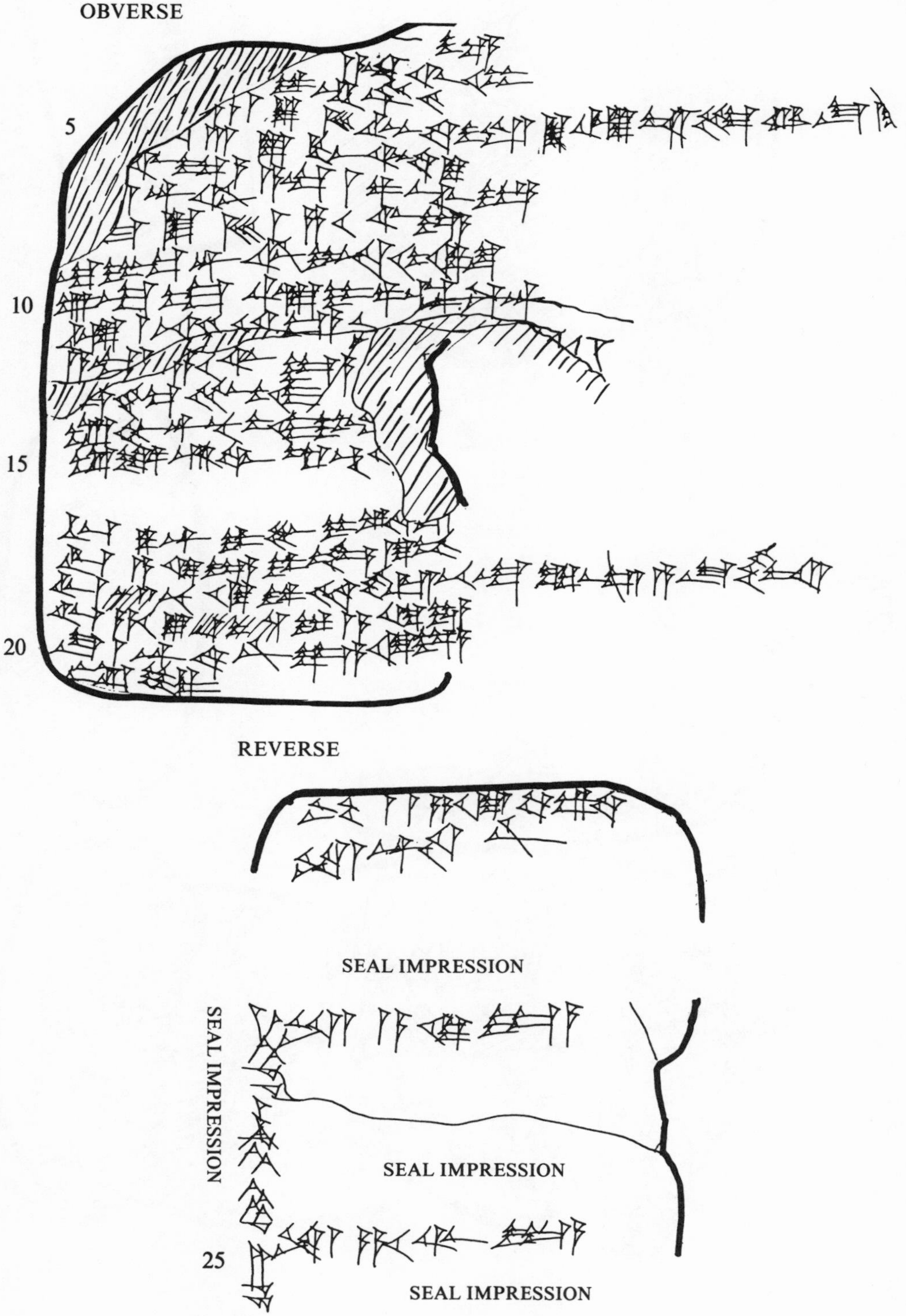
OBVERSE
5
10
15
20
REVERSE
SEAL IMPRESSION
SEAL IMPRESSION
SEAL IMPRESSION
25
SEAL IMPRESSION

262

OBVERSE

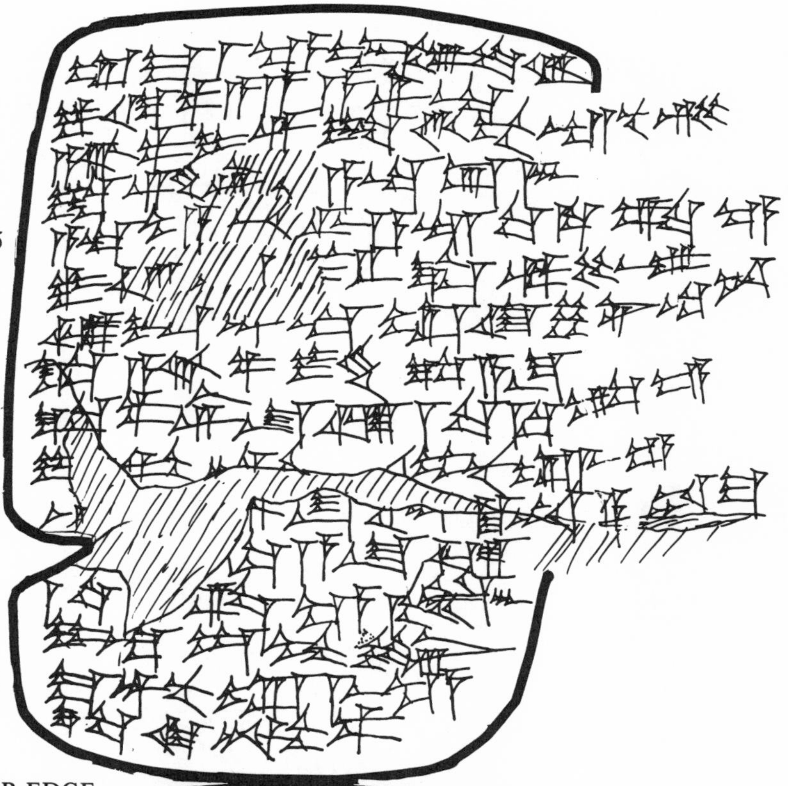

LOWER EDGE

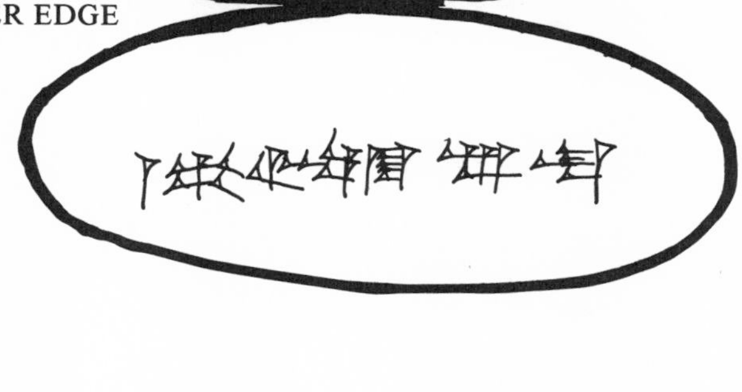

262

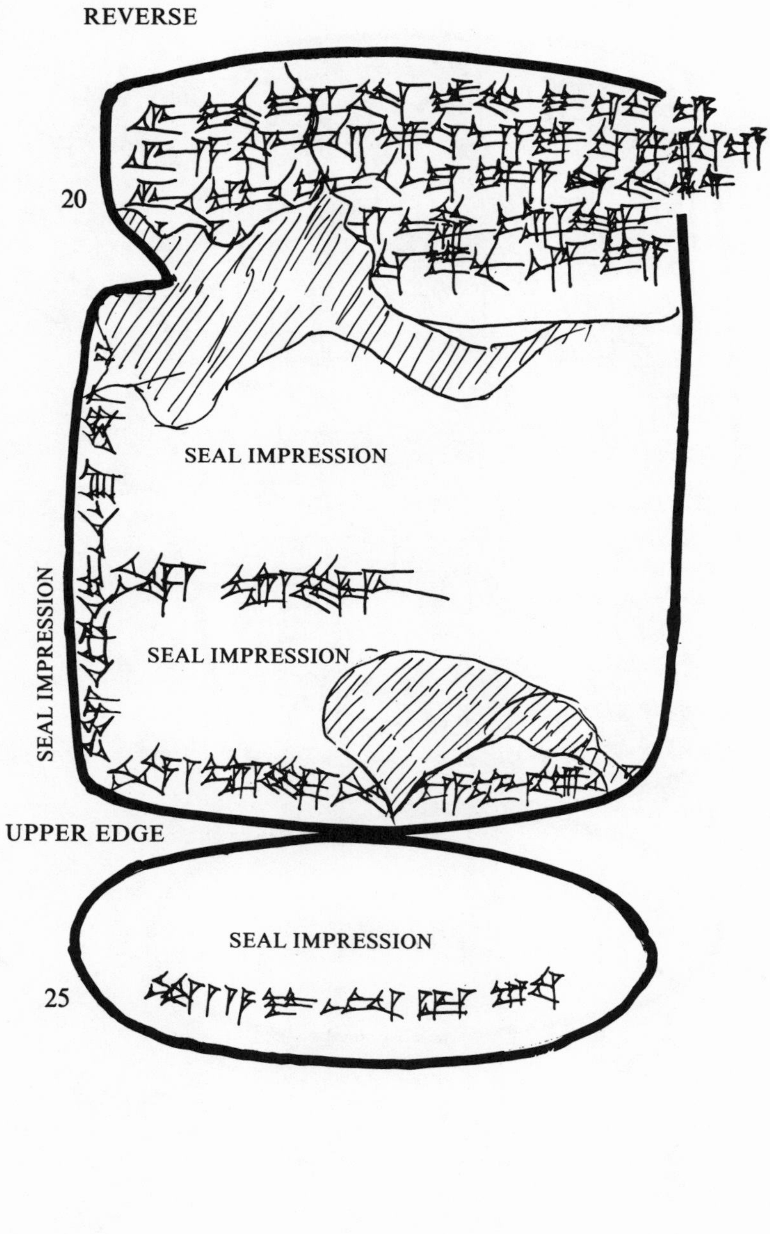
REVERSE
20
SEAL IMPRESSION
SEAL IMPRESSION
SEAL IMPRESSION
UPPER EDGE
SEAL IMPRESSION
25

264

OBVERSE

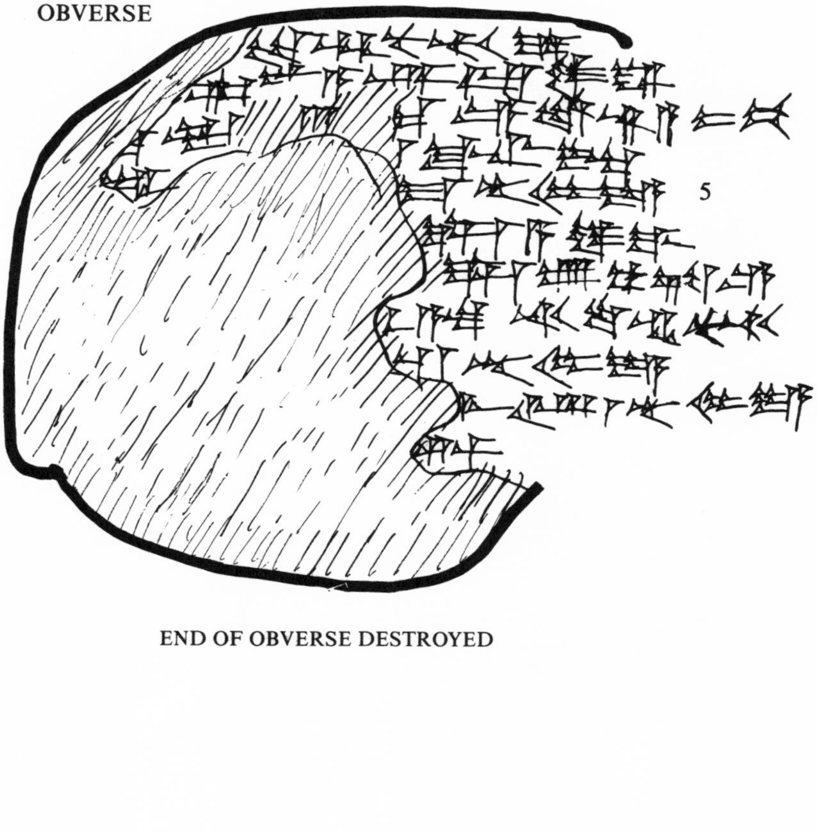

END OF OBVERSE DESTROYED

264

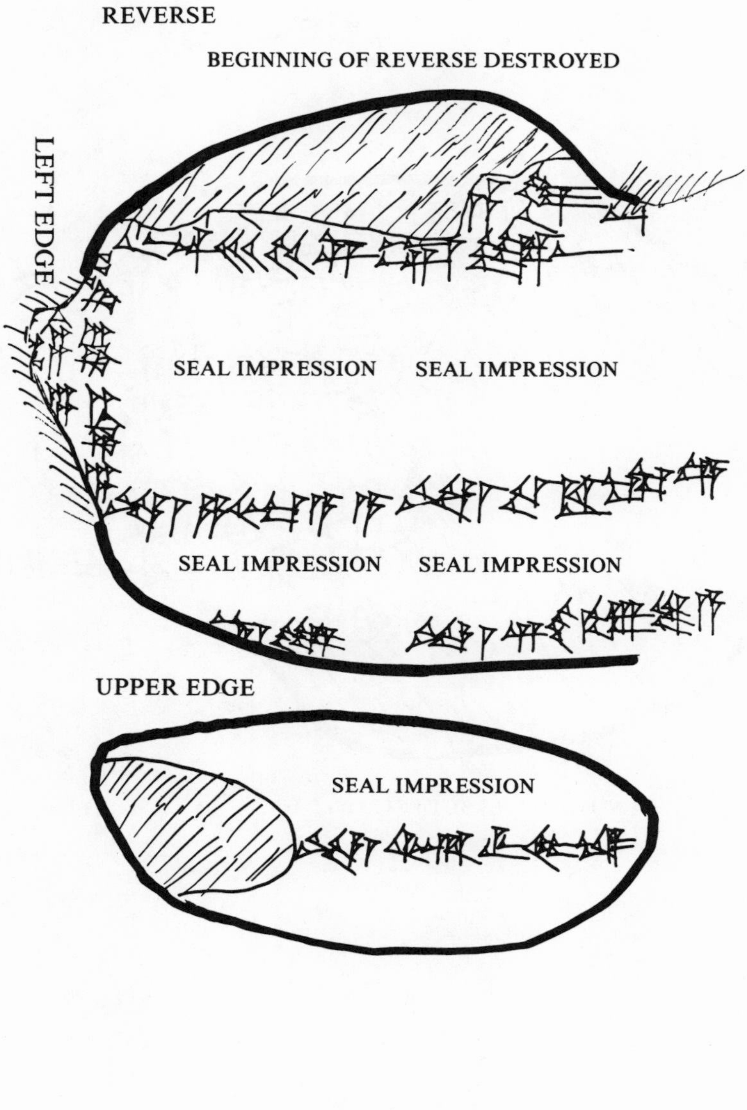
REVERSE
BEGINNING OF REVERSE DESTROYED
LEFT EDGE
SEAL IMPRESSION
SEAL IMPRESSION
SEAL IMPRESSION
SEAL IMPRESSION
UPPER EDGE
SEAL IMPRESSION

267

OBVERSE

BEGINNING OF OBVERSE DESTROYED

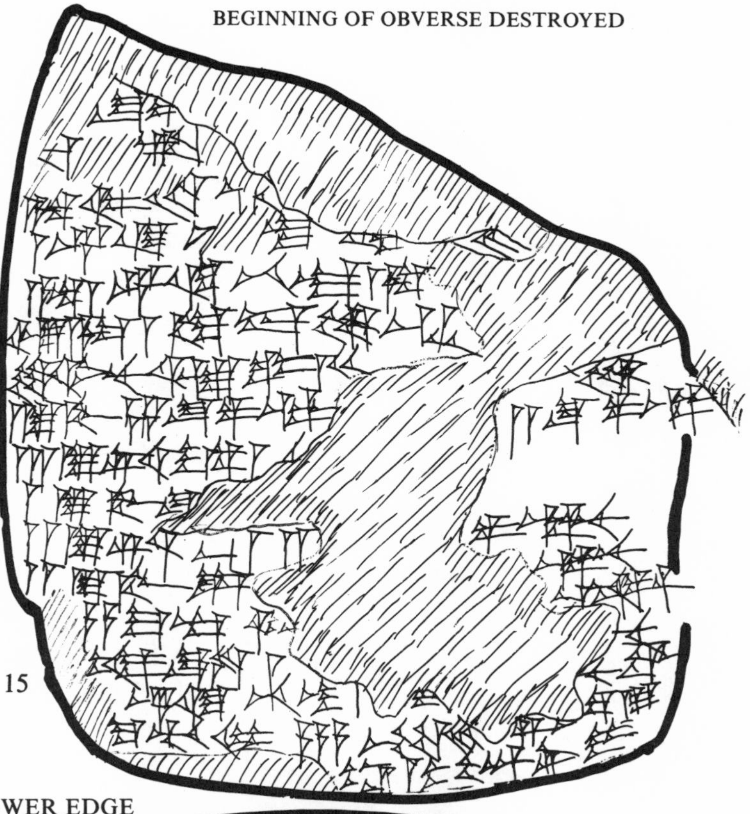

LOWER EDGE

267

REVERSE

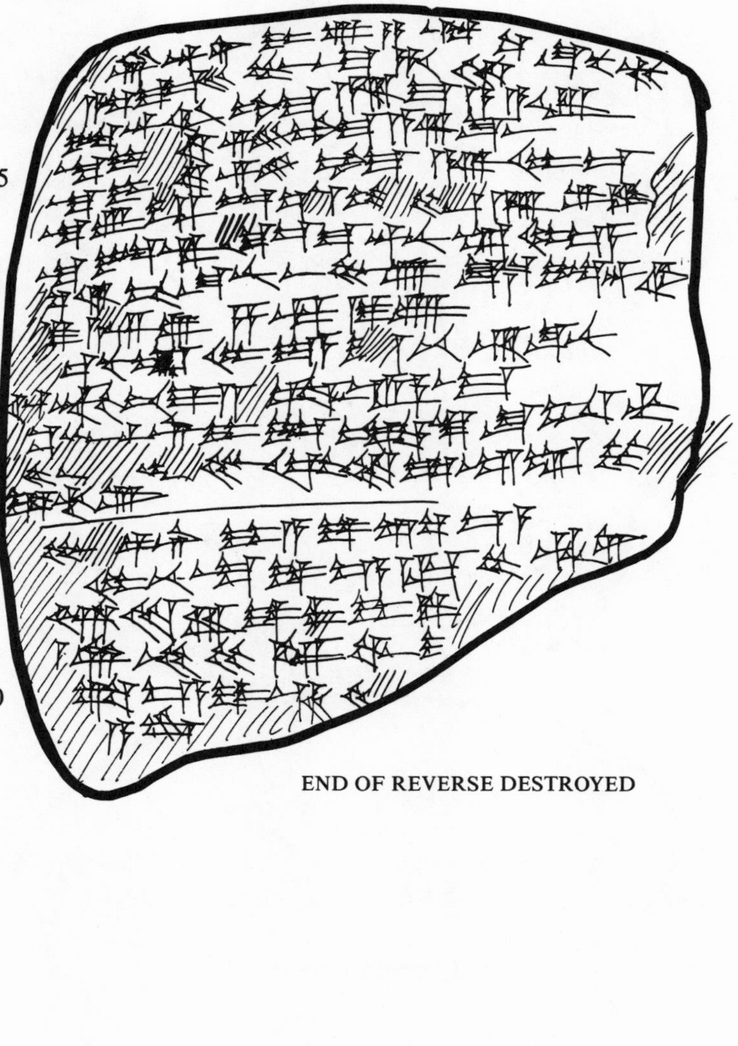

END OF REVERSE DESTROYED

268

OBVERSE BEGINNING OF OBVERSE DESTROYED

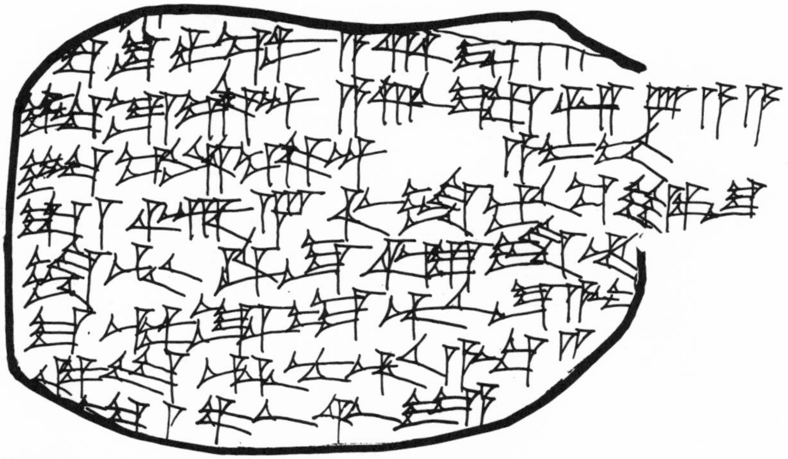

LOWER EDGE

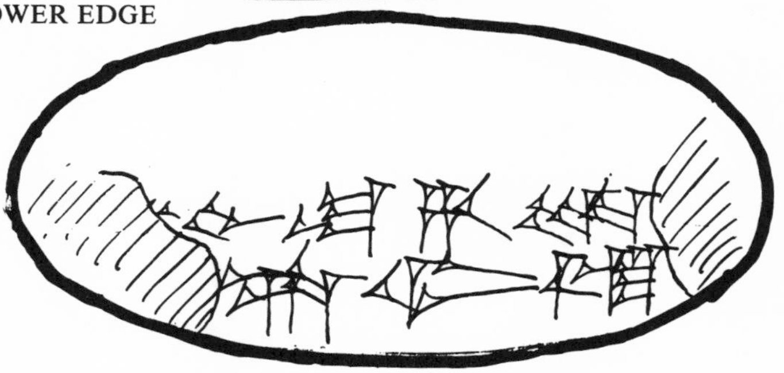

REVERSE

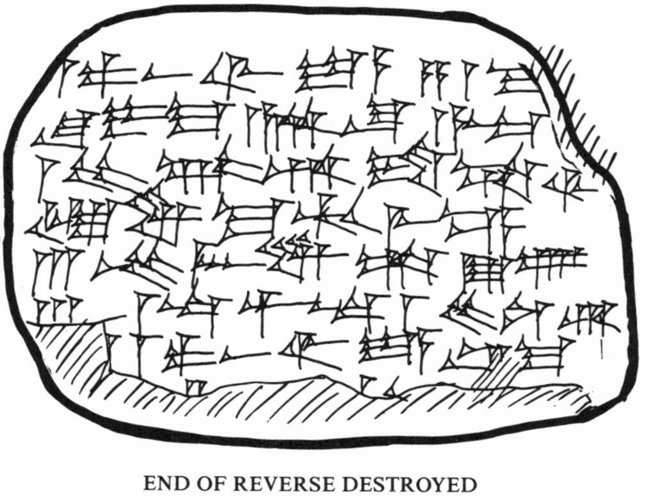

END OF REVERSE DESTROYED

273

OBVERSE

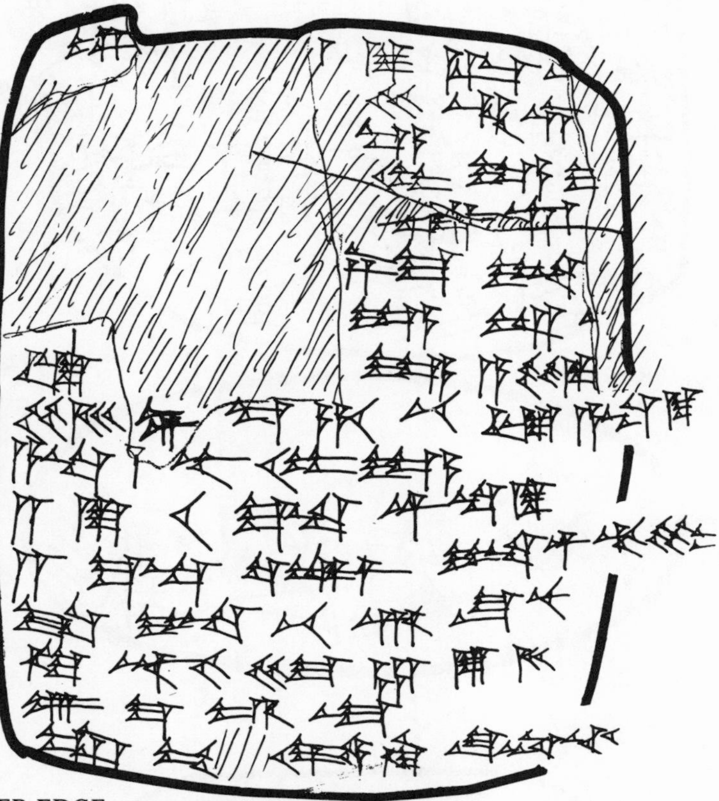

LOWER EDGE

273

REVERSE

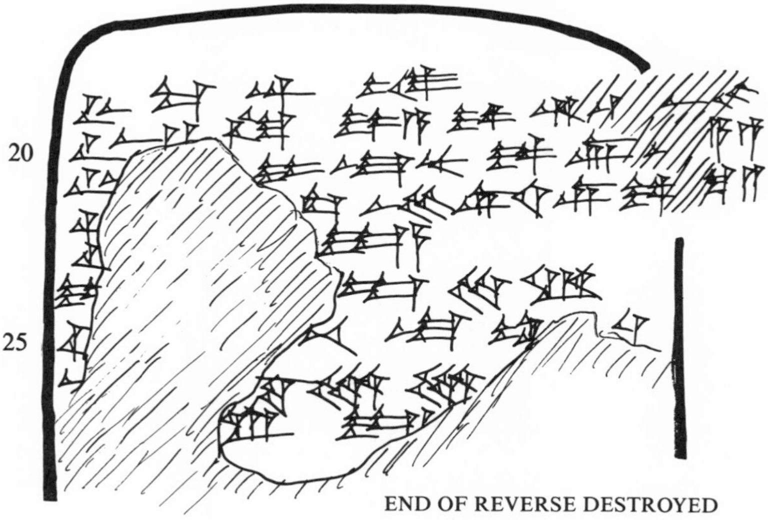

UPPER EDGE

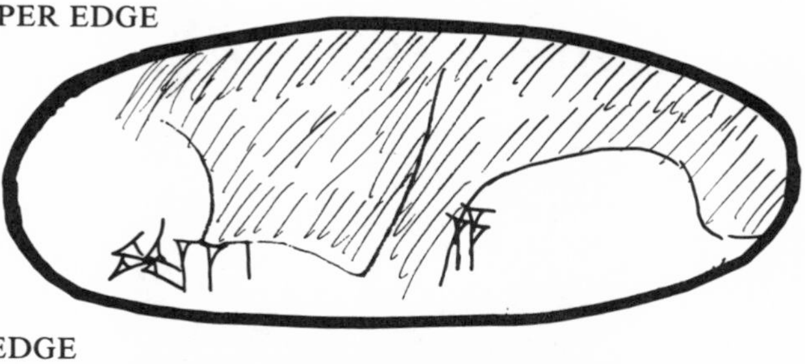

LEFT EDGE

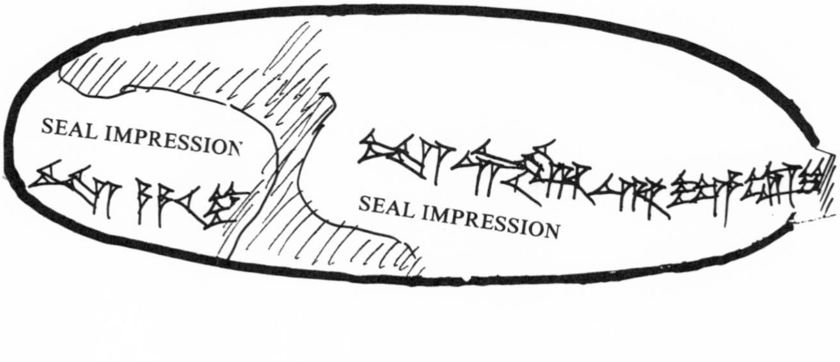

275

OBVERSE

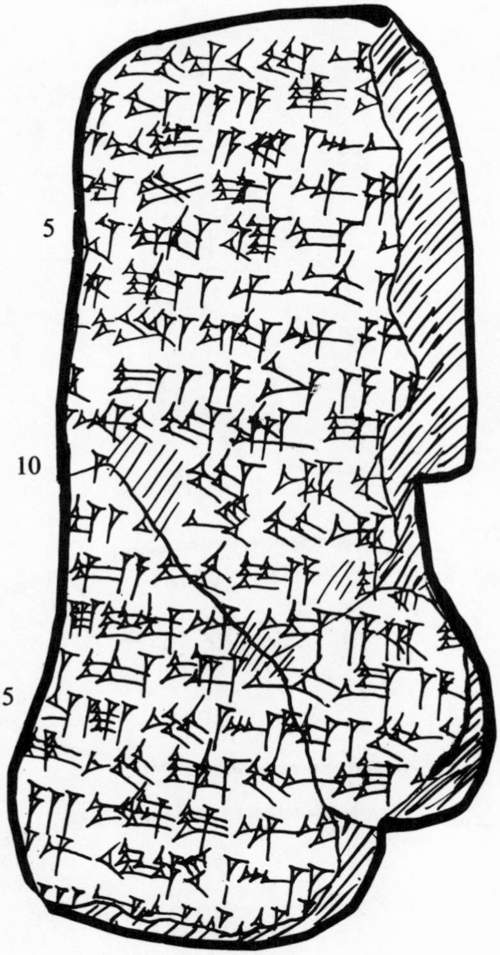

END OF OBVERSE DESTROYED

REVERSE DESTROYED

279

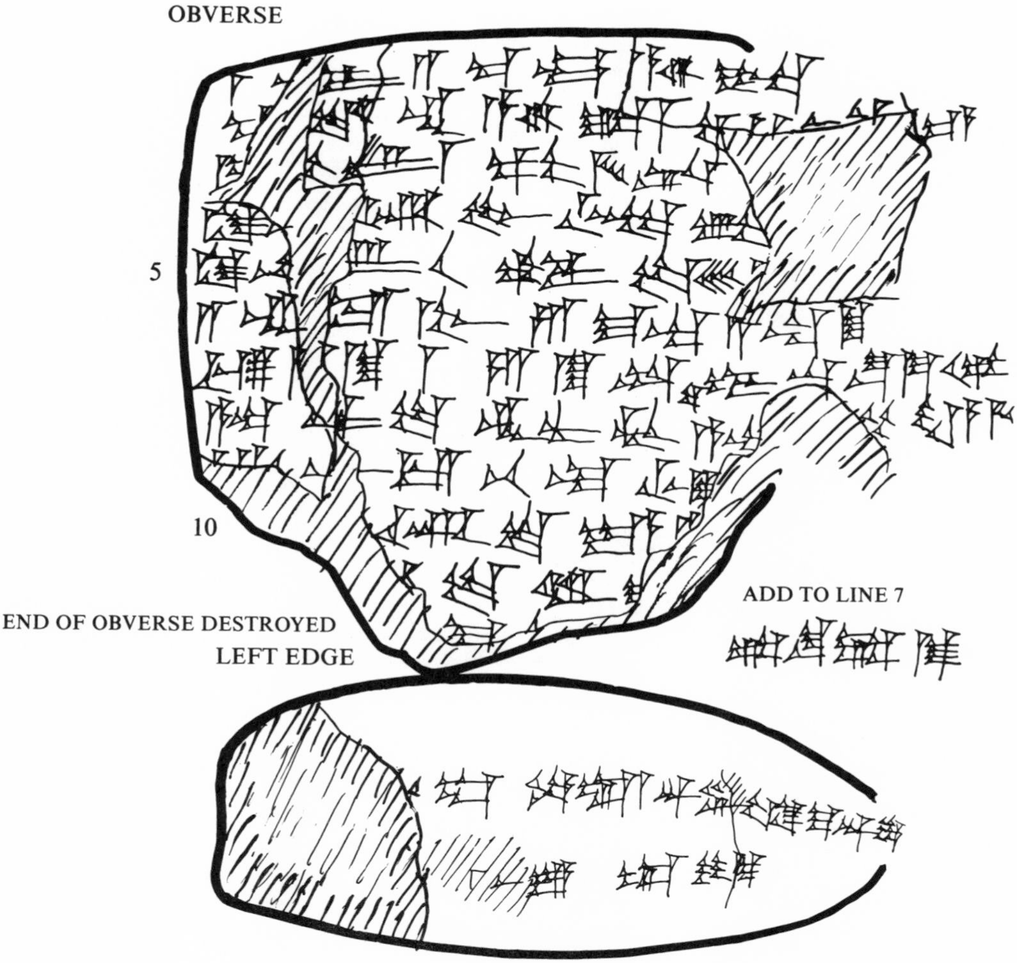

279

REVERSE

BEGINNING OF REVERSE DESTROYED

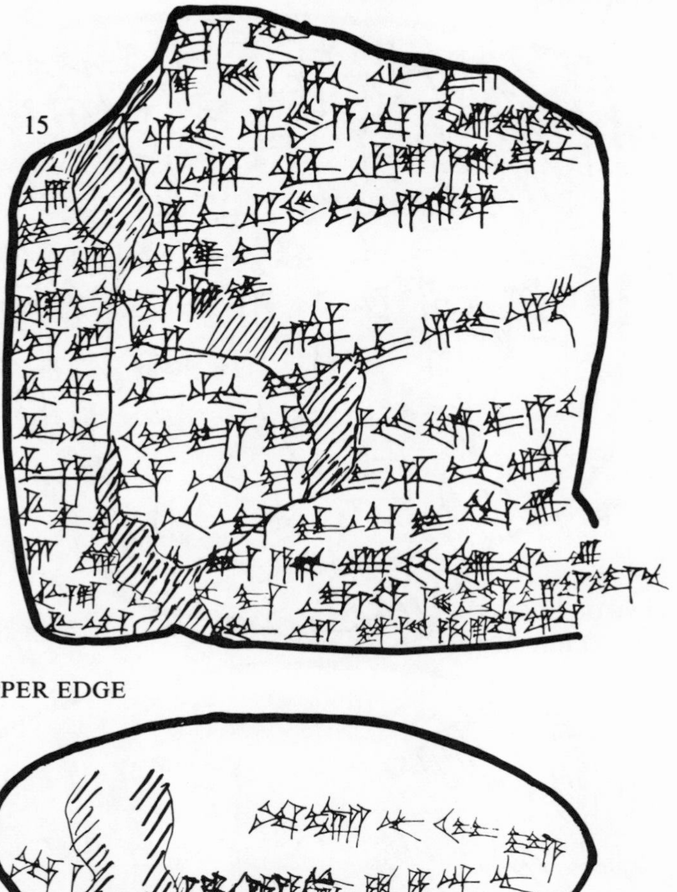

UPPER EDGE

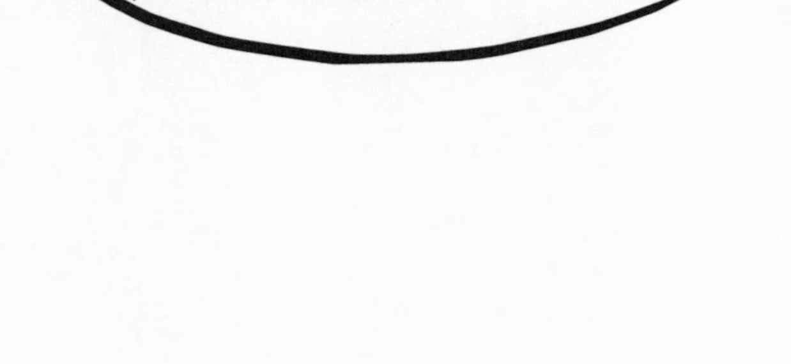

283

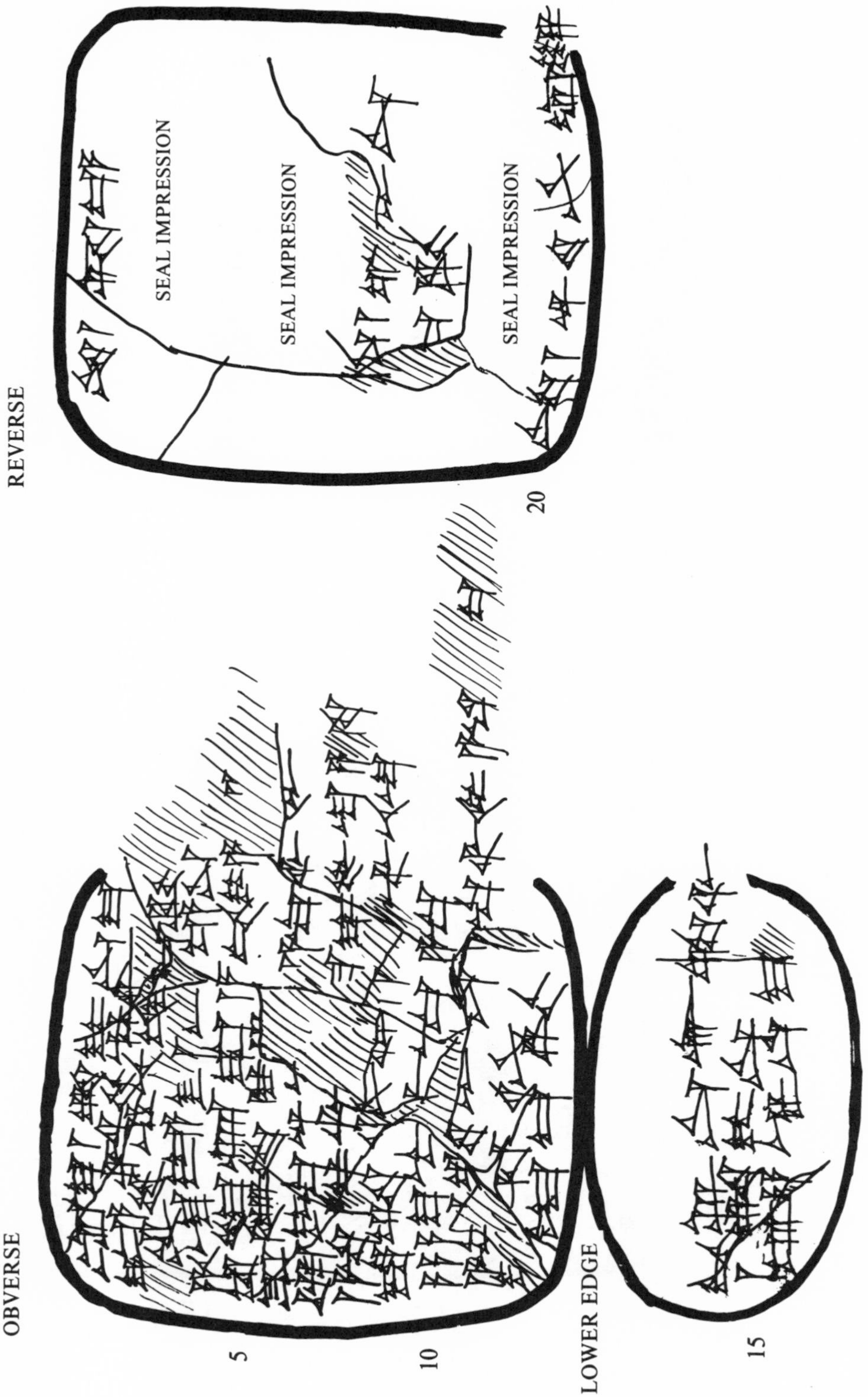
OBVERSE
5
10
LOWER EDGE
15
REVERSE
20
SEAL IMPRESSION
SEAL IMPRESSION
SEAL IMPRESSION

289

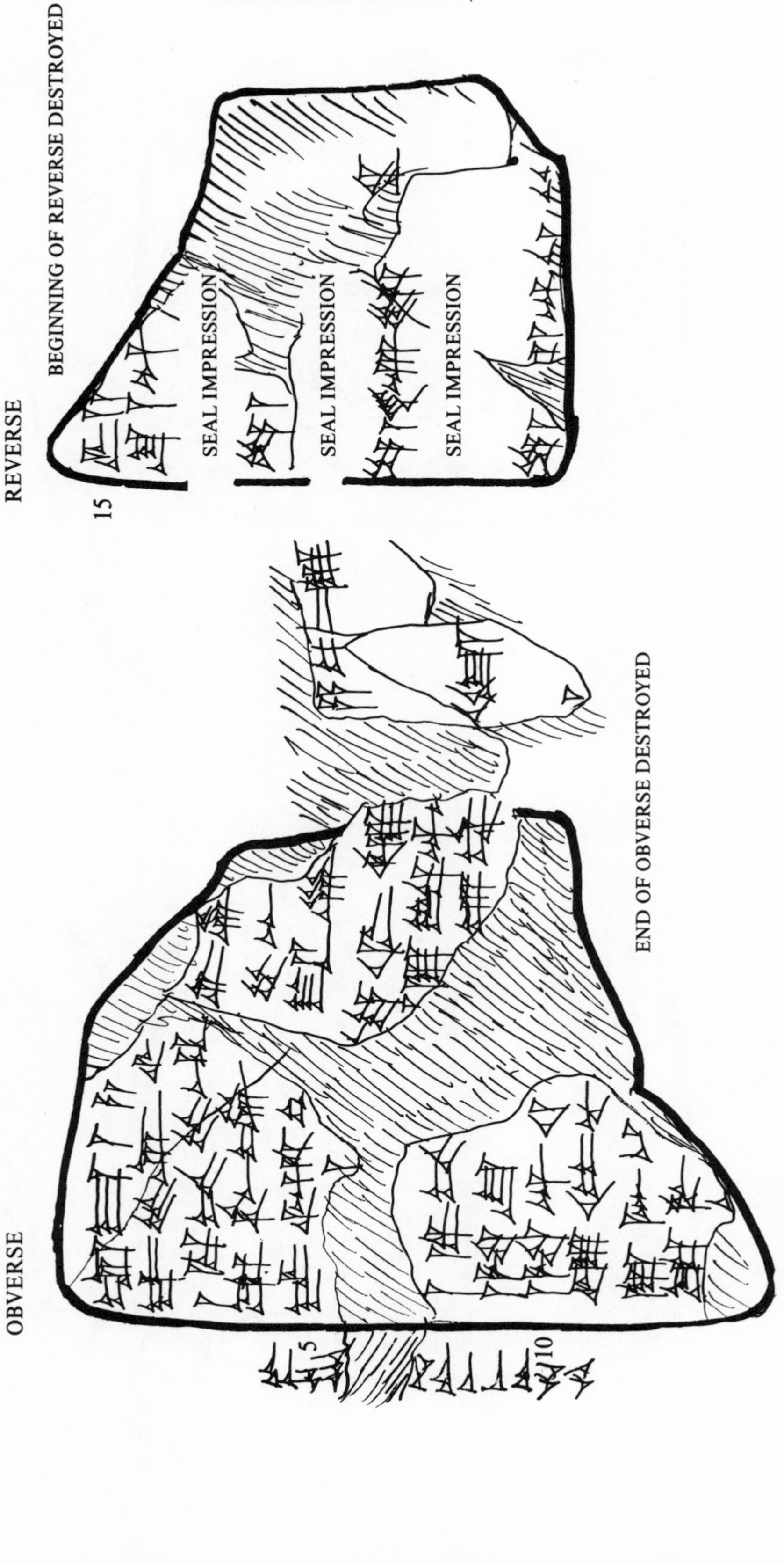
OBVERSE
5
10
END OF OBVERSE DESTROYED
REVERSE
15
BEGINNING OF REVERSE DESTROYED
SEAL IMPRESSION
SEAL IMPRESSION
SEAL IMPRESSION

291

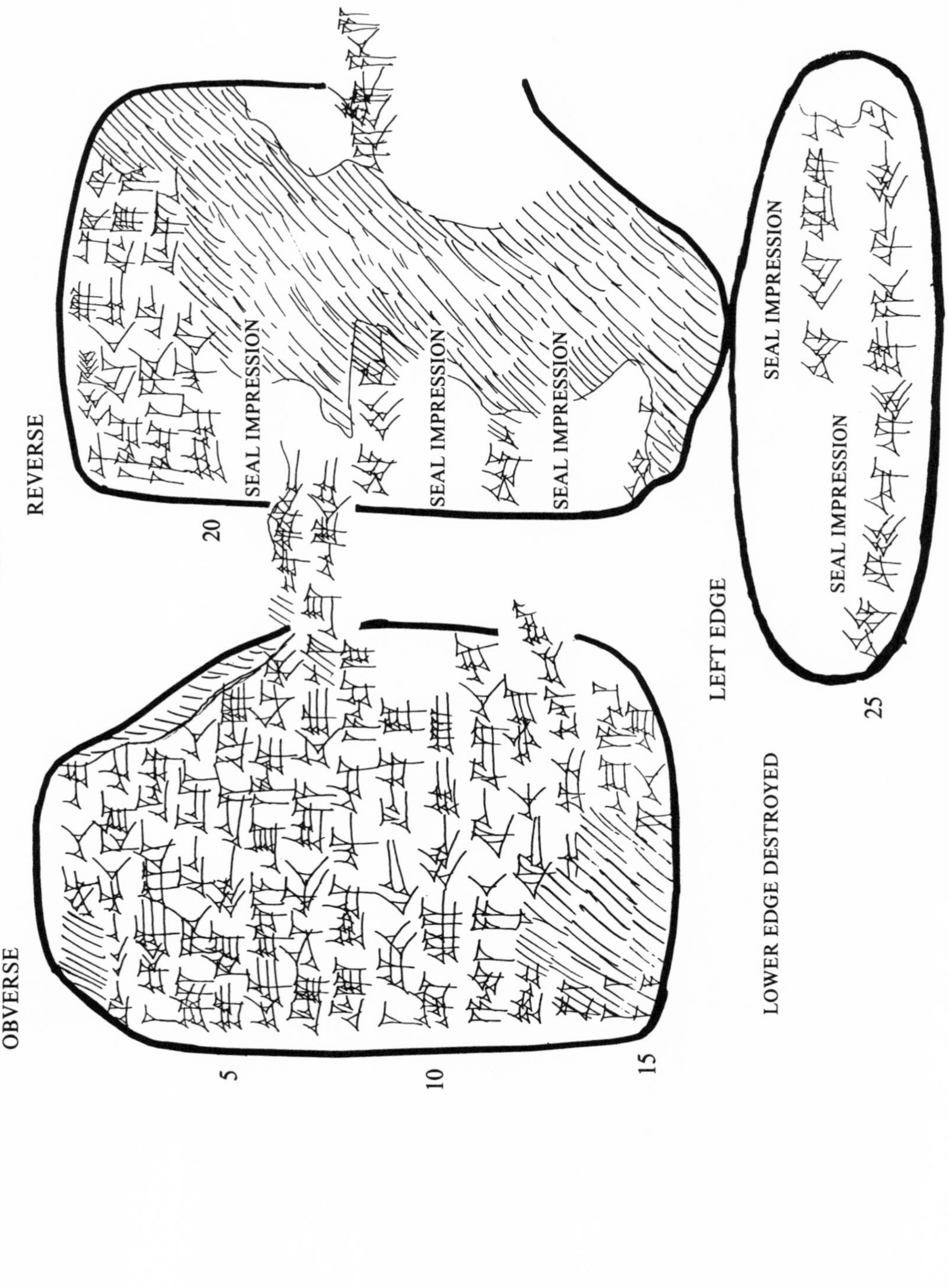
OBVERSE
REVERSE
SEAL IMPRESSION
SEAL IMPRESSION
SEAL IMPRESSION
LEFT EDGE
SEAL IMPRESSION
SEAL IMPRESSION
LOWER EDGE DESTROYED

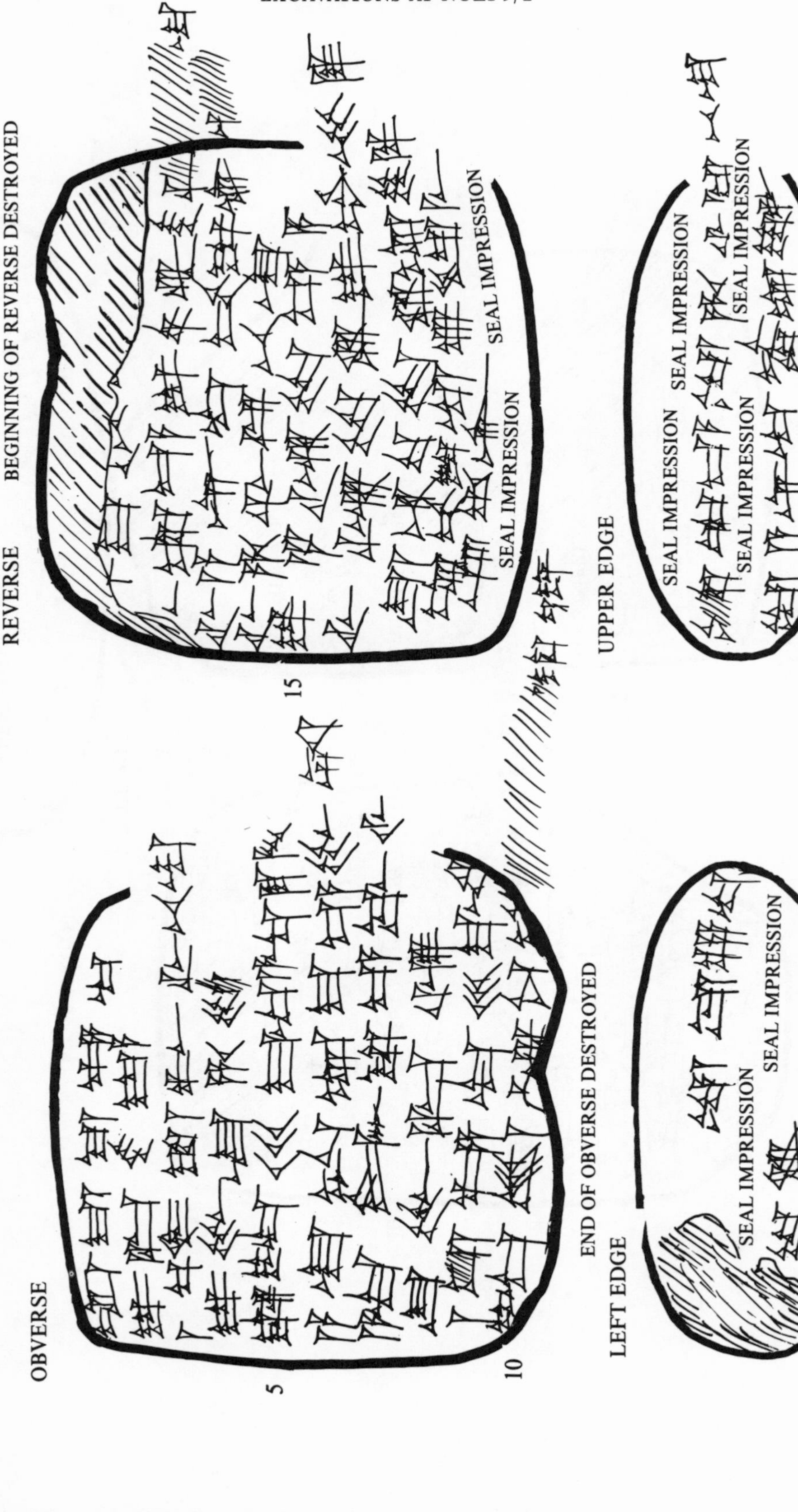

292

OBVERSE

REVERSE   BEGINNING OF REVERSE DESTROYED

SEAL IMPRESSION

SEAL IMPRESSION

5

10

15

END OF OBVERSE DESTROYED

UPPER EDGE

SEAL IMPRESSION   SEAL IMPRESSION

SEAL IMPRESSION

SEAL IMPRESSION

LEFT EDGE

SEAL IMPRESSION

SEAL IMPRESSION

297

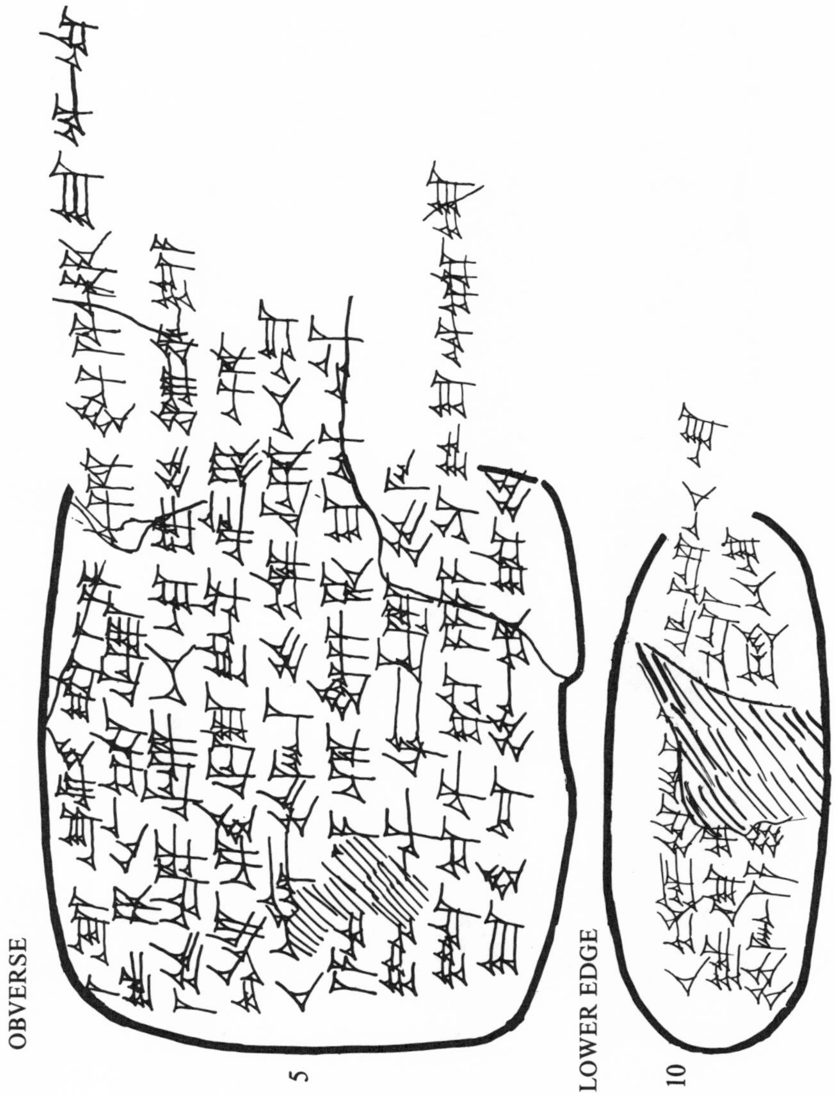

297

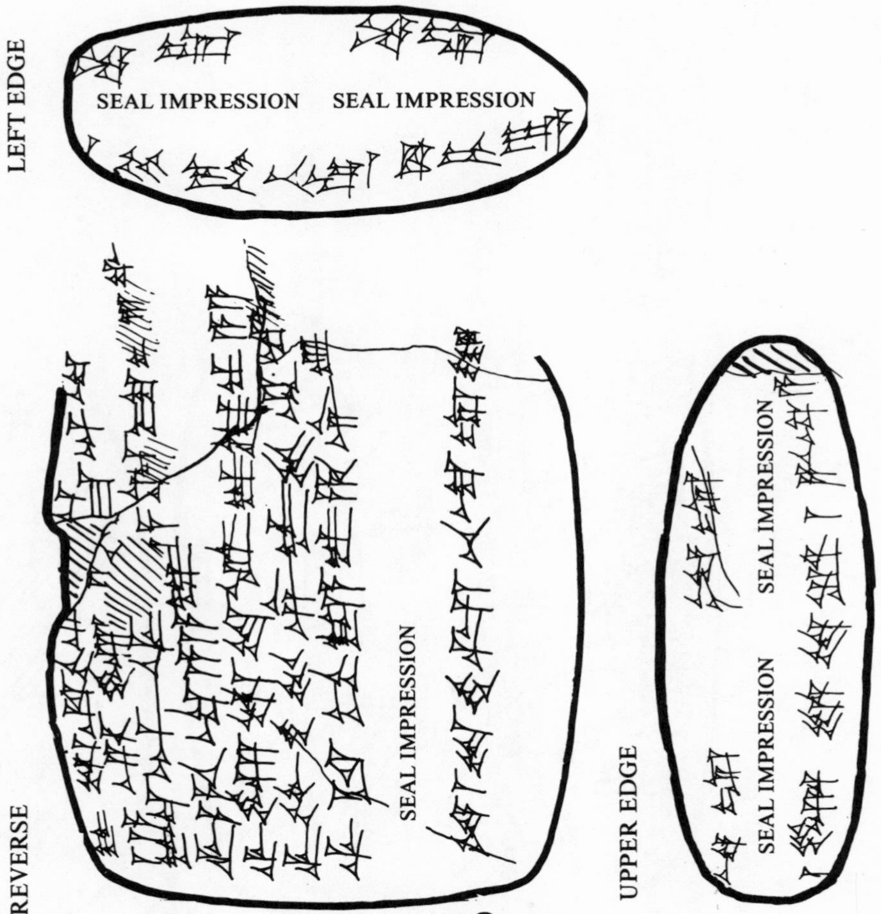
LEFT EDGE
SEAL IMPRESSION
SEAL IMPRESSION
REVERSE
SEAL IMPRESSION
UPPER EDGE
SEAL IMPRESSION
SEAL IMPRESSION

298

OBVERSE

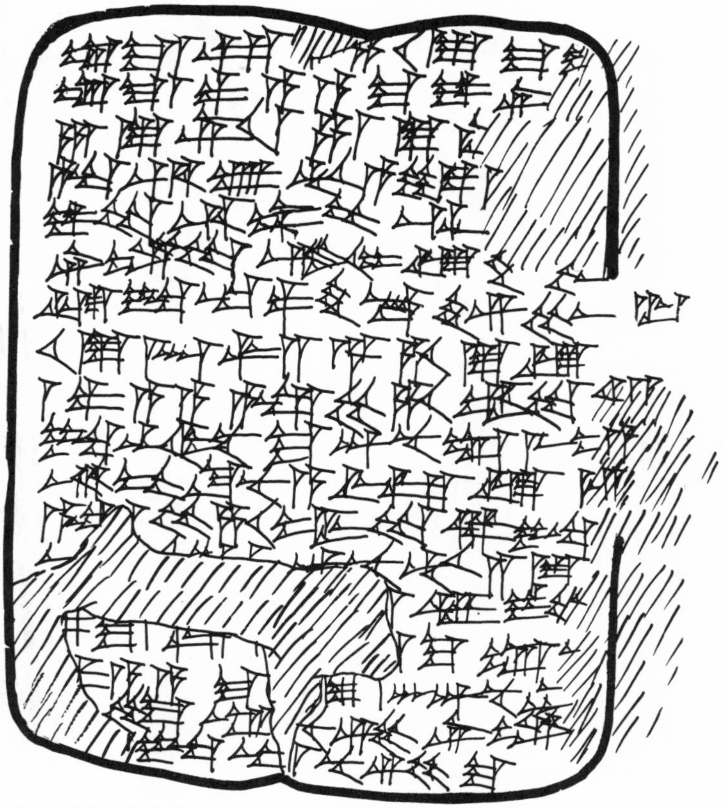

LOWER EDGE

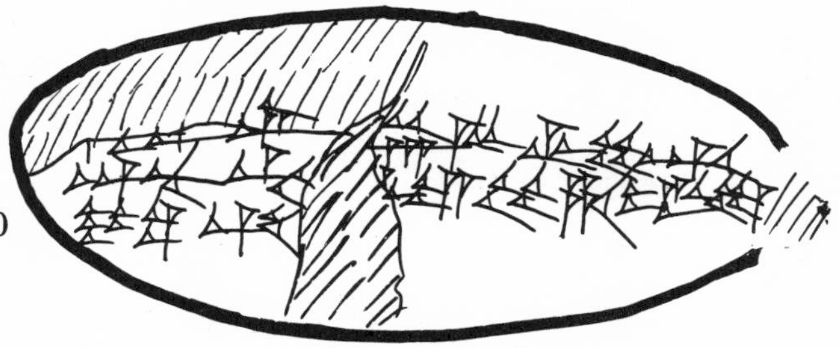

298

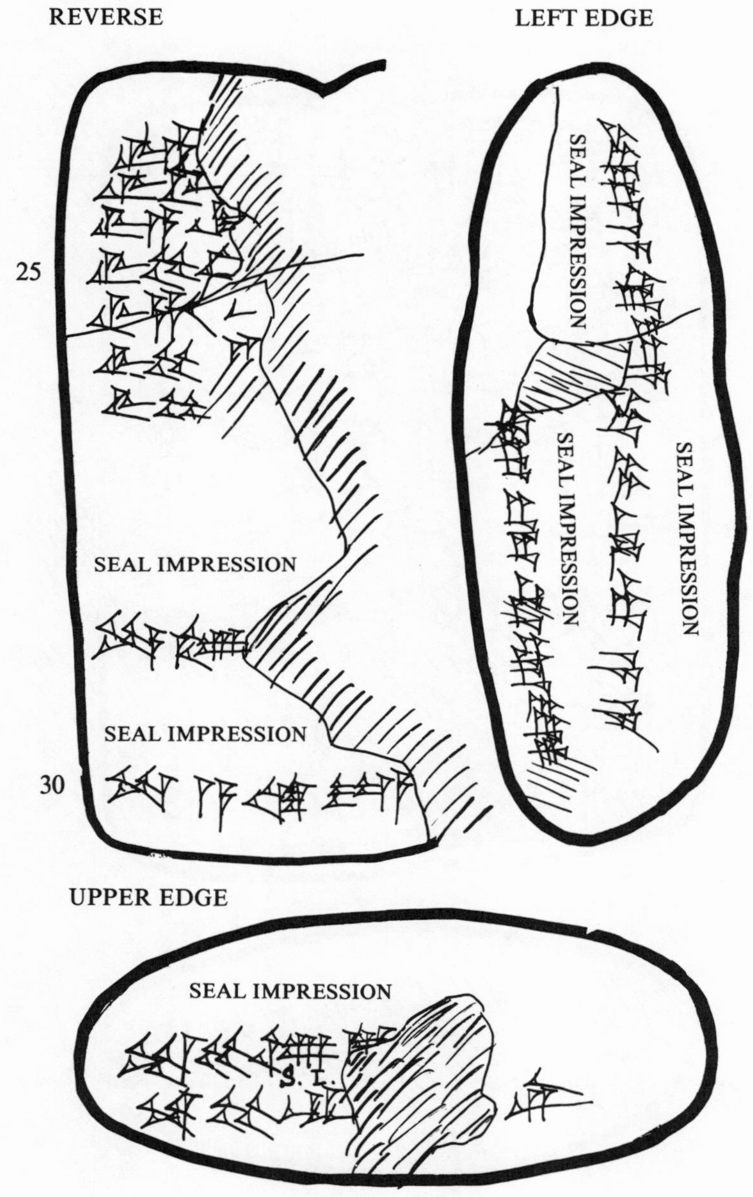
REVERSE
LEFT EDGE
25
SEAL IMPRESSION
SEAL IMPRESSION
SEAL IMPRESSION
SEAL IMPRESSION
SEAL IMPRESSION
30
UPPER EDGE
SEAL IMPRESSION
S. I.

299

OBVERSE

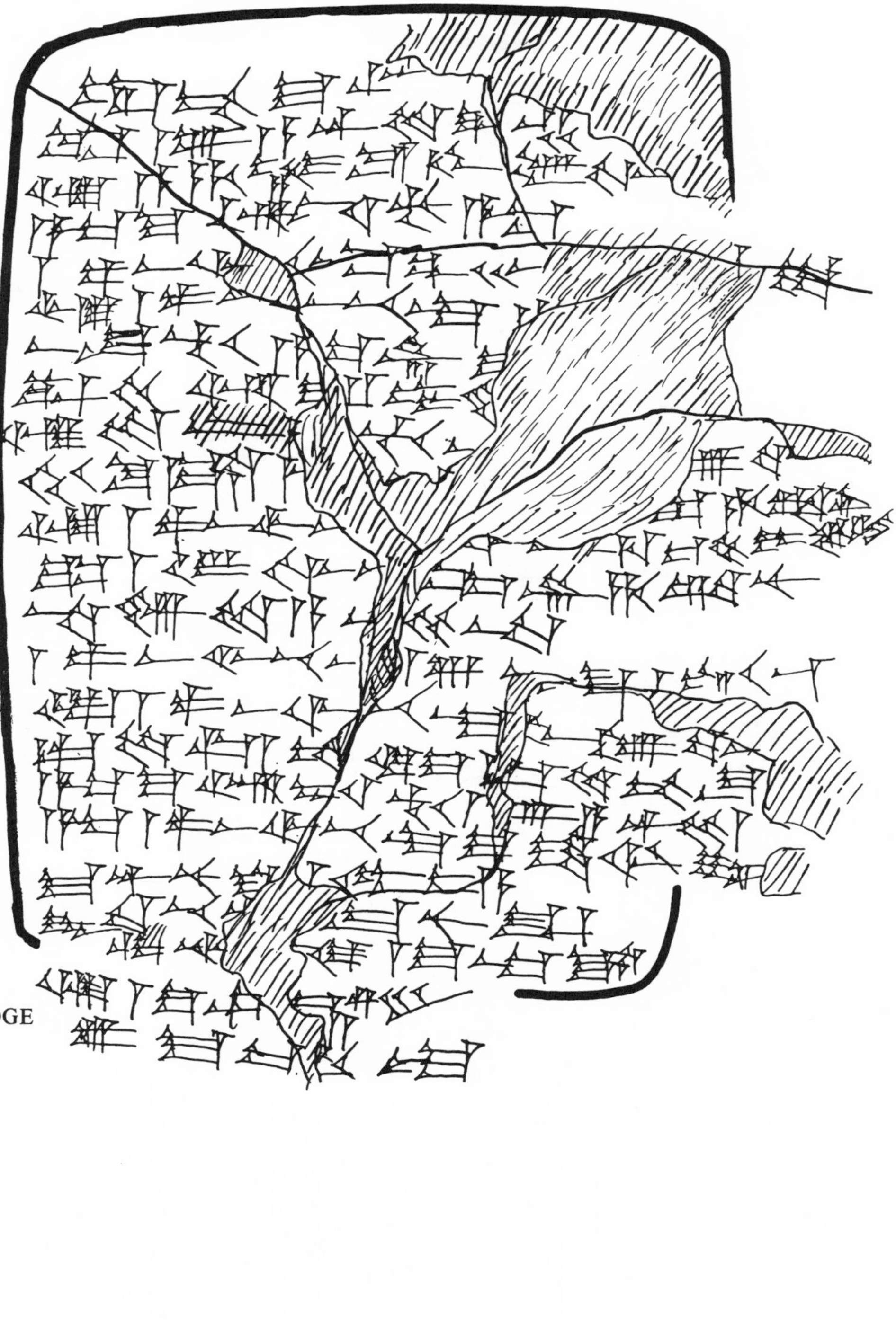

LOWER EDGE

299

REVERSE

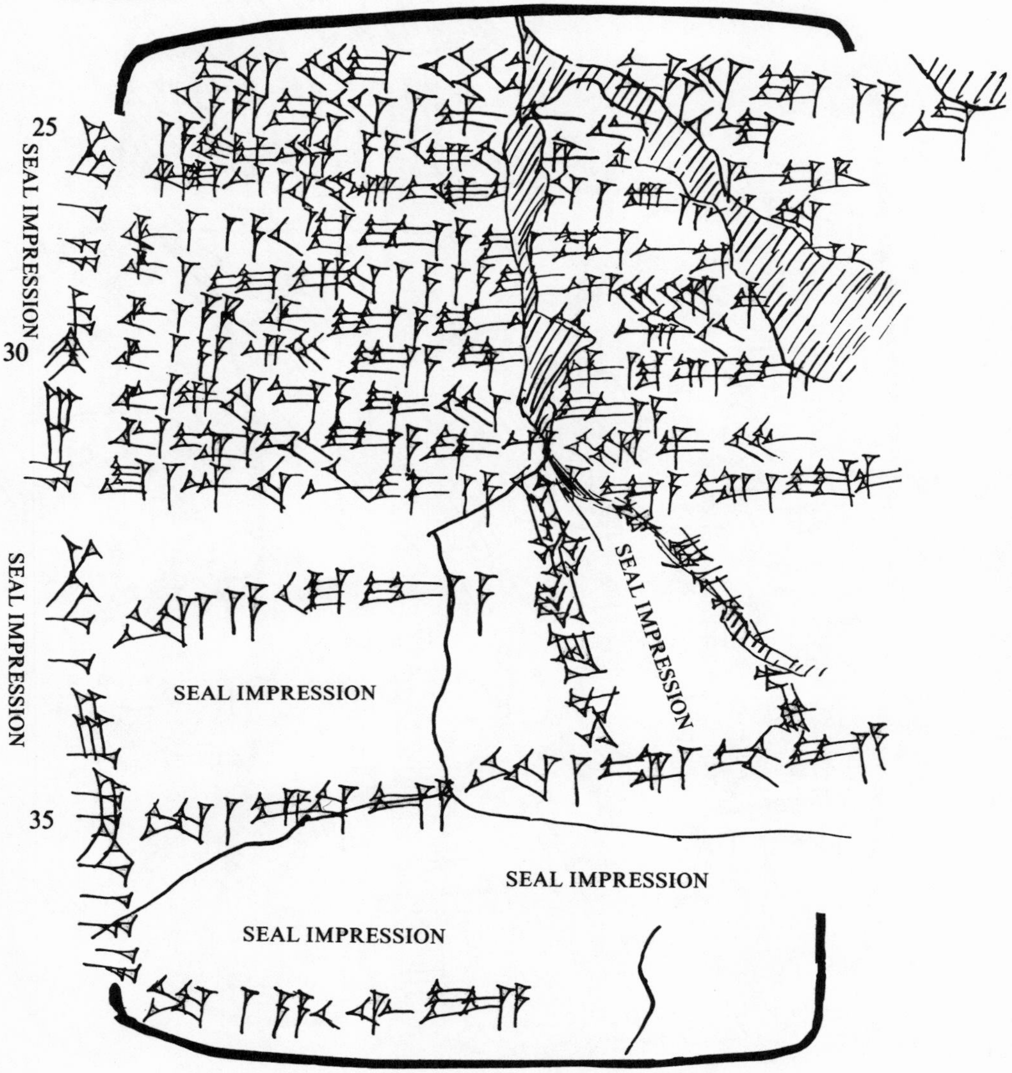
SEAL IMPRESSION
SEAL IMPRESSION
SEAL IMPRESSION
SEAL IMPRESSION
SEAL IMPRESSION
SEAL IMPRESSION

301

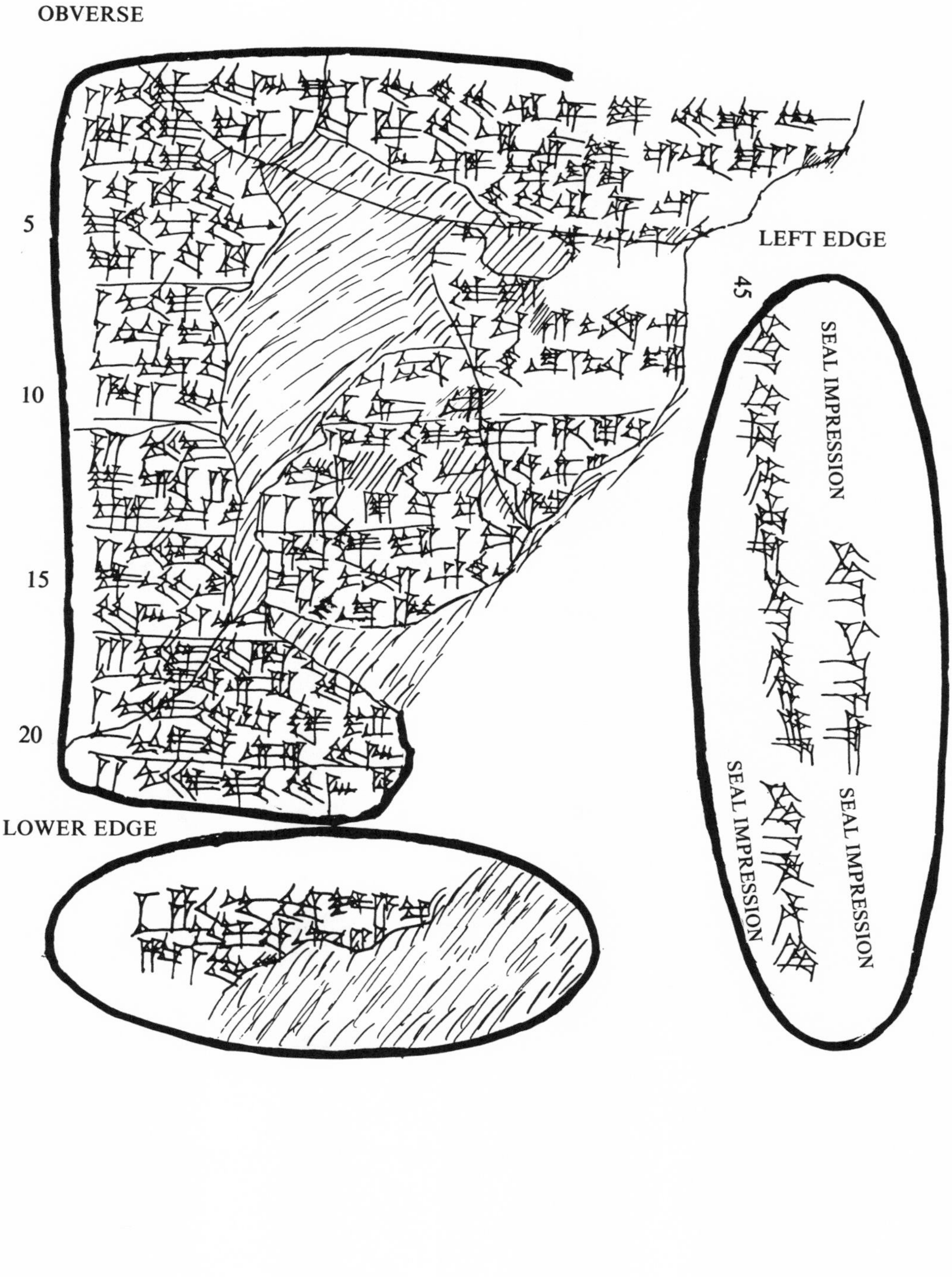
OBVERSE
5
10
15
20
LOWER EDGE
LEFT EDGE
45
SEAL IMPRESSION
SEAL IMPRESSION
SEAL IMPRESSION

301

REVERSE

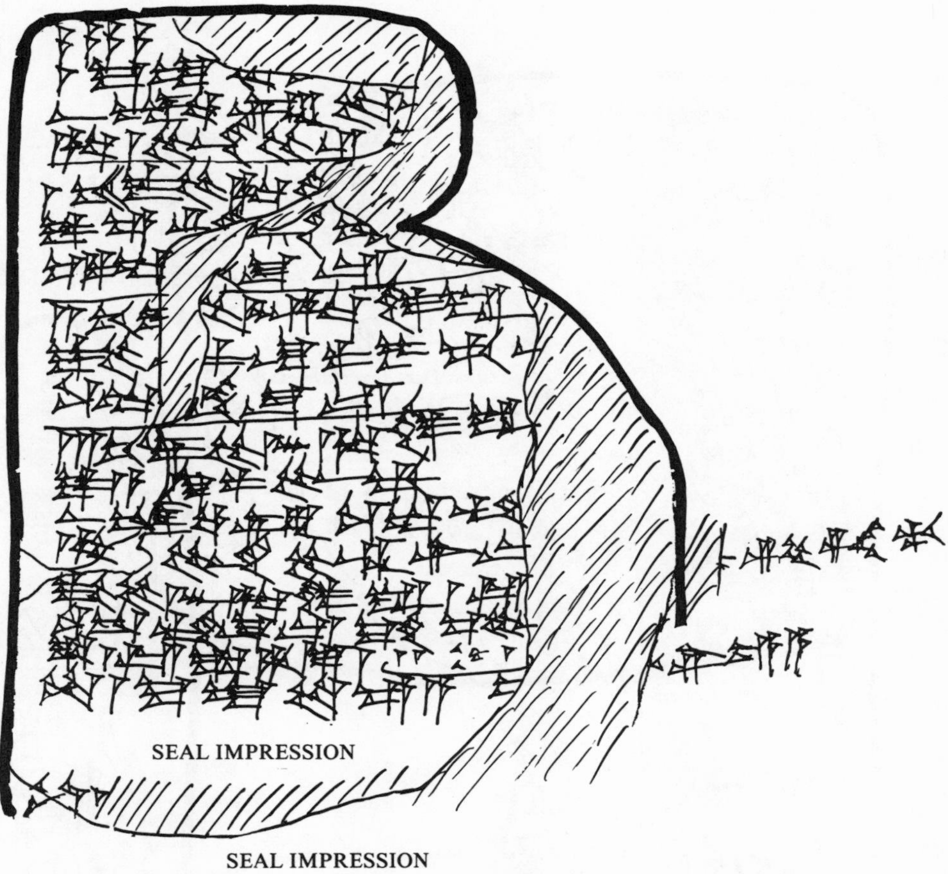

UPPER EDGE

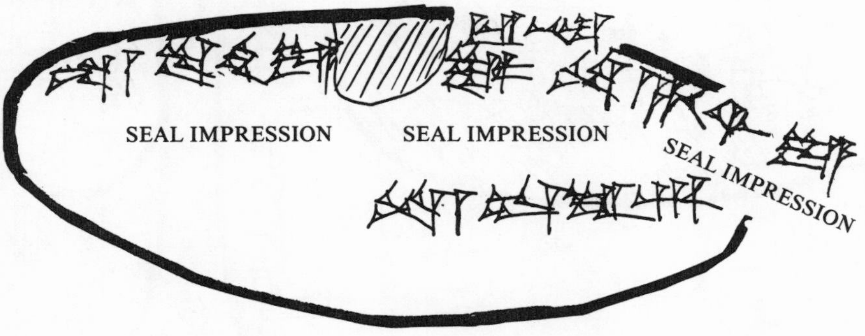

321

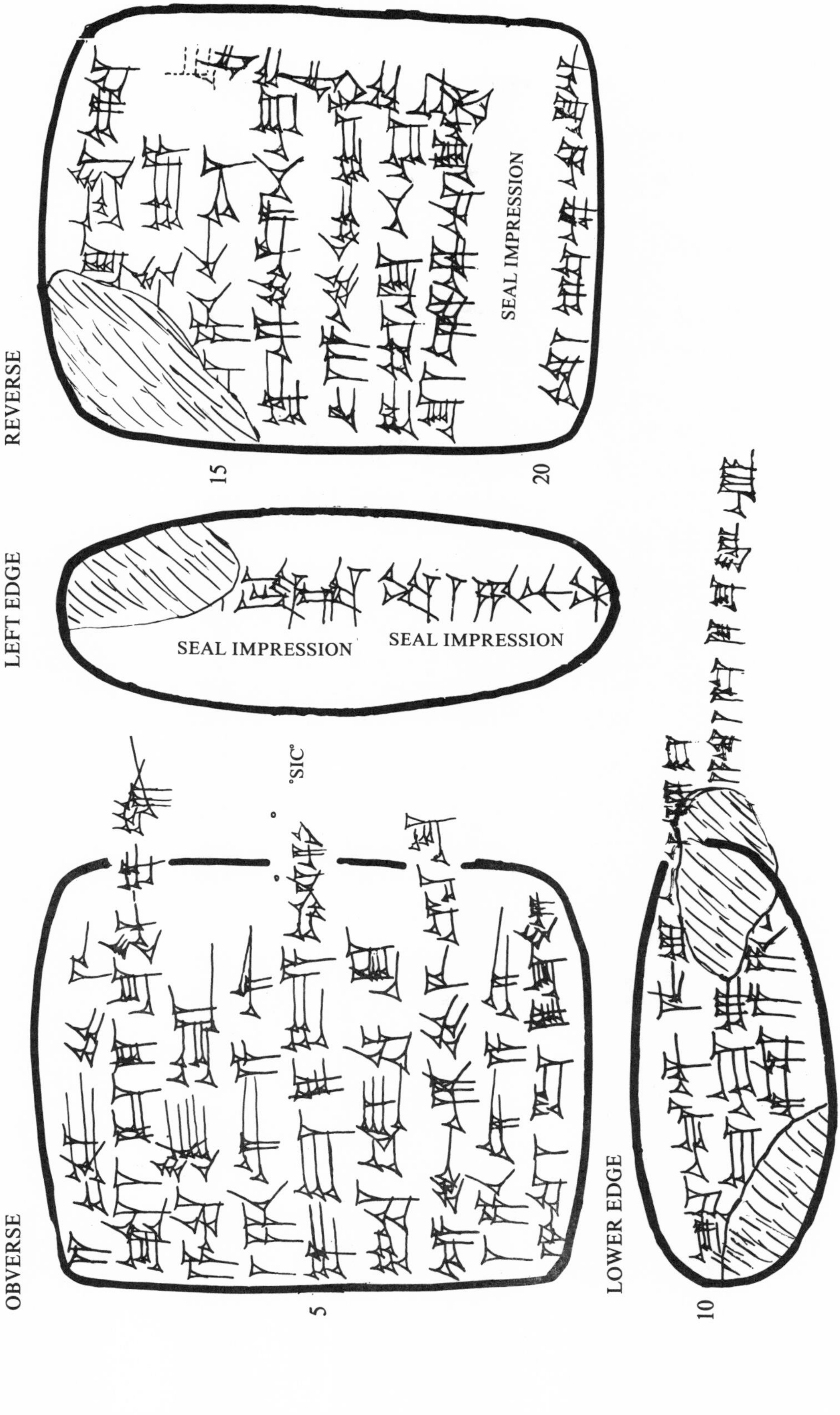
OBVERSE
5
'SIC'
LOWER EDGE
10
LEFT EDGE
SEAL IMPRESSION
SEAL IMPRESSION
REVERSE
15
SEAL IMPRESSION
20

322

OBVERSE

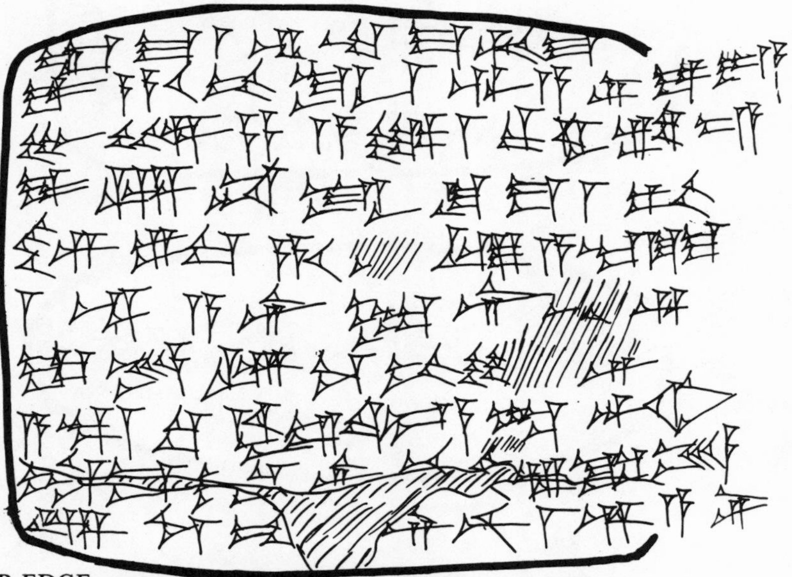

LOWER EDGE

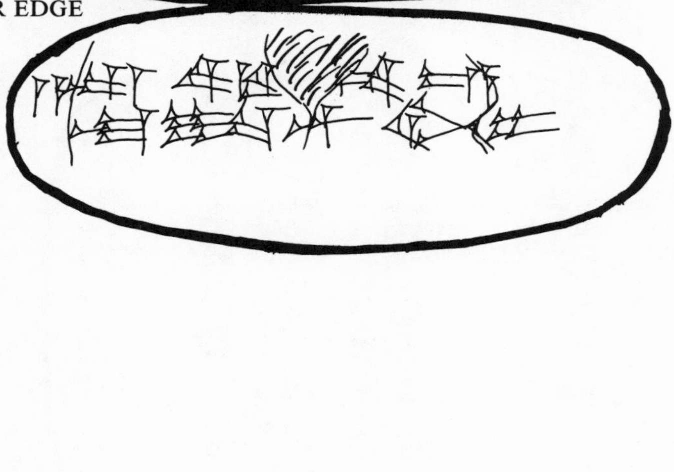

322

REVERSE

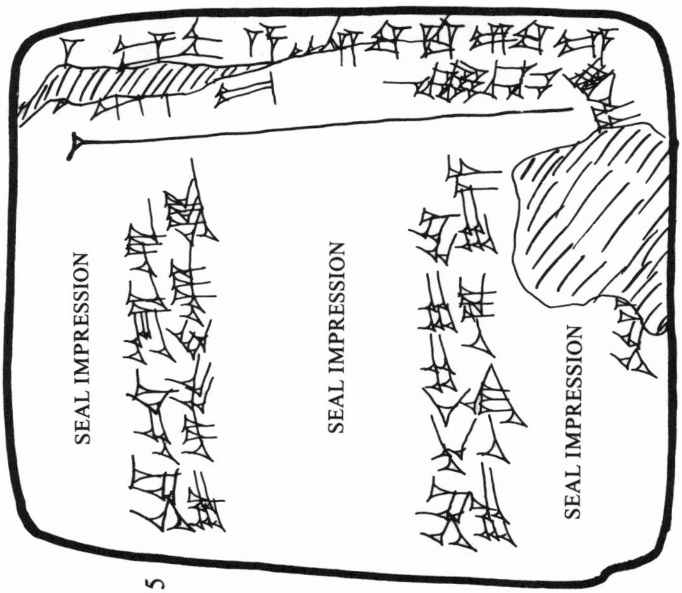

UPPER EDGE

323

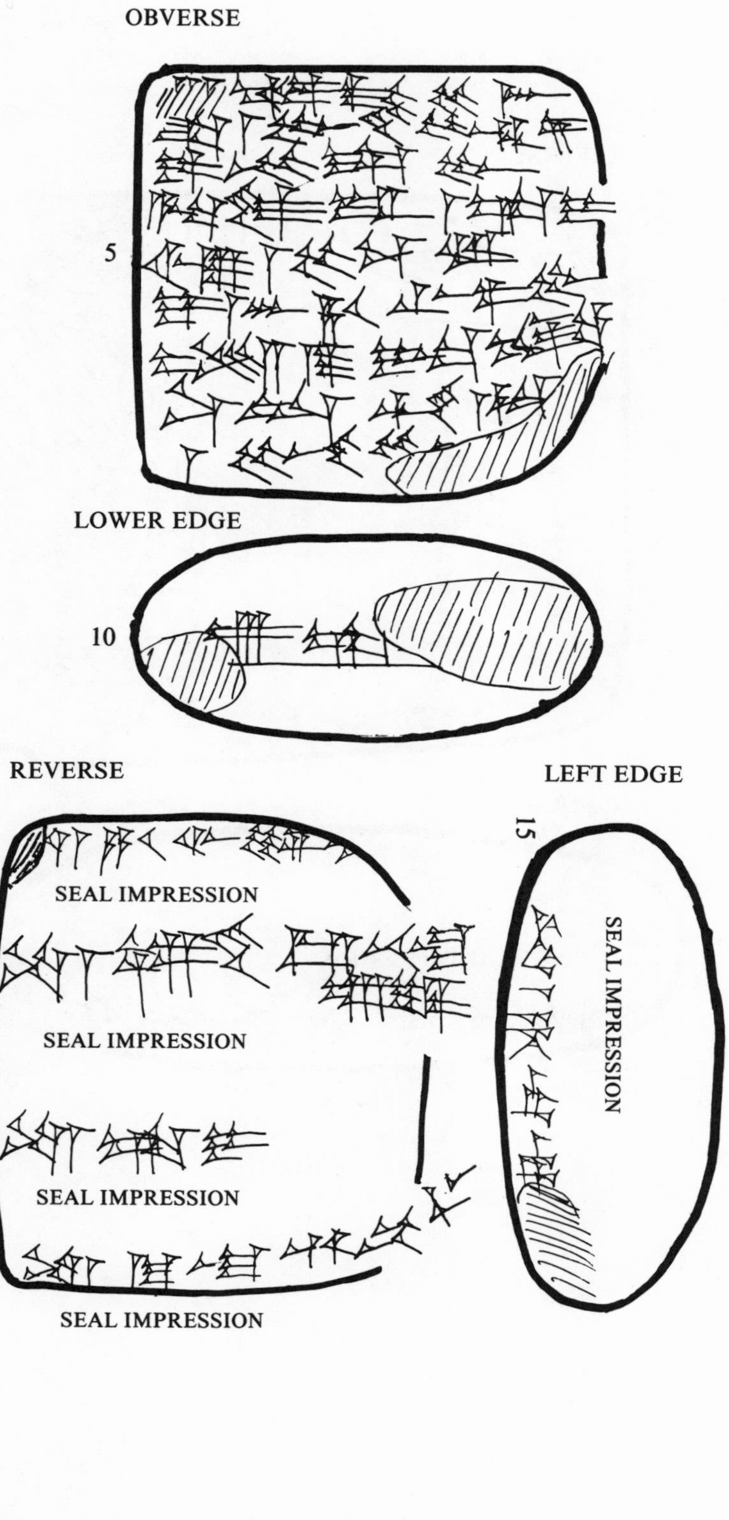
OBVERSE
5
LOWER EDGE
10
REVERSE
LEFT EDGE
15
SEAL IMPRESSION
SEAL IMPRESSION
SEAL IMPRESSION
SEAL IMPRESSION
SEAL IMPRESSION

324

OBVERSE

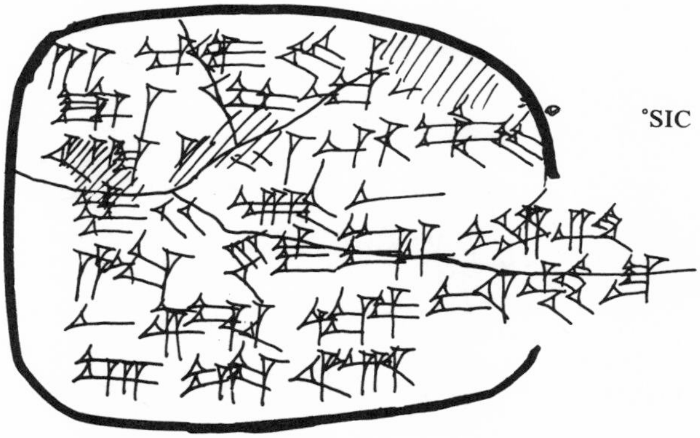

REVERSE

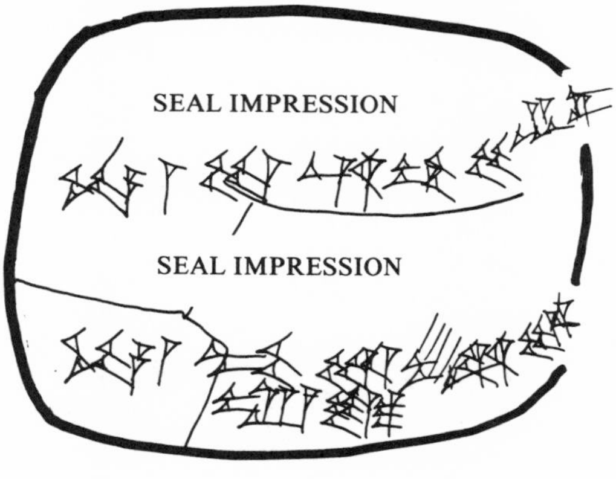

UPPER EDGE

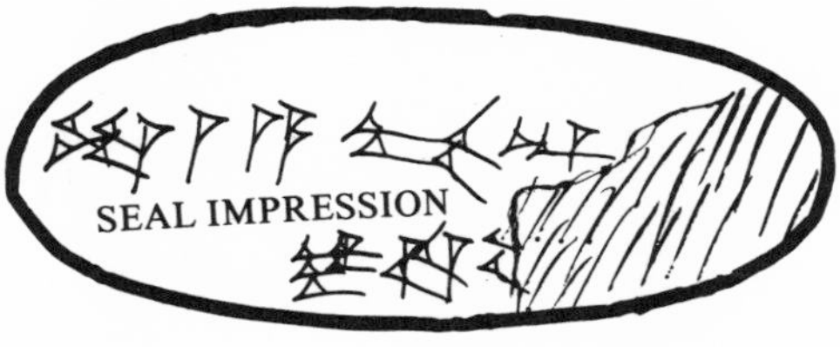

325

OBVERSE

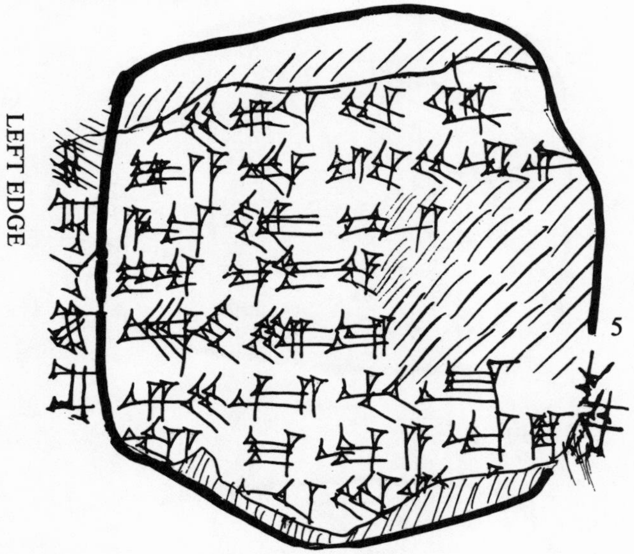

END OF OBVERSE DESTROYED

REVERSE

BEGINNING OF REVERSE DESTROYED

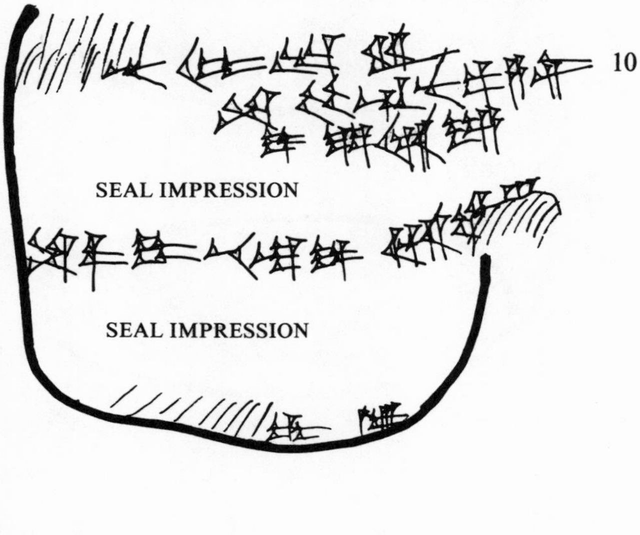

326

OBVERSE

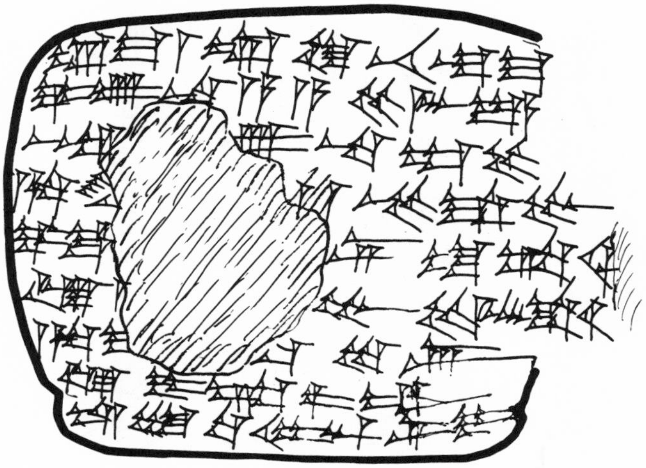

REVERSE

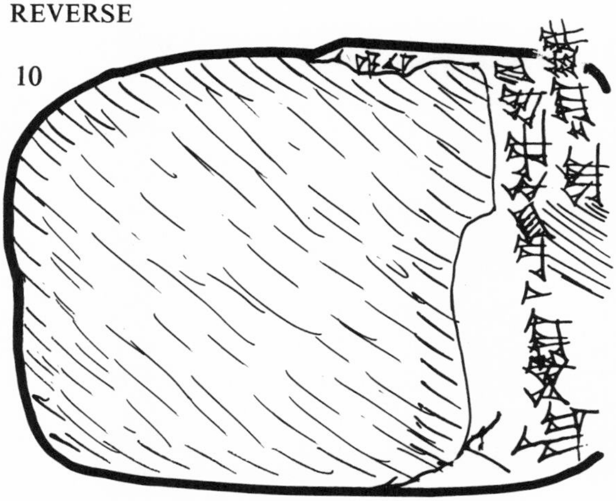

327

OBVERSE

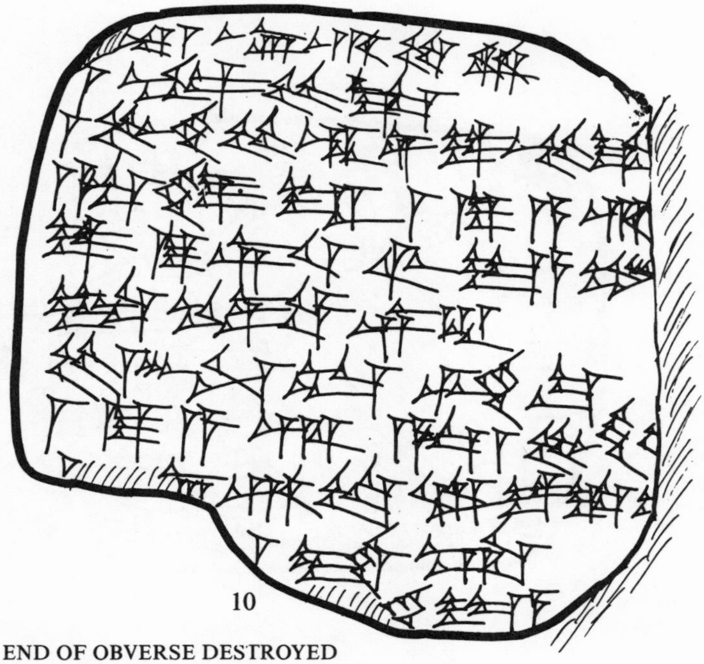

END OF OBVERSE DESTROYED

REVERSE

BEGINNING OF REVERSE DESTROYED

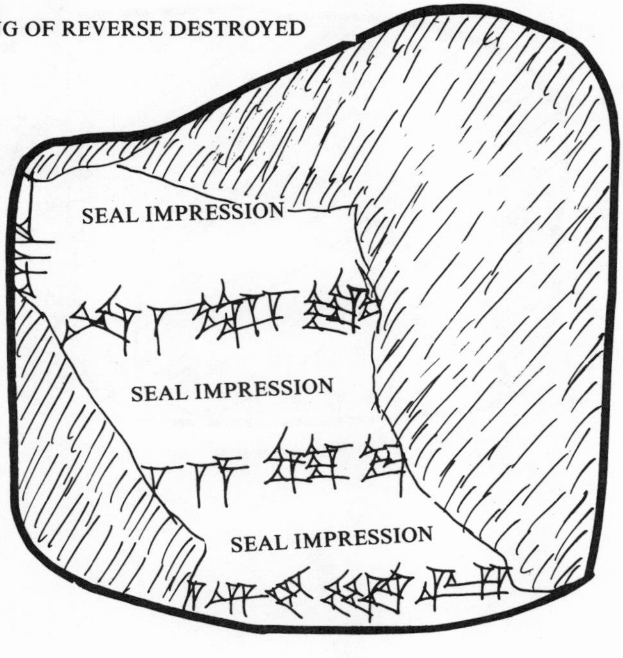

329

OBVERSE

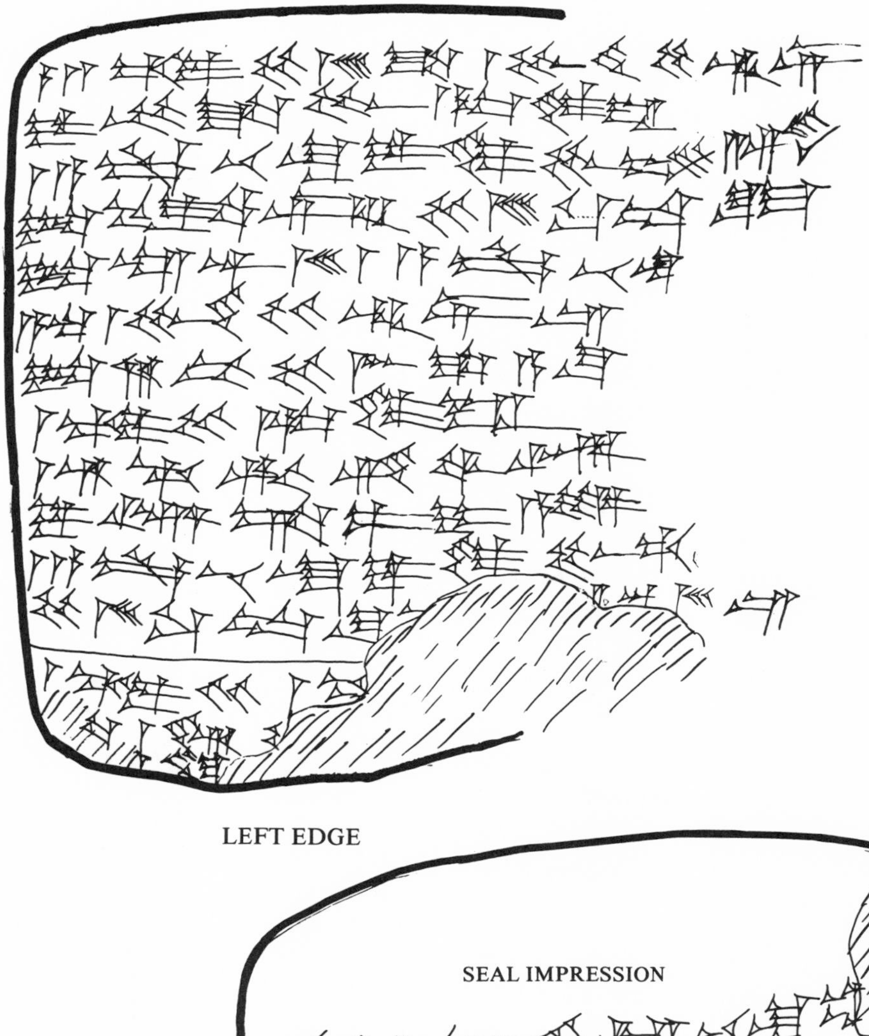

LEFT EDGE

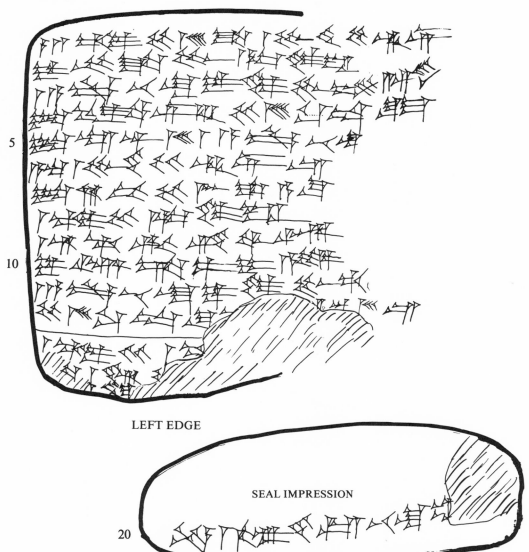

329

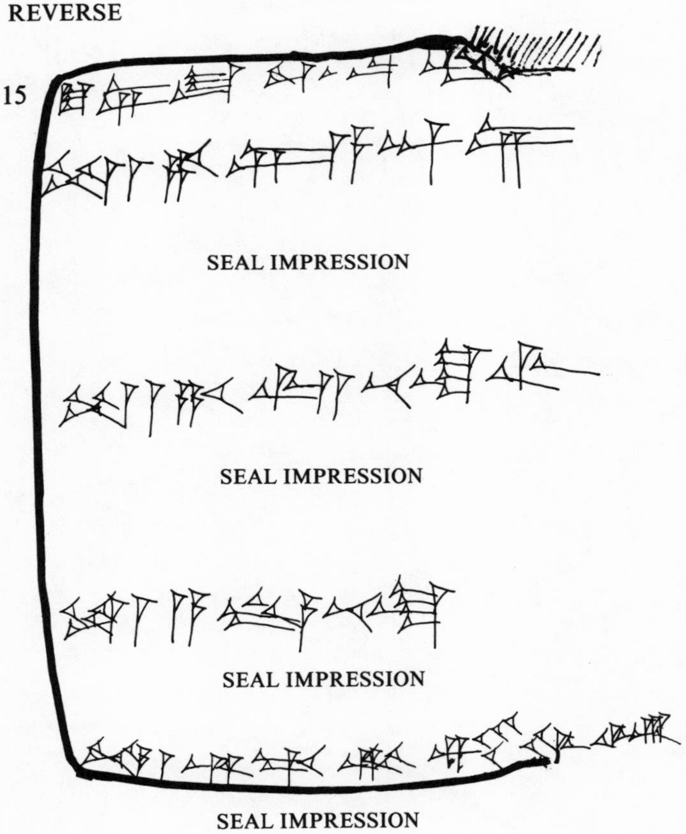
REVERSE
15
SEAL IMPRESSION
SEAL IMPRESSION
SEAL IMPRESSION
SEAL IMPRESSION

331

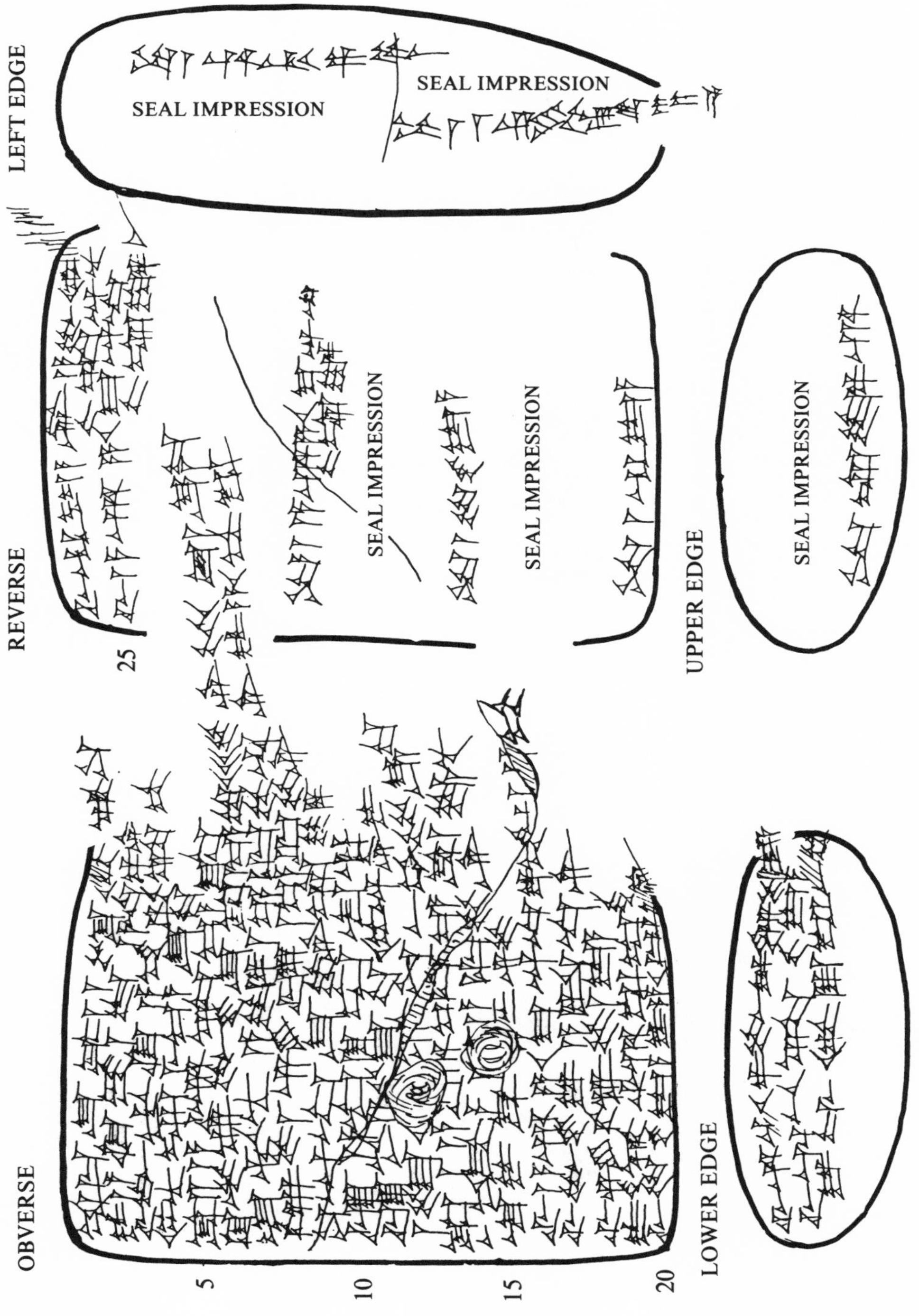
OBVERSE
LOWER EDGE
REVERSE
UPPER EDGE
LEFT EDGE
SEAL IMPRESSION
SEAL IMPRESSION
SEAL IMPRESSION
SEAL IMPRESSION
SEAL IMPRESSION

333

OBVERSE

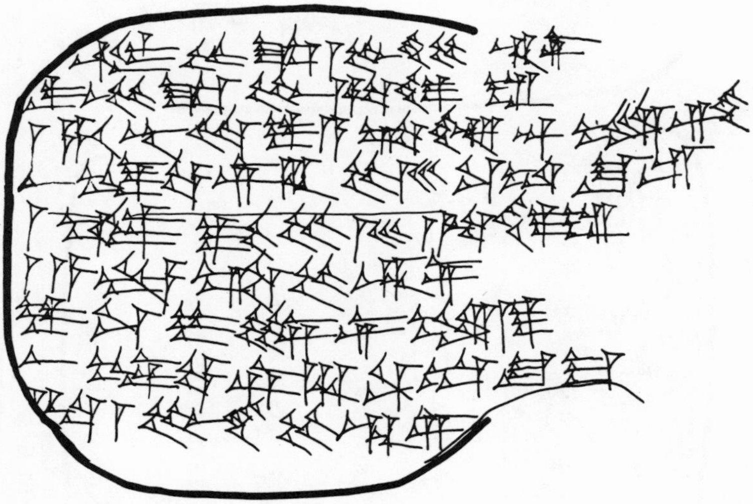

REVERSE

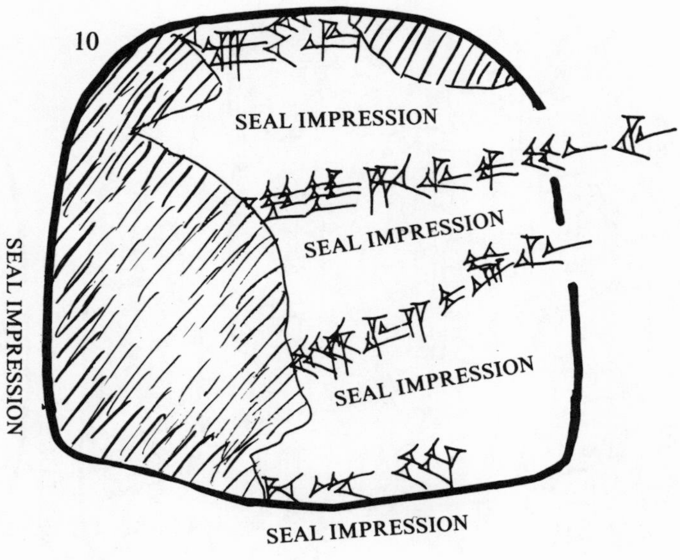

334

OBVERSE

°SIC

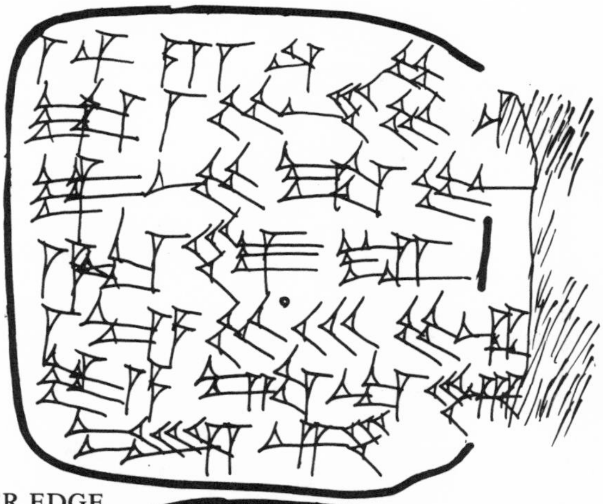

LOWER EDGE

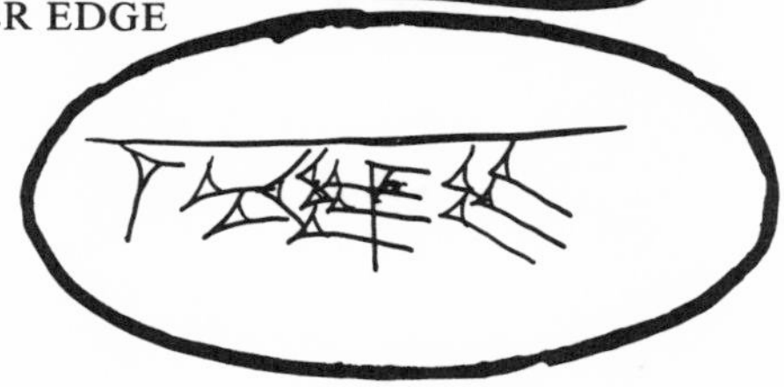

REVERSE

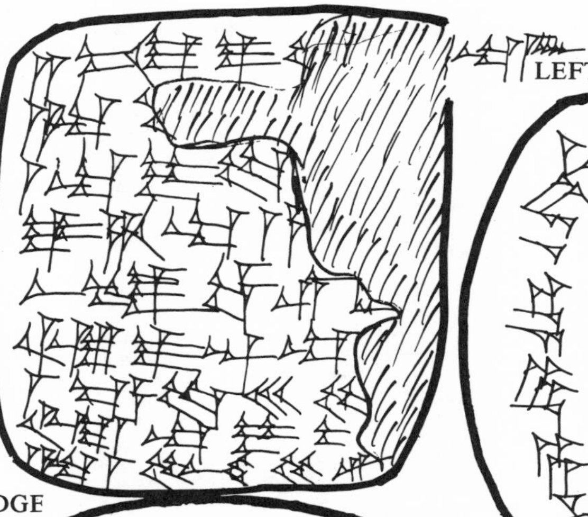

LEFT EDGE

UPPER EDGE

336

OBVERSE

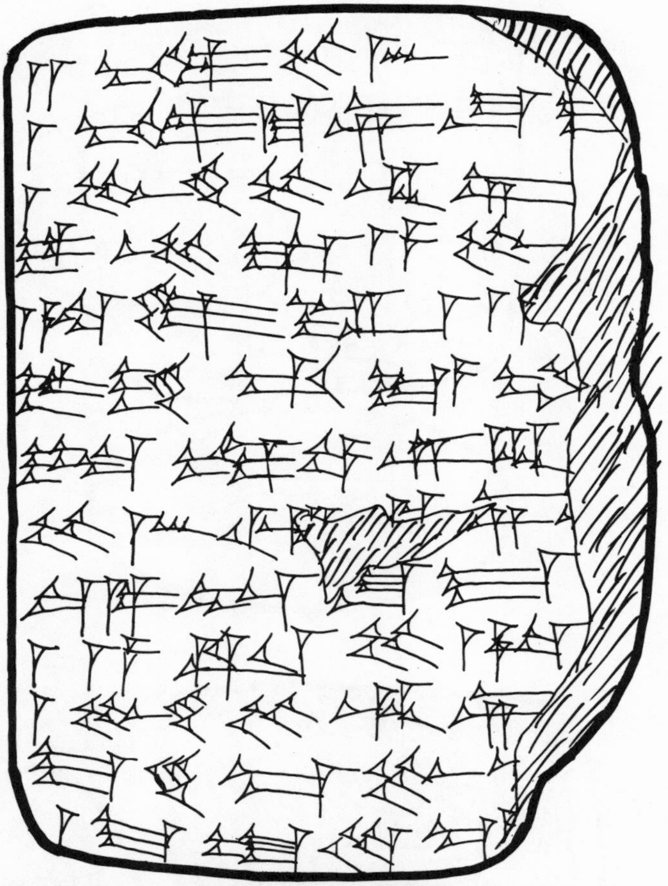

LOWER EDGE

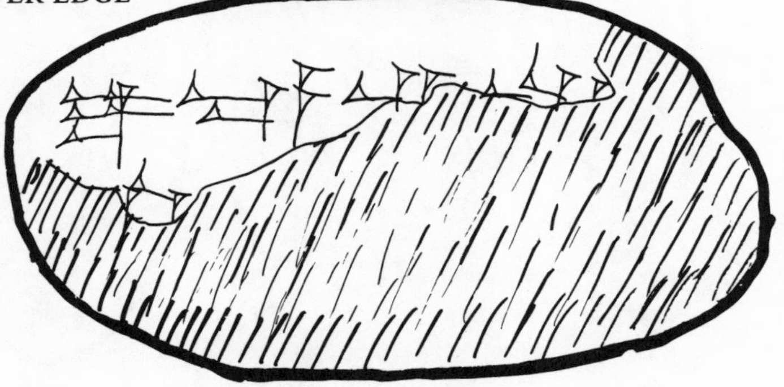

336

REVERSE

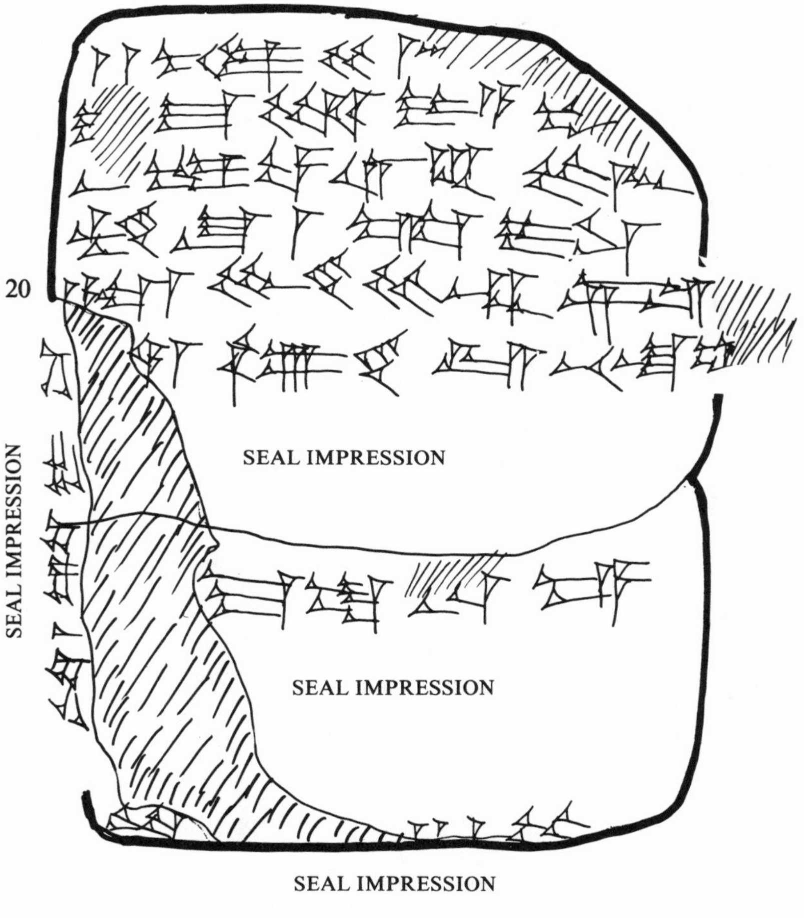
20
SEAL IMPRESSION
SEAL IMPRESSION
SEAL IMPRESSION
SEAL IMPRESSION

337

OBVERSE

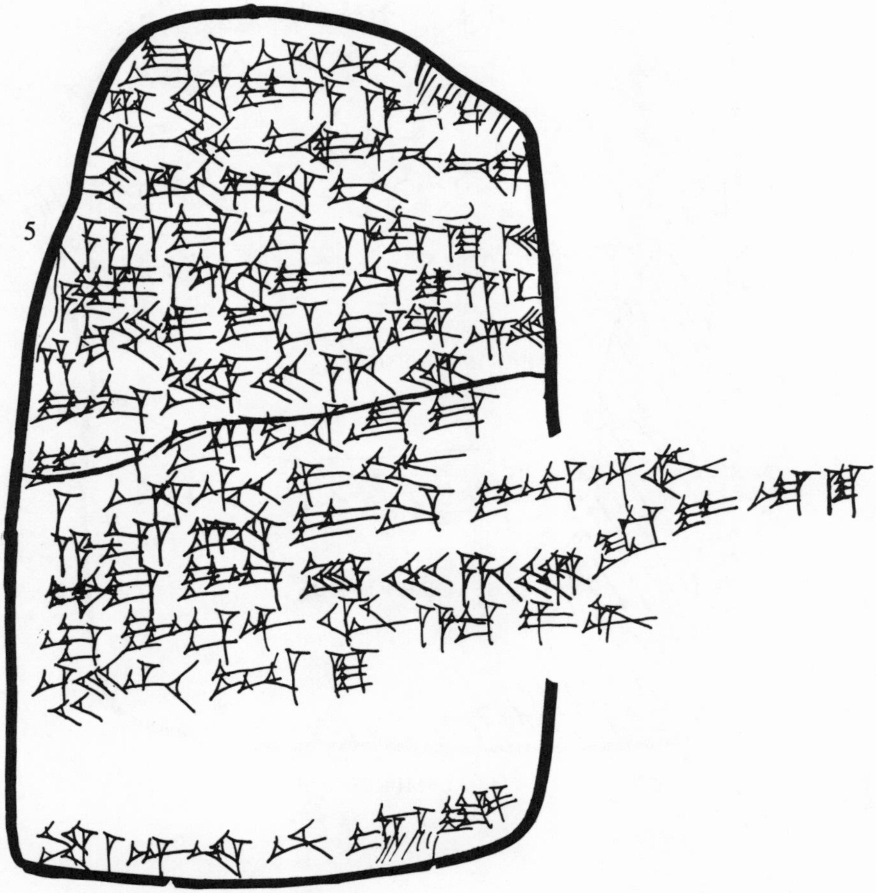

SEAL IMPRESSION

337

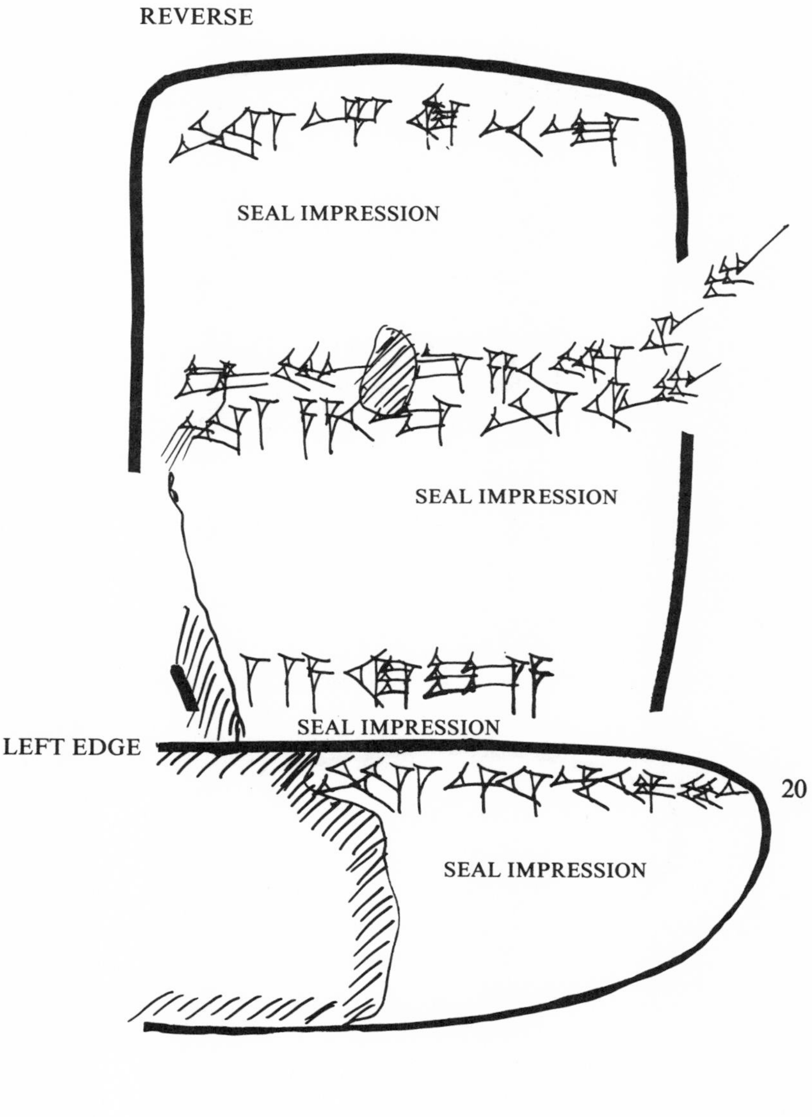
REVERSE
SEAL IMPRESSION
SEAL IMPRESSION
SEAL IMPRESSION
LEFT EDGE
20
SEAL IMPRESSION

338

OBVERSE

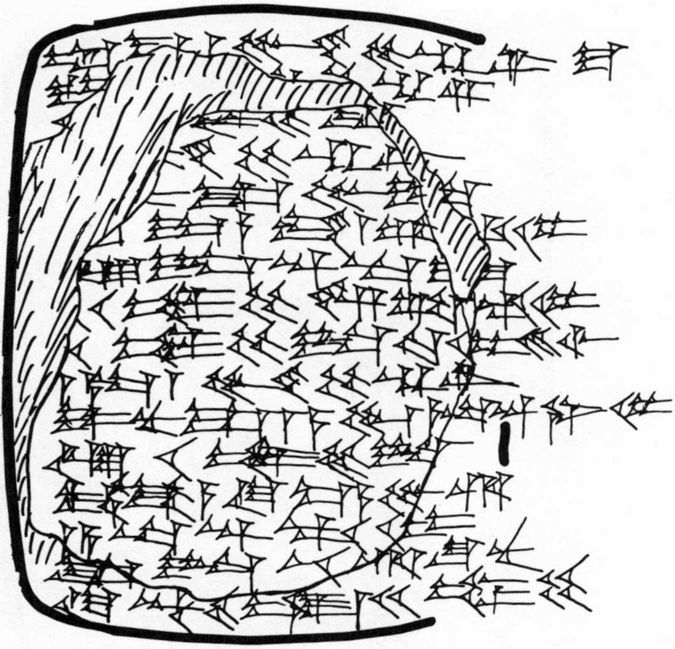

LOWER EDGE

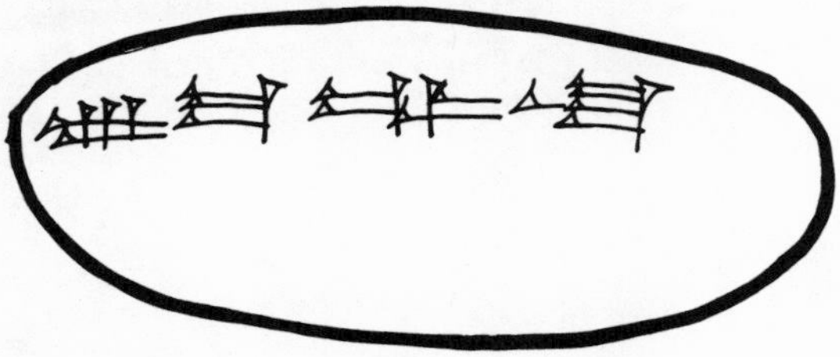

338

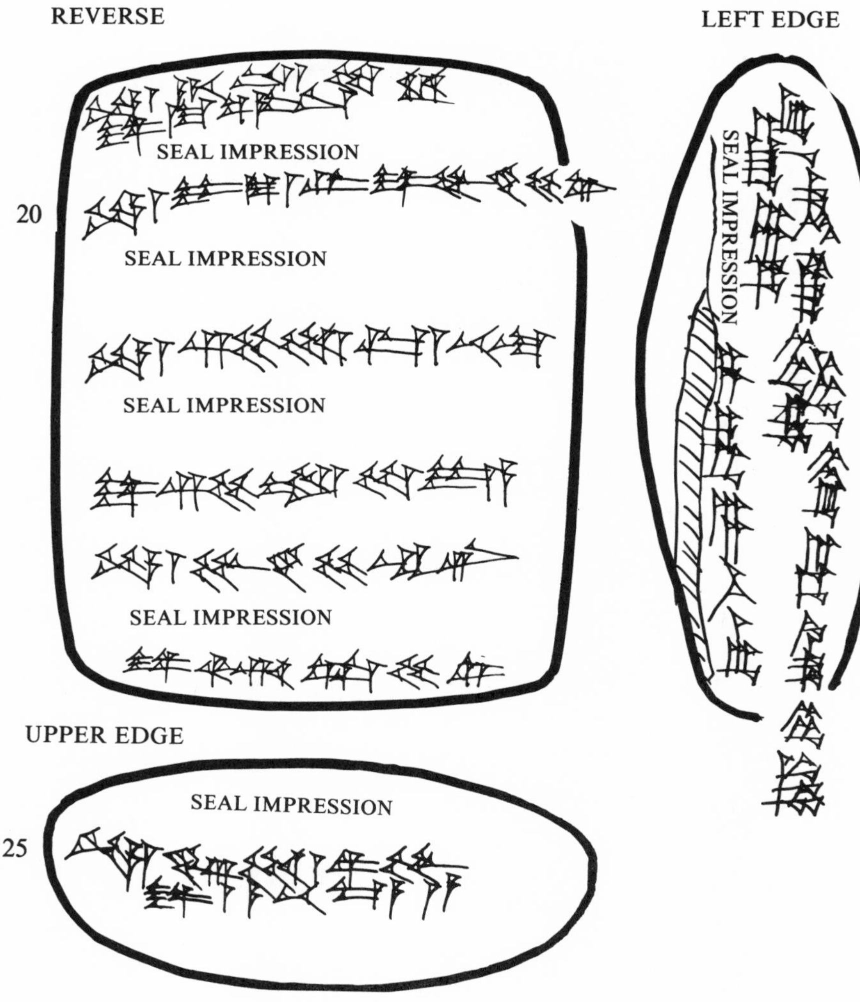
REVERSE
LEFT EDGE
SEAL IMPRESSION
SEAL IMPRESSION
SEAL IMPRESSION
SEAL IMPRESSION
SEAL IMPRESSION
UPPER EDGE
SEAL IMPRESSION

339

OBVERSE

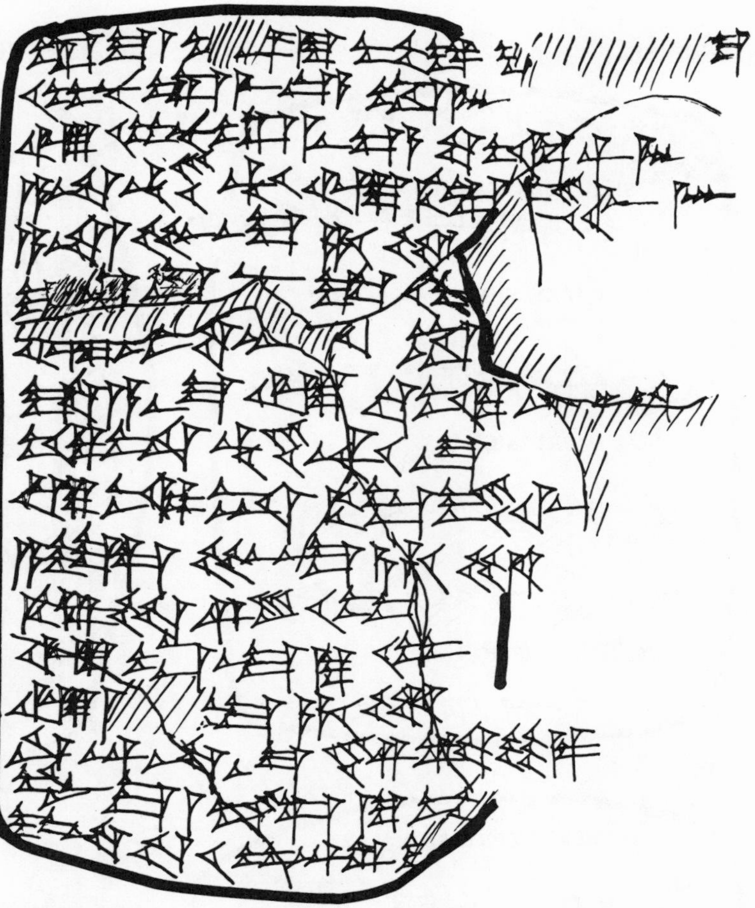

LOWER EDGE

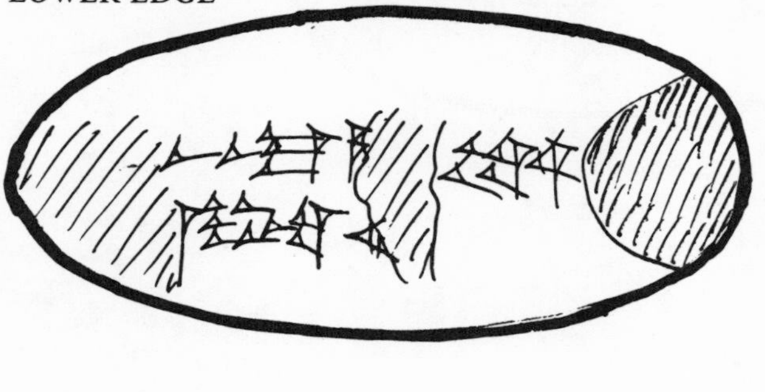

339

REVERSE

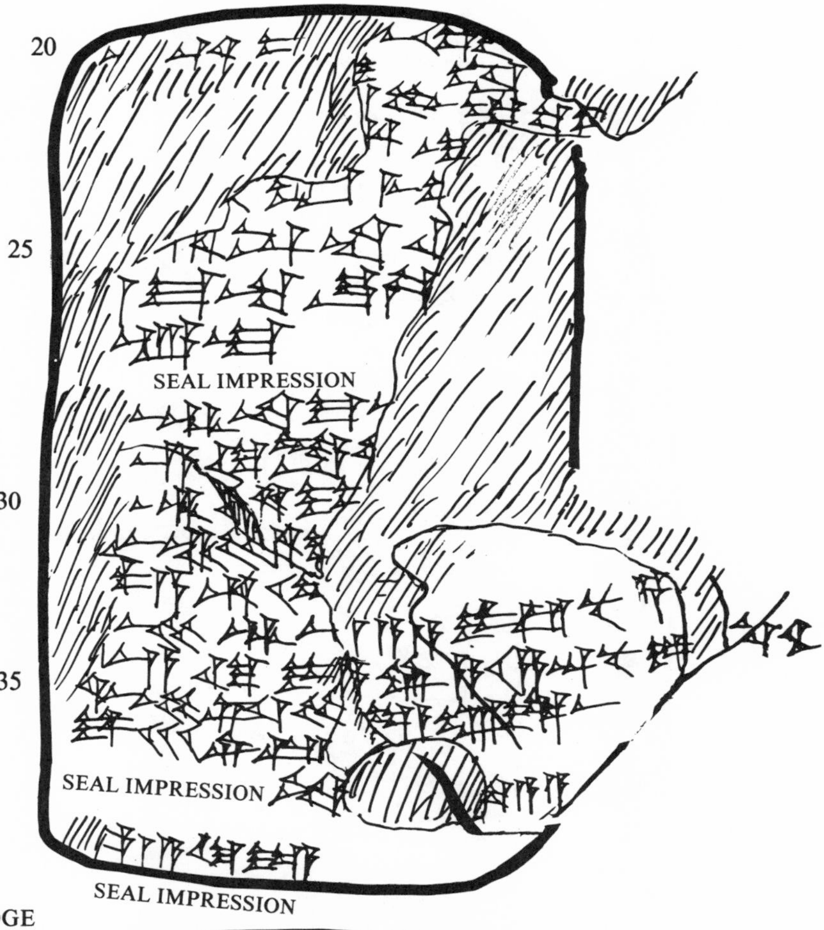

LEFT EDGE

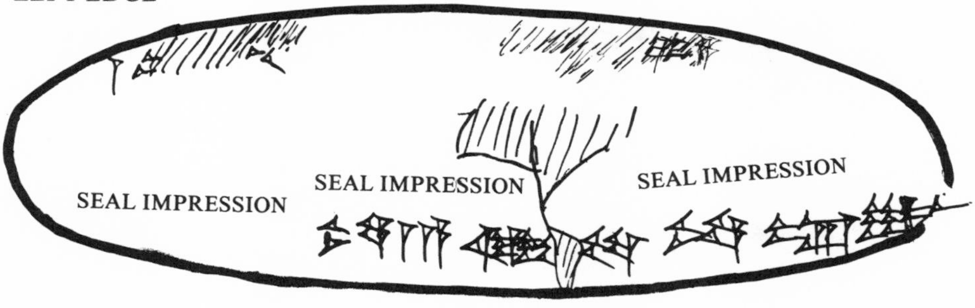

340

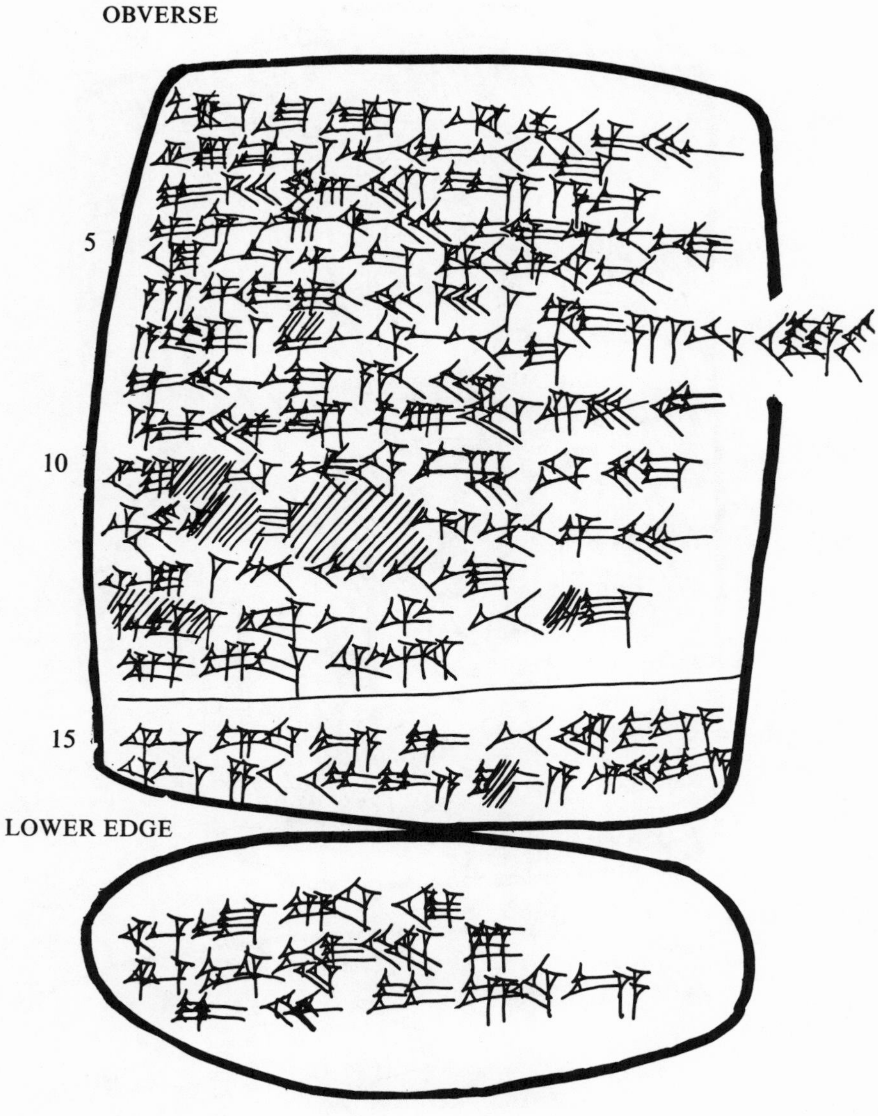

340

REVERSE

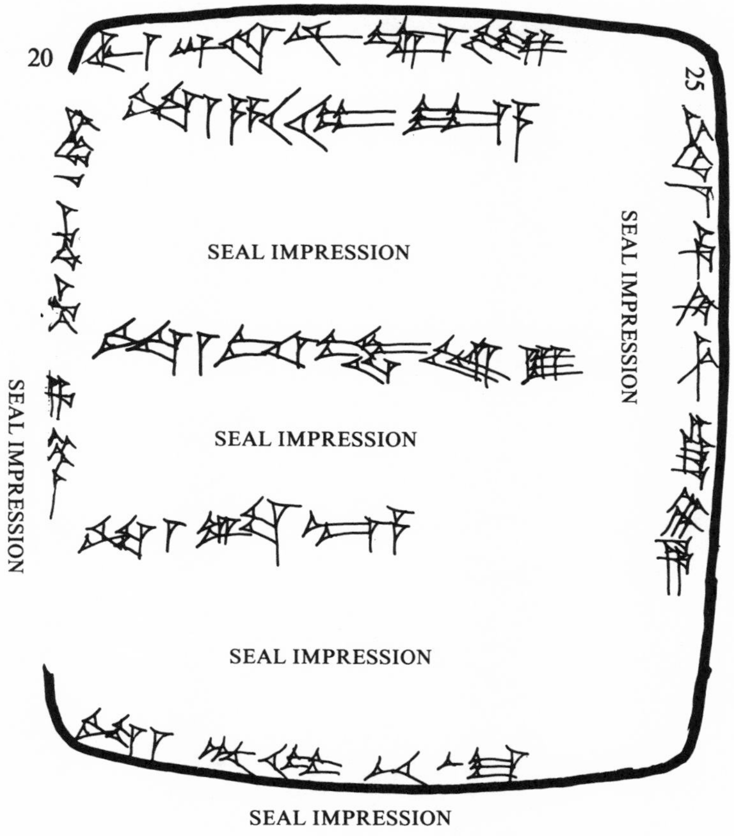
20
25
SEAL IMPRESSION
SEAL IMPRESSION
SEAL IMPRESSION
SEAL IMPRESSION
SEAL IMPRESSION
SEAL IMPRESSION

341

OBVERSE

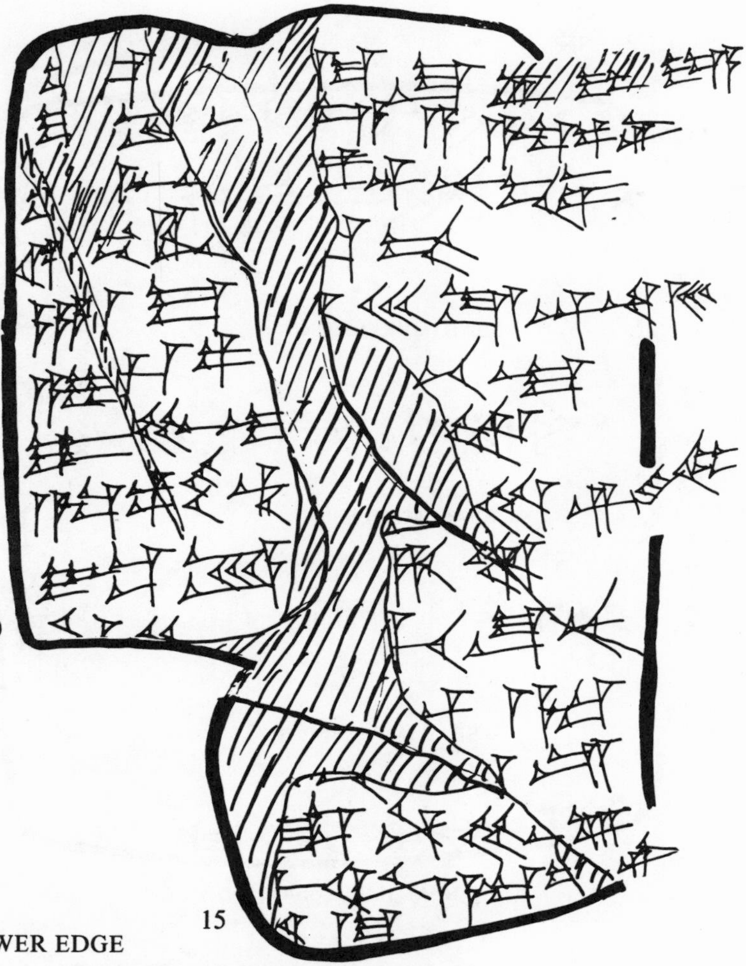

LOWER EDGE

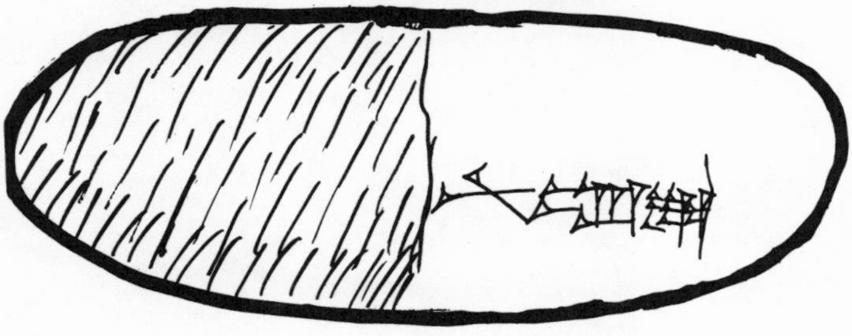

341

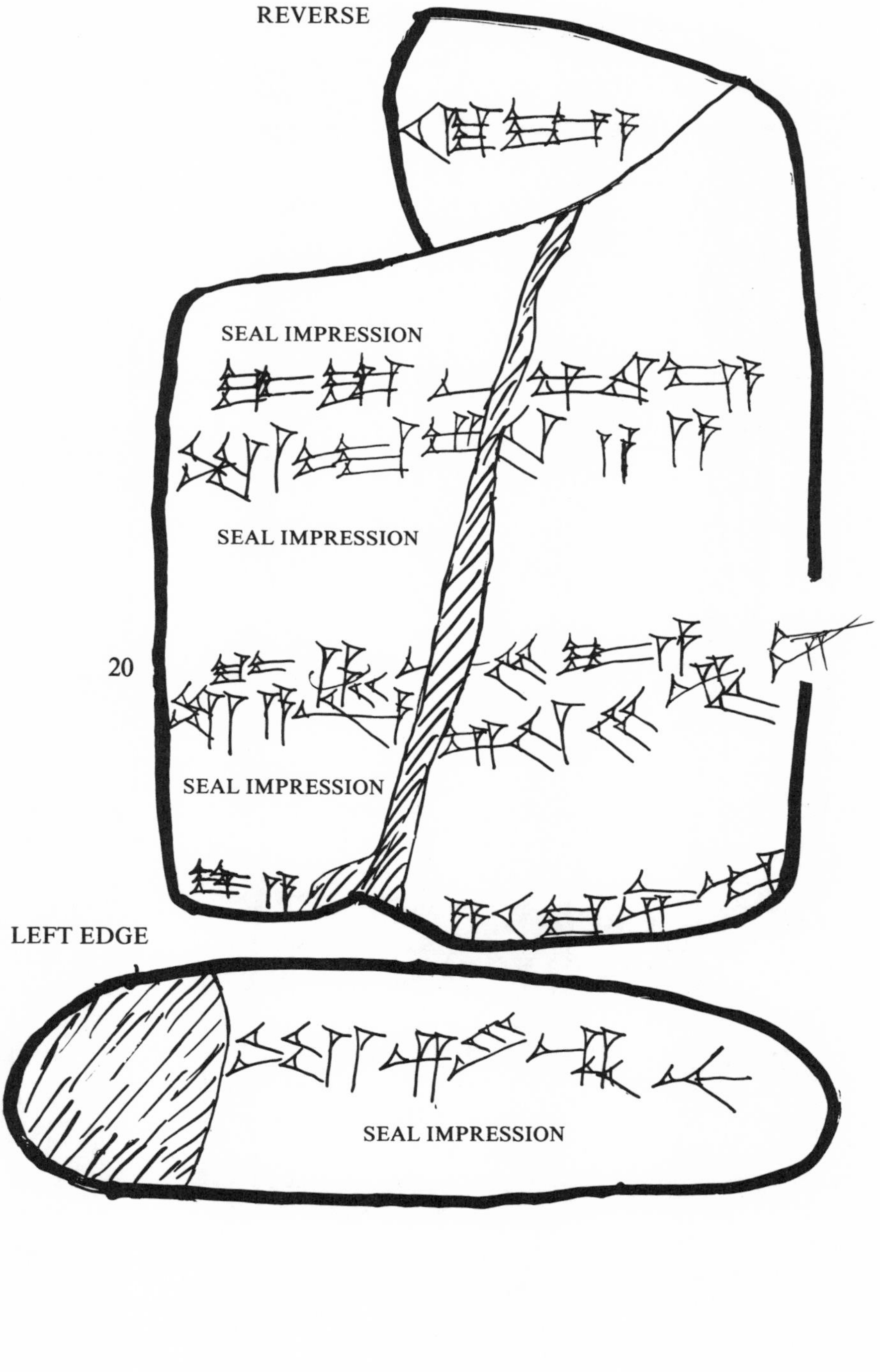
REVERSE
SEAL IMPRESSION
SEAL IMPRESSION
20
SEAL IMPRESSION
LEFT EDGE
SEAL IMPRESSION

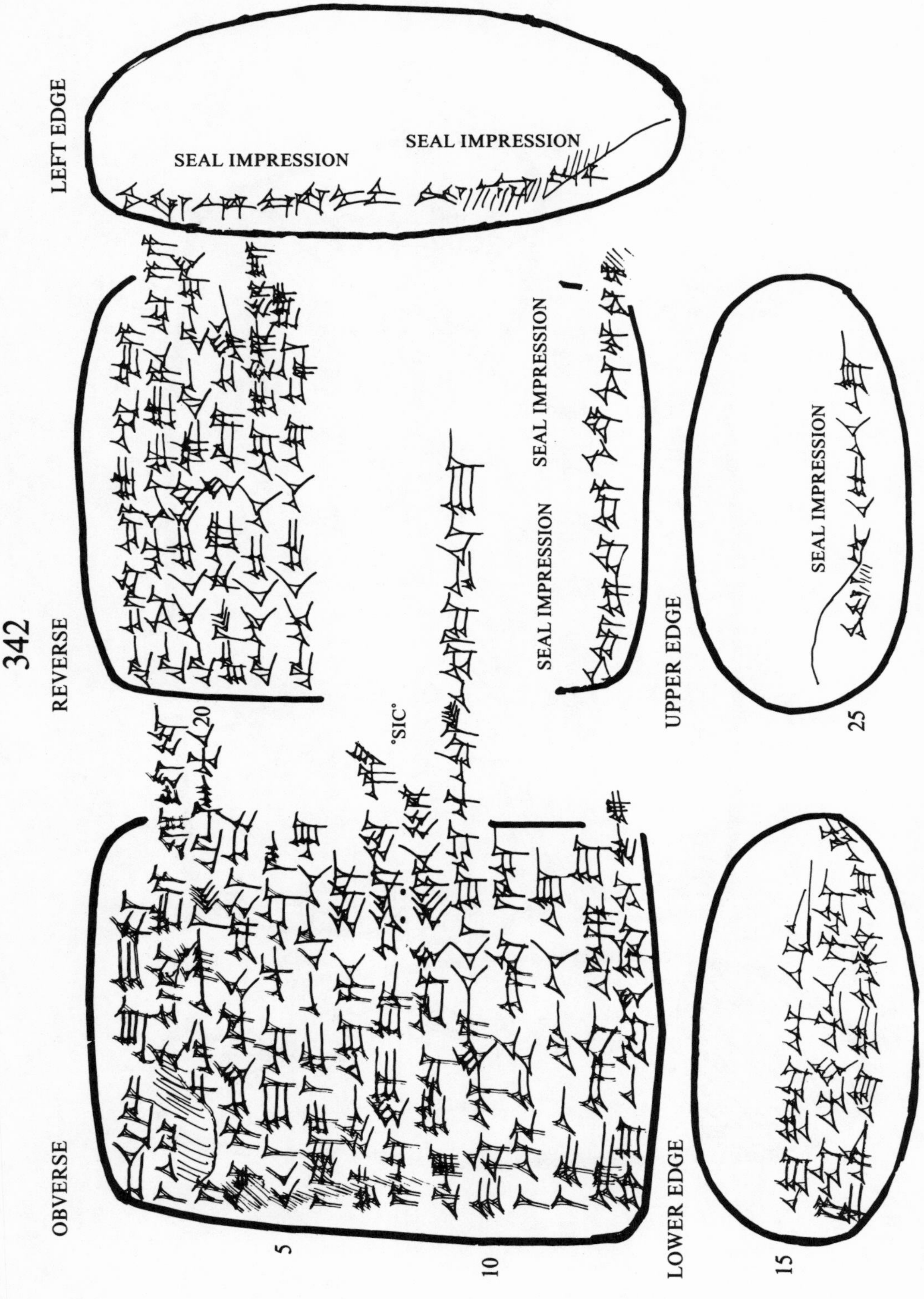

342
OBVERSE
REVERSE
LEFT EDGE
LOWER EDGE
UPPER EDGE
SEAL IMPRESSION
SEAL IMPRESSION
SEAL IMPRESSION
SEAL IMPRESSION
SEAL IMPRESSION
SEAL IMPRESSION
'SIC'
5
10
15
20
25

343

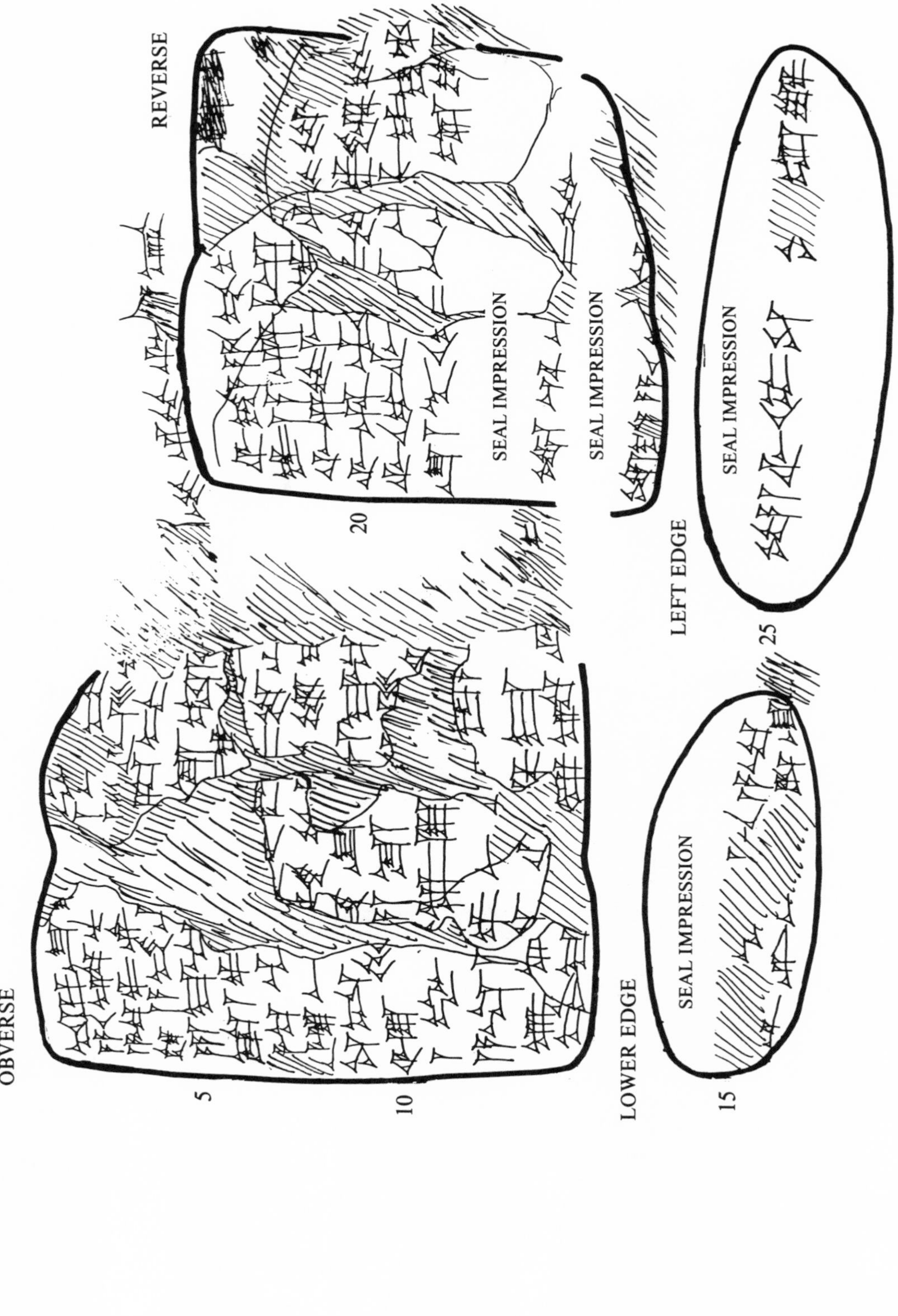
OBVERSE
REVERSE
LOWER EDGE
LEFT EDGE
SEAL IMPRESSION
SEAL IMPRESSION
SEAL IMPRESSION
SEAL IMPRESSION

344

OBVERSE

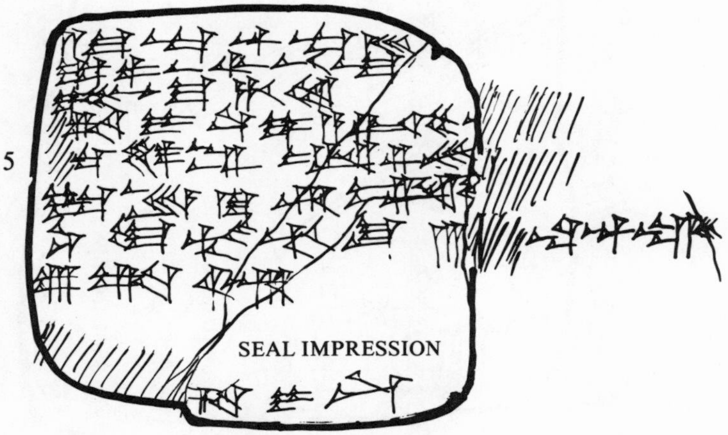

REVERSE

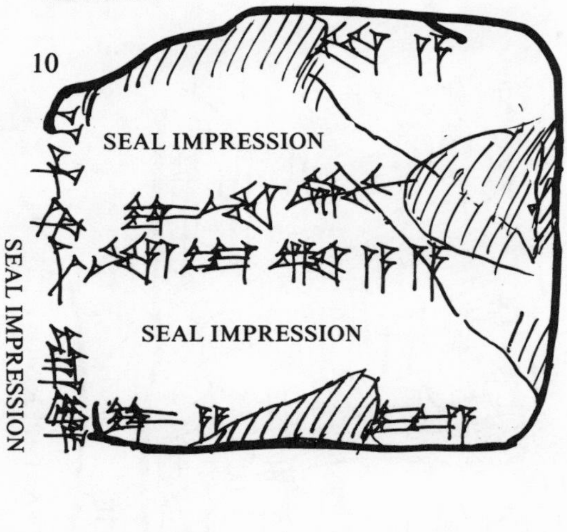

345

OBVERSE

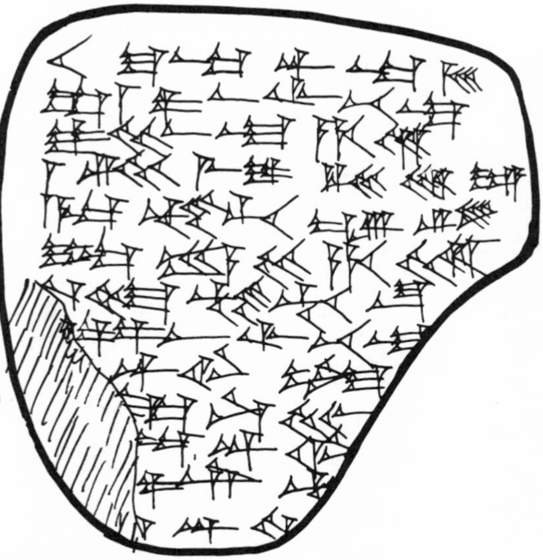

LOWER EDGE

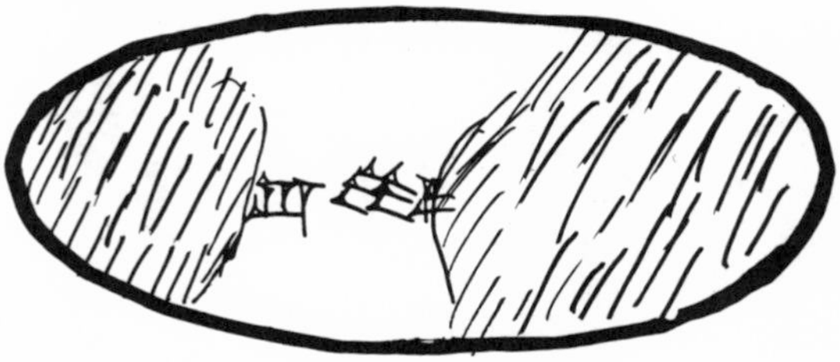

REVERSE

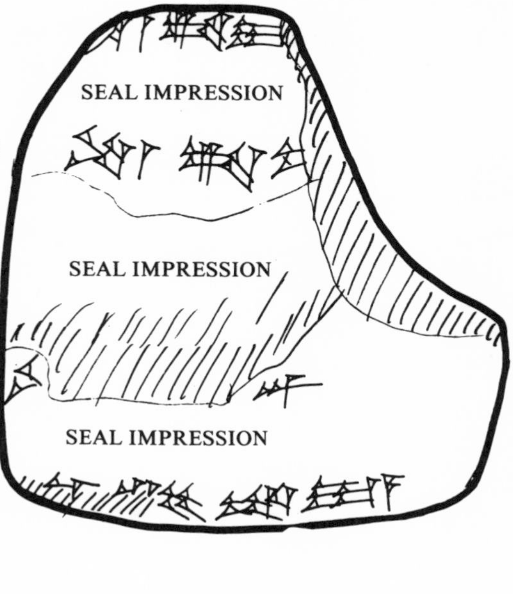

346

OBVERSE

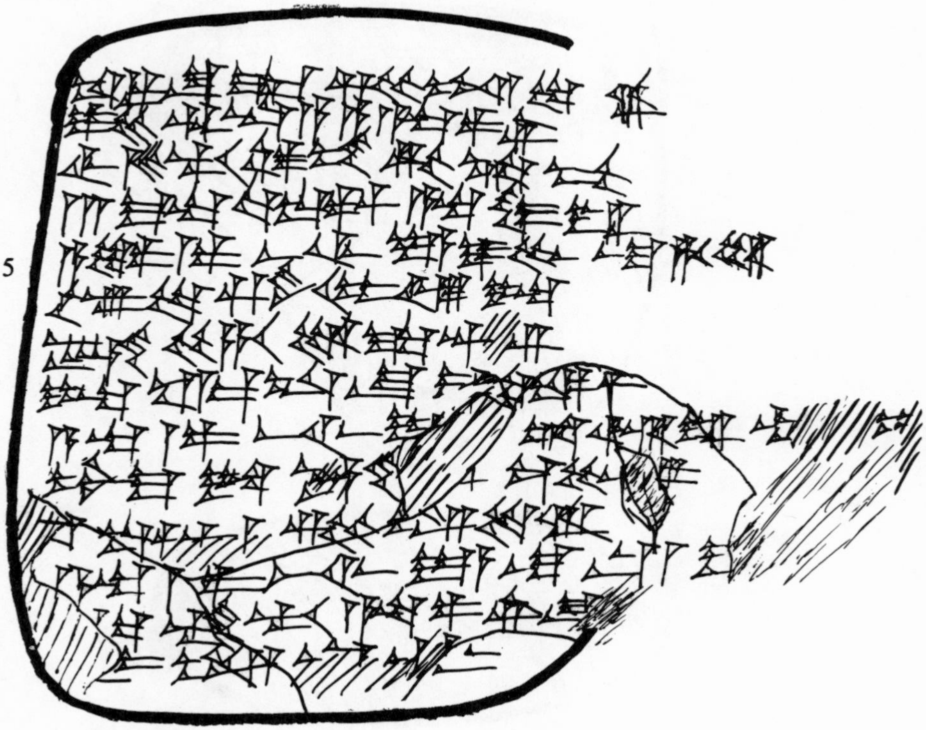

LEFT EDGE

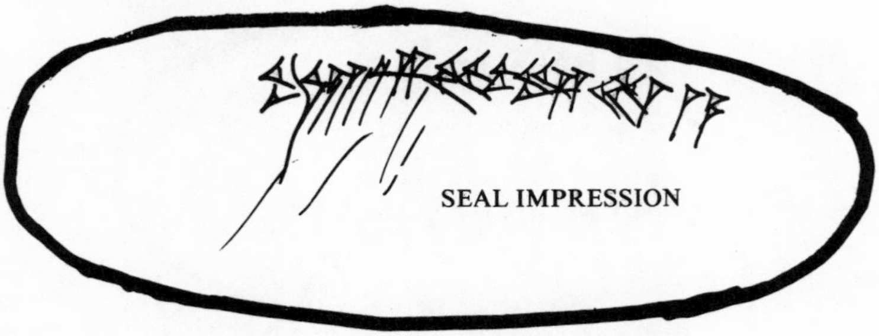

SEAL IMPRESSION

346

REVERSE

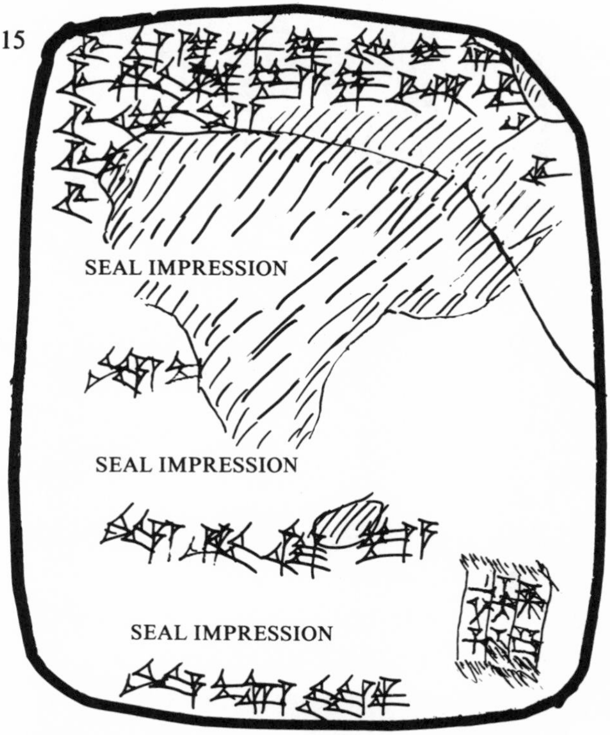

UPPER EDGE

347

OBVERSE

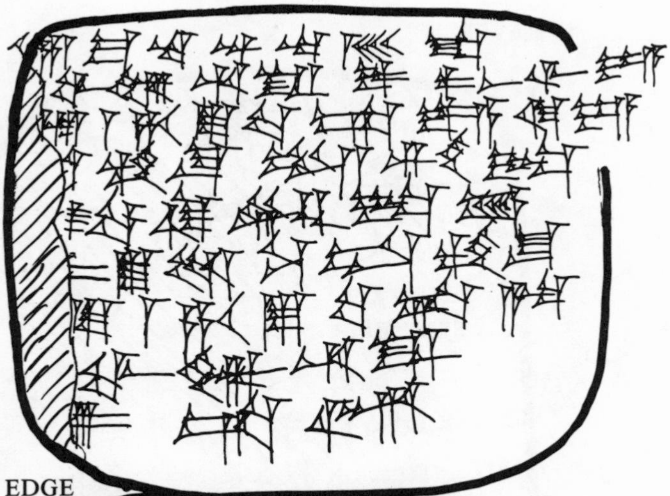

LOWER EDGE

REVERSE

SEAL IMPRESSION

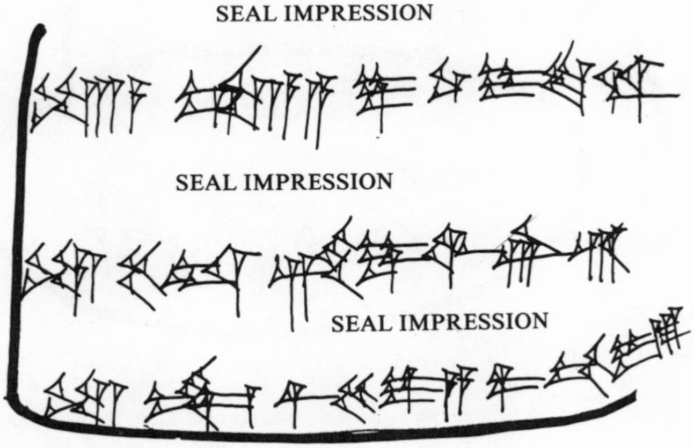

LEFT EDGE

348

OBVERSE

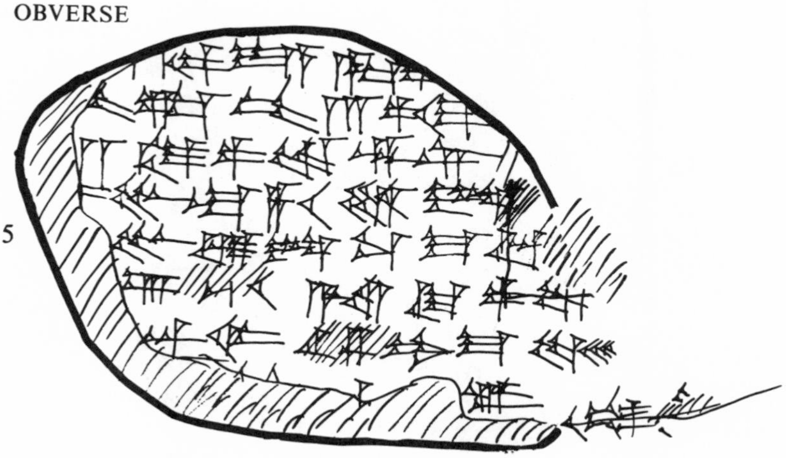

END OF OBVERSE DESTROYED

REVERSE

SEAL IMPRESSION

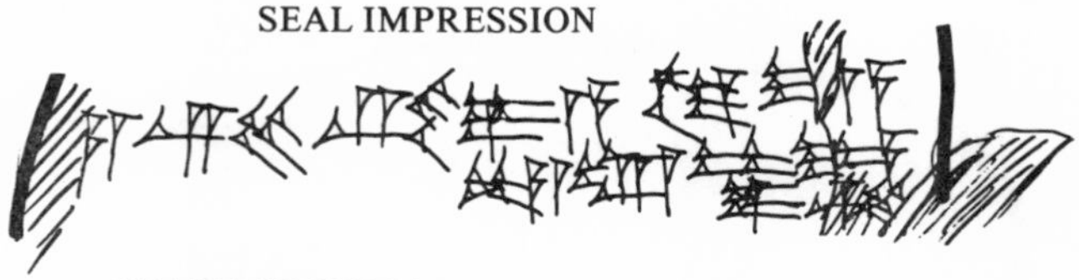

SEAL IMPRESSION

349

OBVERSE

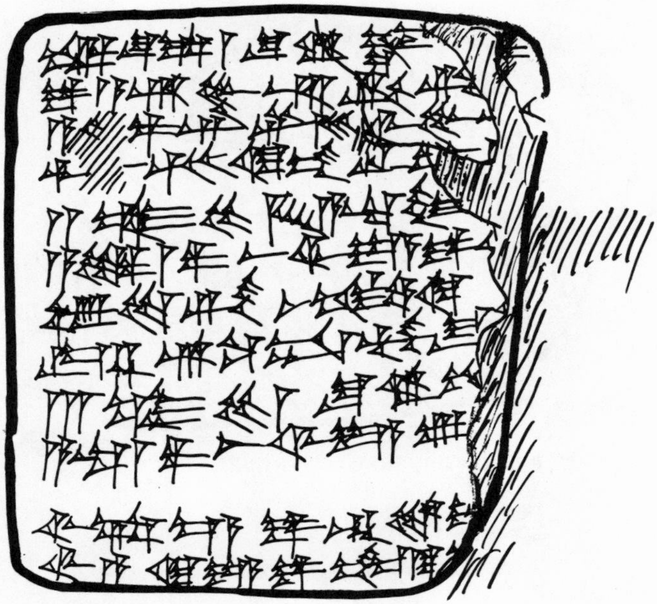

LOWER EDGE

349

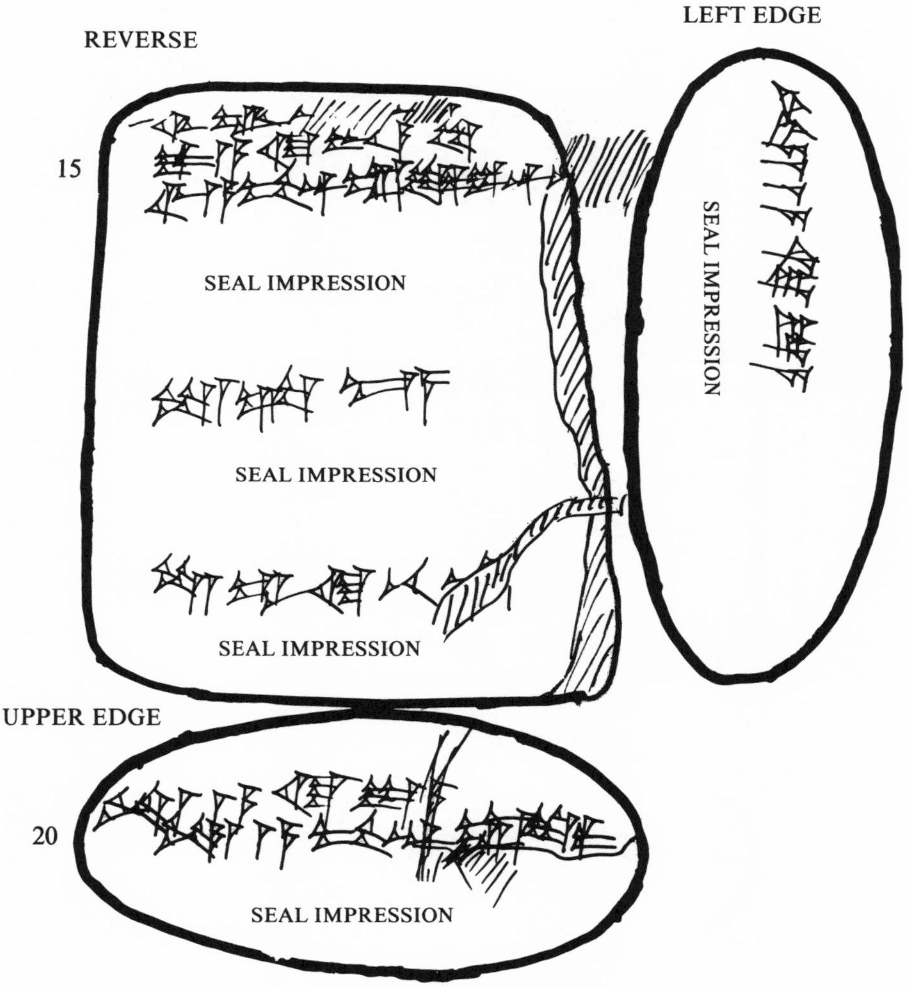
REVERSE
LEFT EDGE
15
SEAL IMPRESSION
SEAL IMPRESSION
SEAL IMPRESSION
SEAL IMPRESSION
UPPER EDGE
20
SEAL IMPRESSION

352

OBVERSE

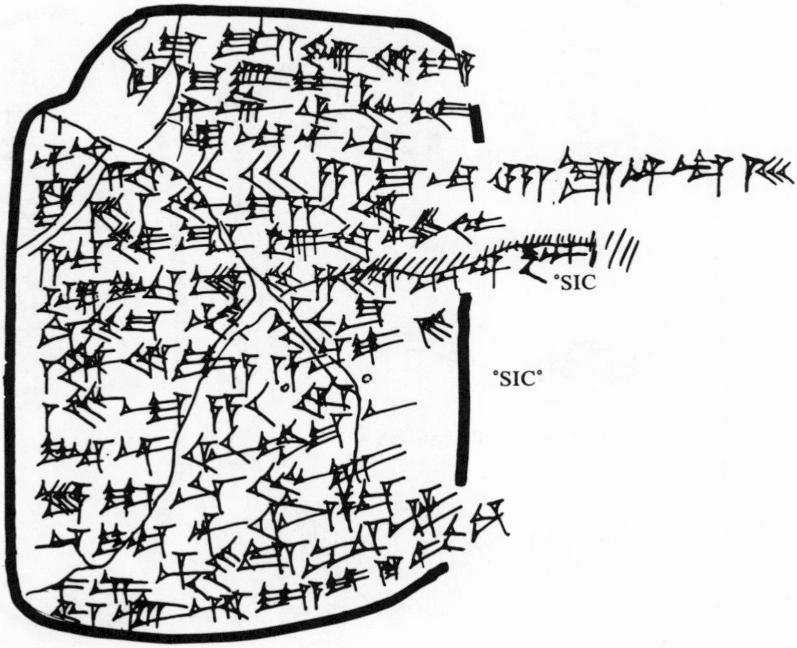

LOWER EDGE

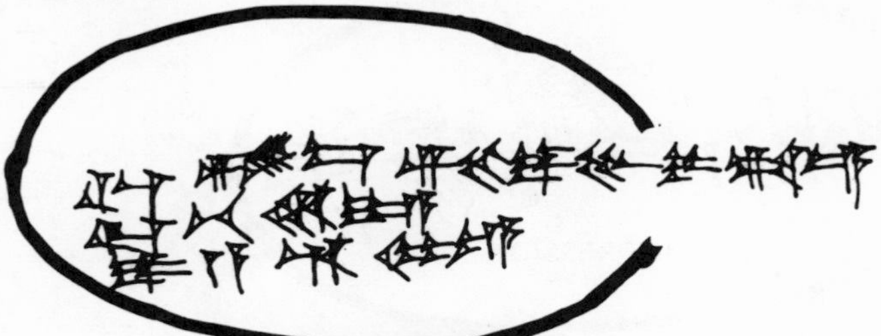

352

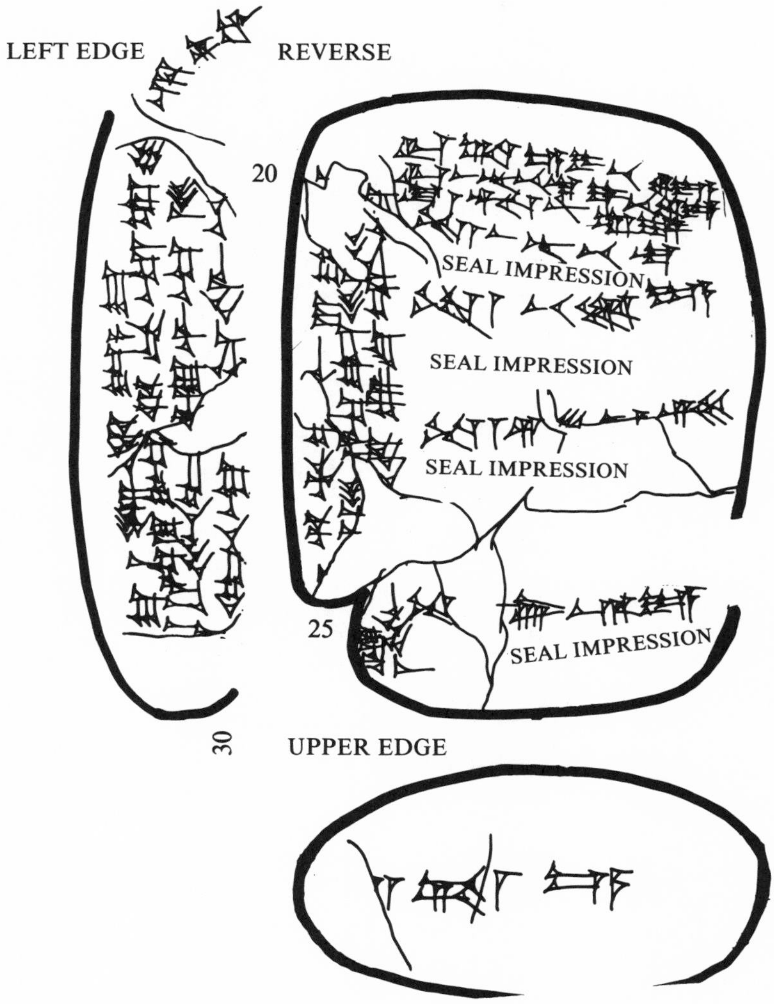
LEFT EDGE
REVERSE
20
SEAL IMPRESSION
SEAL IMPRESSION
SEAL IMPRESSION
25
SEAL IMPRESSION
30
UPPER EDGE

353

OBVERSE

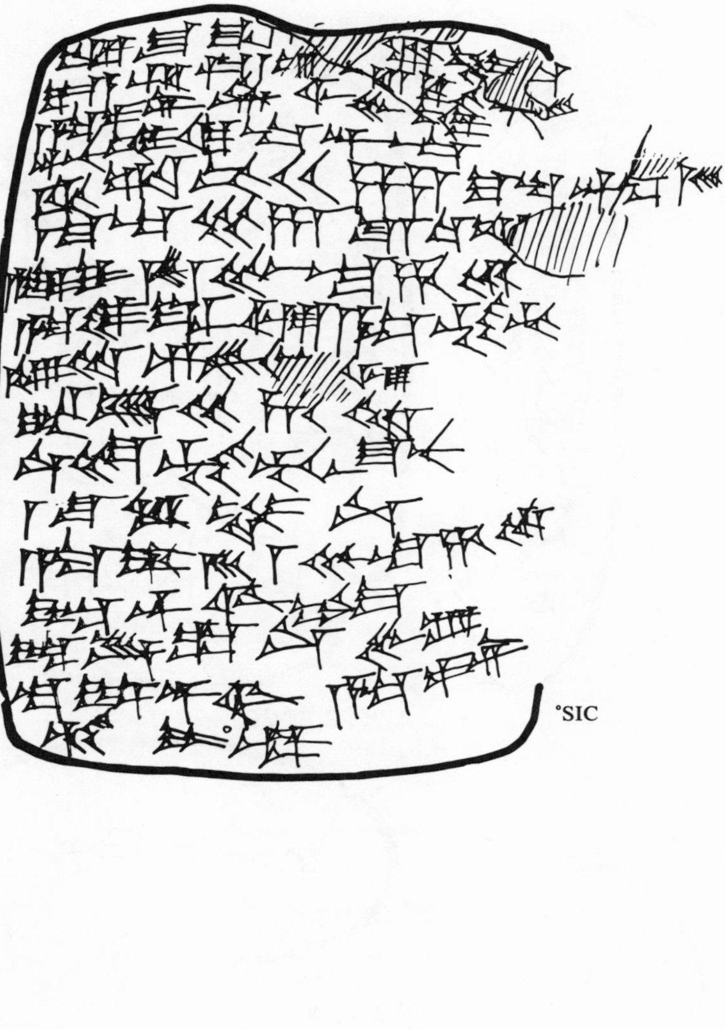

°SIC

353

REVERSE

BEGINNING OF REVERSE DESTROYED

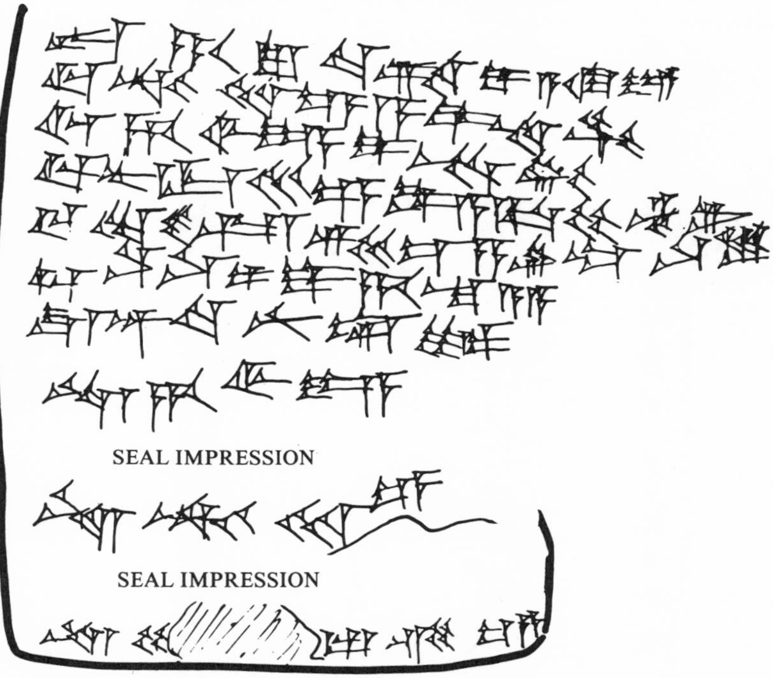

SEAL IMPRESSION

LEFT EDGE

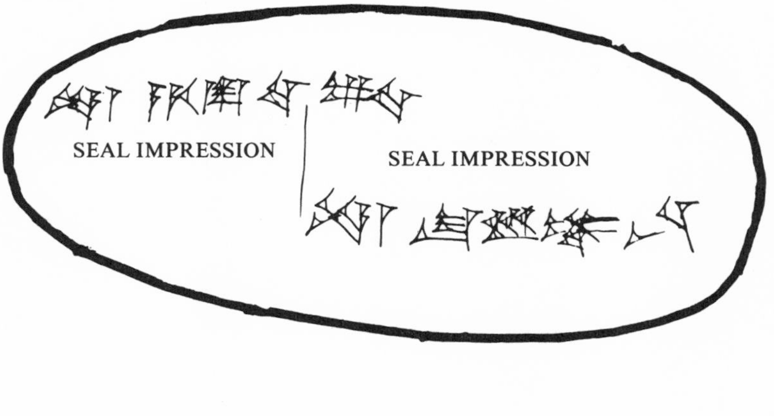

354

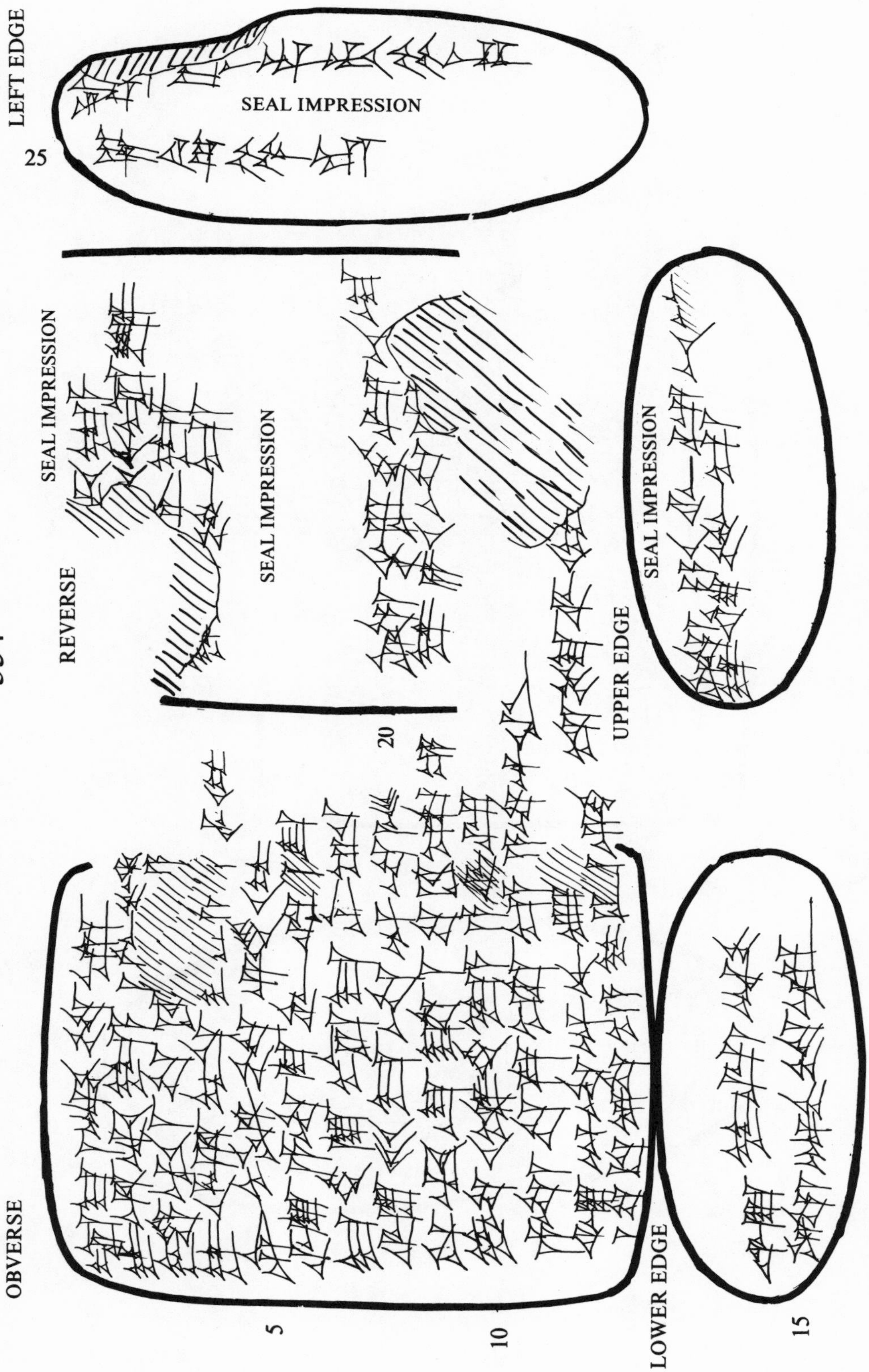
LEFT EDGE
SEAL IMPRESSION
REVERSE
SEAL IMPRESSION
SEAL IMPRESSION
UPPER EDGE
SEAL IMPRESSION
OBVERSE
LOWER EDGE

356

OBVERSE

BEGINNING OF OBVERSE DESTROYED

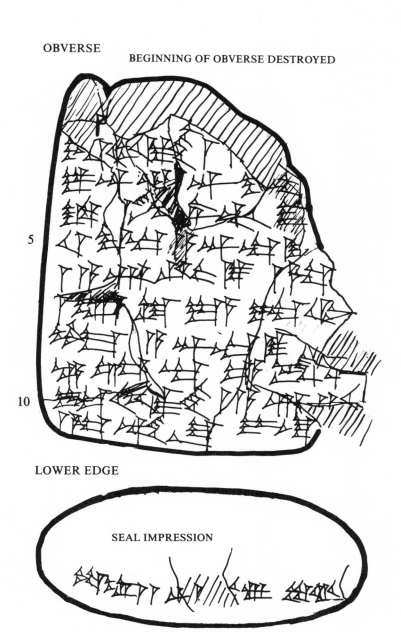

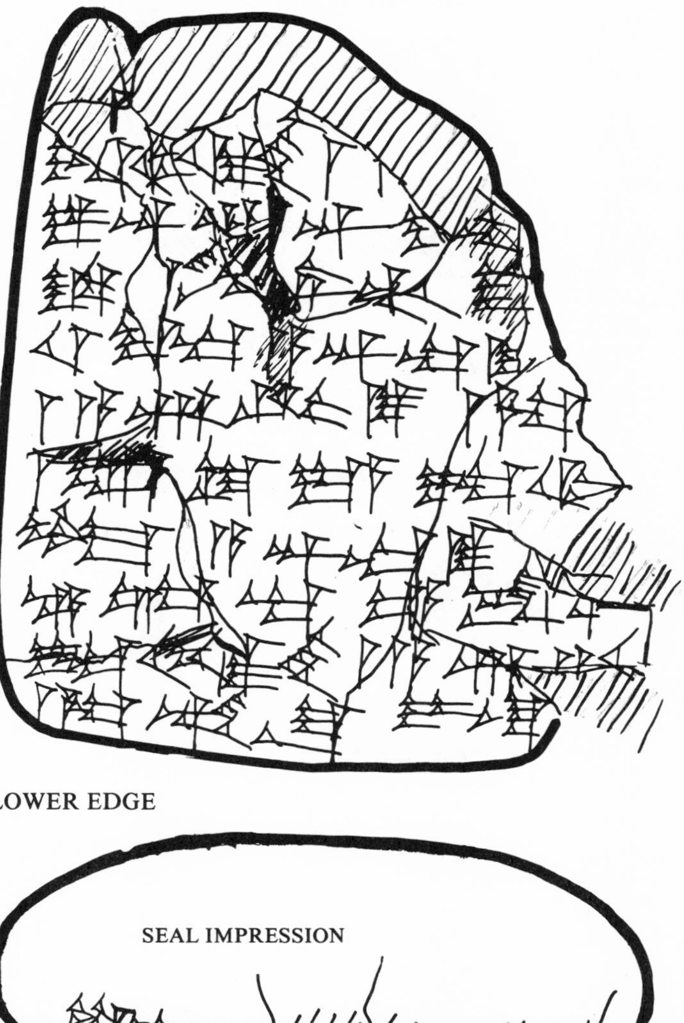

LOWER EDGE

356

REVERSE

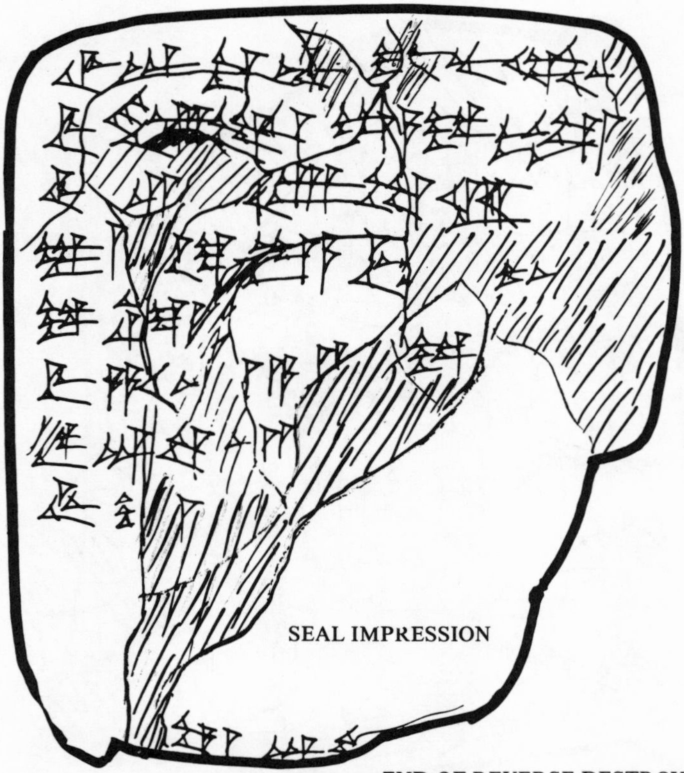

END OF REVERSE DESTROYED

LEFT EDGE

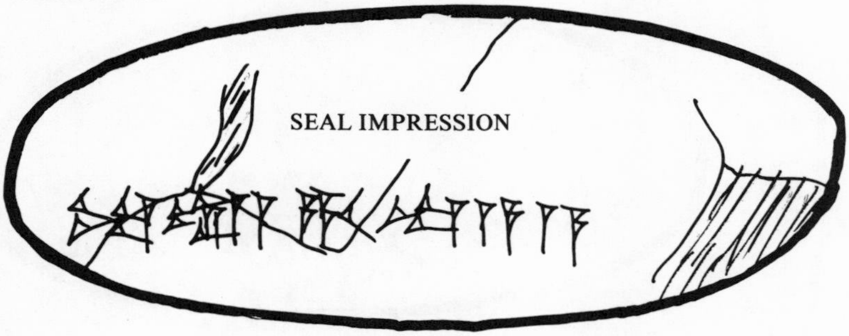

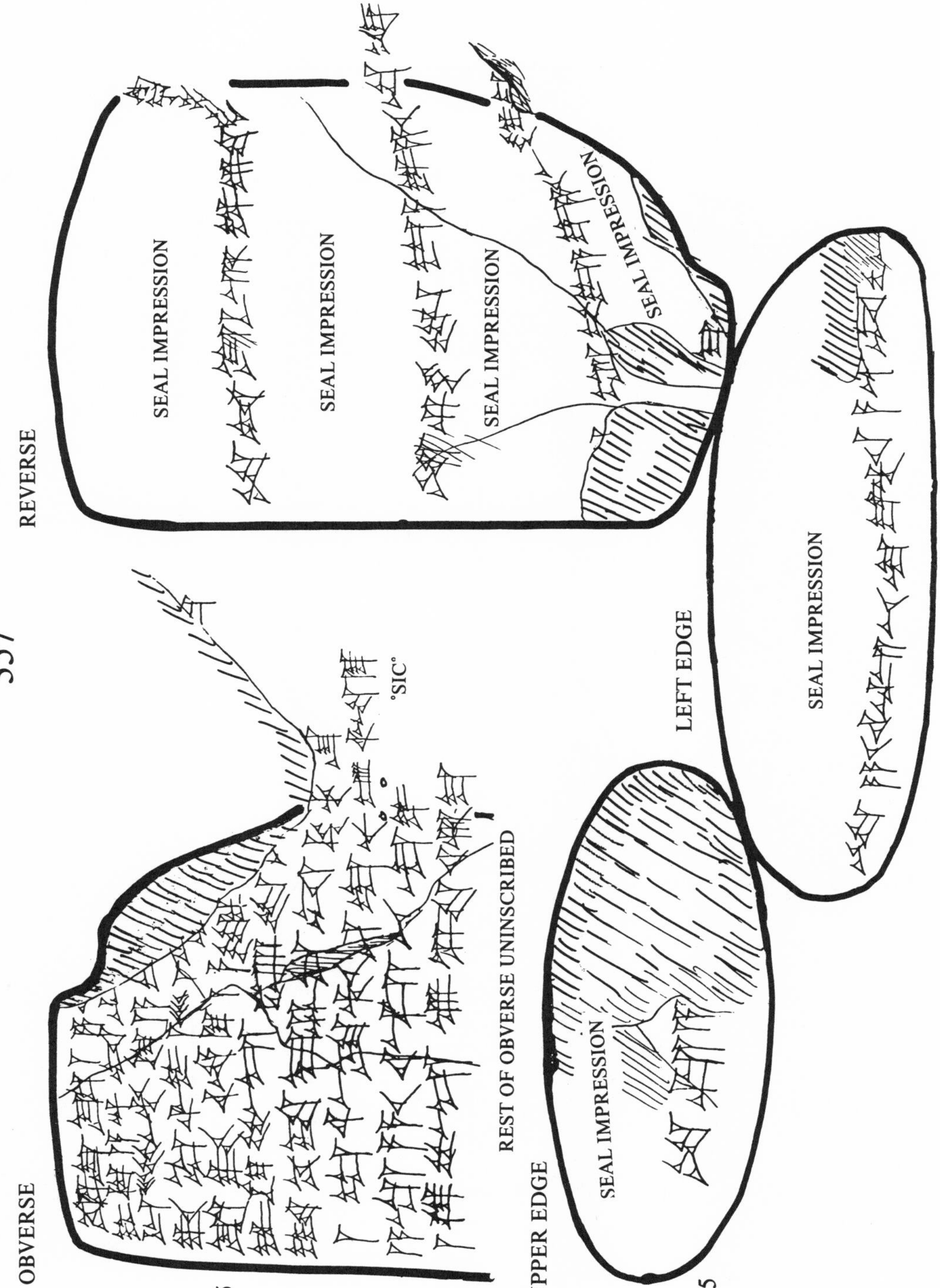
357
OBVERSE
5
10
'SIC'
REST OF OBVERSE UNINSCRIBED
UPPER EDGE
15
SEAL IMPRESSION
REVERSE
SEAL IMPRESSION
SEAL IMPRESSION
SEAL IMPRESSION
SEAL IMPRESSION
LEFT EDGE
SEAL IMPRESSION

358

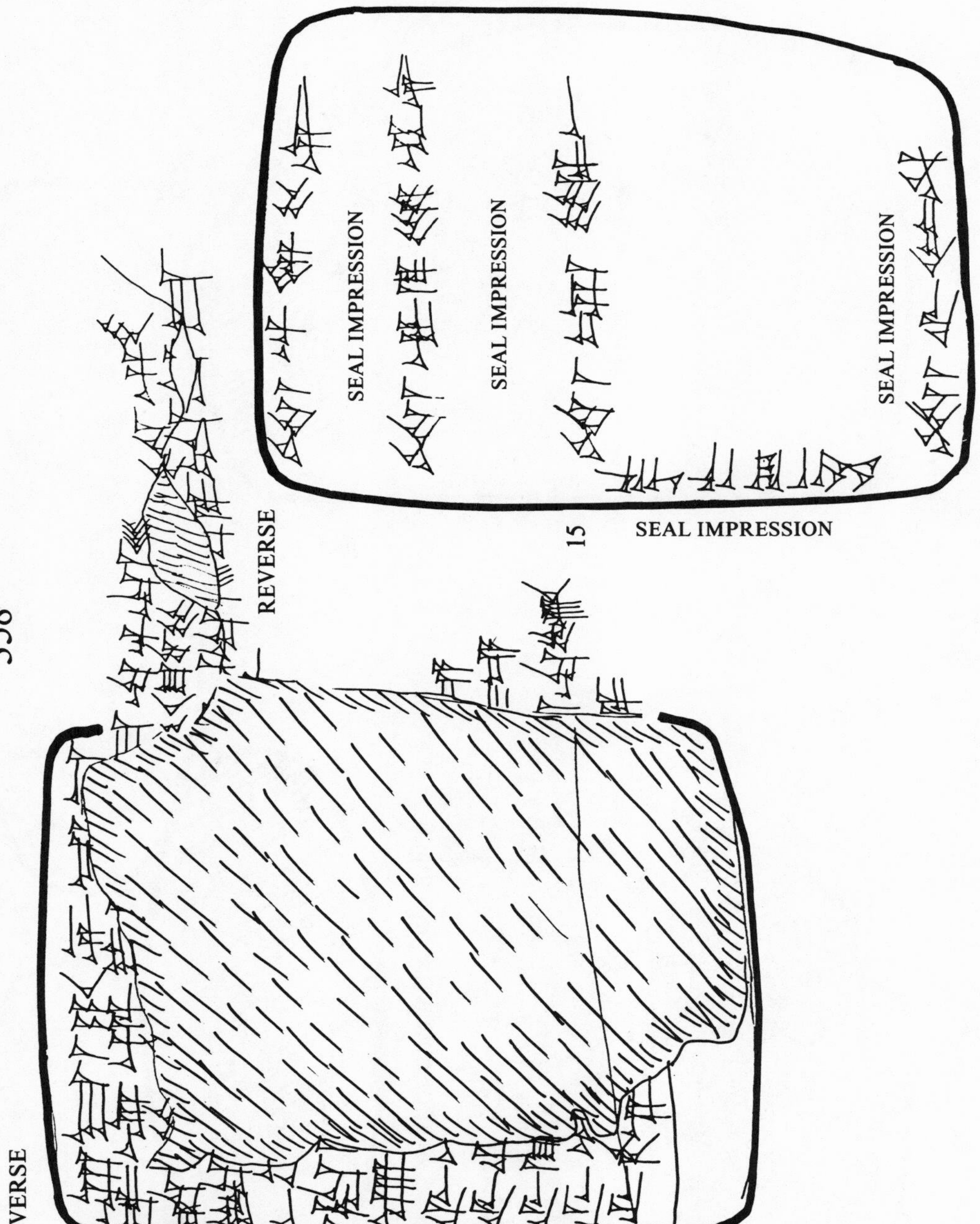
OBVERSE
REVERSE
SEAL IMPRESSION
SEAL IMPRESSION
SEAL IMPRESSION
SEAL IMPRESSION

359

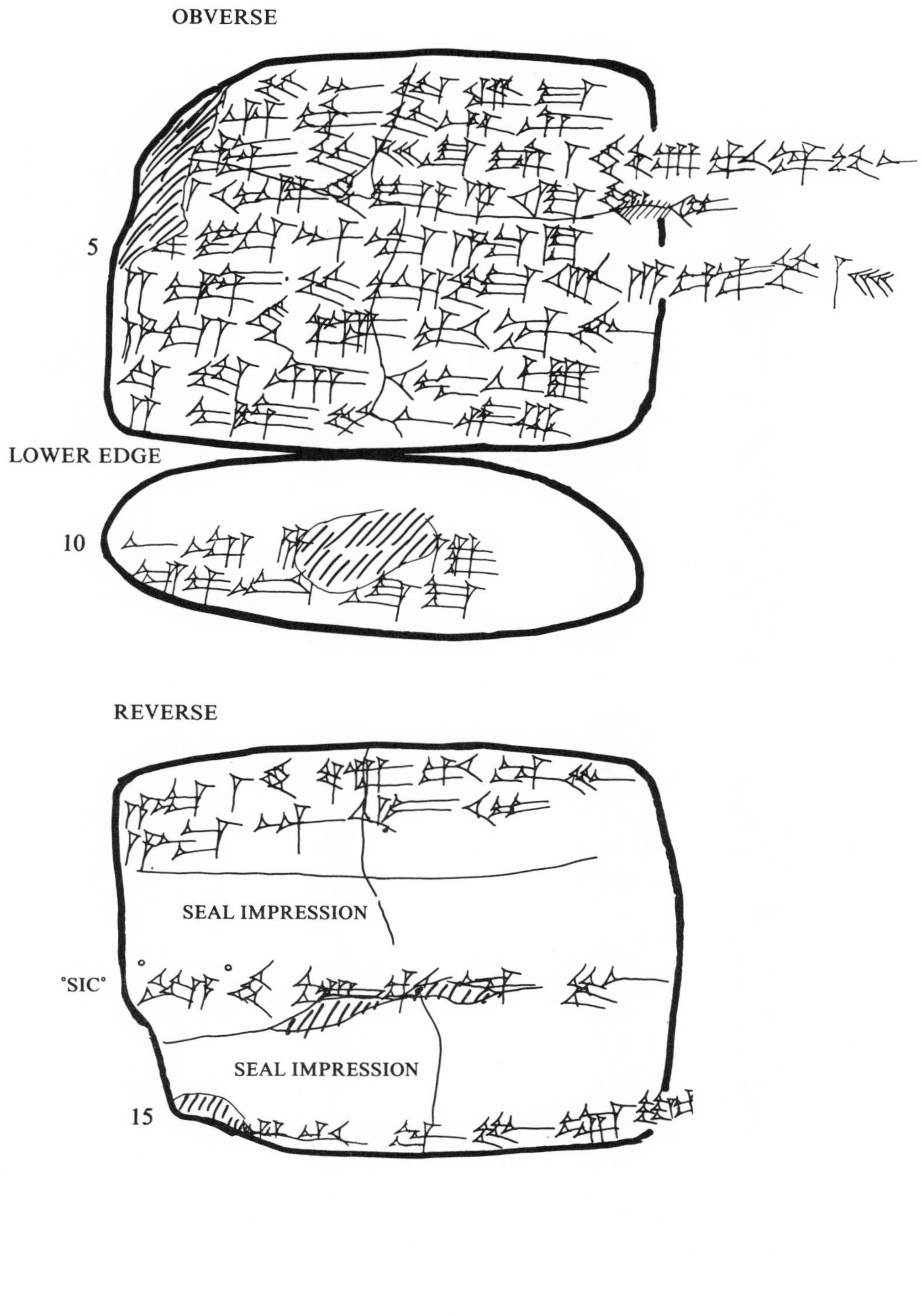
OBVERSE
5
LOWER EDGE
10
REVERSE
SEAL IMPRESSION
°SIC°
SEAL IMPRESSION
15

360

OBVERSE

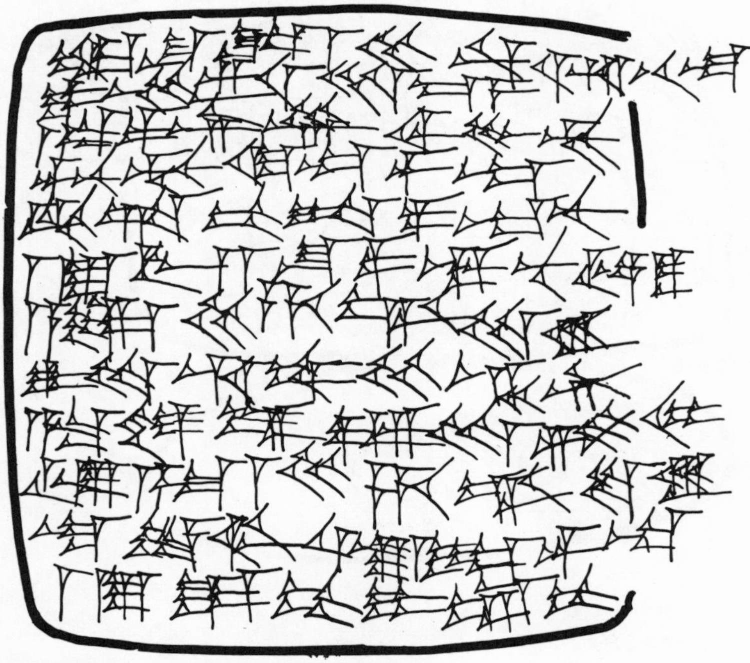

LOWER EDGE

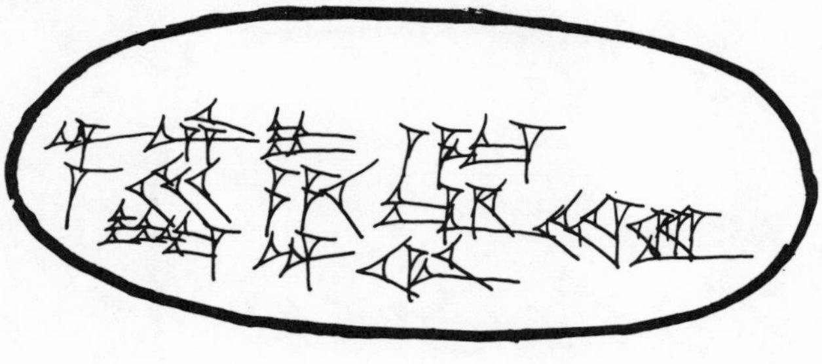

360

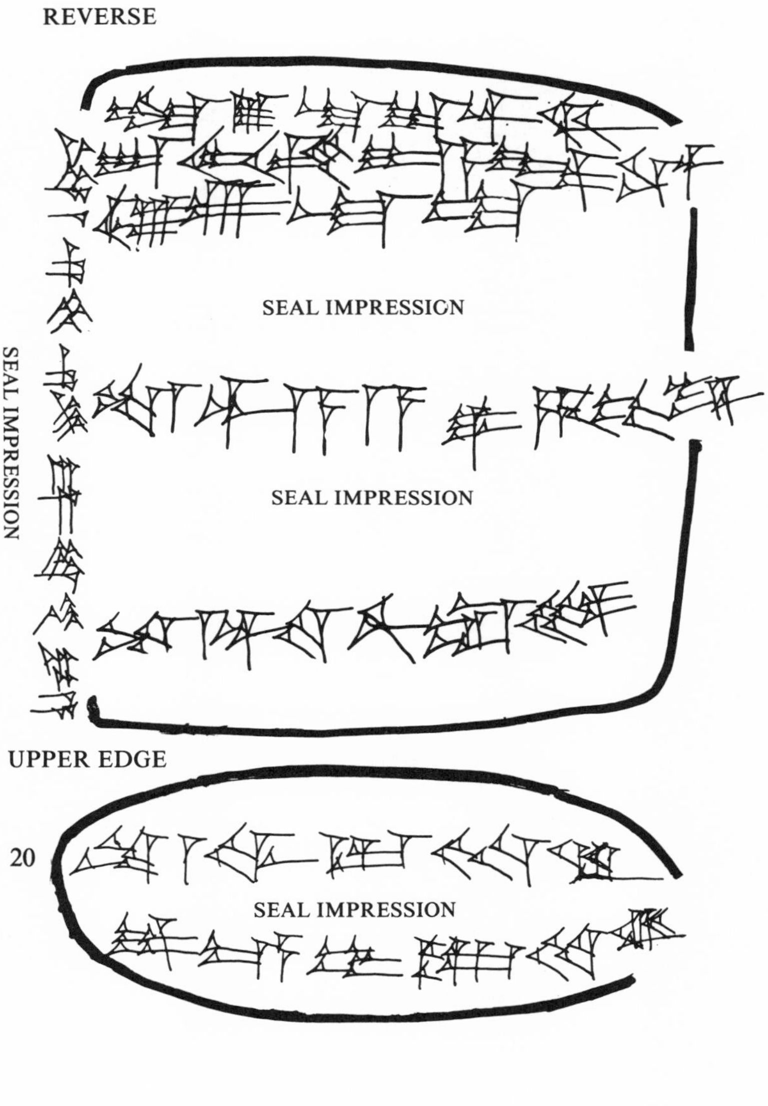
REVERSE
SEAL IMPRESSION
SEAL IMPRESSION
SEAL IMPRESSION
UPPER EDGE
20
SEAL IMPRESSION

362

OBVERSE

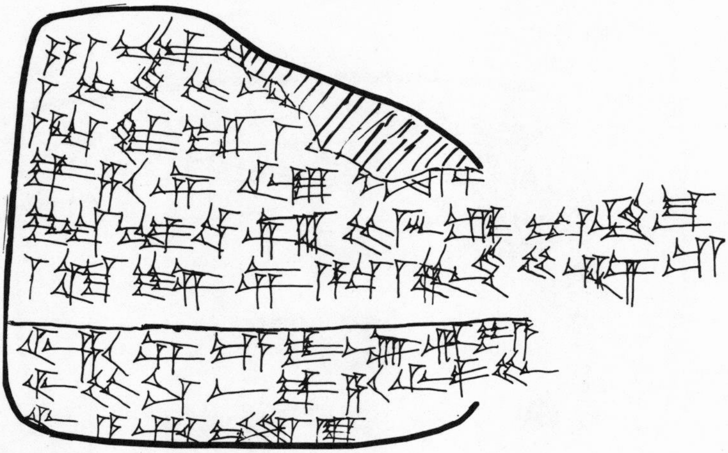

LOWER EDGE

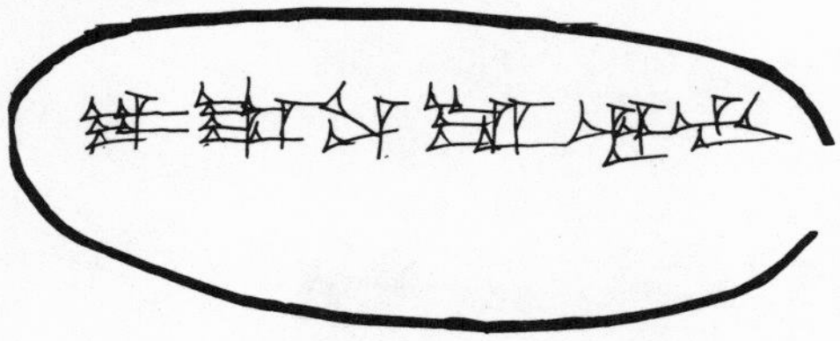

REVERSE

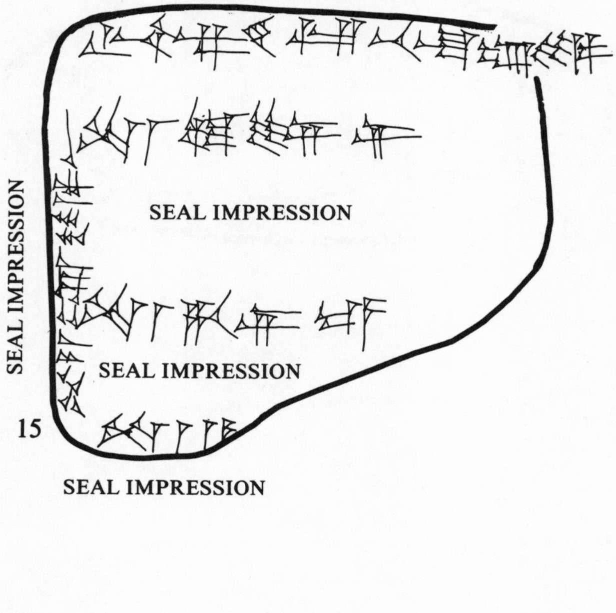

SEAL IMPRESSION

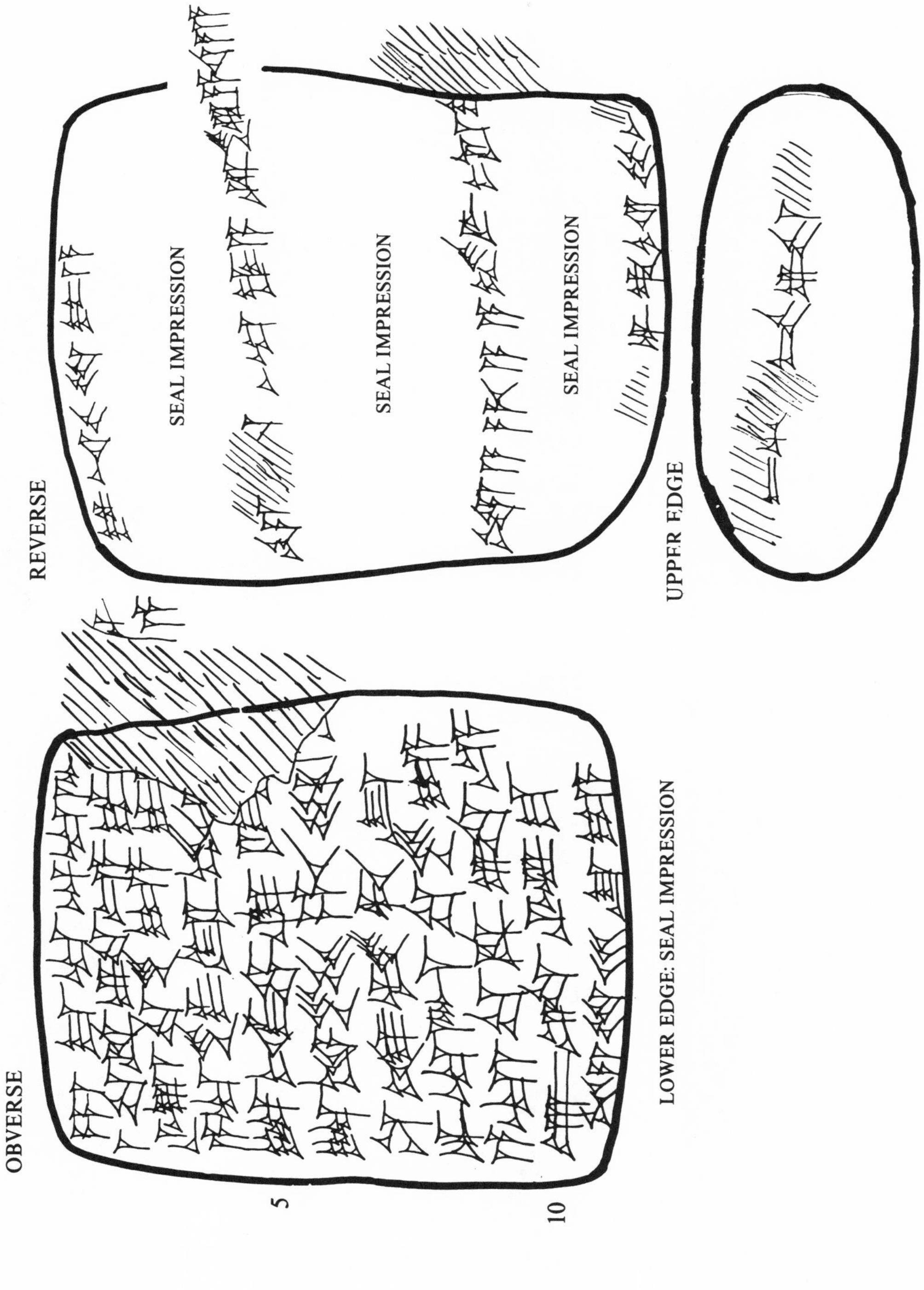
363
OBVERSE
LOWER EDGE: SEAL IMPRESSION
REVERSE
SEAL IMPRESSION
SEAL IMPRESSION
SEAL IMPRESSION
UPPER EDGE

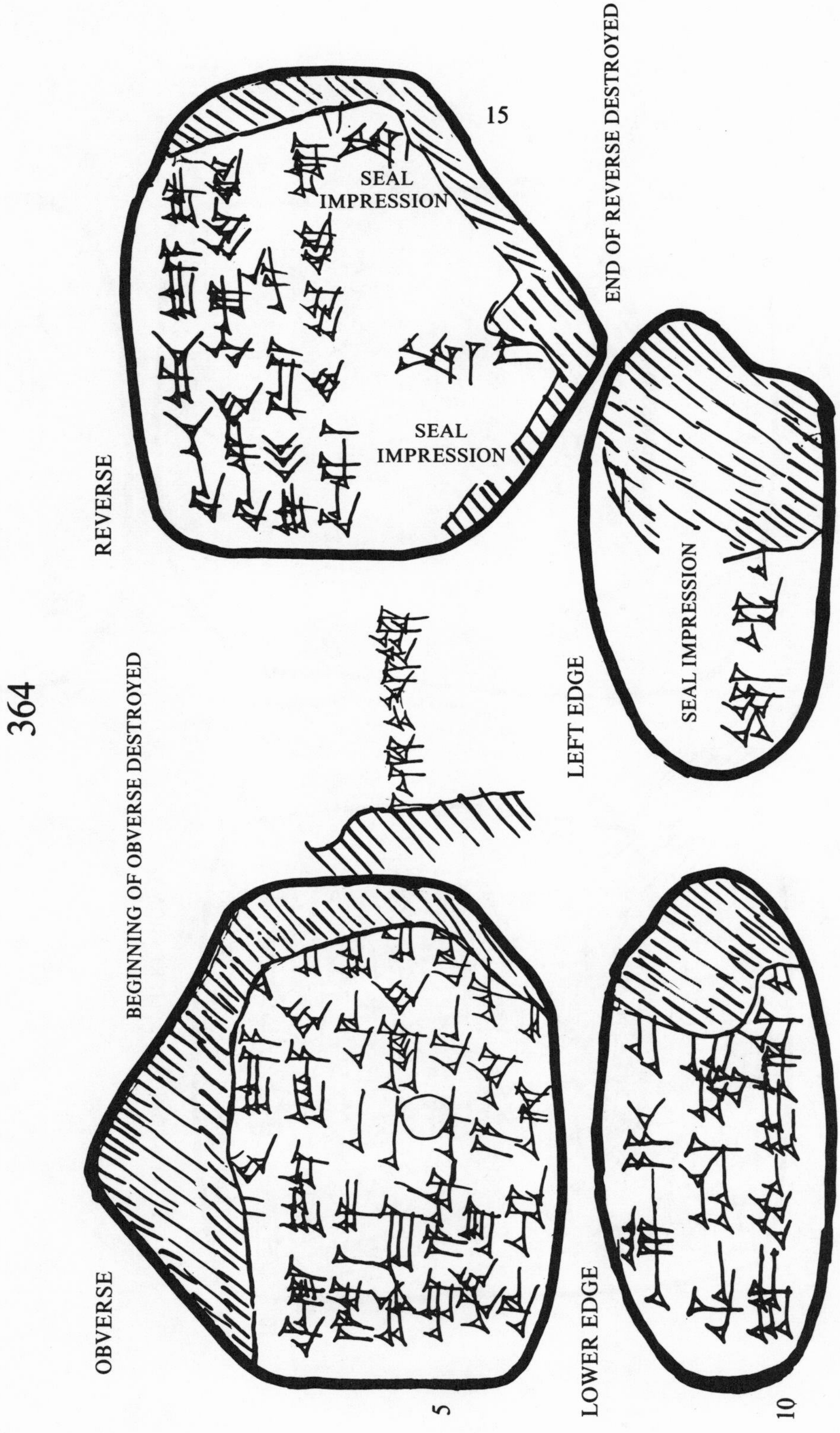
364
OBVERSE
BEGINNING OF OBVERSE DESTROYED
5
LOWER EDGE
10
LEFT EDGE
SEAL IMPRESSION
REVERSE
SEAL IMPRESSION
SEAL IMPRESSION
15
END OF REVERSE DESTROYED

371

OBVERSE

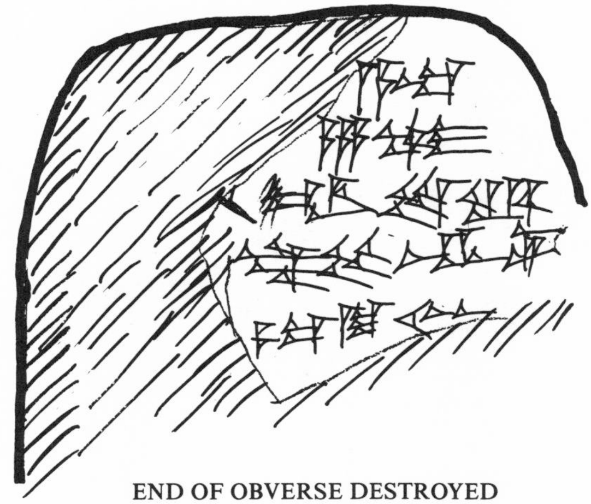

END OF OBVERSE DESTROYED

REVERSE

BEGINNING OF REVERSE DESTROYED

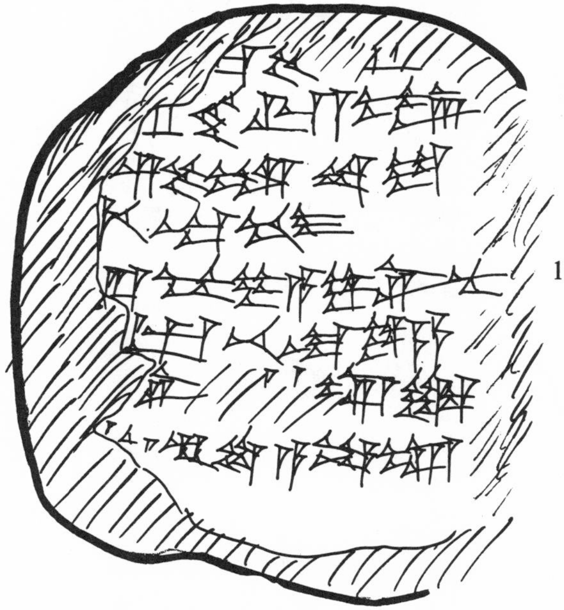

END OF REVERSE DESTROYED

374

OBVERSE

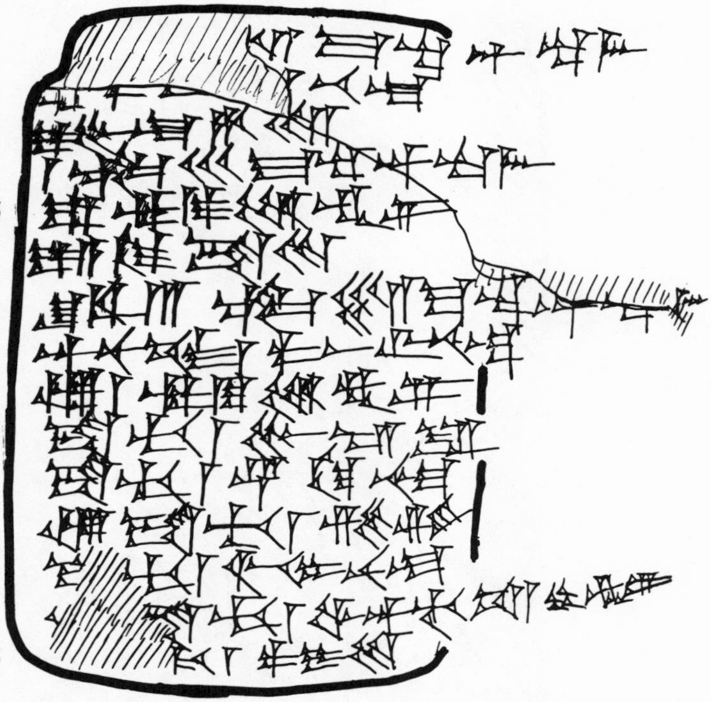

LOWER EDGE

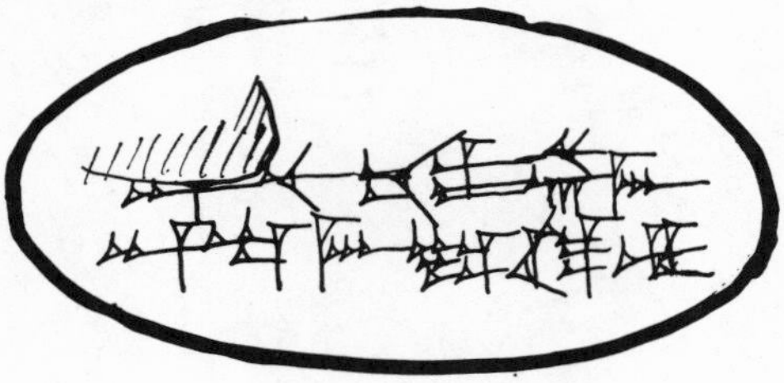

374

REVERSE

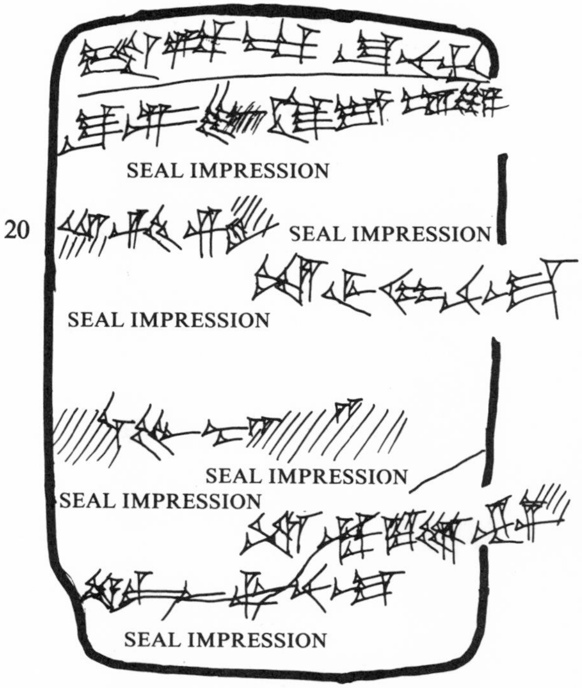

UPPER EDGE

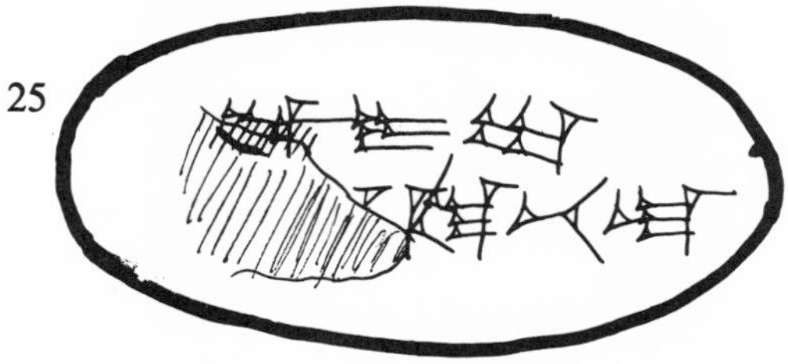

LEFT EDGE

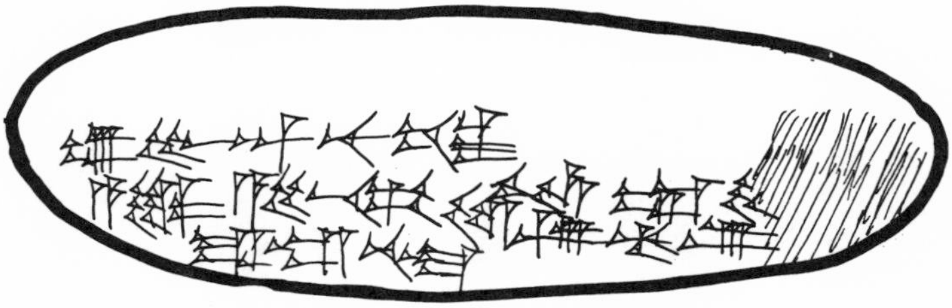

384

OBVERSE

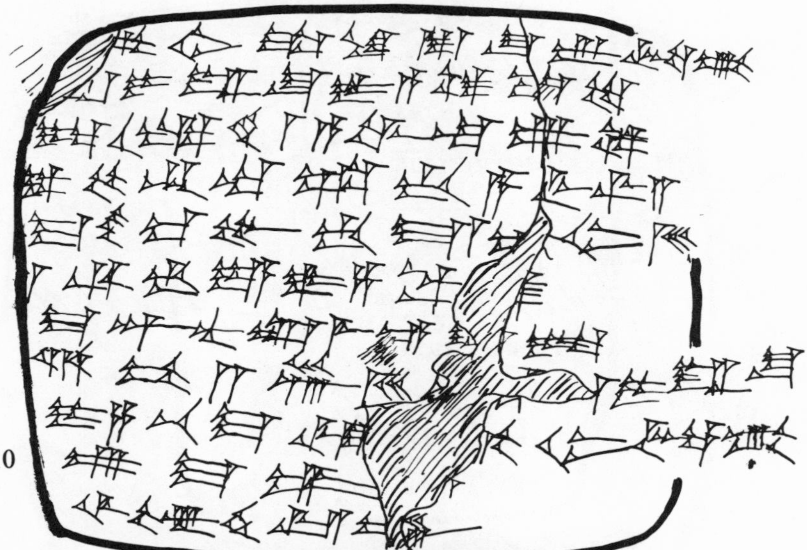

LOWER EDGE

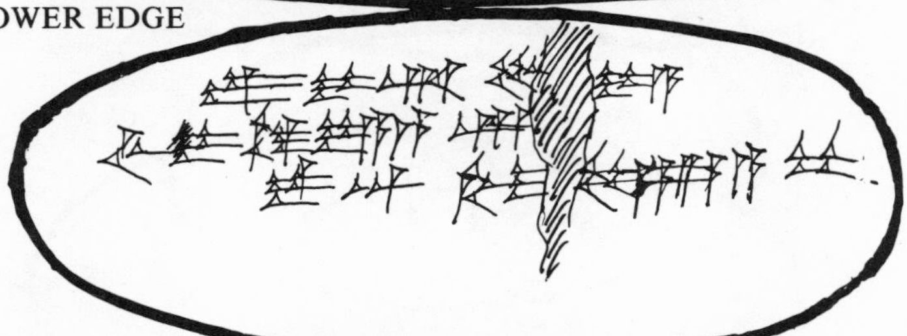

384

REVERSE

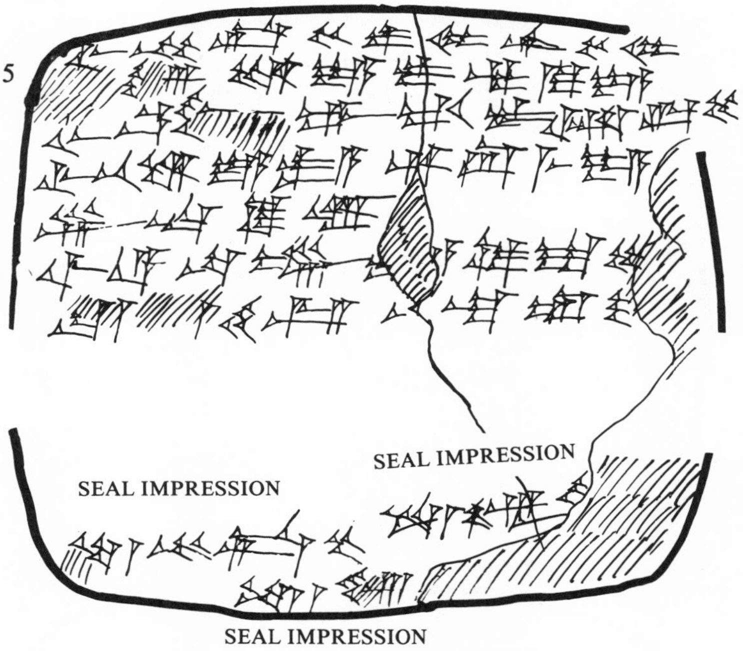

LEFT EDGE

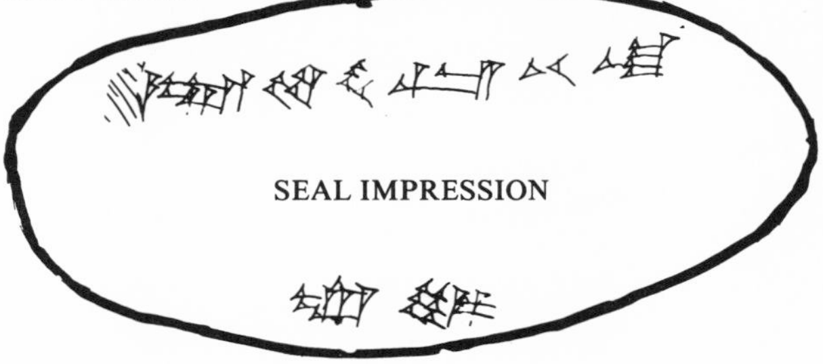

387

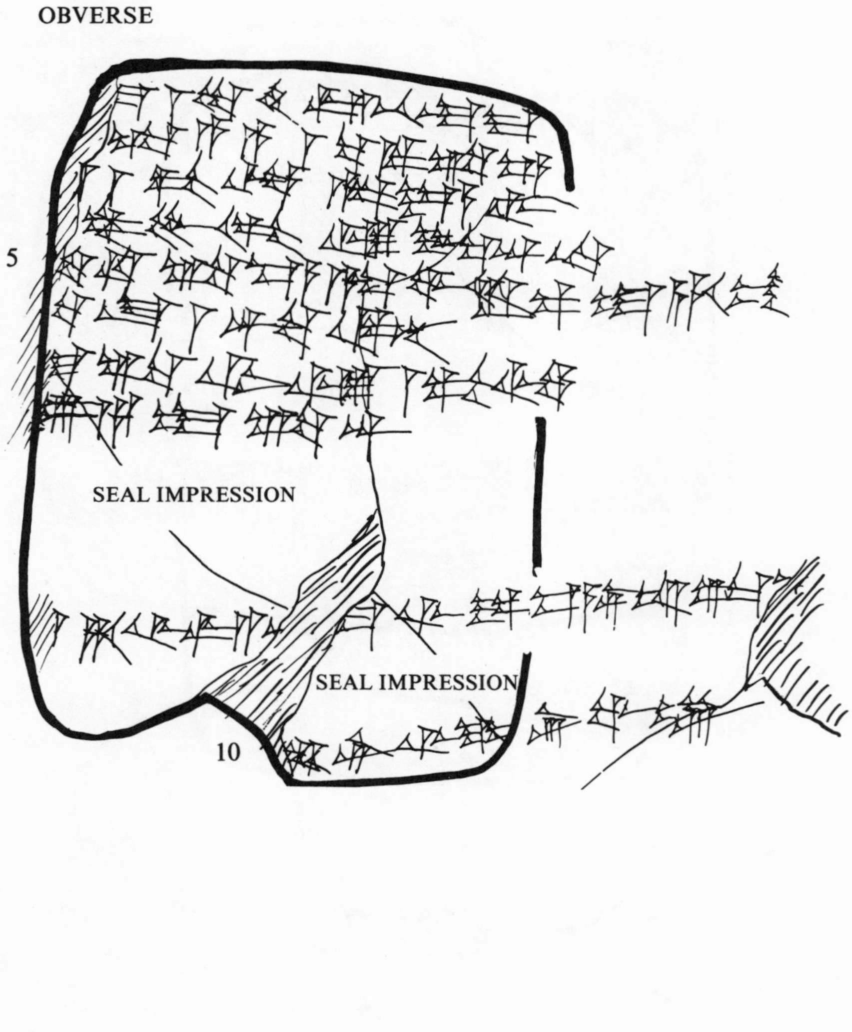

387

REVERSE

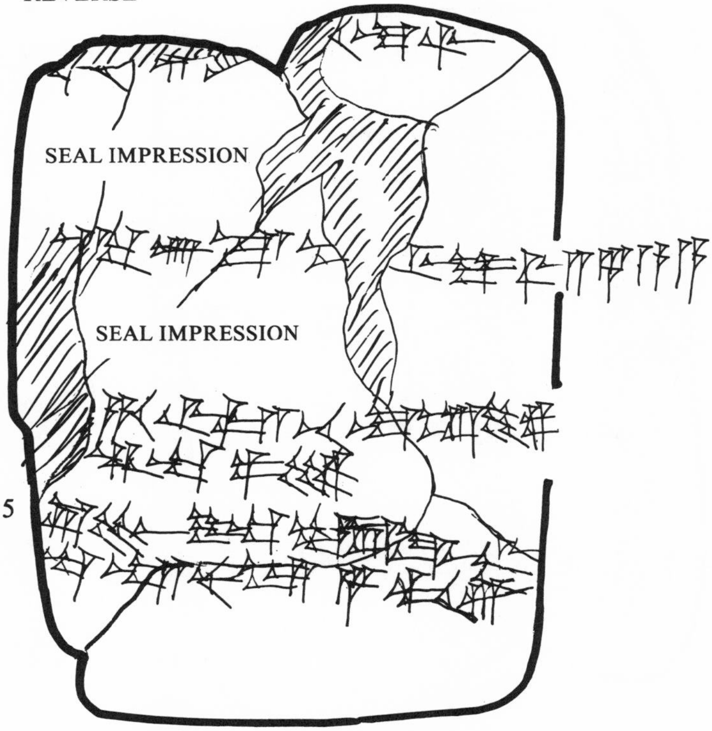

391

OBVERSE

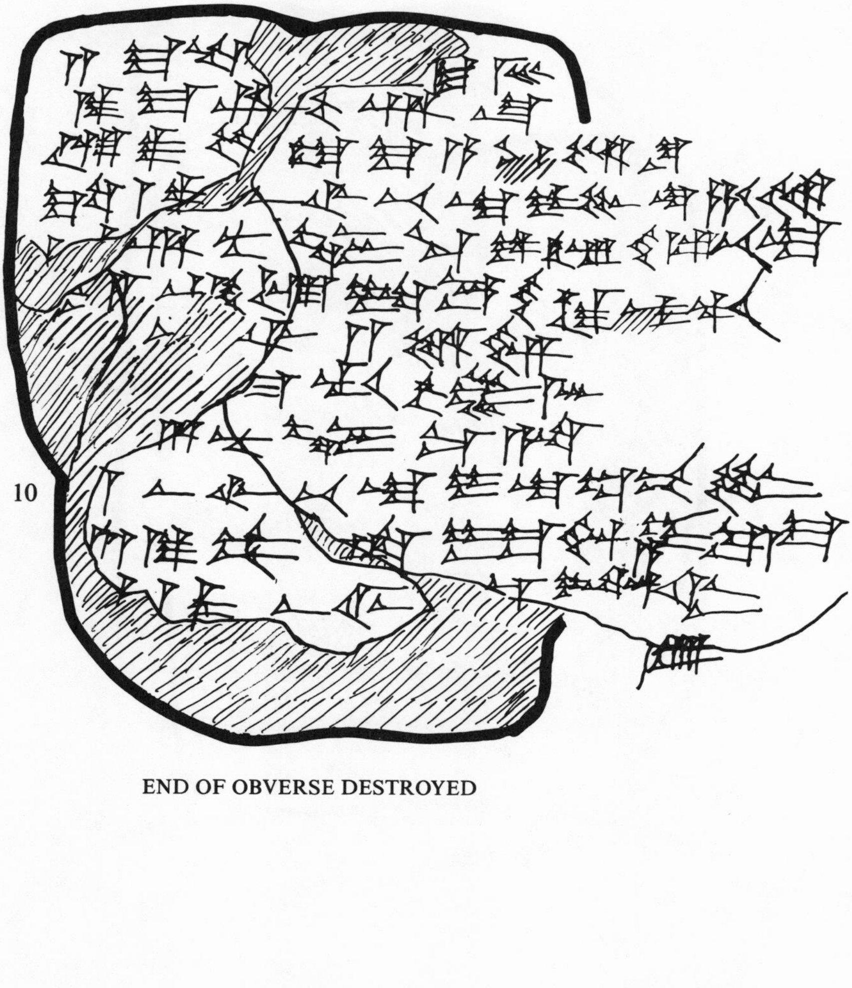

END OF OBVERSE DESTROYED

391

REVERSE

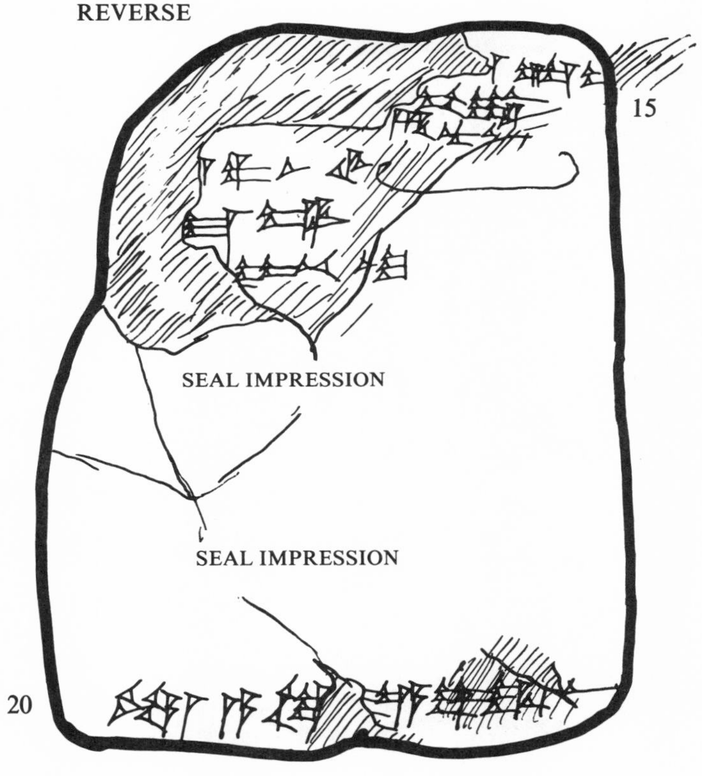

LEFT EDGE

392

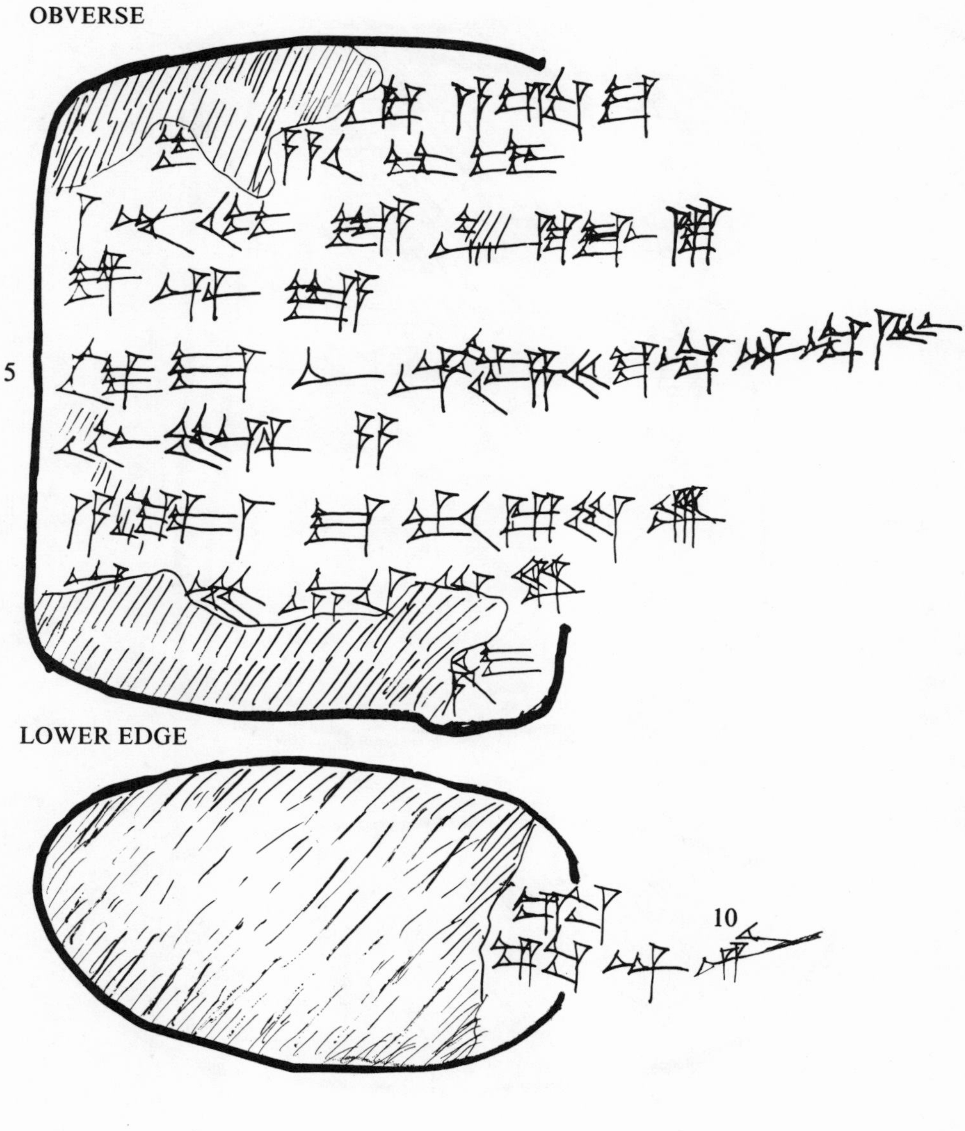

392

REVERSE

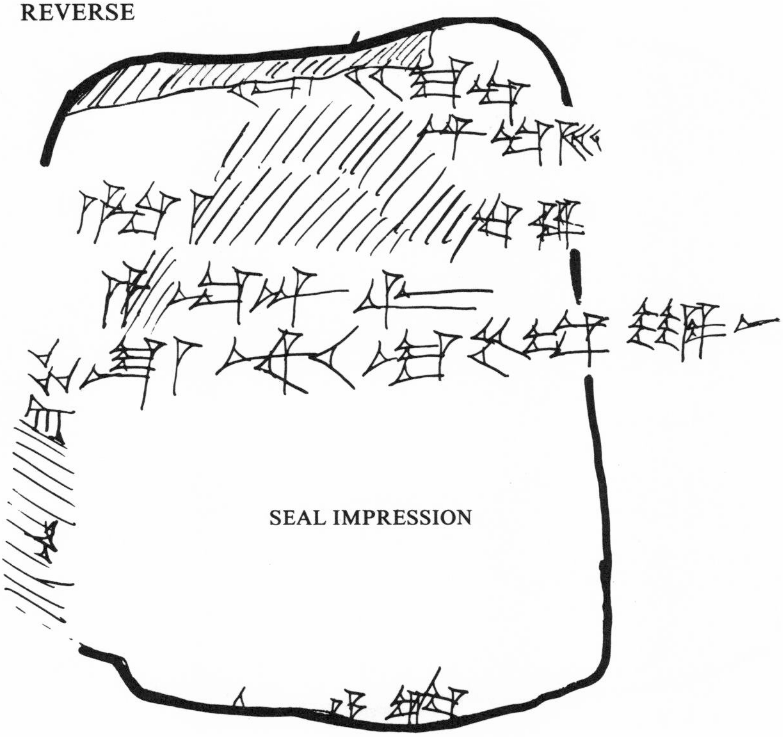

393

OBVERSE

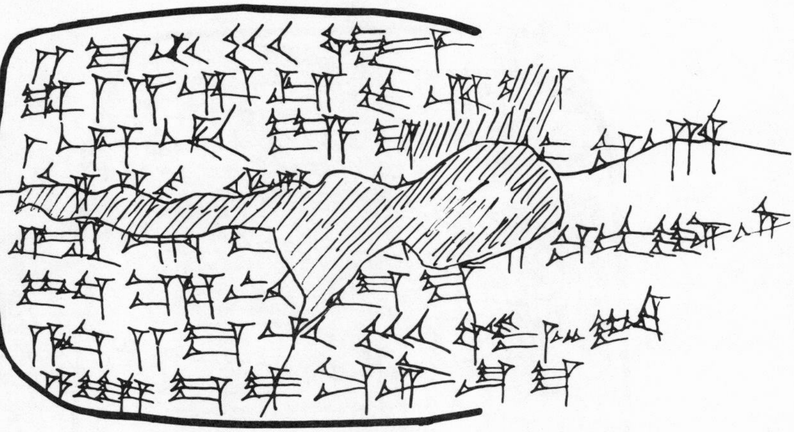

LOWER EDGE

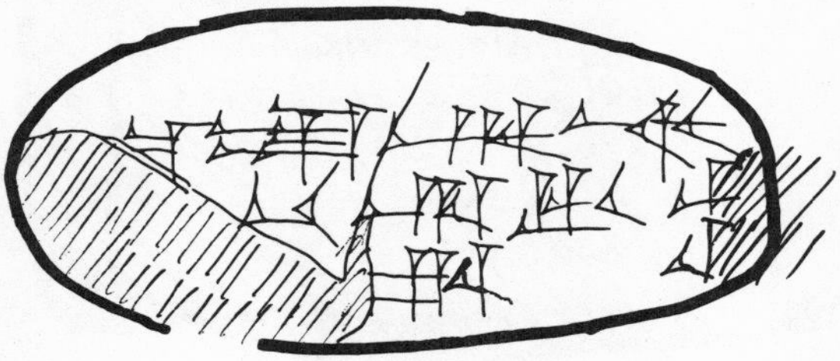

REVERSE

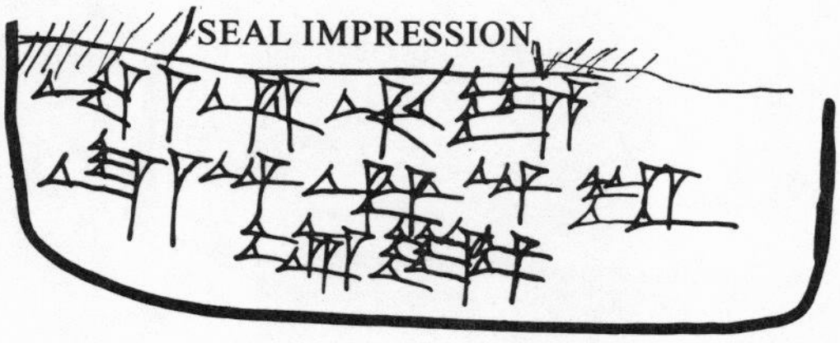

395

OBVERSE

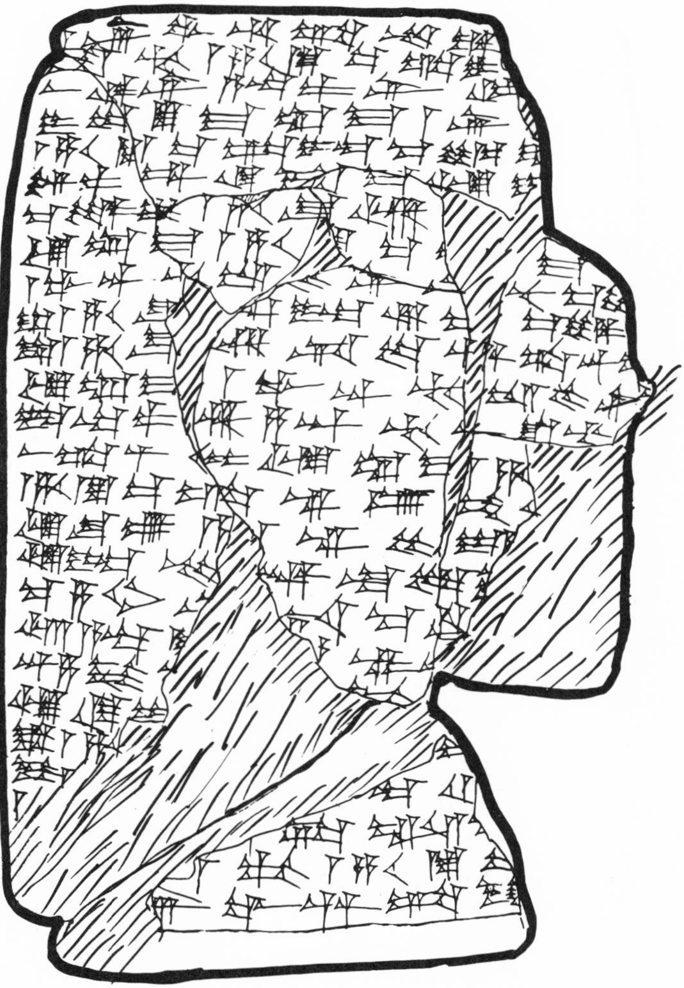

395

REVERSE

SEAL IMPRESSION

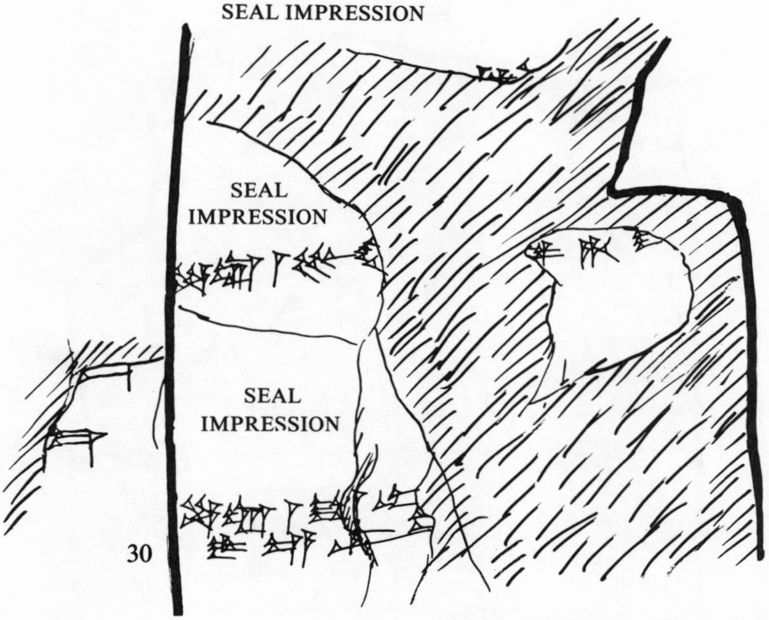

REST OF REVERSE UNINSCRIBED

LEFT EDGE

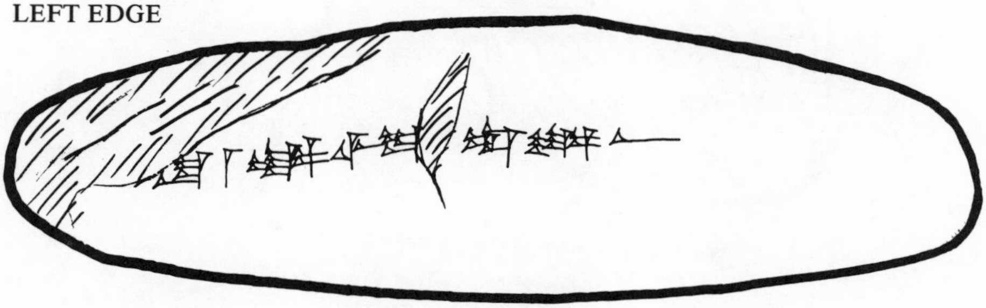

401

OBVERSE

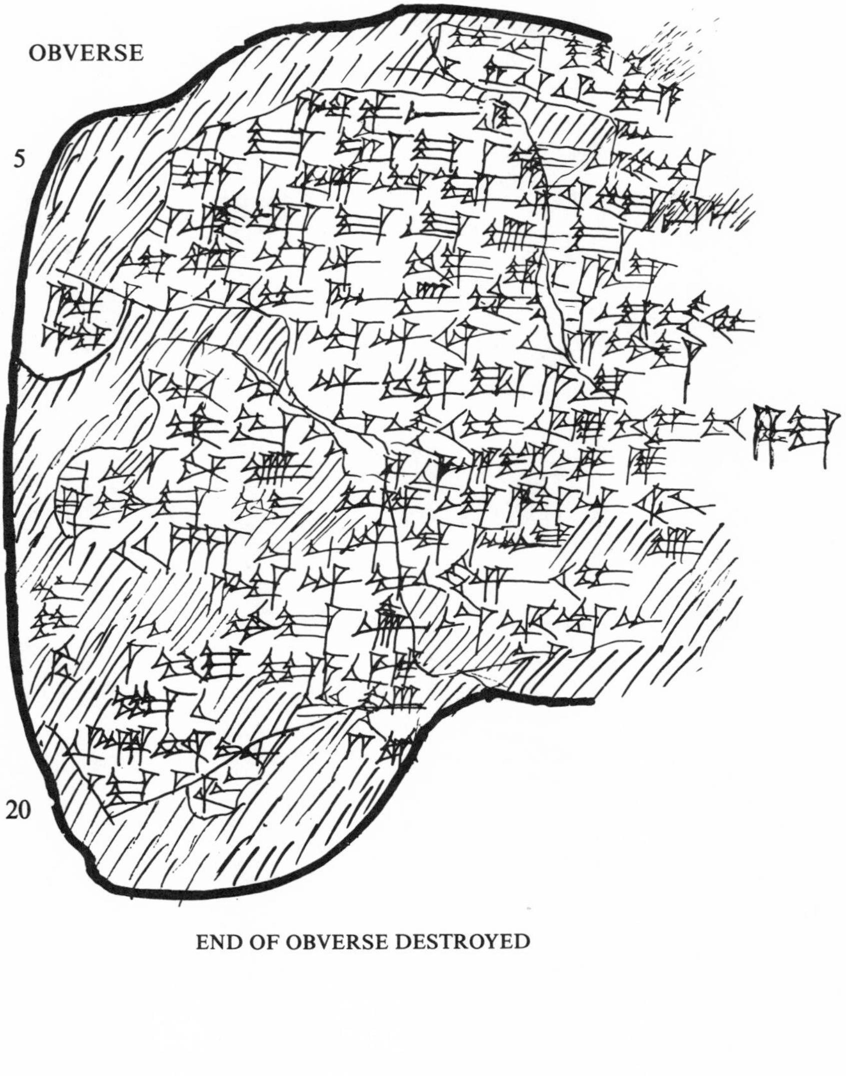

END OF OBVERSE DESTROYED

401

REVERSE

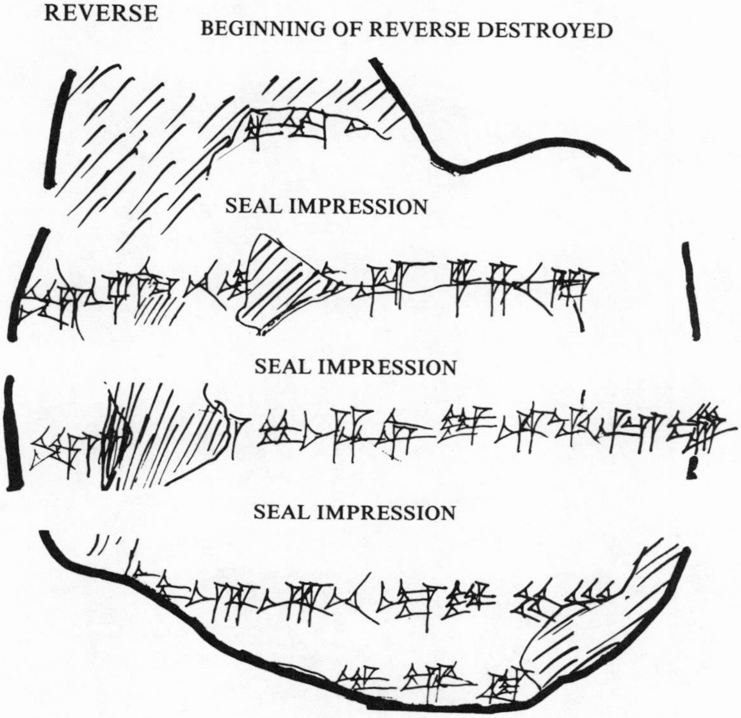

LEFT EDGE

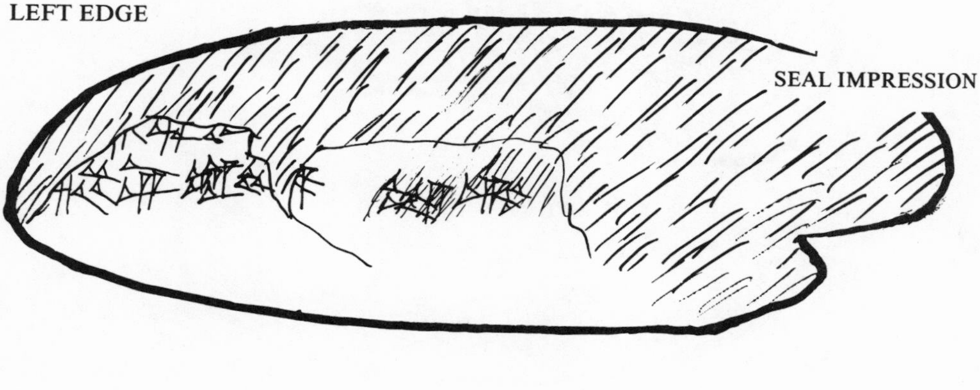

419

OBVERSE

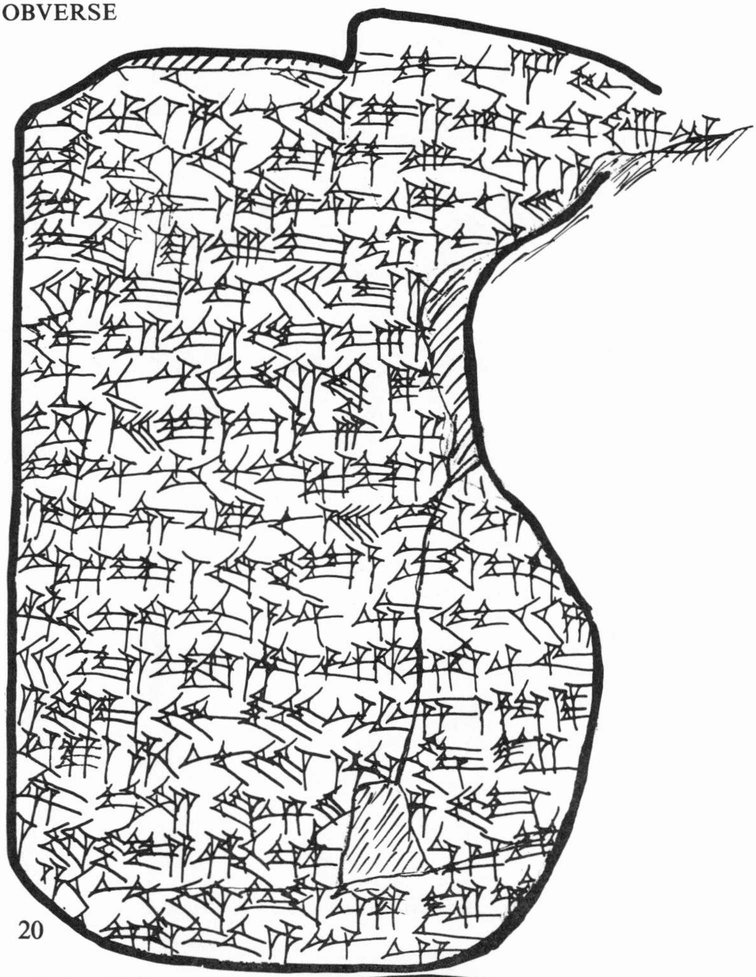

LOWER EDGE

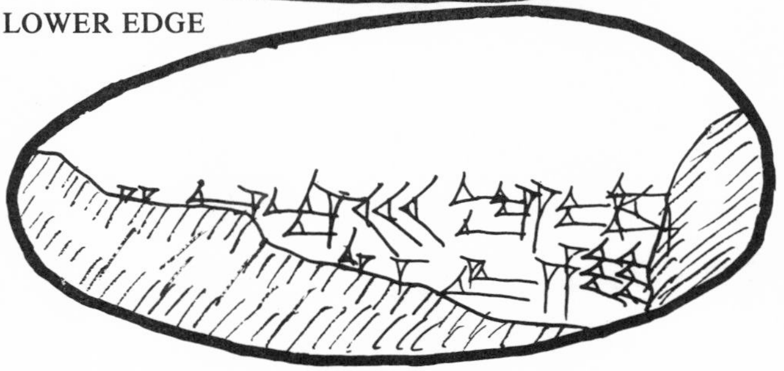

419

REVERSE

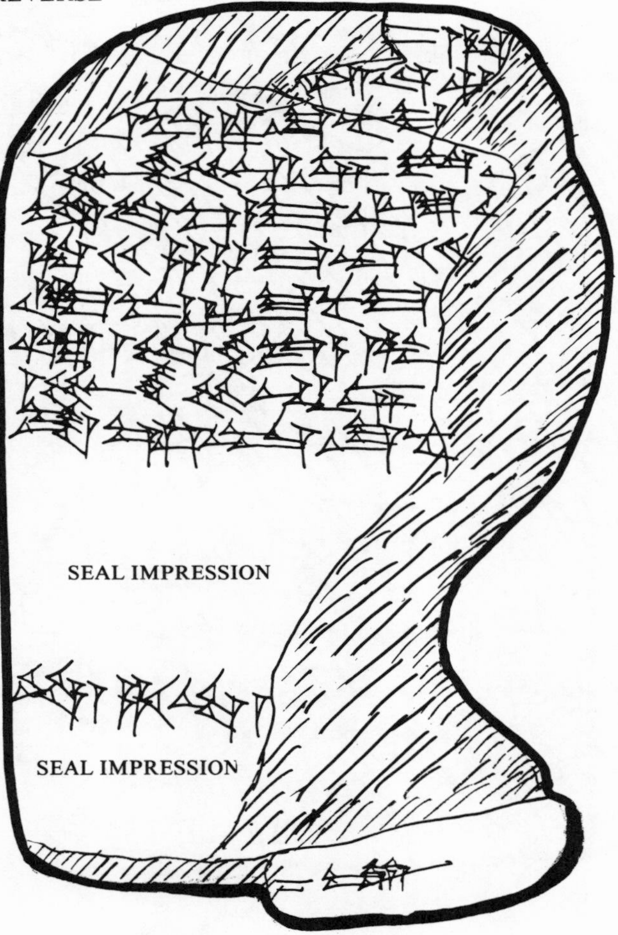

LEFT EDGE

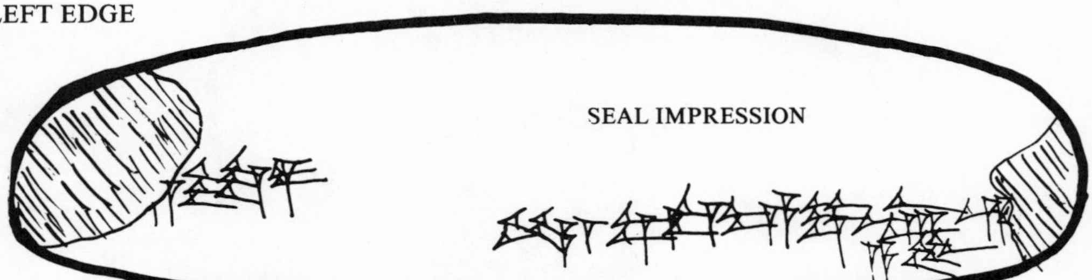

421

OBVERSE

BEGINNING OF OBVERSE DESTROYED

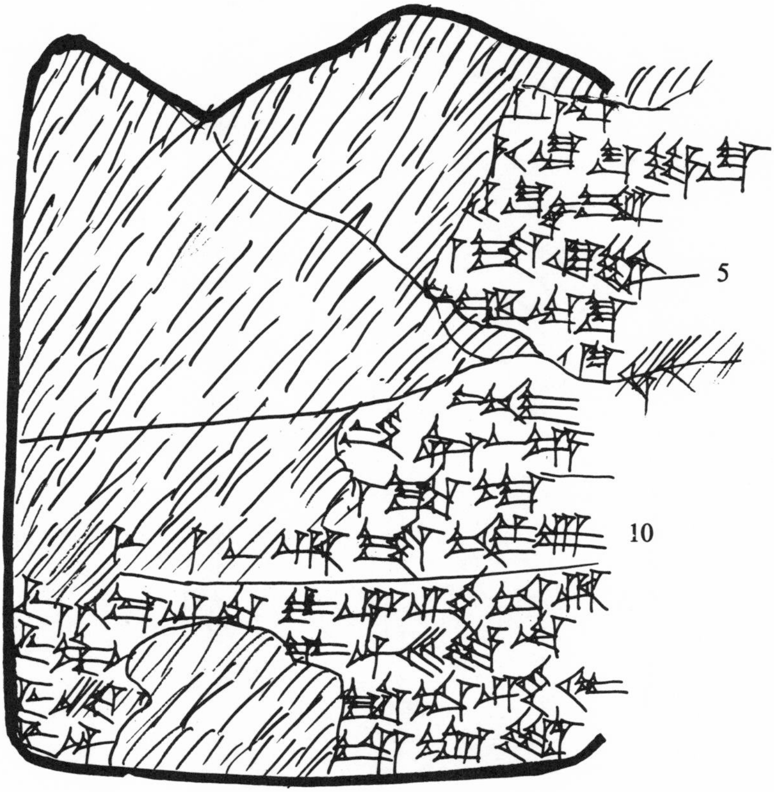

REVERSE

SEAL IMPRESSION

REST OF REVERSE UNINSCRIBED

440

OBVERSE

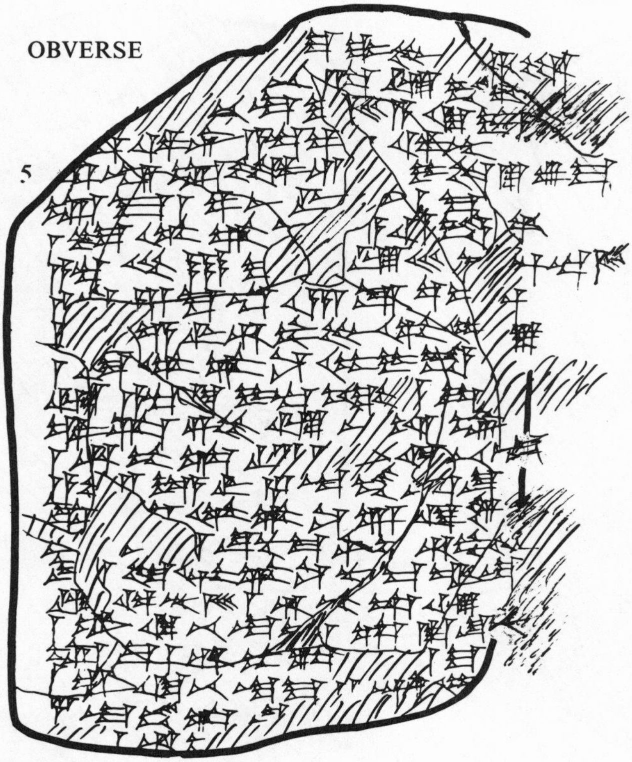

LOWER EDGE

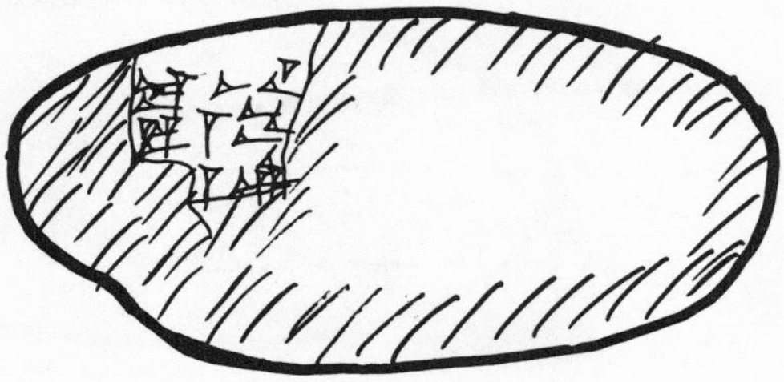

440

LEFT EDGE

REVERSE

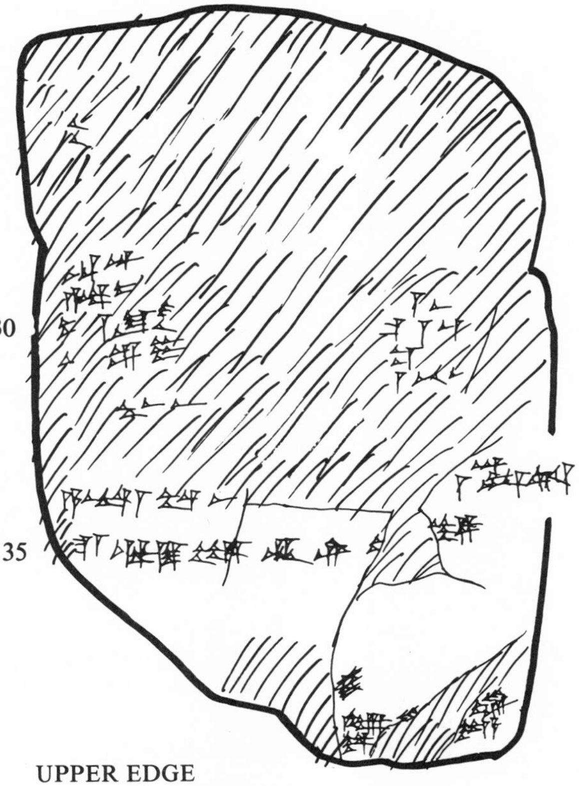

UPPER EDGE

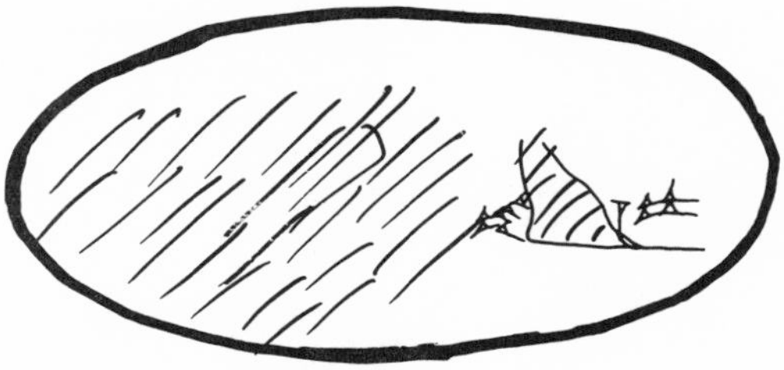

441

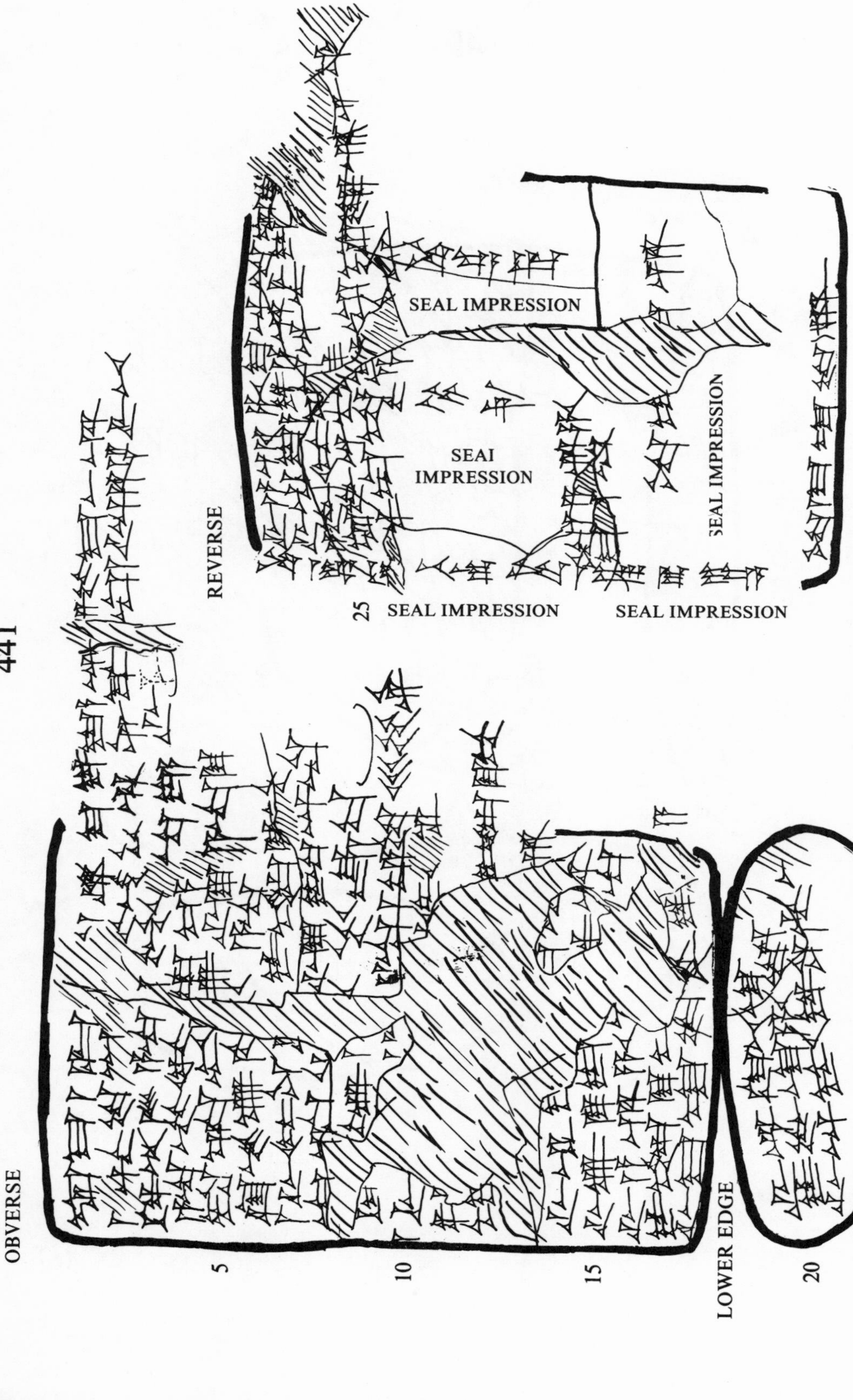
OBVERSE
LOWER EDGE
REVERSE
SEAL IMPRESSION
SEAI IMPRESSION
SEAL IMPRESSION
SEAL IMPRESSION
SEAL IMPRESSION
SEAL IMPRESSION

450

OBVERSE

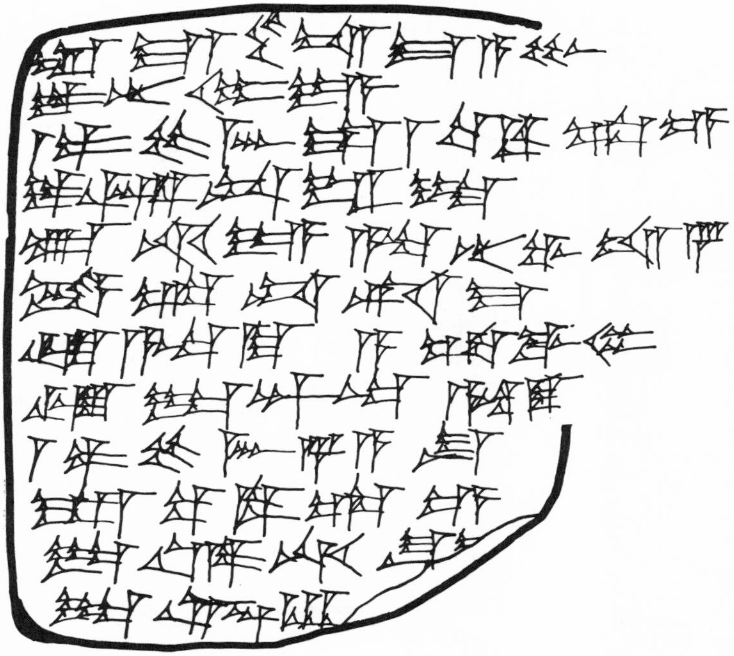

LOWER EDGE

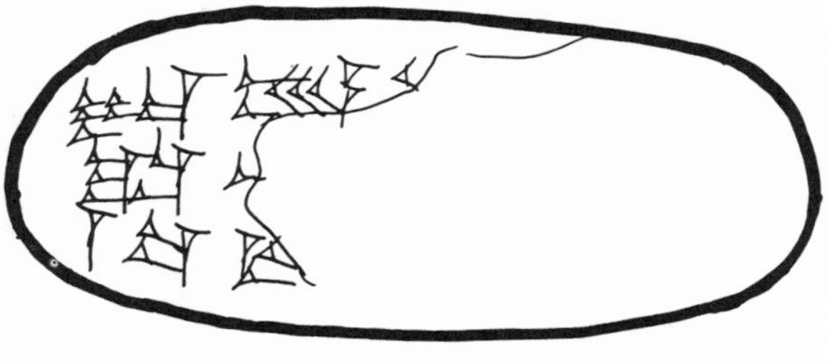

450

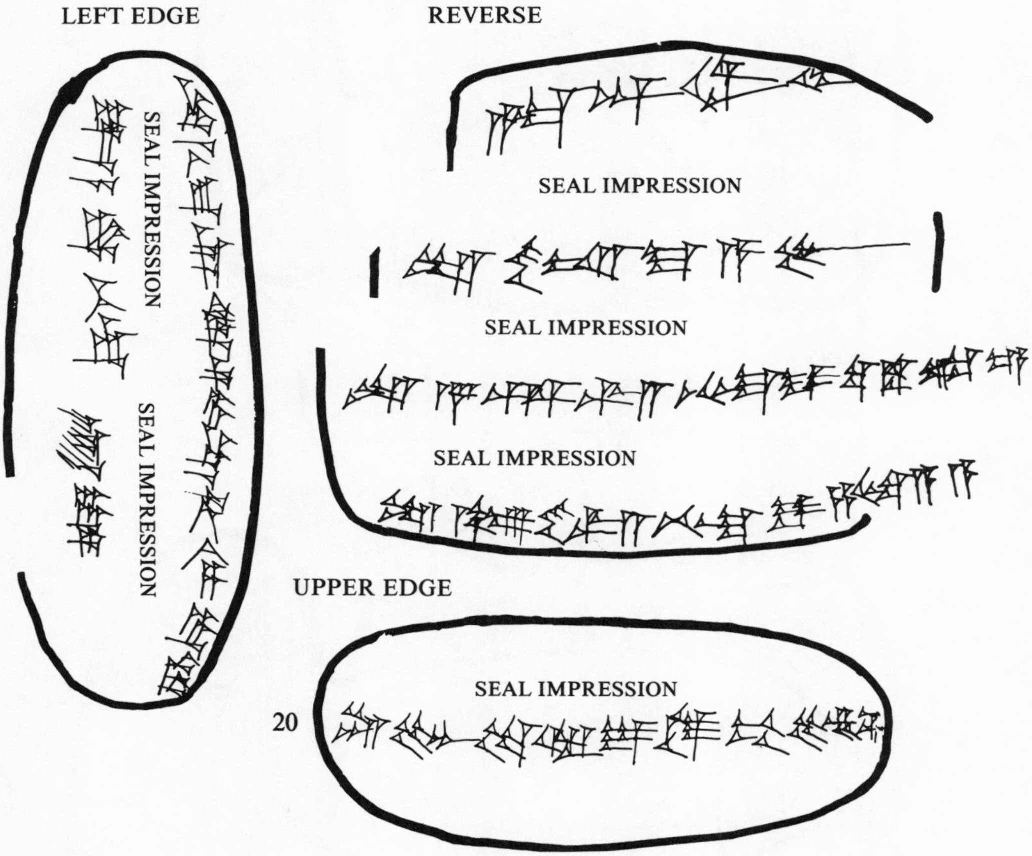
LEFT EDGE
REVERSE
SEAL IMPRESSION
SEAL IMPRESSION
SEAL IMPRESSION
SEAL IMPRESSION
SEAL IMPRESSION
SEAL IMPRESSION
UPPER EDGE
SEAL IMPRESSION
20

452

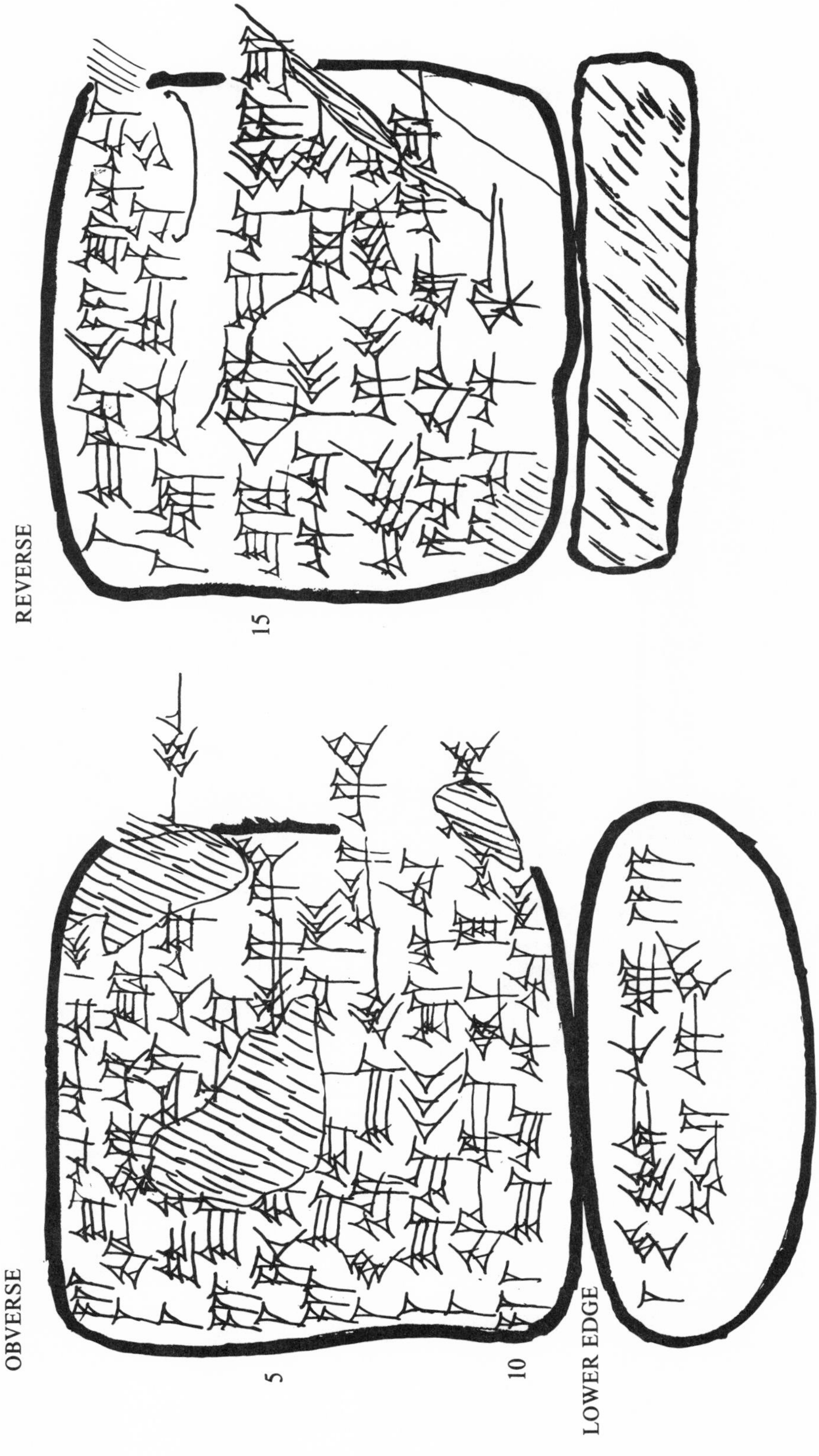

455

OBVERSE

BEGINNING OF OBVERSE DESTROYED

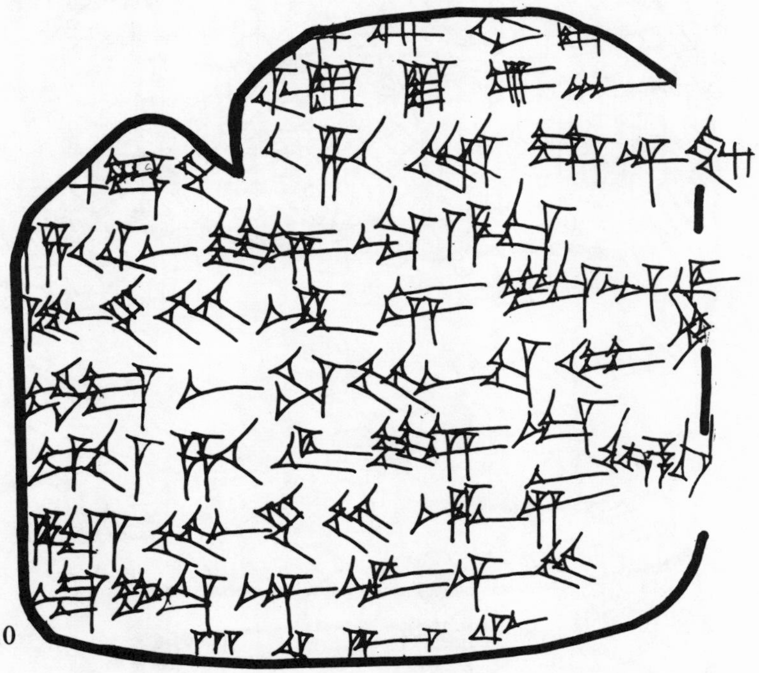

END OF OBVERSE DESTROYED

REVERSE DESTROYED

458

OBVERSE

BEGINNING OF OBVERSE DESTROYED

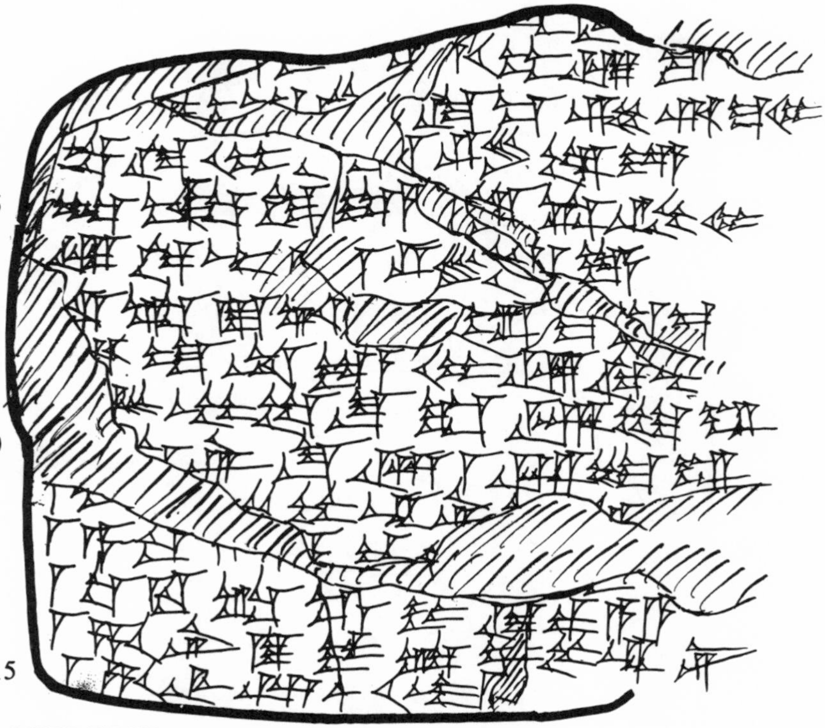

LOWER EDGE

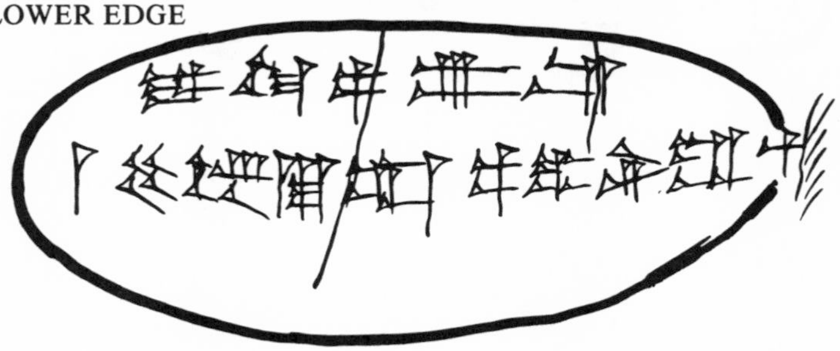

458

REVERSE

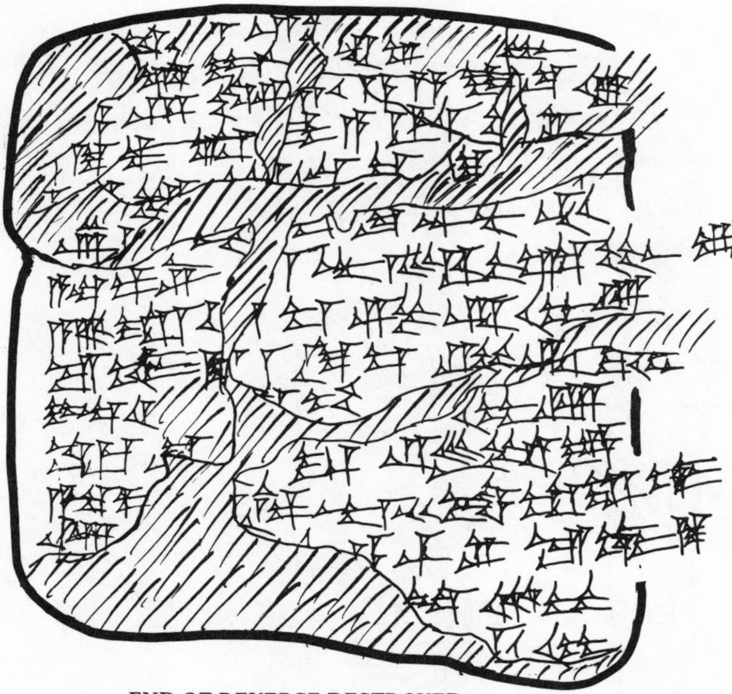

END OF REVERSE DESTROYED

LEFT EDGE

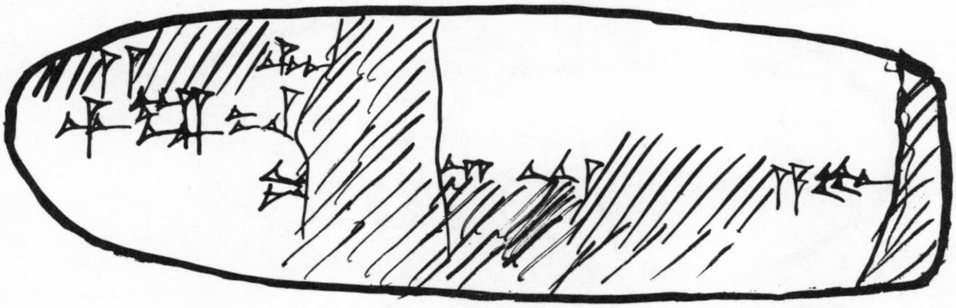

477

OBVERSE

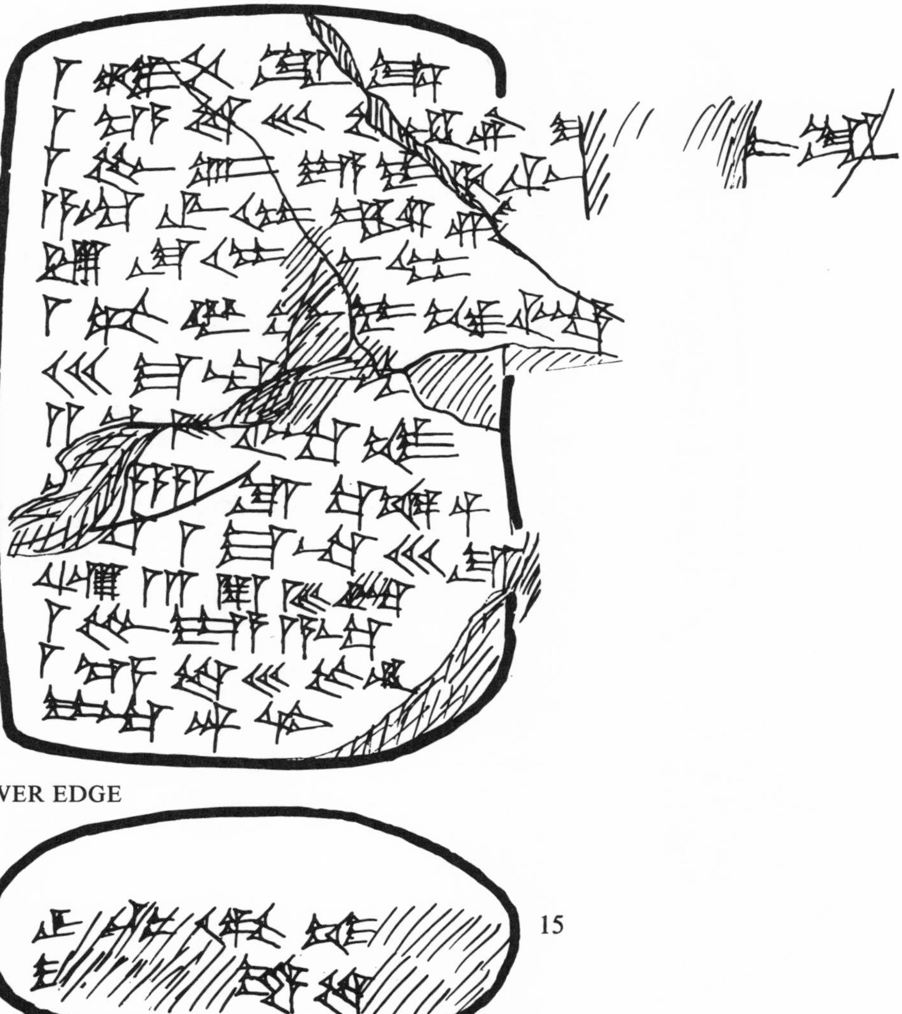

LOWER EDGE

477

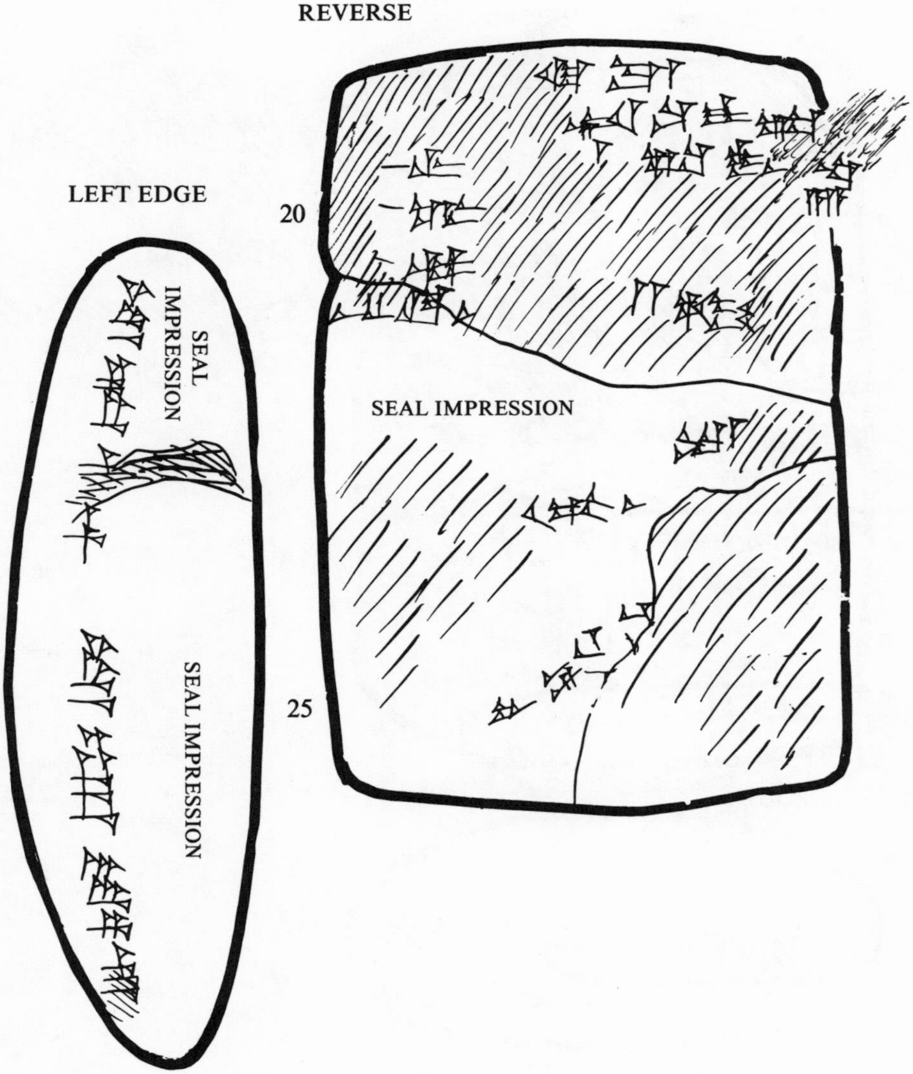
REVERSE
LEFT EDGE
20
SEAL IMPRESSION
SEAL IMPRESSION
SEAL IMPRESSION
25

478

OBVERSE

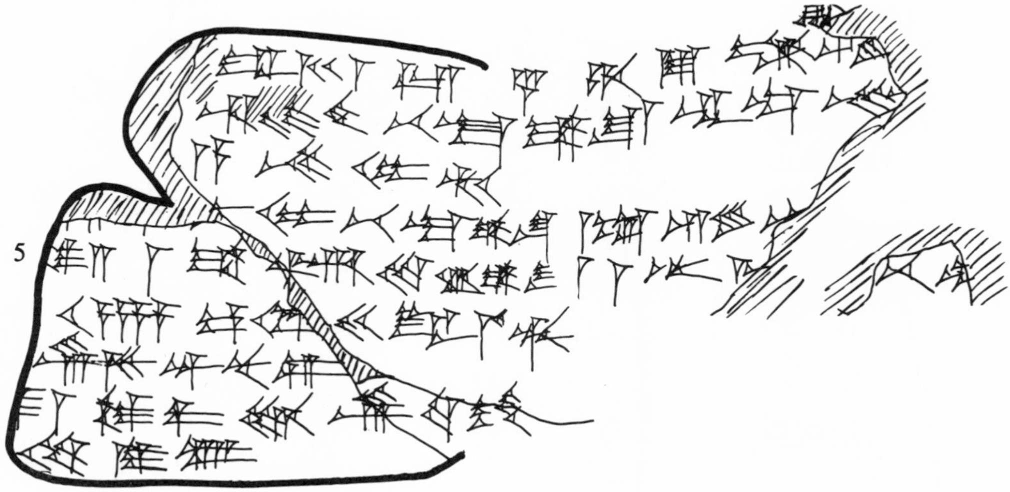

SEAL IMPRESSION

REVERSE

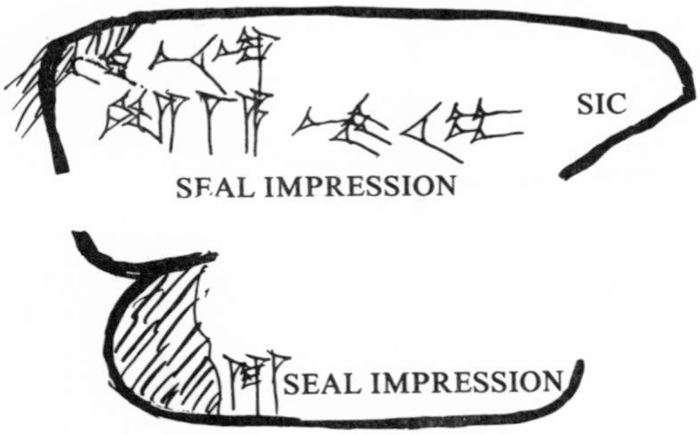

490

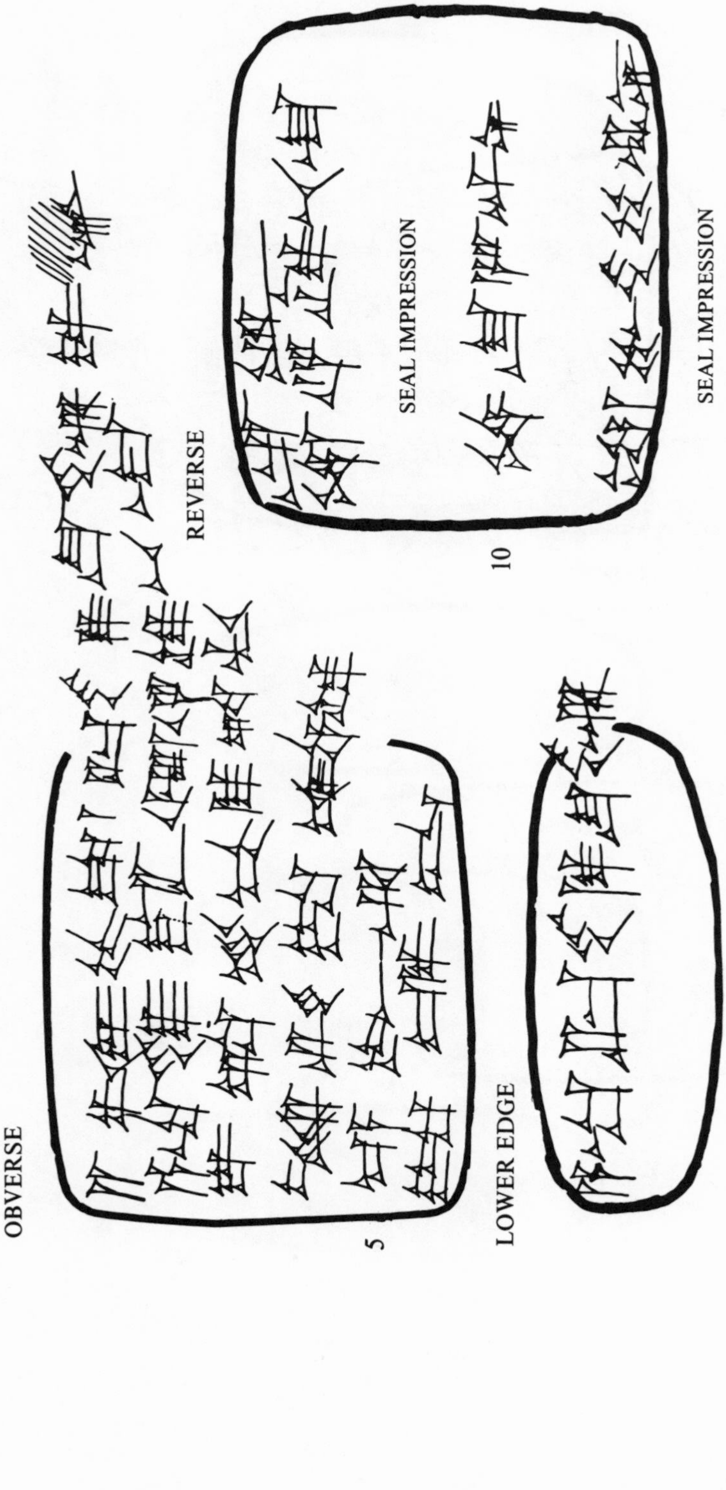
OBVERSE
5
LOWER EDGE
REVERSE
10
SEAL IMPRESSION
SEAL IMPRESSION

493

OBVERSE

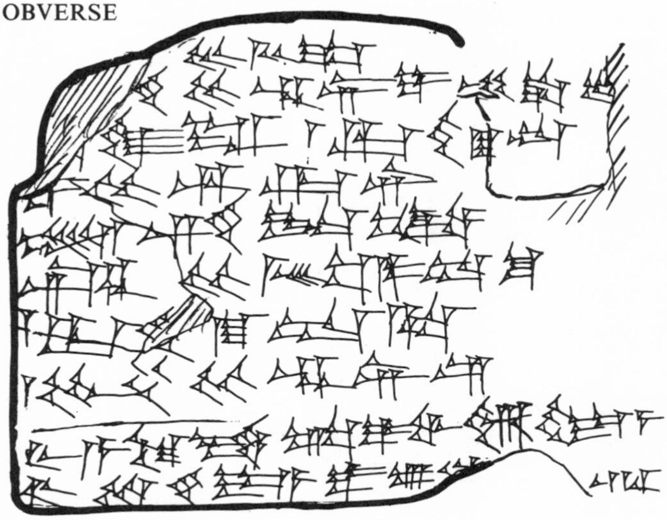

LOWER EDGE

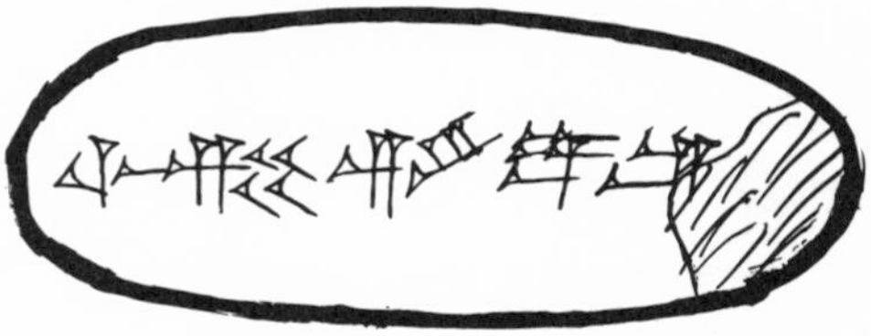

REVERSE

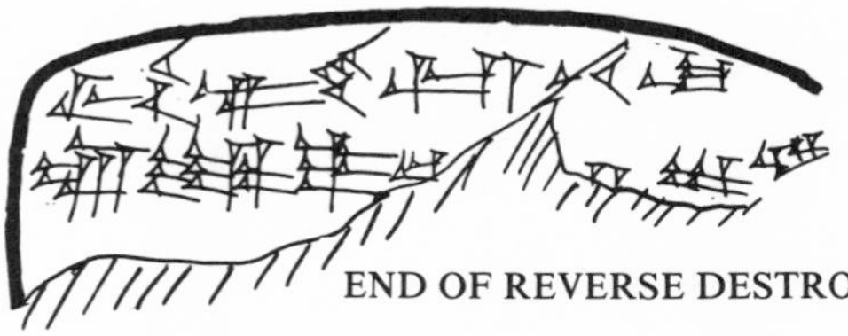

END OF REVERSE DESTROYED

LEFT EDGE

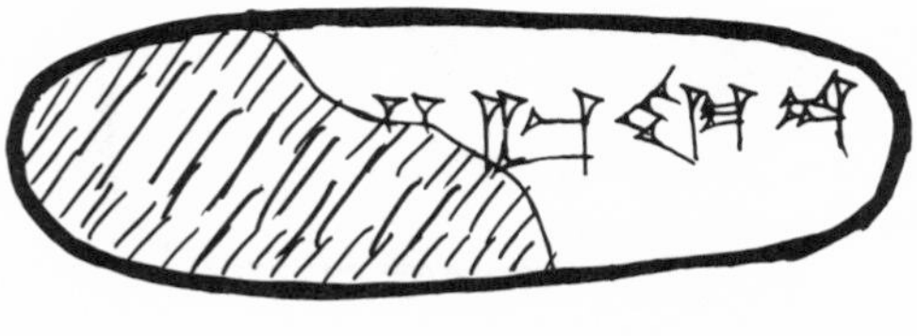

505

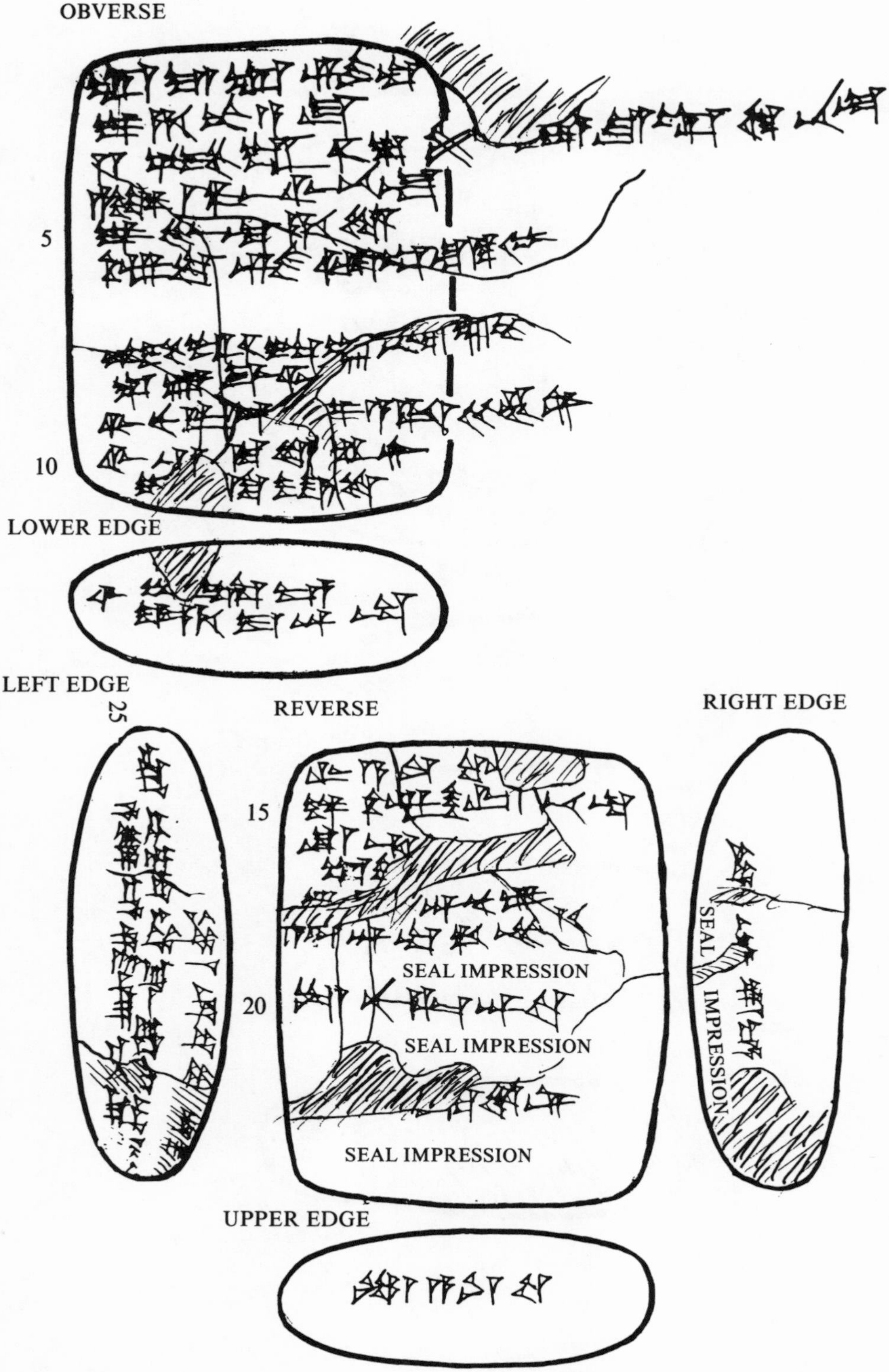
OBVERSE
5
10
LOWER EDGE
LEFT EDGE
25
REVERSE
RIGHT EDGE
15
20
SEAL IMPRESSION
SEAL IMPRESSION
SEAL IMPRESSION
SEAL IMPRESSION
UPPER EDGE

512

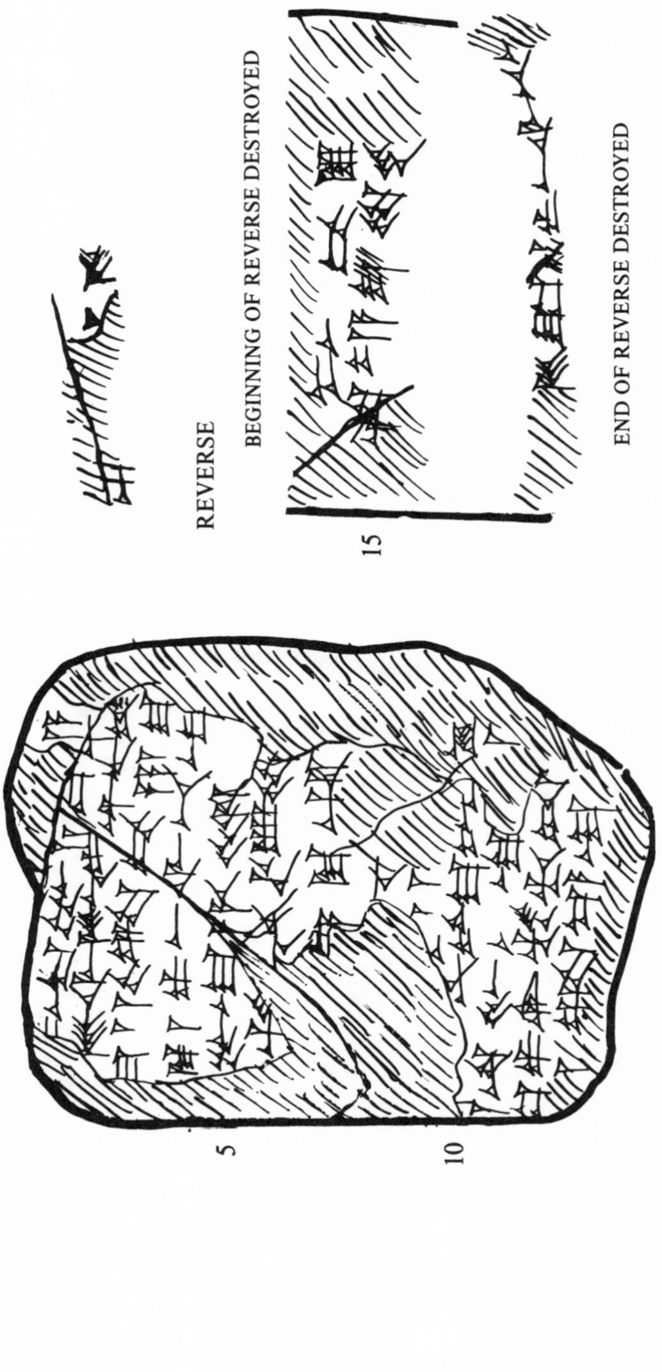
OBVERSE
REVERSE
BEGINNING OF REVERSE DESTROYED
END OF REVERSE DESTROYED

513

OBVERSE

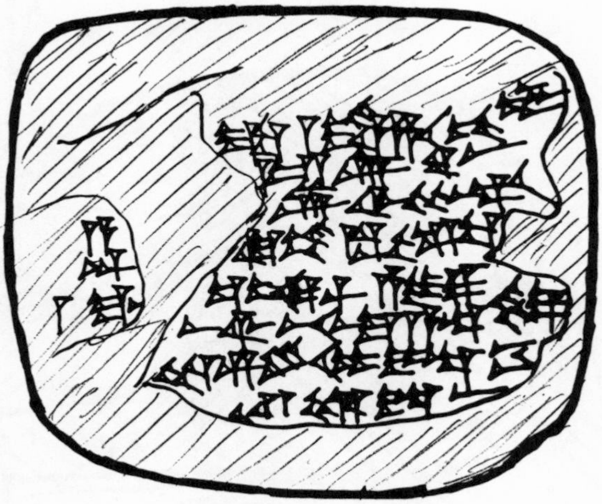

REVERSE

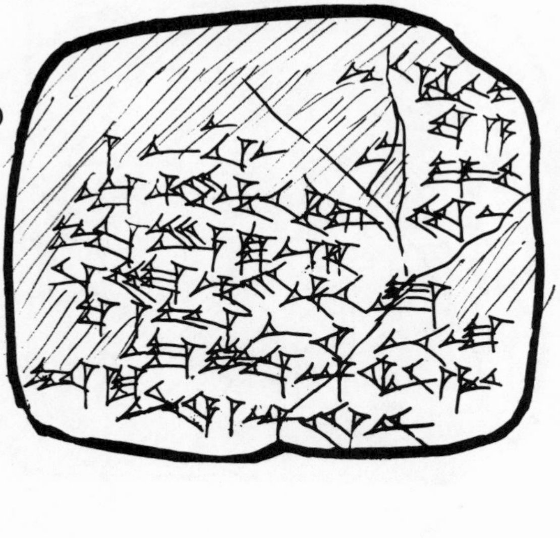

515

OBVERSE

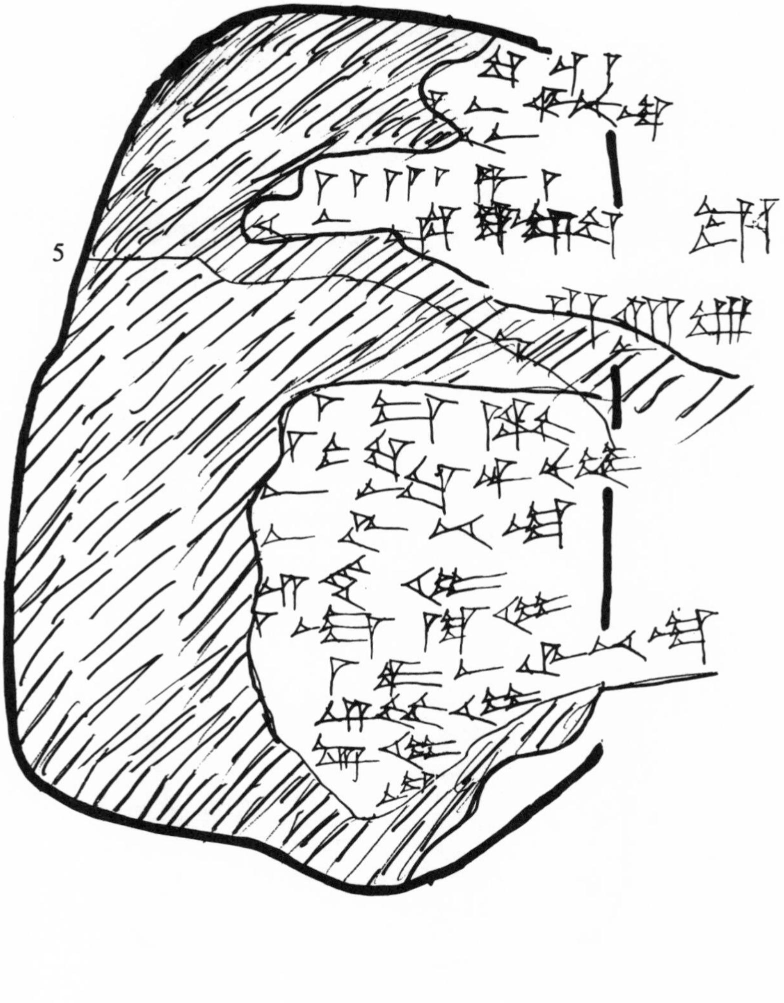

515

REVERSE

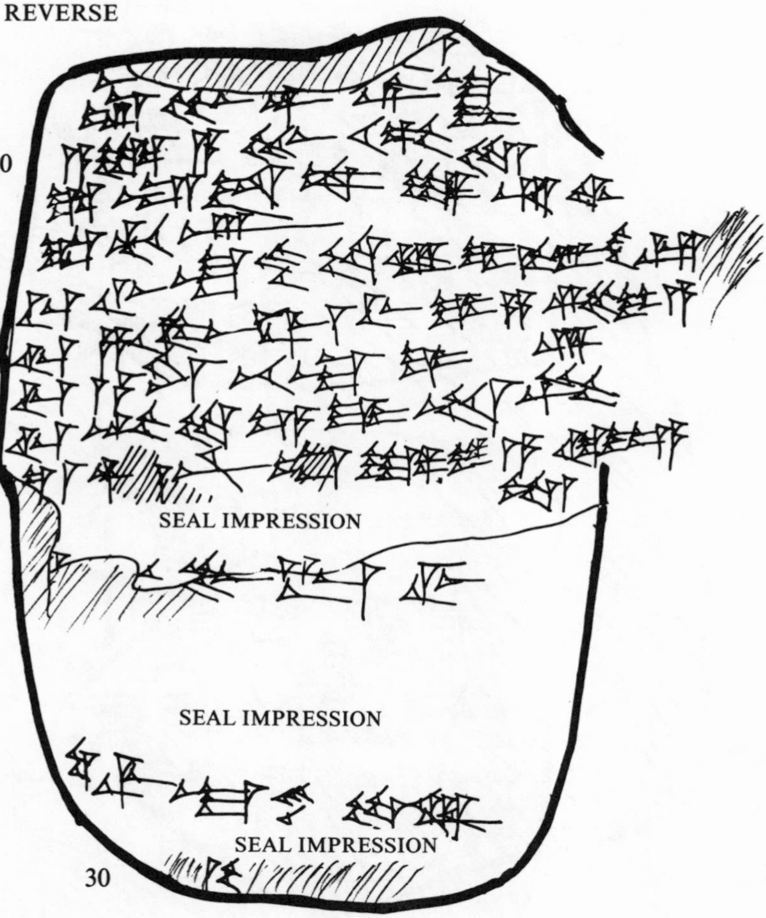
SEAL IMPRESSION
SEAL IMPRESSION
SEAL IMPRESSION

524

OBVERSE

BEGINNING OF OBVERSE DESTROYED

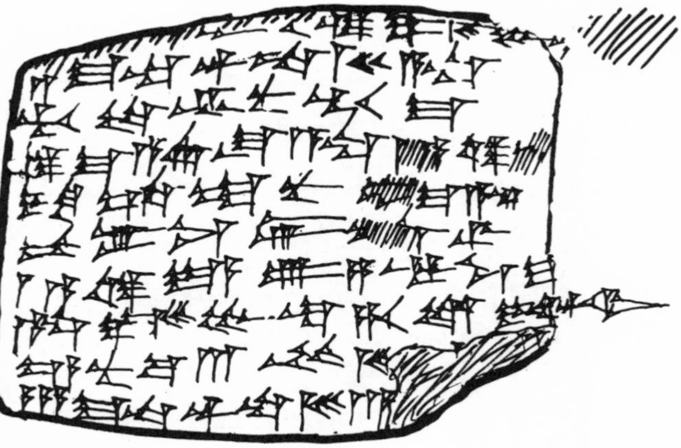

LOWER EDGE

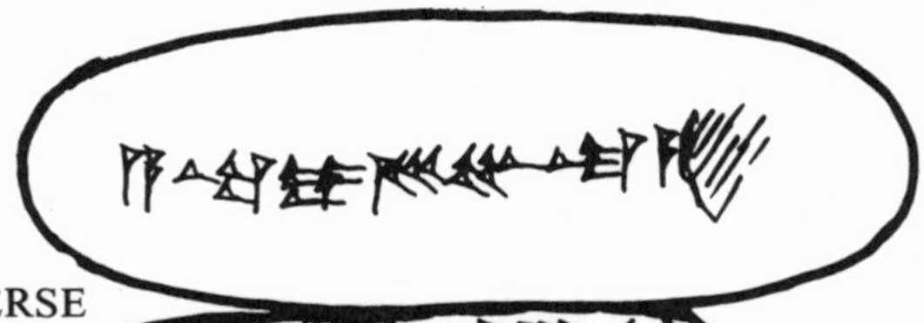

LEFT EDGE

REVERSE

525

OBVERSE

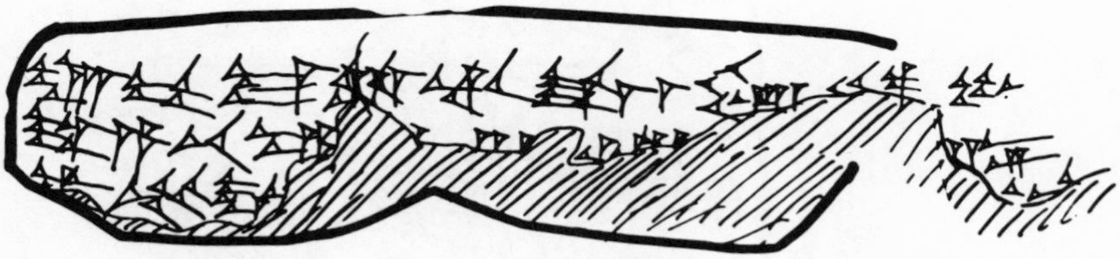

END OF OBVERSE DESTROYED

REVERSE

BEGINNING OF REVERSE DESTROYED

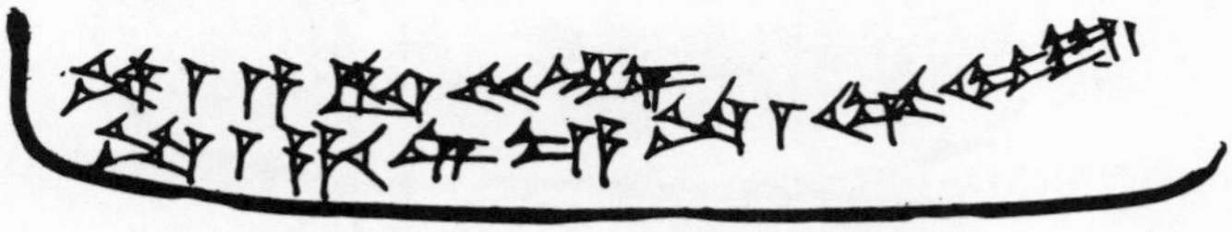

526

OBVERSE

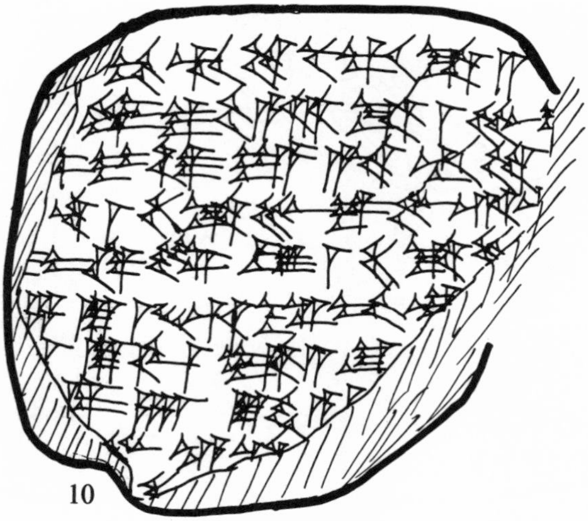

END OF OBVERSE DESTROYED

REVERSE DESTROYED

527

OBVERSE

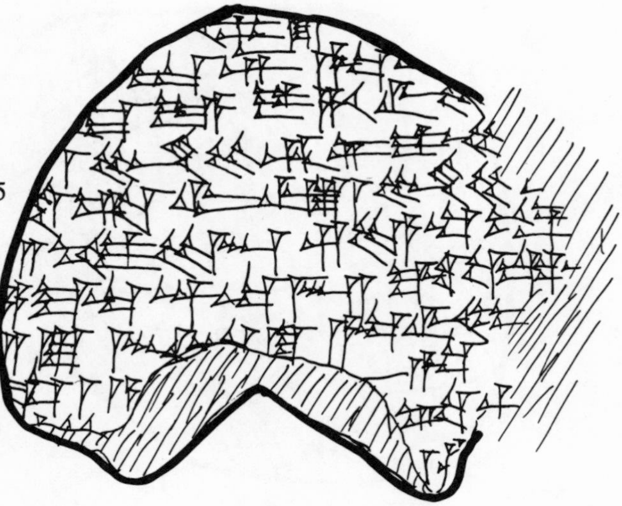

END OF OBVERSE DESTROYED

REVERSE DESTROYED

528

OBVERSE BEGINNING OF OBVERSE DESTROYED

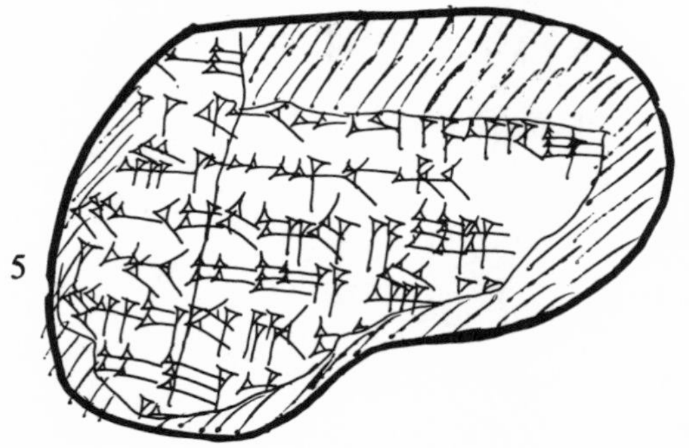

END OF OBVERSE DESTROYED

REVERSE DESTROYED

529

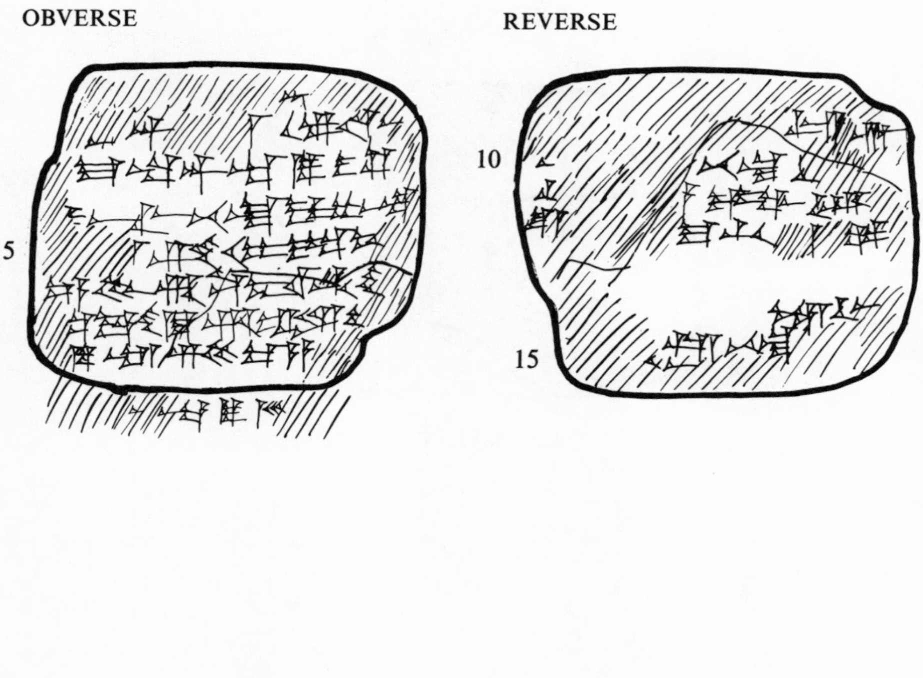

Index to Text References in SCCNH 2

SCOTT NOEGEL

RS

h.10:4	51n358
15.10:5	334n20
20.123	331n3
20.149	331n3; 334n20
24.253:7	54n392 = (U 5 V 13)
24.254:4	53n382
24.254:9	43n327 = (U 5 L 3)
24.261:8	56n407
24.261:15	48n327 = (U 5 L 1)
24.264: + 280:27	49n337
24.278:9	53n380
24.284:11	48n327
24.295:6	48n327 = (U 5 L 4)
25.284:5	54n383

SH

808:9′	10n42
809	10n43
813	54n389
867:10	8n29
867:8	8n29
915:15–17	44n307

SMN

	168; 168n6; 194; 341; 348; 349
59	188n72
64	180n48
69	180n48
150	177n40
183	188n72
770	342
855	350
961	342
1100	79
1103	342
1159	342
1187	199
1232	342
1265	342
1272	342
1373	79
1380	77n4
1529	342
1530	342
1536	342
1537	342
1540	342
1552	342
1561	342
1570	342
1584	342
1584	345; 347; 348
1586	342
1588	342
1591	342
1593	342
1594	342; 350
1595	342
1605	342
1607	342
1608	342
1610	342
1612	342
1615	342
1620	342
1622	342
1623	342
1624	342
1625	342
1627	342
1630	342
1631	342; 350
1632	342
1639	342
1641	342
1646	342
1647	342
1648	342
1651	342
1652	342
1653	342
1655	342; 352; 354
1657	342
1658	342
1660	342
1661	342
1662	342
1663	342
1665	342
1666	342
1667	342
1670	342
1672	342